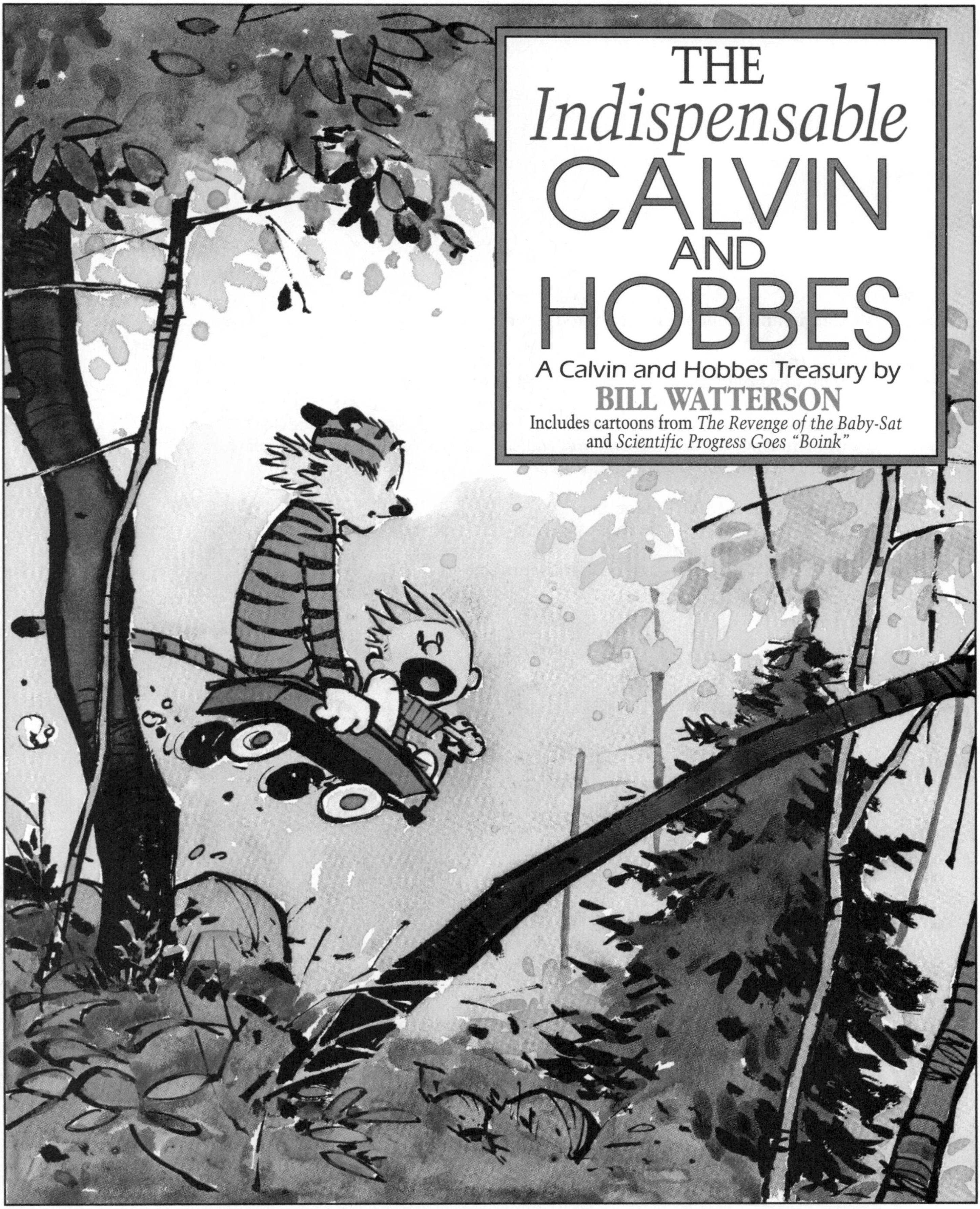

THE *Indispensable* CALVIN AND HOBBES

A Calvin and Hobbes Treasury by

BILL WATTERSON

Includes cartoons from *The Revenge of the Baby-Sat* and *Scientific Progress Goes "Boink"*

Andrews and McMeel ▪ A Universal Press Syndicate Company ▪ Kansas City

Calvin and Hobbes is distributed internationally by Universal Press Syndicate.

ISBN: 0-8362-1898-1 (paperback)
0-8362-1703-9 (hardback)

Library of Congress Catalog Card Number: 92-72247 (paperback)
92-72248 (hardback)

I made a big decision a little while ago.
I don't remember what it was, which prob'ly goes to show
That many times a simple choice can prove to be essential
Even though it often might appear inconsequential.

I must have been distracted when I left my home because
Left or right I'm sure I went. (I wonder which it was!)
Anyway, I never veered: I walked in that direction
Utterly absorbed, it seems, in quiet introspection.

For no reason I can think of, I've wandered far astray.
And that is how I got to where I find myself today.

Explorers are we, intrepid and bold,
Out in the wild, amongst wonders untold.
Equipped with our wits, a map, and a snack,
We're searching for fun and we're on the right track!

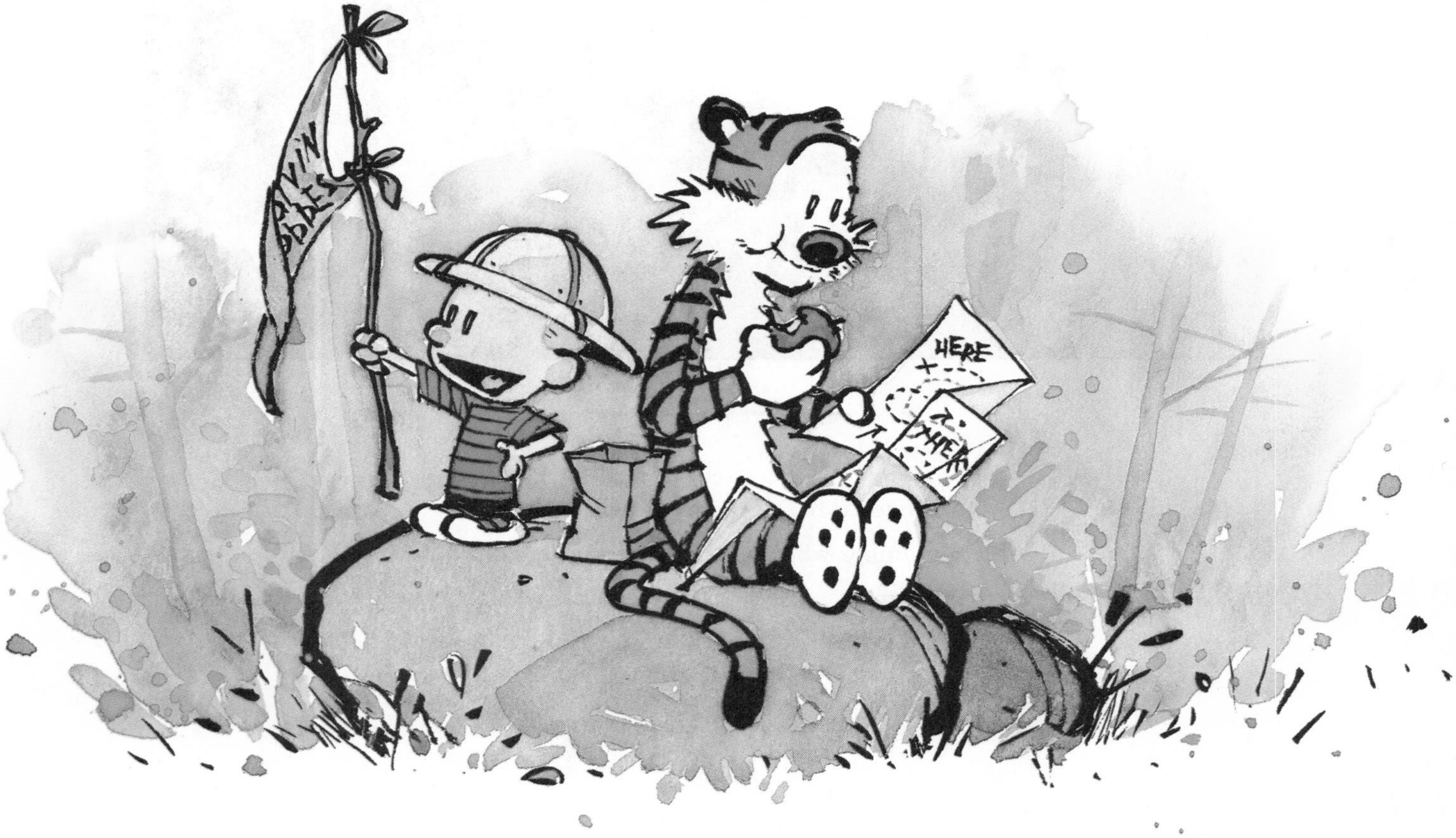
HERE

My mother has eyes on the back of her head!
I don't quite believe it, but that's what she said.
She explained that she'd been so uniquely endowed
To catch me when I did Things Not Allowed.
I think she must also have eyes on her rear.
I've noticed her hindsight is unusually clear.

At night my mind does not much care
If what it thinks is here or there.
It tells me stories it invents
And makes up things that don't make sense.
I don't know why it does this stuff.
The real world seems quite weird enough.

What if my bones were in a museum,
Where aliens paid good money to see 'em?
And suppose that they'd put me together all wrong,
Sticking bones on to bones where they didn't belong!

Imagine phalanges, pelvis, and spine
Welded to mandibles that once had been mine!
With each misassemblage, the error compounded,
The aliens would draw back in terror, astounded!

Their textbooks would show me in grim illustration,
The most hideous thing ever seen in creation!
The museum would commission a model in plaster
Of ME, to be called, "Evolution's Disaster"!

And paleontologists there would debate
Dozens of theories to help postulate
How man survived for those thousands of years
With teeth-covered arms growing out of his ears!

Oh, I hope that I'm never in such manner displayed,
No matter HOW much to see me the aliens paid.

I did not want to go with them.
Alas, I had no choice.
This was made quite clear to me
In threat'ning tones of voice.

I protested mightily
And scrambled 'cross the floor.
But though I grabbed the furniture,
They dragged me out the door.

In the car, I screamed and moaned.
I cried my red eyes dry.
The window down, I yelled for help
To people we passed by.

Mom and Dad can make the rules
And certain things forbid,
But I can make them wish that they
Had never had a kid.

Now I'm in bed,
The sheets pulled to my head.
My tiger is here making Zs.
He's furry and hot.
He takes up a lot
Of the bed and he's hogging the breeze.

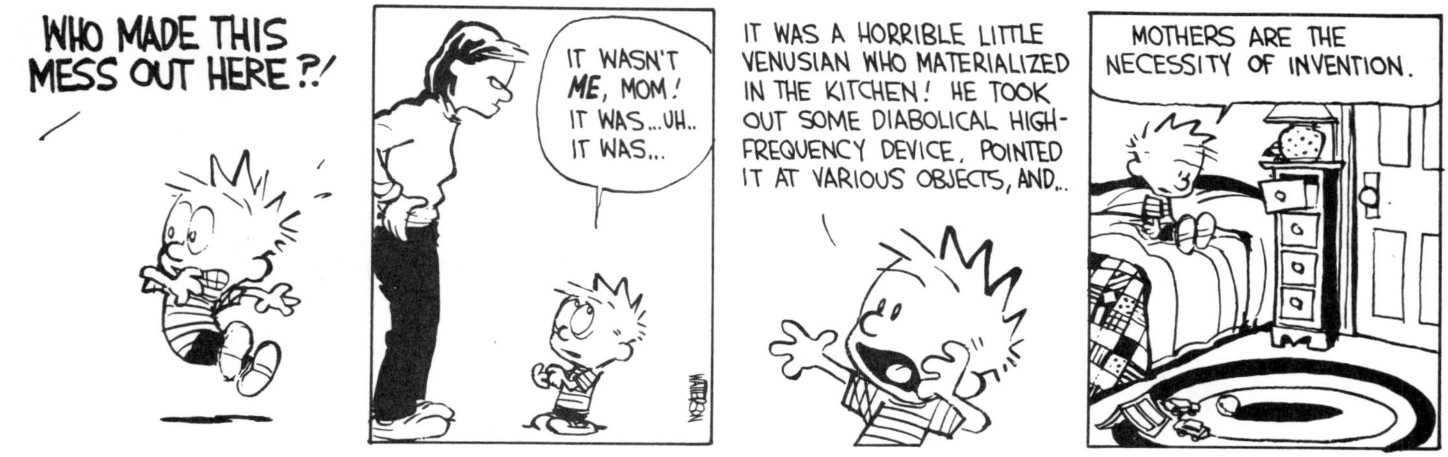
WHO MADE THIS MESS OUT HERE ?!
IT WASN'T ME, MOM! IT WAS...UH.. IT WAS...
IT WAS A HORRIBLE LITTLE VENUSIAN WHO MATERIALIZED IN THE KITCHEN! HE TOOK OUT SOME DIABOLICAL HIGH-FREQUENCY DEVICE, POINTED IT AT VARIOUS OBJECTS, AND...
MOTHERS ARE THE NECESSITY OF INVENTION.

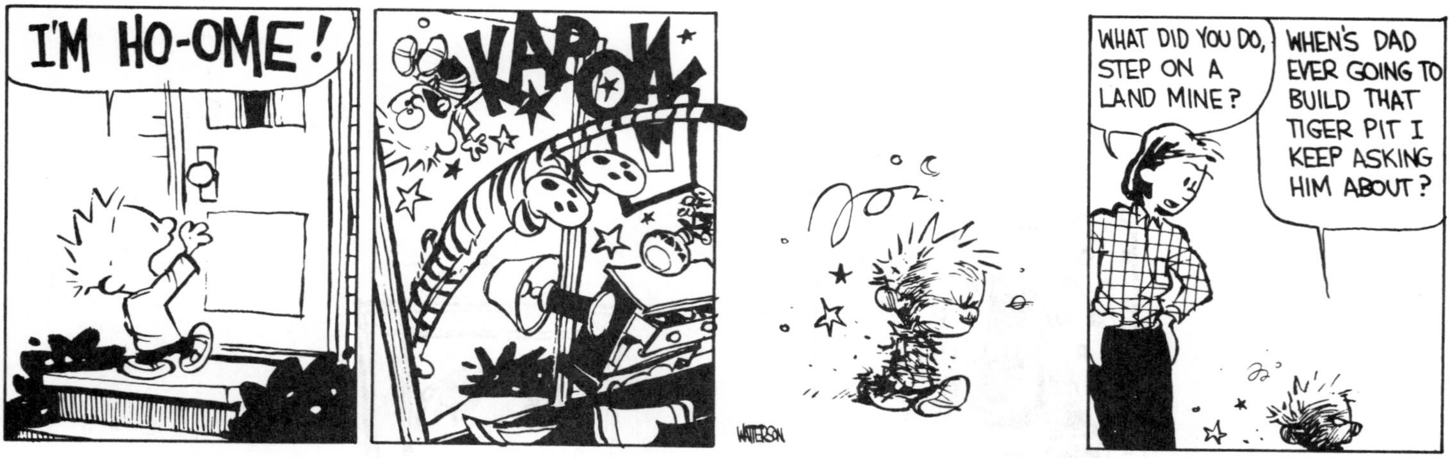
I'M HO-OME!
KAPOW
WHAT DID YOU DO, STEP ON A LAND MINE?
WHEN'S DAD EVER GOING TO BUILD THAT TIGER PIT I KEEP ASKING HIM ABOUT?

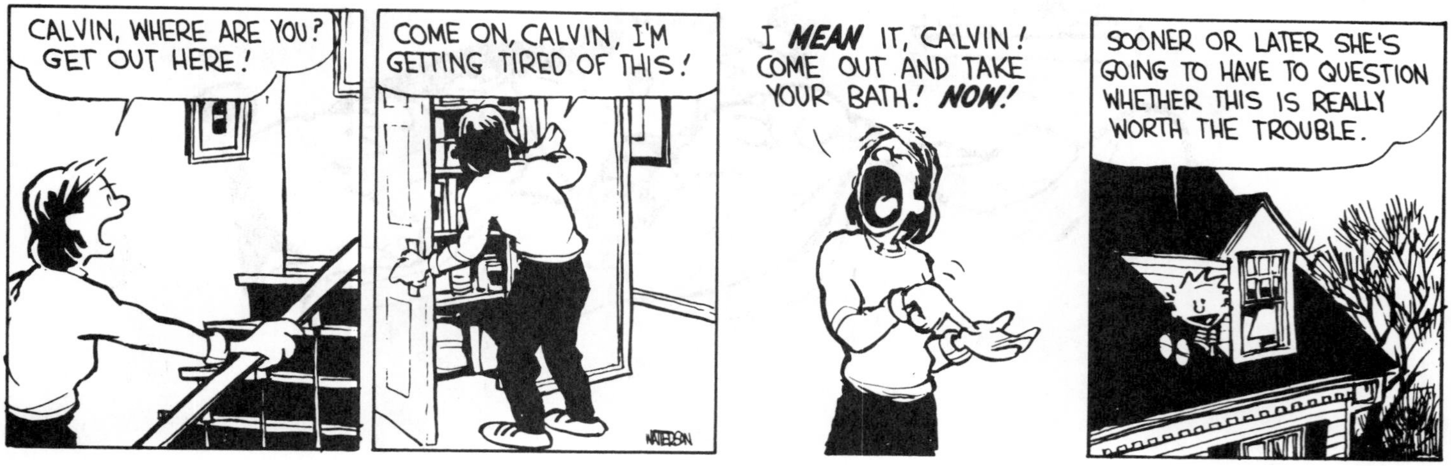
CALVIN, WHERE ARE YOU? GET OUT HERE!
COME ON, CALVIN, I'M GETTING TIRED OF THIS!
I MEAN IT, CALVIN! COME OUT AND TAKE YOUR BATH! NOW!
SOONER OR LATER SHE'S GOING TO HAVE TO QUESTION WHETHER THIS IS REALLY WORTH THE TROUBLE.

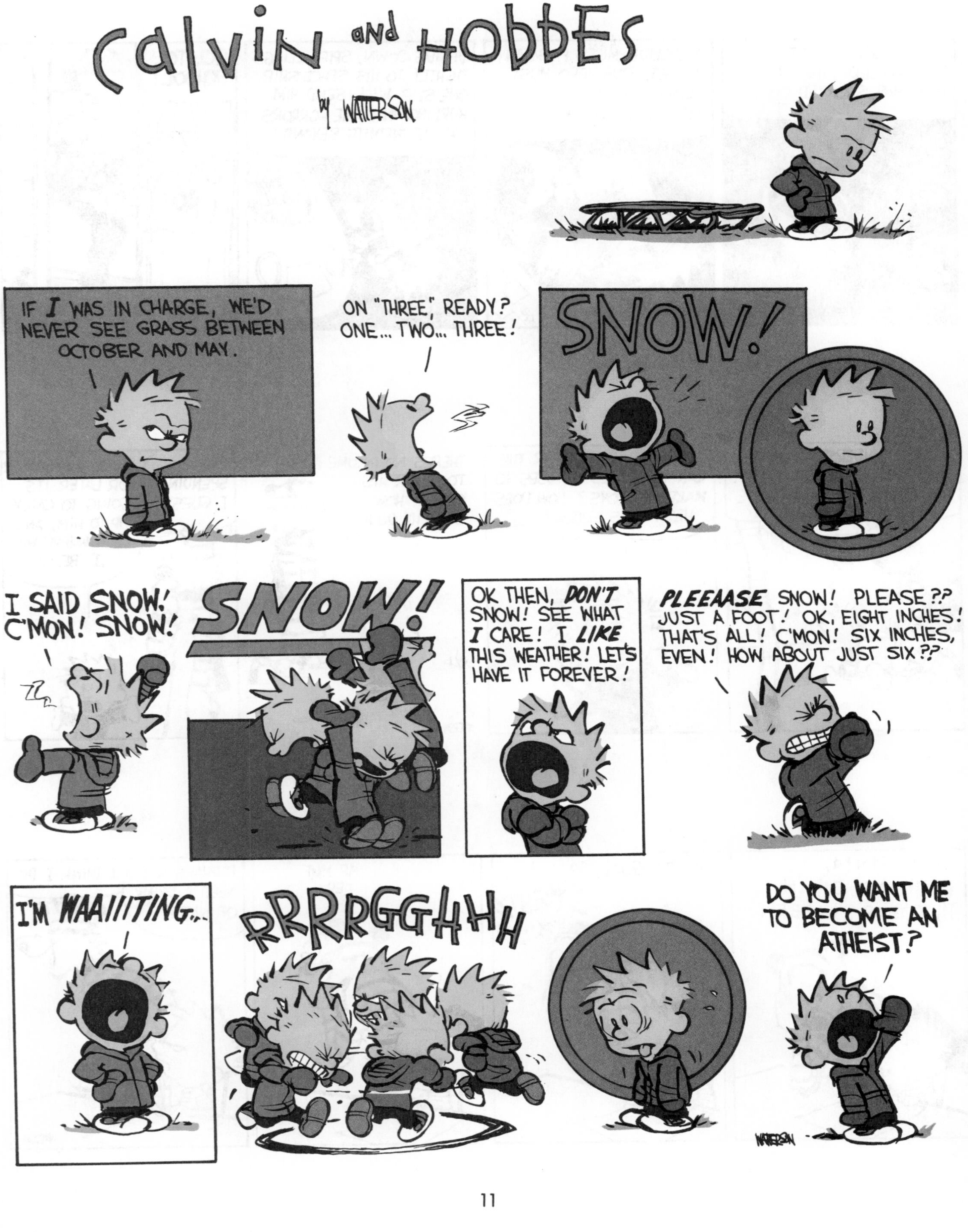
Calvin and HOBBES
by WATTERSON
IF I WAS IN CHARGE, WE'D NEVER SEE GRASS BETWEEN OCTOBER AND MAY.
ON "THREE," READY? ONE... TWO... THREE!
SNOW!
I SAID SNOW! C'MON! SNOW!
SNOW!
OK THEN, DON'T SNOW! SEE WHAT I CARE! I LIKE THIS WEATHER! LET'S HAVE IT FOREVER!
PLEEAASE SNOW! PLEASE?? JUST A FOOT! OK, EIGHT INCHES! THAT'S ALL! C'MON! SIX INCHES, EVEN! HOW ABOUT JUST SIX??
I'M WAAIIITING...
RRRRGGHHH
DO YOU WANT ME TO BECOME AN ATHEIST?
WATTERSON

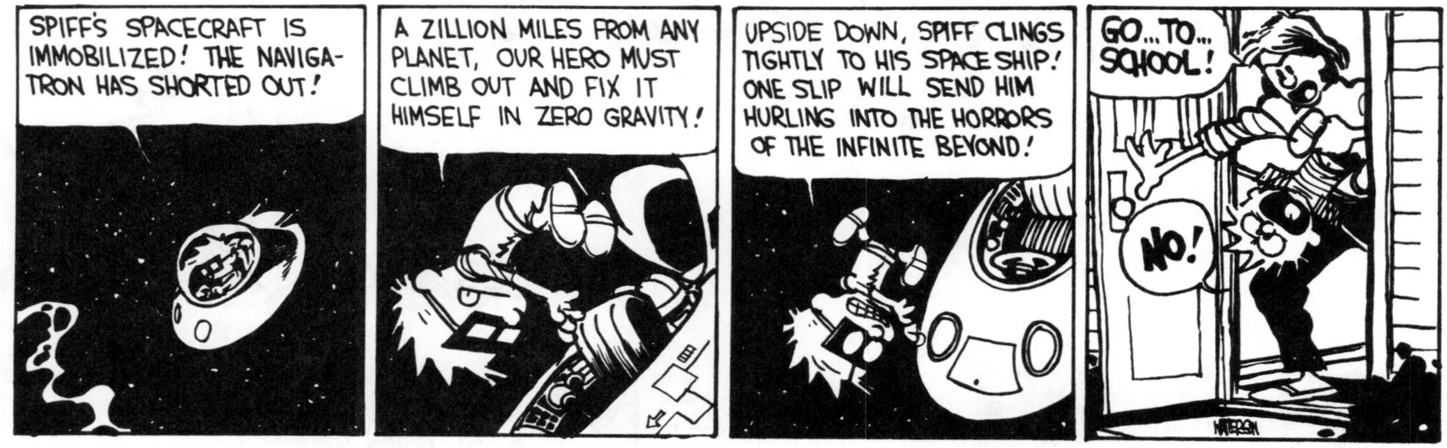
SPIFF'S SPACECRAFT IS IMMOBILIZED! THE NAVIGA-TRON HAS SHORTED OUT!
A ZILLION MILES FROM ANY PLANET, OUR HERO MUST CLIMB OUT AND FIX IT HIMSELF IN ZERO GRAVITY!
UPSIDE DOWN, SPIFF CLINGS TIGHTLY TO HIS SPACE SHIP! ONE SLIP WILL SEND HIM HURLING INTO THE HORRORS OF THE INFINITE BEYOND!
GO... TO... SCHOOL!
NO!

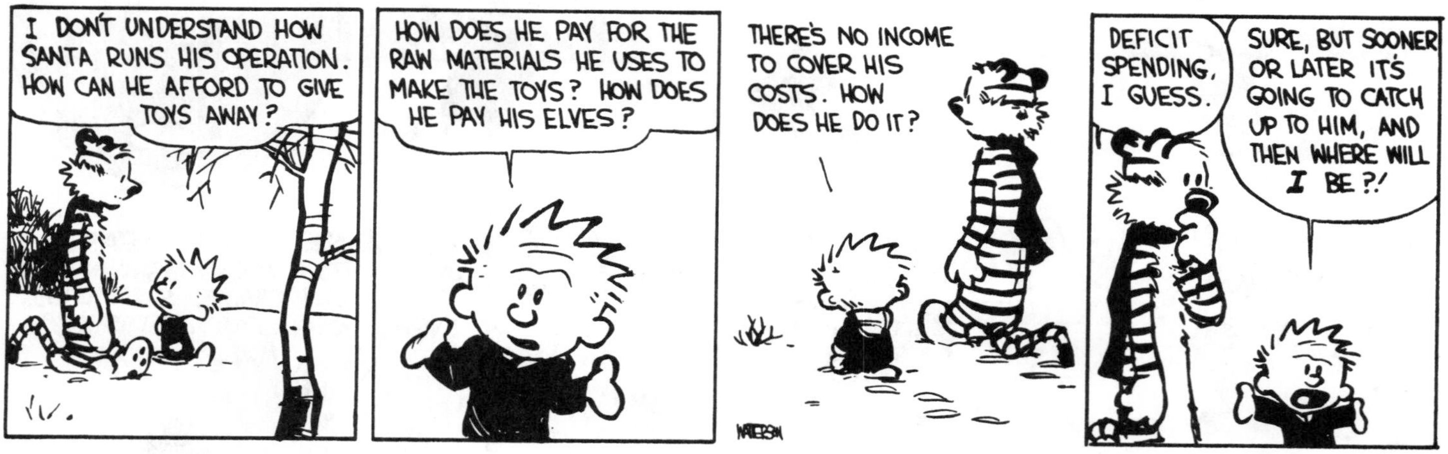
I DON'T UNDERSTAND HOW SANTA RUNS HIS OPERATION. HOW CAN HE AFFORD TO GIVE TOYS AWAY?
HOW DOES HE PAY FOR THE RAW MATERIALS HE USES TO MAKE THE TOYS? HOW DOES HE PAY HIS ELVES?
THERE'S NO INCOME TO COVER HIS COSTS. HOW DOES HE DO IT?
DEFICIT SPENDING, I GUESS.
SURE, BUT SOONER OR LATER IT'S GOING TO CATCH UP TO HIM, AND THEN WHERE WILL I BE?!

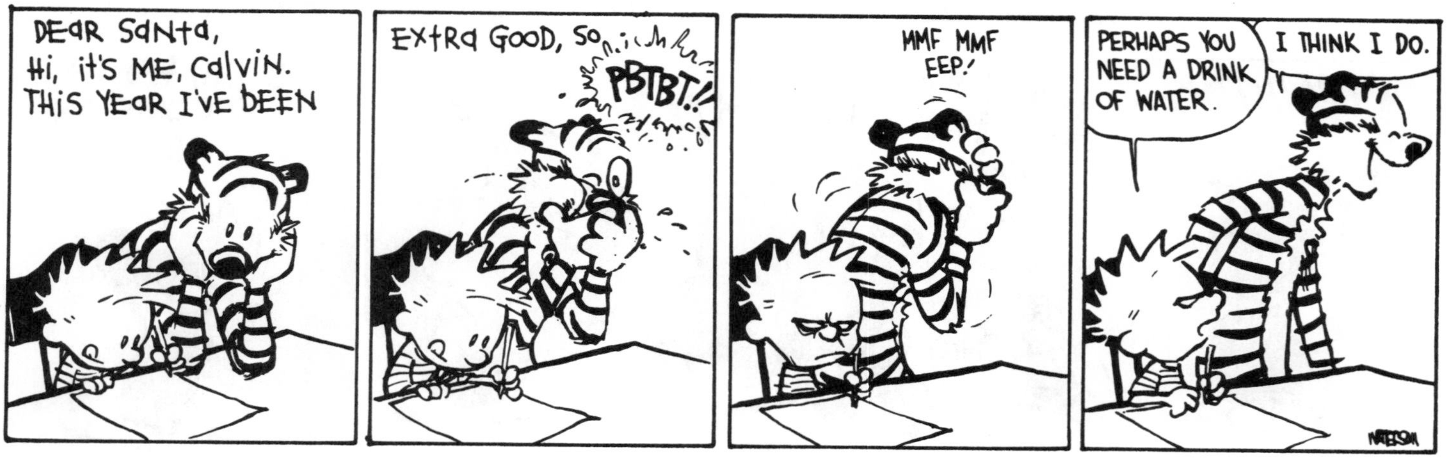
Dear Santa,
Hi, it's ME, Calvin.
THis YEar I'VE BEEN
Extra GOOD, so
PBTBT!!
MMF MMF EEP!
PERHAPS YOU NEED A DRINK OF WATER.
I THINK I DO.

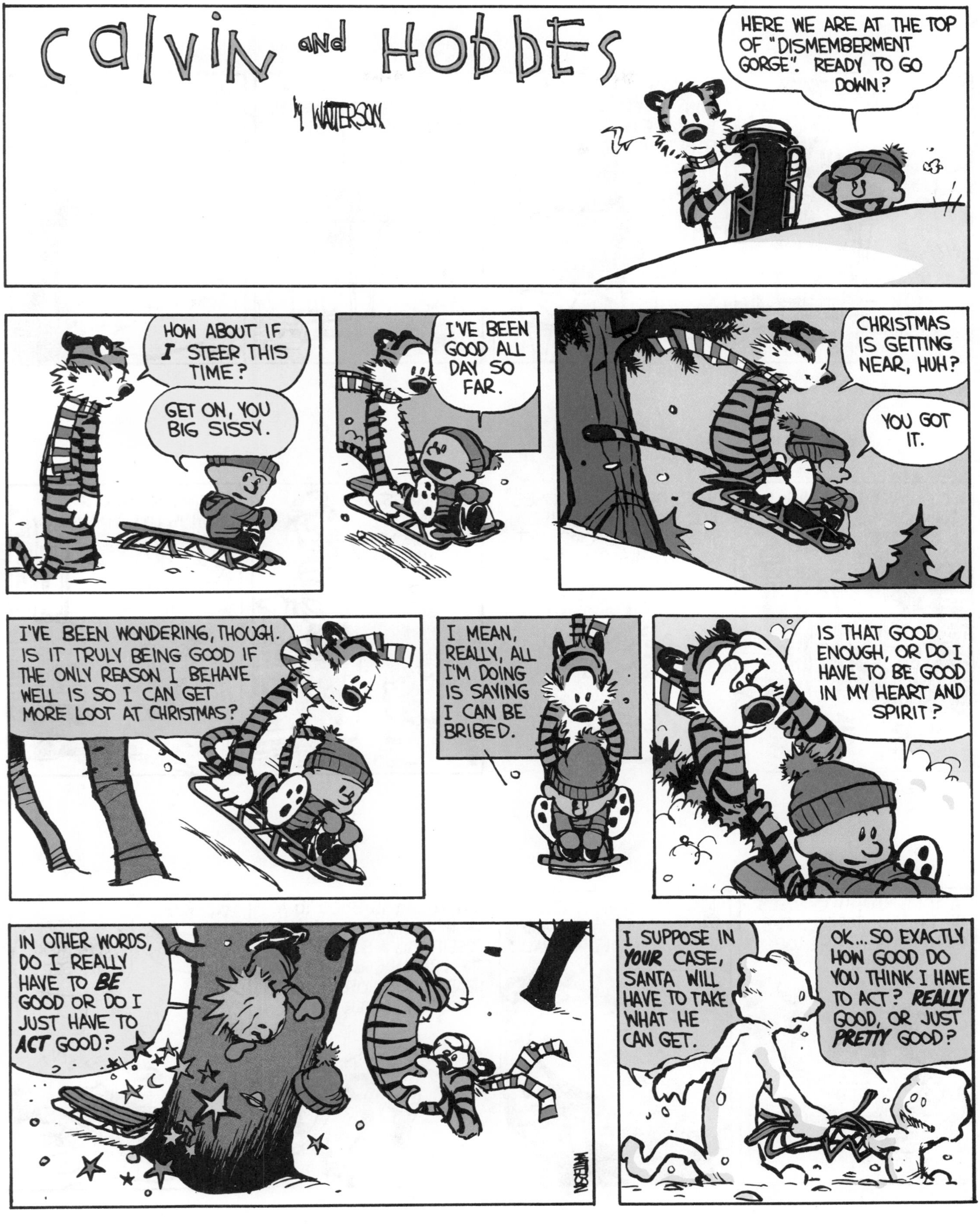
Calvin and HOBBES
by WATTERSON
HERE WE ARE AT THE TOP OF "DISMEMBERMENT GORGE". READY TO GO DOWN?
HOW ABOUT IF I STEER THIS TIME?
GET ON, YOU BIG SISSY.
I'VE BEEN GOOD ALL DAY SO FAR.
CHRISTMAS IS GETTING NEAR, HUH?
YOU GOT IT.
I'VE BEEN WONDERING, THOUGH. IS IT TRULY BEING GOOD IF THE ONLY REASON I BEHAVE WELL IS SO I CAN GET MORE LOOT AT CHRISTMAS?
I MEAN, REALLY, ALL I'M DOING IS SAYING I CAN BE BRIBED.
IS THAT GOOD ENOUGH, OR DO I HAVE TO BE GOOD IN MY HEART AND SPIRIT?
IN OTHER WORDS, DO I REALLY HAVE TO BE GOOD OR DO I JUST HAVE TO ACT GOOD?
I SUPPOSE IN YOUR CASE, SANTA WILL HAVE TO TAKE WHAT HE CAN GET.
OK... SO EXACTLY HOW GOOD DO YOU THINK I HAVE TO ACT? REALLY GOOD, OR JUST PRETTY GOOD?
WATTERSON

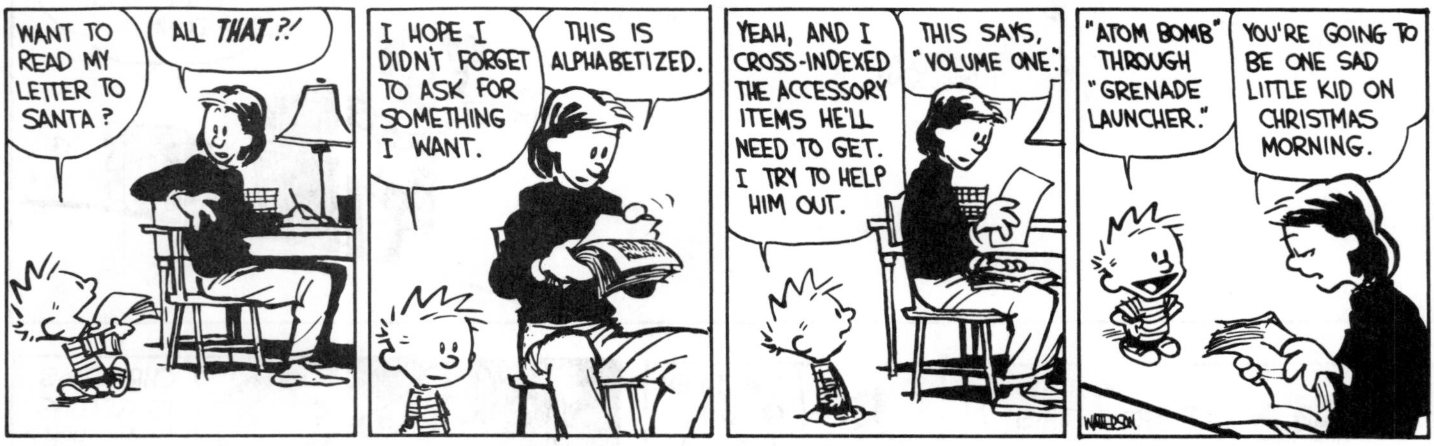
WANT TO READ MY LETTER TO SANTA ?
ALL THAT ?!
I HOPE I DIDN'T FORGET TO ASK FOR SOMETHING I WANT.
THIS IS ALPHABETIZED.
YEAH, AND I CROSS-INDEXED THE ACCESSORY ITEMS HE'LL NEED TO GET. I TRY TO HELP HIM OUT.
THIS SAYS, "VOLUME ONE."
"ATOM BOMB" THROUGH "GRENADE LAUNCHER."
YOU'RE GOING TO BE ONE SAD LITTLE KID ON CHRISTMAS MORNING.
WATTERSON

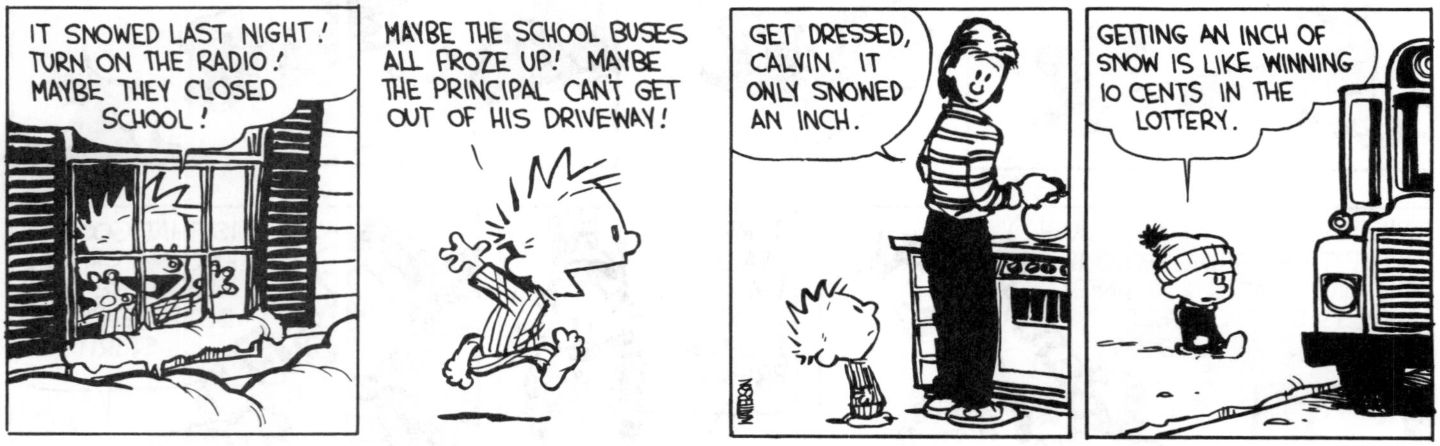
IT SNOWED LAST NIGHT! TURN ON THE RADIO! MAYBE THEY CLOSED SCHOOL!
MAYBE THE SCHOOL BUSES ALL FROZE UP! MAYBE THE PRINCIPAL CAN'T GET OUT OF HIS DRIVEWAY!
GET DRESSED, CALVIN. IT ONLY SNOWED AN INCH.
WATTERSON
GETTING AN INCH OF SNOW IS LIKE WINNING 10 CENTS IN THE LOTTERY.

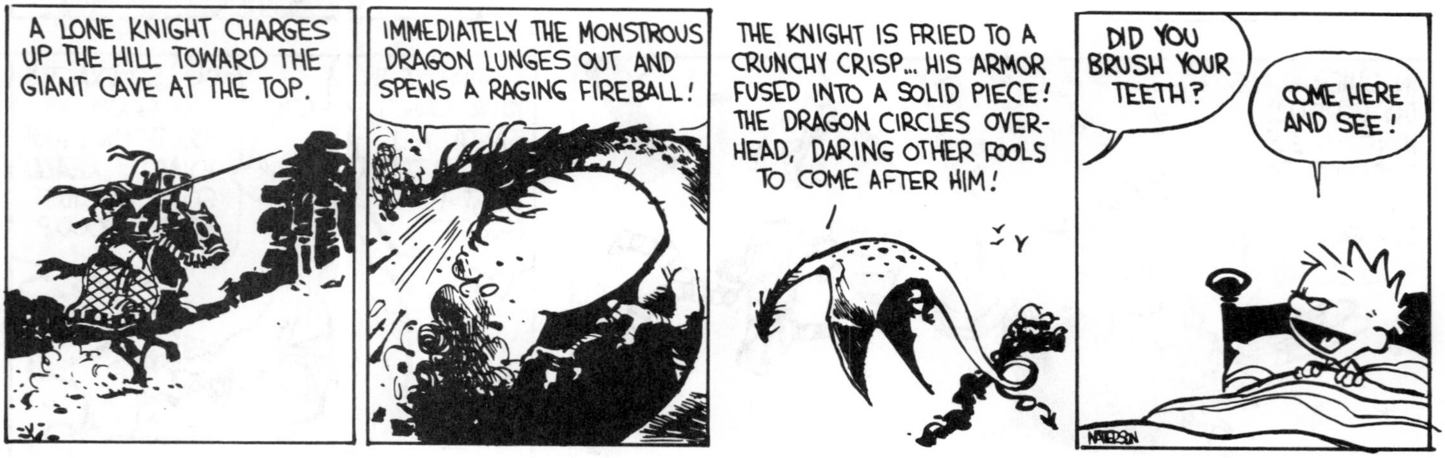
A LONE KNIGHT CHARGES UP THE HILL TOWARD THE GIANT CAVE AT THE TOP.
IMMEDIATELY THE MONSTROUS DRAGON LUNGES OUT AND SPEWS A RAGING FIREBALL!
THE KNIGHT IS FRIED TO A CRUNCHY CRISP... HIS ARMOR FUSED INTO A SOLID PIECE! THE DRAGON CIRCLES OVER-HEAD, DARING OTHER FOOLS TO COME AFTER HIM!
DID YOU BRUSH YOUR TEETH?
COME HERE AND SEE!
WATTERSON

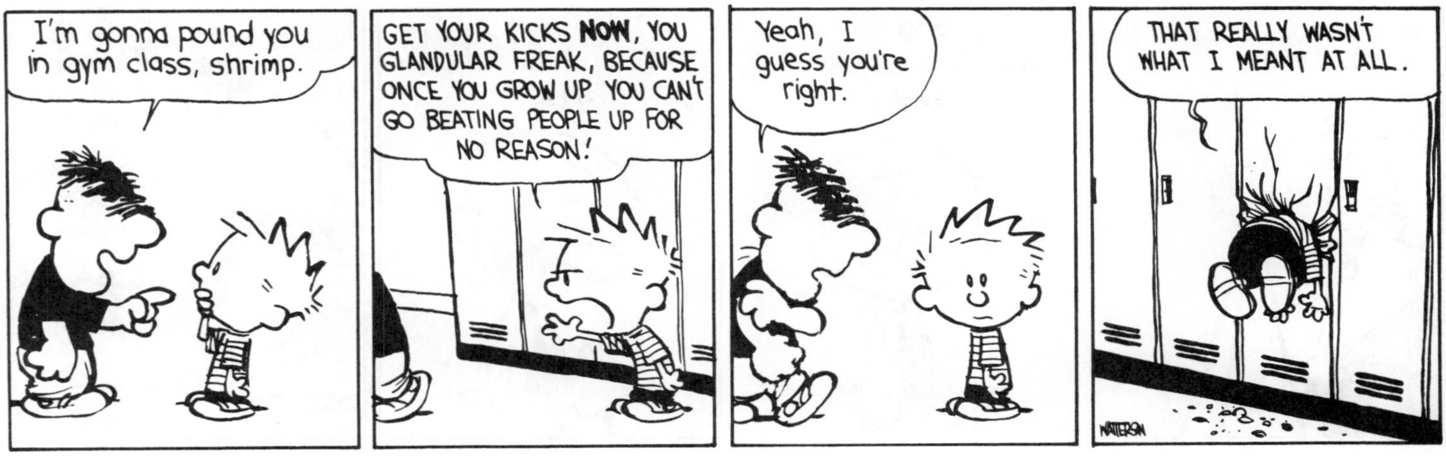
I'm gonna pound you in gym class, shrimp.
GET YOUR KICKS **NOW**, YOU GLANDULAR FREAK, BECAUSE ONCE YOU GROW UP YOU CAN'T GO BEATING PEOPLE UP FOR NO REASON!
Yeah, I guess you're right.
THAT REALLY WASN'T WHAT I MEANT AT ALL.
WATTERSON

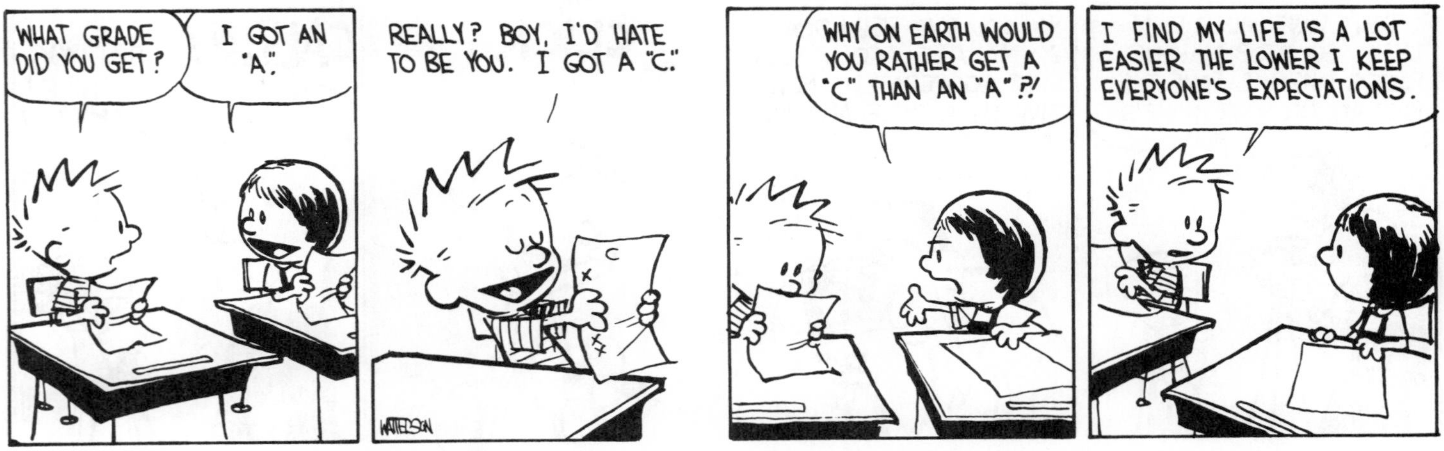
WHAT GRADE DID YOU GET?
I GOT AN "A".
REALLY? BOY, I'D HATE TO BE YOU. I GOT A "C."
WATTERSON
WHY ON EARTH WOULD YOU RATHER GET A "C" THAN AN "A"?!
I FIND MY LIFE IS A LOT EASIER THE LOWER I KEEP EVERYONE'S EXPECTATIONS.

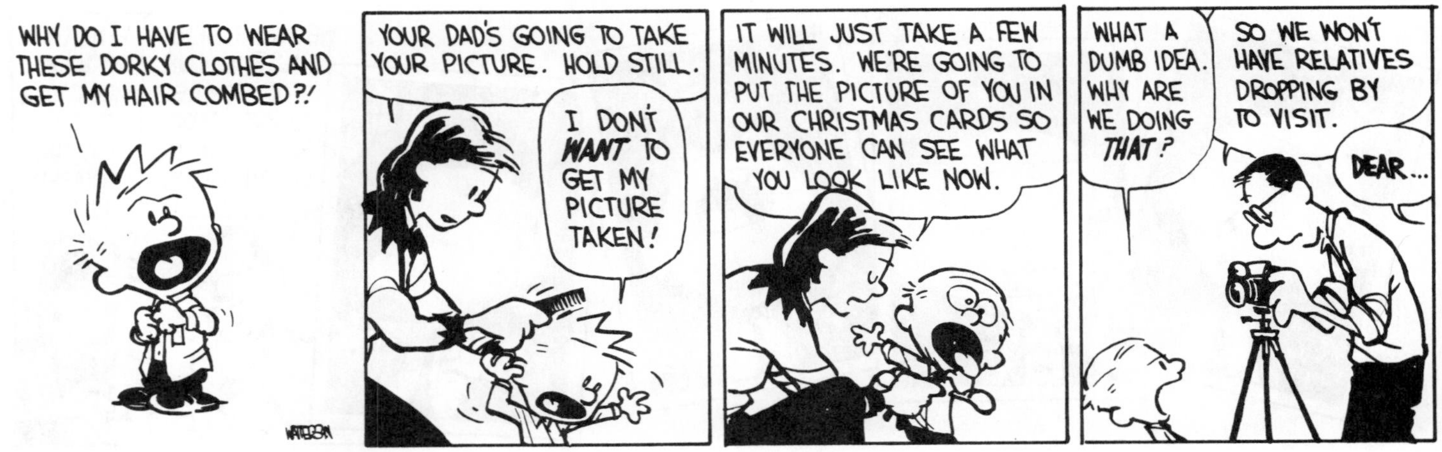
WHY DO I HAVE TO WEAR THESE DORKY CLOTHES AND GET MY HAIR COMBED?!
WATTERSON
YOUR DAD'S GOING TO TAKE YOUR PICTURE. HOLD STILL.
I DON'T *WANT* TO GET MY PICTURE TAKEN!
IT WILL JUST TAKE A FEW MINUTES. WE'RE GOING TO PUT THE PICTURE OF YOU IN OUR CHRISTMAS CARDS SO EVERYONE CAN SEE WHAT YOU LOOK LIKE NOW.
WHAT A DUMB IDEA. WHY ARE WE DOING *THAT*?
SO WE WON'T HAVE RELATIVES DROPPING BY TO VISIT.
DEAR...

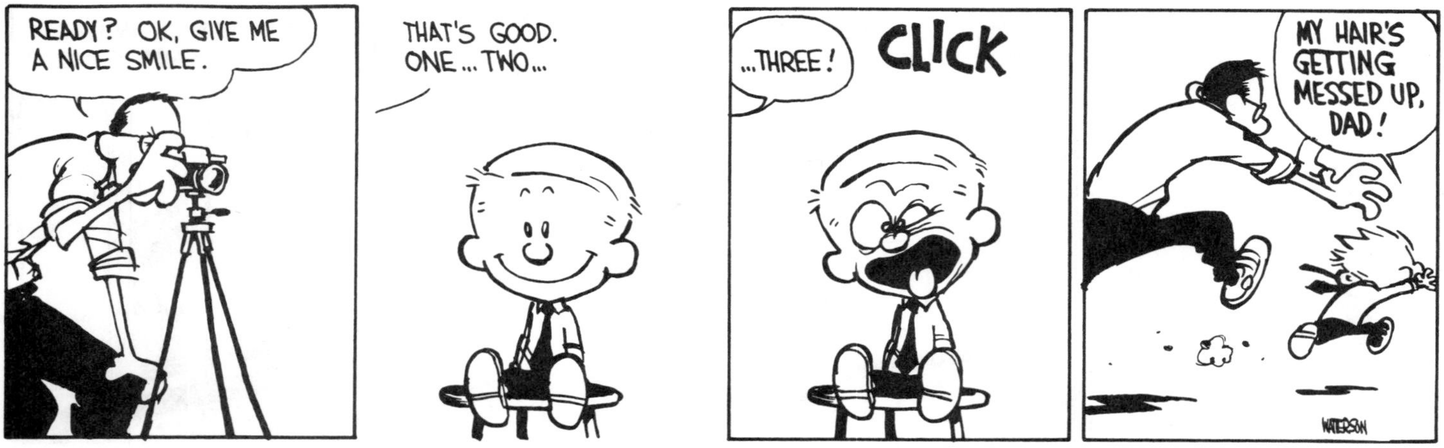
READY? OK, GIVE ME A NICE SMILE.
THAT'S GOOD. ONE... TWO...
...THREE!
CLICK
MY HAIR'S GETTING MESSED UP, DAD!

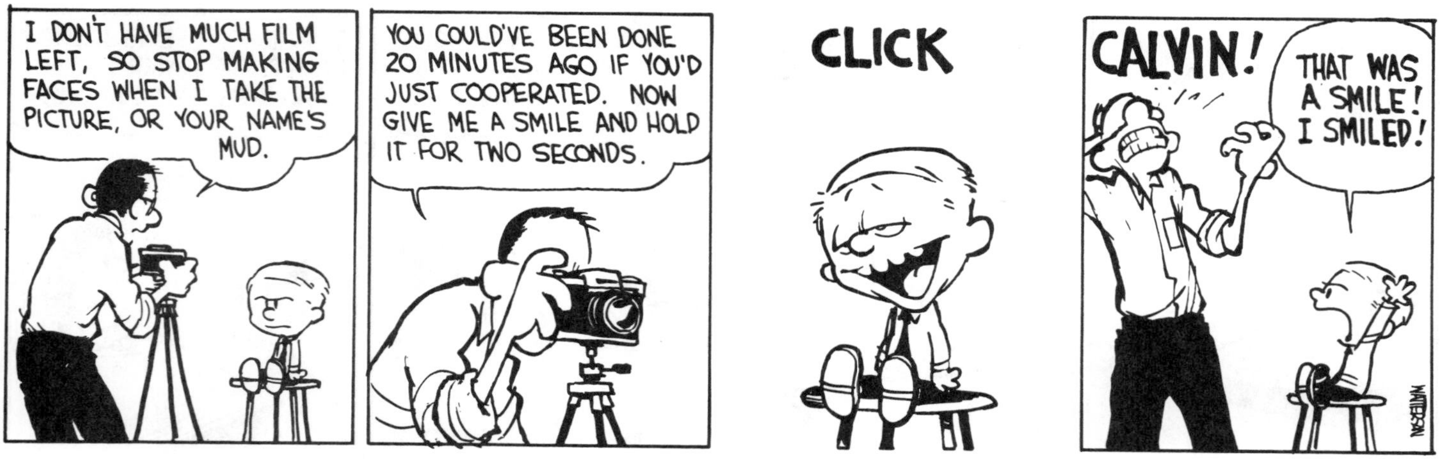
I DON'T HAVE MUCH FILM LEFT, SO STOP MAKING FACES WHEN I TAKE THE PICTURE, OR YOUR NAME'S MUD.
YOU COULD'VE BEEN DONE 20 MINUTES AGO IF YOU'D JUST COOPERATED. NOW GIVE ME A SMILE AND HOLD IT FOR TWO SECONDS.
CLICK
CALVIN!
THAT WAS A SMILE! I SMILED!

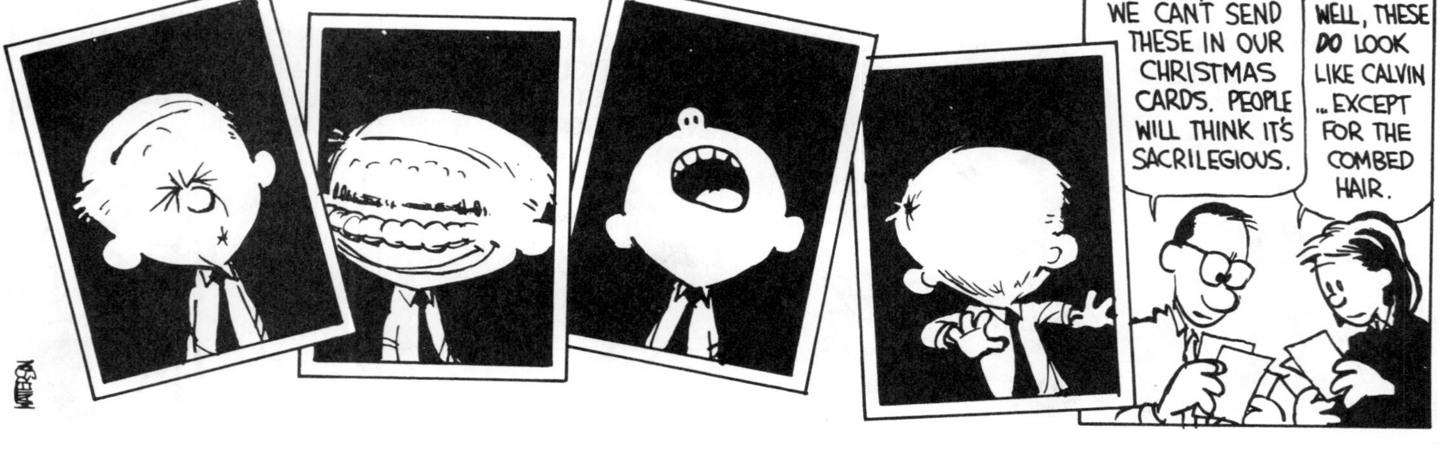
WE CAN'T SEND THESE IN OUR CHRISTMAS CARDS. PEOPLE WILL THINK IT'S SACRILEGIOUS.
WELL, THESE DO LOOK LIKE CALVIN ...EXCEPT FOR THE COMBED HAIR.

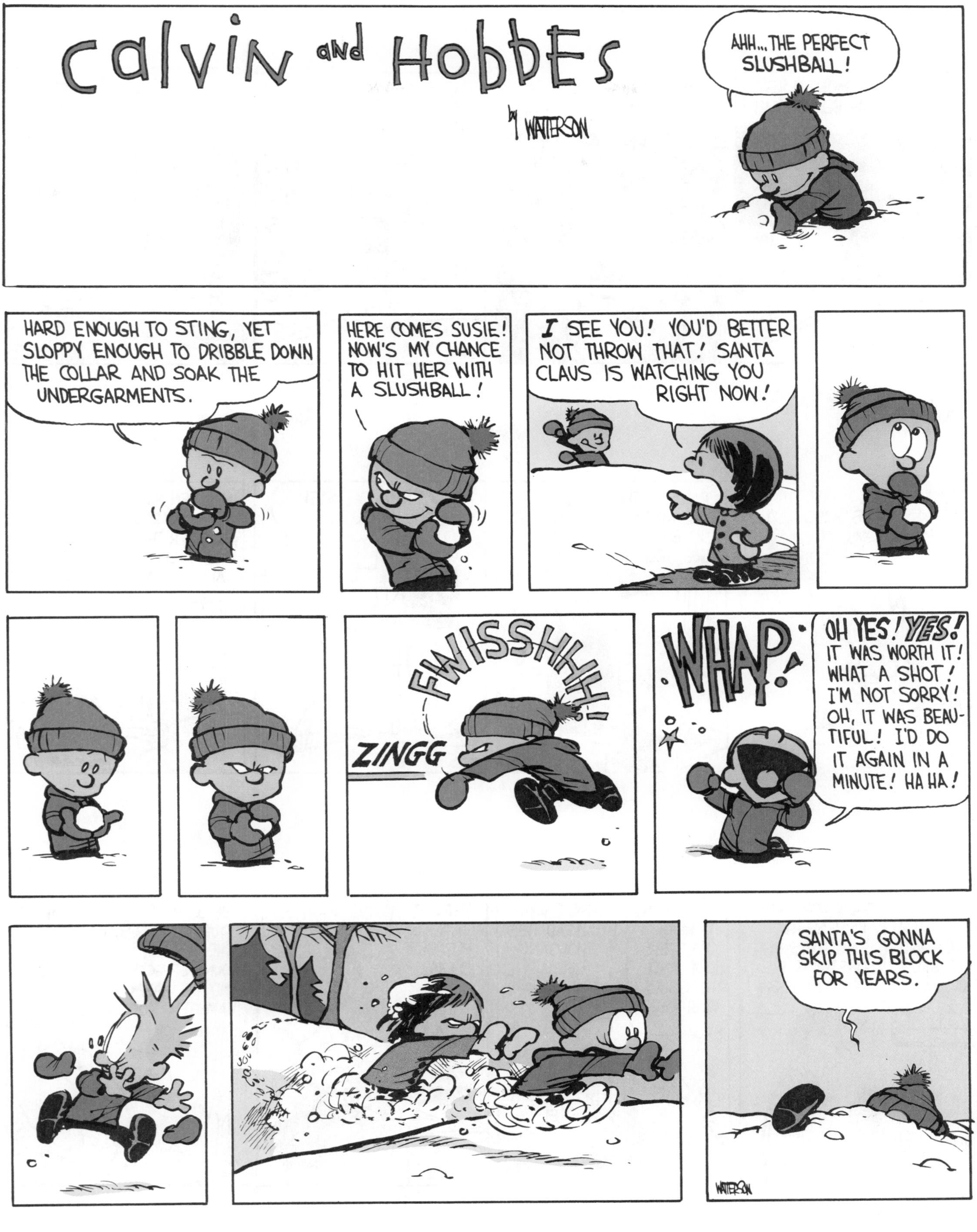

Calvin and Hobbes
by WATTERSON
AHH... THE PERFECT SLUSHBALL!
HARD ENOUGH TO STING, YET SLOPPY ENOUGH TO DRIBBLE DOWN THE COLLAR AND SOAK THE UNDERGARMENTS.
HERE COMES SUSIE! NOW'S MY CHANCE TO HIT HER WITH A SLUSHBALL!
I SEE YOU! YOU'D BETTER NOT THROW THAT! SANTA CLAUS IS WATCHING YOU RIGHT NOW!
FWISSHHH!
ZINGG
WHAP!
OH YES! YES! IT WAS WORTH IT! WHAT A SHOT! I'M NOT SORRY! OH, IT WAS BEAUTIFUL! I'D DO IT AGAIN IN A MINUTE! HA HA!
SANTA'S GONNA SKIP THIS BLOCK FOR YEARS.
WATTERSON

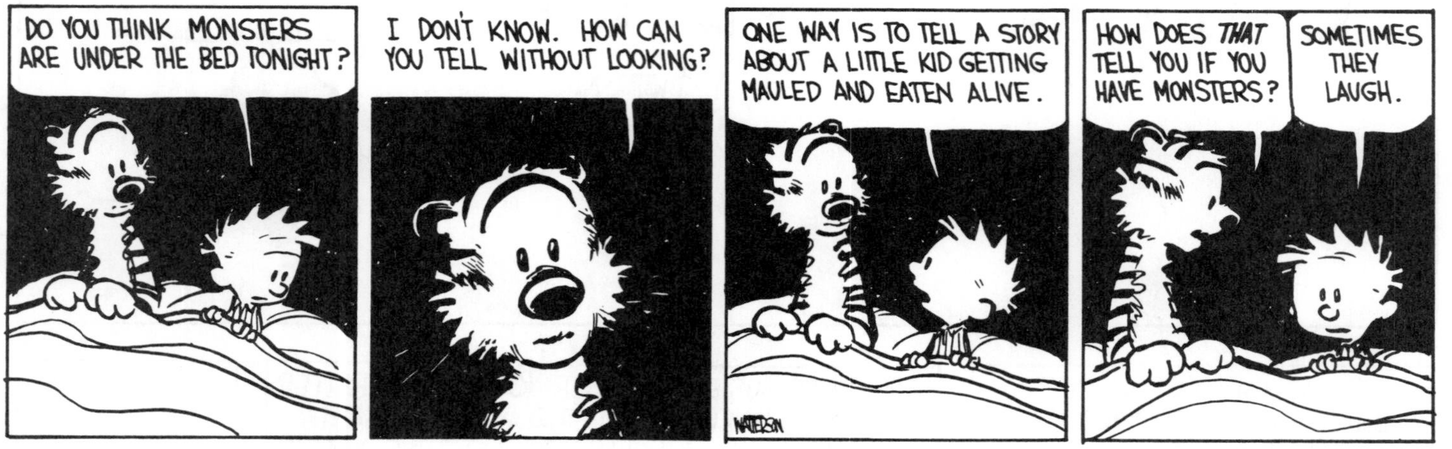
DO YOU THINK MONSTERS ARE UNDER THE BED TONIGHT?
I DON'T KNOW. HOW CAN YOU TELL WITHOUT LOOKING?
ONE WAY IS TO TELL A STORY ABOUT A LITTLE KID GETTING MAULED AND EATEN ALIVE.
HOW DOES *THAT* TELL YOU IF YOU HAVE MONSTERS?
SOMETIMES THEY LAUGH.

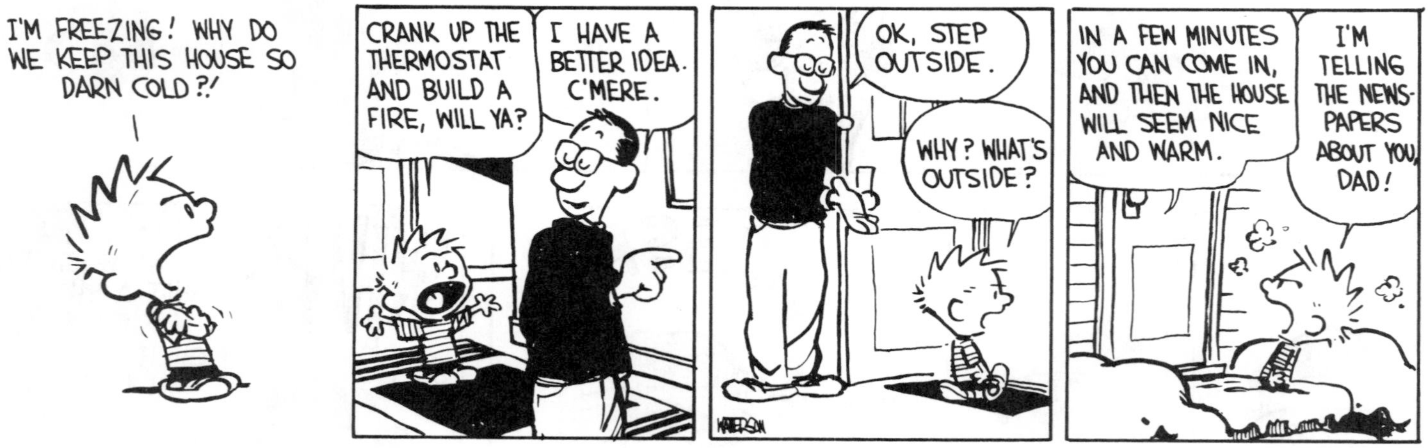
I'M FREEZING! WHY DO WE KEEP THIS HOUSE SO DARN COLD?!
CRANK UP THE THERMOSTAT AND BUILD A FIRE, WILL YA?
I HAVE A BETTER IDEA. C'MERE.
OK, STEP OUTSIDE.
WHY? WHAT'S OUTSIDE?
IN A FEW MINUTES YOU CAN COME IN, AND THEN THE HOUSE WILL SEEM NICE AND WARM.
I'M TELLING THE NEWSPAPERS ABOUT YOU, DAD!

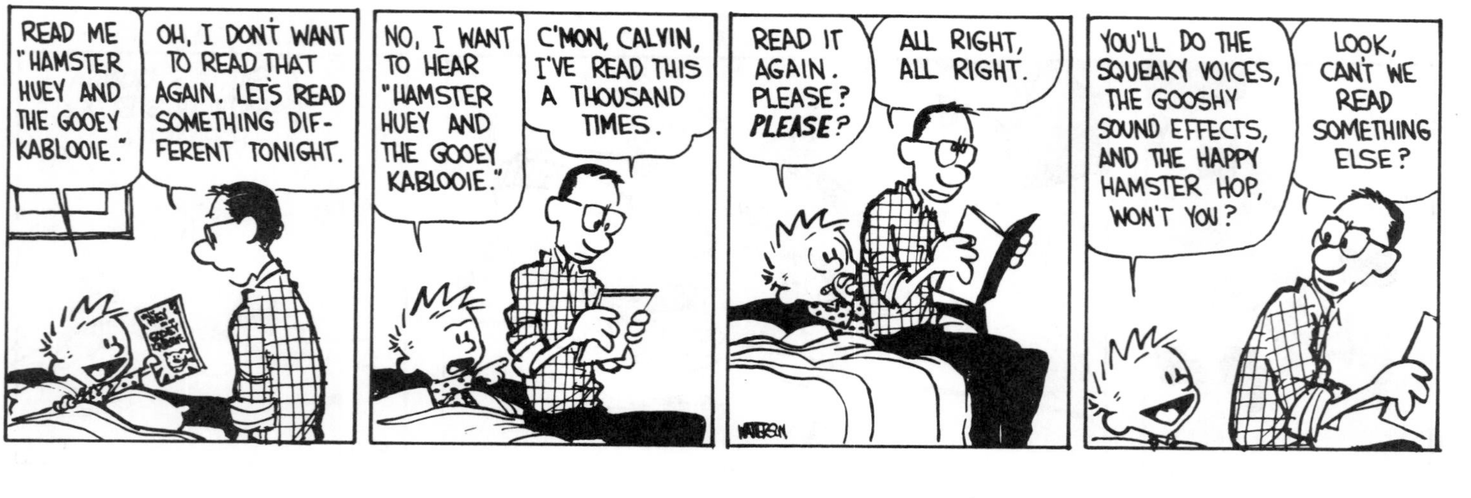
READ ME "HAMSTER HUEY AND THE GOOEY KABLOOIE."
OH, I DON'T WANT TO READ THAT AGAIN. LET'S READ SOMETHING DIFFERENT TONIGHT.
NO, I WANT TO HEAR "HAMSTER HUEY AND THE GOOEY KABLOOIE."
C'MON, CALVIN, I'VE READ THIS A THOUSAND TIMES.
READ IT AGAIN. PLEASE? *PLEASE*?
ALL RIGHT, ALL RIGHT.
YOU'LL DO THE SQUEAKY VOICES, THE GOOSHY SOUND EFFECTS, AND THE HAPPY HAMSTER HOP, WON'T YOU?
LOOK, CAN'T WE READ SOMETHING ELSE?

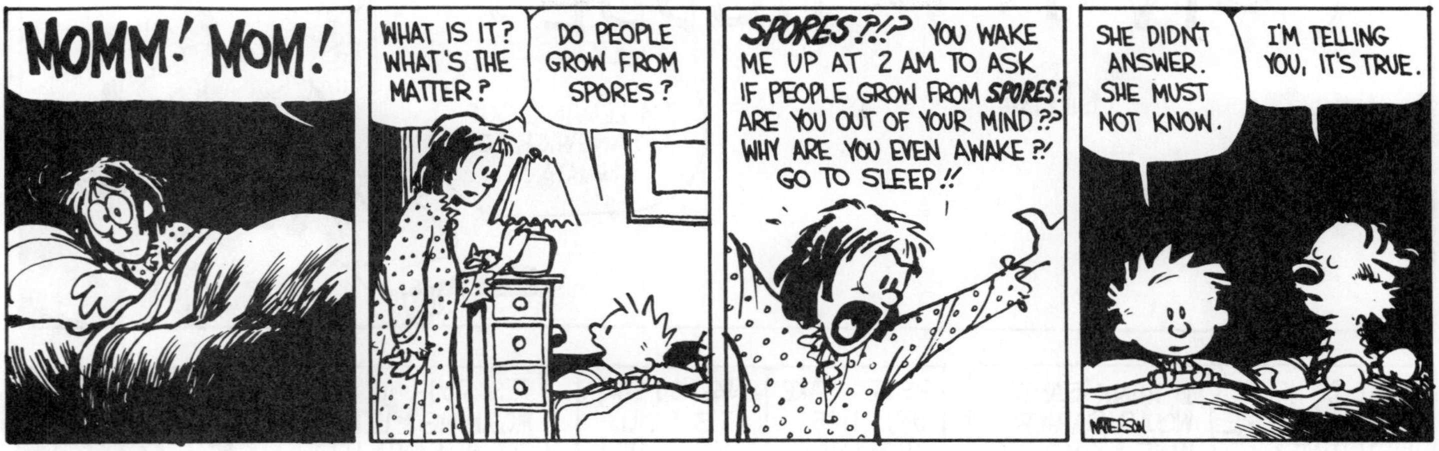
MOMM! MOM!
WHAT IS IT? WHAT'S THE MATTER?
DO PEOPLE GROW FROM SPORES?
SPORES?!? YOU WAKE ME UP AT 2 AM. TO ASK IF PEOPLE GROW FROM SPORES?! ARE YOU OUT OF YOUR MIND?!? WHY ARE YOU EVEN AWAKE?! GO TO SLEEP!!
SHE DIDN'T ANSWER. SHE MUST NOT KNOW.
I'M TELLING YOU, IT'S TRUE.

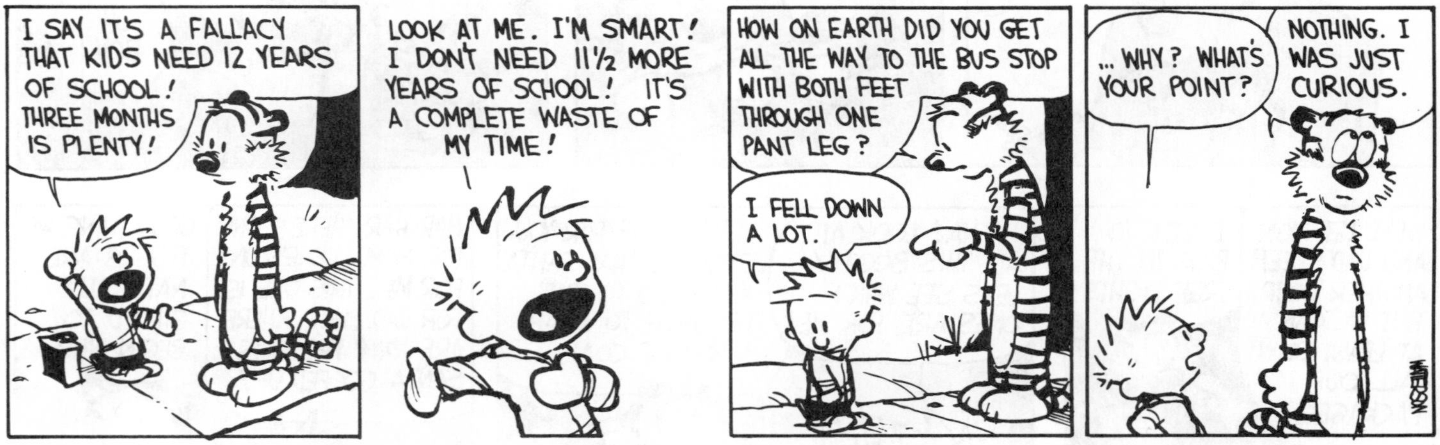
I SAY IT'S A FALLACY THAT KIDS NEED 12 YEARS OF SCHOOL! THREE MONTHS IS PLENTY!
LOOK AT ME. I'M SMART! I DON'T NEED 11½ MORE YEARS OF SCHOOL! IT'S A COMPLETE WASTE OF MY TIME!
HOW ON EARTH DID YOU GET ALL THE WAY TO THE BUS STOP WITH BOTH FEET THROUGH ONE PANT LEG?
I FELL DOWN A LOT.
... WHY? WHAT'S YOUR POINT?
NOTHING. I WAS JUST CURIOUS.

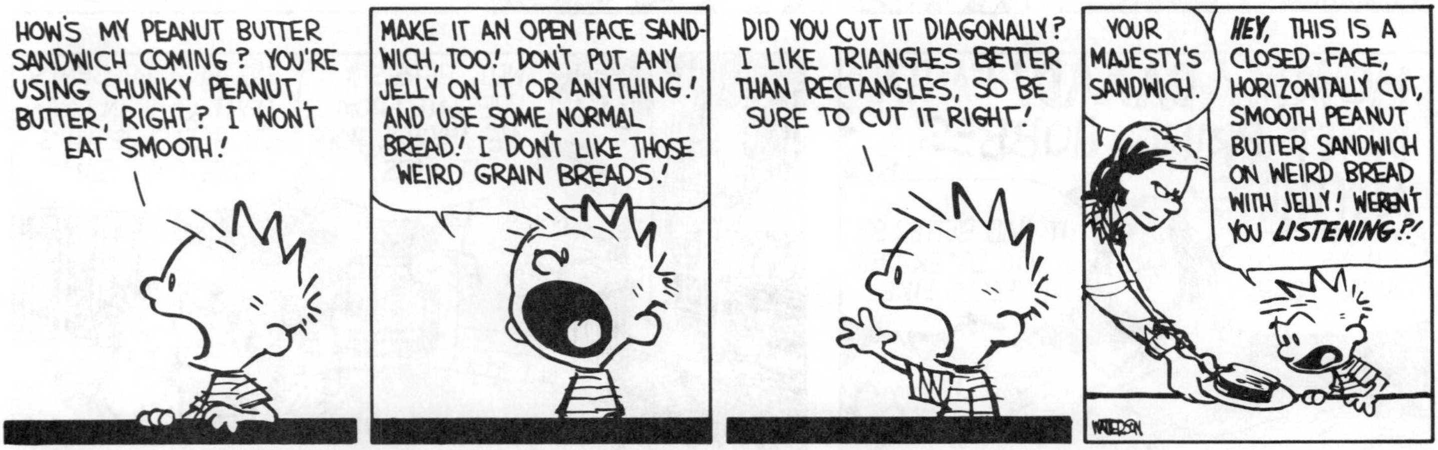
HOW'S MY PEANUT BUTTER SANDWICH COMING? YOU'RE USING CHUNKY PEANUT BUTTER, RIGHT? I WON'T EAT SMOOTH!
MAKE IT AN OPEN FACE SANDWICH, TOO! DON'T PUT ANY JELLY ON IT OR ANYTHING! AND USE SOME NORMAL BREAD! I DON'T LIKE THOSE WEIRD GRAIN BREADS!
DID YOU CUT IT DIAGONALLY? I LIKE TRIANGLES BETTER THAN RECTANGLES, SO BE SURE TO CUT IT RIGHT!
YOUR MAJESTY'S SANDWICH.
HEY, THIS IS A CLOSED-FACE, HORIZONTALLY CUT, SMOOTH PEANUT BUTTER SANDWICH ON WEIRD BREAD WITH JELLY! WEREN'T YOU LISTENING?!

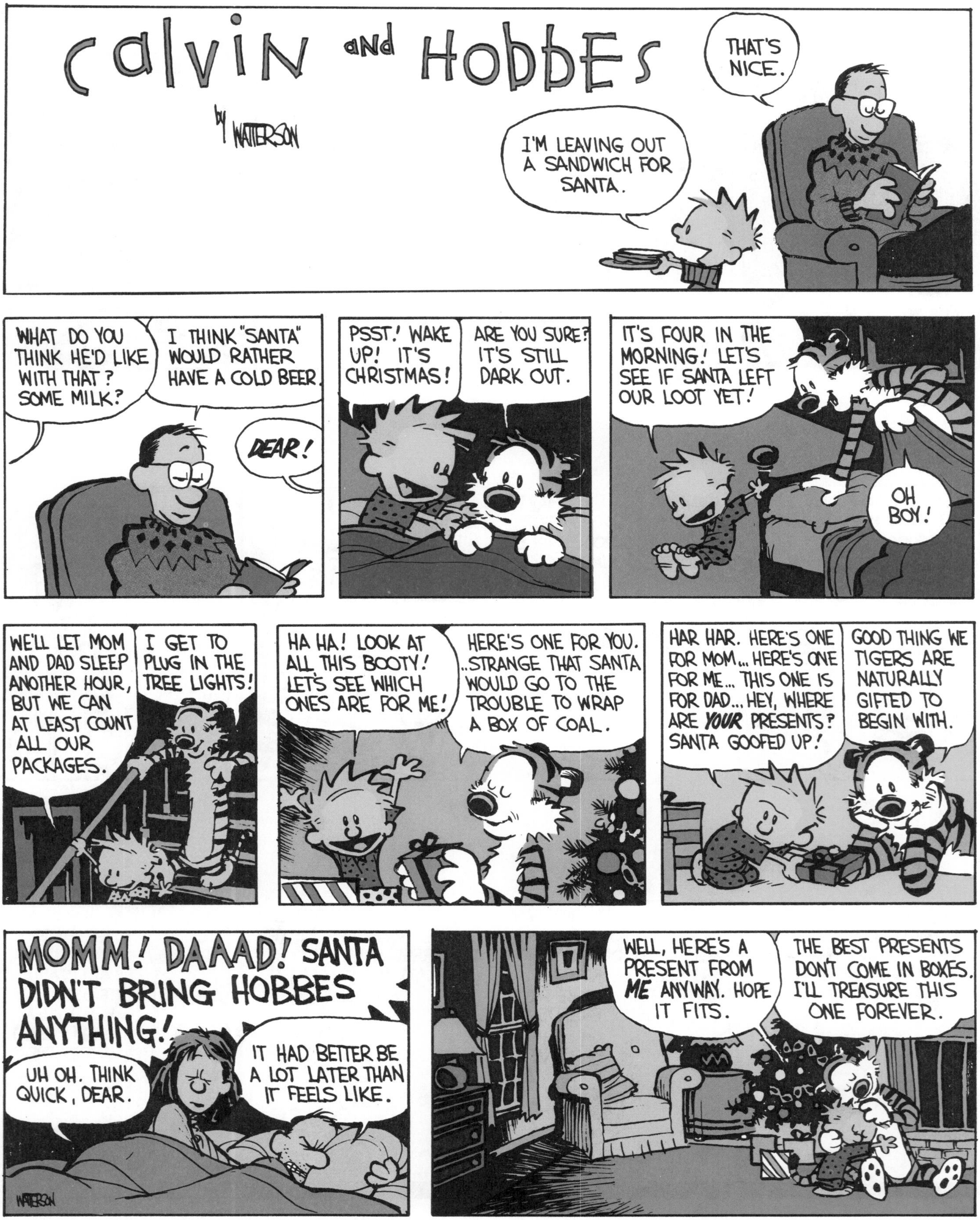
Calvin and Hobbes
by WATTERSON
I'M LEAVING OUT A SANDWICH FOR SANTA.
THAT'S NICE.
WHAT DO YOU THINK HE'D LIKE WITH THAT? SOME MILK?
I THINK "SANTA" WOULD RATHER HAVE A COLD BEER.
DEAR!
PSST! WAKE UP! IT'S CHRISTMAS!
ARE YOU SURE? IT'S STILL DARK OUT.
IT'S FOUR IN THE MORNING! LET'S SEE IF SANTA LEFT OUR LOOT YET!
OH BOY!
WE'LL LET MOM AND DAD SLEEP ANOTHER HOUR, BUT WE CAN AT LEAST COUNT ALL OUR PACKAGES.
I GET TO PLUG IN THE TREE LIGHTS!
HA HA! LOOK AT ALL THIS BOOTY! LET'S SEE WHICH ONES ARE FOR ME!
HERE'S ONE FOR YOU. ..STRANGE THAT SANTA WOULD GO TO THE TROUBLE TO WRAP A BOX OF COAL.
HAR HAR. HERE'S ONE FOR MOM... HERE'S ONE FOR ME... THIS ONE IS FOR DAD... HEY, WHERE ARE YOUR PRESENTS? SANTA GOOFED UP!
GOOD THING WE TIGERS ARE NATURALLY GIFTED TO BEGIN WITH.
MOMM! DAAAD! SANTA DIDN'T BRING HOBBES ANYTHING!
UH OH. THINK QUICK, DEAR.
IT HAD BETTER BE A LOT LATER THAN IT FEELS LIKE.
WATTERSON
WELL, HERE'S A PRESENT FROM ME ANYWAY. HOPE IT FITS.
THE BEST PRESENTS DON'T COME IN BOXES. I'LL TREASURE THIS ONE FOREVER.

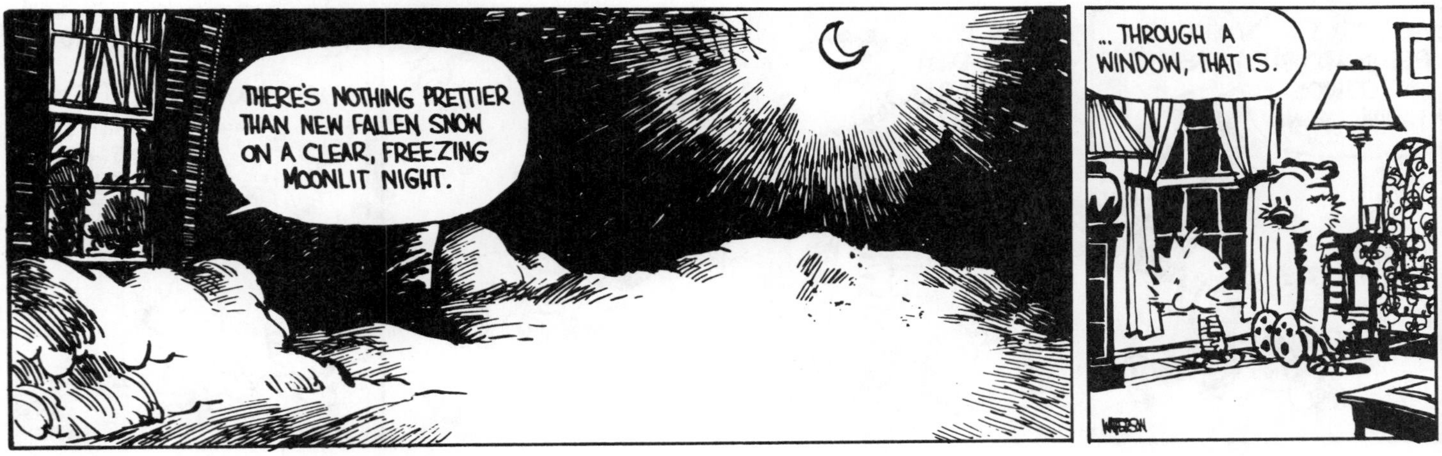
THERE'S NOTHING PRETTIER THAN NEW FALLEN SNOW ON A CLEAR, FREEZING MOONLIT NIGHT.
... THROUGH A WINDOW, THAT IS.

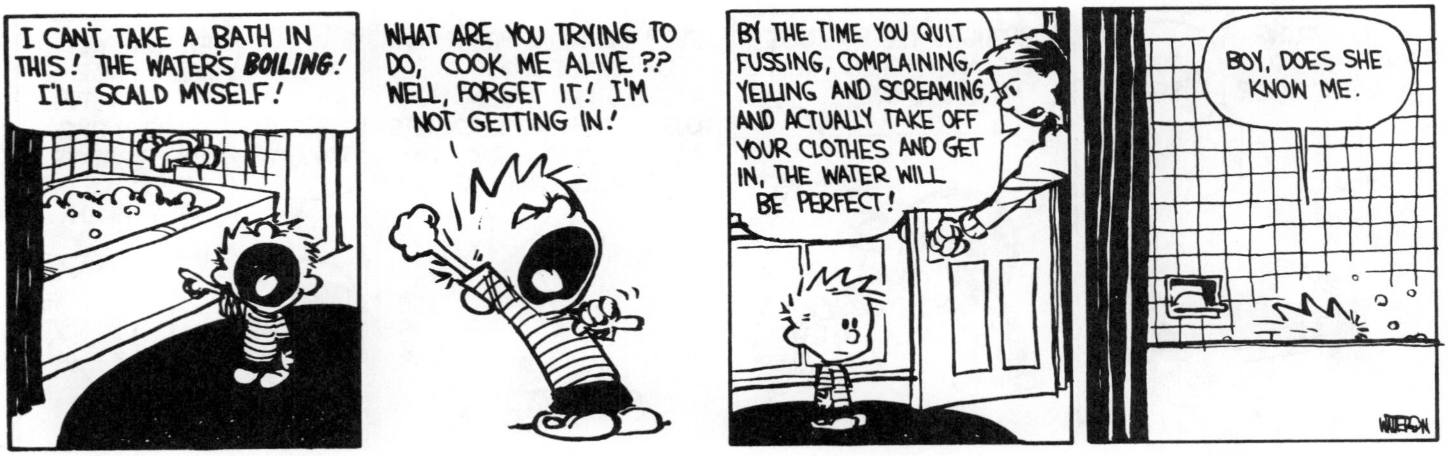
I CAN'T TAKE A BATH IN THIS! THE WATER'S BOILING! I'LL SCALD MYSELF!
WHAT ARE YOU TRYING TO DO, COOK ME ALIVE?? WELL, FORGET IT! I'M NOT GETTING IN!
BY THE TIME YOU QUIT FUSSING, COMPLAINING, YELLING AND SCREAMING, AND ACTUALLY TAKE OFF YOUR CLOTHES AND GET IN, THE WATER WILL BE PERFECT!
BOY, DOES SHE KNOW ME.

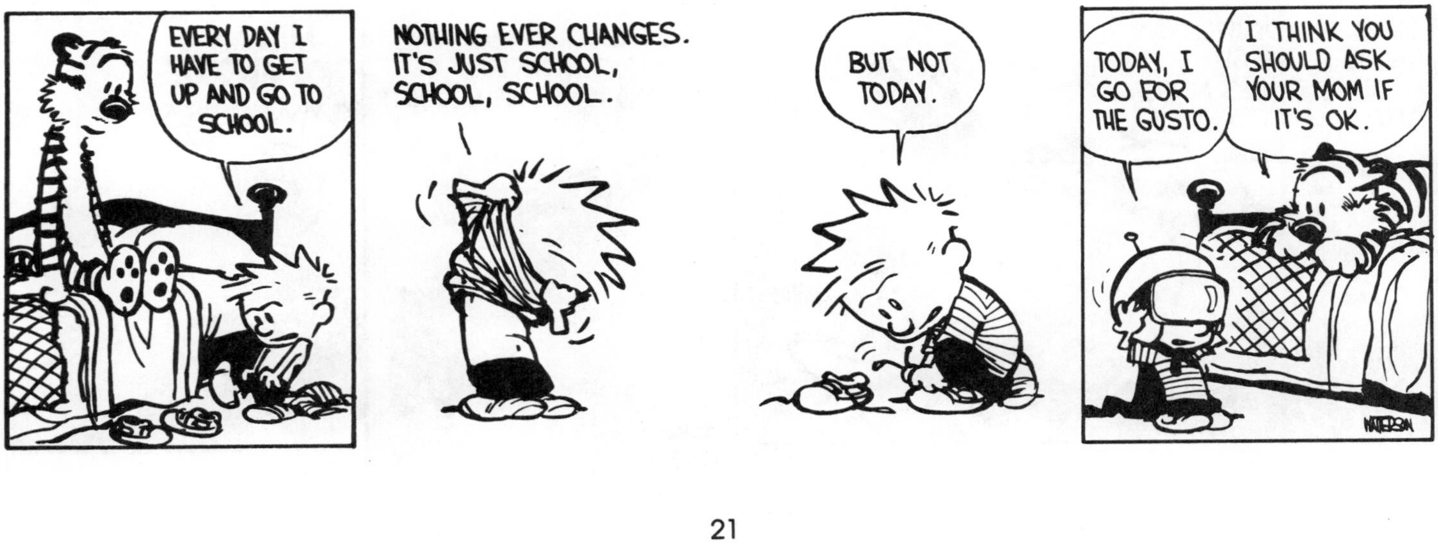
EVERY DAY I HAVE TO GET UP AND GO TO SCHOOL.
NOTHING EVER CHANGES. IT'S JUST SCHOOL, SCHOOL, SCHOOL.
BUT NOT TODAY.
TODAY, I GO FOR THE GUSTO.
I THINK YOU SHOULD ASK YOUR MOM IF IT'S OK.

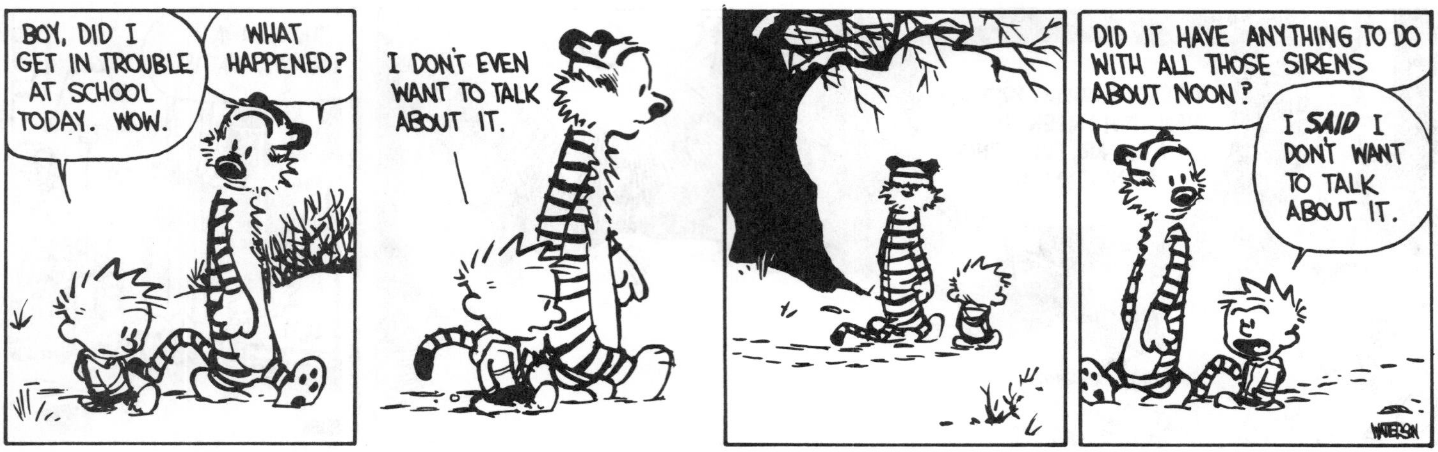
BOY, DID I GET IN TROUBLE AT SCHOOL TODAY. WOW.
WHAT HAPPENED?
I DON'T EVEN WANT TO TALK ABOUT IT.
DID IT HAVE ANYTHING TO DO WITH ALL THOSE SIRENS ABOUT NOON?
I **SAID** I DON'T WANT TO TALK ABOUT IT.
WATERSON

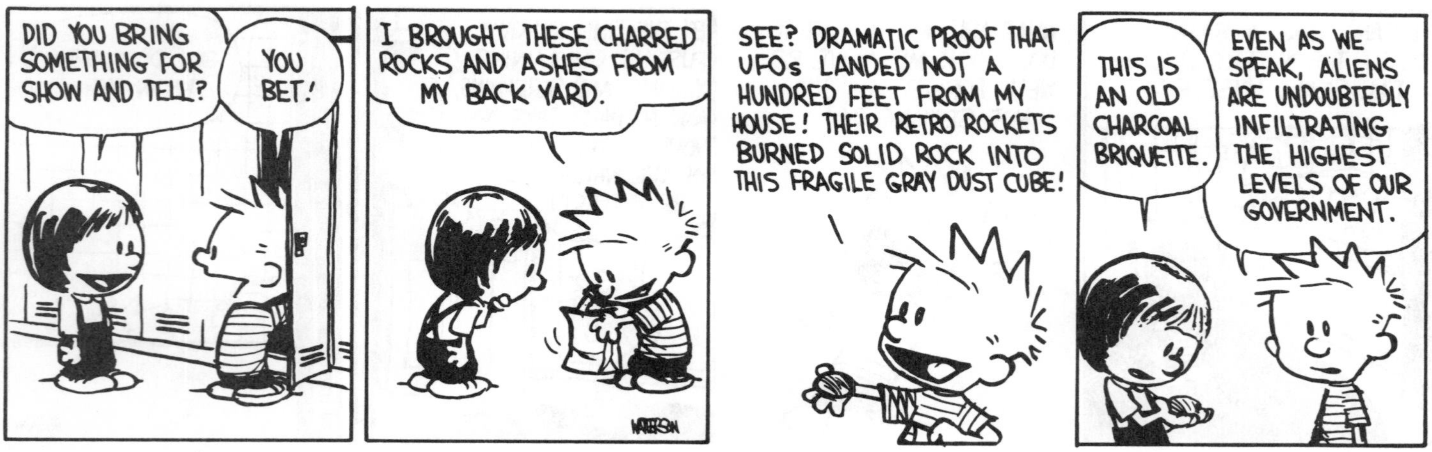
DID YOU BRING SOMETHING FOR SHOW AND TELL?
YOU BET!
I BROUGHT THESE CHARRED ROCKS AND ASHES FROM MY BACK YARD.
WATERSON
SEE? DRAMATIC PROOF THAT UFOs LANDED NOT A HUNDRED FEET FROM MY HOUSE! THEIR RETRO ROCKETS BURNED SOLID ROCK INTO THIS FRAGILE GRAY DUST CUBE!
THIS IS AN OLD CHARCOAL BRIQUETTE.
EVEN AS WE SPEAK, ALIENS ARE UNDOUBTEDLY INFILTRATING THE HIGHEST LEVELS OF OUR GOVERNMENT.

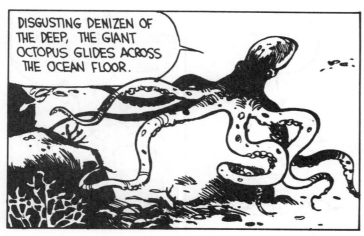

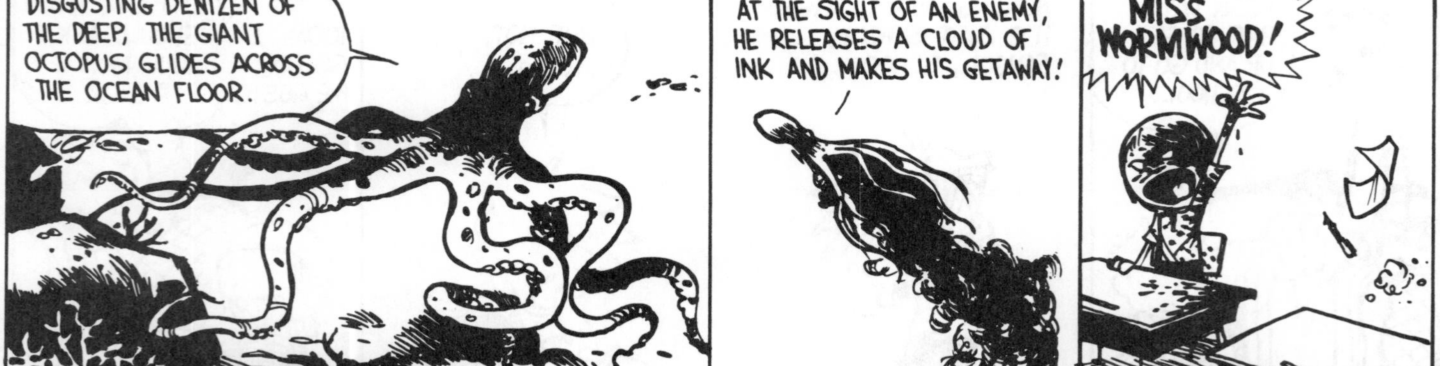
DISGUSTING DENIZEN OF THE DEEP, THE GIANT OCTOPUS GLIDES ACROSS THE OCEAN FLOOR.
WATERSON
AT THE SIGHT OF AN ENEMY, HE RELEASES A CLOUD OF INK AND MAKES HIS GETAWAY!
MISS WORMWOOD!

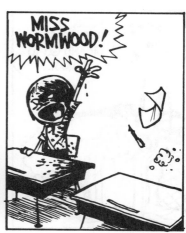

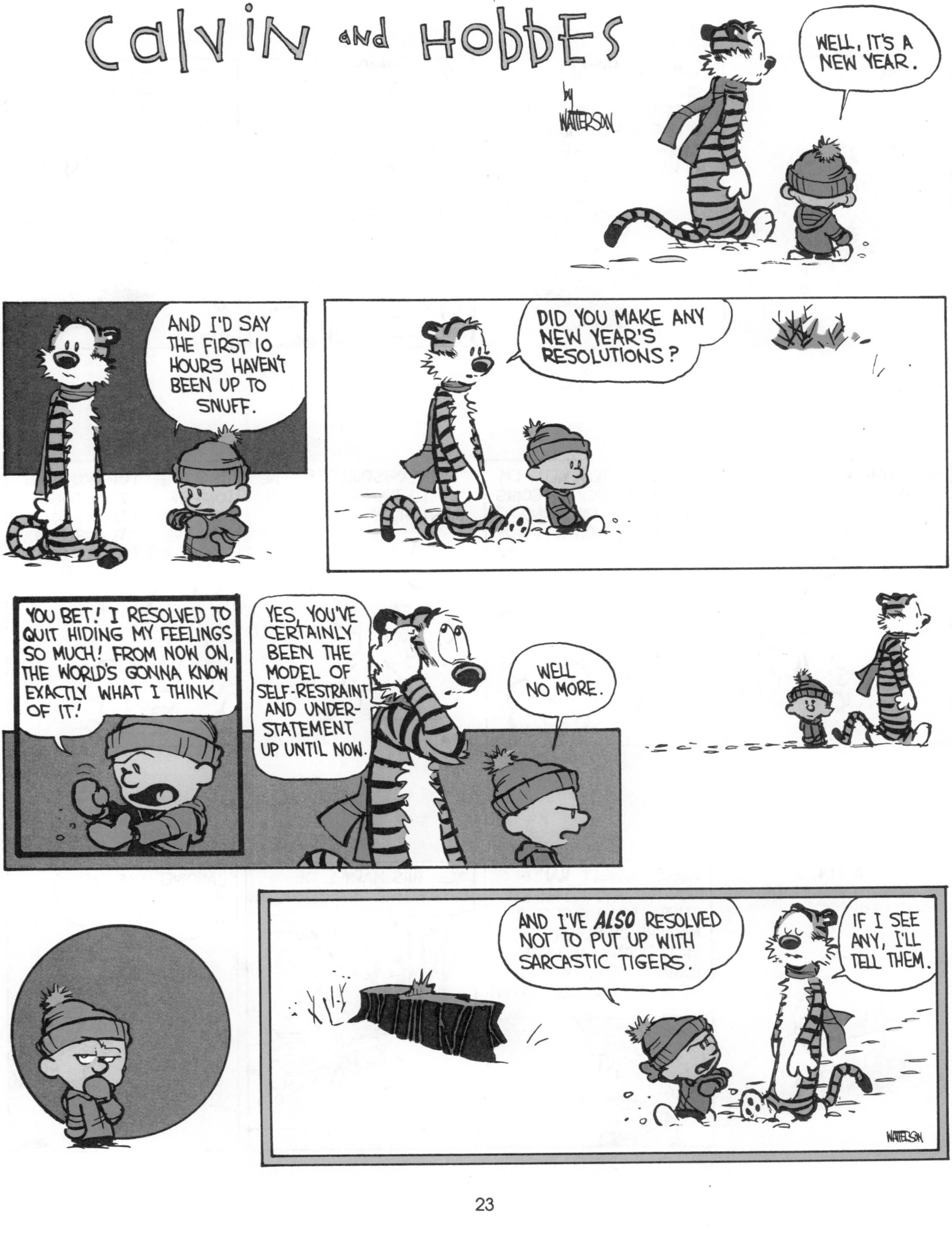
Calvin and Hobbes
by WATTERSON
WELL, IT'S A NEW YEAR.
AND I'D SAY THE FIRST 10 HOURS HAVEN'T BEEN UP TO SNUFF.
DID YOU MAKE ANY NEW YEAR'S RESOLUTIONS?
YOU BET! I RESOLVED TO QUIT HIDING MY FEELINGS SO MUCH! FROM NOW ON, THE WORLD'S GONNA KNOW EXACTLY WHAT I THINK OF IT!
YES, YOU'VE CERTAINLY BEEN THE MODEL OF SELF-RESTRAINT AND UNDERSTATEMENT UP UNTIL NOW.
WELL NO MORE.
AND I'VE ALSO RESOLVED NOT TO PUT UP WITH SARCASTIC TIGERS.
IF I SEE ANY, I'LL TELL THEM.
WATTERSON

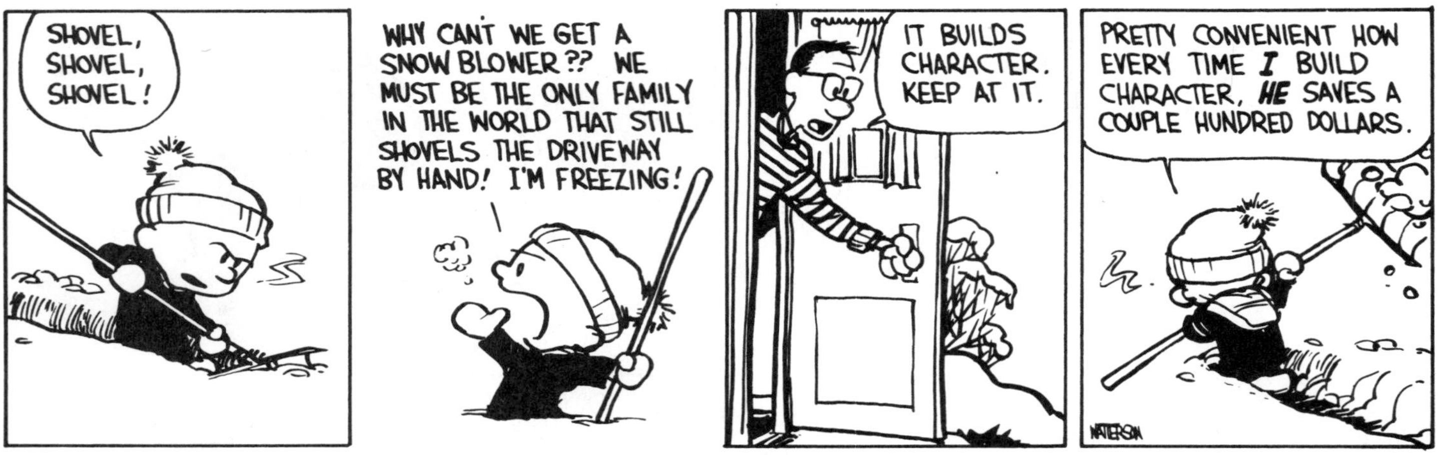
SHOVEL, SHOVEL, SHOVEL!
WHY CAN'T WE GET A SNOW BLOWER?? WE MUST BE THE ONLY FAMILY IN THE WORLD THAT STILL SHOVELS THE DRIVEWAY BY HAND! I'M FREEZING!
IT BUILDS CHARACTER. KEEP AT IT.
PRETTY CONVENIENT HOW EVERY TIME *I* BUILD CHARACTER, ***HE*** SAVES A COUPLE HUNDRED DOLLARS.
WATERSON

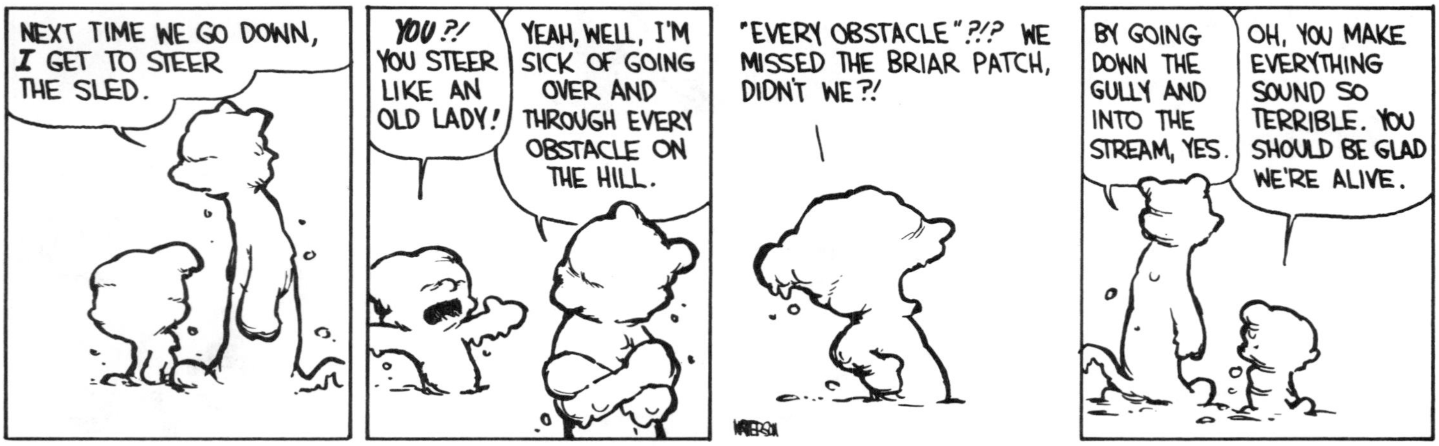
NEXT TIME WE GO DOWN, *I* GET TO STEER THE SLED.
YOU?! YOU STEER LIKE AN OLD LADY!
YEAH, WELL, I'M SICK OF GOING OVER AND THROUGH EVERY OBSTACLE ON THE HILL.
"EVERY OBSTACLE"?!? WE MISSED THE BRIAR PATCH, DIDN'T WE?!
WATERSON
BY GOING DOWN THE GULLY AND INTO THE STREAM, YES.
OH, YOU MAKE EVERYTHING SOUND SO TERRIBLE. YOU SHOULD BE GLAD WE'RE ALIVE.

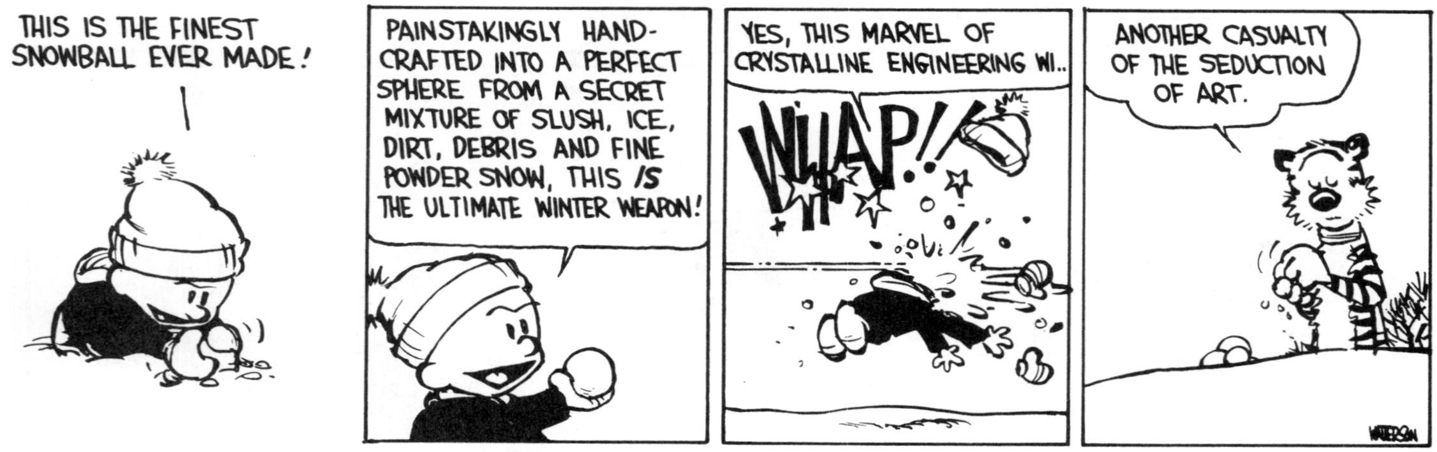
THIS IS THE FINEST SNOWBALL EVER MADE!
PAINSTAKINGLY HAND-CRAFTED INTO A PERFECT SPHERE FROM A SECRET MIXTURE OF SLUSH, ICE, DIRT, DEBRIS AND FINE POWDER SNOW, THIS *IS* THE ULTIMATE WINTER WEAPON!
YES, THIS MARVEL OF CRYSTALLINE ENGINEERING WI..
WHAP!!
ANOTHER CASUALTY OF THE SEDUCTION OF ART.
WATERSON

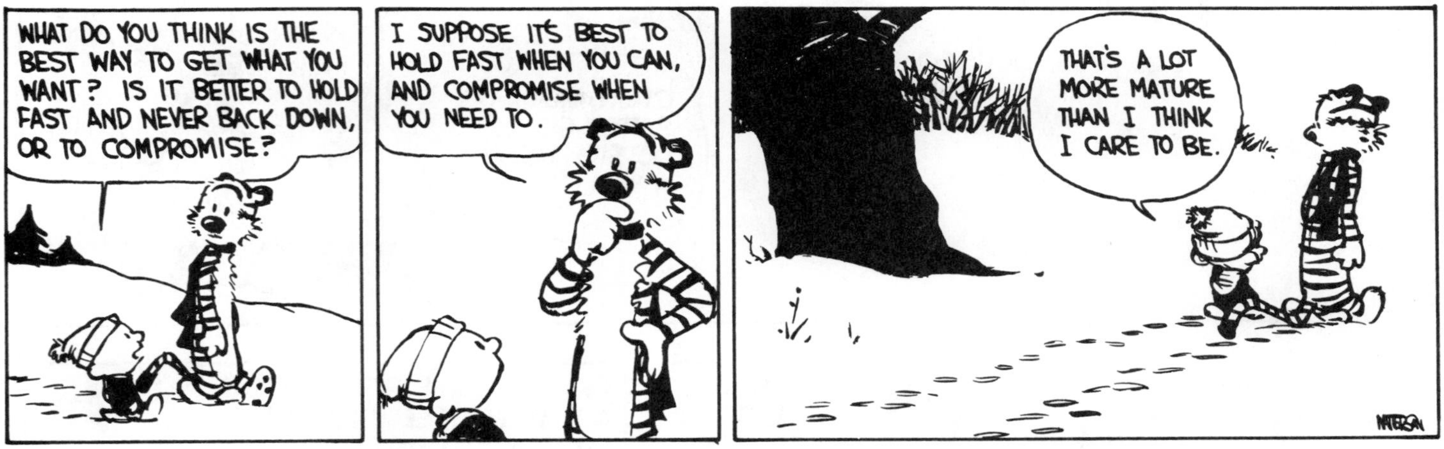
WHAT DO YOU THINK IS THE BEST WAY TO GET WHAT YOU WANT? IS IT BETTER TO HOLD FAST AND NEVER BACK DOWN, OR TO COMPROMISE?
I SUPPOSE IT'S BEST TO HOLD FAST WHEN YOU CAN, AND COMPROMISE WHEN YOU NEED TO.
THAT'S A LOT MORE MATURE THAN I THINK I CARE TO BE.

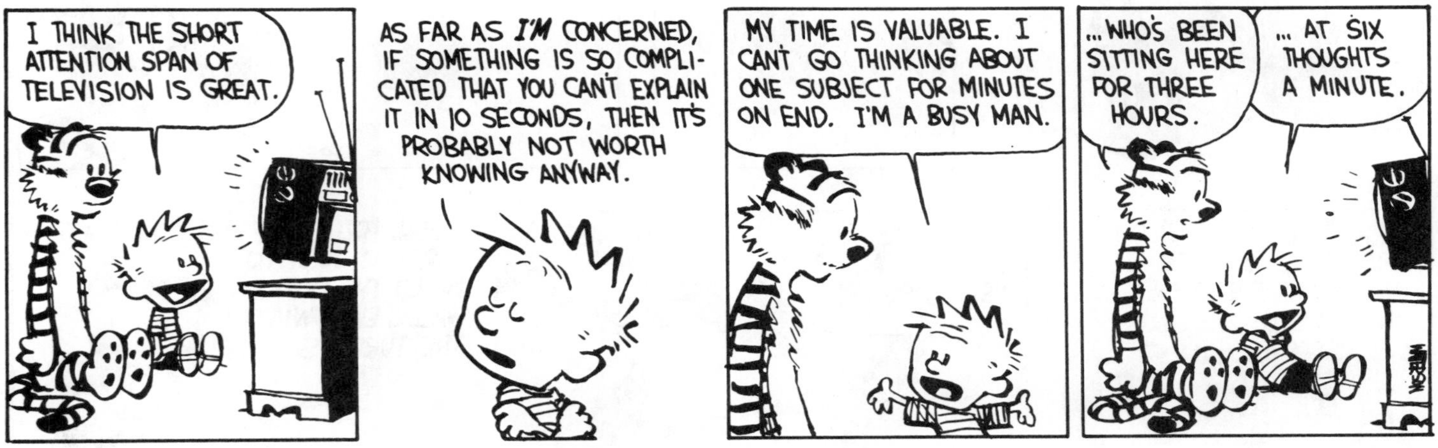
I THINK THE SHORT ATTENTION SPAN OF TELEVISION IS GREAT.
AS FAR AS *I'M* CONCERNED, IF SOMETHING IS SO COMPLICATED THAT YOU CAN'T EXPLAIN IT IN 10 SECONDS, THEN IT'S PROBABLY NOT WORTH KNOWING ANYWAY.
MY TIME IS VALUABLE. I CAN'T GO THINKING ABOUT ONE SUBJECT FOR MINUTES ON END. I'M A BUSY MAN.
...WHO'S BEEN SITTING HERE FOR THREE HOURS.
... AT SIX THOUGHTS A MINUTE.

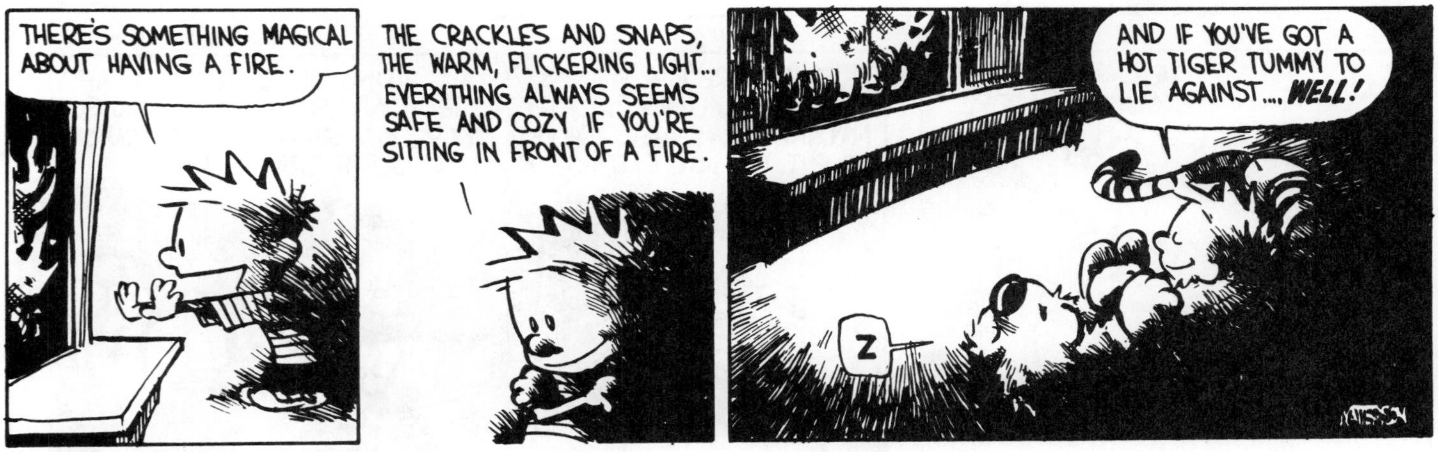
THERE'S SOMETHING MAGICAL ABOUT HAVING A FIRE.
THE CRACKLES AND SNAPS, THE WARM, FLICKERING LIGHT... EVERYTHING ALWAYS SEEMS SAFE AND COZY IF YOU'RE SITTING IN FRONT OF A FIRE.
AND IF YOU'VE GOT A HOT TIGER TUMMY TO LIE AGAINST..., **WELL!**
Z

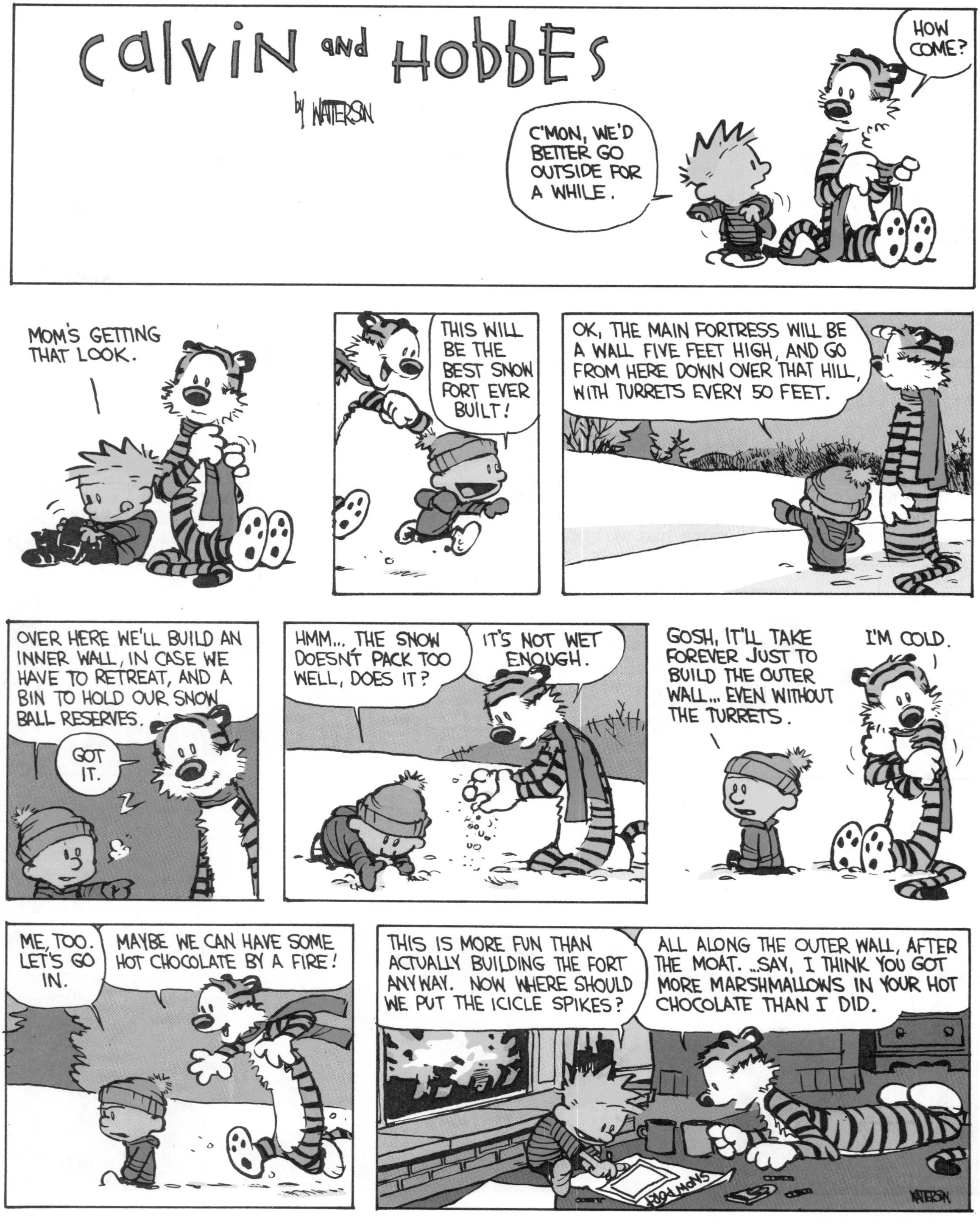

Calvin and Hobbes
by WATTERSON
C'MON, WE'D BETTER GO OUTSIDE FOR A WHILE.
HOW COME?
MOM'S GETTING THAT LOOK.
THIS WILL BE THE BEST SNOW FORT EVER BUILT!
OK, THE MAIN FORTRESS WILL BE A WALL FIVE FEET HIGH, AND GO FROM HERE DOWN OVER THAT HILL, WITH TURRETS EVERY 50 FEET.
OVER HERE WE'LL BUILD AN INNER WALL, IN CASE WE HAVE TO RETREAT, AND A BIN TO HOLD OUR SNOW BALL RESERVES.
GOT IT.
HMM... THE SNOW DOESN'T PACK TOO WELL, DOES IT?
IT'S NOT WET ENOUGH.
GOSH, IT'LL TAKE FOREVER JUST TO BUILD THE OUTER WALL... EVEN WITHOUT THE TURRETS.
I'M COLD.
ME, TOO. LET'S GO IN.
MAYBE WE CAN HAVE SOME HOT CHOCOLATE BY A FIRE!
THIS IS MORE FUN THAN ACTUALLY BUILDING THE FORT ANYWAY. NOW WHERE SHOULD WE PUT THE ICICLE SPIKES?
ALL ALONG THE OUTER WALL, AFTER THE MOAT. ...SAY, I THINK YOU GOT MORE MARSHMALLOWS IN YOUR HOT CHOCOLATE THAN I DID.
SNOW FORT
WATTERSON

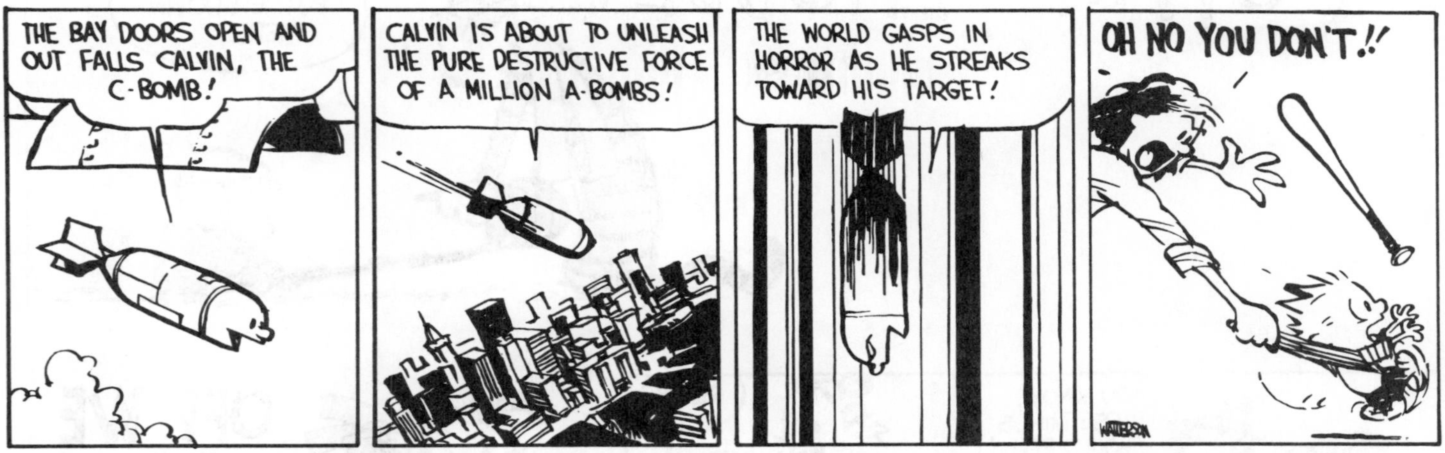
THE BAY DOORS OPEN AND OUT FALLS CALVIN, THE C-BOMB!
CALVIN IS ABOUT TO UNLEASH THE PURE DESTRUCTIVE FORCE OF A MILLION A-BOMBS!
THE WORLD GASPS IN HORROR AS HE STREAKS TOWARD HIS TARGET!
OH NO YOU DON'T.!!

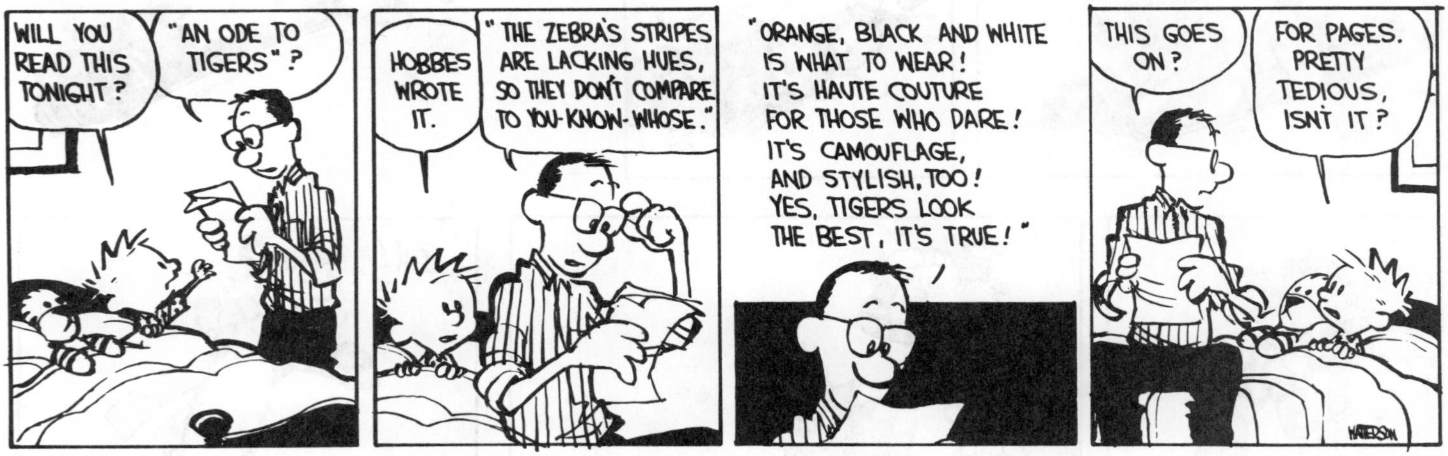
WILL YOU READ THIS TONIGHT?
"AN ODE TO TIGERS"?
HOBBES WROTE IT.
"THE ZEBRA'S STRIPES ARE LACKING HUES, SO THEY DON'T COMPARE TO YOU-KNOW-WHOSE."
"ORANGE, BLACK AND WHITE IS WHAT TO WEAR! IT'S HAUTE COUTURE FOR THOSE WHO DARE! IT'S CAMOUFLAGE, AND STYLISH, TOO! YES, TIGERS LOOK THE BEST, IT'S TRUE!"
THIS GOES ON?
FOR PAGES. PRETTY TEDIOUS, ISN'T IT?

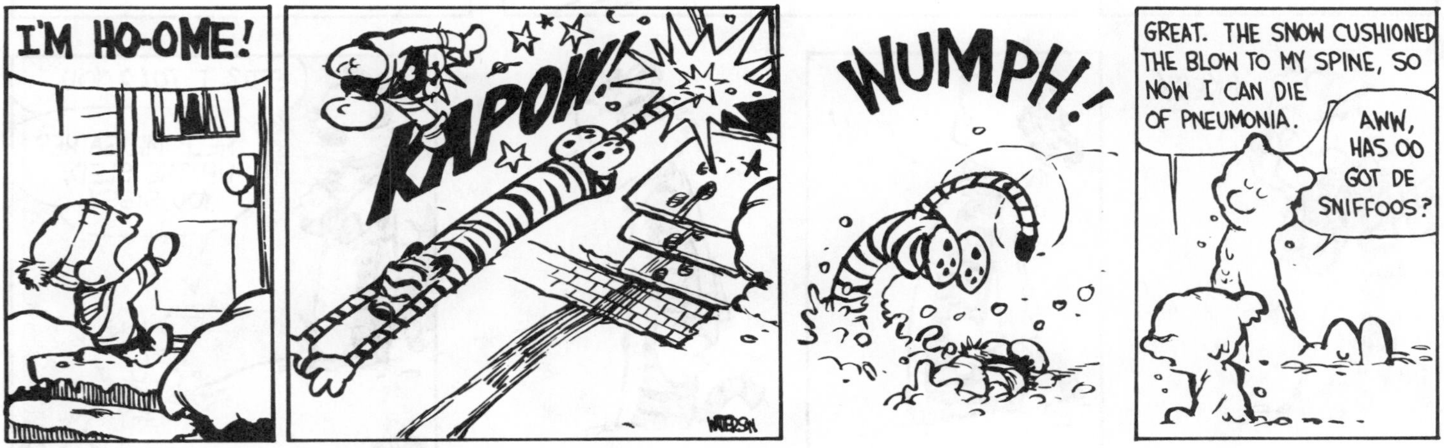
I'M HO-OME!
KAPOW!
WUMPH!
GREAT. THE SNOW CUSHIONED THE BLOW TO MY SPINE, SO NOW I CAN DIE OF PNEUMONIA.
AWW, HAS OO GOT DE SNIFFOOS?

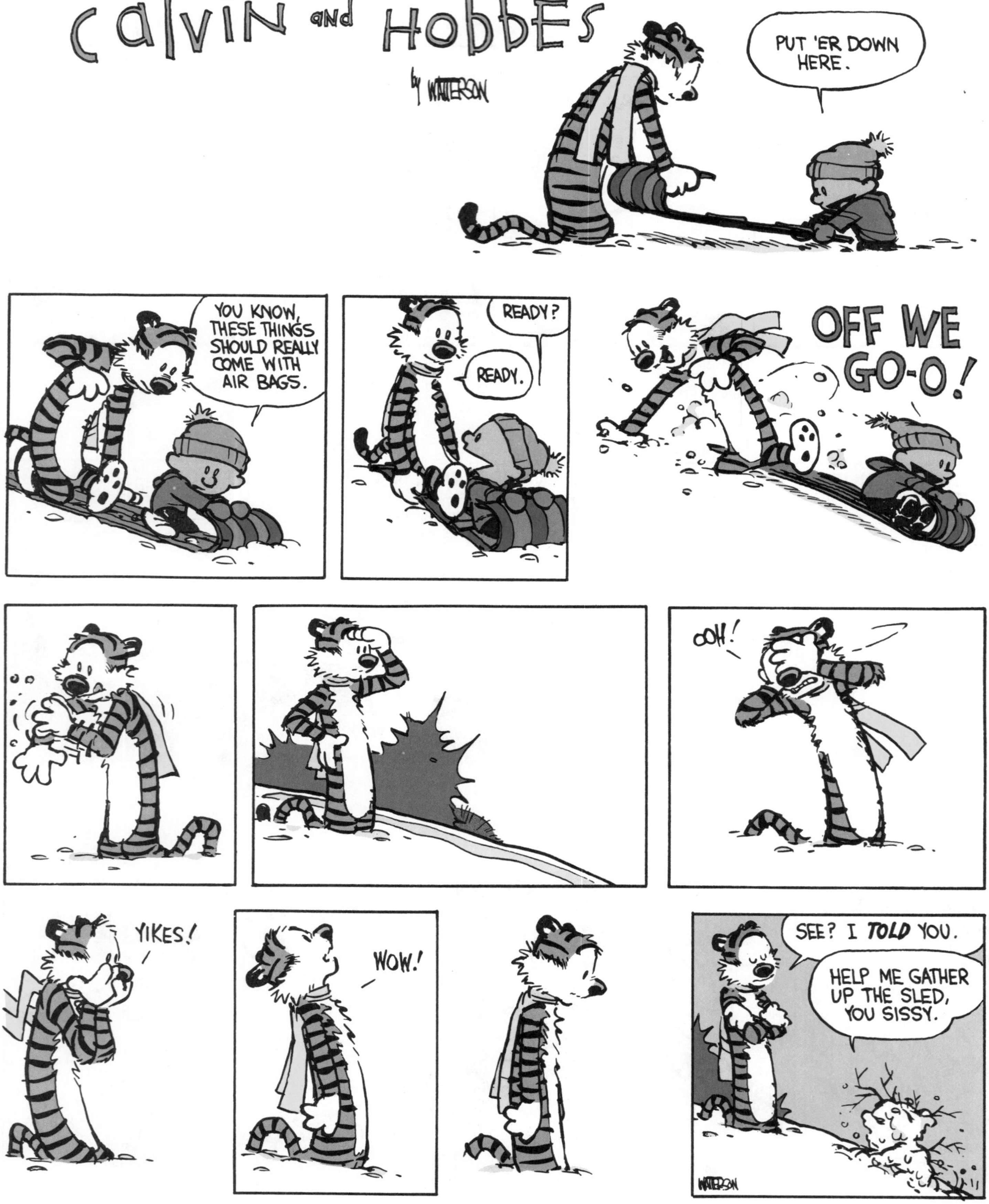
Calvin and Hobbes
by WATTERSON
PUT 'ER DOWN HERE.
YOU KNOW, THESE THINGS SHOULD REALLY COME WITH AIR BAGS.
READY?
READY.
OFF WE GO-O!
OOH!
YIKES!
WOW!
SEE? I TOLD YOU.
HELP ME GATHER UP THE SLED, YOU SISSY.
WATTERSON

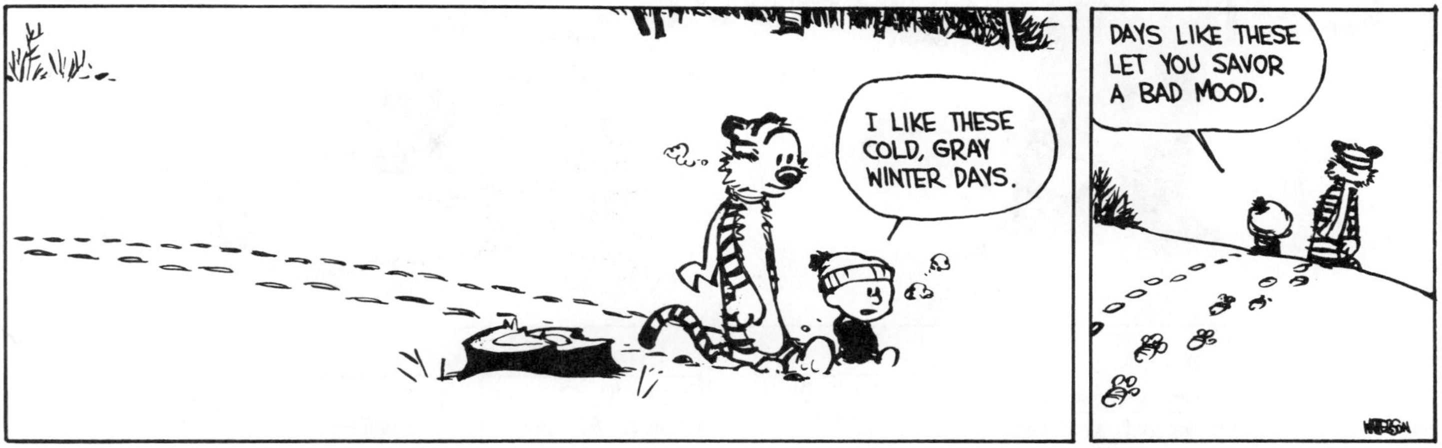
I LIKE THESE COLD, GRAY WINTER DAYS.
DAYS LIKE THESE LET YOU SAVOR A BAD MOOD.
WATTERSON

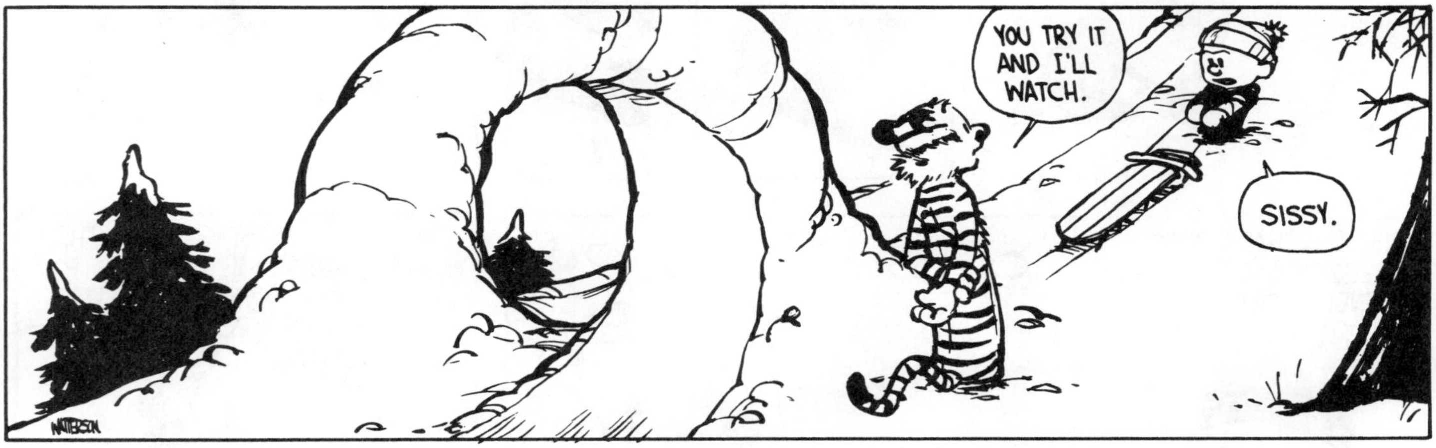
YOU TRY IT AND I'LL WATCH.
SISSY.
WATTERSON

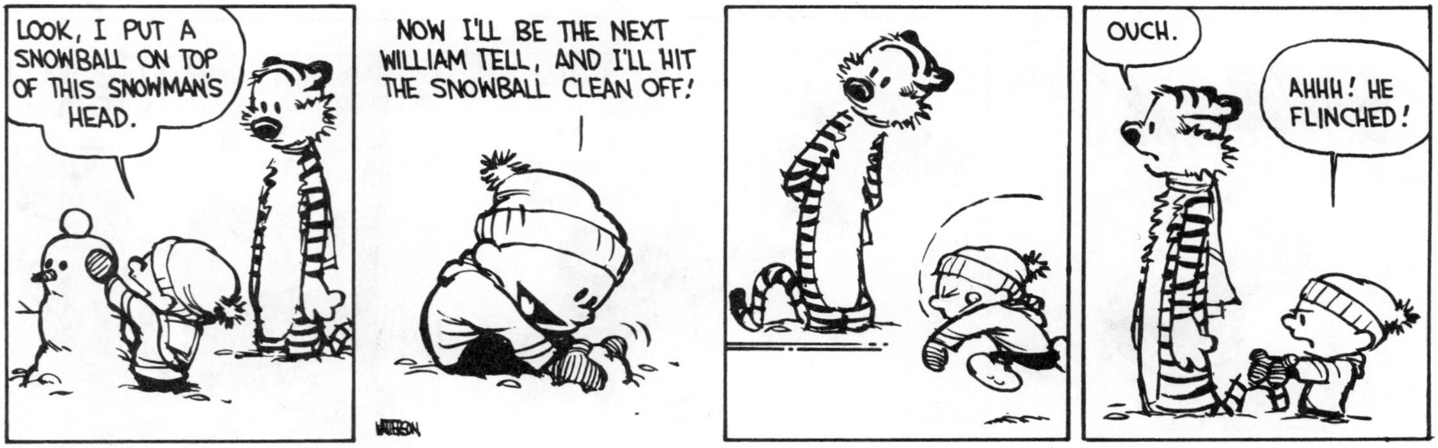
LOOK, I PUT A SNOWBALL ON TOP OF THIS SNOWMAN'S HEAD.
NOW I'LL BE THE NEXT WILLIAM TELL, AND I'LL HIT THE SNOWBALL CLEAN OFF!
WATTERSON
OUCH.
AHHH! HE FLINCHED!

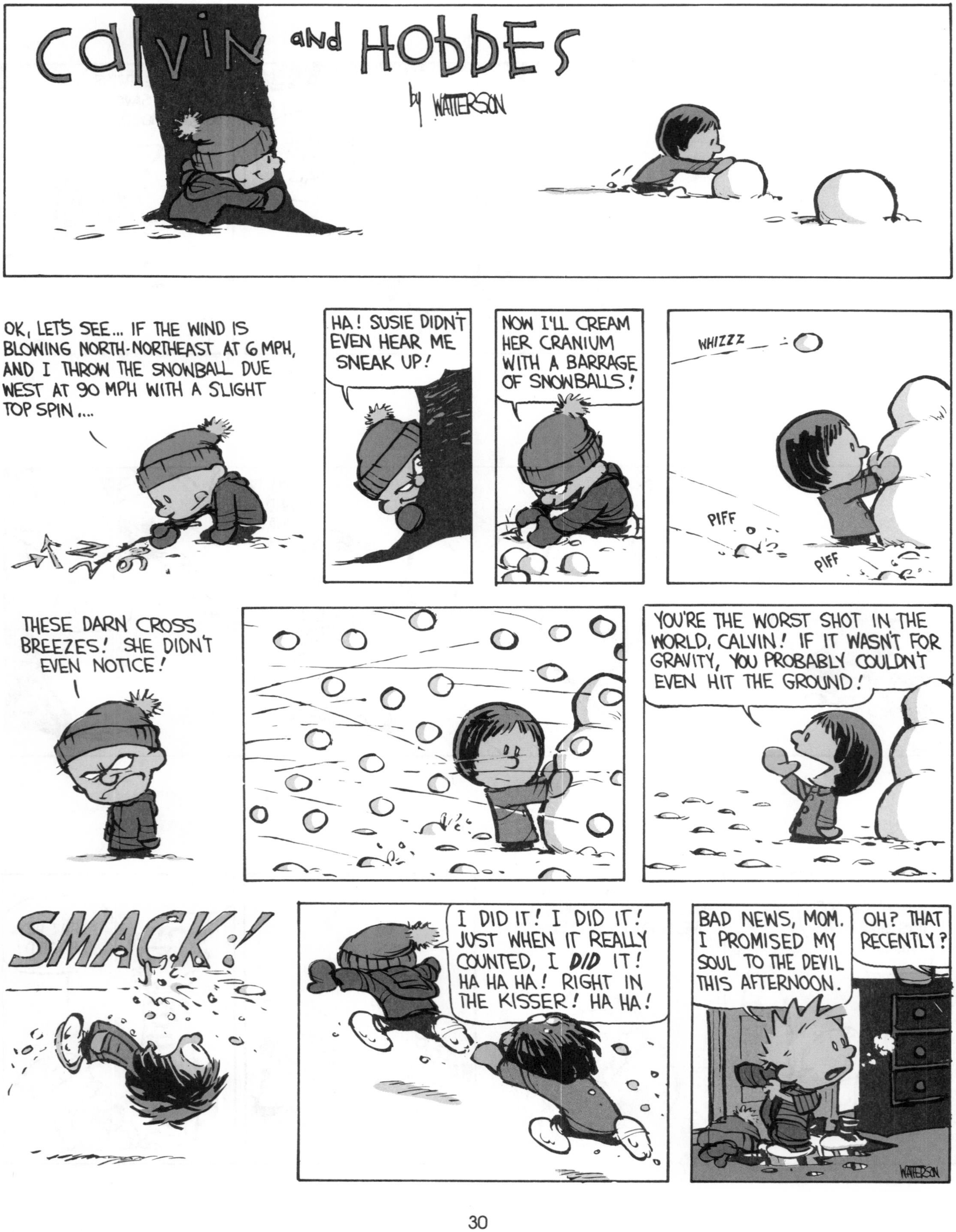
Calvin and Hobbes
by WATTERSON
OK, LET'S SEE... IF THE WIND IS BLOWING NORTH-NORTHEAST AT 6 MPH, AND I THROW THE SNOWBALL DUE WEST AT 90 MPH WITH A SLIGHT TOP SPIN....
HA! SUSIE DIDN'T EVEN HEAR ME SNEAK UP!
NOW I'LL CREAM HER CRANIUM WITH A BARRAGE OF SNOWBALLS!
WHIZZZ
PIFF
PIFF
THESE DARN CROSS BREEZES! SHE DIDN'T EVEN NOTICE!
YOU'RE THE WORST SHOT IN THE WORLD, CALVIN! IF IT WASN'T FOR GRAVITY, YOU PROBABLY COULDN'T EVEN HIT THE GROUND!
SMACK!
I DID IT! I DID IT! JUST WHEN IT REALLY COUNTED, I DID IT! HA HA HA! RIGHT IN THE KISSER! HA HA!
BAD NEWS, MOM. I PROMISED MY SOUL TO THE DEVIL THIS AFTERNOON.
OH? THAT RECENTLY?
WATTERSON

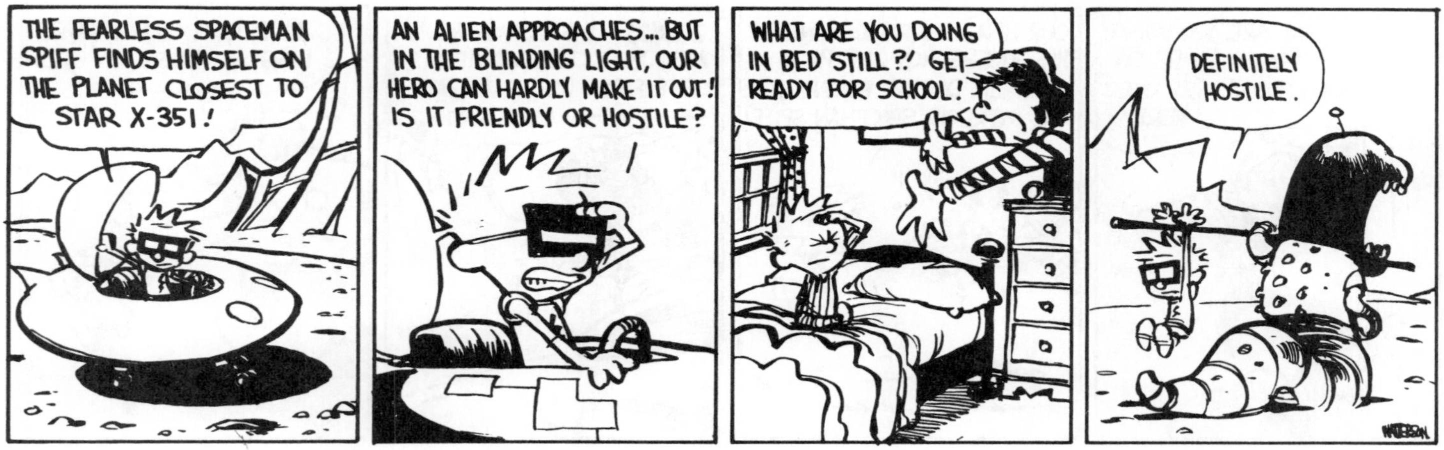
THE FEARLESS SPACEMAN SPIFF FINDS HIMSELF ON THE PLANET CLOSEST TO STAR X-351!
AN ALIEN APPROACHES... BUT IN THE BLINDING LIGHT, OUR HERO CAN HARDLY MAKE IT OUT! IS IT FRIENDLY OR HOSTILE?
WHAT ARE YOU DOING IN BED STILL?! GET READY FOR SCHOOL!
DEFINITELY HOSTILE.

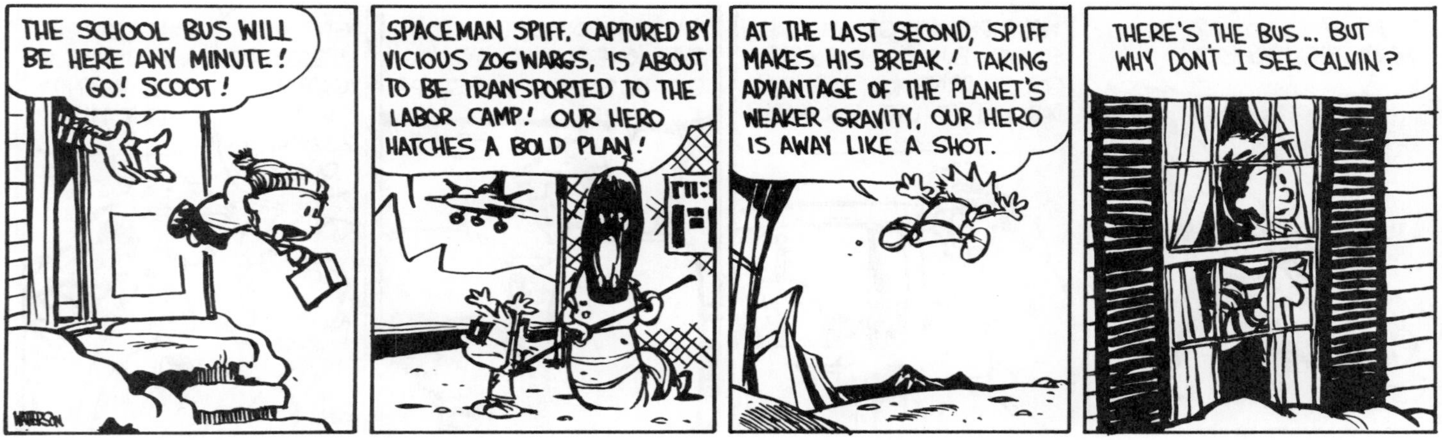
THE SCHOOL BUS WILL BE HERE ANY MINUTE! GO! SCOOT!
SPACEMAN SPIFF, CAPTURED BY VICIOUS ZOGWARGS, IS ABOUT TO BE TRANSPORTED TO THE LABOR CAMP! OUR HERO HATCHES A BOLD PLAN!
AT THE LAST SECOND, SPIFF MAKES HIS BREAK! TAKING ADVANTAGE OF THE PLANET'S WEAKER GRAVITY, OUR HERO IS AWAY LIKE A SHOT.
THERE'S THE BUS.. BUT WHY DON'T I SEE CALVIN?

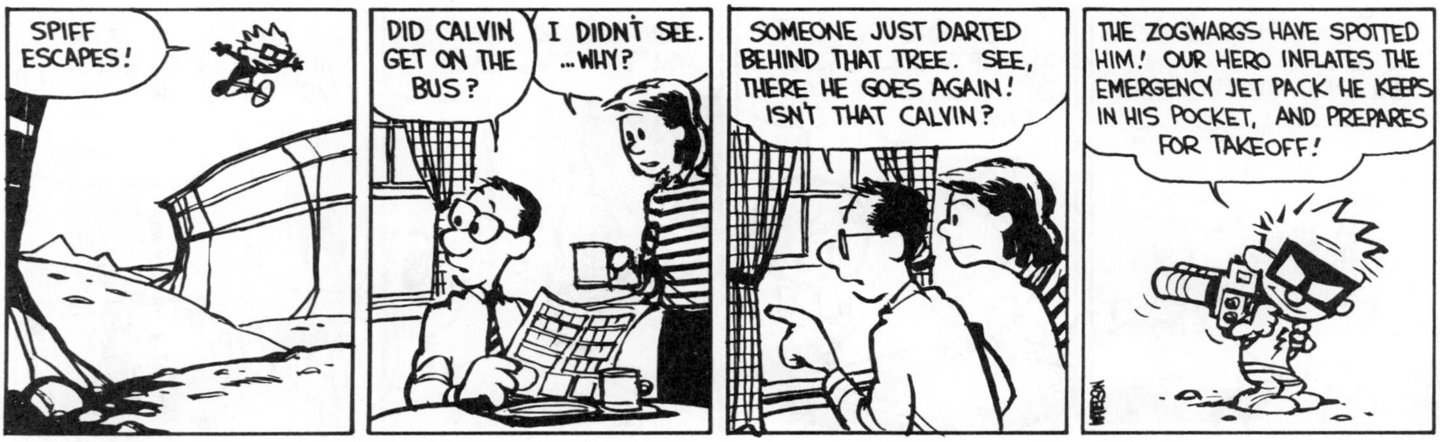
SPIFF ESCAPES!
DID CALVIN GET ON THE BUS?
I DIDN'T SEE. ...WHY?
SOMEONE JUST DARTED BEHIND THAT TREE. SEE, THERE HE GOES AGAIN! ISN'T THAT CALVIN?
THE ZOGWARGS HAVE SPOTTED HIM! OUR HERO INFLATES THE EMERGENCY JET PACK HE KEEPS IN HIS POCKET, AND PREPARES FOR TAKEOFF!

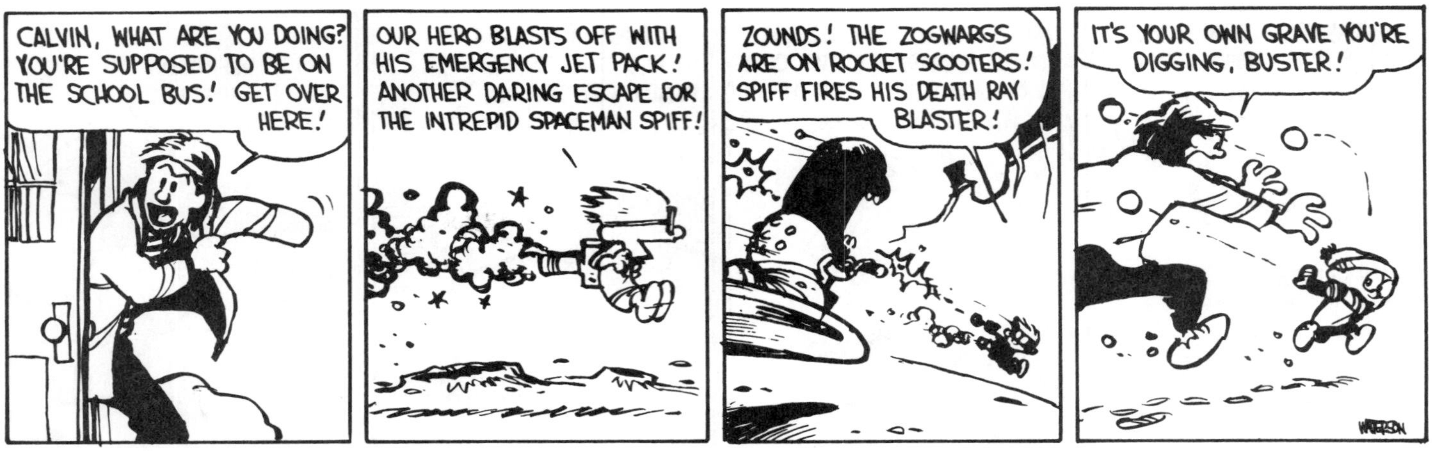
CALVIN, WHAT ARE YOU DOING? YOU'RE SUPPOSED TO BE ON THE SCHOOL BUS! GET OVER HERE!
OUR HERO BLASTS OFF WITH HIS EMERGENCY JET PACK! ANOTHER DARING ESCAPE FOR THE INTREPID SPACEMAN SPIFF!
ZOUNDS! THE ZOGWARGS ARE ON ROCKET SCOOTERS! SPIFF FIRES HIS DEATH RAY BLASTER!
IT'S YOUR OWN GRAVE YOU'RE DIGGING, BUSTER!
WATTERSON

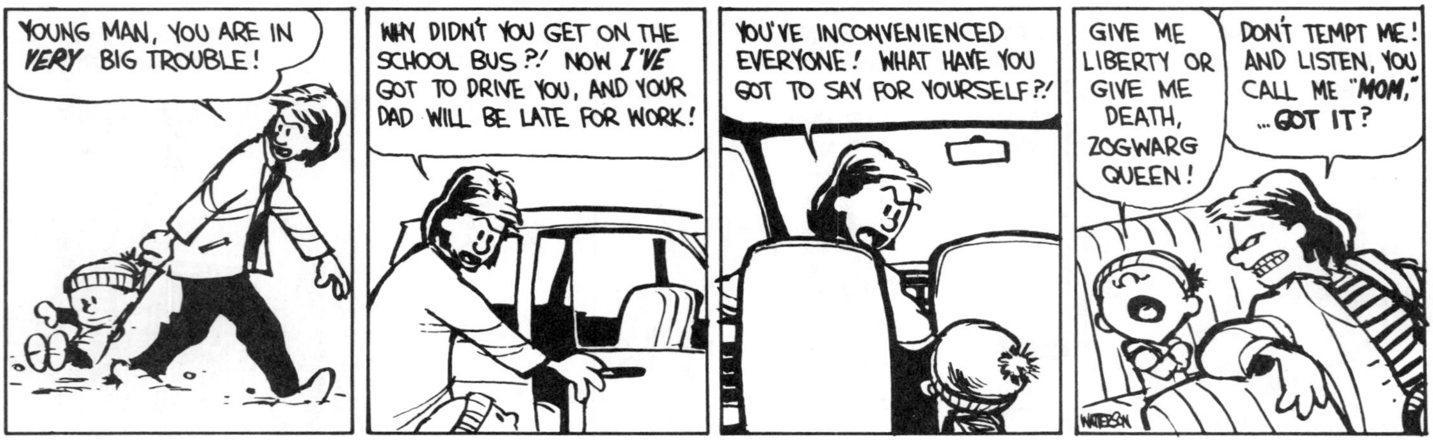
YOUNG MAN, YOU ARE IN VERY BIG TROUBLE!
WHY DIDN'T YOU GET ON THE SCHOOL BUS?! NOW I'VE GOT TO DRIVE YOU, AND YOUR DAD WILL BE LATE FOR WORK!
YOU'VE INCONVENIENCED EVERYONE! WHAT HAVE YOU GOT TO SAY FOR YOURSELF?!
GIVE ME LIBERTY OR GIVE ME DEATH, ZOGWARG QUEEN!
DON'T TEMPT ME! AND LISTEN, YOU CALL ME "MOM," ...GOT IT?
WATTERSON

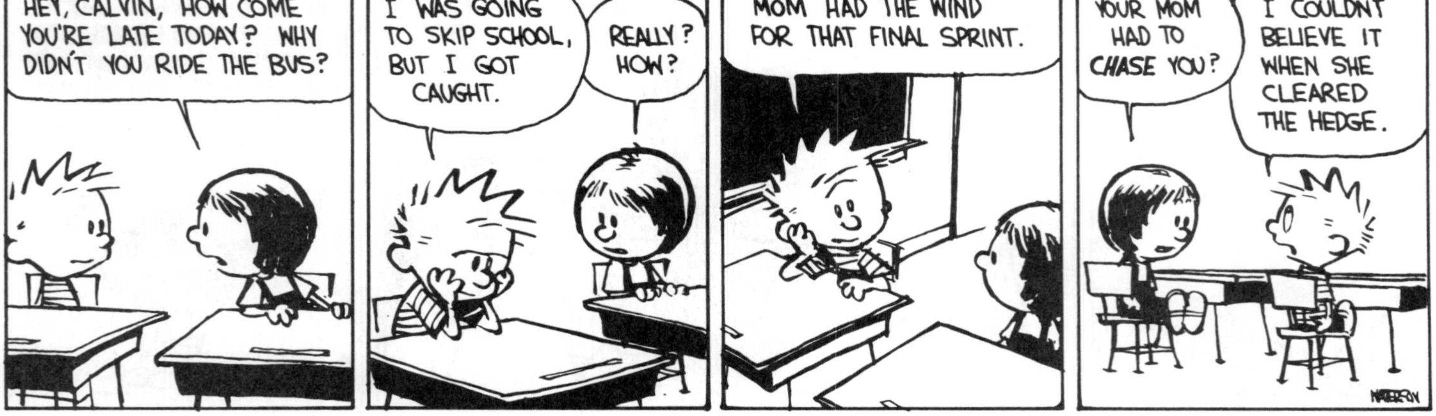
HEY, CALVIN, HOW COME YOU'RE LATE TODAY? WHY DIDN'T YOU RIDE THE BUS?
I WAS GOING TO SKIP SCHOOL, BUT I GOT CAUGHT.
REALLY? HOW?
MOM HAD THE WIND FOR THAT FINAL SPRINT.
YOUR MOM HAD TO CHASE YOU?
I COULDN'T BELIEVE IT WHEN SHE CLEARED THE HEDGE.
WATTERSON

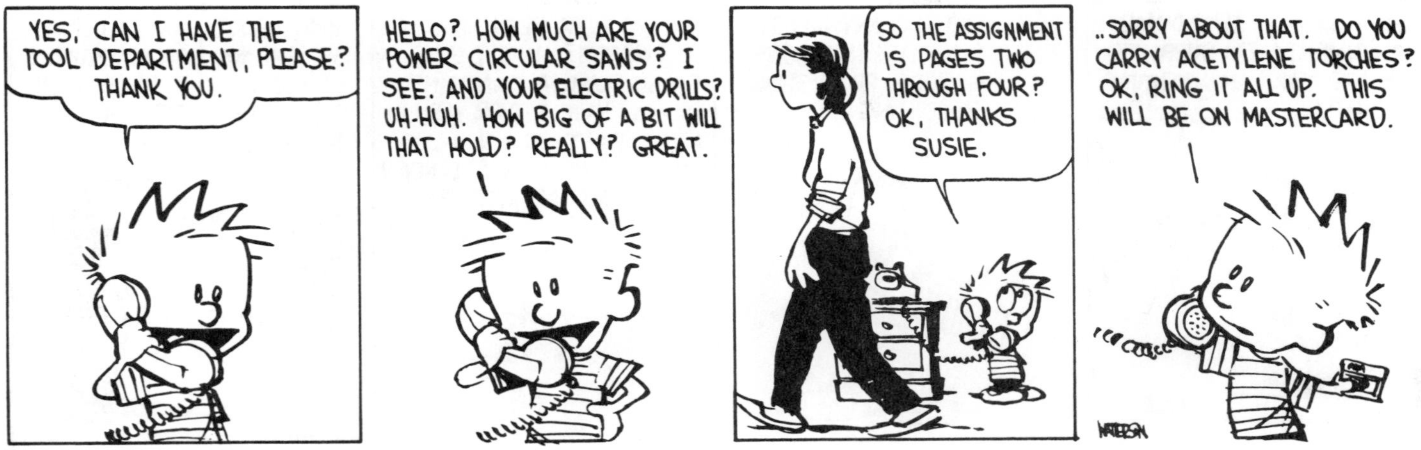
YES, CAN I HAVE THE TOOL DEPARTMENT, PLEASE? THANK YOU.
HELLO? HOW MUCH ARE YOUR POWER CIRCULAR SAWS? I SEE. AND YOUR ELECTRIC DRILLS? UH-HUH. HOW BIG OF A BIT WILL THAT HOLD? REALLY? GREAT.
SO THE ASSIGNMENT IS PAGES TWO THROUGH FOUR? OK, THANKS SUSIE.
..SORRY ABOUT THAT. DO YOU CARRY ACETYLENE TORCHES? OK, RING IT ALL UP. THIS WILL BE ON MASTERCARD.

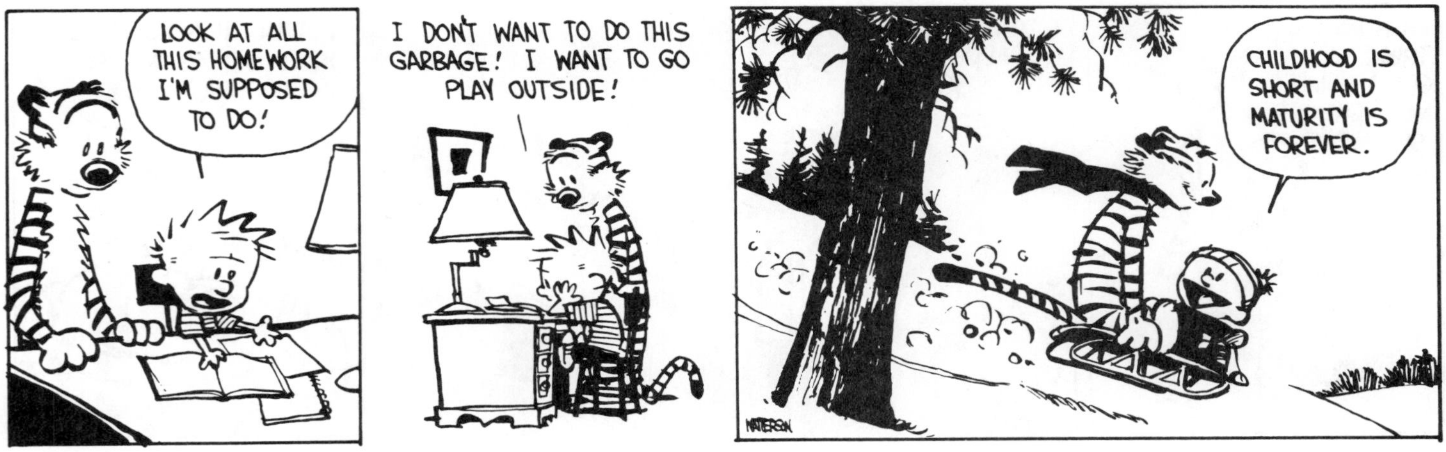
LOOK AT ALL THIS HOMEWORK I'M SUPPOSED TO DO!
I DON'T WANT TO DO THIS GARBAGE! I WANT TO GO PLAY OUTSIDE!
CHILDHOOD IS SHORT AND MATURITY IS FOREVER.

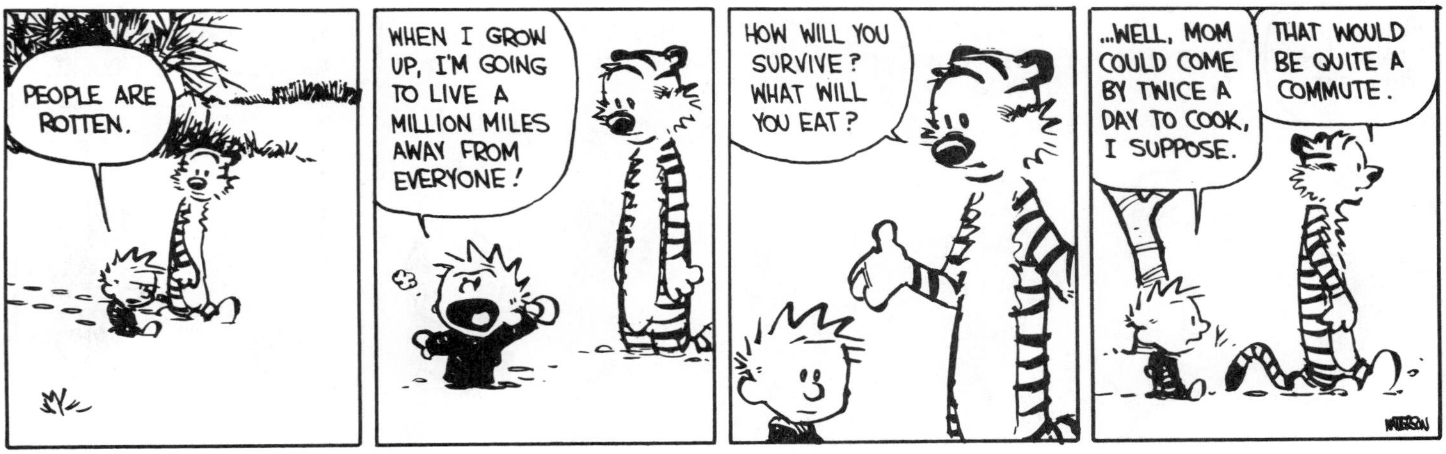
PEOPLE ARE ROTTEN.
WHEN I GROW UP, I'M GOING TO LIVE A MILLION MILES AWAY FROM EVERYONE!
HOW WILL YOU SURVIVE? WHAT WILL YOU EAT?
...WELL, MOM COULD COME BY TWICE A DAY TO COOK, I SUPPOSE.
THAT WOULD BE QUITE A COMMUTE.

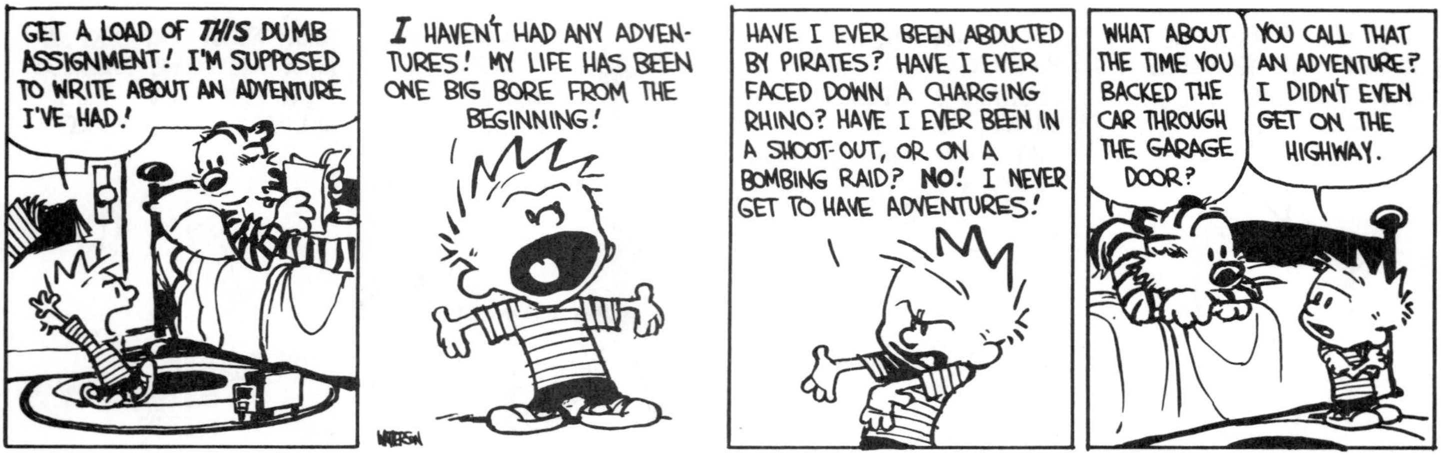
GET A LOAD OF THIS DUMB ASSIGNMENT! I'M SUPPOSED TO WRITE ABOUT AN ADVENTURE I'VE HAD!
I HAVEN'T HAD ANY ADVENTURES! MY LIFE HAS BEEN ONE BIG BORE FROM THE BEGINNING!
HAVE I EVER BEEN ABDUCTED BY PIRATES? HAVE I EVER FACED DOWN A CHARGING RHINO? HAVE I EVER BEEN IN A SHOOT-OUT, OR ON A BOMBING RAID? NO! I NEVER GET TO HAVE ADVENTURES!
WHAT ABOUT THE TIME YOU BACKED THE CAR THROUGH THE GARAGE DOOR?
YOU CALL THAT AN ADVENTURE? I DIDN'T EVEN GET ON THE HIGHWAY.

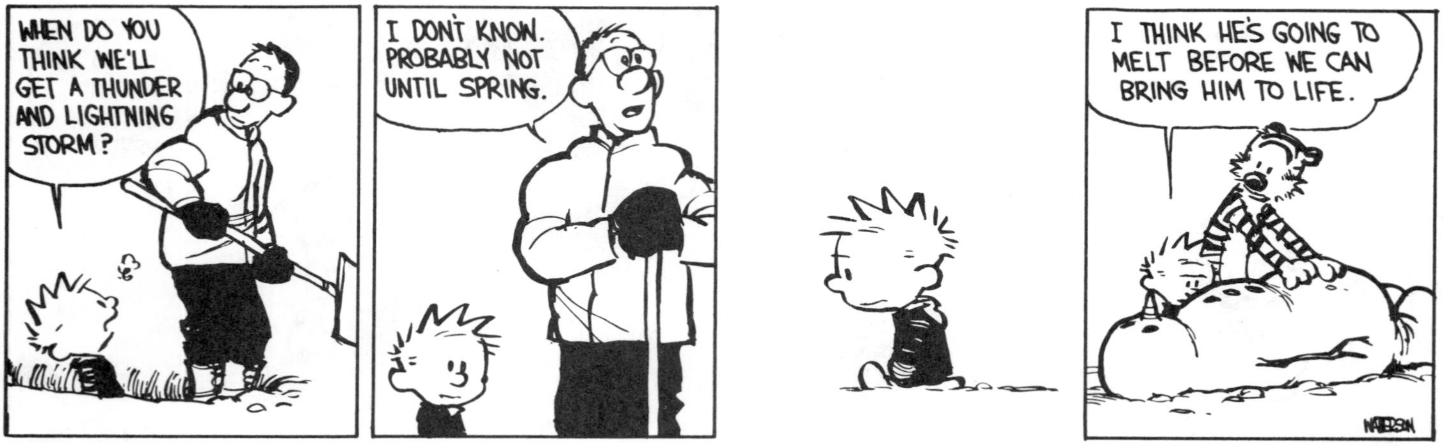
WHEN DO YOU THINK WE'LL GET A THUNDER AND LIGHTNING STORM?
I DON'T KNOW. PROBABLY NOT UNTIL SPRING.
I THINK HE'S GOING TO MELT BEFORE WE CAN BRING HIM TO LIFE.

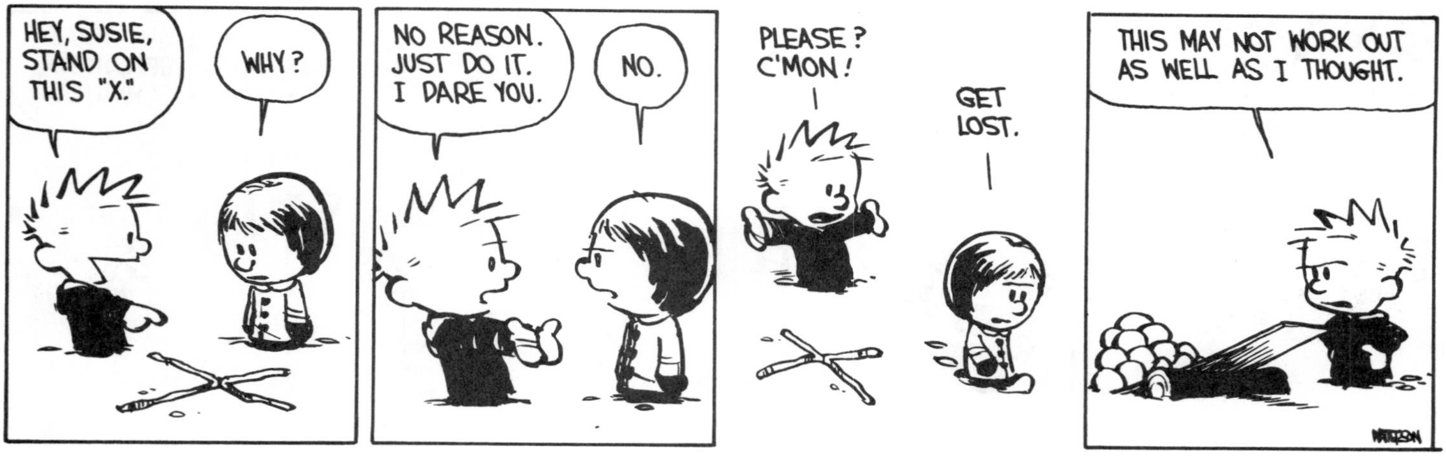
HEY, SUSIE, STAND ON THIS "X."
WHY?
NO REASON. JUST DO IT. I DARE YOU.
NO.
PLEASE? C'MON!
GET LOST.
THIS MAY NOT WORK OUT AS WELL AS I THOUGHT.

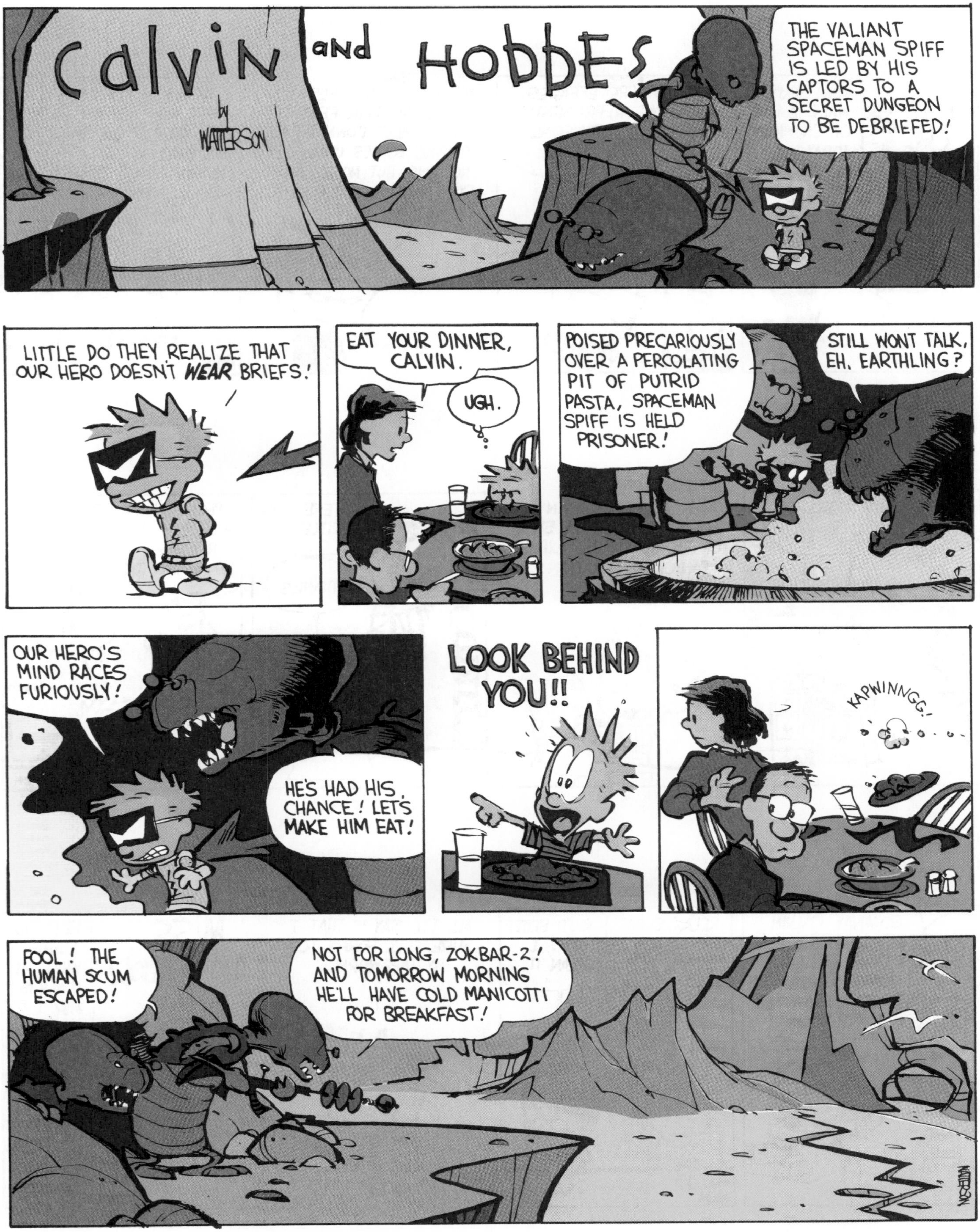
Calvin and HOBBES
by WATTERSON
THE VALIANT SPACEMAN SPIFF IS LED BY HIS CAPTORS TO A SECRET DUNGEON TO BE DEBRIEFED!
LITTLE DO THEY REALIZE THAT OUR HERO DOESN'T WEAR BRIEFS!
EAT YOUR DINNER, CALVIN.
UGH.
POISED PRECARIOUSLY OVER A PERCOLATING PIT OF PUTRID PASTA, SPACEMAN SPIFF IS HELD PRISONER!
STILL WONT TALK, EH, EARTHLING?
OUR HERO'S MIND RACES FURIOUSLY!
HE'S HAD HIS CHANCE! LET'S MAKE HIM EAT!
LOOK BEHIND YOU!!
KAPWINNGG!
FOOL! THE HUMAN SCUM ESCAPED!
NOT FOR LONG, ZOKBAR-2! AND TOMORROW MORNING HE'LL HAVE COLD MANICOTTI FOR BREAKFAST!
WATTERSON

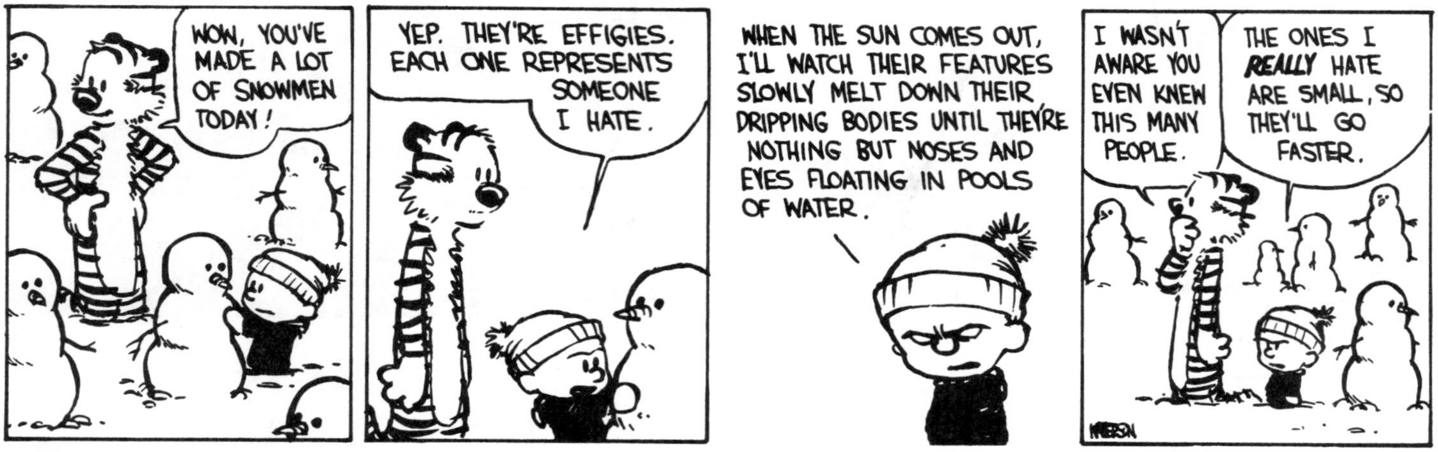
WOW, YOU'VE MADE A LOT OF SNOWMEN TODAY!
YEP. THEY'RE EFFIGIES. EACH ONE REPRESENTS SOMEONE I HATE.
WHEN THE SUN COMES OUT, I'LL WATCH THEIR FEATURES SLOWLY MELT DOWN THEIR DRIPPING BODIES UNTIL THEY'RE NOTHING BUT NOSES AND EYES FLOATING IN POOLS OF WATER.
I WASN'T AWARE YOU EVEN KNEW THIS MANY PEOPLE.
THE ONES I ***REALLY*** HATE ARE SMALL, SO THEY'LL GO FASTER.

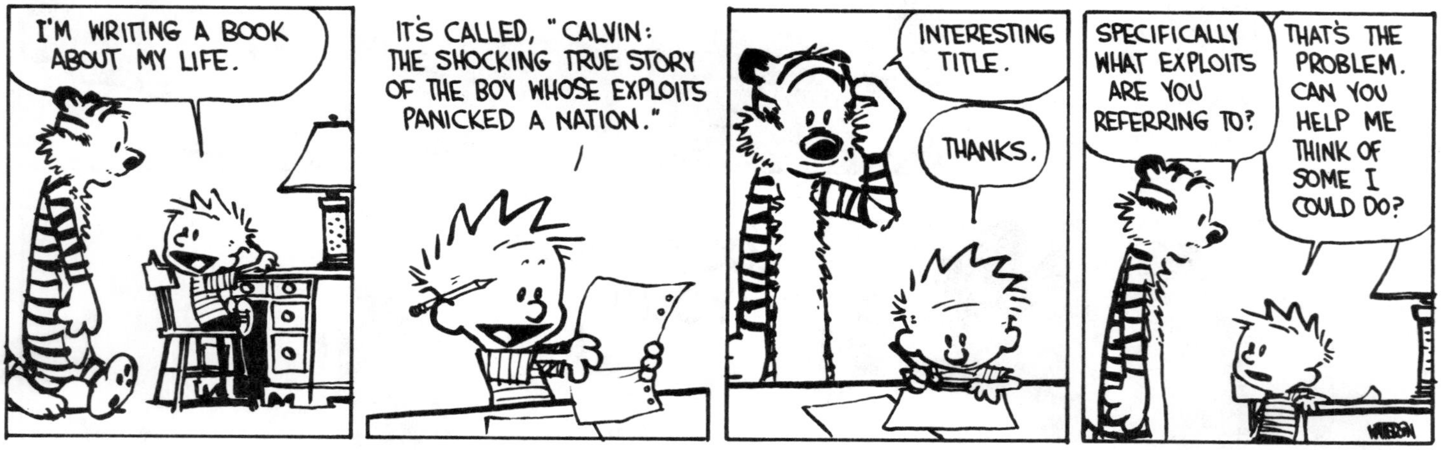
I'M WRITING A BOOK ABOUT MY LIFE.
IT'S CALLED, "CALVIN: THE SHOCKING TRUE STORY OF THE BOY WHOSE EXPLOITS PANICKED A NATION."
INTERESTING TITLE.
THANKS.
SPECIFICALLY WHAT EXPLOITS ARE YOU REFERRING TO?
THAT'S THE PROBLEM. CAN YOU HELP ME THINK OF SOME I COULD DO?

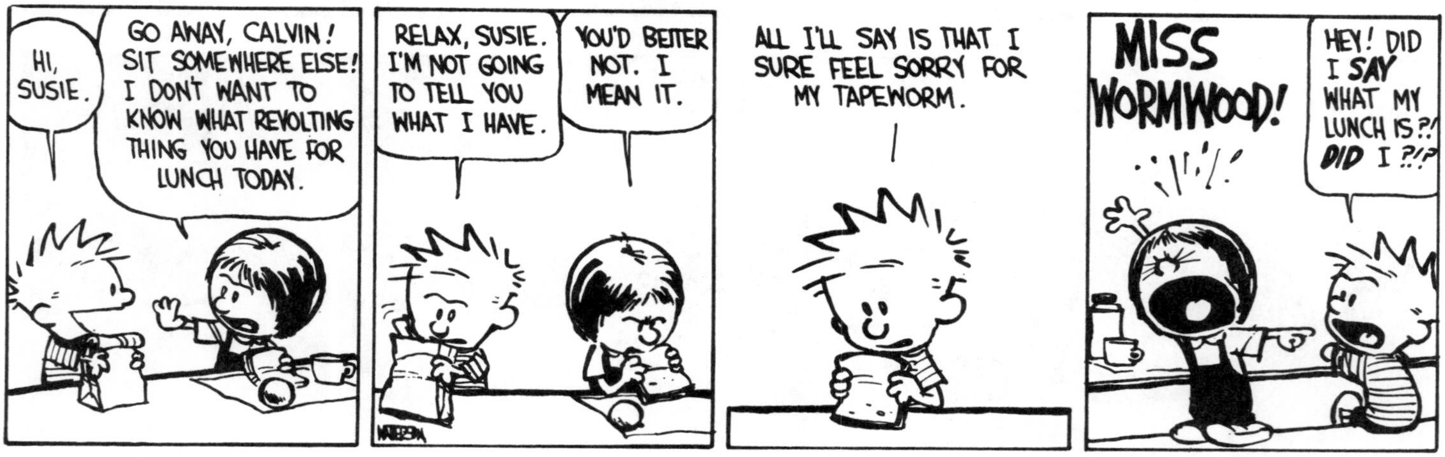
HI, SUSIE.
GO AWAY, CALVIN! SIT SOMEWHERE ELSE! I DON'T WANT TO KNOW WHAT REVOLTING THING YOU HAVE FOR LUNCH TODAY.
RELAX, SUSIE. I'M NOT GOING TO TELL YOU WHAT I HAVE.
YOU'D BETTER NOT. I MEAN IT.
ALL I'LL SAY IS THAT I SURE FEEL SORRY FOR MY TAPEWORM.
MISS WORMWOOD!
HEY! DID I ***SAY*** WHAT MY LUNCH IS?! ***DID*** I?!?

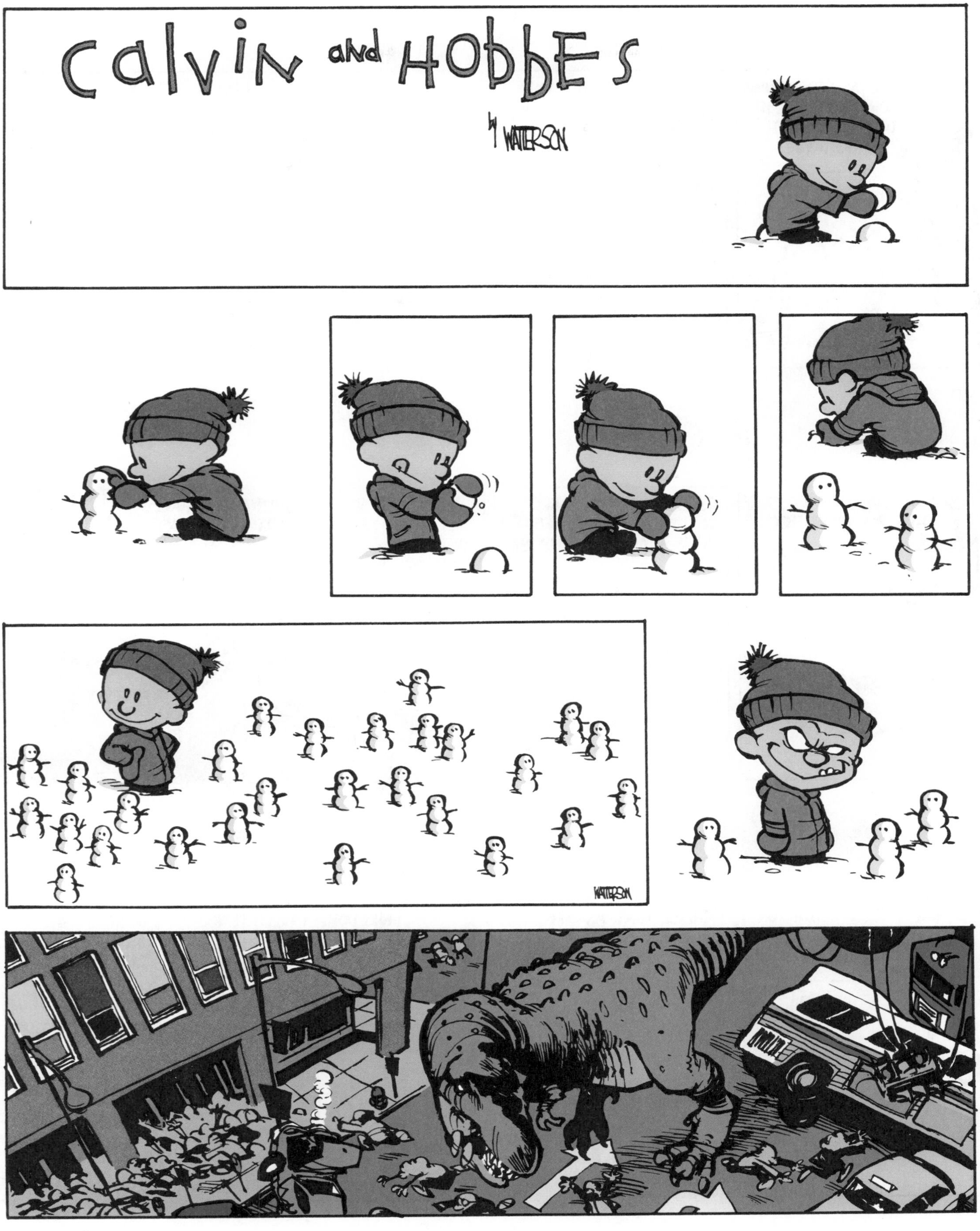

Calvin and HOBBES
by WATTERSON
WATTERSON

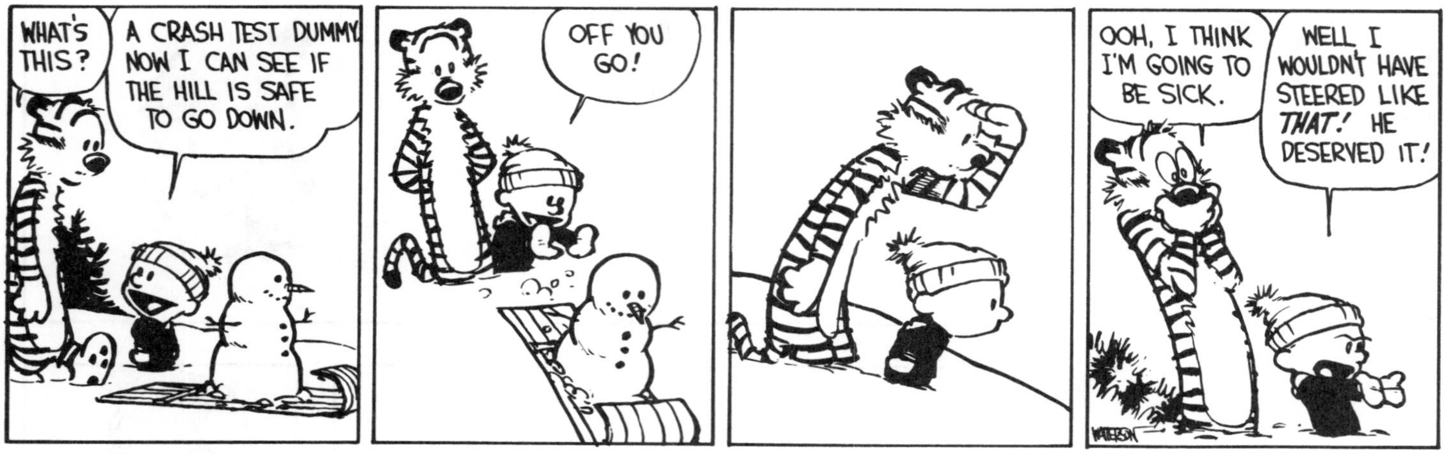
WHAT'S THIS?
A CRASH TEST DUMMY! NOW I CAN SEE IF THE HILL IS SAFE TO GO DOWN.
OFF YOU GO!
OOH, I THINK I'M GOING TO BE SICK.
WELL I WOULDN'T HAVE STEERED LIKE *THAT!* HE DESERVED IT!

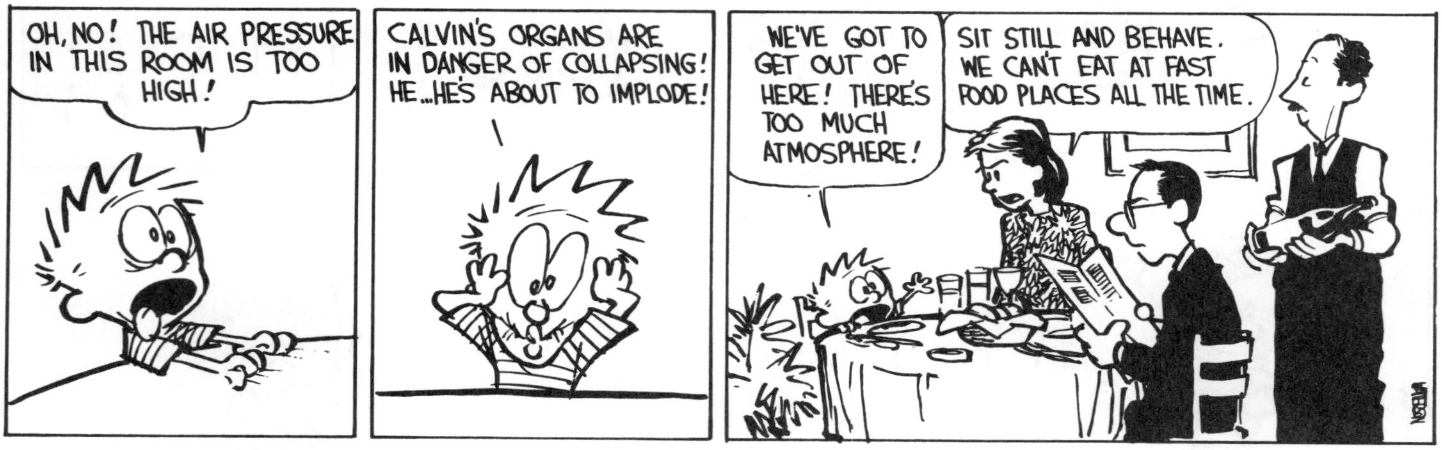
OH, NO! THE AIR PRESSURE IN THIS ROOM IS TOO HIGH!
CALVIN'S ORGANS ARE IN DANGER OF COLLAPSING! HE...HE'S ABOUT TO IMPLODE!
WE'VE GOT TO GET OUT OF HERE! THERE'S TOO MUCH ATMOSPHERE!
SIT STILL AND BEHAVE. WE CAN'T EAT AT FAST FOOD PLACES ALL THE TIME.

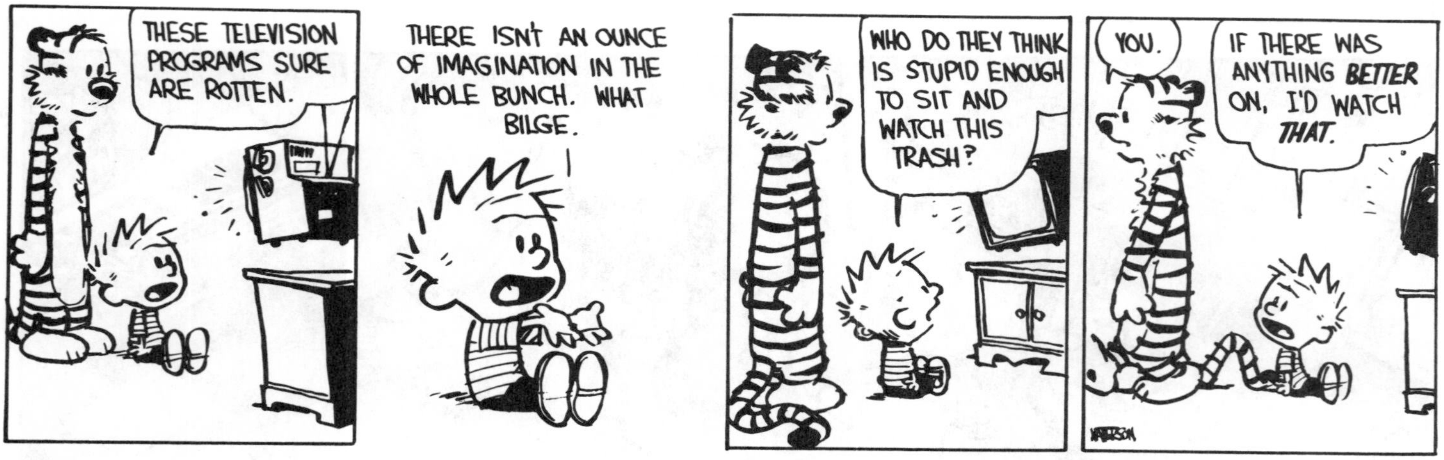
THESE TELEVISION PROGRAMS SURE ARE ROTTEN.
THERE ISN'T AN OUNCE OF IMAGINATION IN THE WHOLE BUNCH. WHAT BILGE.
WHO DO THEY THINK IS STUPID ENOUGH TO SIT AND WATCH THIS TRASH?
YOU.
IF THERE WAS ANYTHING **BETTER** ON, I'D WATCH ***THAT.***

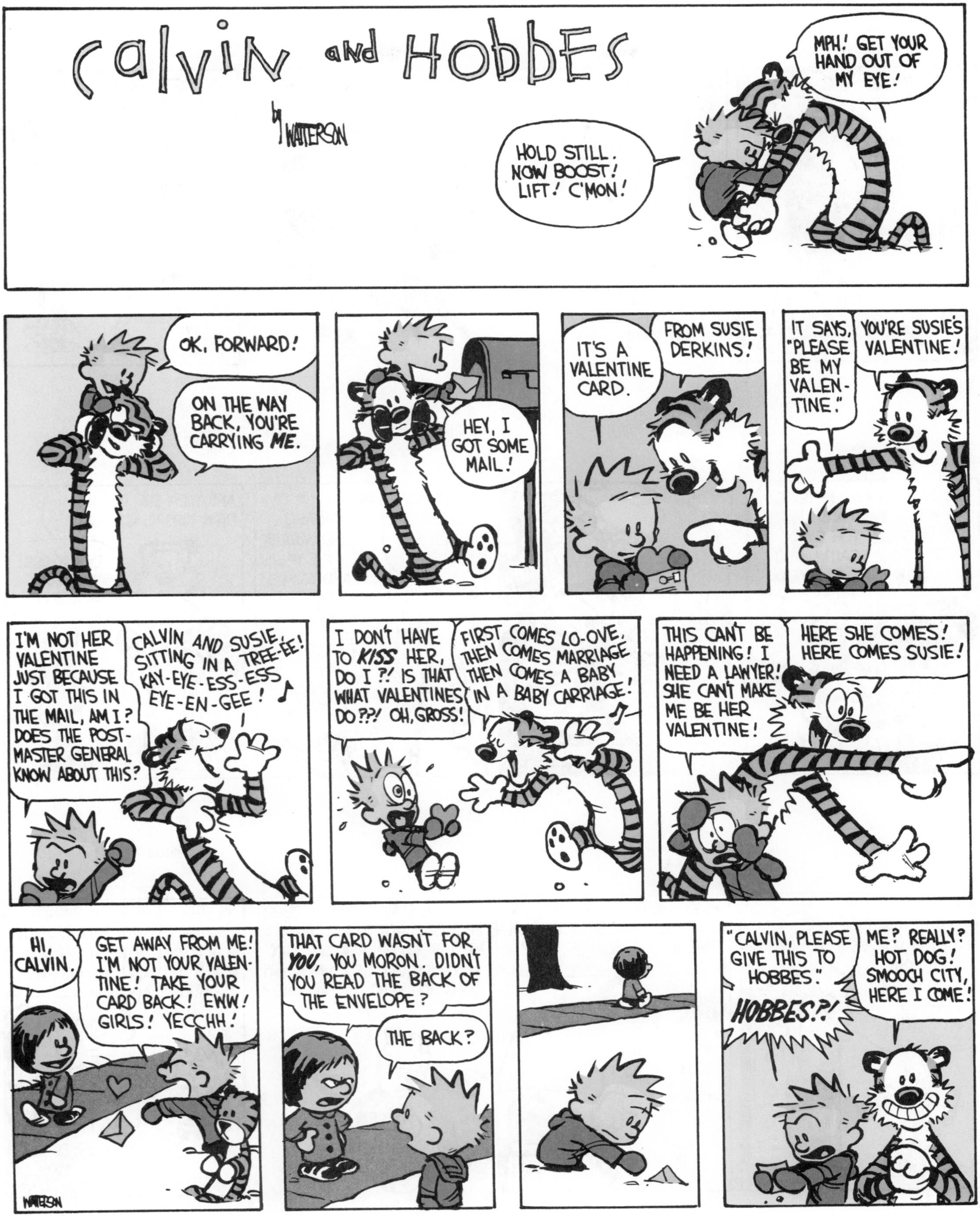
Calvin and Hobbes
by WATTERSON
MPH! GET YOUR HAND OUT OF MY EYE!
HOLD STILL. NOW BOOST! LIFT! C'MON!
OK, FORWARD!
ON THE WAY BACK, YOU'RE CARRYING ME.
HEY, I GOT SOME MAIL!
IT'S A VALENTINE CARD.
FROM SUSIE DERKINS!
IT SAYS, "PLEASE BE MY VALENTINE."
YOU'RE SUSIE'S VALENTINE!
I'M NOT HER VALENTINE JUST BECAUSE I GOT THIS IN THE MAIL, AM I? DOES THE POSTMASTER GENERAL KNOW ABOUT THIS?
CALVIN AND SUSIE, SITTING IN A TREE-EE! KAY-EYE-ESS-ESS EYE-EN-GEE!
I DON'T HAVE TO KISS HER, DO I?! IS THAT WHAT VALENTINES DO?!? OH, GROSS!
FIRST COMES LO-OVE, THEN COMES MARRIAGE THEN COMES A BABY IN A BABY CARRIAGE!
THIS CAN'T BE HAPPENING! I NEED A LAWYER! SHE CAN'T MAKE ME BE HER VALENTINE!
HERE SHE COMES! HERE COMES SUSIE!
HI, CALVIN.
GET AWAY FROM ME! I'M NOT YOUR VALENTINE! TAKE YOUR CARD BACK! EWW! GIRLS! YECCHH!
WATTERSON
THAT CARD WASN'T FOR YOU, YOU MORON. DIDN'T YOU READ THE BACK OF THE ENVELOPE?
THE BACK?
"CALVIN, PLEASE GIVE THIS TO HOBBES."
HOBBES?!
ME? REALLY? HOT DOG! SMOOCH CITY, HERE I COME!

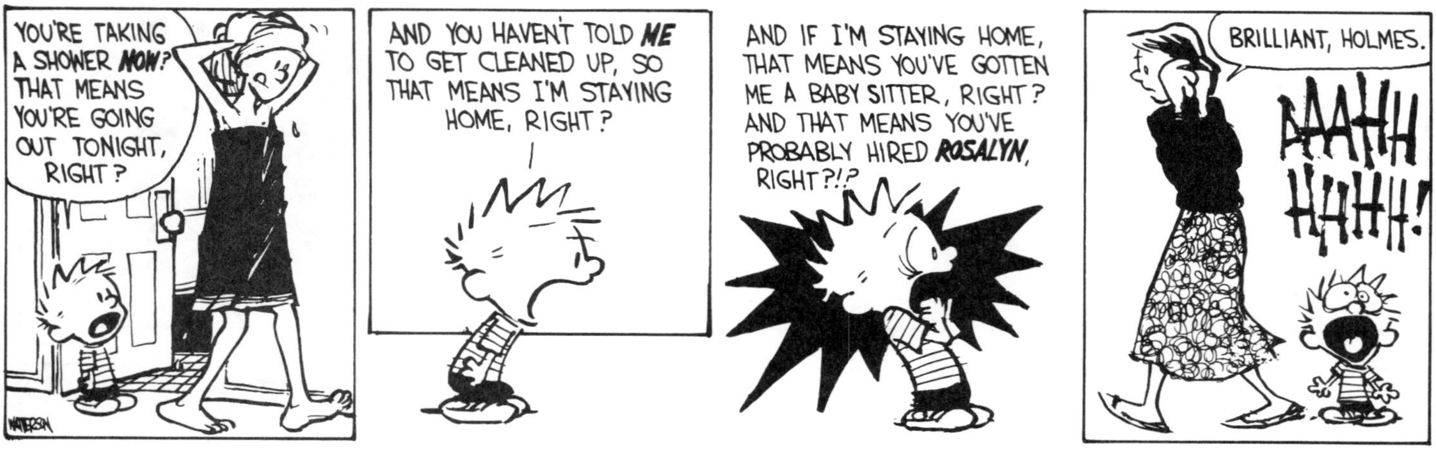
YOU'RE TAKING A SHOWER NOW? THAT MEANS YOU'RE GOING OUT TONIGHT, RIGHT?
AND YOU HAVEN'T TOLD ME TO GET CLEANED UP, SO THAT MEANS I'M STAYING HOME, RIGHT?
AND IF I'M STAYING HOME, THAT MEANS YOU'VE GOTTEN ME A BABY SITTER, RIGHT? AND THAT MEANS YOU'VE PROBABLY HIRED ROSALYN, RIGHT?!?
BRILLIANT, HOLMES.
AAAHH HHHH!

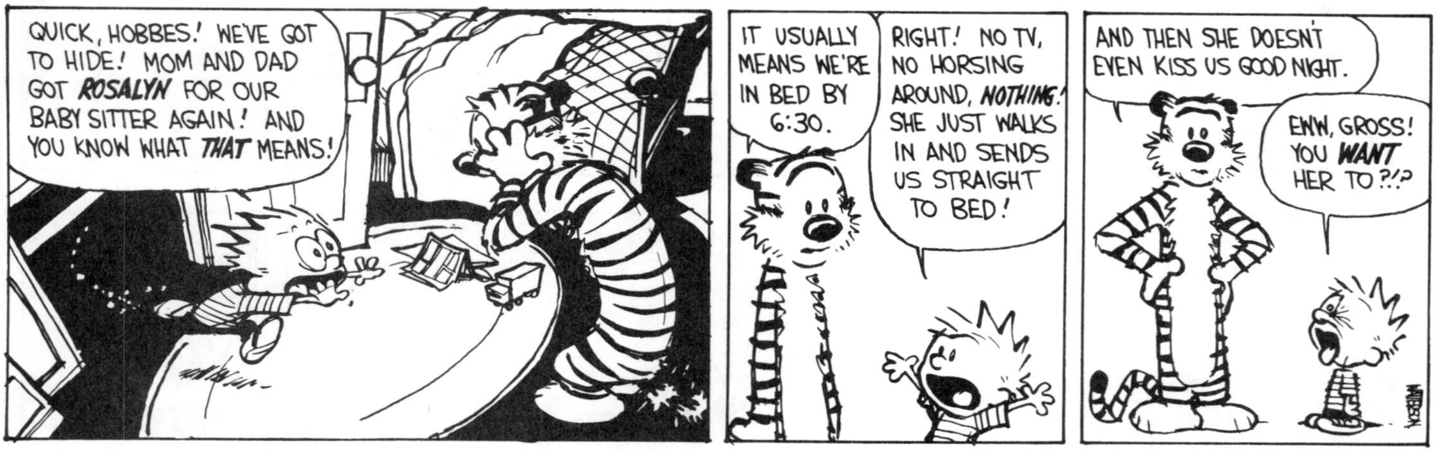
QUICK, HOBBES! WE'VE GOT TO HIDE! MOM AND DAD GOT ROSALYN FOR OUR BABY SITTER AGAIN! AND YOU KNOW WHAT THAT MEANS!
IT USUALLY MEANS WE'RE IN BED BY 6:30.
RIGHT! NO TV, NO HORSING AROUND, NOTHING! SHE JUST WALKS IN AND SENDS US STRAIGHT TO BED!
AND THEN SHE DOESN'T EVEN KISS US GOOD NIGHT.
EWW, GROSS! YOU WANT HER TO?!?

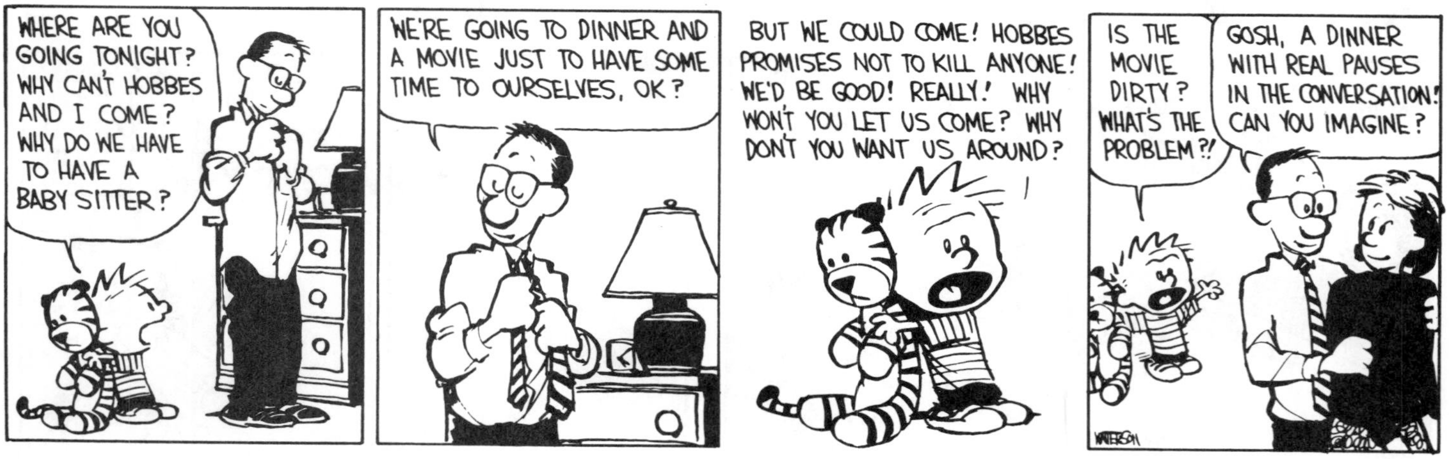
WHERE ARE YOU GOING TONIGHT? WHY CAN'T HOBBES AND I COME? WHY DO WE HAVE TO HAVE A BABY SITTER?
WE'RE GOING TO DINNER AND A MOVIE JUST TO HAVE SOME TIME TO OURSELVES, OK?
BUT WE COULD COME! HOBBES PROMISES NOT TO KILL ANYONE! WE'D BE GOOD! REALLY! WHY WON'T YOU LET US COME? WHY DON'T YOU WANT US AROUND?
IS THE MOVIE DIRTY? WHAT'S THE PROBLEM?!
GOSH, A DINNER WITH REAL PAUSES IN THE CONVERSATION! CAN YOU IMAGINE?

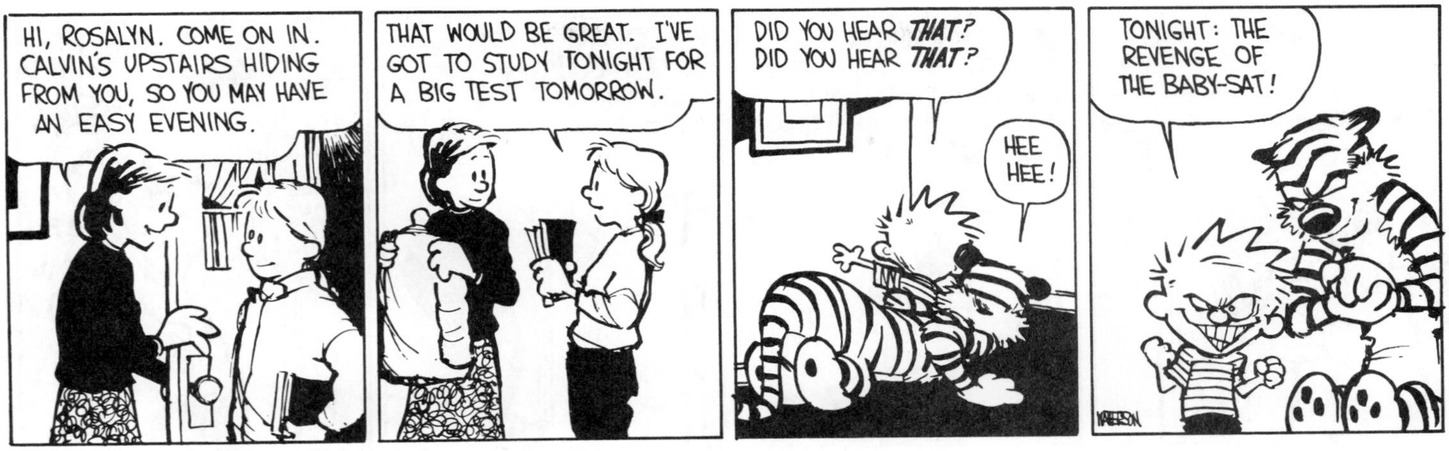
HI, ROSALYN. COME ON IN. CALVIN'S UPSTAIRS HIDING FROM YOU, SO YOU MAY HAVE AN EASY EVENING.
THAT WOULD BE GREAT. I'VE GOT TO STUDY TONIGHT FOR A BIG TEST TOMORROW.
DID YOU HEAR THAT? DID YOU HEAR THAT?
HEE HEE!
TONIGHT: THE REVENGE OF THE BABY-SAT!

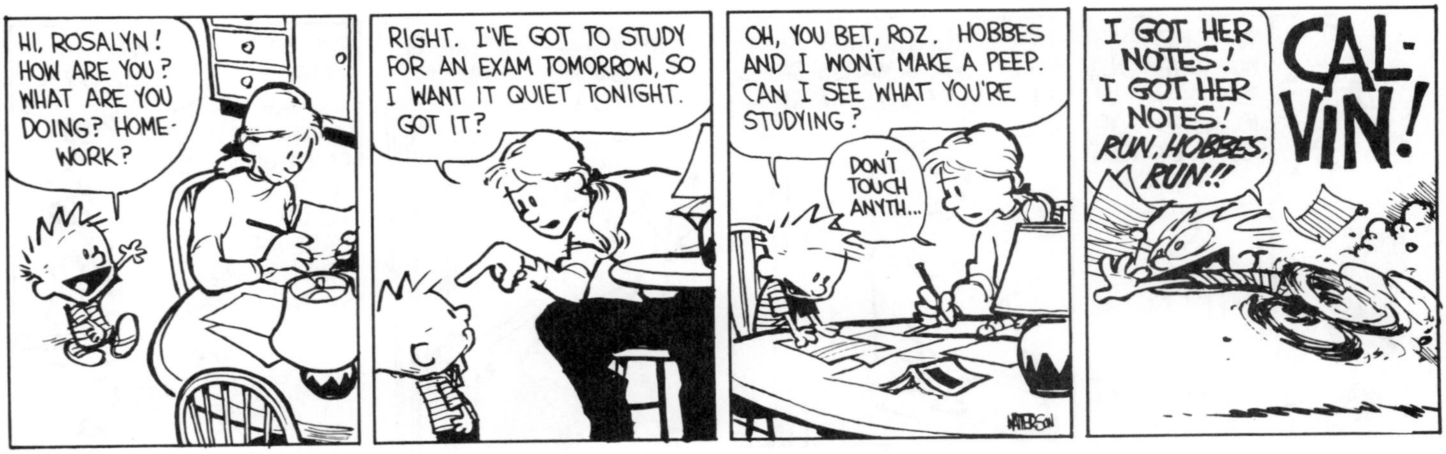
HI, ROSALYN! HOW ARE YOU? WHAT ARE YOU DOING? HOME-WORK?
RIGHT. I'VE GOT TO STUDY FOR AN EXAM TOMORROW, SO I WANT IT QUIET TONIGHT. GOT IT?
OH, YOU BET, ROZ. HOBBES AND I WON'T MAKE A PEEP. CAN I SEE WHAT YOU'RE STUDYING?
DON'T TOUCH ANYTH...
I GOT HER NOTES! I GOT HER NOTES! RUN, HOBBES, RUN!!
CAL-VIN!

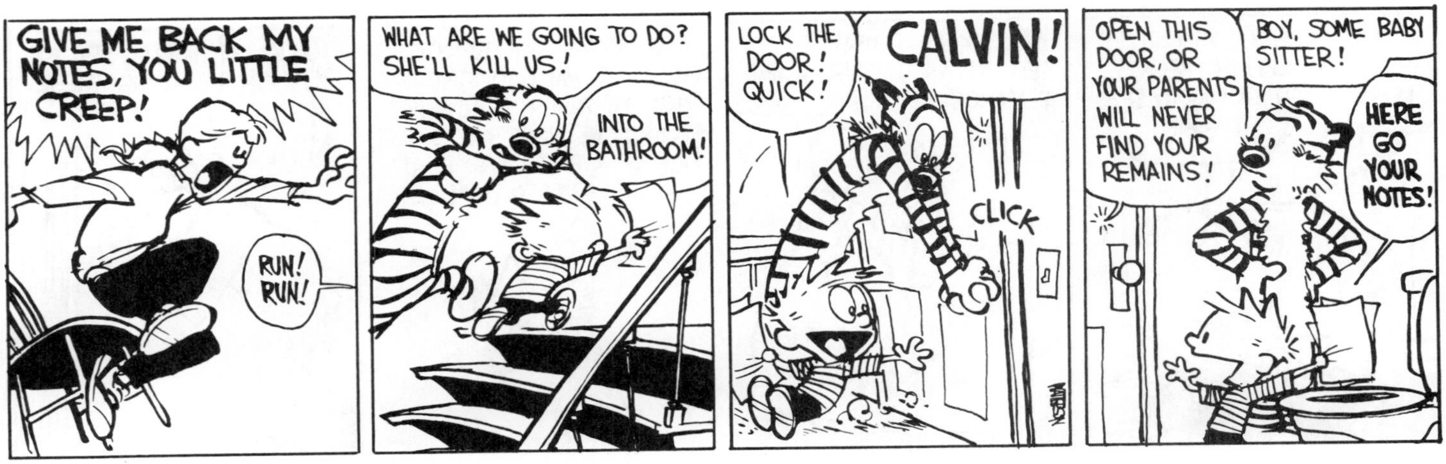
GIVE ME BACK MY NOTES, YOU LITTLE CREEP!
RUN! RUN!
WHAT ARE WE GOING TO DO? SHE'LL KILL US!
INTO THE BATHROOM!
LOCK THE DOOR! QUICK!
CALVIN!
CLICK
OPEN THIS DOOR, OR YOUR PARENTS WILL NEVER FIND YOUR REMAINS!
BOY, SOME BABY SITTER!
HERE GO YOUR NOTES!

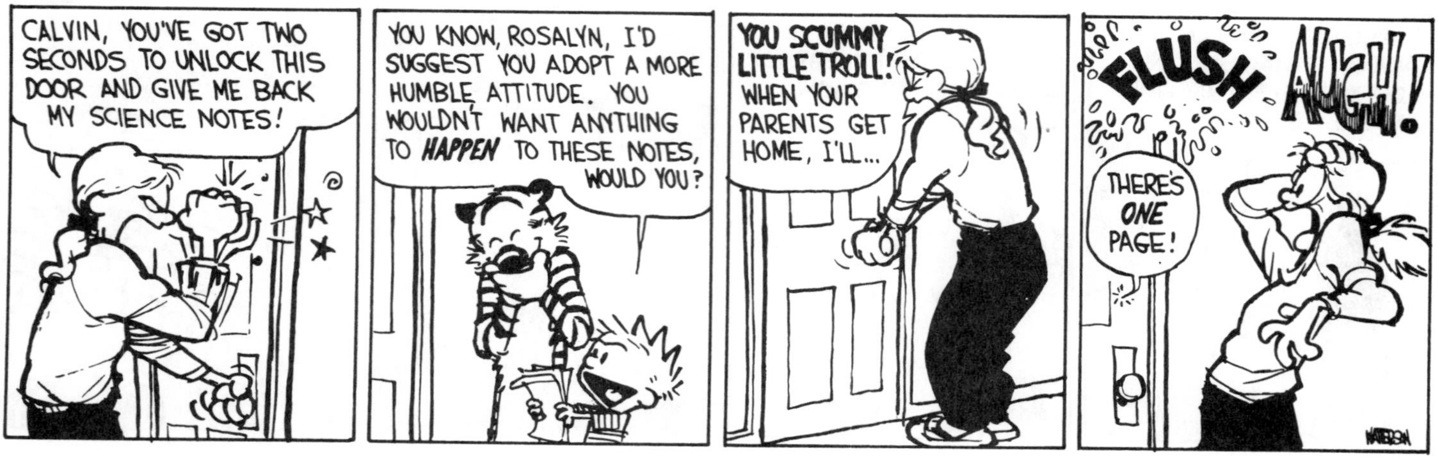
CALVIN, YOU'VE GOT TWO SECONDS TO UNLOCK THIS DOOR AND GIVE ME BACK MY SCIENCE NOTES!
YOU KNOW, ROSALYN, I'D SUGGEST YOU ADOPT A MORE HUMBLE ATTITUDE. YOU WOULDN'T WANT ANYTHING TO HAPPEN TO THESE NOTES, WOULD YOU?
YOU SCUMMY LITTLE TROLL! WHEN YOUR PARENTS GET HOME, I'LL...
FLUSH
AUGH!
THERE'S ONE PAGE!

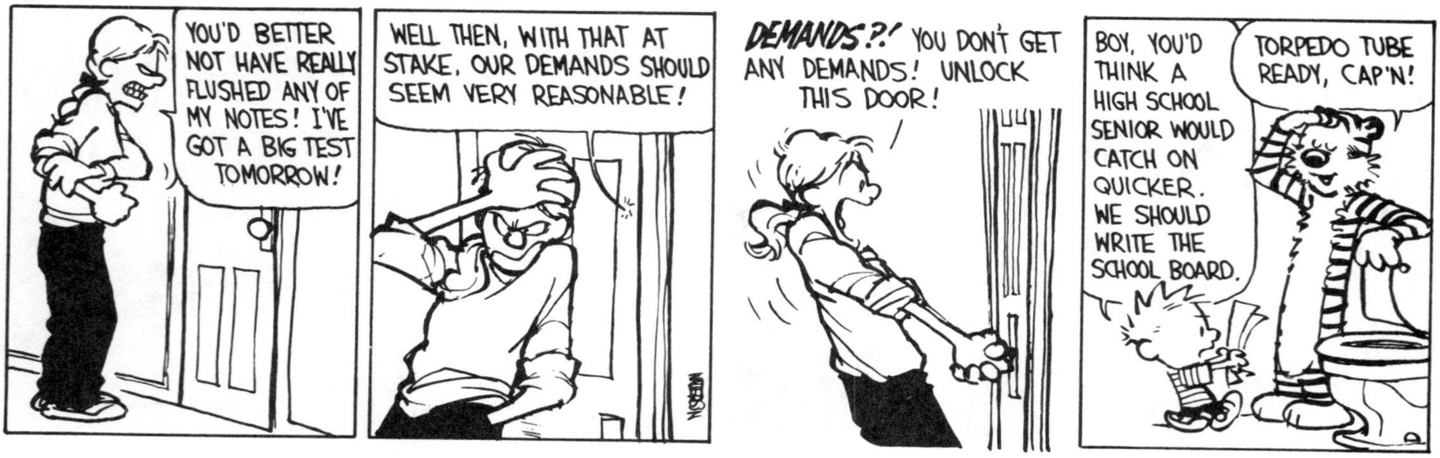
YOU'D BETTER NOT HAVE REALLY FLUSHED ANY OF MY NOTES! I'VE GOT A BIG TEST TOMORROW!
WELL THEN, WITH THAT AT STAKE, OUR DEMANDS SHOULD SEEM VERY REASONABLE!
DEMANDS?! YOU DON'T GET ANY DEMANDS! UNLOCK THIS DOOR!
BOY, YOU'D THINK A HIGH SCHOOL SENIOR WOULD CATCH ON QUICKER. WE SHOULD WRITE THE SCHOOL BOARD.
TORPEDO TUBE READY, CAP'N!

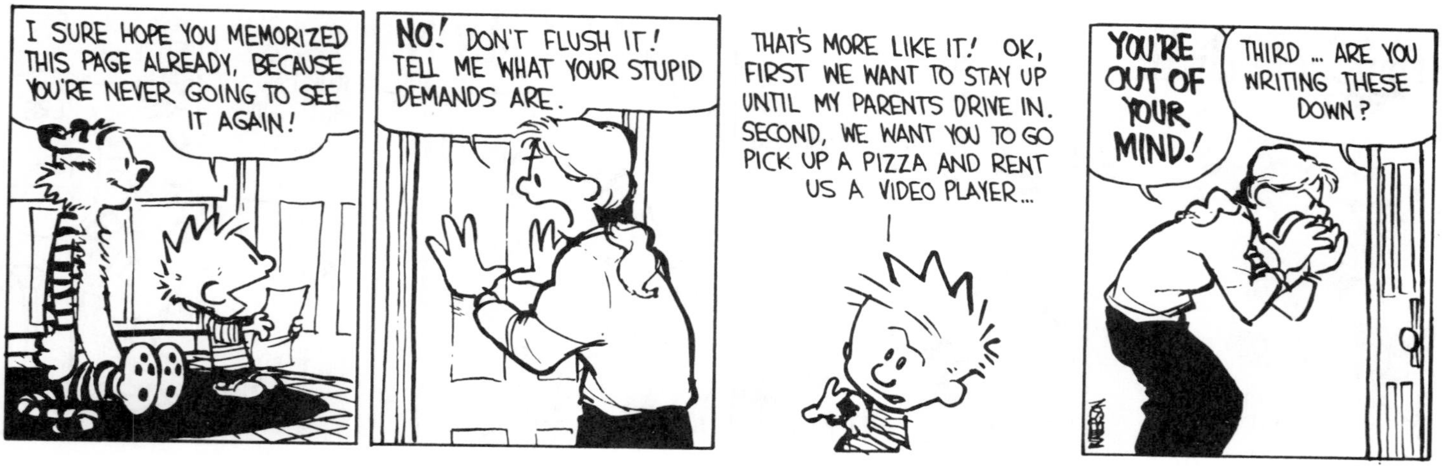
I SURE HOPE YOU MEMORIZED THIS PAGE ALREADY, BECAUSE YOU'RE NEVER GOING TO SEE IT AGAIN!
NO! DON'T FLUSH IT! TELL ME WHAT YOUR STUPID DEMANDS ARE.
THAT'S MORE LIKE IT! OK, FIRST WE WANT TO STAY UP UNTIL MY PARENTS DRIVE IN. SECOND, WE WANT YOU TO GO PICK UP A PIZZA AND RENT US A VIDEO PLAYER...
YOU'RE OUT OF YOUR MIND!
THIRD ... ARE YOU WRITING THESE DOWN?

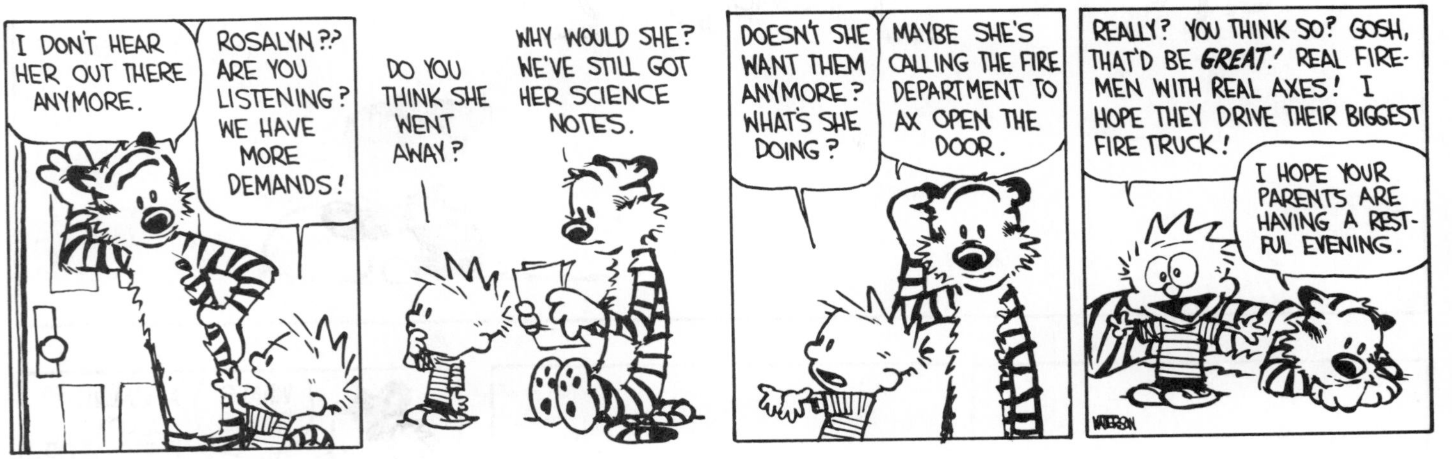
I DON'T HEAR HER OUT THERE ANYMORE.
ROSALYN?? ARE YOU LISTENING? WE HAVE MORE DEMANDS!
DO YOU THINK SHE WENT AWAY?
WHY WOULD SHE? WE'VE STILL GOT HER SCIENCE NOTES.
DOESN'T SHE WANT THEM ANYMORE? WHAT'S SHE DOING?
MAYBE SHE'S CALLING THE FIRE DEPARTMENT TO AX OPEN THE DOOR.
REALLY? YOU THINK SO? GOSH, THAT'D BE GREAT! REAL FIREMEN WITH REAL AXES! I HOPE THEY DRIVE THEIR BIGGEST FIRE TRUCK!
I HOPE YOUR PARENTS ARE HAVING A RESTFUL EVENING.
WATTERSON

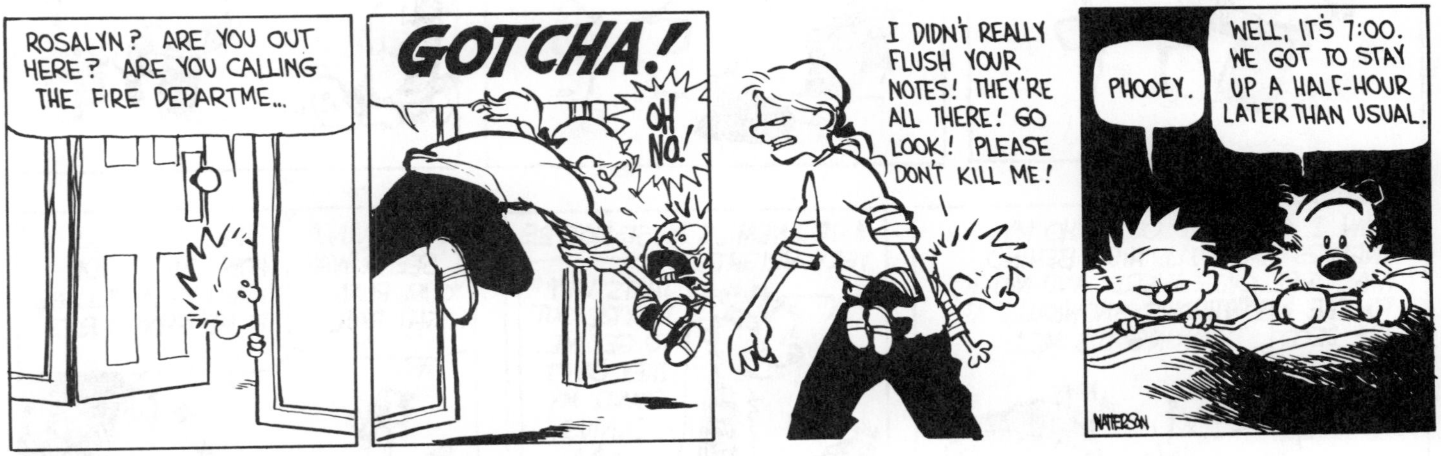
ROSALYN? ARE YOU OUT HERE? ARE YOU CALLING THE FIRE DEPARTME...
GOTCHA!
OH NO!
I DIDN'T REALLY FLUSH YOUR NOTES! THEY'RE ALL THERE! GO LOOK! PLEASE DON'T KILL ME!
PHOOEY.
WELL, IT'S 7:00. WE GOT TO STAY UP A HALF-HOUR LATER THAN USUAL.
WATTERSON

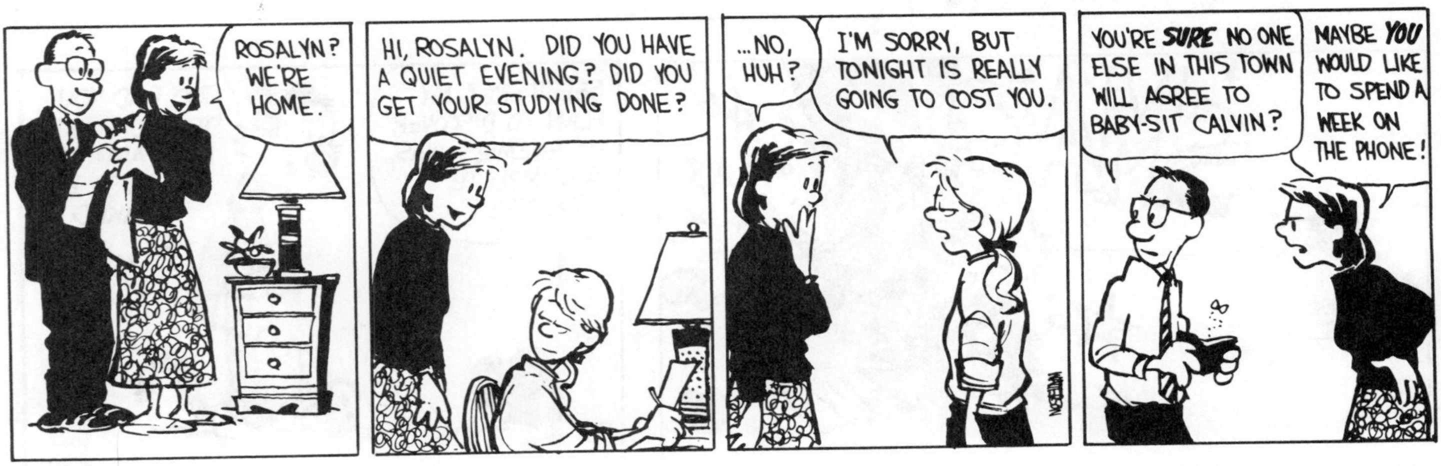
ROSALYN? WE'RE HOME.
HI, ROSALYN. DID YOU HAVE A QUIET EVENING? DID YOU GET YOUR STUDYING DONE?
...NO, HUH?
I'M SORRY, BUT TONIGHT IS REALLY GOING TO COST YOU.
WATTERSON
YOU'RE SURE NO ONE ELSE IN THIS TOWN WILL AGREE TO BABY-SIT CALVIN?
MAYBE YOU WOULD LIKE TO SPEND A WEEK ON THE PHONE!

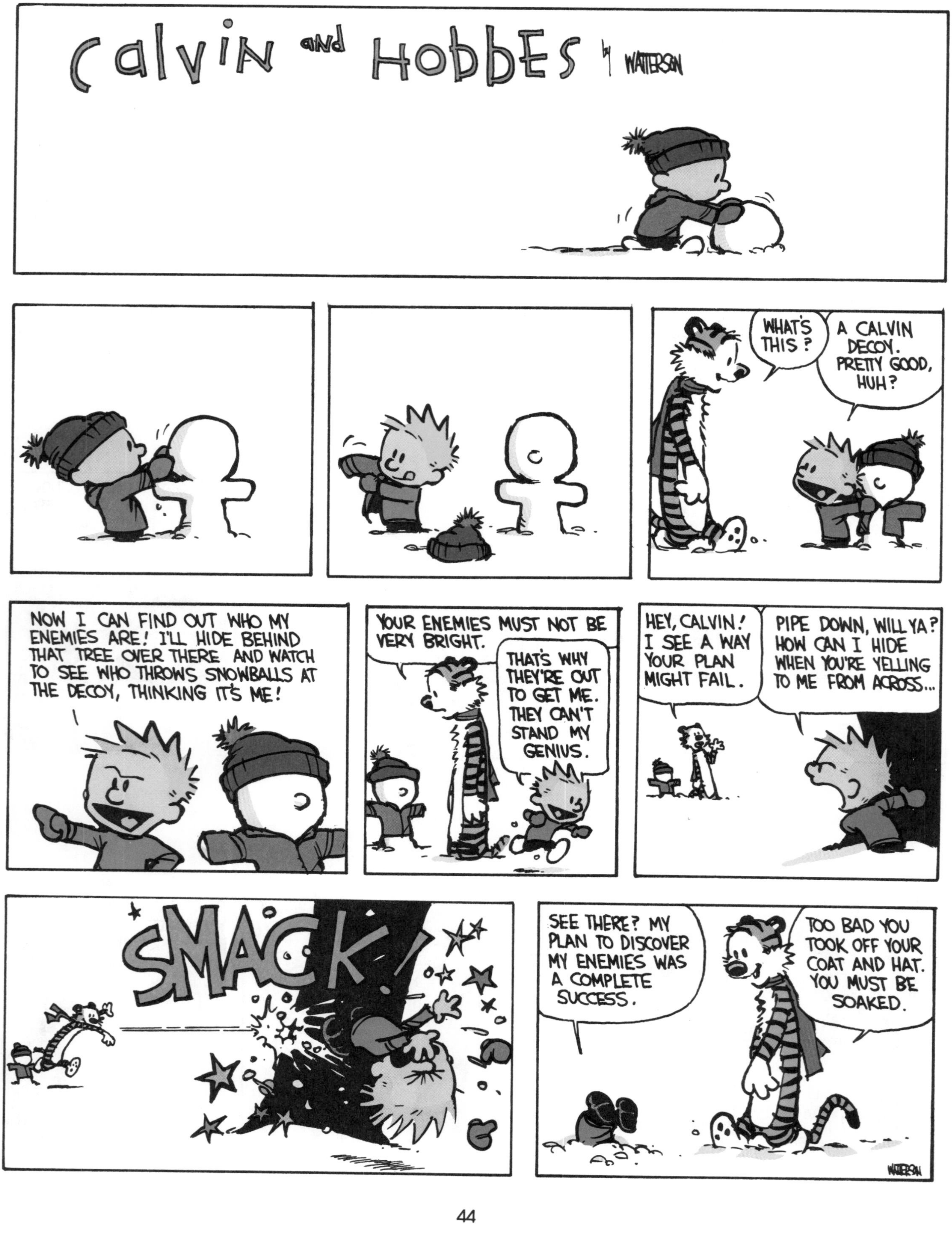
Calvin and Hobbes
by WATTERSON
WHAT'S THIS?
A CALVIN DECOY. PRETTY GOOD, HUH?
NOW I CAN FIND OUT WHO MY ENEMIES ARE! I'LL HIDE BEHIND THAT TREE OVER THERE AND WATCH TO SEE WHO THROWS SNOWBALLS AT THE DECOY, THINKING IT'S ME!
YOUR ENEMIES MUST NOT BE VERY BRIGHT.
THAT'S WHY THEY'RE OUT TO GET ME. THEY CAN'T STAND MY GENIUS.
HEY, CALVIN! I SEE A WAY YOUR PLAN MIGHT FAIL.
PIPE DOWN, WILL YA? HOW CAN I HIDE WHEN YOU'RE YELLING TO ME FROM ACROSS...
SMACK!
SEE THERE? MY PLAN TO DISCOVER MY ENEMIES WAS A COMPLETE SUCCESS.
TOO BAD YOU TOOK OFF YOUR COAT AND HAT. YOU MUST BE SOAKED.
WATTERSON

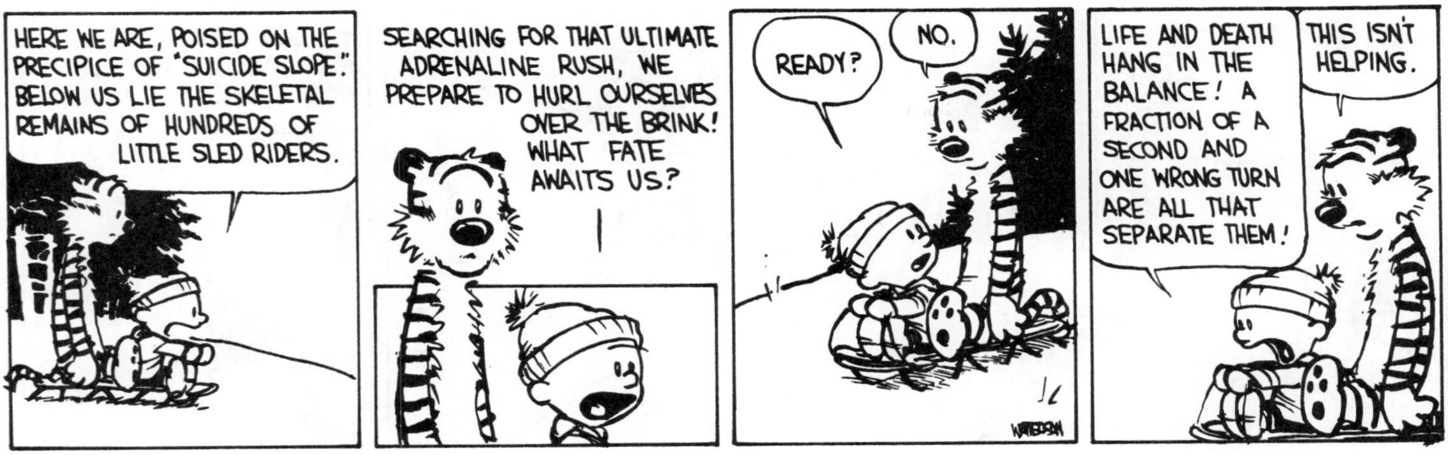
HERE WE ARE, POISED ON THE PRECIPICE OF "SUICIDE SLOPE." BELOW US LIE THE SKELETAL REMAINS OF HUNDREDS OF LITTLE SLED RIDERS.
SEARCHING FOR THAT ULTIMATE ADRENALINE RUSH, WE PREPARE TO HURL OURSELVES OVER THE BRINK! WHAT FATE AWAITS US?
READY?
NO.
LIFE AND DEATH HANG IN THE BALANCE! A FRACTION OF A SECOND AND ONE WRONG TURN ARE ALL THAT SEPARATE THEM!
THIS ISN'T HELPING.

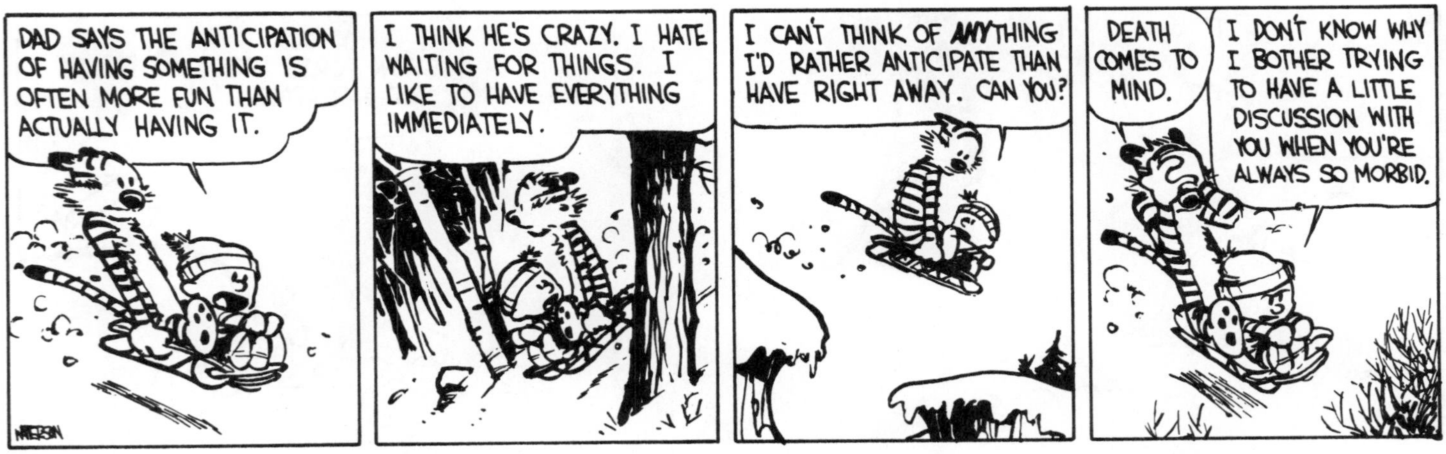
DAD SAYS THE ANTICIPATION OF HAVING SOMETHING IS OFTEN MORE FUN THAN ACTUALLY HAVING IT.
I THINK HE'S CRAZY. I HATE WAITING FOR THINGS. I LIKE TO HAVE EVERYTHING IMMEDIATELY.
I CAN'T THINK OF ANYTHING I'D RATHER ANTICIPATE THAN HAVE RIGHT AWAY. CAN YOU?
DEATH COMES TO MIND.
I DON'T KNOW WHY I BOTHER TRYING TO HAVE A LITTLE DISCUSSION WITH YOU WHEN YOU'RE ALWAYS SO MORBID.

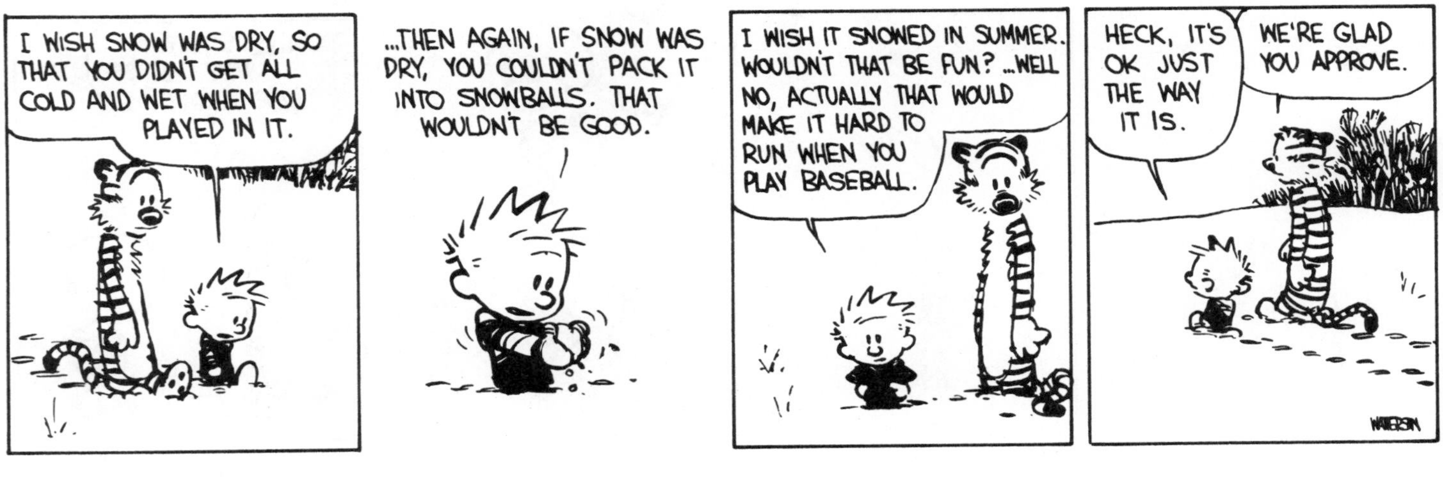
I WISH SNOW WAS DRY, SO THAT YOU DIDN'T GET ALL COLD AND WET WHEN YOU PLAYED IN IT.
...THEN AGAIN, IF SNOW WAS DRY, YOU COULDN'T PACK IT INTO SNOWBALLS. THAT WOULDN'T BE GOOD.
I WISH IT SNOWED IN SUMMER. WOULDN'T THAT BE FUN? ...WELL NO, ACTUALLY THAT WOULD MAKE IT HARD TO RUN WHEN YOU PLAY BASEBALL.
HECK, IT'S OK JUST THE WAY IT IS.
WE'RE GLAD YOU APPROVE.

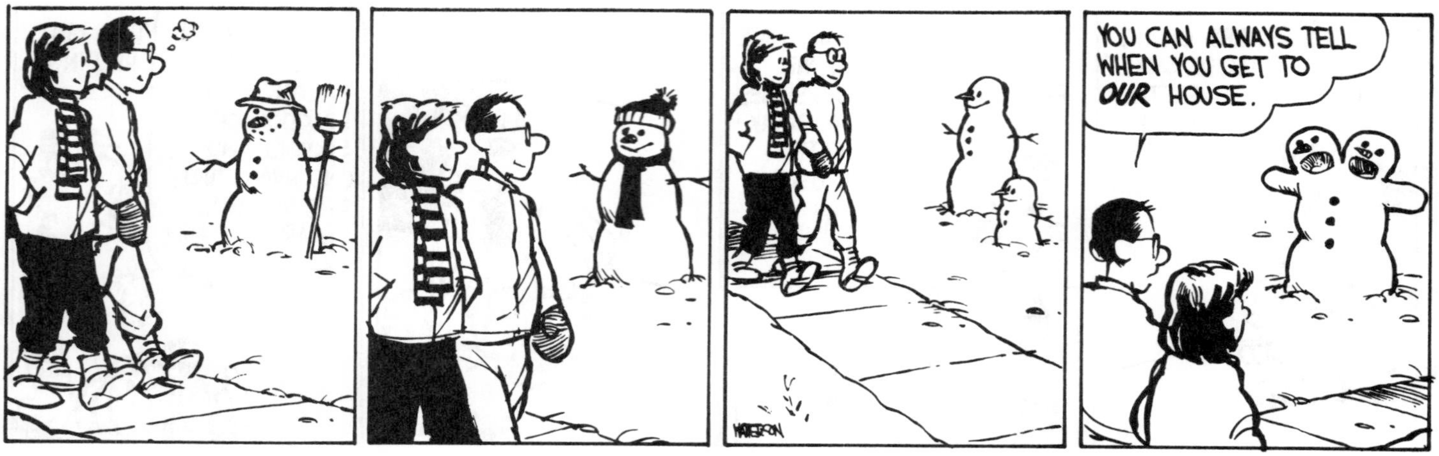
YOU CAN ALWAYS TELL WHEN YOU GET TO OUR HOUSE.

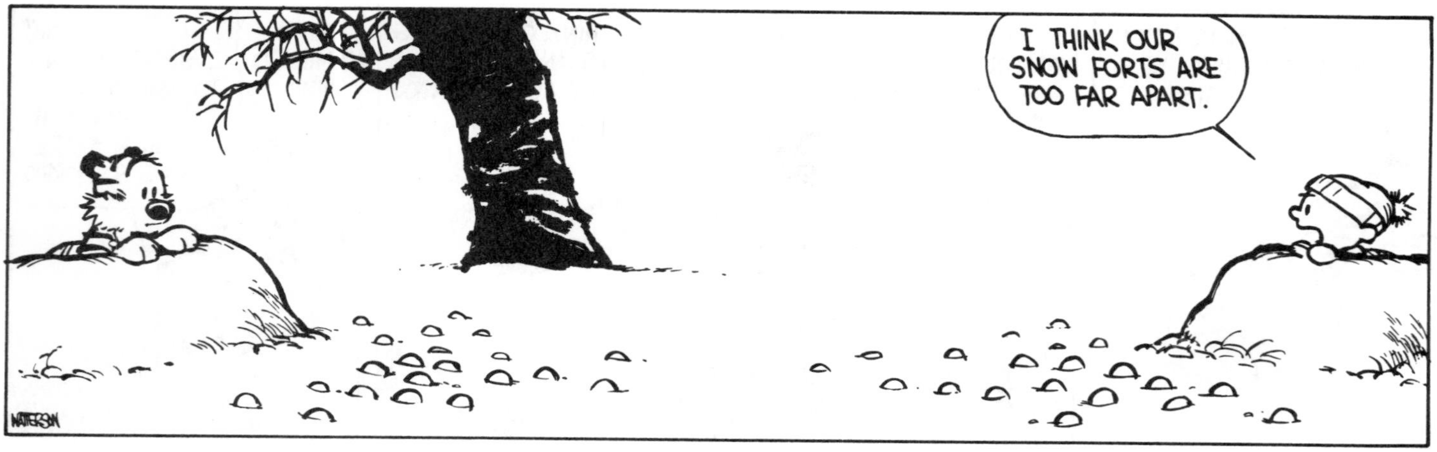
I THINK OUR SNOW FORTS ARE TOO FAR APART.

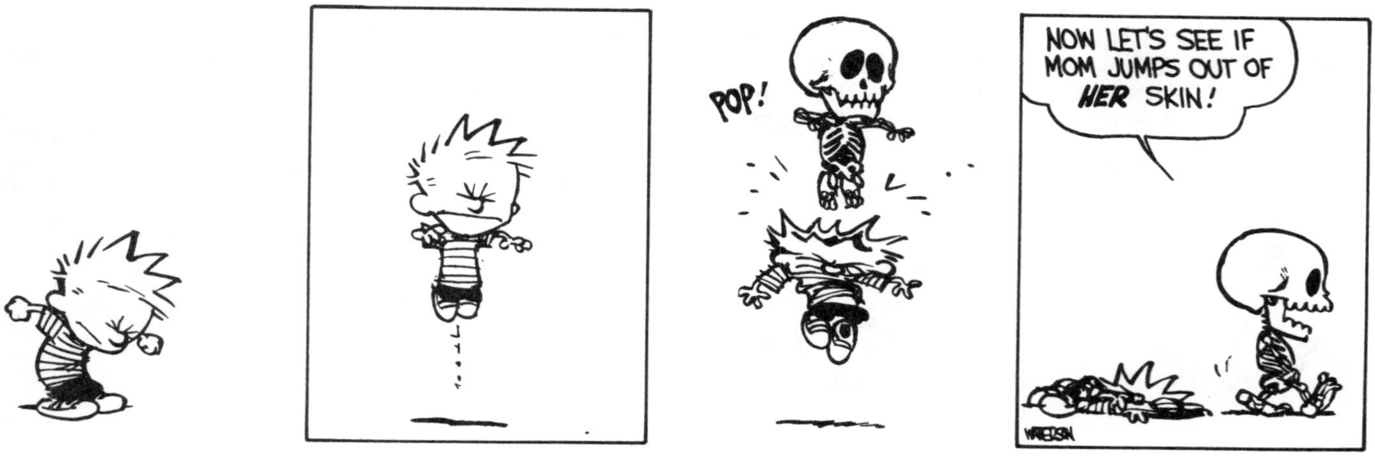
POP!
NOW LET'S SEE IF MOM JUMPS OUT OF HER SKIN!

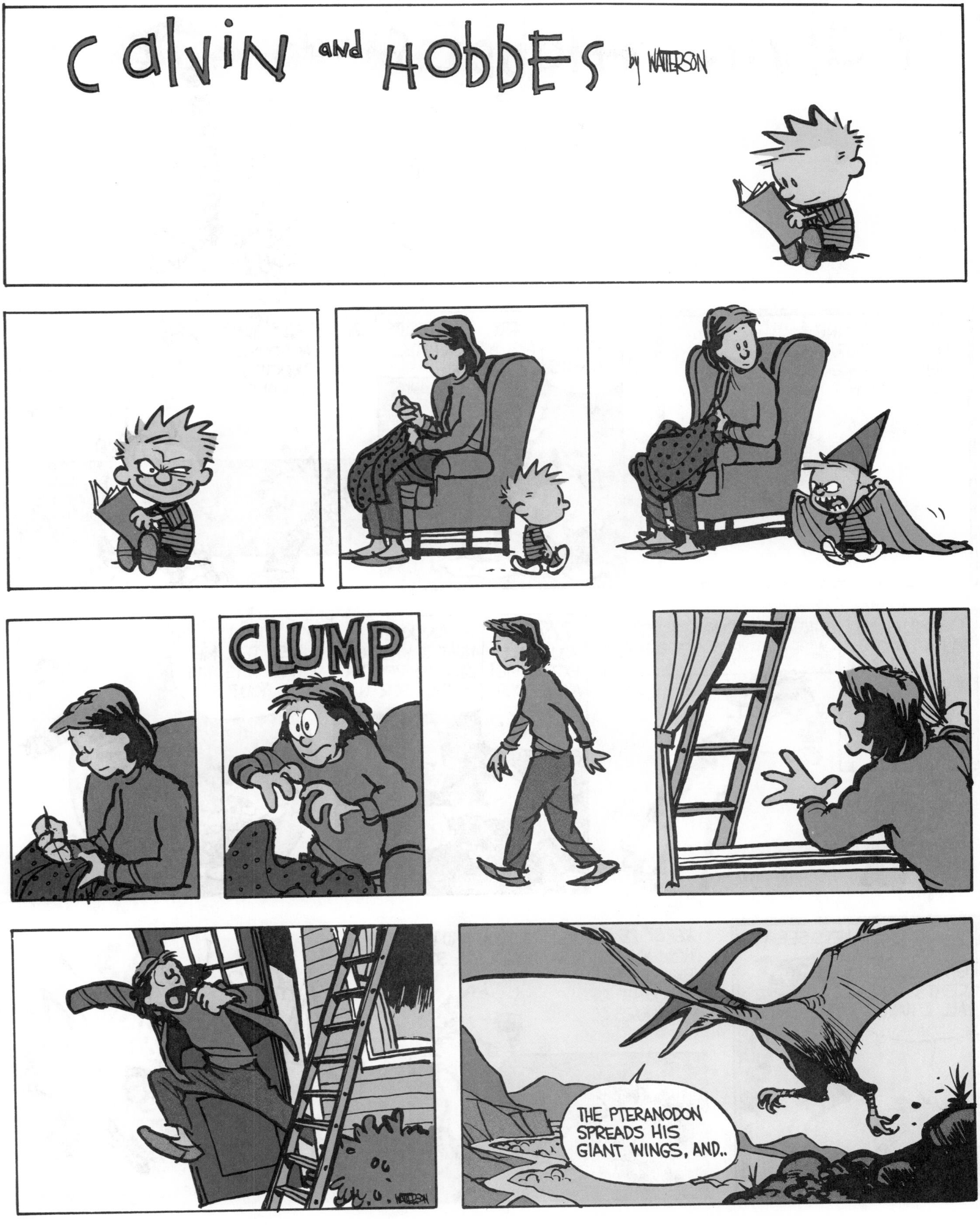
Calvin and HOBBES by WATTERSON
CLUMP
THE PTERANODON SPREADS HIS GIANT WINGS, AND..
WATTERSON

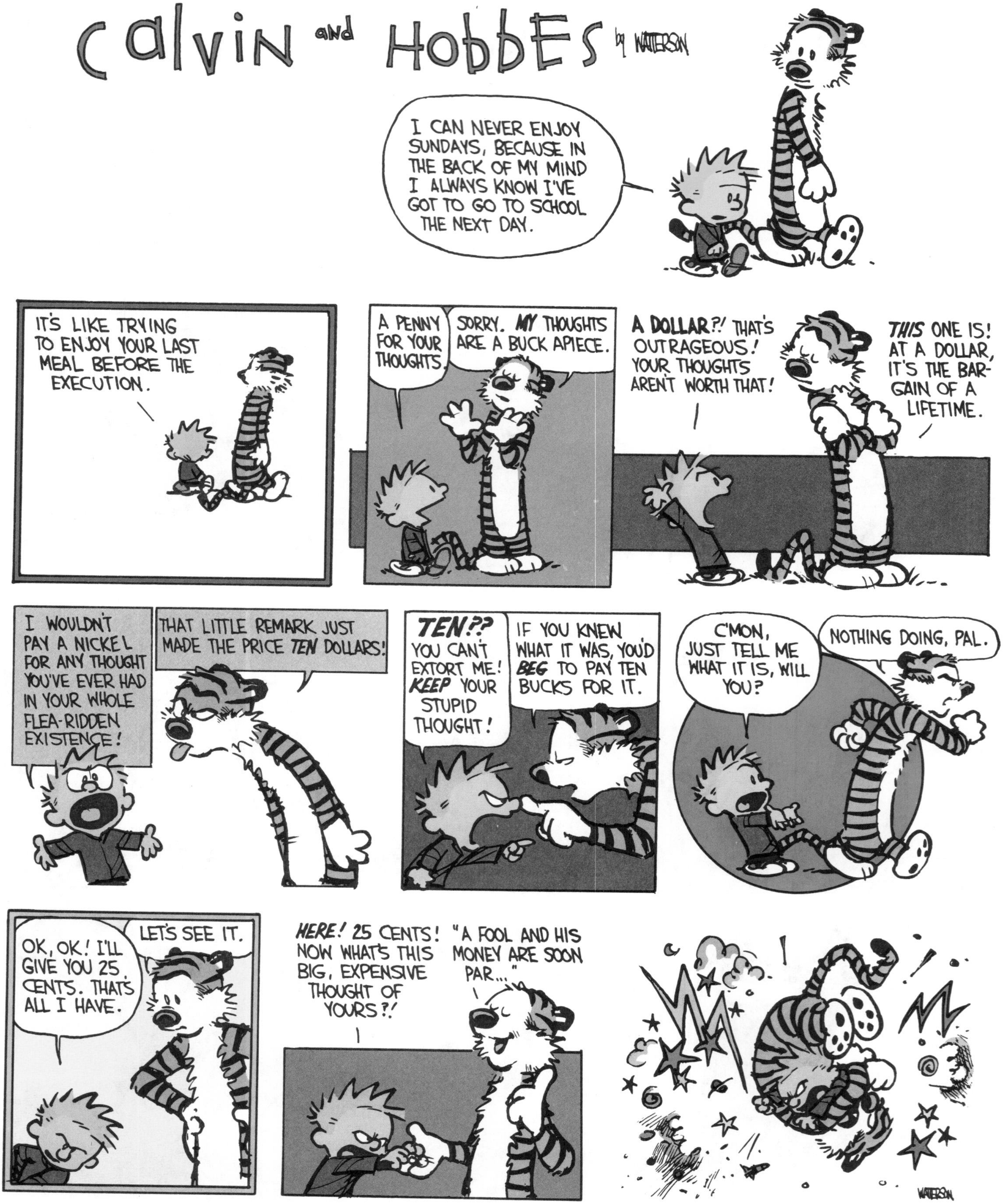
Calvin and HobbES
by WATTERSON
I CAN NEVER ENJOY SUNDAYS, BECAUSE IN THE BACK OF MY MIND I ALWAYS KNOW I'VE GOT TO GO TO SCHOOL THE NEXT DAY.
IT'S LIKE TRYING TO ENJOY YOUR LAST MEAL BEFORE THE EXECUTION.
A PENNY FOR YOUR THOUGHTS.
SORRY. MY THOUGHTS ARE A BUCK APIECE.
A DOLLAR?! THAT'S OUTRAGEOUS! YOUR THOUGHTS AREN'T WORTH THAT!
THIS ONE IS! AT A DOLLAR, IT'S THE BARGAIN OF A LIFETIME.
I WOULDN'T PAY A NICKEL FOR ANY THOUGHT YOU'VE EVER HAD IN YOUR WHOLE FLEA-RIDDEN EXISTENCE!
THAT LITTLE REMARK JUST MADE THE PRICE TEN DOLLARS!
TEN?? YOU CAN'T EXTORT ME! KEEP YOUR STUPID THOUGHT!
IF YOU KNEW WHAT IT WAS, YOU'D BEG TO PAY TEN BUCKS FOR IT.
C'MON, JUST TELL ME WHAT IT IS, WILL YOU?
NOTHING DOING, PAL.
OK, OK! I'LL GIVE YOU 25 CENTS. THAT'S ALL I HAVE.
LET'S SEE IT.
HERE! 25 CENTS! NOW WHAT'S THIS BIG, EXPENSIVE THOUGHT OF YOURS?!
"A FOOL AND HIS MONEY ARE SOON PAR..."
WATTERSON

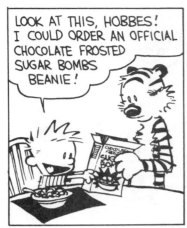

LOOK AT THIS, HOBBES! I COULD ORDER AN OFFICIAL CHOCOLATE FROSTED SUGAR BOMBS BEANIE!
SEE, IT HAS A BATTERY-POWERED PROPELLER ON TOP AND A BIG STAR ON THE FRONT! ISN'T THAT NEAT?
YOU HAVE TO SEND IN FOUR BOX "PROOF OF PURCHASE SEALS" TO GET IT, IT SAYS.
CHOCOLATE FROSTED SUGAR BOMBS
WELL, DON'T JUST STAND THERE, OR THIS'LL TAKE FOREVER.
UGH. THIS STUFF ALWAYS MAKES MY HEART SKIP.

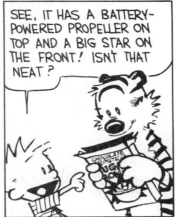

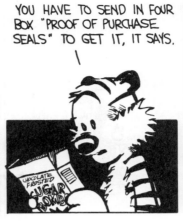

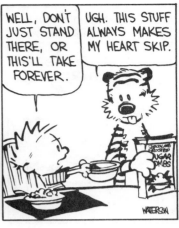

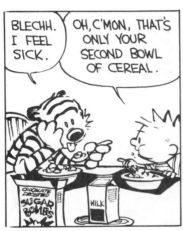

BLECHH. I FEEL SICK.
OH, C'MON, THAT'S ONLY YOUR SECOND BOWL OF CEREAL.
CHOCOLATE FROSTED SUGAR BOMBS
MILK
THIS STUFF IS PURE SUGAR.
BUT IT'S **FORTIFIED** WITH EIGHT ESSENTIAL VITAMINS, SO IT'S GOOD FOR YOU.
GIVE ME A BREAK. THIS IS LIKE EATING A BOWL OF MILK DUDS.
LOOK, IT SAYS RIGHT ON THE BOX, "PART OF A WHOLESOME, NUTRITIOUS, BALANCED BREAKFAST."
AND THEY SHOW A GUY EATING FIVE GRAPEFRUITS, A DOZEN BRAN MUFFINS...
YOU KNOW WHY YOU SHAKE LIKE THAT? VITAMIN DEFICIENCY, I'LL BET.

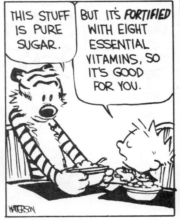

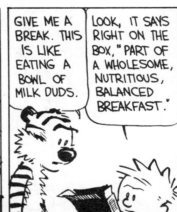

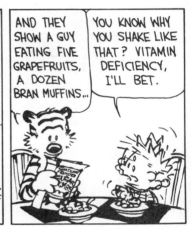

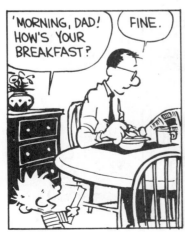

'MORNING, DAD! HOW'S YOUR BREAKFAST?
FINE.
OATMEAL, HUH? A BOWL OF PASTY, BLAND, COLORLESS SLUDGE.
YES. WHY DON'T YOU GO DESCRIBE YOUR **OWN** FOOD SOMEWHERE ELSE?
I'LL BET YOU'D RATHER HAVE A BOWL OF TASTY, LIP-SMACKING, CRUNCHY-ON-THE-OUTSIDE, CHEWY-ON-THE-INSIDE, CHOCOLATE FROSTED SUGAR BOMBS! CAN I POUR YOU SOME?
CHOCOLATE FROSTED SUGAR BOMBS
NO, THANKS. I'M TRYING TO REACH MIDDLE AGE.
WHAT ARE **YOU** HAVING, MOM? BORING OLD TOAST AND TEA?
YOU WANT THE BEANIE, **YOU** EAT THE CEREAL, CALVIN.

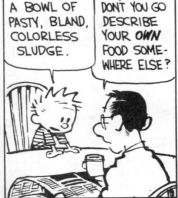

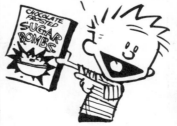

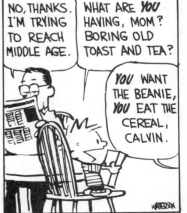

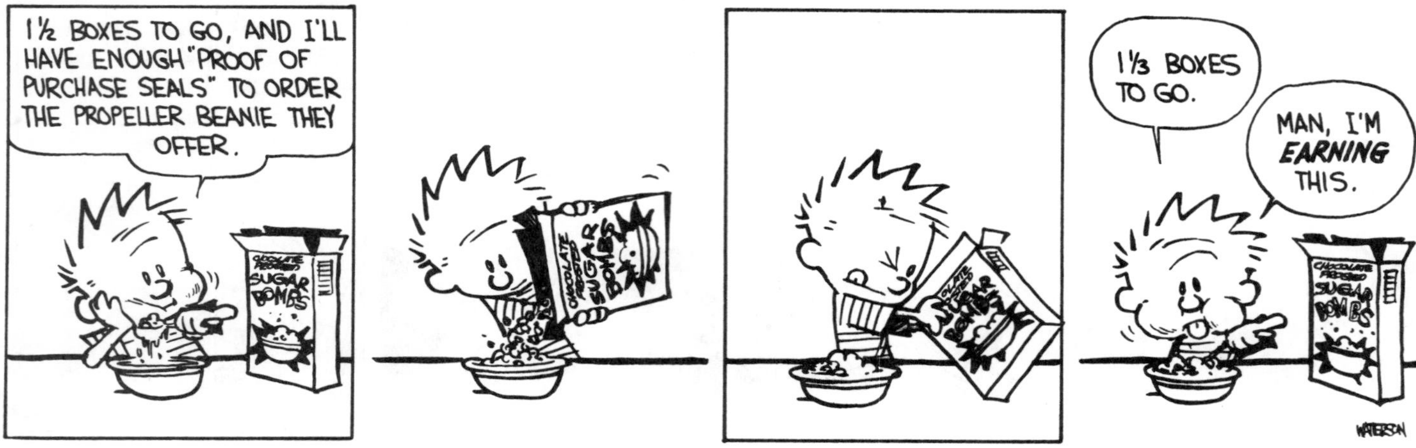
1½ BOXES TO GO, AND I'LL HAVE ENOUGH "PROOF OF PURCHASE SEALS" TO ORDER THE PROPELLER BEANIE THEY OFFER.
1⅓ BOXES TO GO.
MAN, I'M *EARNING* THIS.

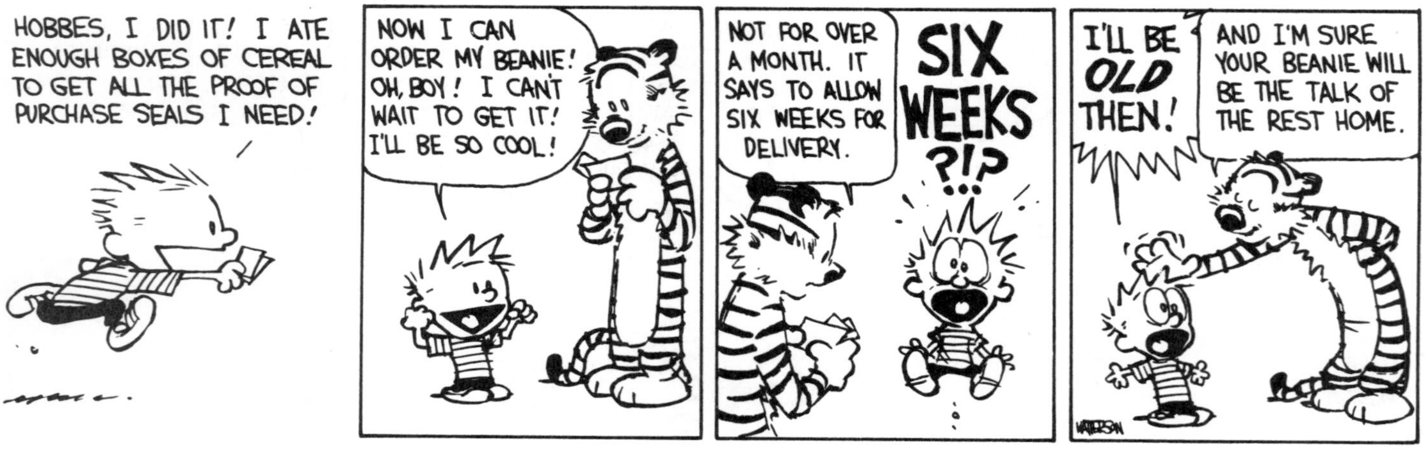
HOBBES, I DID IT! I ATE ENOUGH BOXES OF CEREAL TO GET ALL THE PROOF OF PURCHASE SEALS I NEED!
NOW I CAN ORDER MY BEANIE! OH, BOY! I CAN'T WAIT TO GET IT! I'LL BE SO COOL!
NOT FOR OVER A MONTH. IT SAYS TO ALLOW SIX WEEKS FOR DELIVERY.
SIX WEEKS ?!?
I'LL BE *OLD* THEN!
AND I'M SURE YOUR BEANIE WILL BE THE TALK OF THE REST HOME.

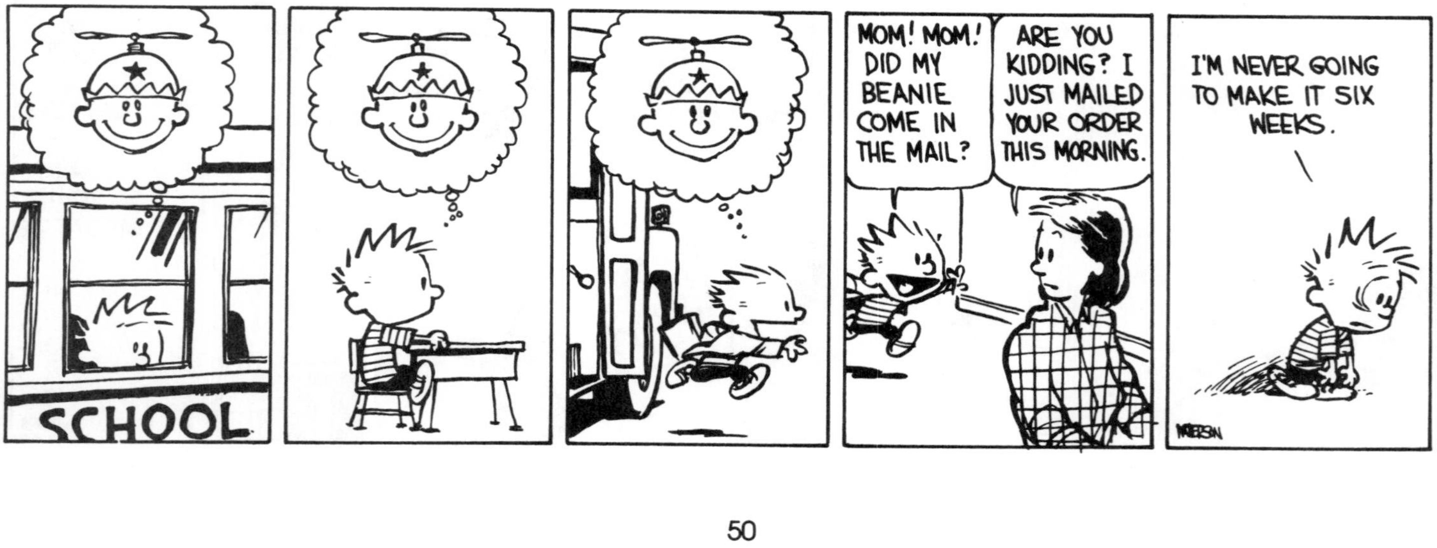
SCHOOL
MOM! MOM! DID MY BEANIE COME IN THE MAIL?
ARE YOU KIDDING? I JUST MAILED YOUR ORDER THIS MORNING.
I'M NEVER GOING TO MAKE IT SIX WEEKS.

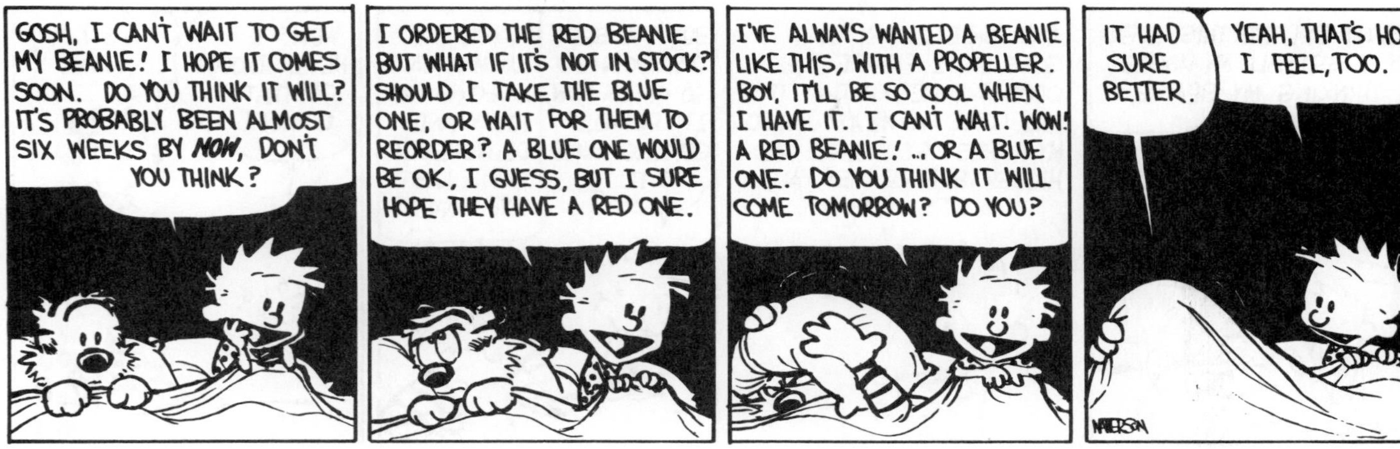
GOSH, I CAN'T WAIT TO GET MY BEANIE! I HOPE IT COMES SOON. DO YOU THINK IT WILL? IT'S PROBABLY BEEN ALMOST SIX WEEKS BY *NOW*, DON'T YOU THINK?
I ORDERED THE RED BEANIE. BUT WHAT IF IT'S NOT IN STOCK? SHOULD I TAKE THE BLUE ONE, OR WAIT FOR THEM TO REORDER? A BLUE ONE WOULD BE OK, I GUESS, BUT I SURE HOPE THEY HAVE A RED ONE.
I'VE ALWAYS WANTED A BEANIE LIKE THIS, WITH A PROPELLER. BOY, IT'LL BE SO COOL WHEN I HAVE IT. I CAN'T WAIT. WOW! A RED BEANIE! ...OR A BLUE ONE. DO YOU THINK IT WILL COME TOMORROW? DO YOU?
IT HAD SURE BETTER.
YEAH, THAT'S HOW I FEEL, TOO.

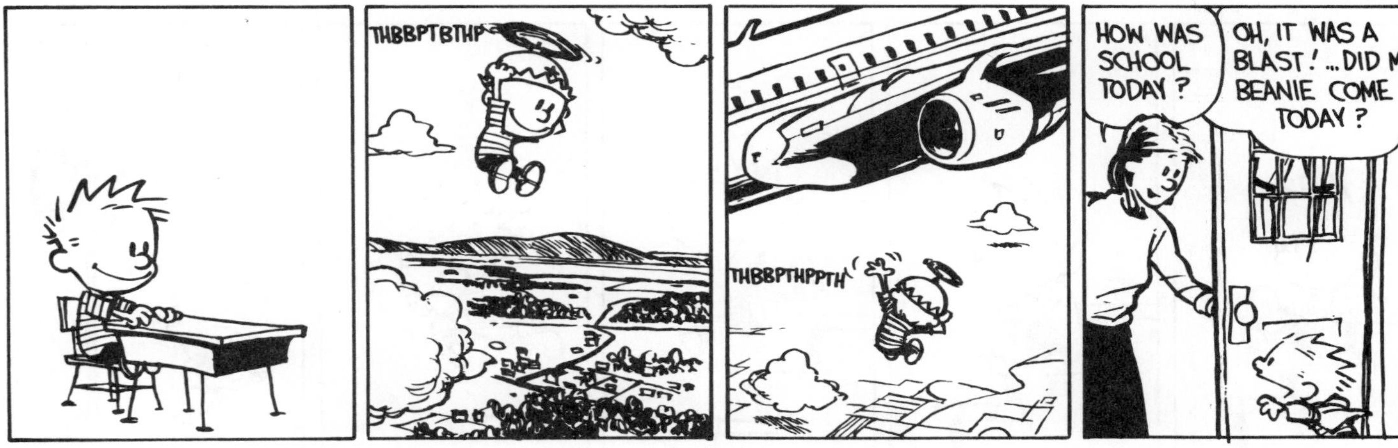
THBBPTBTHP
THBBPTHPPTH
HOW WAS SCHOOL TODAY?
OH, IT WAS A BLAST! ...DID MY BEANIE COME TODAY?

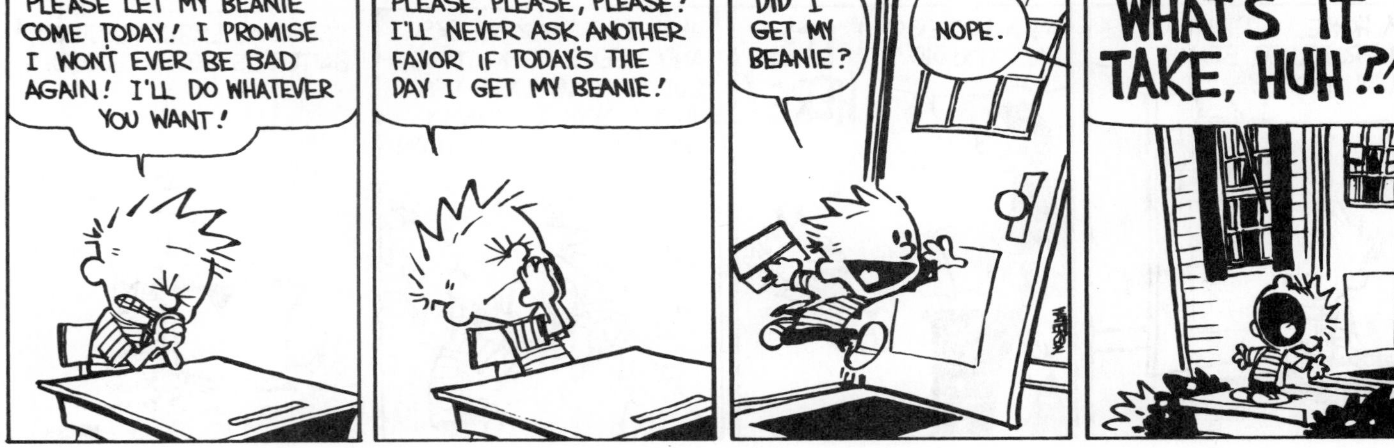
PLEASE LET MY BEANIE COME TODAY! I PROMISE I WON'T EVER BE BAD AGAIN! I'LL DO WHATEVER YOU WANT!
PLEASE, PLEASE, PLEASE! I'LL NEVER ASK ANOTHER FAVOR IF TODAY'S THE DAY I GET MY BEANIE!
DID I GET MY BEANIE?
NOPE.
WHAT'S IT TAKE, HUH ?!

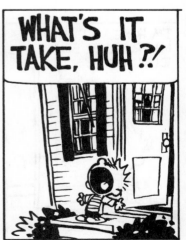

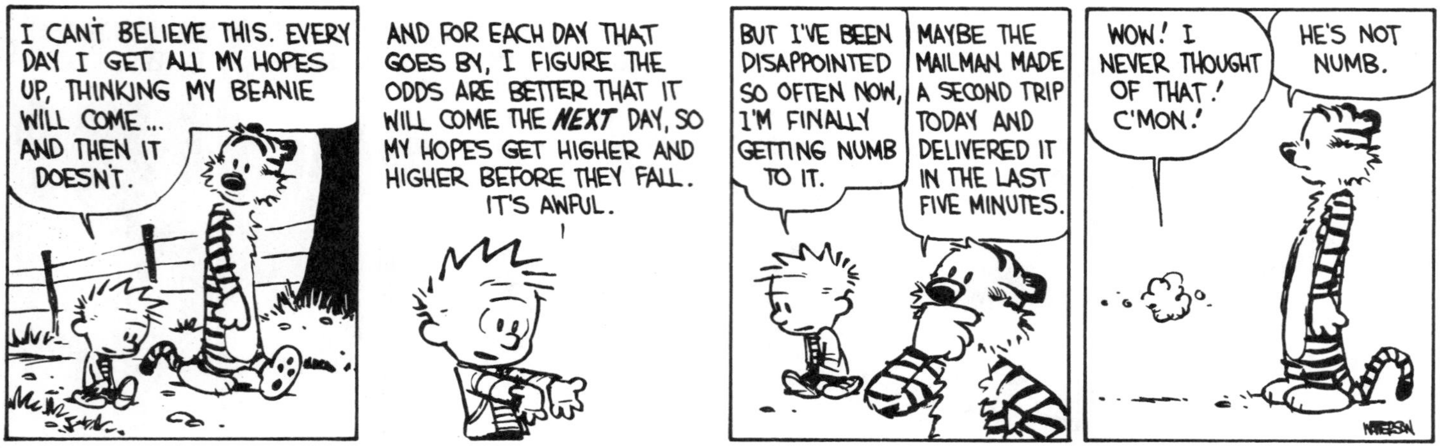
I CAN'T BELIEVE THIS. EVERY DAY I GET ALL MY HOPES UP, THINKING MY BEANIE WILL COME... AND THEN IT DOESN'T.
AND FOR EACH DAY THAT GOES BY, I FIGURE THE ODDS ARE BETTER THAT IT WILL COME THE NEXT DAY, SO MY HOPES GET HIGHER AND HIGHER BEFORE THEY FALL. IT'S AWFUL.
BUT I'VE BEEN DISAPPOINTED SO OFTEN NOW, I'M FINALLY GETTING NUMB TO IT.
MAYBE THE MAILMAN MADE A SECOND TRIP TODAY AND DELIVERED IT IN THE LAST FIVE MINUTES.
WOW! I NEVER THOUGHT OF THAT! C'MON!
HE'S NOT NUMB.

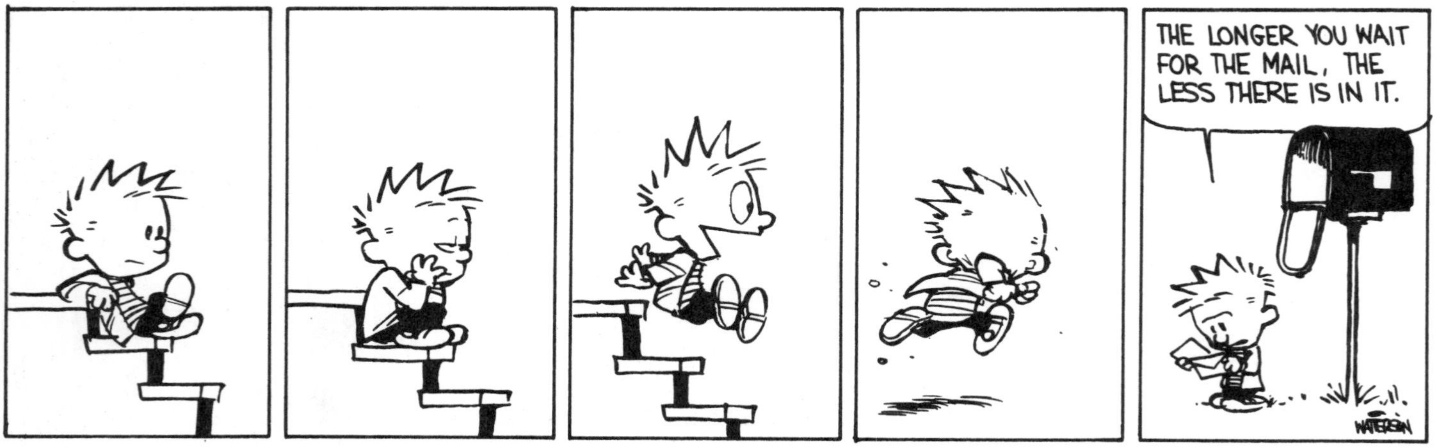
THE LONGER YOU WAIT FOR THE MAIL, THE LESS THERE IS IN IT.

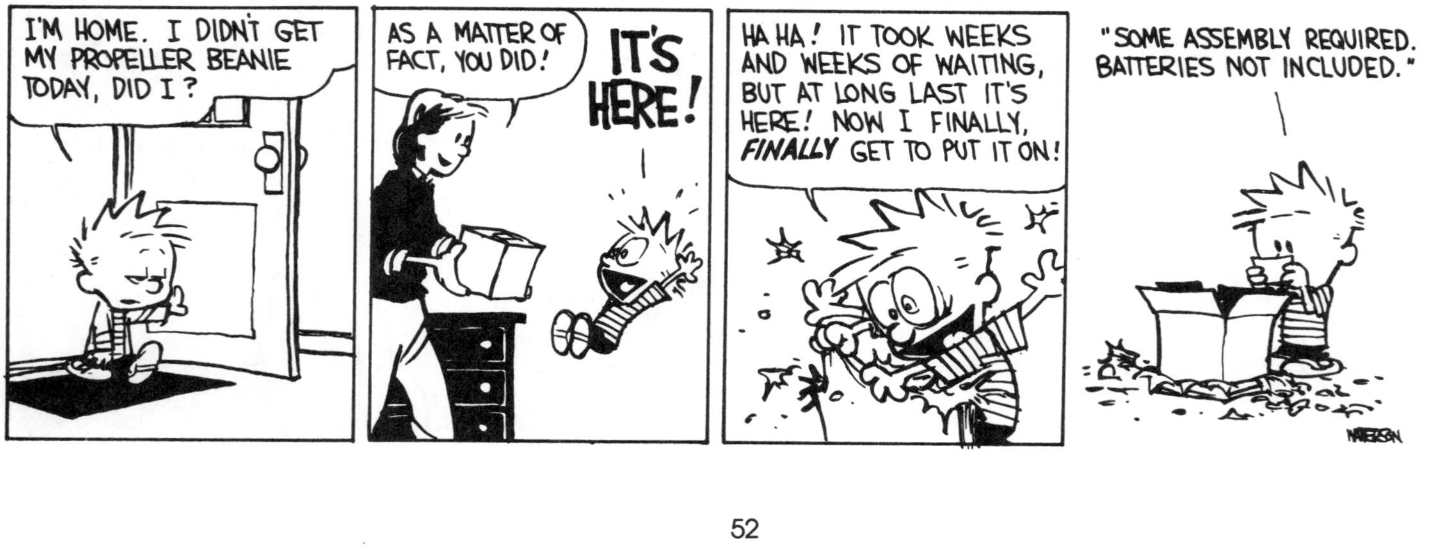
I'M HOME. I DIDN'T GET MY PROPELLER BEANIE TODAY, DID I?
AS A MATTER OF FACT, YOU DID!
IT'S HERE!
HA HA! IT TOOK WEEKS AND WEEKS OF WAITING, BUT AT LONG LAST IT'S HERE! NOW I FINALLY, FINALLY GET TO PUT IT ON!
"SOME ASSEMBLY REQUIRED. BATTERIES NOT INCLUDED."

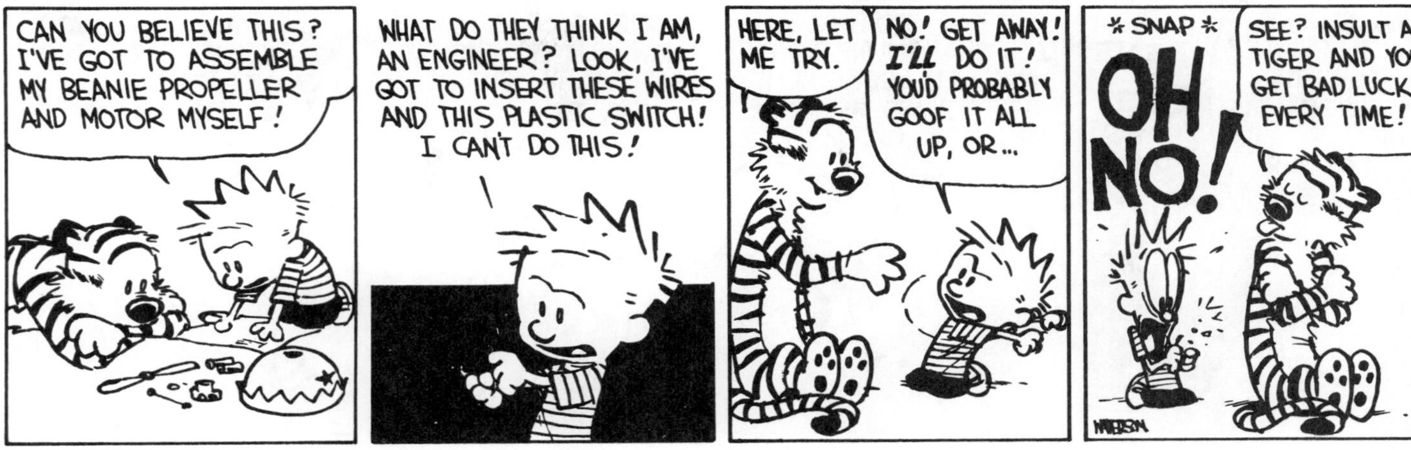
CAN YOU BELIEVE THIS? I'VE GOT TO ASSEMBLE MY BEANIE PROPELLER AND MOTOR MYSELF!
WHAT DO THEY THINK I AM, AN ENGINEER? LOOK, I'VE GOT TO INSERT THESE WIRES AND THIS PLASTIC SWITCH! I CAN'T DO THIS!
HERE, LET ME TRY.
NO! GET AWAY! I'LL DO IT! YOU'D PROBABLY GOOF IT ALL UP, OR...
SNAP
OH NO!
SEE? INSULT A TIGER AND YOU GET BAD LUCK! EVERY TIME!

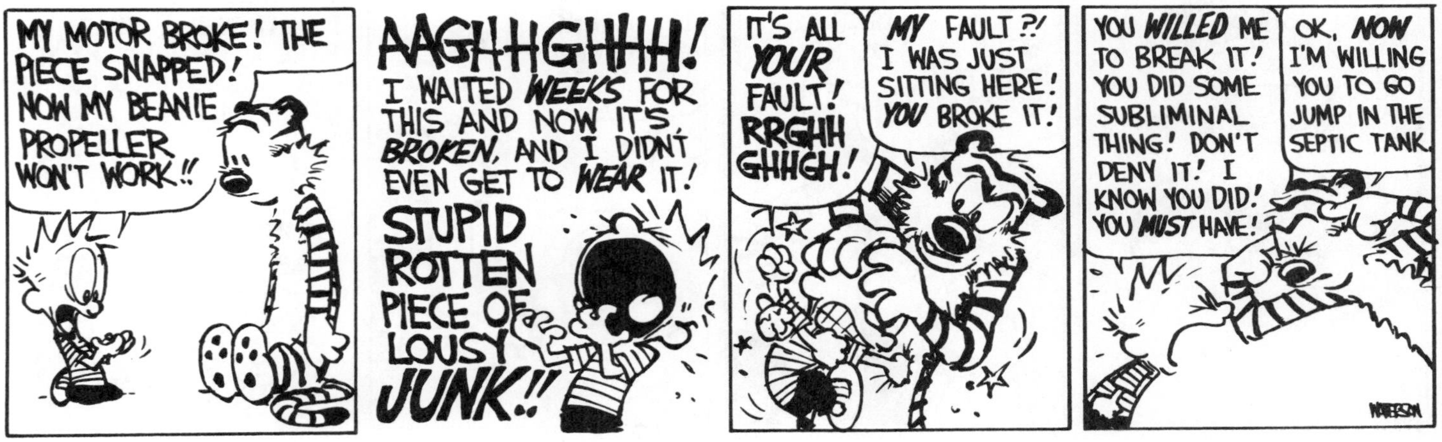
MY MOTOR BROKE! THE PIECE SNAPPED! NOW MY BEANIE PROPELLER WON'T WORK!!
AAGHHGHHH! I WAITED WEEKS FOR THIS AND NOW IT'S BROKEN, AND I DIDN'T EVEN GET TO WEAR IT!
STUPID ROTTEN PIECE OF LOUSY JUNK!!
IT'S ALL YOUR FAULT! RRGHH GHHGH!
MY FAULT?! I WAS JUST SITTING HERE! YOU BROKE IT!
YOU WILLED ME TO BREAK IT! YOU DID SOME SUBLIMINAL THING! DON'T DENY IT! I KNOW YOU DID! YOU MUST HAVE!
OK, NOW I'M WILLING YOU TO GO JUMP IN THE SEPTIC TANK.

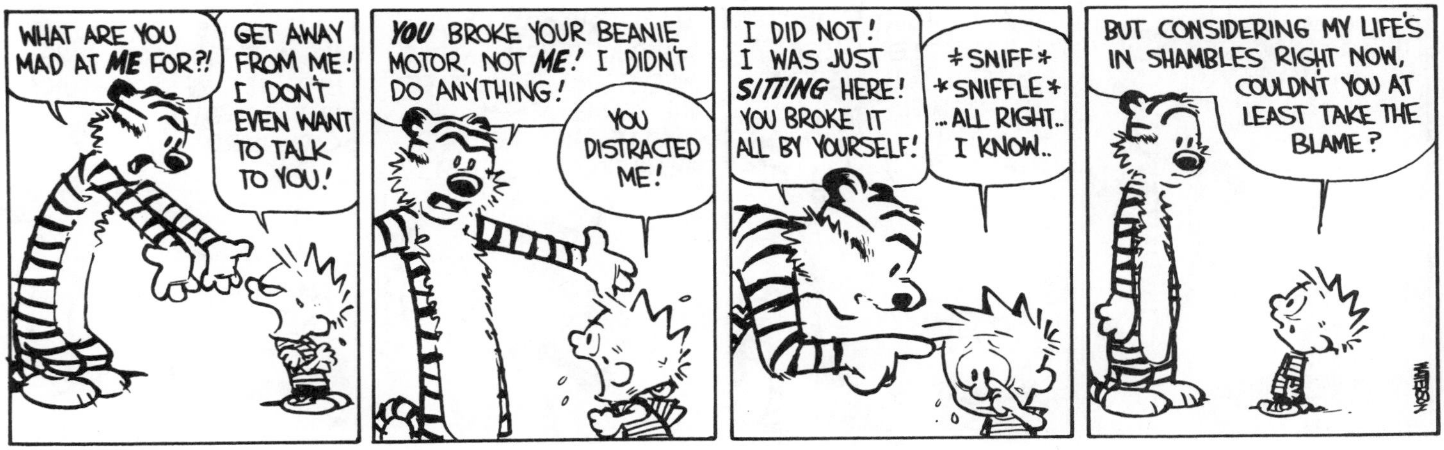
WHAT ARE YOU MAD AT ME FOR?!
GET AWAY FROM ME! I DON'T EVEN WANT TO TALK TO YOU!
YOU BROKE YOUR BEANIE MOTOR, NOT ME! I DIDN'T DO ANYTHING!
YOU DISTRACTED ME!
I DID NOT! I WAS JUST SITTING HERE! YOU BROKE IT ALL BY YOURSELF!
SNIFF *SNIFFLE* ...ALL RIGHT.. I KNOW..
BUT CONSIDERING MY LIFE'S IN SHAMBLES RIGHT NOW, COULDN'T YOU AT LEAST TAKE THE BLAME?

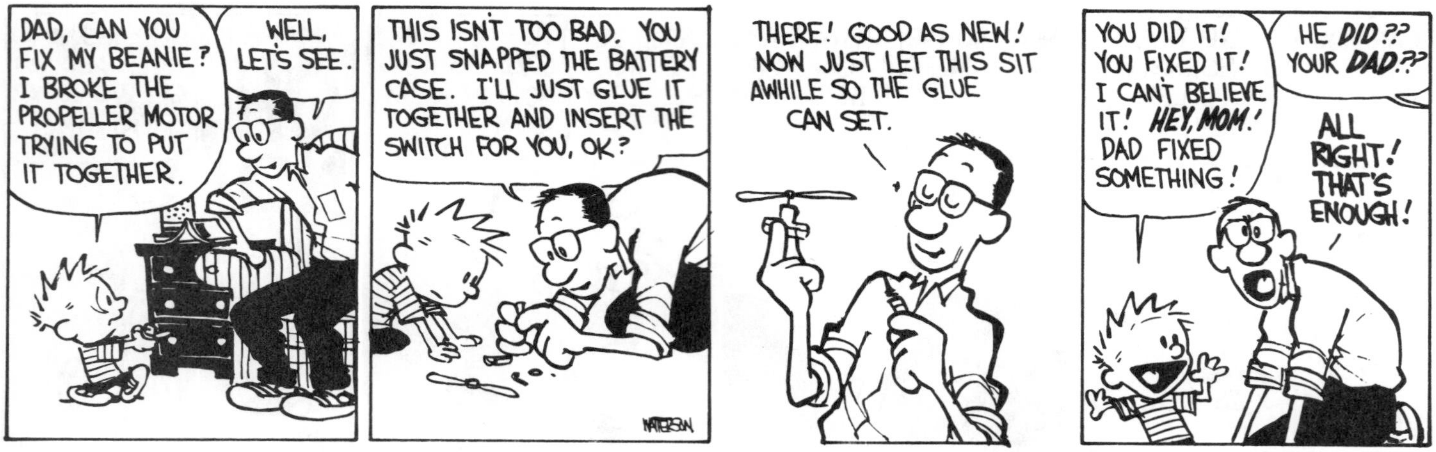
DAD, CAN YOU FIX MY BEANIE? I BROKE THE PROPELLER MOTOR TRYING TO PUT IT TOGETHER.
WELL, LET'S SEE.
THIS ISN'T TOO BAD. YOU JUST SNAPPED THE BATTERY CASE. I'LL JUST GLUE IT TOGETHER AND INSERT THE SWITCH FOR YOU, OK?
WATERSON
THERE! GOOD AS NEW! NOW JUST LET THIS SIT AWHILE SO THE GLUE CAN SET.
YOU DID IT! YOU FIXED IT! I CAN'T BELIEVE IT! HEY, MOM! DAD FIXED SOMETHING!
HE DID?? YOUR DAD??
ALL RIGHT! THAT'S ENOUGH!

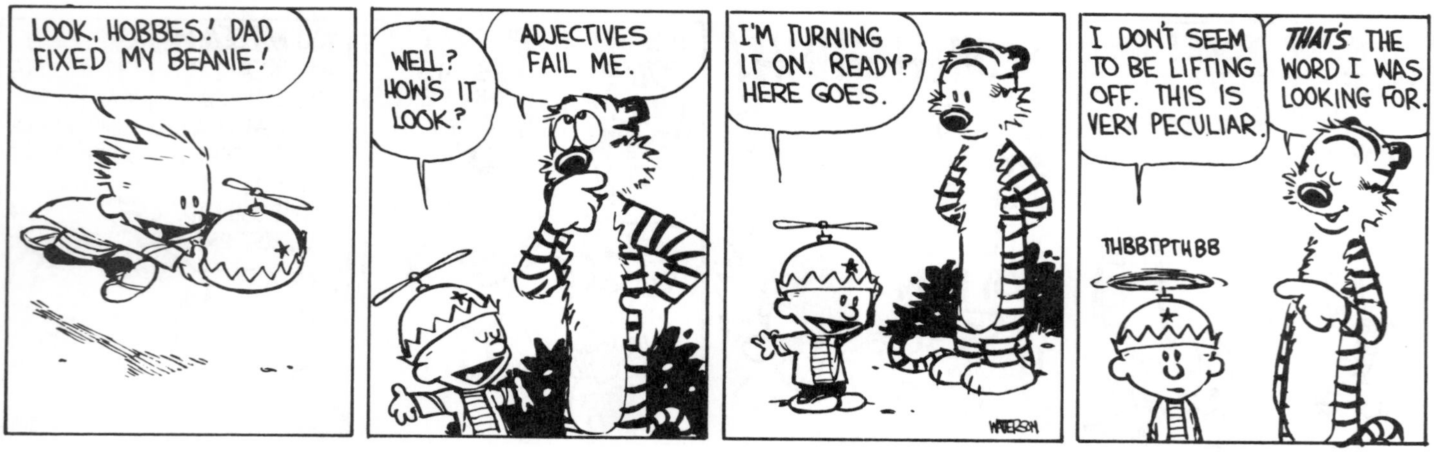
LOOK, HOBBES! DAD FIXED MY BEANIE!
WELL? HOW'S IT LOOK?
ADJECTIVES FAIL ME.
I'M TURNING IT ON. READY? HERE GOES.
WATERSON
I DON'T SEEM TO BE LIFTING OFF. THIS IS VERY PECULIAR.
THAT'S THE WORD I WAS LOOKING FOR.
THBBTPTHBB

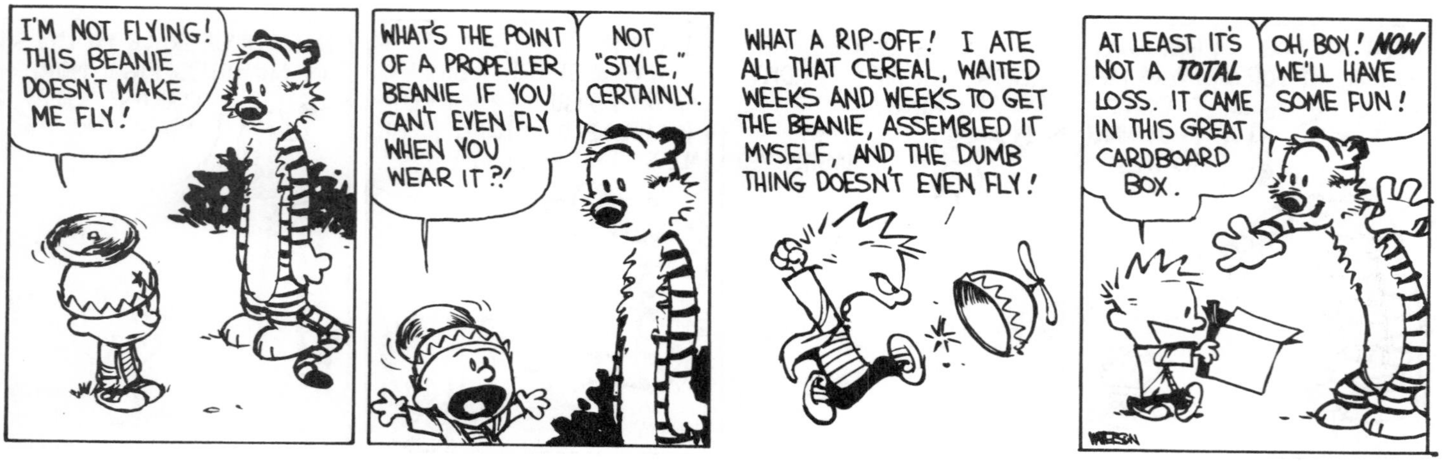
I'M NOT FLYING! THIS BEANIE DOESN'T MAKE ME FLY!
WHAT'S THE POINT OF A PROPELLER BEANIE IF YOU CAN'T EVEN FLY WHEN YOU WEAR IT?!
NOT "STYLE," CERTAINLY.
WHAT A RIP-OFF! I ATE ALL THAT CEREAL, WAITED WEEKS AND WEEKS TO GET THE BEANIE, ASSEMBLED IT MYSELF, AND THE DUMB THING DOESN'T EVEN FLY!
AT LEAST IT'S NOT A TOTAL LOSS. IT CAME IN THIS GREAT CARDBOARD BOX.
OH, BOY! NOW WE'LL HAVE SOME FUN!
WATERSON

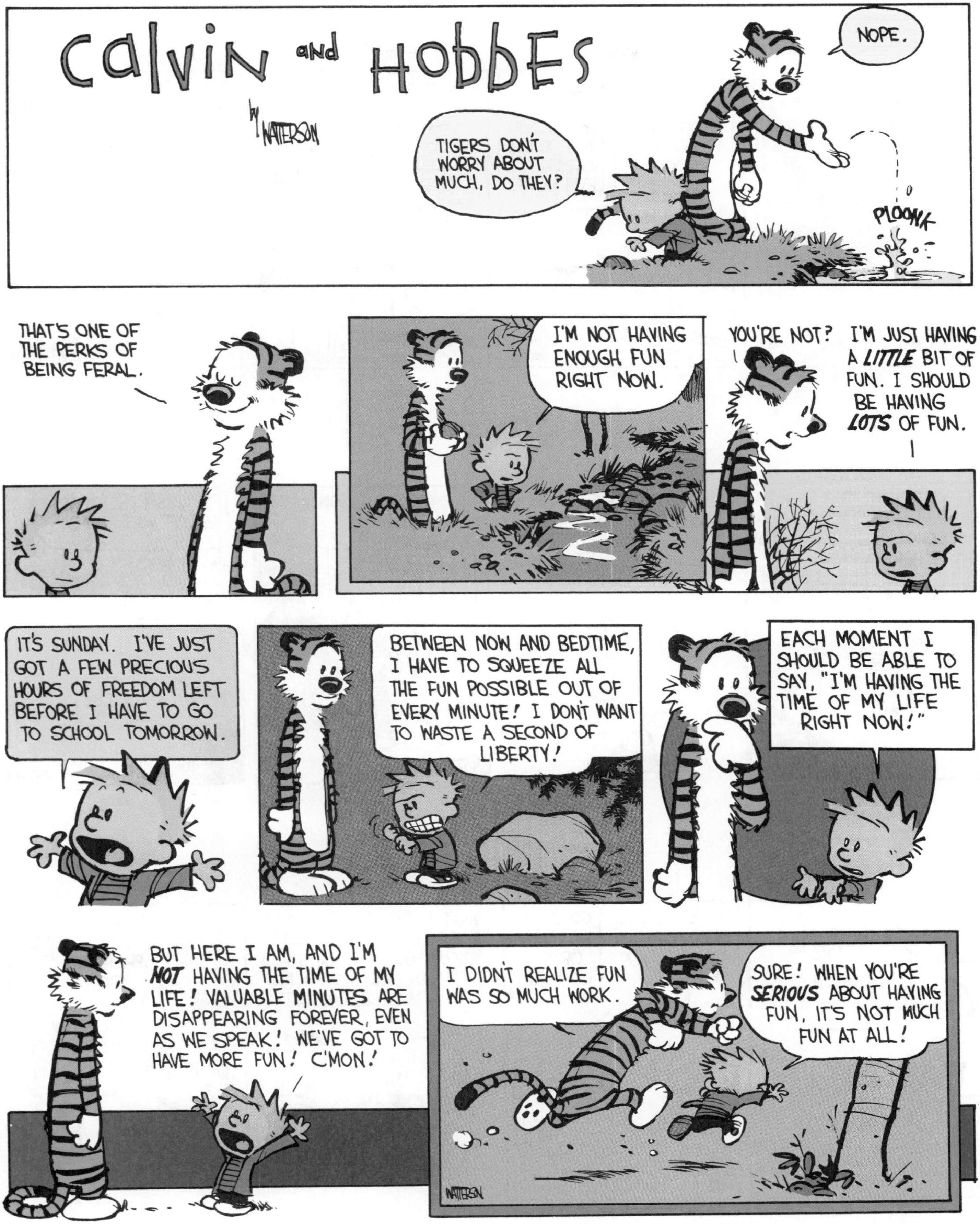
Calvin and HOBBES
by WATTERSON
TIGERS DON'T WORRY ABOUT MUCH, DO THEY?
NOPE.
PLOONK
THAT'S ONE OF THE PERKS OF BEING FERAL.
I'M NOT HAVING ENOUGH FUN RIGHT NOW.
YOU'RE NOT?
I'M JUST HAVING A LITTLE BIT OF FUN. I SHOULD BE HAVING LOTS OF FUN.
IT'S SUNDAY. I'VE JUST GOT A FEW PRECIOUS HOURS OF FREEDOM LEFT BEFORE I HAVE TO GO TO SCHOOL TOMORROW.
BETWEEN NOW AND BEDTIME, I HAVE TO SQUEEZE ALL THE FUN POSSIBLE OUT OF EVERY MINUTE! I DON'T WANT TO WASTE A SECOND OF LIBERTY!
EACH MOMENT I SHOULD BE ABLE TO SAY, "I'M HAVING THE TIME OF MY LIFE RIGHT NOW!"
BUT HERE I AM, AND I'M NOT HAVING THE TIME OF MY LIFE! VALUABLE MINUTES ARE DISAPPEARING FOREVER, EVEN AS WE SPEAK! WE'VE GOT TO HAVE MORE FUN! C'MON!
I DIDN'T REALIZE FUN WAS SO MUCH WORK.
SURE! WHEN YOU'RE SERIOUS ABOUT HAVING FUN, IT'S NOT MUCH FUN AT ALL!
WATTERSON

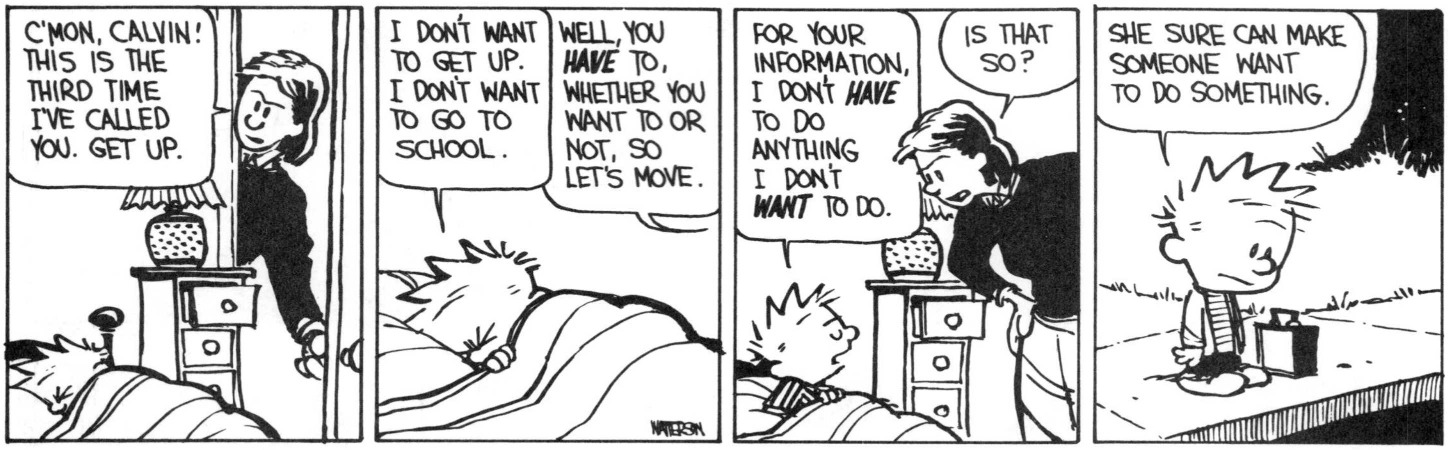
C'MON, CALVIN! THIS IS THE THIRD TIME I'VE CALLED YOU. GET UP.
I DON'T WANT TO GET UP. I DON'T WANT TO GO TO SCHOOL.
WELL, YOU *HAVE* TO, WHETHER YOU WANT TO OR NOT, SO LET'S MOVE.
FOR YOUR INFORMATION, I DON'T *HAVE* TO DO ANYTHING I DON'T *WANT* TO DO.
IS THAT SO?
SHE SURE CAN MAKE SOMEONE WANT TO DO SOMETHING.

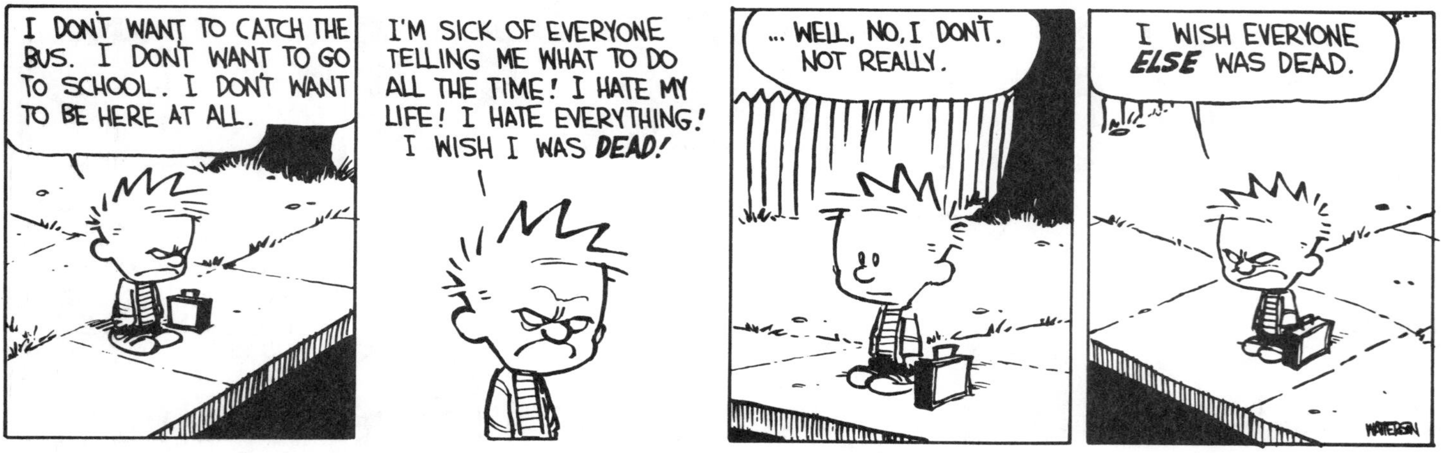
I DON'T WANT TO CATCH THE BUS. I DON'T WANT TO GO TO SCHOOL. I DON'T WANT TO BE HERE AT ALL.
I'M SICK OF EVERYONE TELLING ME WHAT TO DO ALL THE TIME! I HATE MY LIFE! I HATE EVERYTHING! I WISH I WAS *DEAD!*
... WELL, NO, I DON'T. NOT REALLY.
I WISH EVERYONE *ELSE* WAS DEAD.

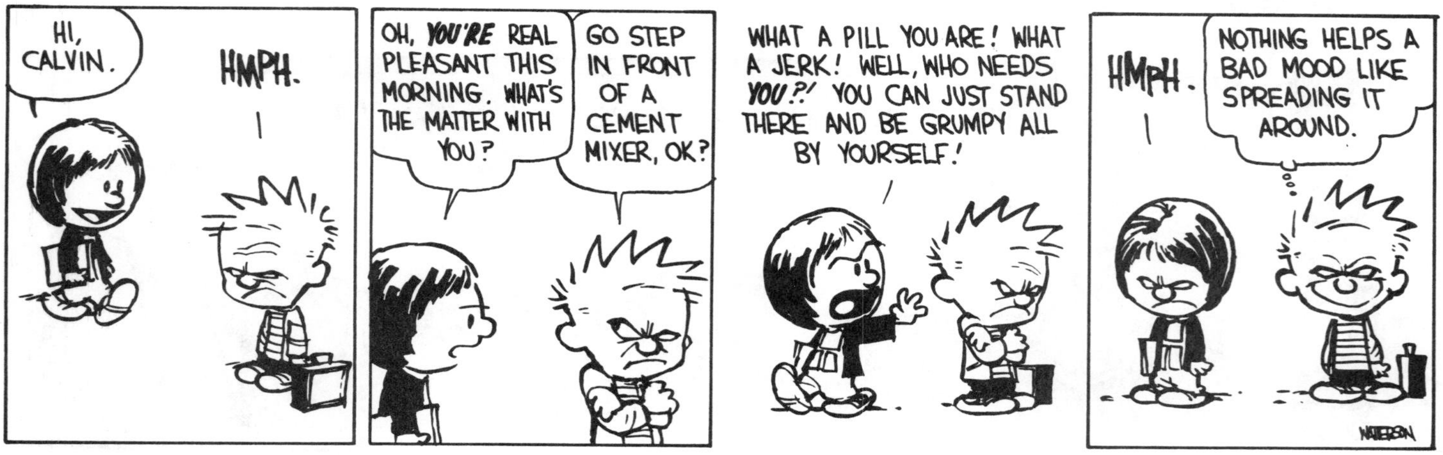
HI, CALVIN.
HMPH.
OH, *YOU'RE* REAL PLEASANT THIS MORNING. WHAT'S THE MATTER WITH YOU?
GO STEP IN FRONT OF A CEMENT MIXER, OK?
WHAT A PILL YOU ARE! WHAT A JERK! WELL, WHO NEEDS *YOU?!* YOU CAN JUST STAND THERE AND BE GRUMPY ALL BY YOURSELF!
HMPH.
NOTHING HELPS A BAD MOOD LIKE SPREADING IT AROUND.

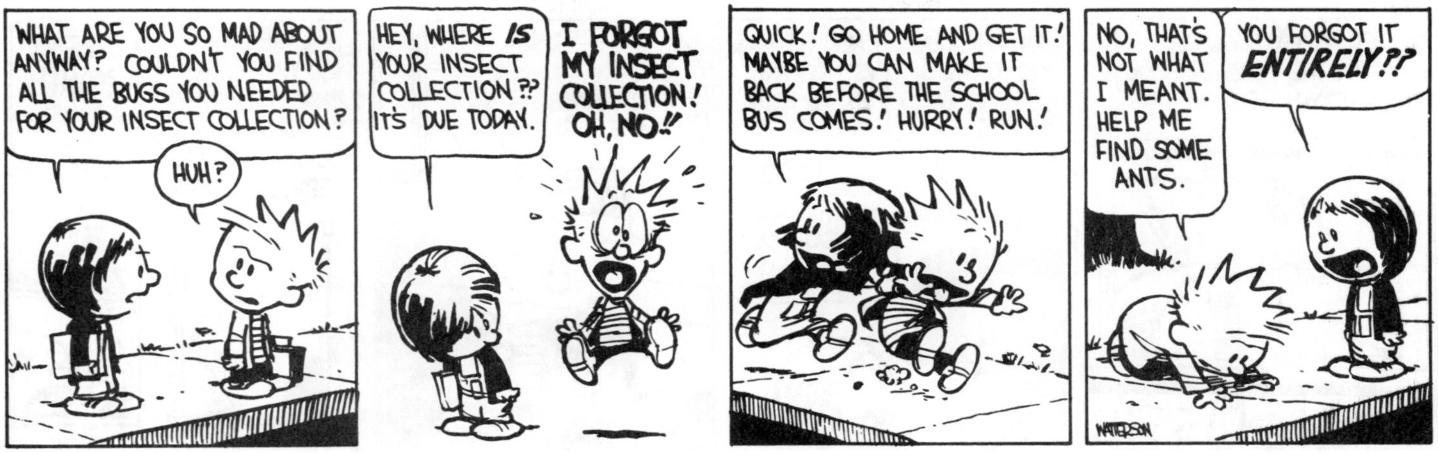
WHAT ARE YOU SO MAD ABOUT ANYWAY? COULDN'T YOU FIND ALL THE BUGS YOU NEEDED FOR YOUR INSECT COLLECTION?
HUH?
HEY, WHERE *IS* YOUR INSECT COLLECTION?? IT'S DUE TODAY.
I FORGOT MY INSECT COLLECTION! OH, NO!!
QUICK! GO HOME AND GET IT! MAYBE YOU CAN MAKE IT BACK BEFORE THE SCHOOL BUS COMES! HURRY! RUN!
NO, THAT'S NOT WHAT I MEANT. HELP ME FIND SOME ANTS.
YOU FORGOT IT *ENTIRELY*??
WATTERSON

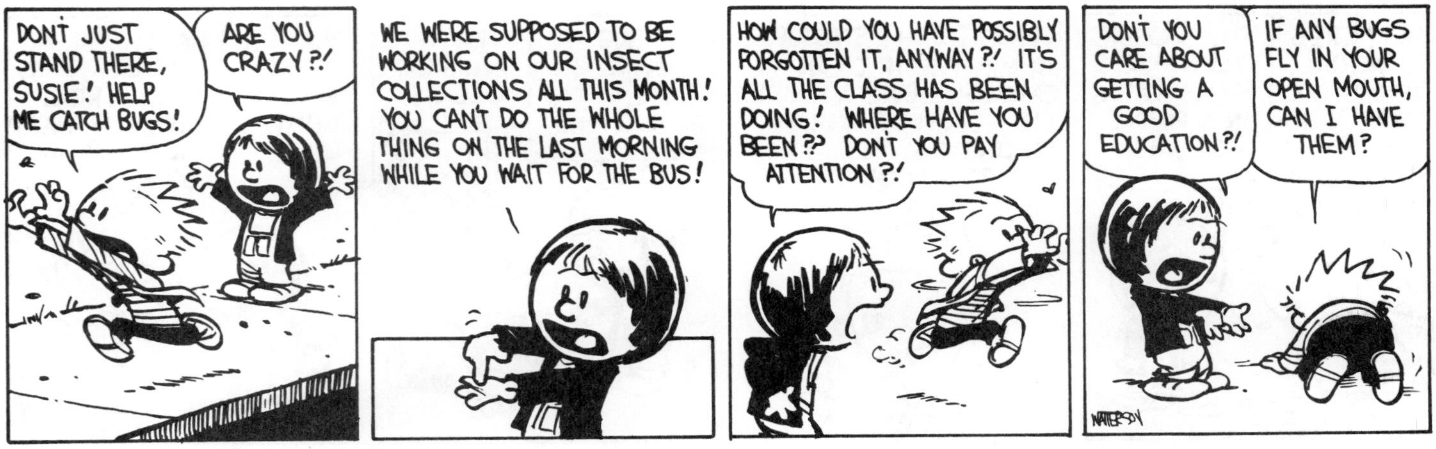
DON'T JUST STAND THERE, SUSIE! HELP ME CATCH BUGS!
ARE YOU CRAZY?!
WE WERE SUPPOSED TO BE WORKING ON OUR INSECT COLLECTIONS ALL THIS MONTH! YOU CAN'T DO THE WHOLE THING ON THE LAST MORNING WHILE YOU WAIT FOR THE BUS!
HOW COULD YOU HAVE POSSIBLY FORGOTTEN IT, ANYWAY?! IT'S ALL THE CLASS HAS BEEN DOING! WHERE HAVE YOU BEEN?? DON'T YOU PAY ATTENTION?!
DON'T YOU CARE ABOUT GETTING A GOOD EDUCATION?!
IF ANY BUGS FLY IN YOUR OPEN MOUTH, CAN I HAVE THEM?
WATTERSON

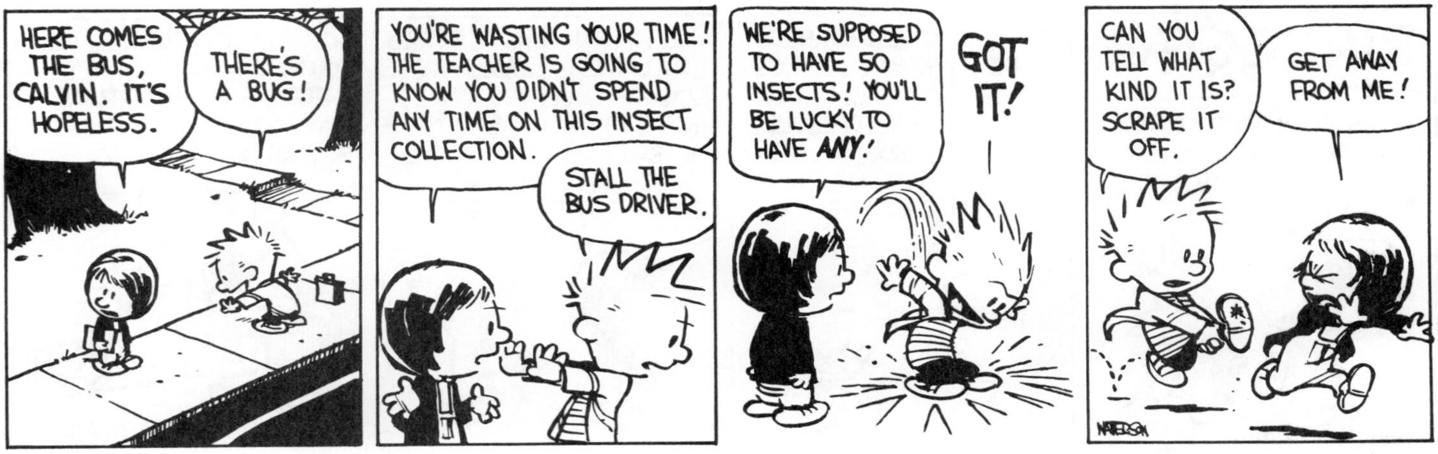
HERE COMES THE BUS, CALVIN. IT'S HOPELESS.
THERE'S A BUG!
YOU'RE WASTING YOUR TIME! THE TEACHER IS GOING TO KNOW YOU DIDN'T SPEND ANY TIME ON THIS INSECT COLLECTION.
STALL THE BUS DRIVER.
WE'RE SUPPOSED TO HAVE 50 INSECTS! YOU'LL BE LUCKY TO HAVE *ANY*!
GOT IT!
CAN YOU TELL WHAT KIND IT IS? SCRAPE IT OFF.
GET AWAY FROM ME!
WATTERSON

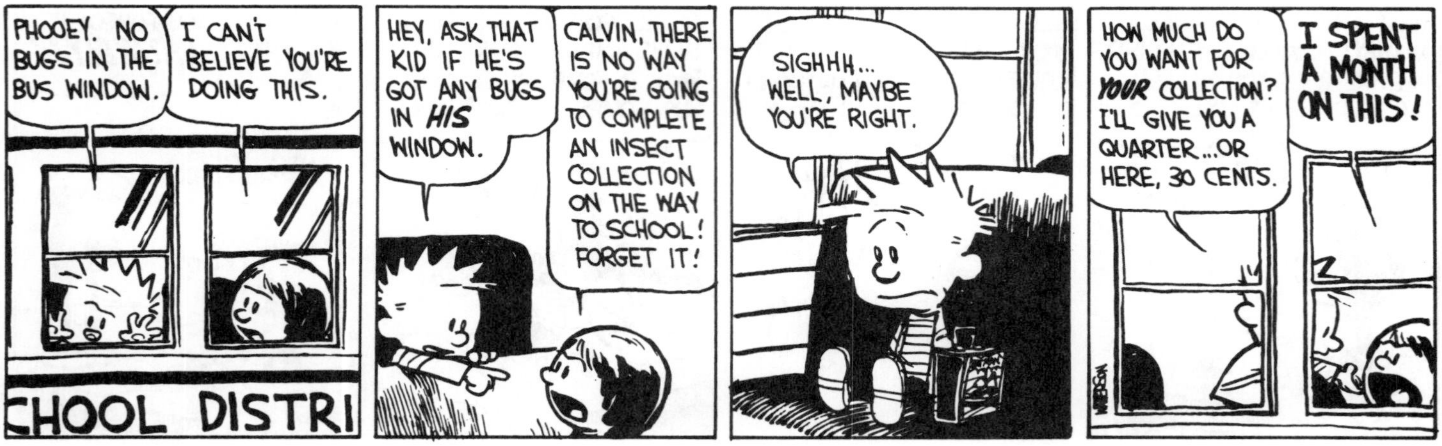
PHOOEY. NO BUGS IN THE BUS WINDOW.
I CAN'T BELIEVE YOU'RE DOING THIS.
CHOOL DISTRI
HEY, ASK THAT KID IF HE'S GOT ANY BUGS IN ***HIS*** WINDOW.
CALVIN, THERE IS NO WAY YOU'RE GOING TO COMPLETE AN INSECT COLLECTION ON THE WAY TO SCHOOL! FORGET IT!
SIGHHH... WELL, MAYBE YOU'RE RIGHT.
HOW MUCH DO YOU WANT FOR ***YOUR*** COLLECTION? I'LL GIVE YOU A QUARTER...OR HERE, 30 CENTS.
I SPENT A MONTH ON THIS!

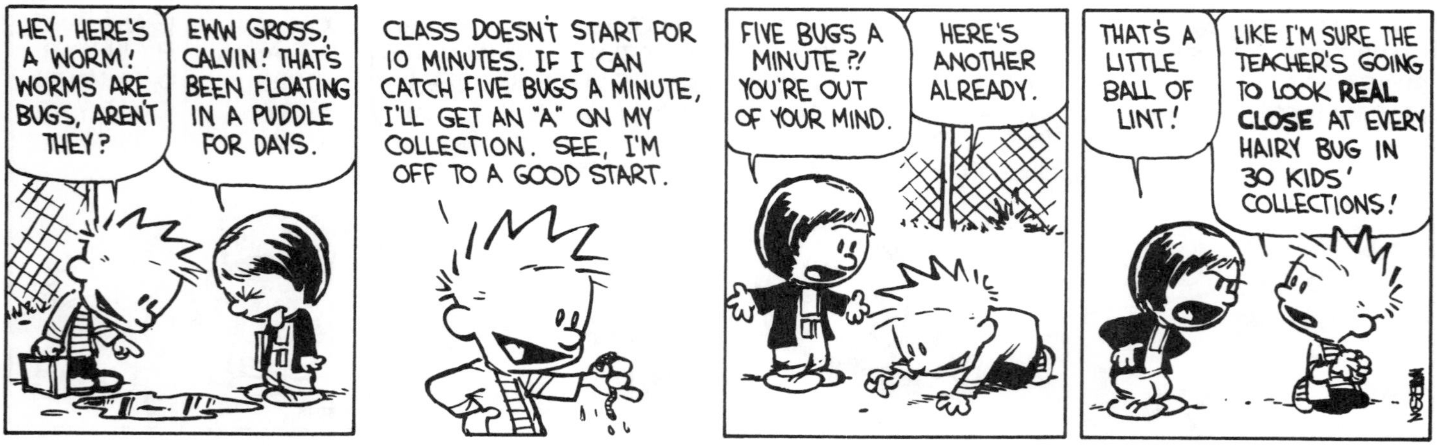
HEY, HERE'S A WORM! WORMS ARE BUGS, AREN'T THEY?
EWW GROSS, CALVIN! THAT'S BEEN FLOATING IN A PUDDLE FOR DAYS.
CLASS DOESN'T START FOR 10 MINUTES. IF I CAN CATCH FIVE BUGS A MINUTE, I'LL GET AN "A" ON MY COLLECTION. SEE, I'M OFF TO A GOOD START.
FIVE BUGS A MINUTE ?! YOU'RE OUT OF YOUR MIND.
HERE'S ANOTHER ALREADY.
THAT'S A LITTLE BALL OF LINT!
LIKE I'M SURE THE TEACHER'S GOING TO LOOK **REAL CLOSE** AT EVERY HAIRY BUG IN 30 KIDS' COLLECTIONS!

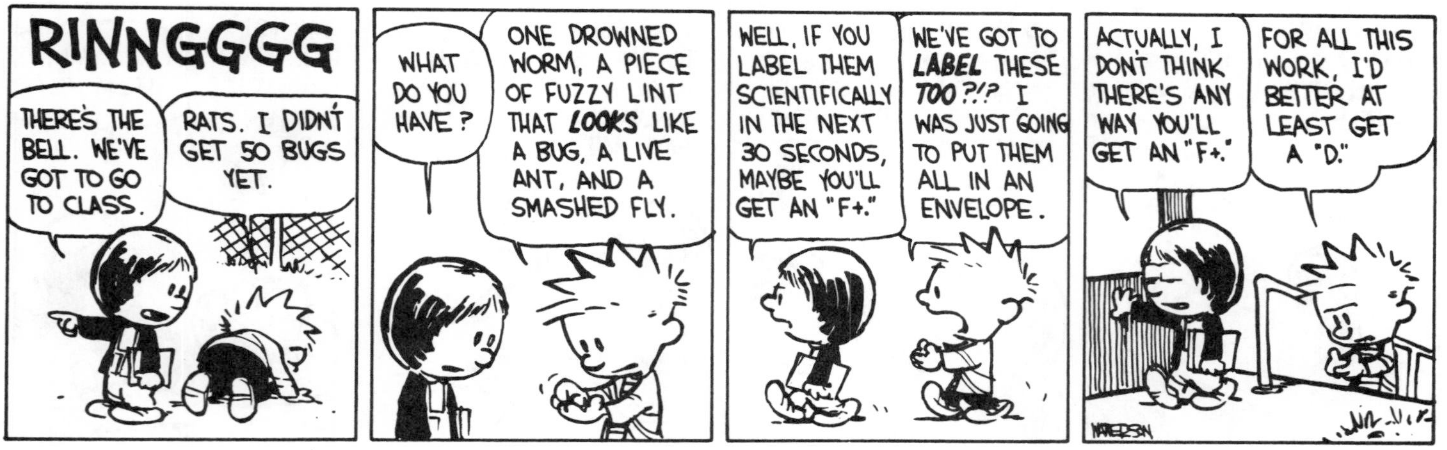
RINNGGGG
THERE'S THE BELL. WE'VE GOT TO GO TO CLASS.
RATS. I DIDN'T GET 50 BUGS YET.
WHAT DO YOU HAVE?
ONE DROWNED WORM, A PIECE OF FUZZY LINT THAT ***LOOKS*** LIKE A BUG, A LIVE ANT, AND A SMASHED FLY.
WELL, IF YOU LABEL THEM SCIENTIFICALLY IN THE NEXT 30 SECONDS, MAYBE YOU'LL GET AN "F+."
WE'VE GOT TO ***LABEL*** THESE ***TOO*** ?!? I WAS JUST GOING TO PUT THEM ALL IN AN ENVELOPE.
ACTUALLY, I DON'T THINK THERE'S ANY WAY YOU'LL GET AN "F+."
FOR ALL THIS WORK, I'D BETTER AT LEAST GET A "D."

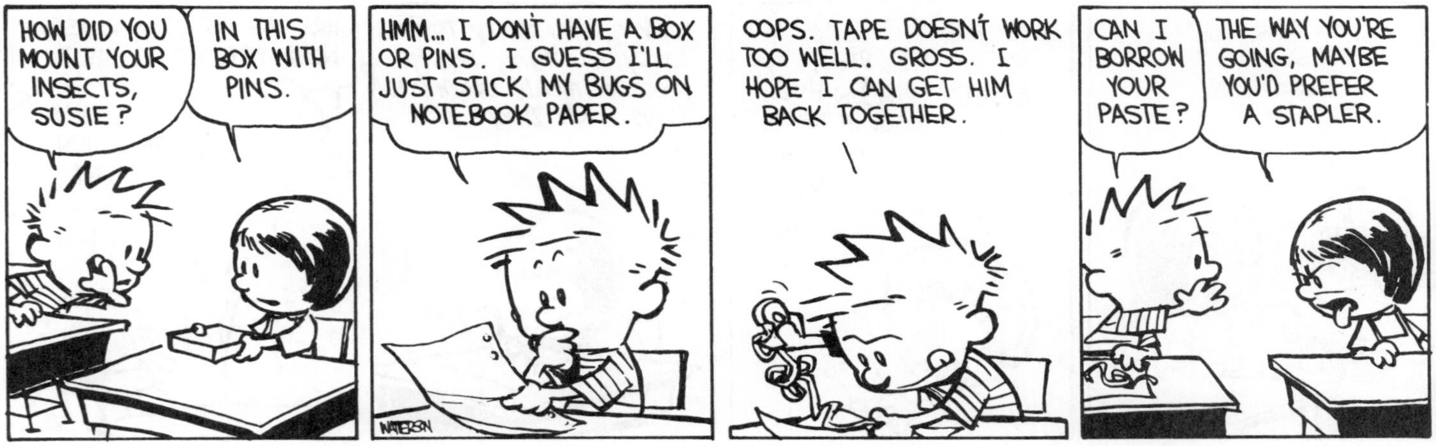
HOW DID YOU MOUNT YOUR INSECTS, SUSIE?
IN THIS BOX WITH PINS.
HMM... I DON'T HAVE A BOX OR PINS. I GUESS I'LL JUST STICK MY BUGS ON NOTEBOOK PAPER.
OOPS. TAPE DOESN'T WORK TOO WELL. GROSS. I HOPE I CAN GET HIM BACK TOGETHER.
CAN I BORROW YOUR PASTE?
THE WAY YOU'RE GOING, MAYBE YOU'D PREFER A STAPLER.

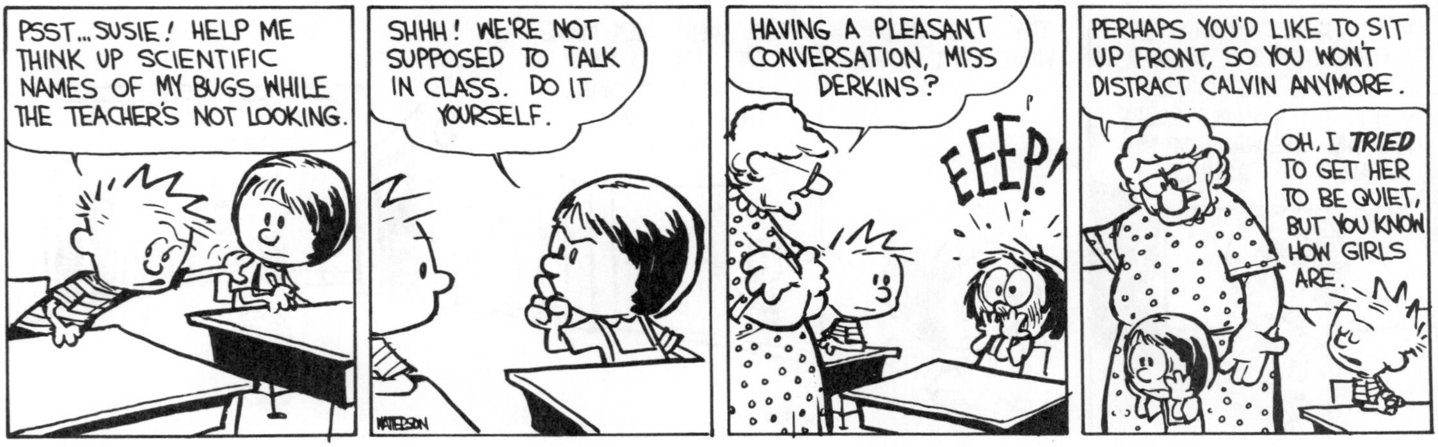
PSST...SUSIE! HELP ME THINK UP SCIENTIFIC NAMES OF MY BUGS WHILE THE TEACHER'S NOT LOOKING.
SHHH! WE'RE NOT SUPPOSED TO TALK IN CLASS. DO IT YOURSELF.
HAVING A PLEASANT CONVERSATION, MISS DERKINS?
EEEP!
PERHAPS YOU'D LIKE TO SIT UP FRONT, SO YOU WON'T DISTRACT CALVIN ANYMORE.
OH, I TRIED TO GET HER TO BE QUIET, BUT YOU KNOW HOW GIRLS ARE.

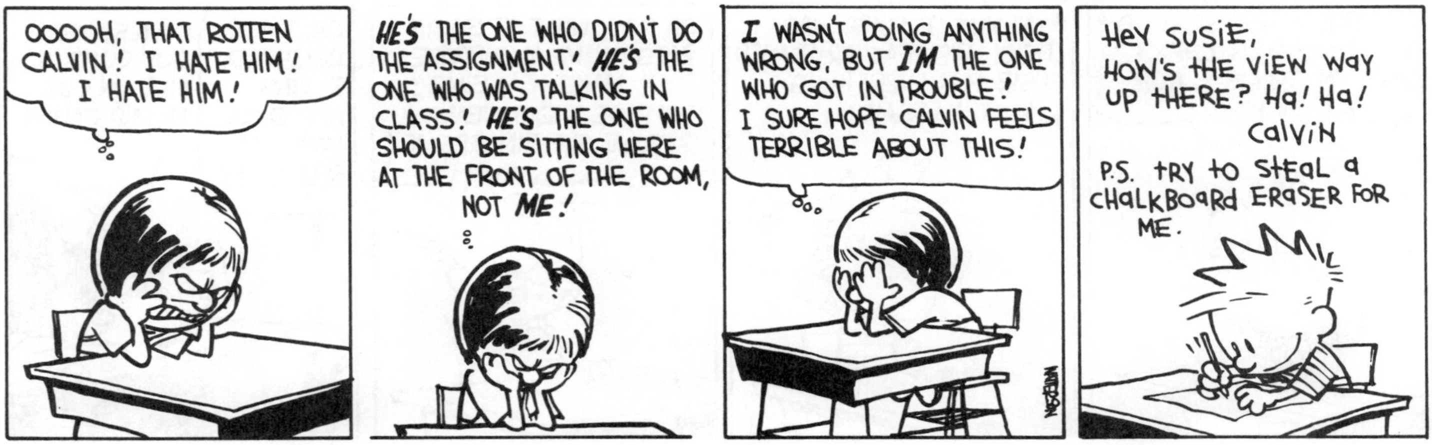
OOOOH, THAT ROTTEN CALVIN! I HATE HIM! I HATE HIM!
HE'S THE ONE WHO DIDN'T DO THE ASSIGNMENT! HE'S THE ONE WHO WAS TALKING IN CLASS! HE'S THE ONE WHO SHOULD BE SITTING HERE AT THE FRONT OF THE ROOM, NOT ME!
I WASN'T DOING ANYTHING WRONG, BUT I'M THE ONE WHO GOT IN TROUBLE! I SURE HOPE CALVIN FEELS TERRIBLE ABOUT THIS!
Hey SUSIE, HOW'S THE VIEW WAY UP THERE? Ha! Ha! CALVIN
P.S. TRY TO STEAL A CHALKBOARD ERASER FOR ME.

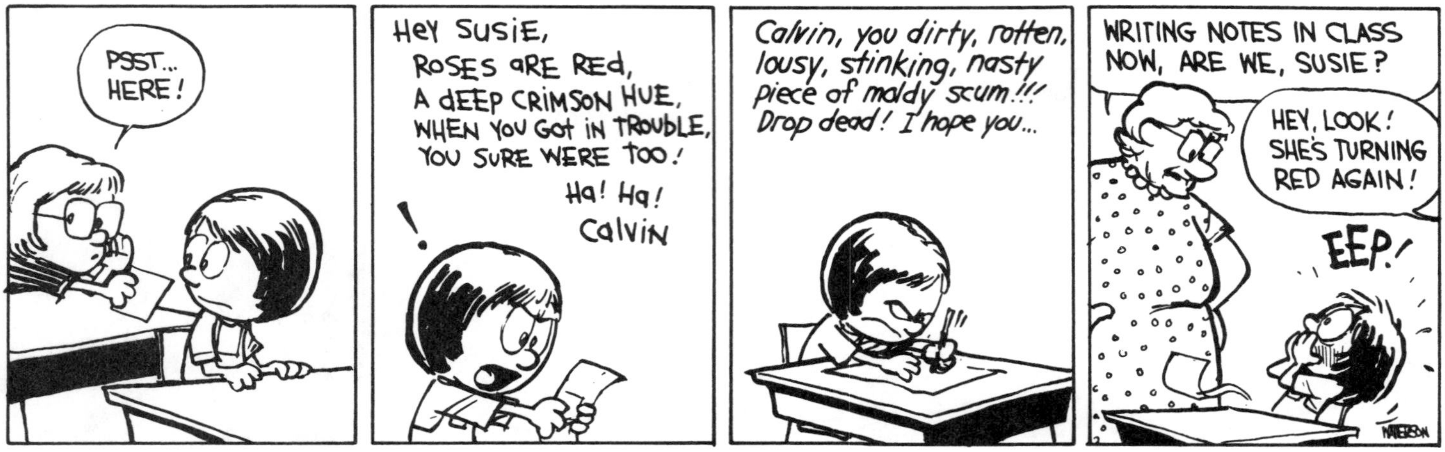
PSST... HERE!
Hey SUSiE,
ROSES aRE REd,
A dEEP CRIMSON HUE,
WHEN YOU GOt iN TROUBLE,
YOU SURE WERE TOO!
Ha! Ha!
Calvin
!
Calvin, you dirty, rotten, lousy, stinking, nasty piece of moldy scum!!! Drop dead! I hope you...
WRITING NOTES IN CLASS NOW, ARE WE, SUSIE?
HEY, LOOK! SHE'S TURNING RED AGAIN!
EEP!

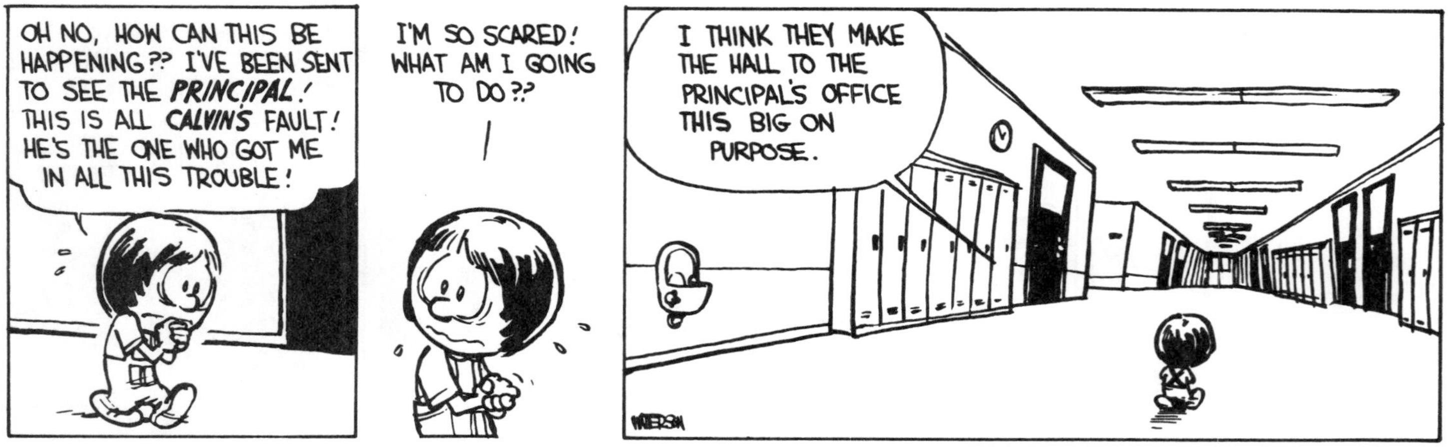
OH NO, HOW CAN THIS BE HAPPENING?? I'VE BEEN SENT TO SEE THE PRINCIPAL! THIS IS ALL CALVIN'S FAULT! HE'S THE ONE WHO GOT ME IN ALL THIS TROUBLE!
I'M SO SCARED! WHAT AM I GOING TO DO??
I THINK THEY MAKE THE HALL TO THE PRINCIPAL'S OFFICE THIS BIG ON PURPOSE.

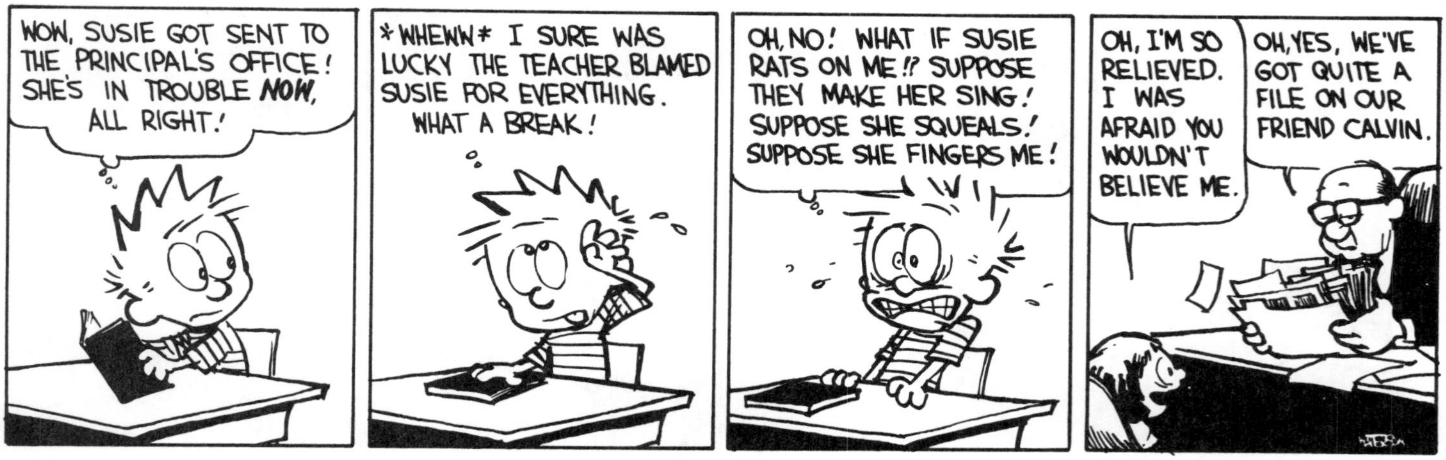
WOW, SUSIE GOT SENT TO THE PRINCIPAL'S OFFICE! SHE'S IN TROUBLE NOW, ALL RIGHT!
WHEWW I SURE WAS LUCKY THE TEACHER BLAMED SUSIE FOR EVERYTHING. WHAT A BREAK!
OH, NO! WHAT IF SUSIE RATS ON ME!? SUPPOSE THEY MAKE HER SING! SUPPOSE SHE SQUEALS! SUPPOSE SHE FINGERS ME!
OH, I'M SO RELIEVED. I WAS AFRAID YOU WOULDN'T BELIEVE ME.
OH, YES, WE'VE GOT QUITE A FILE ON OUR FRIEND CALVIN.

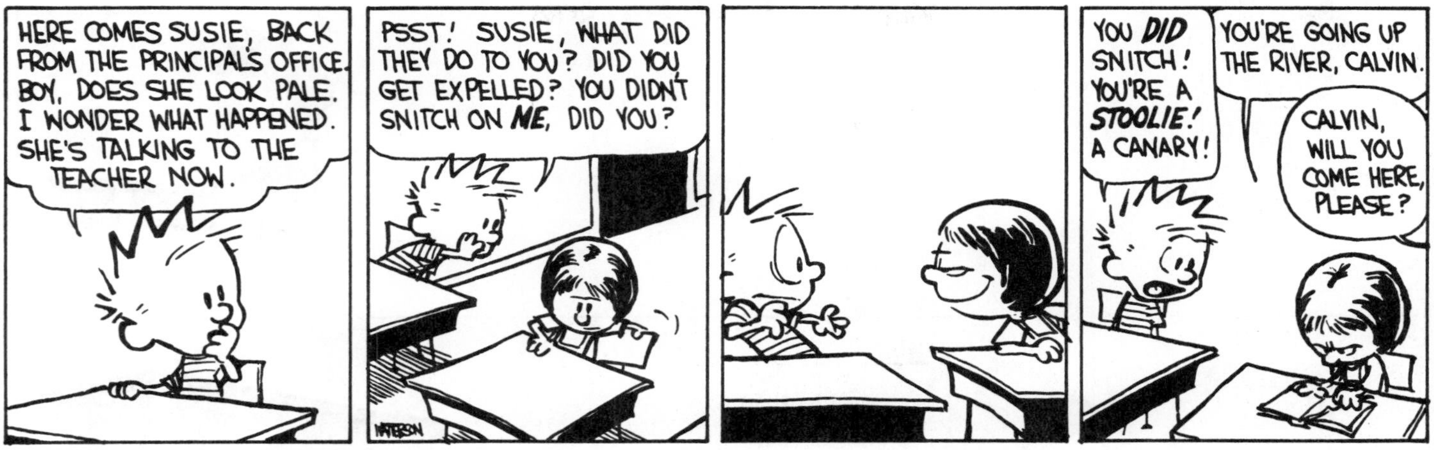
HERE COMES SUSIE, BACK FROM THE PRINCIPAL'S OFFICE. BOY, DOES SHE LOOK PALE. I WONDER WHAT HAPPENED. SHE'S TALKING TO THE TEACHER NOW.
PSST! SUSIE, WHAT DID THEY DO TO YOU? DID YOU GET EXPELLED? YOU DIDN'T SNITCH ON ME, DID YOU?
YOU DID SNITCH! YOU'RE A STOOLIE! A CANARY!
YOU'RE GOING UP THE RIVER, CALVIN.
CALVIN, WILL YOU COME HERE, PLEASE?
WATTERSON

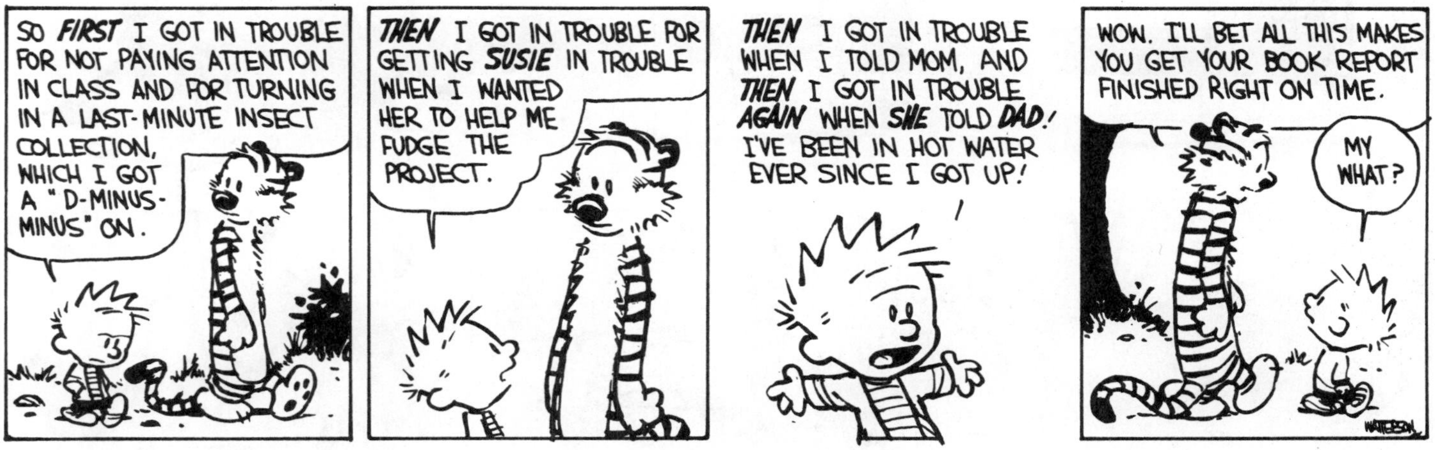
SO FIRST I GOT IN TROUBLE FOR NOT PAYING ATTENTION IN CLASS AND FOR TURNING IN A LAST-MINUTE INSECT COLLECTION, WHICH I GOT A "D-MINUS-MINUS" ON.
THEN I GOT IN TROUBLE FOR GETTING SUSIE IN TROUBLE WHEN I WANTED HER TO HELP ME FUDGE THE PROJECT.
THEN I GOT IN TROUBLE WHEN I TOLD MOM, AND THEN I GOT IN TROUBLE AGAIN WHEN SHE TOLD DAD! I'VE BEEN IN HOT WATER EVER SINCE I GOT UP!
WOW. I'LL BET ALL THIS MAKES YOU GET YOUR BOOK REPORT FINISHED RIGHT ON TIME.
MY WHAT?
WATTERSON

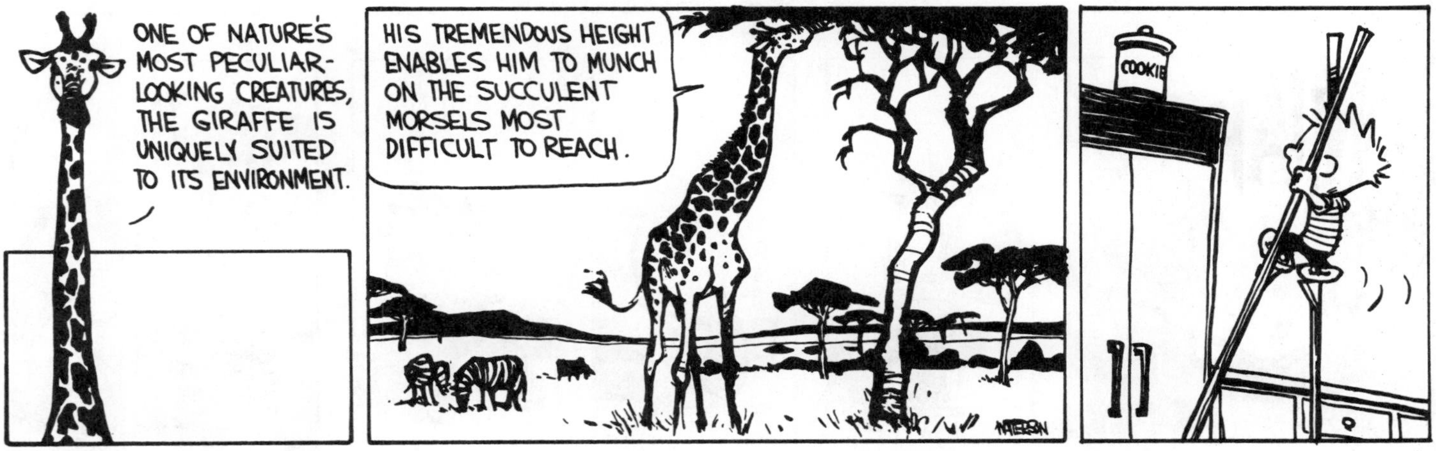
ONE OF NATURE'S MOST PECULIAR-LOOKING CREATURES, THE GIRAFFE IS UNIQUELY SUITED TO ITS ENVIRONMENT.
HIS TREMENDOUS HEIGHT ENABLES HIM TO MUNCH ON THE SUCCULENT MORSELS MOST DIFFICULT TO REACH.
WATTERSON
COOKIE

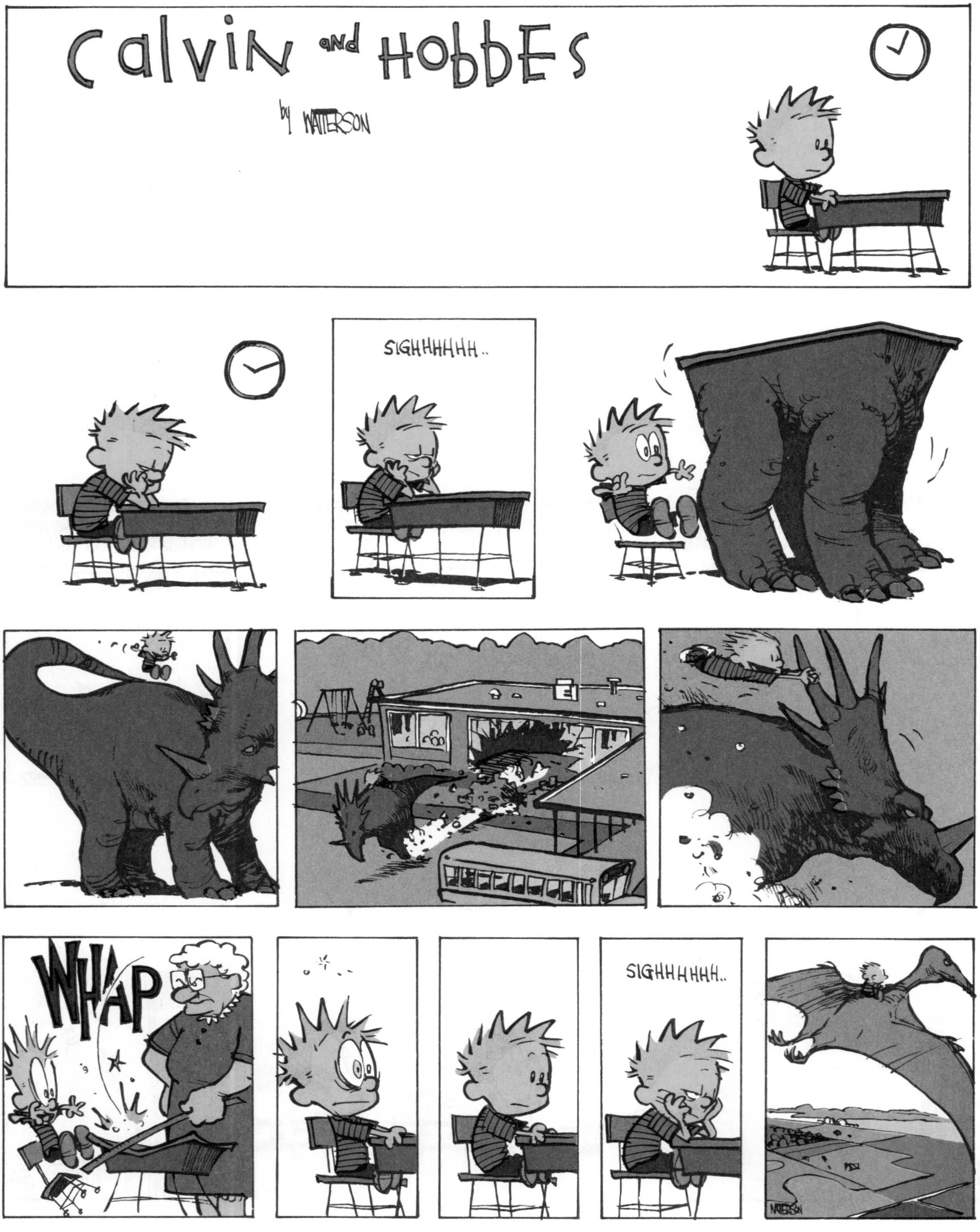
Calvin and HOBBES
by WATTERSON
SIGHHHHHH..
WHAP
SIGHHHHHH..
WATTERSON

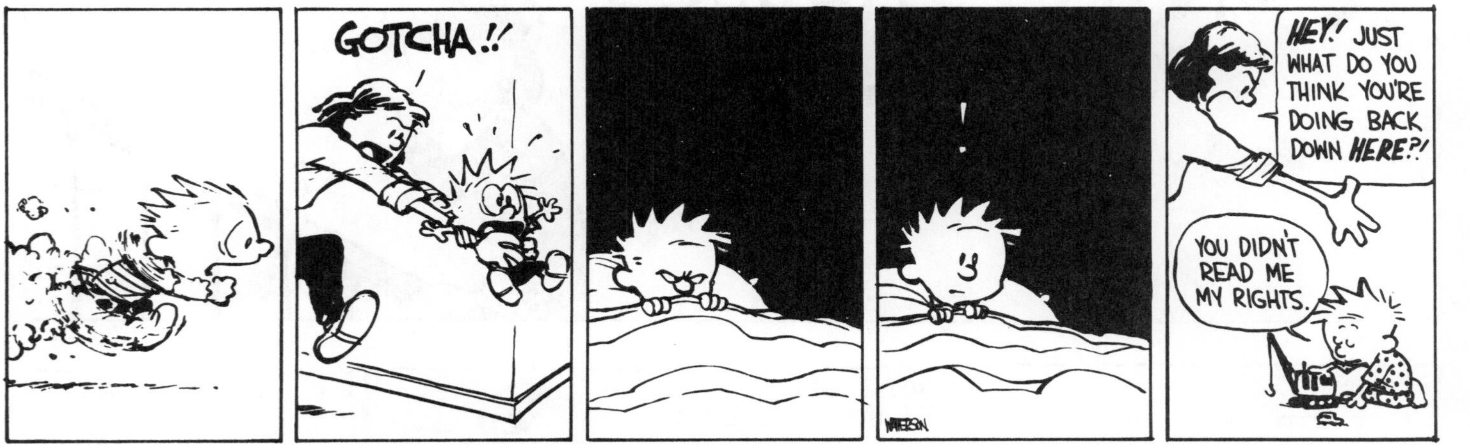
GOTCHA!!
!
HEY! JUST WHAT DO YOU THINK YOU'RE DOING BACK DOWN HERE?!
YOU DIDN'T READ ME MY RIGHTS.

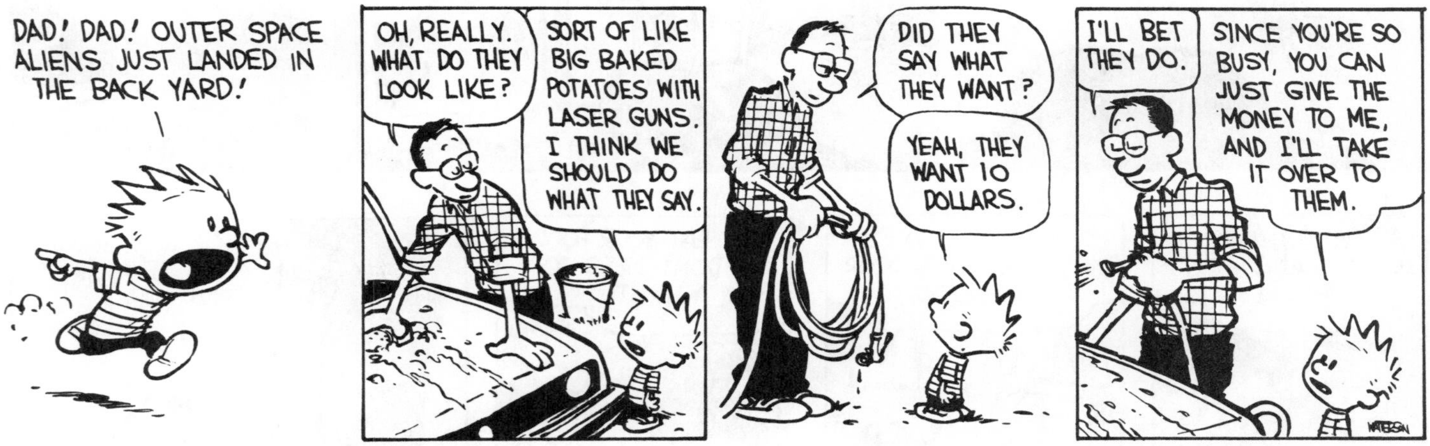
DAD! DAD! OUTER SPACE ALIENS JUST LANDED IN THE BACK YARD!
OH, REALLY. WHAT DO THEY LOOK LIKE?
SORT OF LIKE BIG BAKED POTATOES WITH LASER GUNS. I THINK WE SHOULD DO WHAT THEY SAY.
DID THEY SAY WHAT THEY WANT?
YEAH, THEY WANT 10 DOLLARS.
I'LL BET THEY DO.
SINCE YOU'RE SO BUSY, YOU CAN JUST GIVE THE MONEY TO ME, AND I'LL TAKE IT OVER TO THEM.

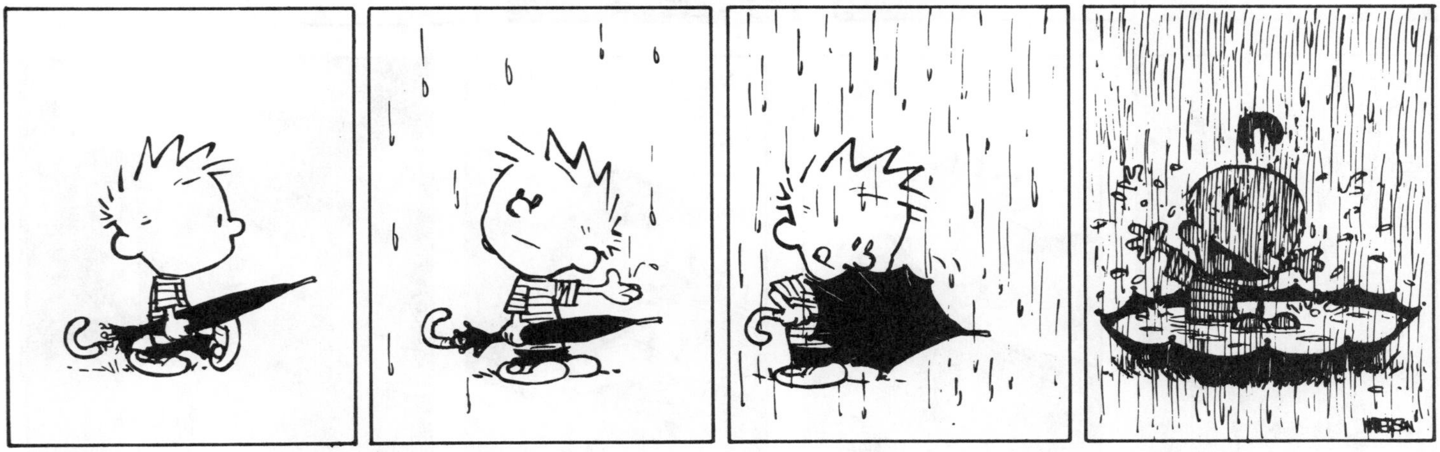

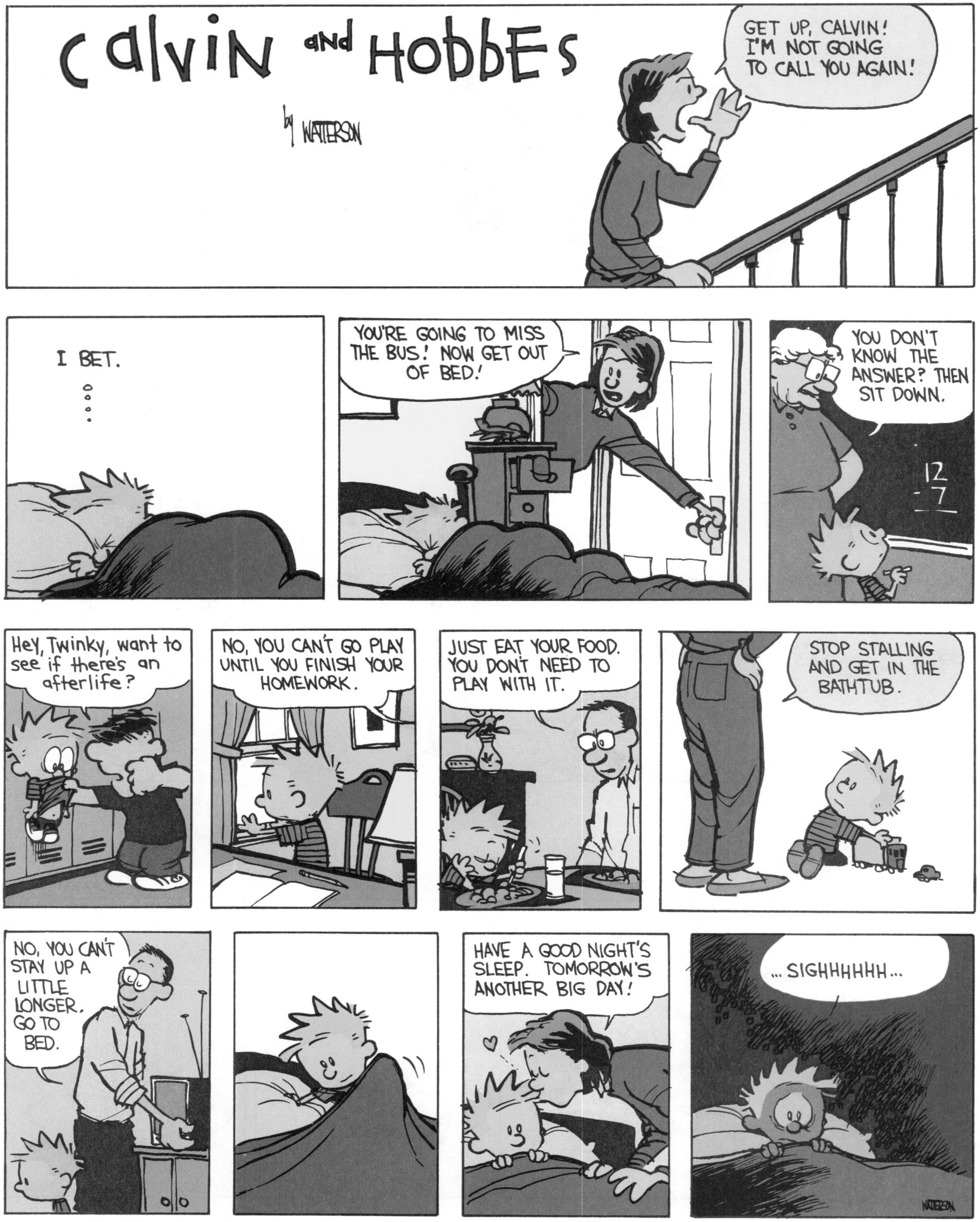
Calvin and HOBBES
by WATTERSON
GET UP, CALVIN! I'M NOT GOING TO CALL YOU AGAIN!
I BET.
YOU'RE GOING TO MISS THE BUS! NOW GET OUT OF BED!
YOU DON'T KNOW THE ANSWER? THEN SIT DOWN.
12
- 7
Hey, Twinky, want to see if there's an afterlife?
NO, YOU CAN'T GO PLAY UNTIL YOU FINISH YOUR HOMEWORK.
JUST EAT YOUR FOOD. YOU DON'T NEED TO PLAY WITH IT.
STOP STALLING AND GET IN THE BATHTUB.
NO, YOU CAN'T STAY UP A LITTLE LONGER. GO TO BED.
HAVE A GOOD NIGHT'S SLEEP. TOMORROW'S ANOTHER BIG DAY!
...SIGHHHHHH...
WATTERSON

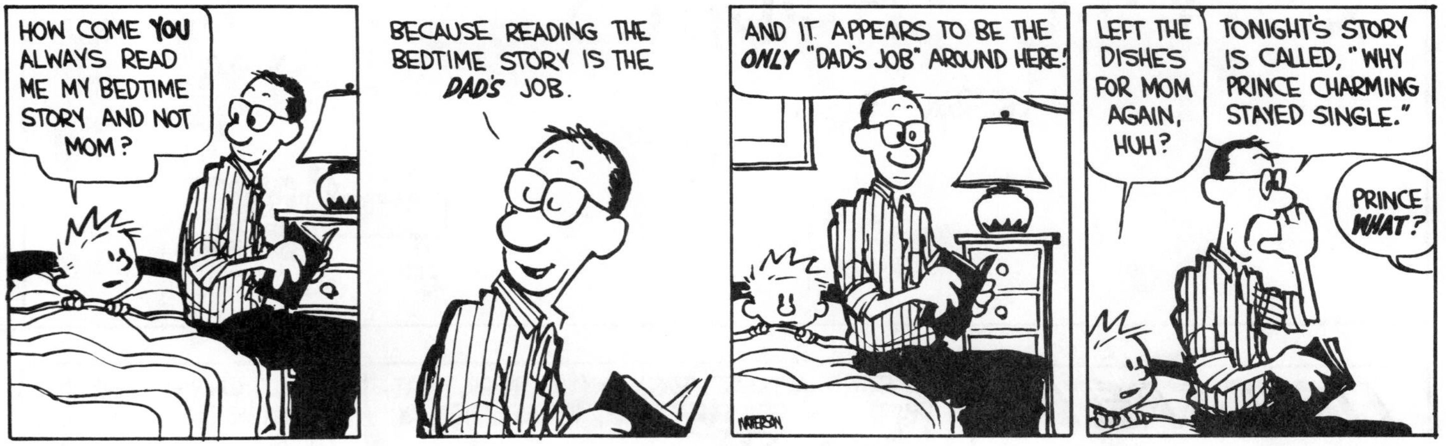
HOW COME **YOU** ALWAYS READ ME MY BEDTIME STORY AND NOT MOM?
BECAUSE READING THE BEDTIME STORY IS THE ***DAD'S*** JOB.
AND IT APPEARS TO BE THE ***ONLY*** "DAD'S JOB" AROUND HERE!
LEFT THE DISHES FOR MOM AGAIN, HUH?
TONIGHT'S STORY IS CALLED, "WHY PRINCE CHARMING STAYED SINGLE."
PRINCE ***WHAT***?

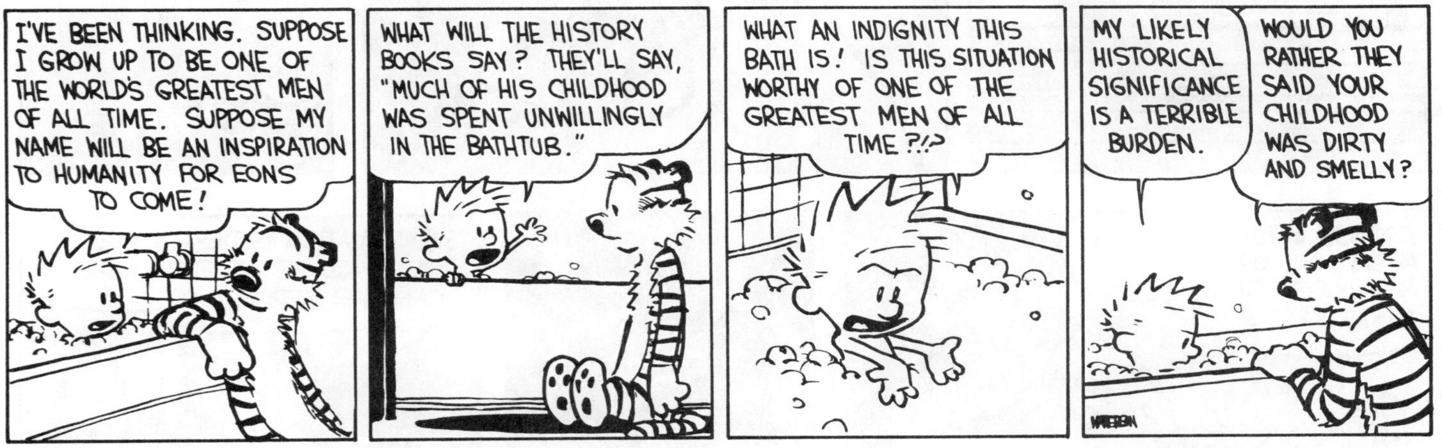
I'VE BEEN THINKING. SUPPOSE I GROW UP TO BE ONE OF THE WORLD'S GREATEST MEN OF ALL TIME. SUPPOSE MY NAME WILL BE AN INSPIRATION TO HUMANITY FOR EONS TO COME!
WHAT WILL THE HISTORY BOOKS SAY? THEY'LL SAY, "MUCH OF HIS CHILDHOOD WAS SPENT UNWILLINGLY IN THE BATHTUB."
WHAT AN INDIGNITY THIS BATH IS! IS THIS SITUATION WORTHY OF ONE OF THE GREATEST MEN OF ALL TIME?!?
MY LIKELY HISTORICAL SIGNIFICANCE IS A TERRIBLE BURDEN.
WOULD YOU RATHER THEY SAID YOUR CHILDHOOD WAS DIRTY AND SMELLY?

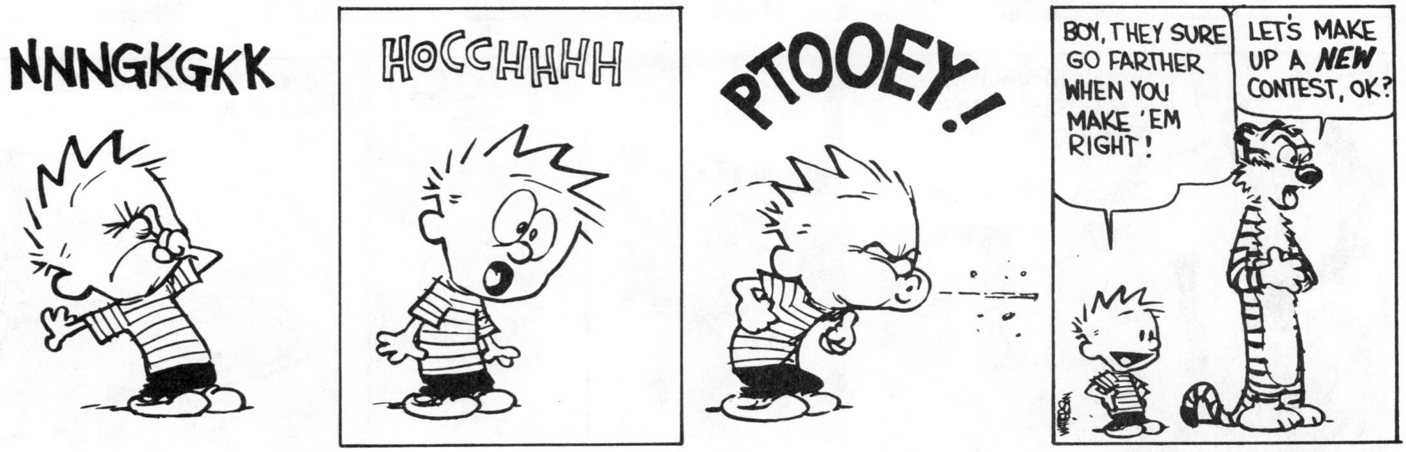
NNNGKGKK
HOCCHHHH
PTOOEY!
BOY, THEY SURE GO FARTHER WHEN YOU MAKE 'EM RIGHT!
LET'S MAKE UP A ***NEW*** CONTEST, OK?

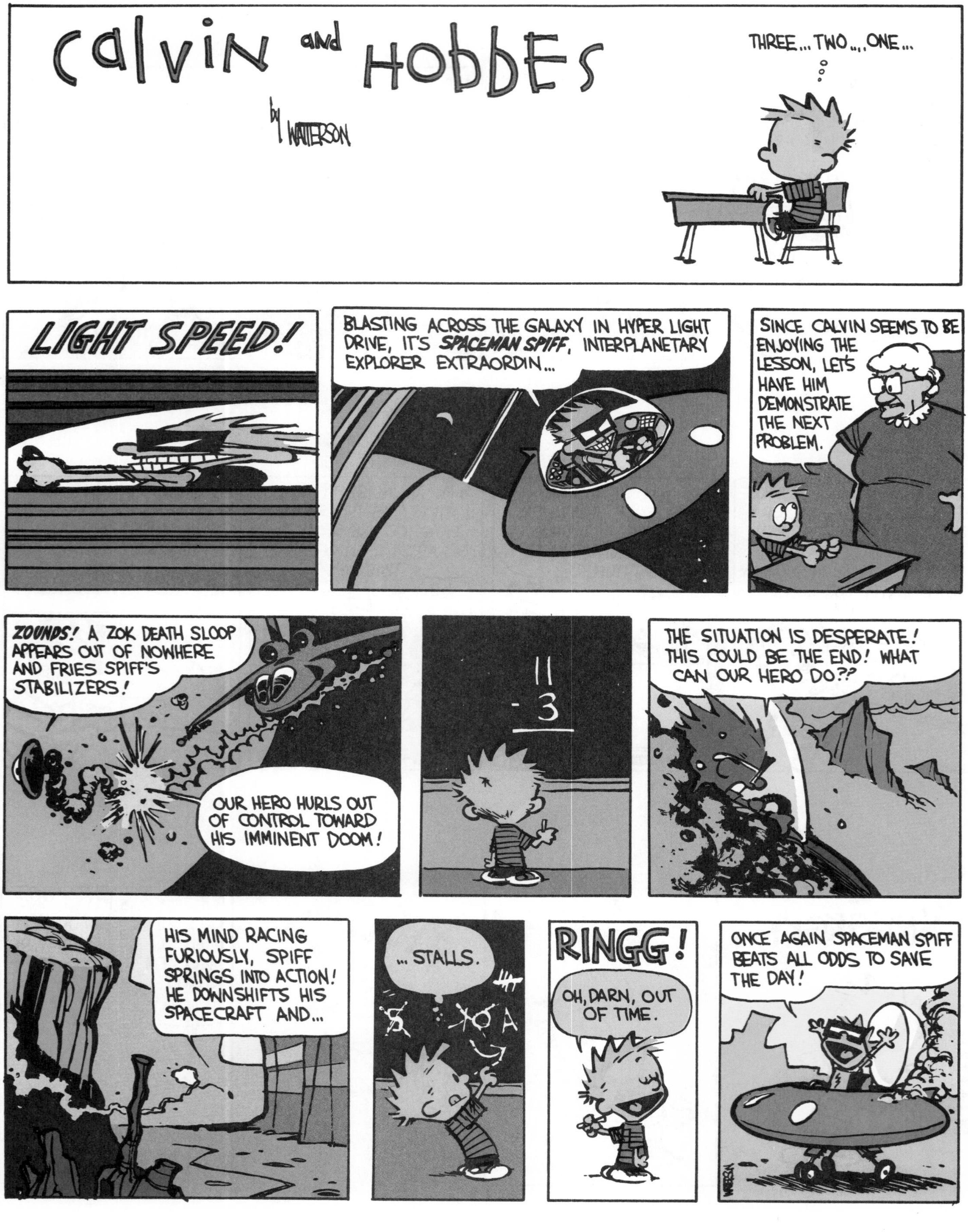
Calvin and HOBBES
by WATTERSON
THREE... TWO... ONE...
LIGHT SPEED!
BLASTING ACROSS THE GALAXY IN HYPER LIGHT DRIVE, IT'S SPACEMAN SPIFF, INTERPLANETARY EXPLORER EXTRAORDIN...
SINCE CALVIN SEEMS TO BE ENJOYING THE LESSON, LET'S HAVE HIM DEMONSTRATE THE NEXT PROBLEM.
ZOUNDS! A ZOK DEATH SLOOP APPEARS OUT OF NOWHERE AND FRIES SPIFF'S STABILIZERS!
OUR HERO HURLS OUT OF CONTROL TOWARD HIS IMMINENT DOOM!
11
- 3
THE SITUATION IS DESPERATE! THIS COULD BE THE END! WHAT CAN OUR HERO DO?!?
HIS MIND RACING FURIOUSLY, SPIFF SPRINGS INTO ACTION! HE DOWNSHIFTS HIS SPACECRAFT AND...
... STALLS.
RINGG!
OH, DARN, OUT OF TIME.
ONCE AGAIN SPACEMAN SPIFF BEATS ALL ODDS TO SAVE THE DAY!
WATTERSON

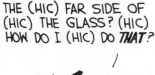

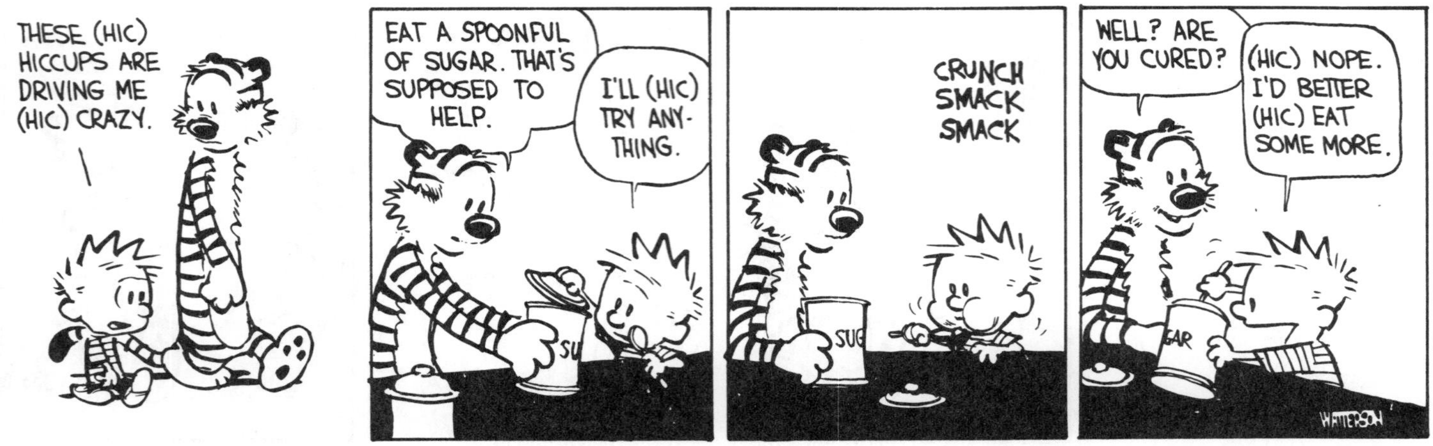
THESE (HIC) HICCUPS ARE DRIVING ME (HIC) CRAZY.
EAT A SPOONFUL OF SUGAR. THAT'S SUPPOSED TO HELP.
I'LL (HIC) TRY ANY-THING.
SU
CRUNCH SMACK SMACK
SUG
WELL? ARE YOU CURED?
(HIC) NOPE. I'D BETTER (HIC) EAT SOME MORE.
GAR
WATTERSON

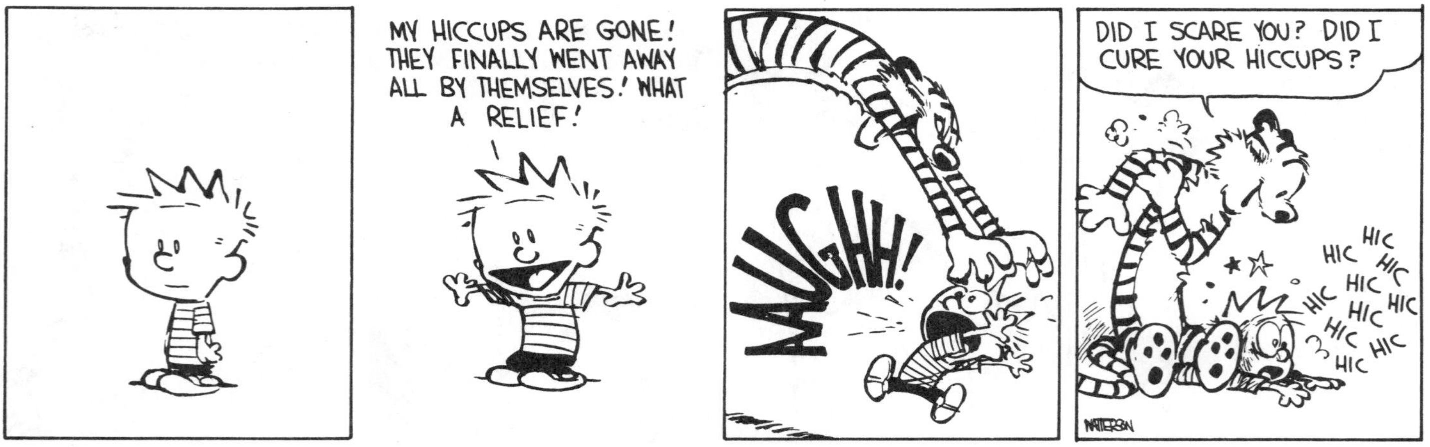
MY HICCUPS ARE GONE! THEY FINALLY WENT AWAY ALL BY THEMSELVES! WHAT A RELIEF!
MAUGHH!
DID I SCARE YOU? DID I CURE YOUR HICCUPS?
HIC HIC HIC HIC HIC HIC HIC HIC HIC HIC HIC
WATTERSON

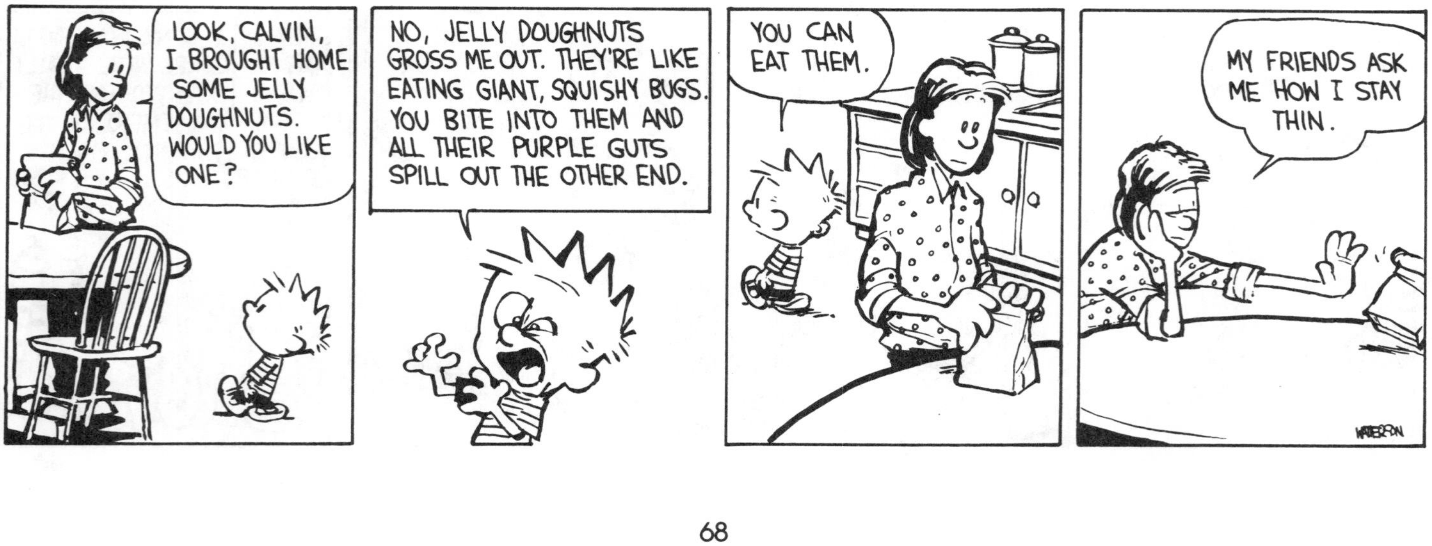
LOOK, CALVIN, I BROUGHT HOME SOME JELLY DOUGHNUTS. WOULD YOU LIKE ONE?
NO, JELLY DOUGHNUTS GROSS ME OUT. THEY'RE LIKE EATING GIANT, SQUISHY BUGS. YOU BITE INTO THEM AND ALL THEIR PURPLE GUTS SPILL OUT THE OTHER END.
YOU CAN EAT THEM.
MY FRIENDS ASK ME HOW I STAY THIN.
WATTERSON

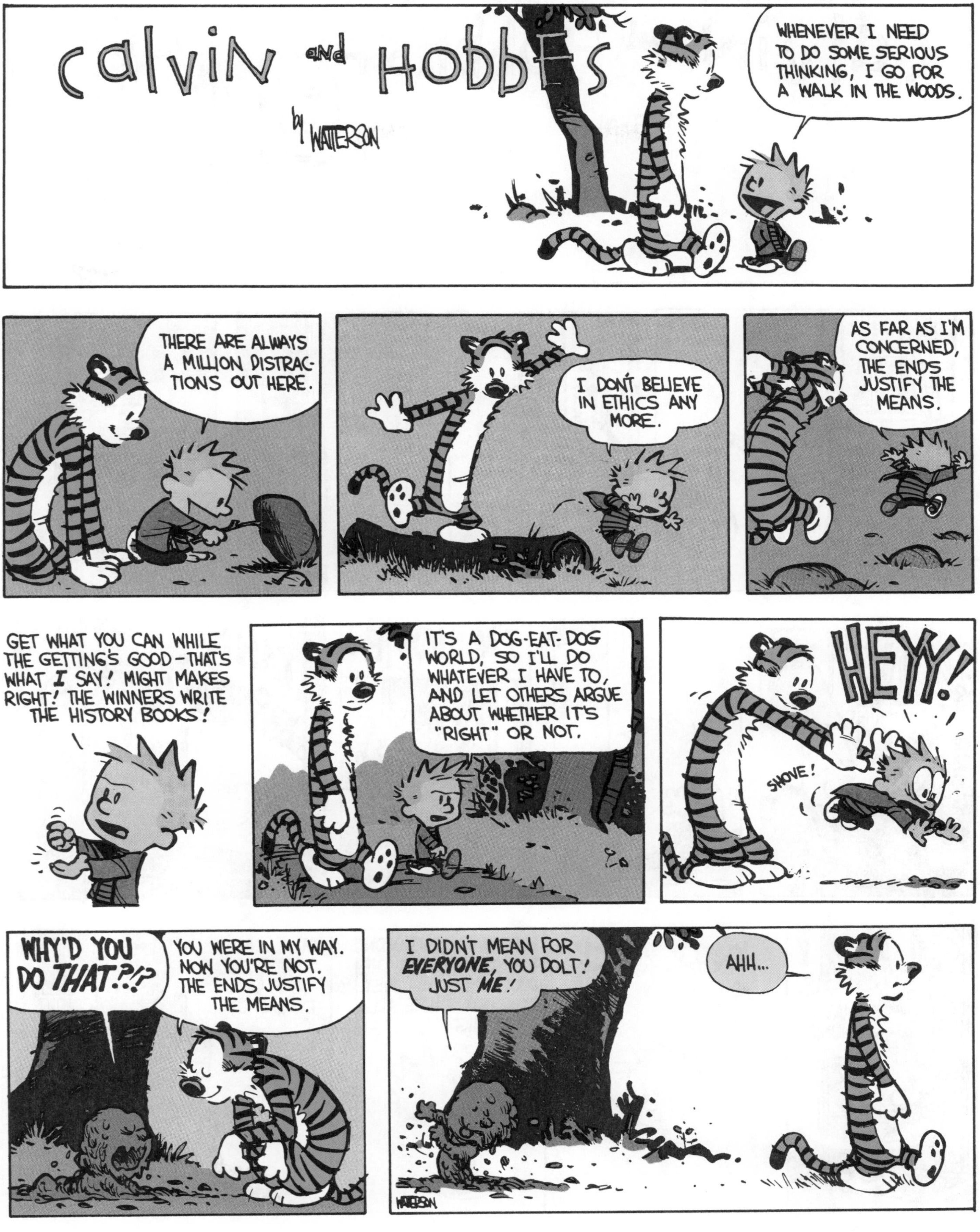
Calvin and HOBBES
by WATTERSON
WHENEVER I NEED TO DO SOME SERIOUS THINKING, I GO FOR A WALK IN THE WOODS.
THERE ARE ALWAYS A MILLION DISTRACTIONS OUT HERE.
I DON'T BELIEVE IN ETHICS ANY MORE.
AS FAR AS I'M CONCERNED, THE ENDS JUSTIFY THE MEANS.
GET WHAT YOU CAN WHILE THE GETTING'S GOOD - THAT'S WHAT I SAY! MIGHT MAKES RIGHT! THE WINNERS WRITE THE HISTORY BOOKS!
IT'S A DOG-EAT-DOG WORLD, SO I'LL DO WHATEVER I HAVE TO, AND LET OTHERS ARGUE ABOUT WHETHER IT'S "RIGHT" OR NOT.
HEYY!
SHOVE!
WHY'D YOU DO THAT?!?
YOU WERE IN MY WAY. NOW YOU'RE NOT. THE ENDS JUSTIFY THE MEANS.
I DIDN'T MEAN FOR EVERYONE, YOU DOLT! JUST ME!
AHH...
WATTERSON

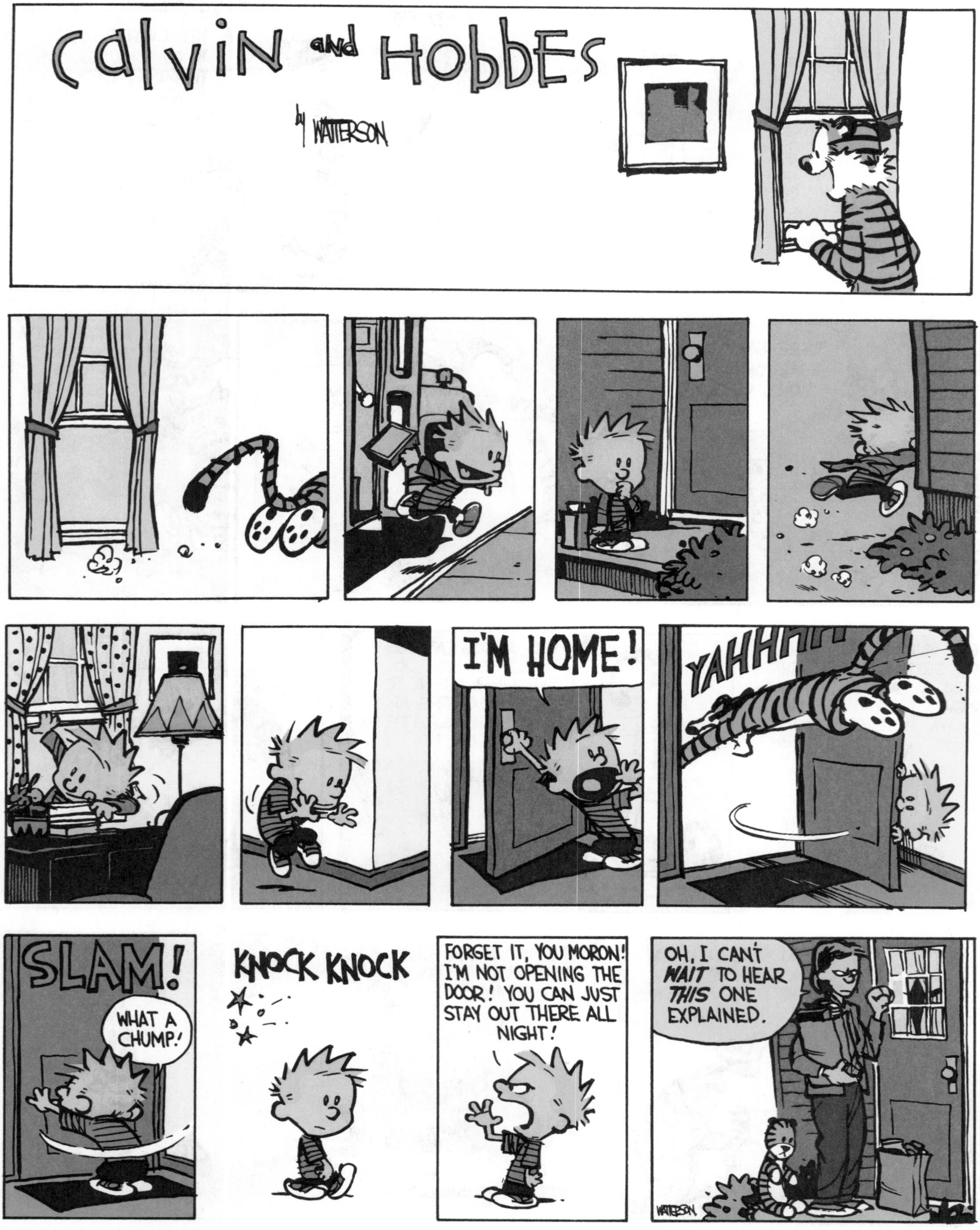
Calvin and Hobbes
by WATTERSON
I'M HOME!
YAHHHH
SLAM!
WHAT A CHUMP!
KNOCK KNOCK
FORGET IT, YOU MORON! I'M NOT OPENING THE DOOR! YOU CAN JUST STAY OUT THERE ALL NIGHT!
OH, I CAN'T WAIT TO HEAR THIS ONE EXPLAINED.
WATTERSON

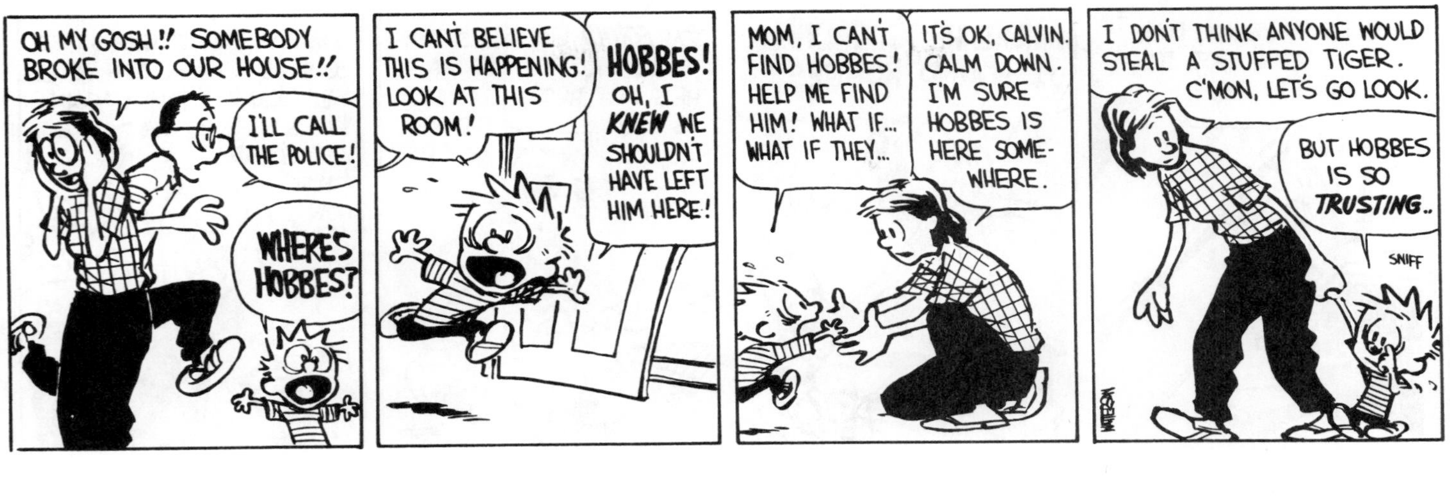
OH MY GOSH!! SOMEBODY BROKE INTO OUR HOUSE!!
I'LL CALL THE POLICE!
WHERE'S HOBBES?
I CAN'T BELIEVE THIS IS HAPPENING! LOOK AT THIS ROOM!
HOBBES! OH, I KNEW WE SHOULDN'T HAVE LEFT HIM HERE!
MOM, I CAN'T FIND HOBBES! HELP ME FIND HIM! WHAT IF... WHAT IF THEY...
IT'S OK, CALVIN. CALM DOWN. I'M SURE HOBBES IS HERE SOMEWHERE.
I DON'T THINK ANYONE WOULD STEAL A STUFFED TIGER. C'MON, LET'S GO LOOK.
BUT HOBBES IS SO TRUSTING..
SNIFF

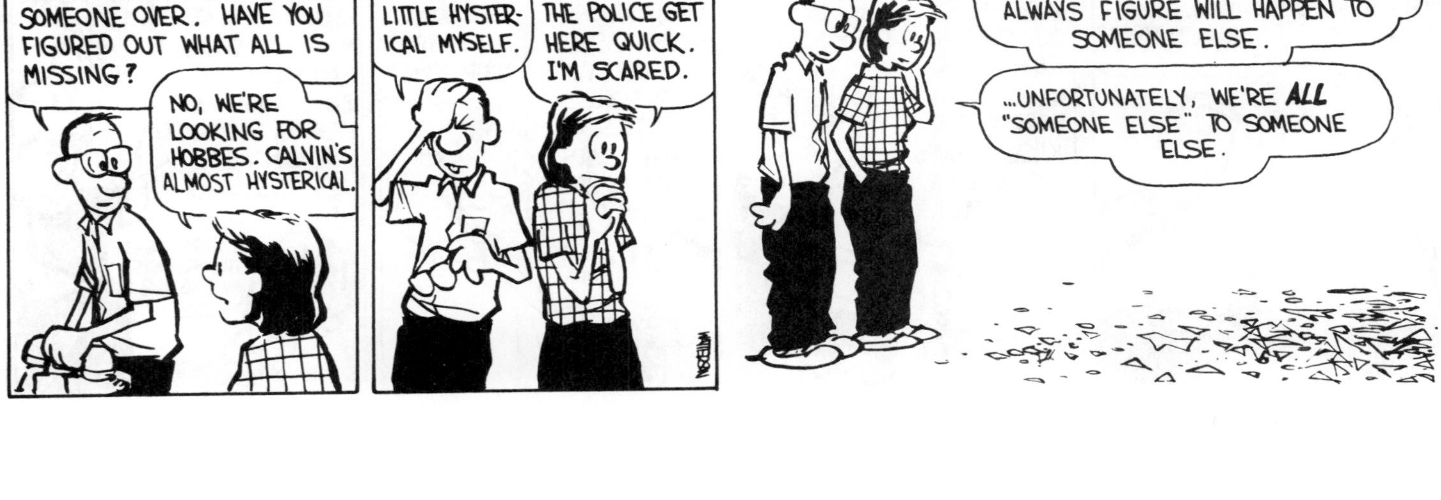
THE POLICE SAY THEY'LL SEND SOMEONE OVER. HAVE YOU FIGURED OUT WHAT ALL IS MISSING?
NO, WE'RE LOOKING FOR HOBBES. CALVIN'S ALMOST HYSTERICAL.
I FEEL A LITTLE HYSTERICAL MYSELF.
OOH.. I HOPE THE POLICE GET HERE QUICK. I'M SCARED.
THIS IS ONE OF THOSE THINGS YOU ALWAYS FIGURE WILL HAPPEN TO SOMEONE ELSE.
...UNFORTUNATELY, WE'RE ALL "SOMEONE ELSE" TO SOMEONE ELSE.

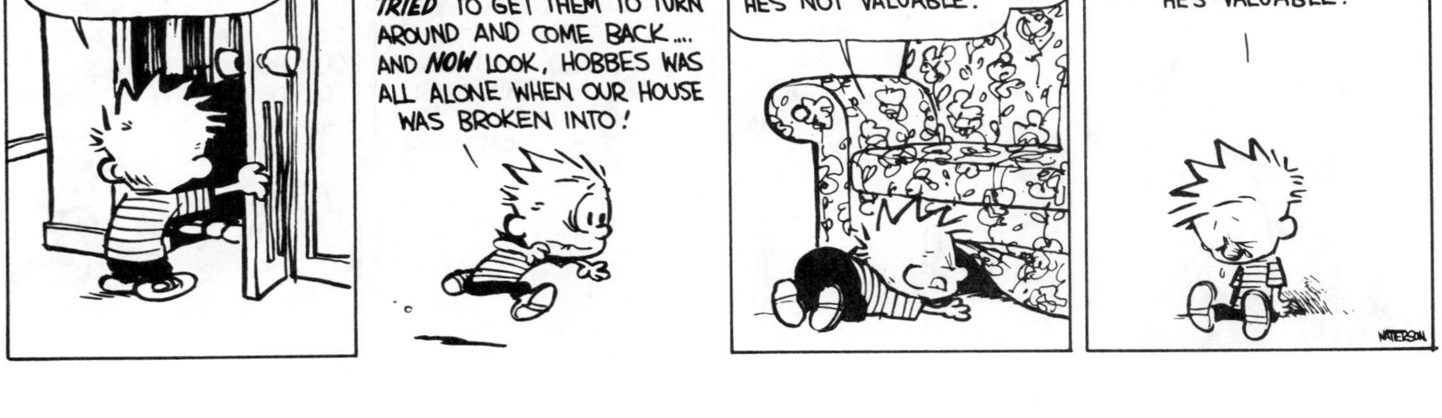
HOBBES? HOBBES? WHERE ARE YOU??
I TOLD MOM AND DAD WE LEFT HOBBES BEHIND.... I TRIED TO GET THEM TO TURN AROUND AND COME BACK.... AND NOW LOOK, HOBBES WAS ALL ALONE WHEN OUR HOUSE WAS BROKEN INTO!
MOM SAYS HOBBES WOULDN'T HAVE BEEN STOLEN BECAUSE HE'S NOT VALUABLE.
...(SNIFF) WELL, I THINK HE'S VALUABLE.

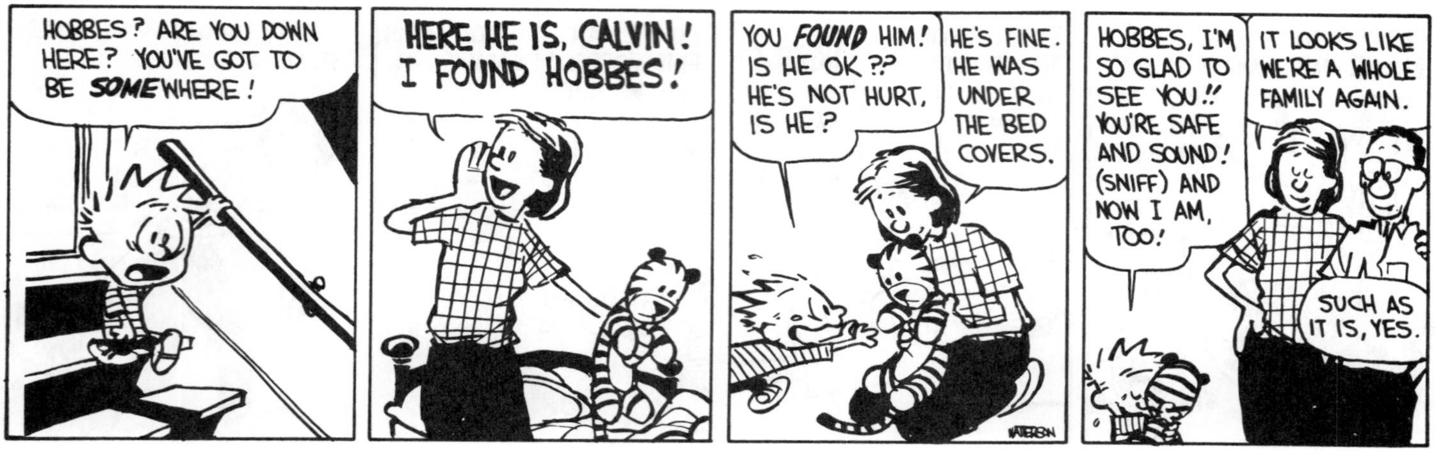
HOBBES? ARE YOU DOWN HERE? YOU'VE GOT TO BE **SOME**WHERE!
HERE HE IS, CALVIN! I FOUND HOBBES!
YOU **FOUND** HIM! IS HE OK?? HE'S NOT HURT, IS HE?
HE'S FINE. HE WAS UNDER THE BED COVERS.
HOBBES, I'M SO GLAD TO SEE YOU!! YOU'RE SAFE AND SOUND! (SNIFF) AND NOW I AM, TOO!
IT LOOKS LIKE WE'RE A WHOLE FAMILY AGAIN.
SUCH AS IT IS, YES.

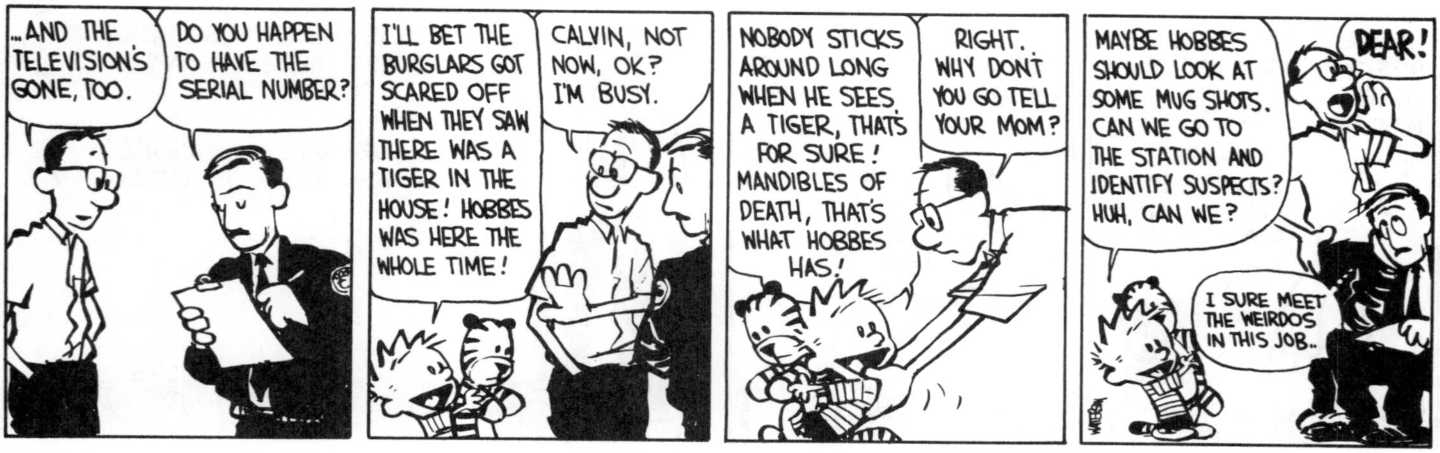
...AND THE TELEVISION'S GONE, TOO.
DO YOU HAPPEN TO HAVE THE SERIAL NUMBER?
I'LL BET THE BURGLARS GOT SCARED OFF WHEN THEY SAW THERE WAS A TIGER IN THE HOUSE! HOBBES WAS HERE THE WHOLE TIME!
CALVIN, NOT NOW, OK? I'M BUSY.
NOBODY STICKS AROUND LONG WHEN HE SEES A TIGER, THAT'S FOR SURE! MANDIBLES OF DEATH, THAT'S WHAT HOBBES HAS!
RIGHT. WHY DON'T YOU GO TELL YOUR MOM?
MAYBE HOBBES SHOULD LOOK AT SOME MUG SHOTS. CAN WE GO TO THE STATION AND IDENTIFY SUSPECTS? HUH, CAN WE?
DEAR!
I SURE MEET THE WEIRDOS IN THIS JOB..

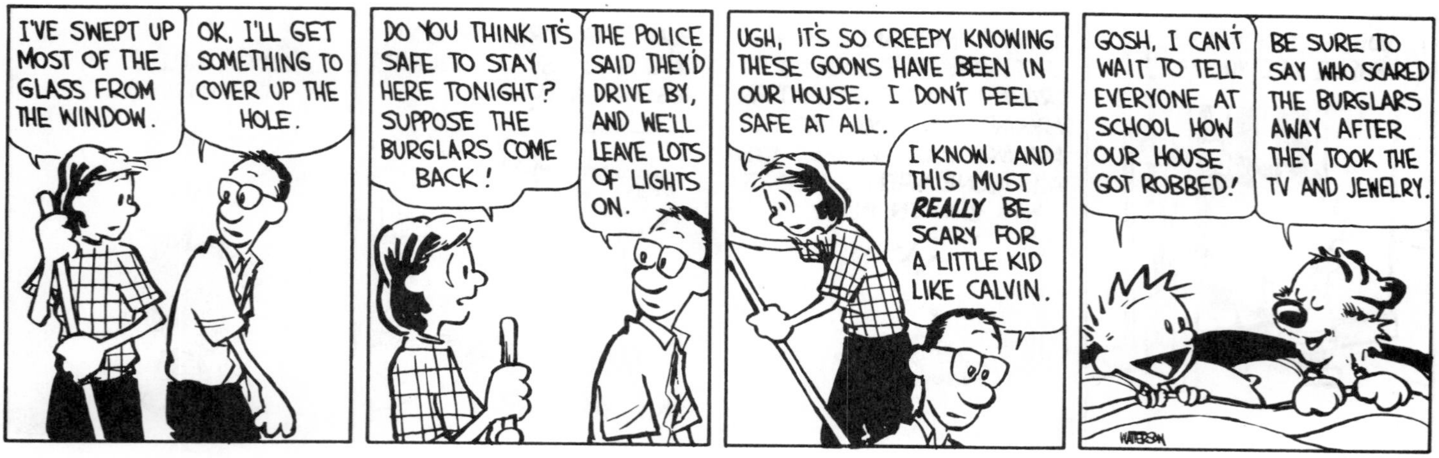
I'VE SWEPT UP MOST OF THE GLASS FROM THE WINDOW.
OK, I'LL GET SOMETHING TO COVER UP THE HOLE.
DO YOU THINK IT'S SAFE TO STAY HERE TONIGHT? SUPPOSE THE BURGLARS COME BACK!
THE POLICE SAID THEY'D DRIVE BY, AND WE'LL LEAVE LOTS OF LIGHTS ON.
UGH, IT'S SO CREEPY KNOWING THESE GOONS HAVE BEEN IN OUR HOUSE. I DON'T FEEL SAFE AT ALL.
I KNOW. AND THIS MUST **REALLY** BE SCARY FOR A LITTLE KID LIKE CALVIN.
GOSH, I CAN'T WAIT TO TELL EVERYONE AT SCHOOL HOW OUR HOUSE GOT ROBBED!
BE SURE TO SAY WHO SCARED THE BURGLARS AWAY AFTER THEY TOOK THE TV AND JEWELRY.

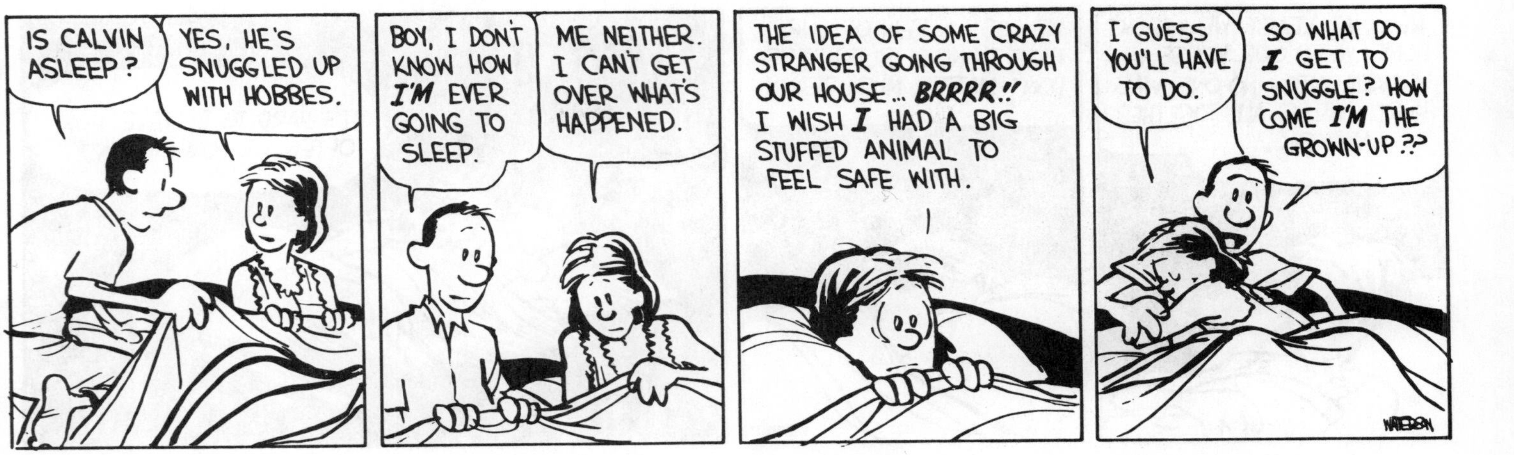
IS CALVIN ASLEEP?
YES, HE'S SNUGGLED UP WITH HOBBES.
BOY, I DON'T KNOW HOW I'M EVER GOING TO SLEEP.
ME NEITHER. I CAN'T GET OVER WHAT'S HAPPENED.
THE IDEA OF SOME CRAZY STRANGER GOING THROUGH OUR HOUSE... BRRRR!! I WISH I HAD A BIG STUFFED ANIMAL TO FEEL SAFE WITH.
I GUESS YOU'LL HAVE TO DO.
SO WHAT DO I GET TO SNUGGLE? HOW COME I'M THE GROWN-UP ??
WATTERSON

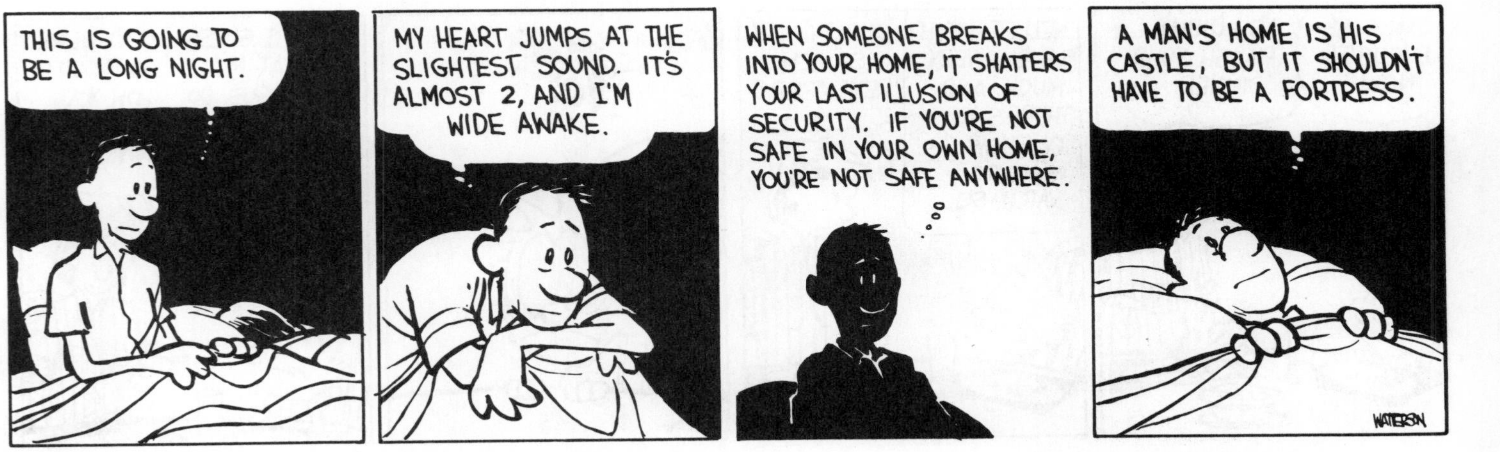
THIS IS GOING TO BE A LONG NIGHT.
MY HEART JUMPS AT THE SLIGHTEST SOUND. IT'S ALMOST 2, AND I'M WIDE AWAKE.
WHEN SOMEONE BREAKS INTO YOUR HOME, IT SHATTERS YOUR LAST ILLUSION OF SECURITY. IF YOU'RE NOT SAFE IN YOUR OWN HOME, YOU'RE NOT SAFE ANYWHERE.
A MAN'S HOME IS HIS CASTLE, BUT IT SHOULDN'T HAVE TO BE A FORTRESS.
WATTERSON

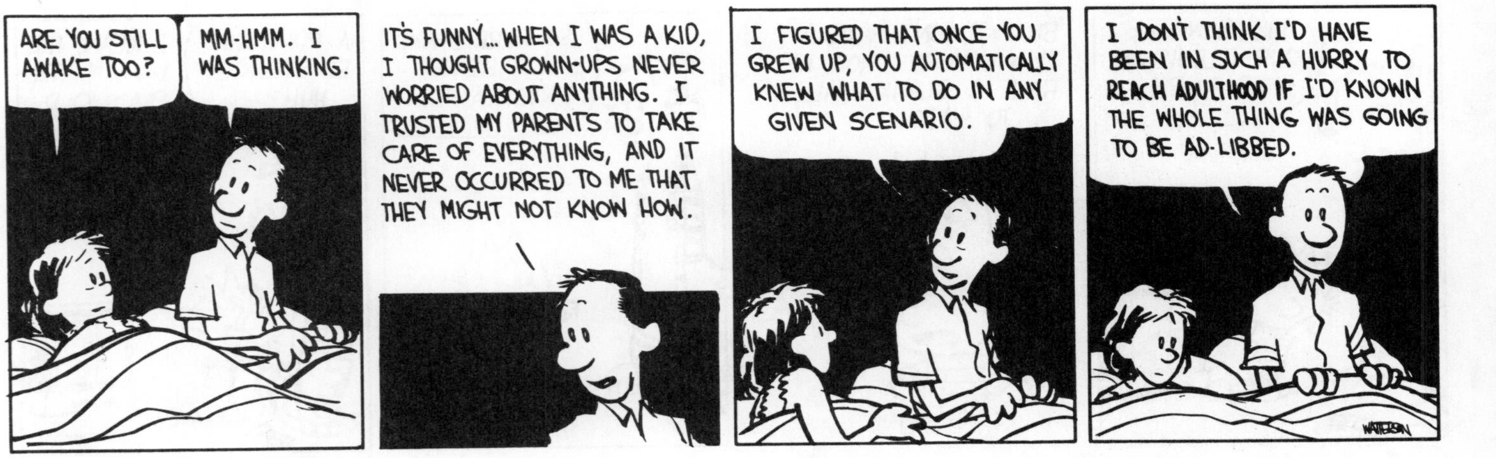
ARE YOU STILL AWAKE TOO?
MM-HMM. I WAS THINKING.
IT'S FUNNY... WHEN I WAS A KID, I THOUGHT GROWN-UPS NEVER WORRIED ABOUT ANYTHING. I TRUSTED MY PARENTS TO TAKE CARE OF EVERYTHING, AND IT NEVER OCCURRED TO ME THAT THEY MIGHT NOT KNOW HOW.
I FIGURED THAT ONCE YOU GREW UP, YOU AUTOMATICALLY KNEW WHAT TO DO IN ANY GIVEN SCENARIO.
I DON'T THINK I'D HAVE BEEN IN SUCH A HURRY TO REACH ADULTHOOD IF I'D KNOWN THE WHOLE THING WAS GOING TO BE AD-LIBBED.
WATTERSON

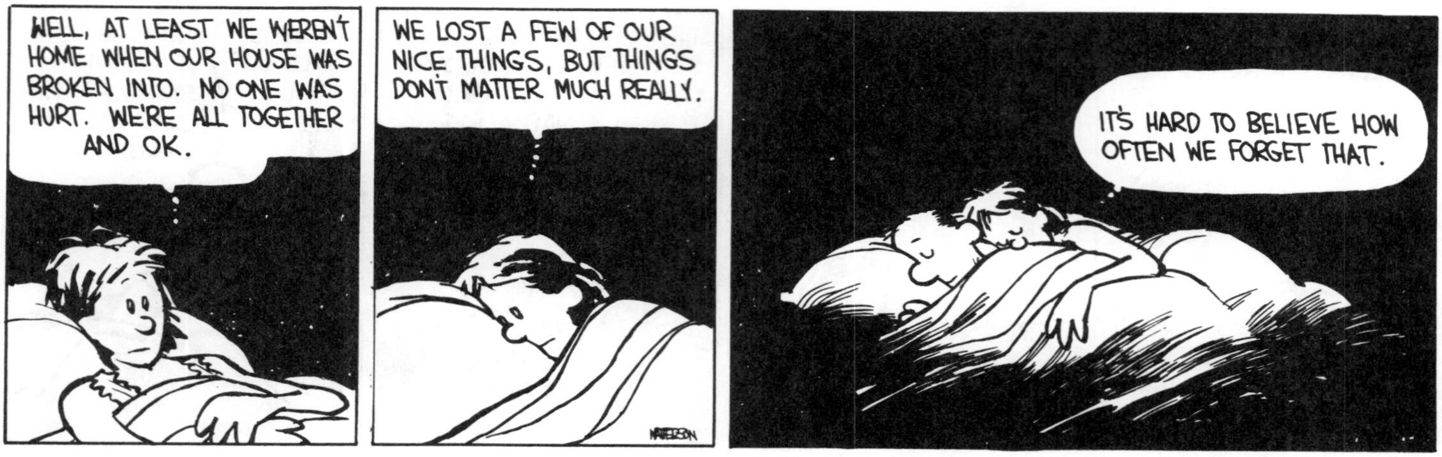
WELL, AT LEAST WE WEREN'T HOME WHEN OUR HOUSE WAS BROKEN INTO. NO ONE WAS HURT. WE'RE ALL TOGETHER AND OK.
WE LOST A FEW OF OUR NICE THINGS, BUT THINGS DON'T MATTER MUCH REALLY.
IT'S HARD TO BELIEVE HOW OFTEN WE FORGET THAT.
WATTERSON

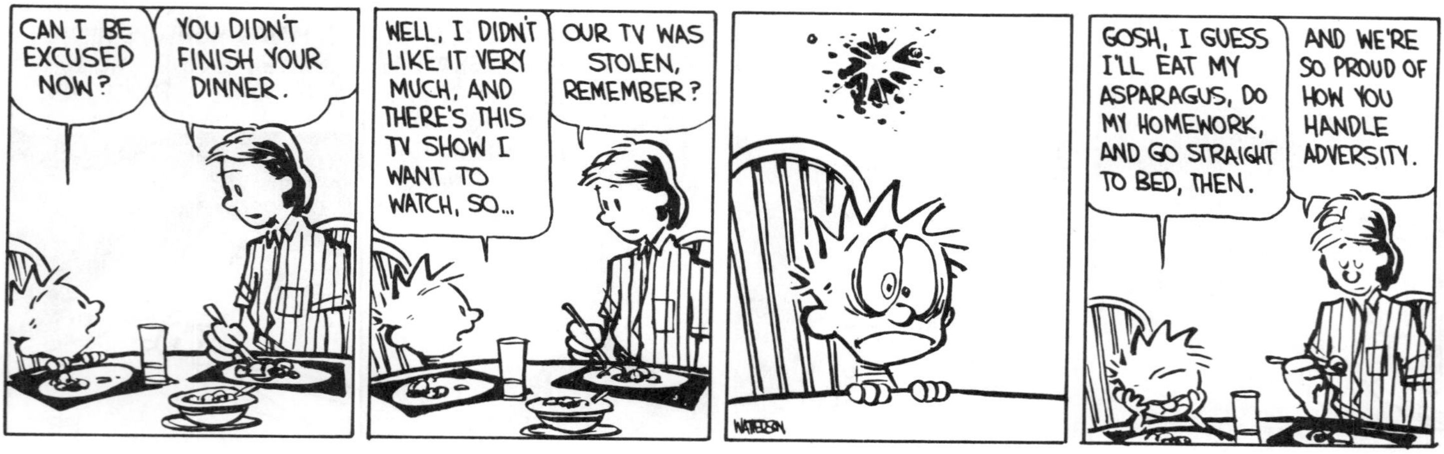
CAN I BE EXCUSED NOW?
YOU DIDN'T FINISH YOUR DINNER.
WELL, I DIDN'T LIKE IT VERY MUCH, AND THERE'S THIS TV SHOW I WANT TO WATCH, SO...
OUR TV WAS STOLEN, REMEMBER?
WATTERSON
GOSH, I GUESS I'LL EAT MY ASPARAGUS, DO MY HOMEWORK, AND GO STRAIGHT TO BED, THEN.
AND WE'RE SO PROUD OF HOW YOU HANDLE ADVERSITY.

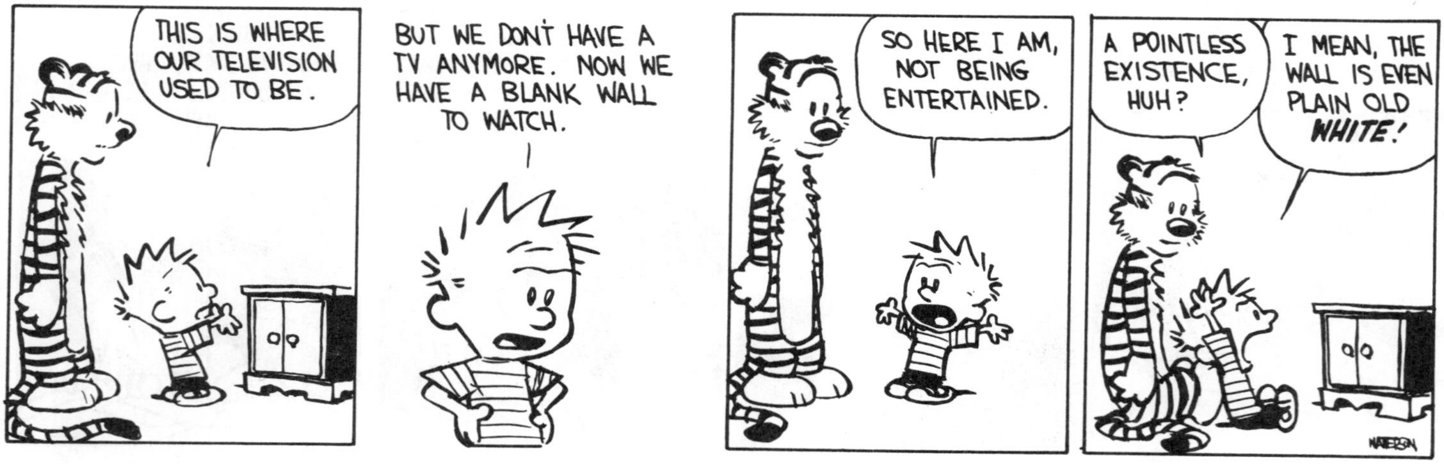
THIS IS WHERE OUR TELEVISION USED TO BE.
BUT WE DON'T HAVE A TV ANYMORE. NOW WE HAVE A BLANK WALL TO WATCH.
SO HERE I AM, NOT BEING ENTERTAINED.
A POINTLESS EXISTENCE, HUH?
I MEAN, THE WALL IS EVEN PLAIN OLD WHITE!
WATTERSON

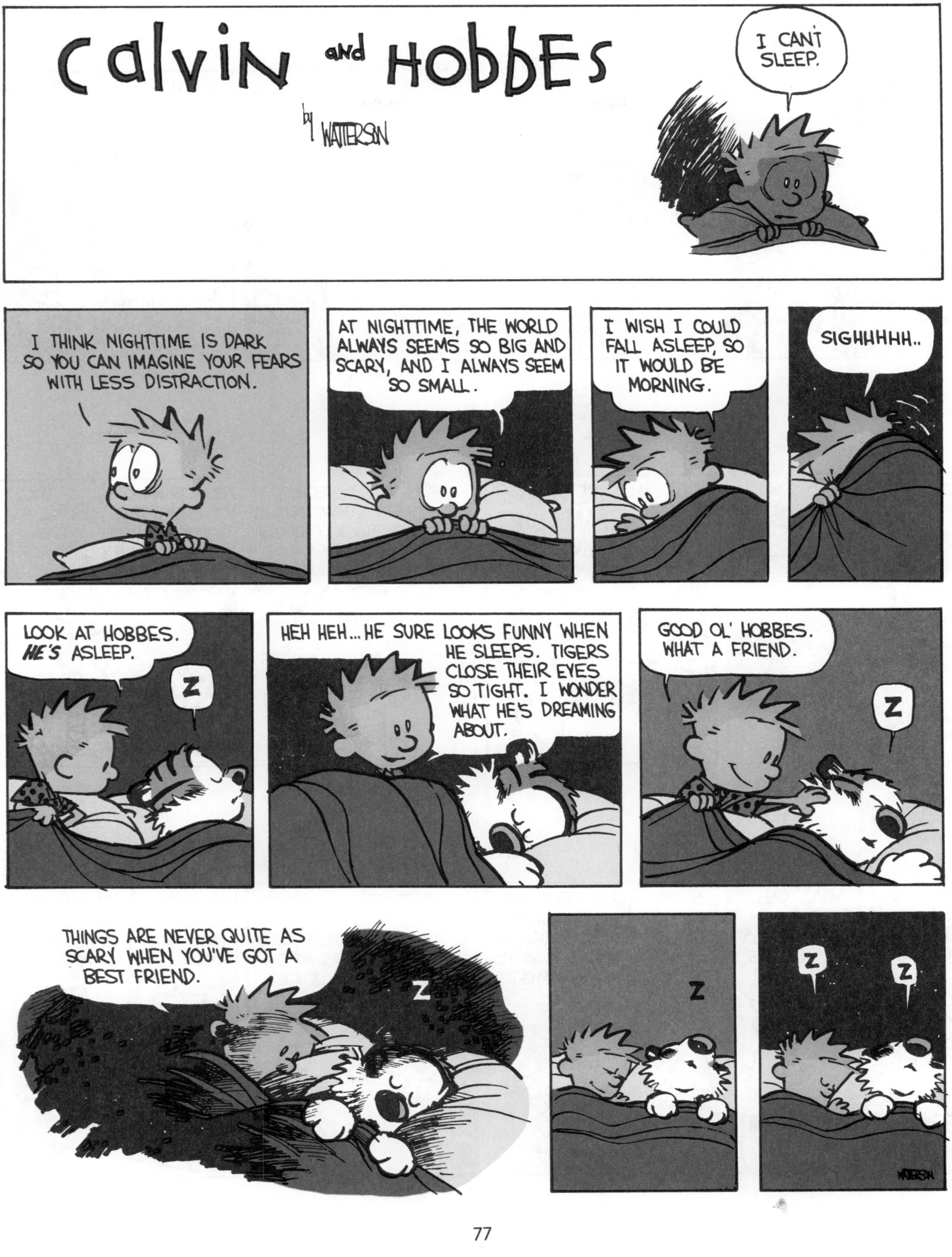
Calvin and HOBBES
by WATTERSON
I CAN'T SLEEP.
I THINK NIGHTTIME IS DARK SO YOU CAN IMAGINE YOUR FEARS WITH LESS DISTRACTION.
AT NIGHTTIME, THE WORLD ALWAYS SEEMS SO BIG AND SCARY, AND I ALWAYS SEEM SO SMALL.
I WISH I COULD FALL ASLEEP, SO IT WOULD BE MORNING.
SIGHHHHH..
LOOK AT HOBBES. HE'S ASLEEP.
Z
HEH HEH... HE SURE LOOKS FUNNY WHEN HE SLEEPS. TIGERS CLOSE THEIR EYES SO TIGHT. I WONDER WHAT HE'S DREAMING ABOUT.
GOOD OL' HOBBES. WHAT A FRIEND.
Z
THINGS ARE NEVER QUITE AS SCARY WHEN YOU'VE GOT A BEST FRIEND.
Z
Z
Z
Z
WATTERSON

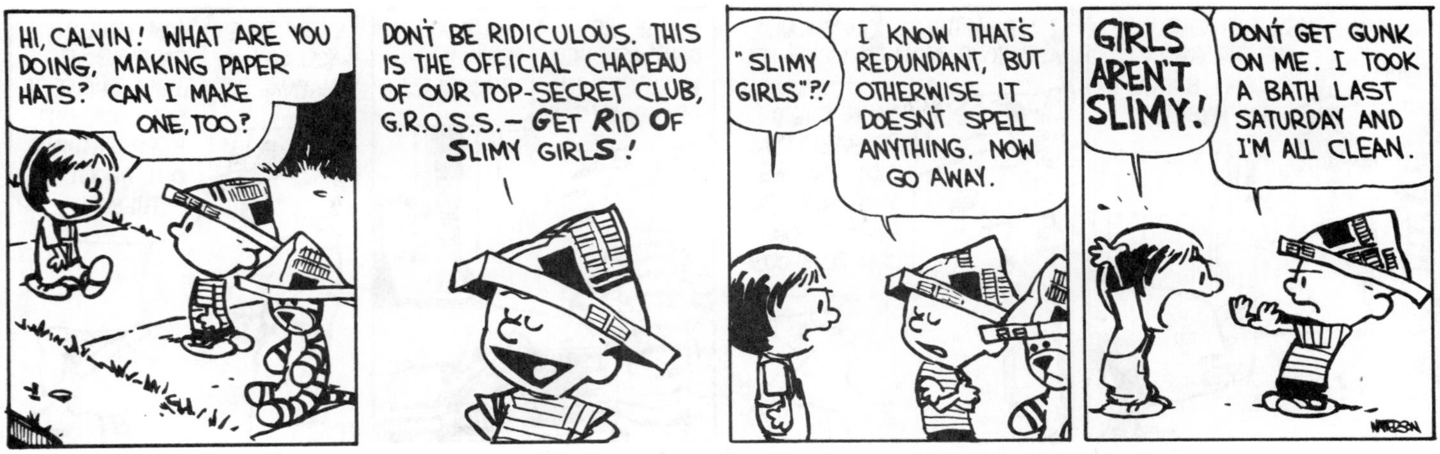
HI, CALVIN! WHAT ARE YOU DOING, MAKING PAPER HATS? CAN I MAKE ONE, TOO?
DON'T BE RIDICULOUS. THIS IS THE OFFICIAL CHAPEAU OF OUR TOP-SECRET CLUB, G.R.O.S.S.- GET RID OF SLIMY GIRLS!
"SLIMY GIRLS"?!
I KNOW THAT'S REDUNDANT, BUT OTHERWISE IT DOESN'T SPELL ANYTHING. NOW GO AWAY.
GIRLS AREN'T SLIMY!
DON'T GET GUNK ON ME. I TOOK A BATH LAST SATURDAY AND I'M ALL CLEAN.

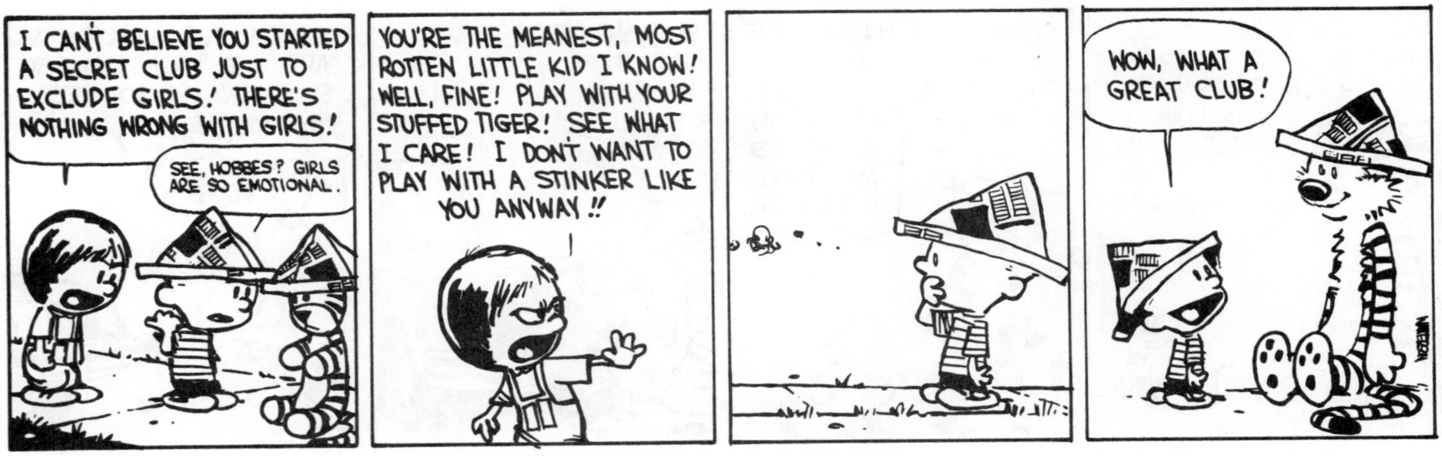
I CAN'T BELIEVE YOU STARTED A SECRET CLUB JUST TO EXCLUDE GIRLS! THERE'S NOTHING WRONG WITH GIRLS!
SEE, HOBBES? GIRLS ARE SO EMOTIONAL.
YOU'RE THE MEANEST, MOST ROTTEN LITTLE KID I KNOW! WELL, FINE! PLAY WITH YOUR STUFFED TIGER! SEE WHAT I CARE! I DON'T WANT TO PLAY WITH A STINKER LIKE YOU ANYWAY!!
WOW, WHAT A GREAT CLUB!

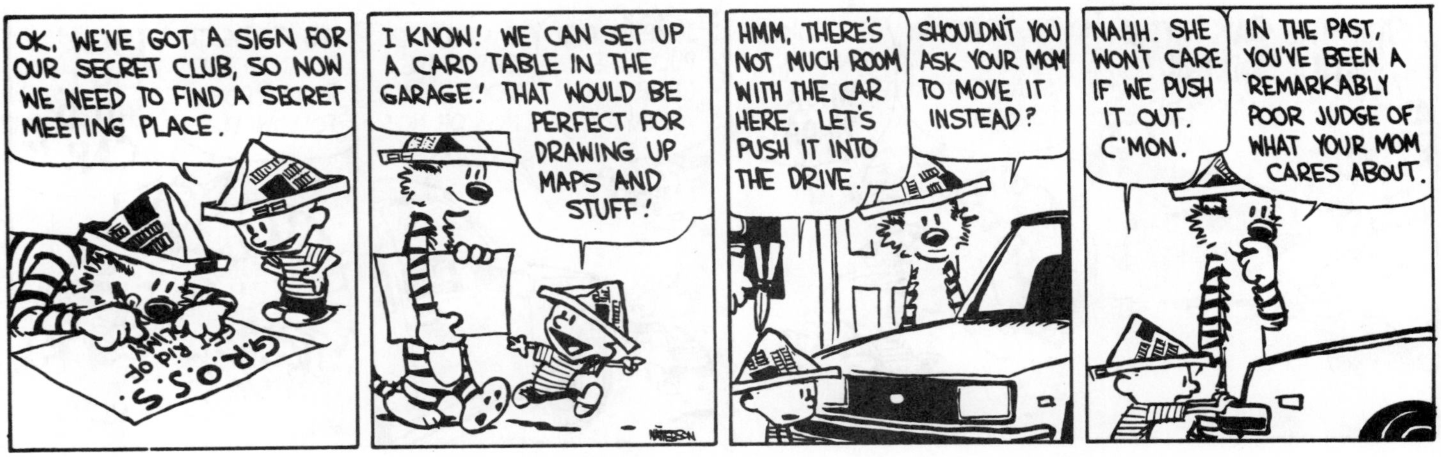
OK, WE'VE GOT A SIGN FOR OUR SECRET CLUB, SO NOW WE NEED TO FIND A SECRET MEETING PLACE.
G.R.O.S.S.
I KNOW! WE CAN SET UP A CARD TABLE IN THE GARAGE! THAT WOULD BE PERFECT FOR DRAWING UP MAPS AND STUFF!
HMM, THERE'S NOT MUCH ROOM WITH THE CAR HERE. LET'S PUSH IT INTO THE DRIVE.
SHOULDN'T YOU ASK YOUR MOM TO MOVE IT INSTEAD?
NAHH. SHE WON'T CARE IF WE PUSH IT OUT. C'MON.
IN THE PAST, YOU'VE BEEN A REMARKABLY POOR JUDGE OF WHAT YOUR MOM CARES ABOUT.

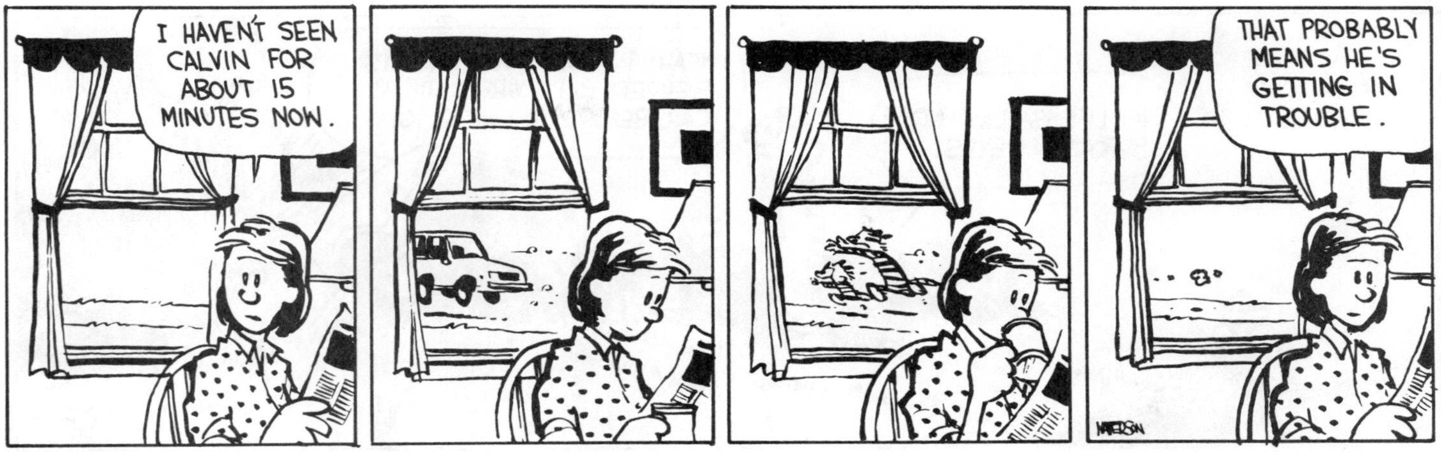
I HAVEN'T SEEN CALVIN FOR ABOUT 15 MINUTES NOW.
THAT PROBABLY MEANS HE'S GETTING IN TROUBLE.

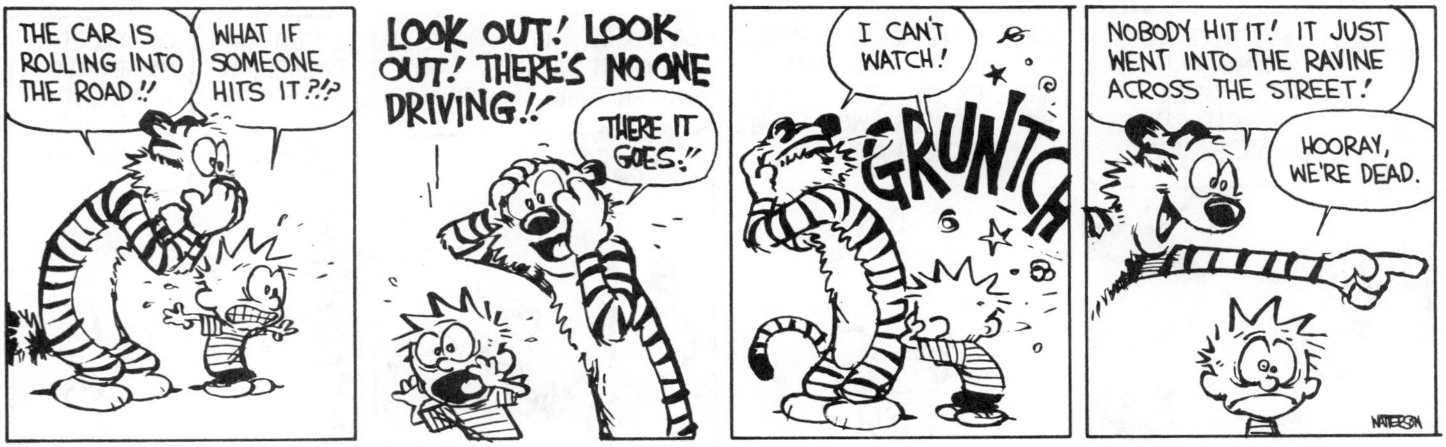
THE CAR IS ROLLING INTO THE ROAD!!
WHAT IF SOMEONE HITS IT?!?
LOOK OUT! LOOK OUT! THERE'S NO ONE DRIVING!!
THERE IT GOES!!
I CAN'T WATCH!
GRUNTCH
NOBODY HIT IT! IT JUST WENT INTO THE RAVINE ACROSS THE STREET!
HOORAY, WE'RE DEAD.

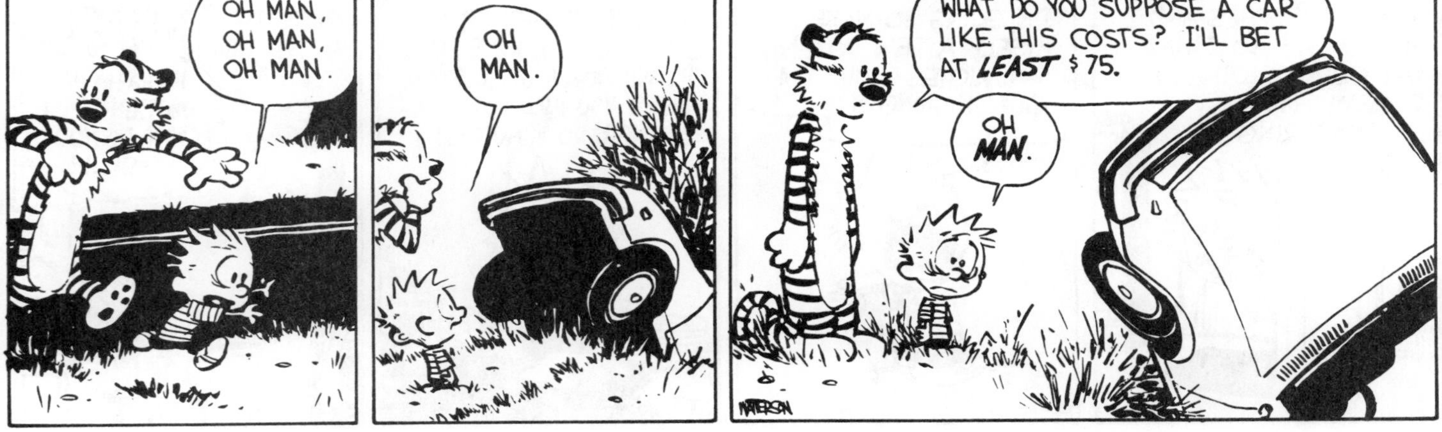
OH MAN, OH MAN, OH MAN.
OH MAN.
WHAT DO YOU SUPPOSE A CAR LIKE THIS COSTS? I'LL BET AT LEAST $75.
OH MAN.

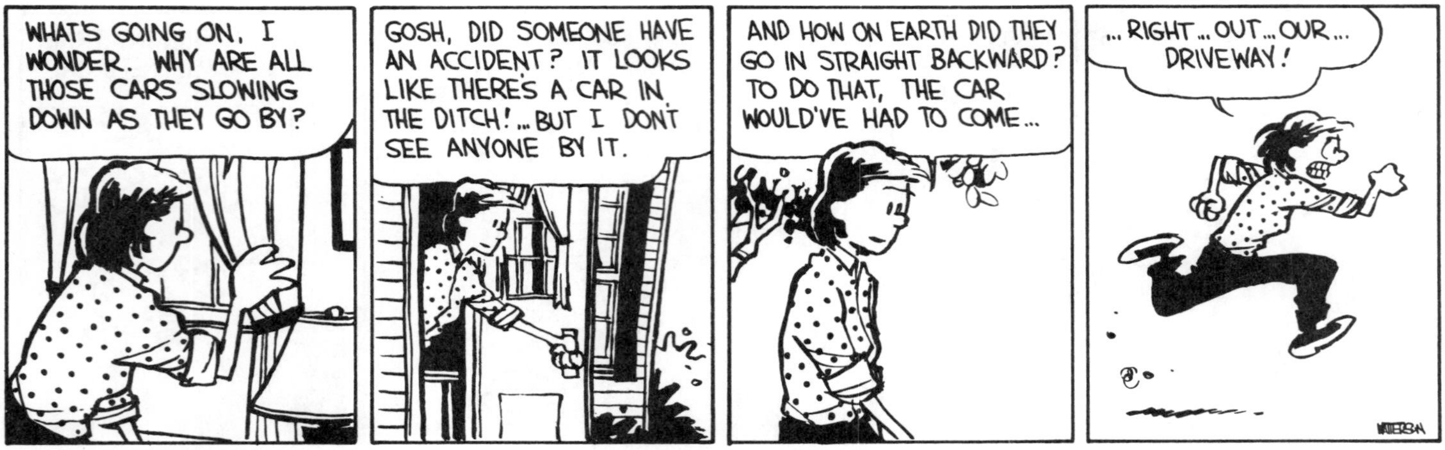
WHAT'S GOING ON, I WONDER. WHY ARE ALL THOSE CARS SLOWING DOWN AS THEY GO BY?
GOSH, DID SOMEONE HAVE AN ACCIDENT? IT LOOKS LIKE THERE'S A CAR IN THE DITCH! ...BUT I DON'T SEE ANYONE BY IT.
AND HOW ON EARTH DID THEY GO IN STRAIGHT BACKWARD? TO DO THAT, THE CAR WOULD'VE HAD TO COME...
...RIGHT...OUT...OUR... DRIVEWAY!

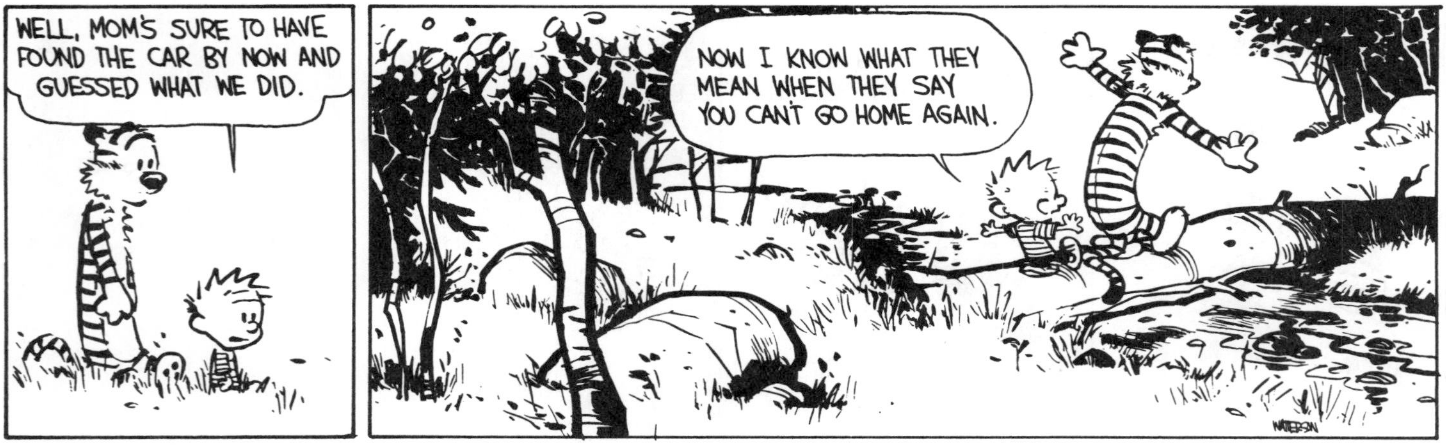
WELL, MOM'S SURE TO HAVE FOUND THE CAR BY NOW AND GUESSED WHAT WE DID.
NOW I KNOW WHAT THEY MEAN WHEN THEY SAY YOU CAN'T GO HOME AGAIN.

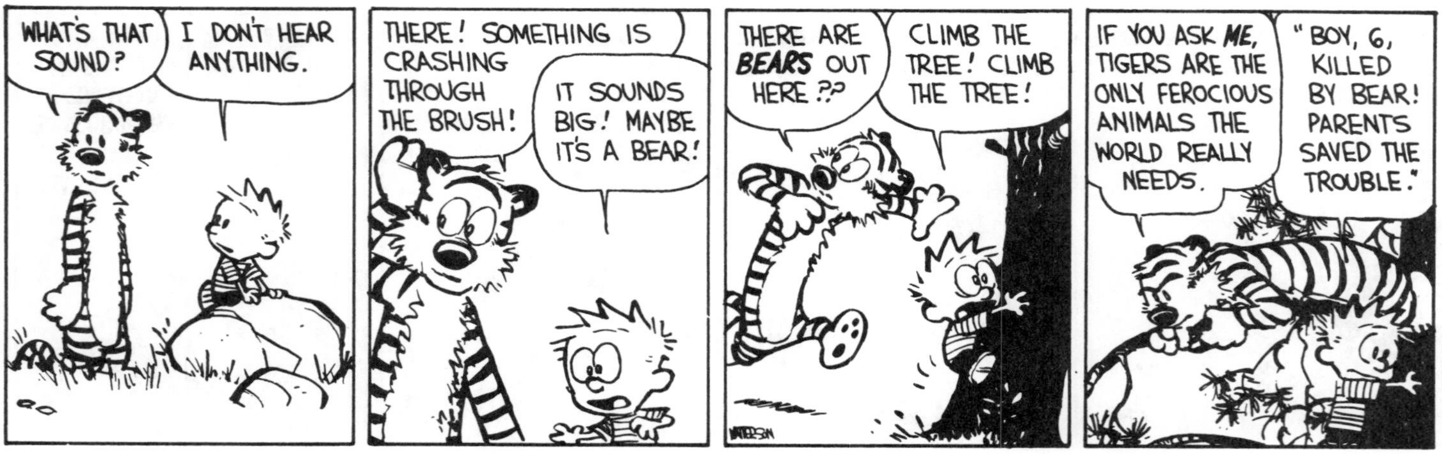
WHAT'S THAT SOUND?
I DON'T HEAR ANYTHING.
THERE! SOMETHING IS CRASHING THROUGH THE BRUSH!
IT SOUNDS BIG! MAYBE IT'S A BEAR!
THERE ARE BEARS OUT HERE?!?
CLIMB THE TREE! CLIMB THE TREE!
IF YOU ASK ME, TIGERS ARE THE ONLY FEROCIOUS ANIMALS THE WORLD REALLY NEEDS.
"BOY, 6, KILLED BY BEAR! PARENTS SAVED THE TROUBLE."

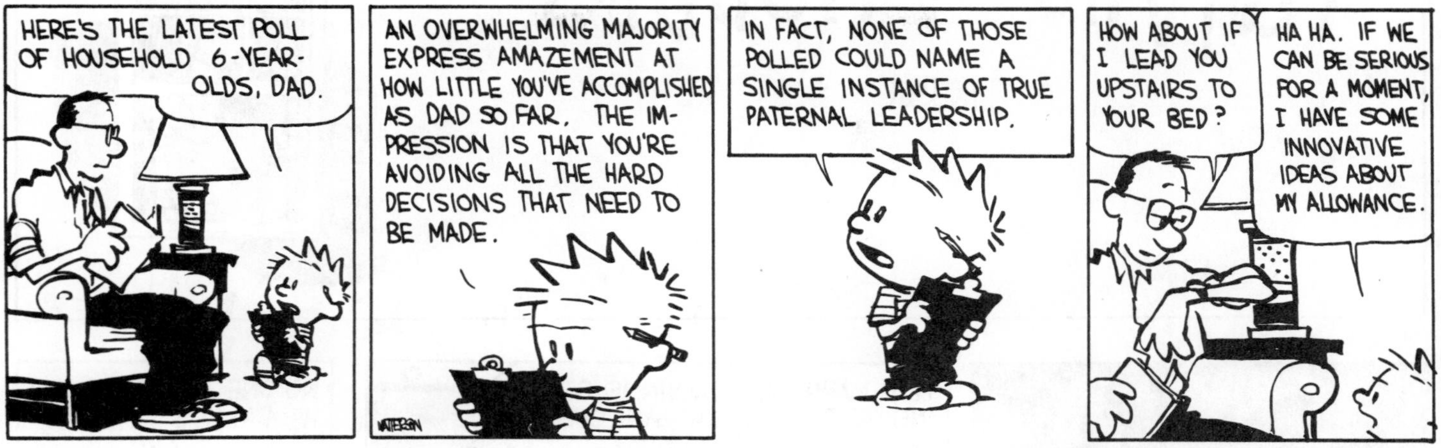
HERE'S THE LATEST POLL OF HOUSEHOLD 6-YEAR-OLDS, DAD.
AN OVERWHELMING MAJORITY EXPRESS AMAZEMENT AT HOW LITTLE YOU'VE ACCOMPLISHED AS DAD SO FAR. THE IMPRESSION IS THAT YOU'RE AVOIDING ALL THE HARD DECISIONS THAT NEED TO BE MADE.
IN FACT, NONE OF THOSE POLLED COULD NAME A SINGLE INSTANCE OF TRUE PATERNAL LEADERSHIP.
HOW ABOUT IF I LEAD YOU UPSTAIRS TO YOUR BED?
HA HA. IF WE CAN BE SERIOUS FOR A MOMENT, I HAVE SOME INNOVATIVE IDEAS ABOUT MY ALLOWANCE.

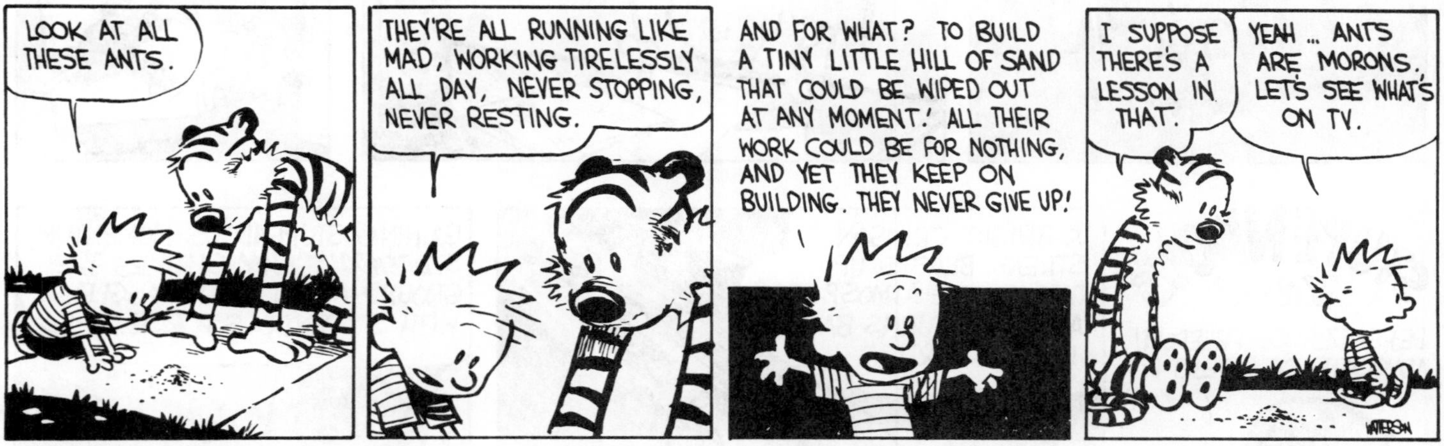
LOOK AT ALL THESE ANTS.
THEY'RE ALL RUNNING LIKE MAD, WORKING TIRELESSLY ALL DAY, NEVER STOPPING, NEVER RESTING.
AND FOR WHAT? TO BUILD A TINY LITTLE HILL OF SAND THAT COULD BE WIPED OUT AT ANY MOMENT! ALL THEIR WORK COULD BE FOR NOTHING, AND YET THEY KEEP ON BUILDING. THEY NEVER GIVE UP!
I SUPPOSE THERE'S A LESSON IN THAT.
YEAH ... ANTS ARE MORONS. LET'S SEE WHAT'S ON TV.

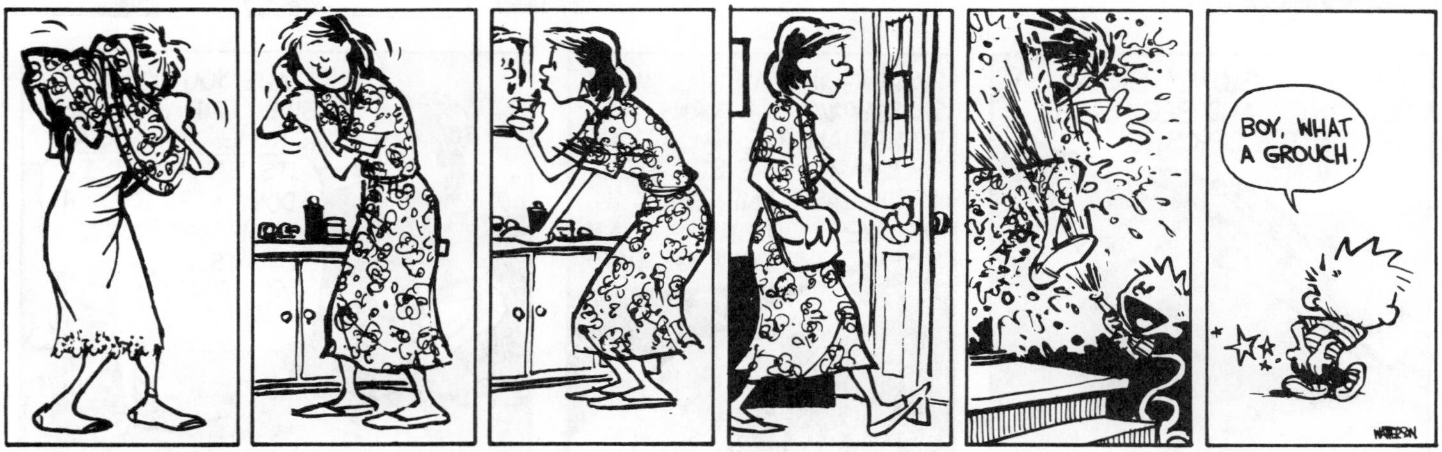
BOY, WHAT A GROUCH.

CALVIN and HOBBES

by WATTERSON

MILD-MANNERED CALVIN IS STUCK INSIDE DOING MATH PROBLEMS ON A BEAUTIFUL SUNDAY.

NO ONE IS WATCHING! HE DASHES INTO HIS CLOSET! *THIS* IS A JOB FOR...

STUPENDOUS MAN!

DEFENDER OF FREEDOM! ADVOCATE OF LIBERTY!

A BRIGHT CRIMSON STREAK BLASTS UP THROUGH THE ATMOSPHERE, AND THEN TURNS BACK TOWARD EARTH!

GAINING STUPENDOUS MOMENTUM, *STUPENDOUS MAN* STRIKES THE GROUND AT AN ACUTE ANGLE WITH STUPENDOUS FORCE!

THE EARTH SLOWLY STOPS ROTATING... AND BEGINS TO TURN IN THE OPPOSITE DIRECTION!

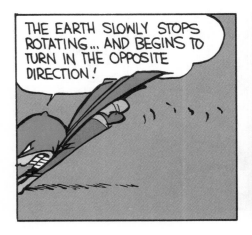

PUSHING WITH ALL HIS MIGHT, *STUPENDOUS MAN* TURNS THE PLANET ALL THE WAY AROUND BACKWARD! THE SUN SETS IN THE EAST AND RISES IN THE WEST! SOON IT'S 10 A.M. THE PREVIOUS DAY!

WHAT ARE YOU DOING OUTSIDE? DID YOU FINISH YOUR HOMEWORK ALREADY?

IT'S SATURDAY! I DON'T NEED TO DO IT UNTIL TOMORROW... *THANKS TO STUPENDOUS MAN!*

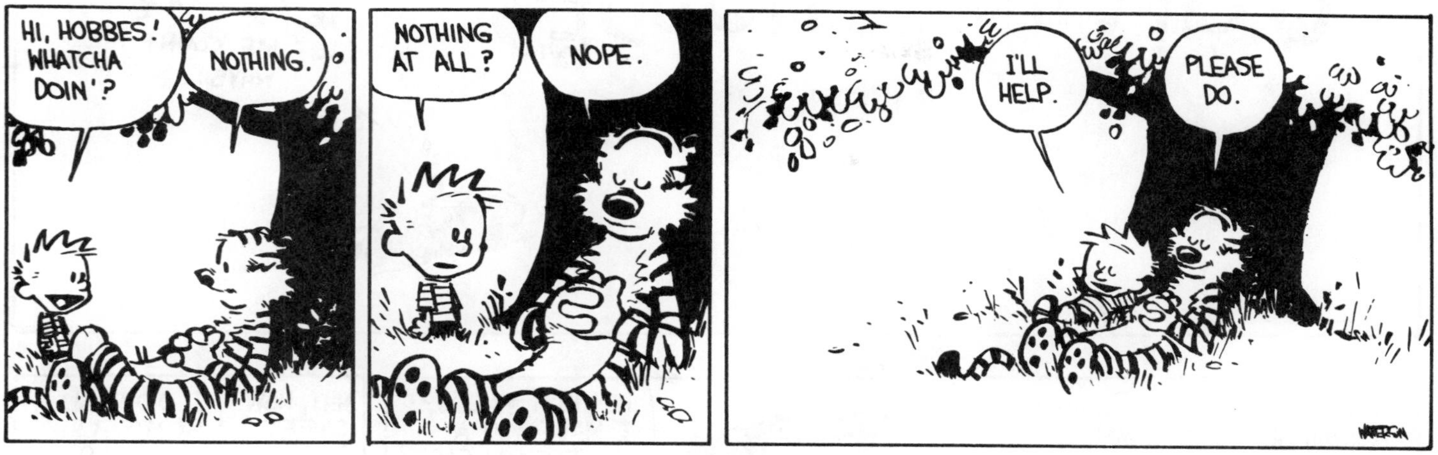
HI, HOBBES! WHATCHA DOIN'?
NOTHING.
NOTHING AT ALL?
NOPE.
I'LL HELP.
PLEASE DO.

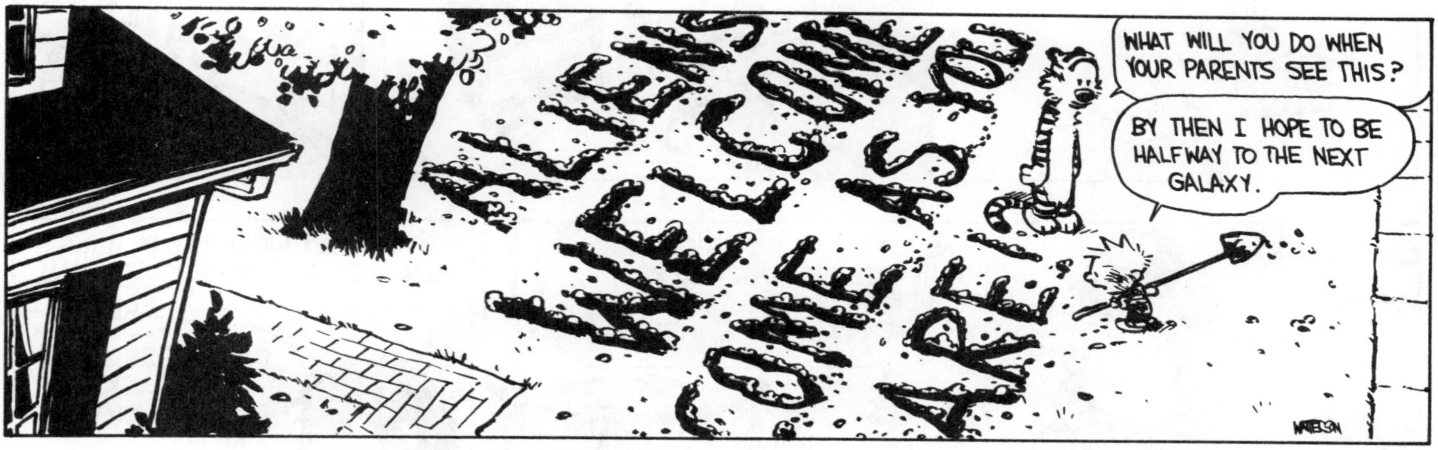
WHAT WILL YOU DO WHEN YOUR PARENTS SEE THIS?
BY THEN I HOPE TO BE HALFWAY TO THE NEXT GALAXY.

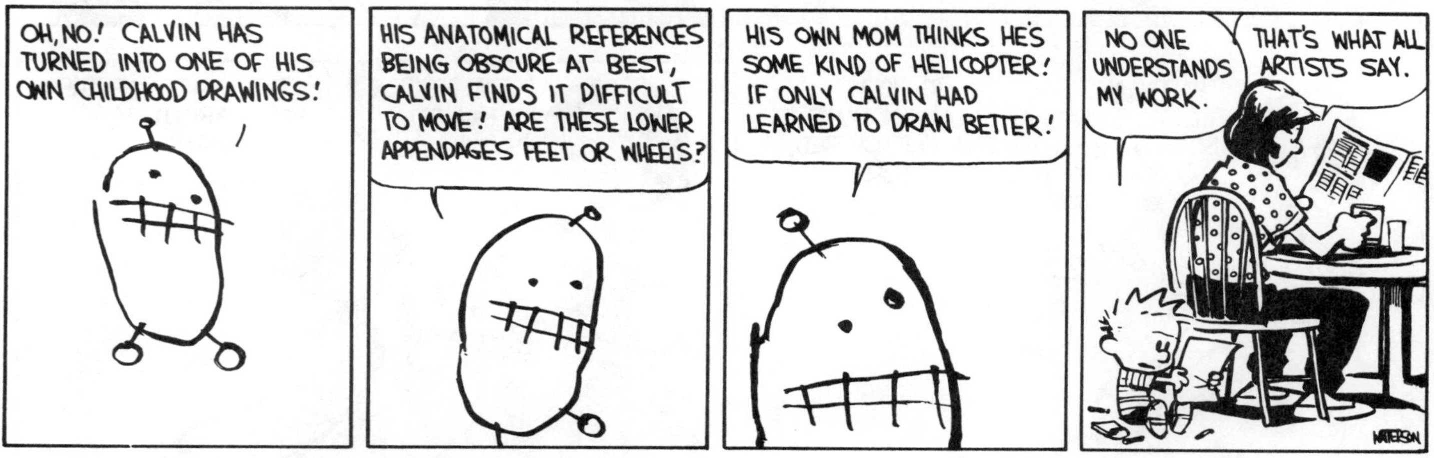
OH, NO! CALVIN HAS TURNED INTO ONE OF HIS OWN CHILDHOOD DRAWINGS!
HIS ANATOMICAL REFERENCES BEING OBSCURE AT BEST, CALVIN FINDS IT DIFFICULT TO MOVE! ARE THESE LOWER APPENDAGES FEET OR WHEELS?
HIS OWN MOM THINKS HE'S SOME KIND OF HELICOPTER! IF ONLY CALVIN HAD LEARNED TO DRAW BETTER!
NO ONE UNDERSTANDS MY WORK.
THAT'S WHAT ALL ARTISTS SAY.

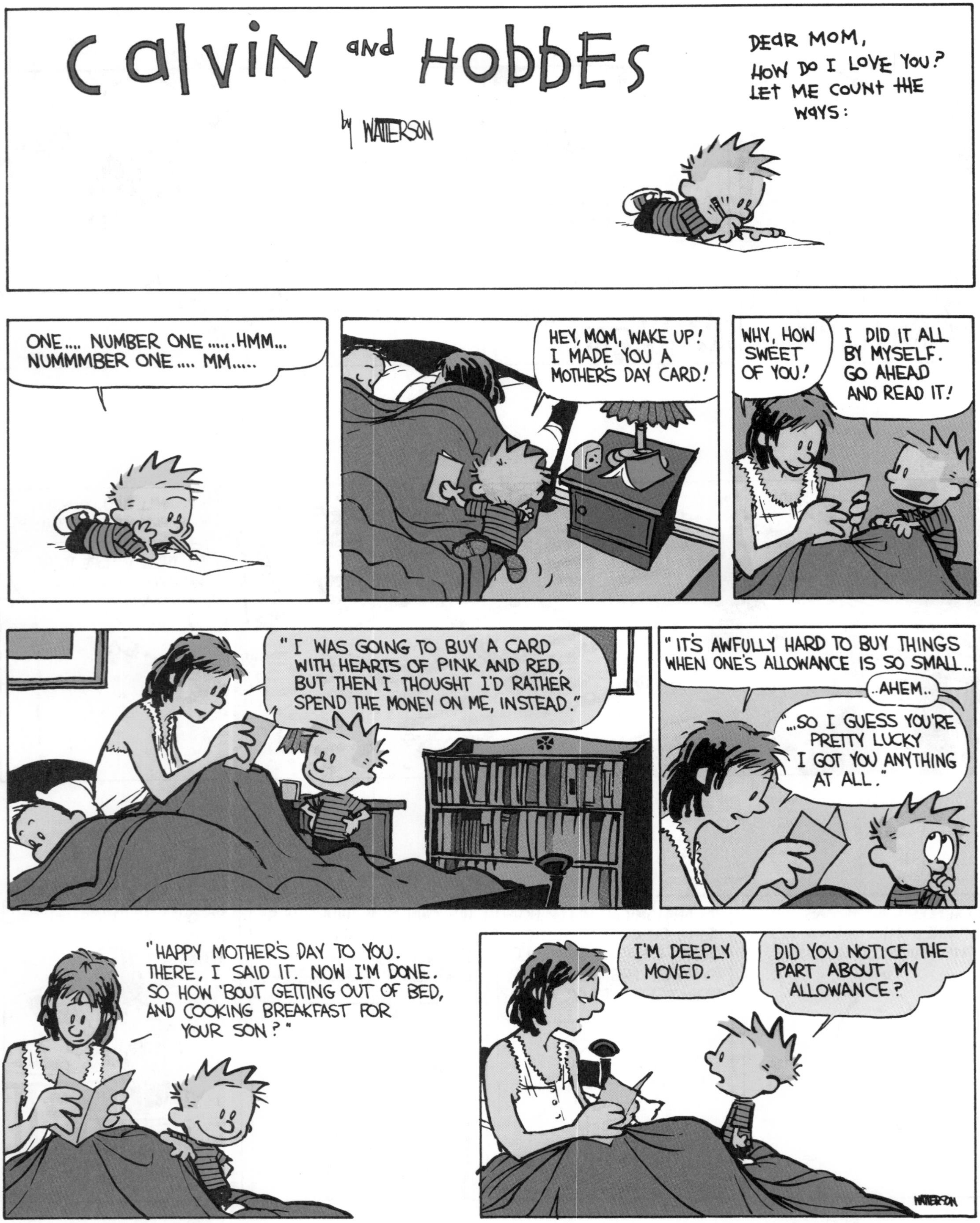
Calvin and Hobbes
by WATTERSON
DEAR MOM,
HOW DO I LOVE YOU? LET ME COUNT THE WAYS:
ONE.... NUMBER ONE......HMM... NUMMMBER ONE..... MM.....
HEY, MOM, WAKE UP! I MADE YOU A MOTHER'S DAY CARD!
WHY, HOW SWEET OF YOU!
I DID IT ALL BY MYSELF. GO AHEAD AND READ IT!
" I WAS GOING TO BUY A CARD WITH HEARTS OF PINK AND RED, BUT THEN I THOUGHT I'D RATHER SPEND THE MONEY ON ME, INSTEAD."
" IT'S AWFULLY HARD TO BUY THINGS WHEN ONE'S ALLOWANCE IS SO SMALL...
..AHEM..
...SO I GUESS YOU'RE PRETTY LUCKY I GOT YOU ANYTHING AT ALL."
"HAPPY MOTHER'S DAY TO YOU. THERE, I SAID IT. NOW I'M DONE. SO HOW 'BOUT GETTING OUT OF BED, AND COOKING BREAKFAST FOR YOUR SON?"
I'M DEEPLY MOVED.
DID YOU NOTICE THE PART ABOUT MY ALLOWANCE?
WATTERSON

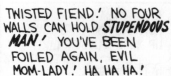

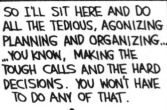

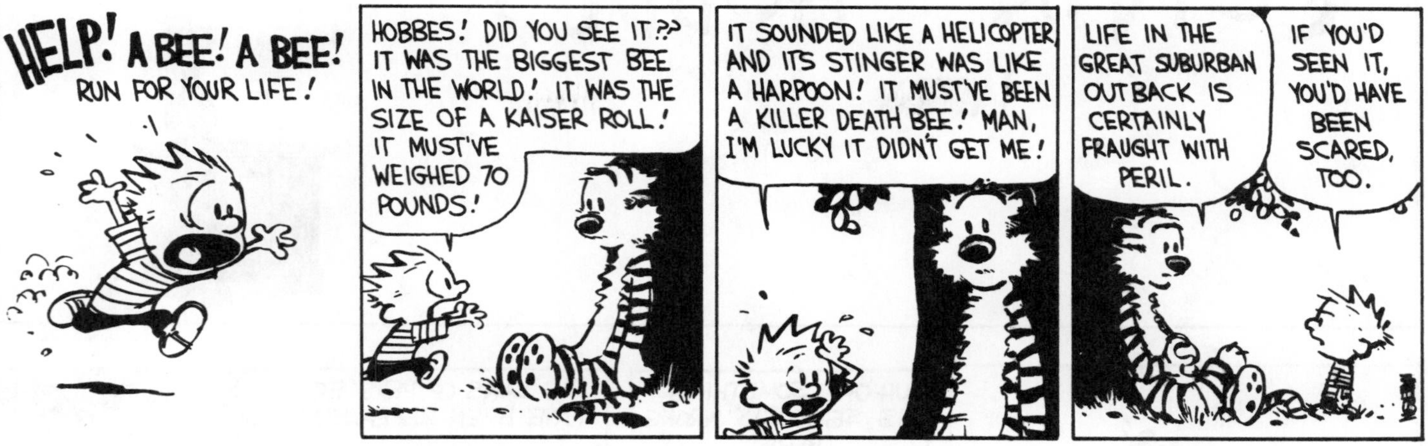
HELP! A BEE! A BEE!
RUN FOR YOUR LIFE!
HOBBES! DID YOU SEE IT?? IT WAS THE BIGGEST BEE IN THE WORLD! IT WAS THE SIZE OF A KAISER ROLL! IT MUST'VE WEIGHED 70 POUNDS!
IT SOUNDED LIKE A HELICOPTER, AND ITS STINGER WAS LIKE A HARPOON! IT MUST'VE BEEN A KILLER DEATH BEE! MAN, I'M LUCKY IT DIDN'T GET ME!
LIFE IN THE GREAT SUBURBAN OUTBACK IS CERTAINLY FRAUGHT WITH PERIL.
IF YOU'D SEEN IT, YOU'D HAVE BEEN SCARED, TOO.

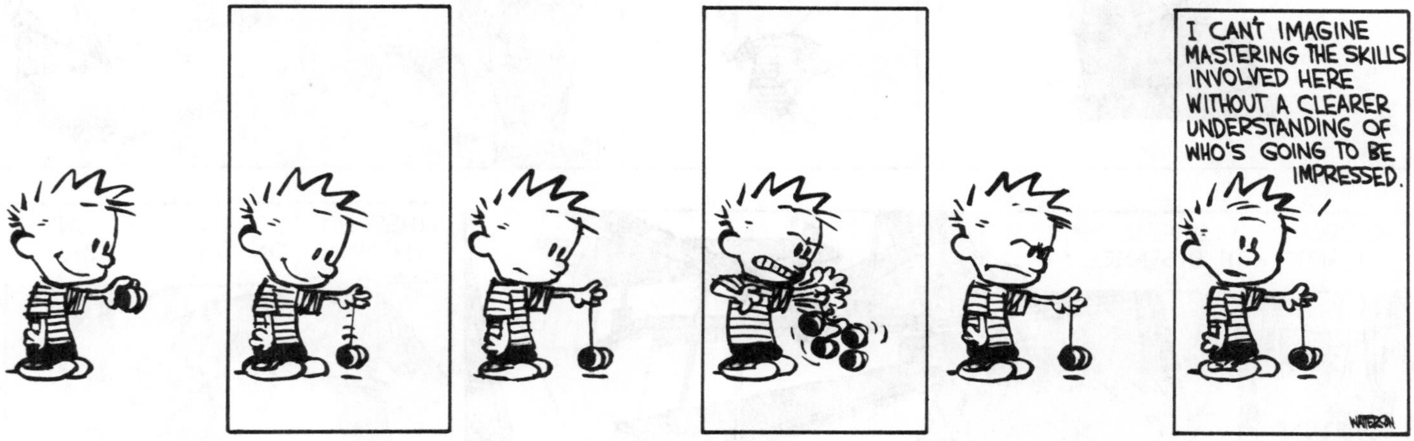
I CAN'T IMAGINE MASTERING THE SKILLS INVOLVED HERE WITHOUT A CLEARER UNDERSTANDING OF WHO'S GOING TO BE IMPRESSED.

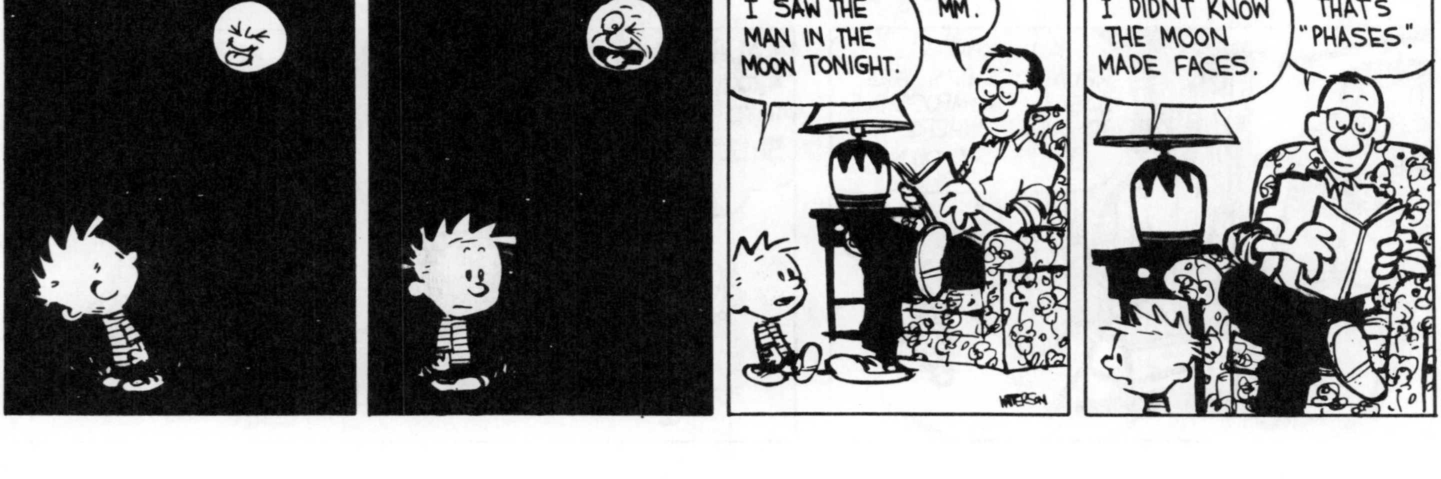
I SAW THE MAN IN THE MOON TONIGHT.
MM.
I DIDN'T KNOW THE MOON MADE FACES.
THAT'S "PHASES".

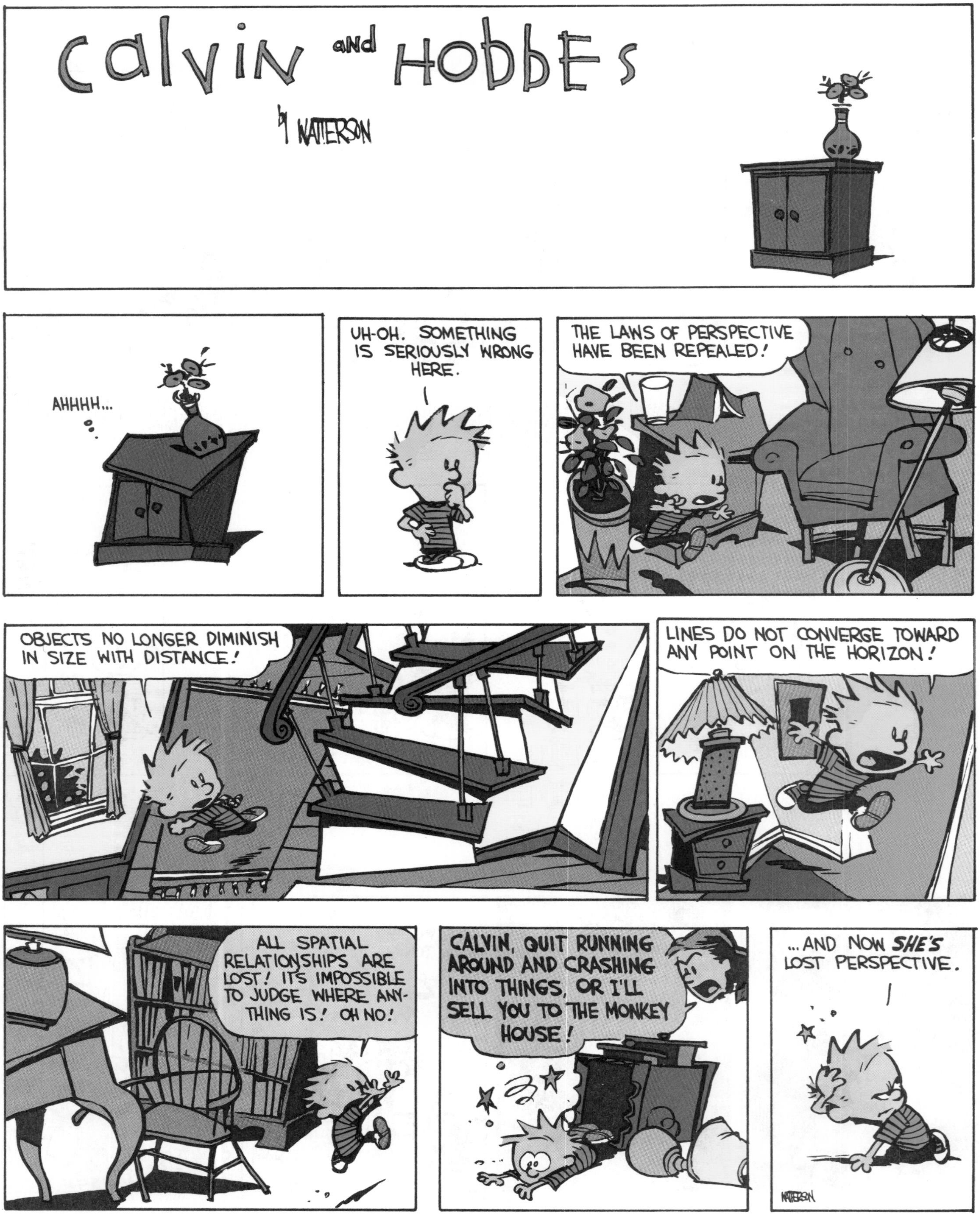
Calvin and Hobbes
by WATTERSON
AHHHH...
UH-OH. SOMETHING IS SERIOUSLY WRONG HERE.
THE LAWS OF PERSPECTIVE HAVE BEEN REPEALED!
OBJECTS NO LONGER DIMINISH IN SIZE WITH DISTANCE!
LINES DO NOT CONVERGE TOWARD ANY POINT ON THE HORIZON!
ALL SPATIAL RELATIONSHIPS ARE LOST! IT'S IMPOSSIBLE TO JUDGE WHERE ANYTHING IS! OH NO!
CALVIN, QUIT RUNNING AROUND AND CRASHING INTO THINGS, OR I'LL SELL YOU TO THE MONKEY HOUSE!
...AND NOW SHE'S LOST PERSPECTIVE.
WATTERSON

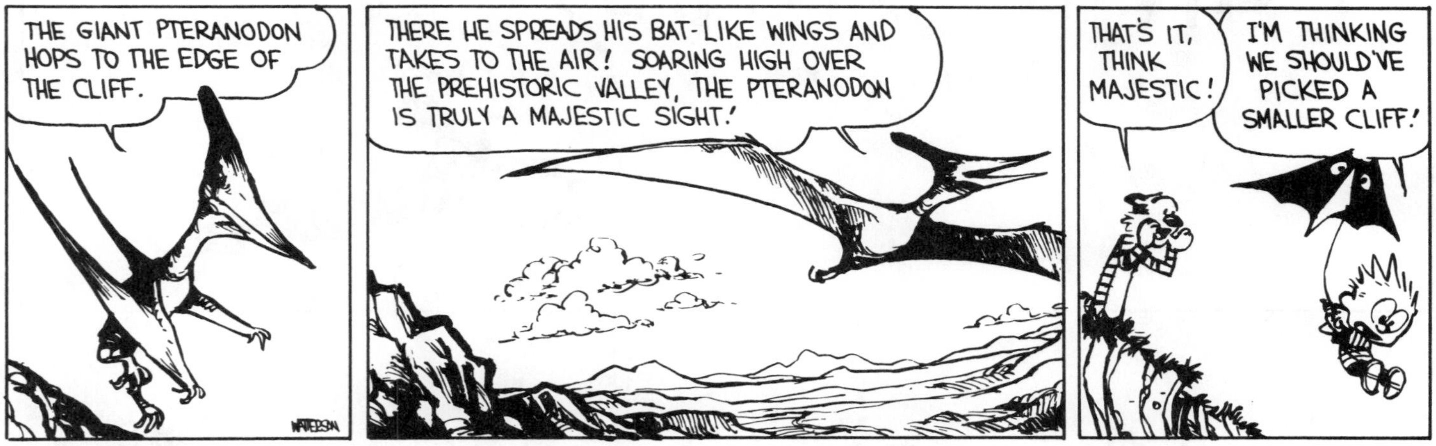
THE GIANT PTERANODON HOPS TO THE EDGE OF THE CLIFF.
THERE HE SPREADS HIS BAT-LIKE WINGS AND TAKES TO THE AIR! SOARING HIGH OVER THE PREHISTORIC VALLEY, THE PTERANODON IS TRULY A MAJESTIC SIGHT!
THAT'S IT, THINK MAJESTIC!
I'M THINKING WE SHOULD'VE PICKED A SMALLER CLIFF!

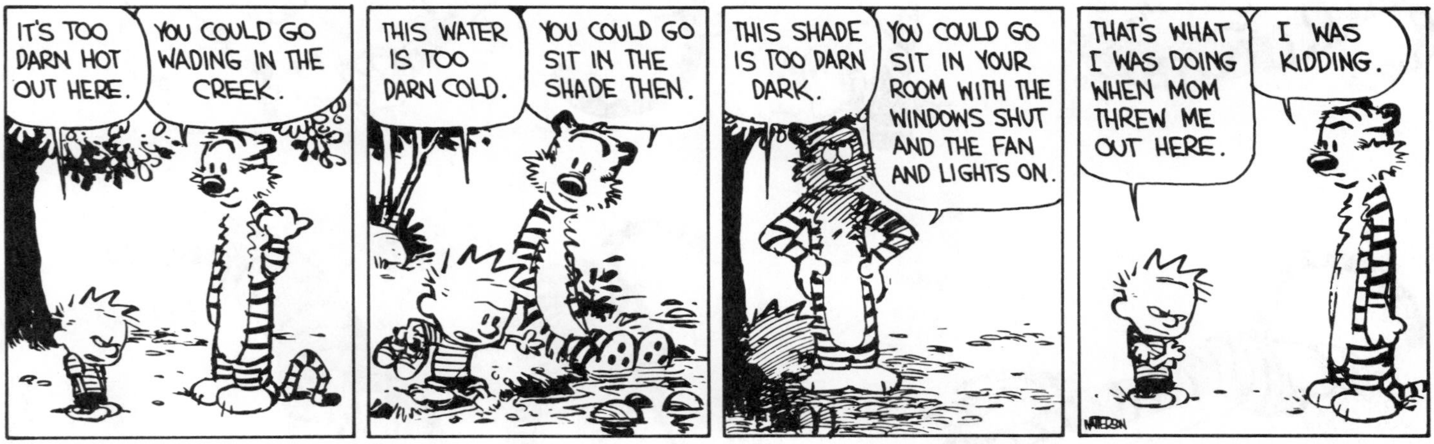
IT'S TOO DARN HOT OUT HERE.
YOU COULD GO WADING IN THE CREEK.
THIS WATER IS TOO DARN COLD.
YOU COULD GO SIT IN THE SHADE THEN.
THIS SHADE IS TOO DARN DARK.
YOU COULD GO SIT IN YOUR ROOM WITH THE WINDOWS SHUT AND THE FAN AND LIGHTS ON.
THAT'S WHAT I WAS DOING WHEN MOM THREW ME OUT HERE.
I WAS KIDDING.

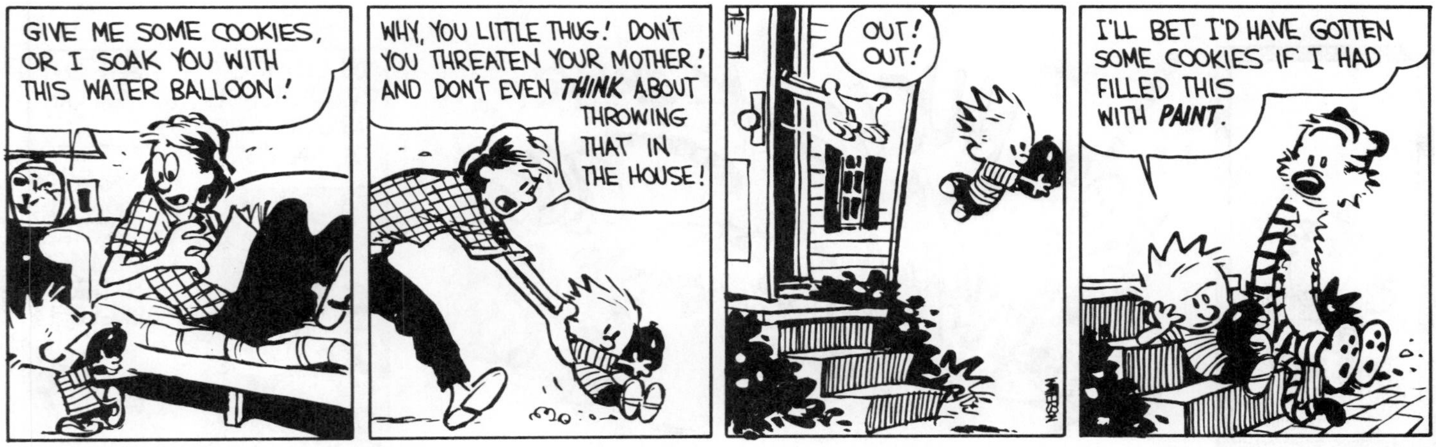
GIVE ME SOME COOKIES, OR I SOAK YOU WITH THIS WATER BALLOON!
WHY, YOU LITTLE THUG! DON'T YOU THREATEN YOUR MOTHER! AND DON'T EVEN THINK ABOUT THROWING THAT IN THE HOUSE!
OUT! OUT!
I'LL BET I'D HAVE GOTTEN SOME COOKIES IF I HAD FILLED THIS WITH PAINT.

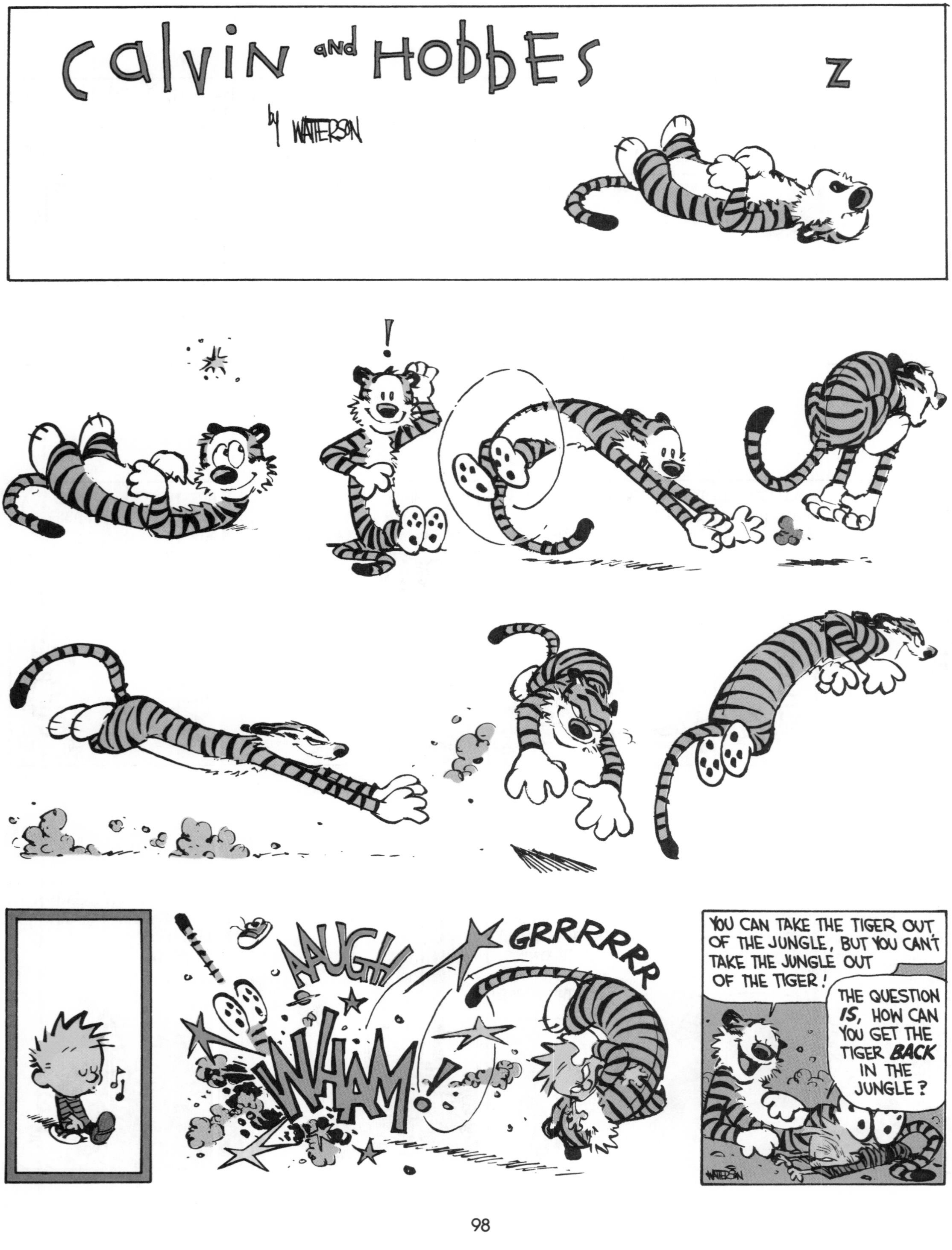
Calvin and HOBBES
by WATTERSON
Z
!
AAUGH
WHAM
GRRRRRR
YOU CAN TAKE THE TIGER OUT OF THE JUNGLE, BUT YOU CAN'T TAKE THE JUNGLE OUT OF THE TIGER!
THE QUESTION IS, HOW CAN YOU GET THE TIGER BACK IN THE JUNGLE?
WATTERSON

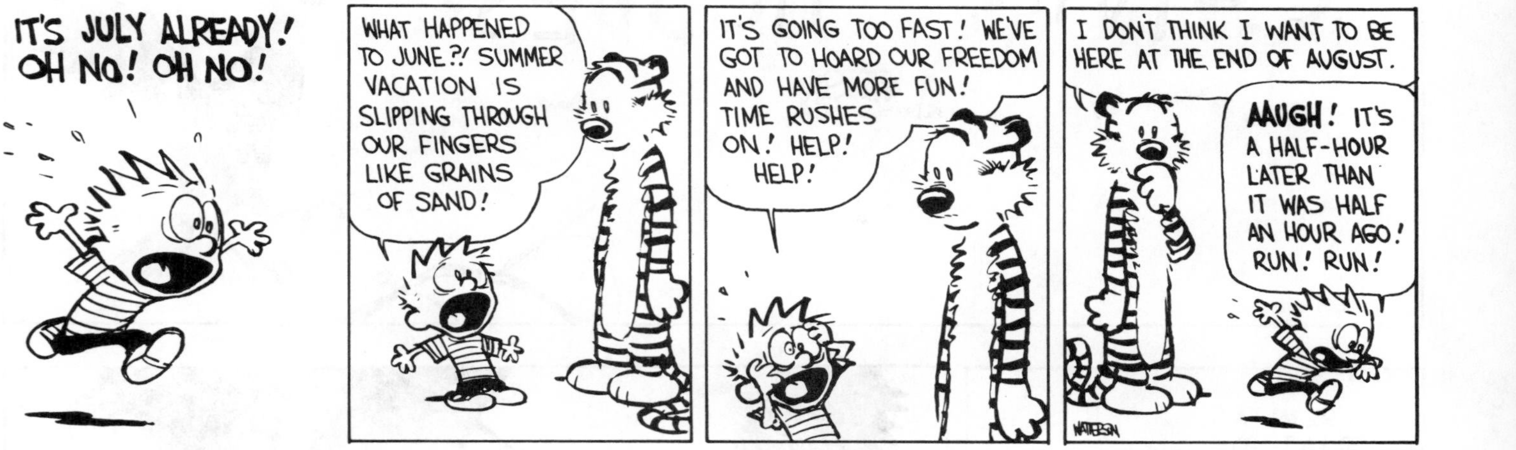
IT'S JULY ALREADY! OH NO! OH NO!
WHAT HAPPENED TO JUNE?! SUMMER VACATION IS SLIPPING THROUGH OUR FINGERS LIKE GRAINS OF SAND!
IT'S GOING TOO FAST! WE'VE GOT TO HOARD OUR FREEDOM AND HAVE MORE FUN! TIME RUSHES ON! HELP! HELP!
I DON'T THINK I WANT TO BE HERE AT THE END OF AUGUST.
AAUGH! IT'S A HALF-HOUR LATER THAN IT WAS HALF AN HOUR AGO! RUN! RUN!

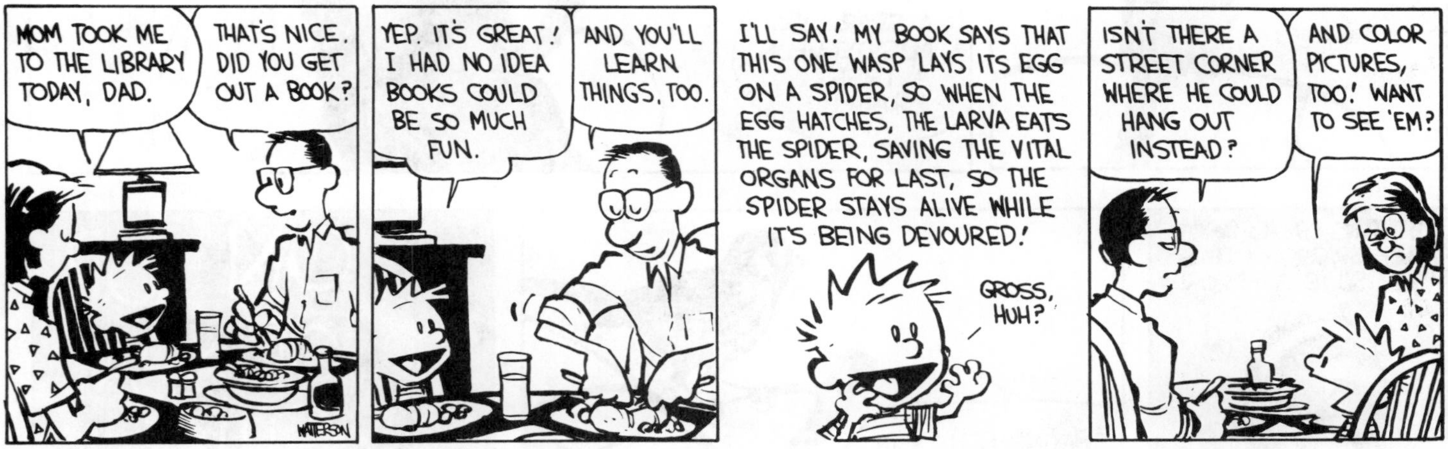
MOM TOOK ME TO THE LIBRARY TODAY, DAD.
THAT'S NICE. DID YOU GET OUT A BOOK?
YEP. IT'S GREAT! I HAD NO IDEA BOOKS COULD BE SO MUCH FUN.
AND YOU'LL LEARN THINGS, TOO.
I'LL SAY! MY BOOK SAYS THAT THIS ONE WASP LAYS ITS EGG ON A SPIDER, SO WHEN THE EGG HATCHES, THE LARVA EATS THE SPIDER, SAVING THE VITAL ORGANS FOR LAST, SO THE SPIDER STAYS ALIVE WHILE IT'S BEING DEVOURED!
GROSS, HUH?
ISN'T THERE A STREET CORNER WHERE HE COULD HANG OUT INSTEAD?
AND COLOR PICTURES, TOO! WANT TO SEE 'EM?

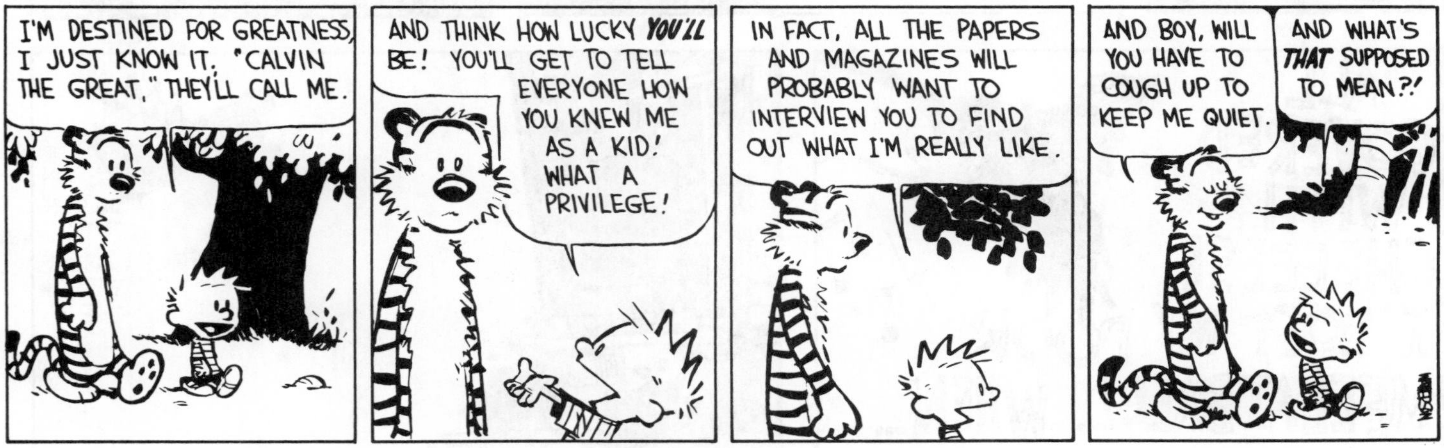
I'M DESTINED FOR GREATNESS, I JUST KNOW IT. "CALVIN THE GREAT," THEY'LL CALL ME.
AND THINK HOW LUCKY YOU'LL BE! YOU'LL GET TO TELL EVERYONE HOW YOU KNEW ME AS A KID! WHAT A PRIVILEGE!
IN FACT, ALL THE PAPERS AND MAGAZINES WILL PROBABLY WANT TO INTERVIEW YOU TO FIND OUT WHAT I'M REALLY LIKE.
AND BOY, WILL YOU HAVE TO COUGH UP TO KEEP ME QUIET.
AND WHAT'S THAT SUPPOSED TO MEAN?!

CalviN and HobbEs

by WATTERSON

DO RE MI FA
SO LA TI DO

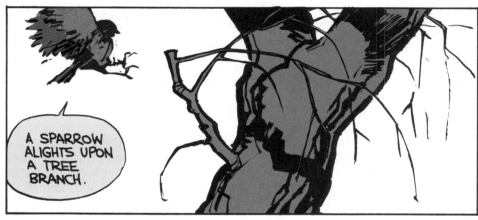

A SPARROW ALIGHTS UPON A TREE BRANCH.

BUT THIS IS NO *ORDINARY* SPARROW! THIS IS A *SONG* SPARROW!

SWAYING GENTLY IN THE BREEZE, HE PREPARES TO BURST FORTH IN RAPTUROUS MELODY!

ON TOP OF SPA-GHETTI

ALL COVERED WITH CHEEEESE, I LOST MY POOR MEEEATBALLL, WHEN...

WATTERSON

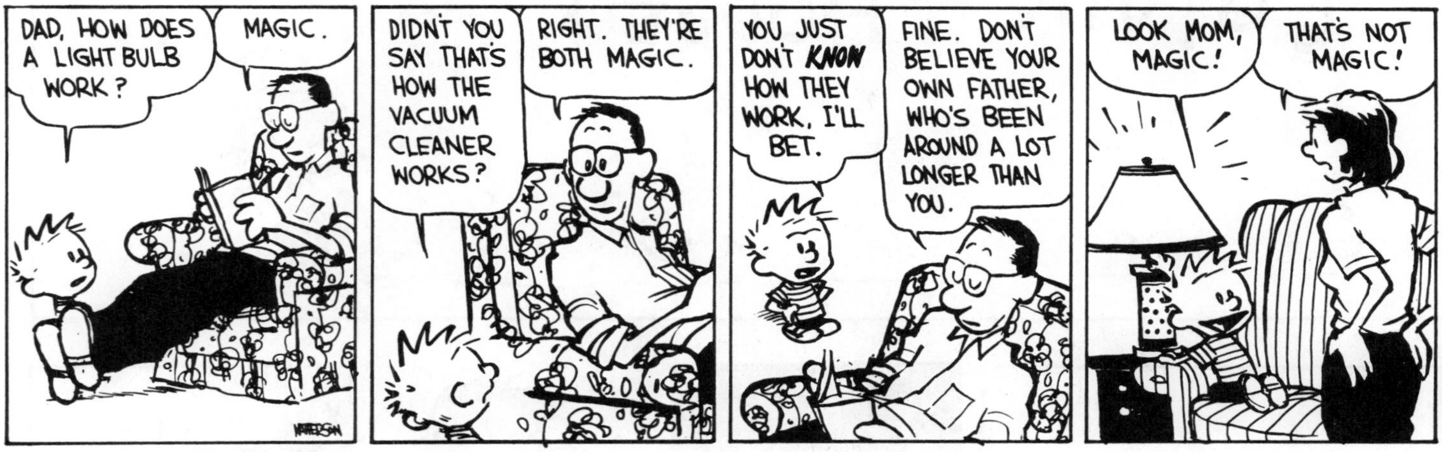
DAD, HOW DOES A LIGHT BULB WORK?
MAGIC.
DIDN'T YOU SAY THAT'S HOW THE VACUUM CLEANER WORKS?
RIGHT. THEY'RE BOTH MAGIC.
YOU JUST DON'T KNOW HOW THEY WORK, I'LL BET.
FINE. DON'T BELIEVE YOUR OWN FATHER, WHO'S BEEN AROUND A LOT LONGER THAN YOU.
LOOK MOM, MAGIC!
THAT'S NOT MAGIC!

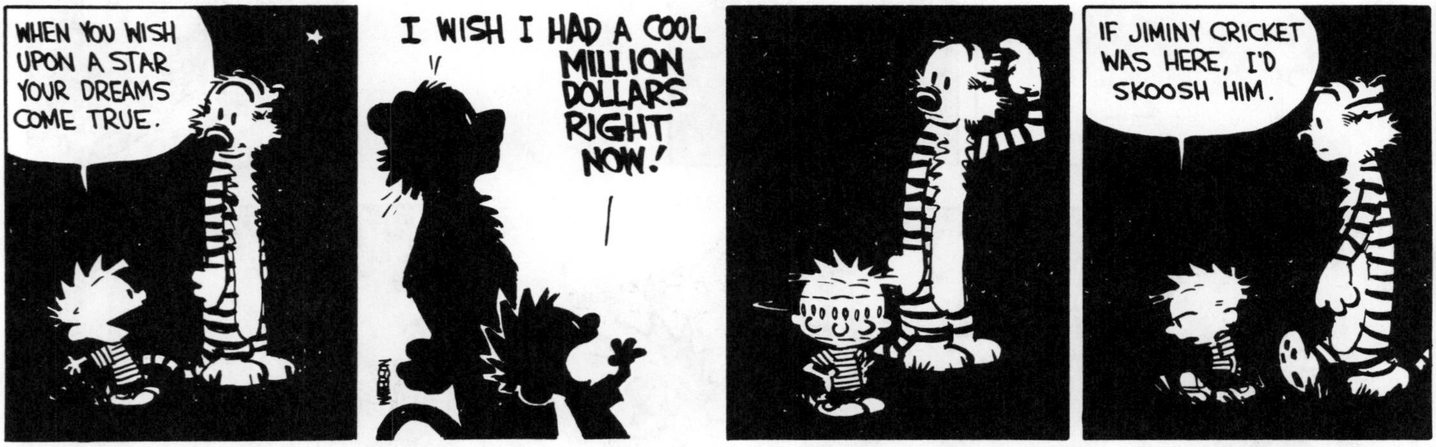
WHEN YOU WISH UPON A STAR YOUR DREAMS COME TRUE.
I WISH I HAD A COOL MILLION DOLLARS RIGHT NOW!
IF JIMINY CRICKET WAS HERE, I'D SKOOSH HIM.

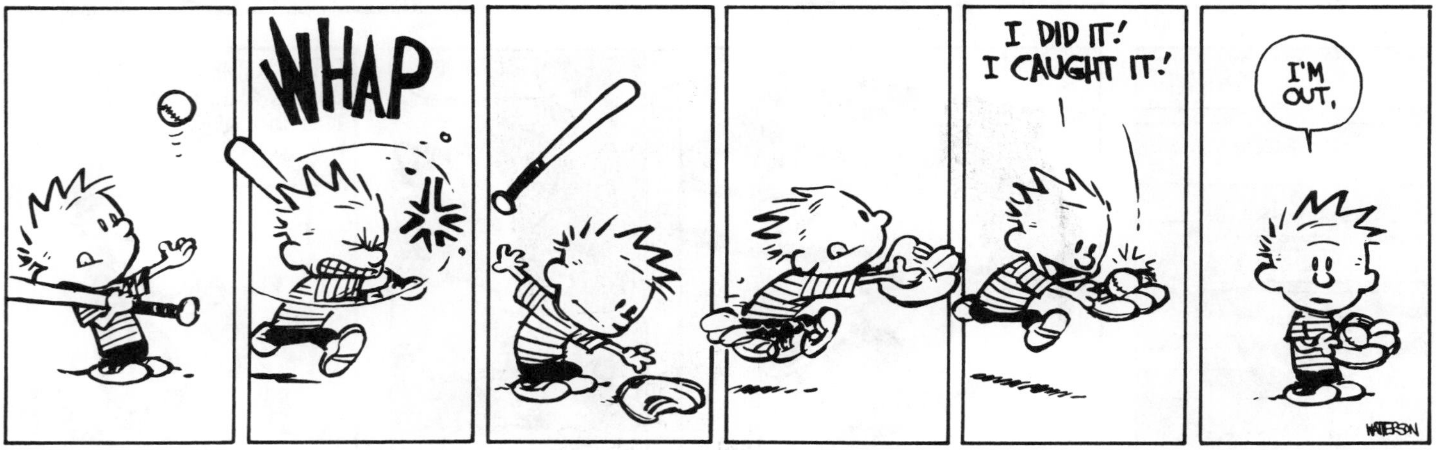
WHAP
I DID IT! I CAUGHT IT!
I'M OUT.

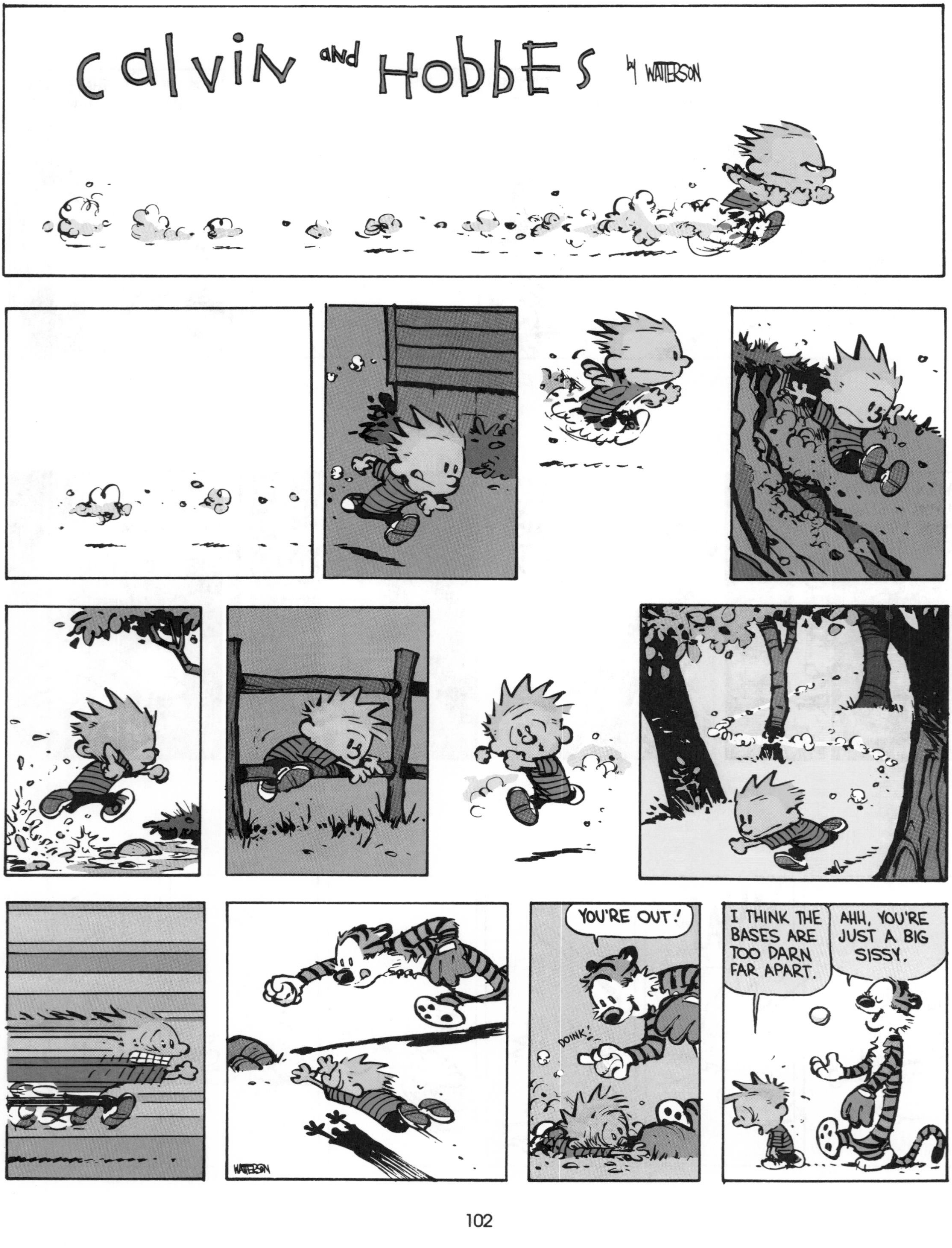
Calvin and Hobbes
by WATTERSON
WATTERSON
YOU'RE OUT!
DOINK!
I THINK THE BASES ARE TOO DARN FAR APART.
AHH, YOU'RE JUST A BIG SISSY.

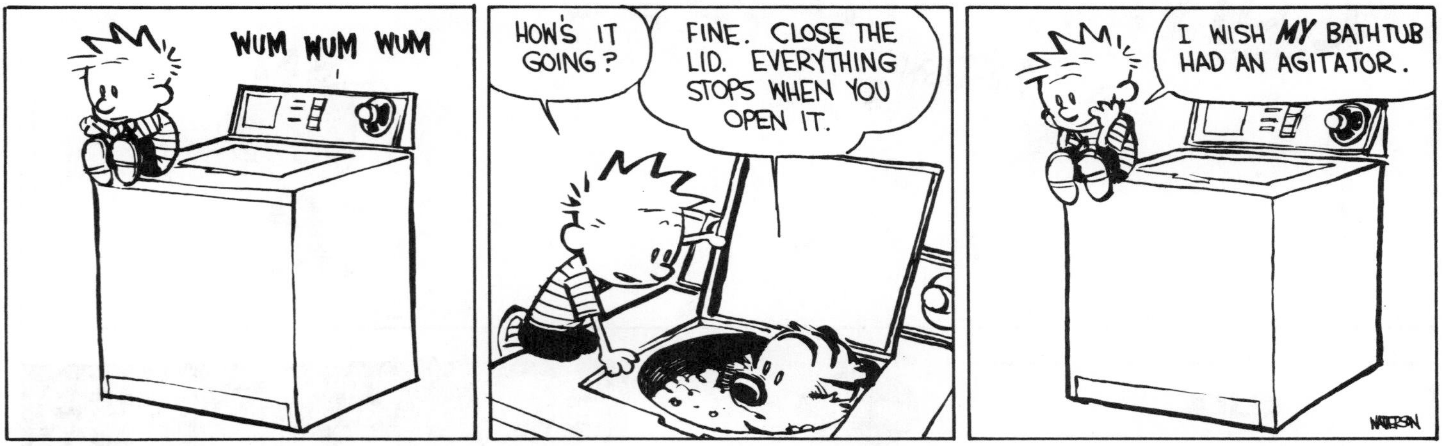
WUM WUM WUM
HOW'S IT GOING?
FINE. CLOSE THE LID. EVERYTHING STOPS WHEN YOU OPEN IT.
I WISH MY BATHTUB HAD AN AGITATOR.
WATTERSON

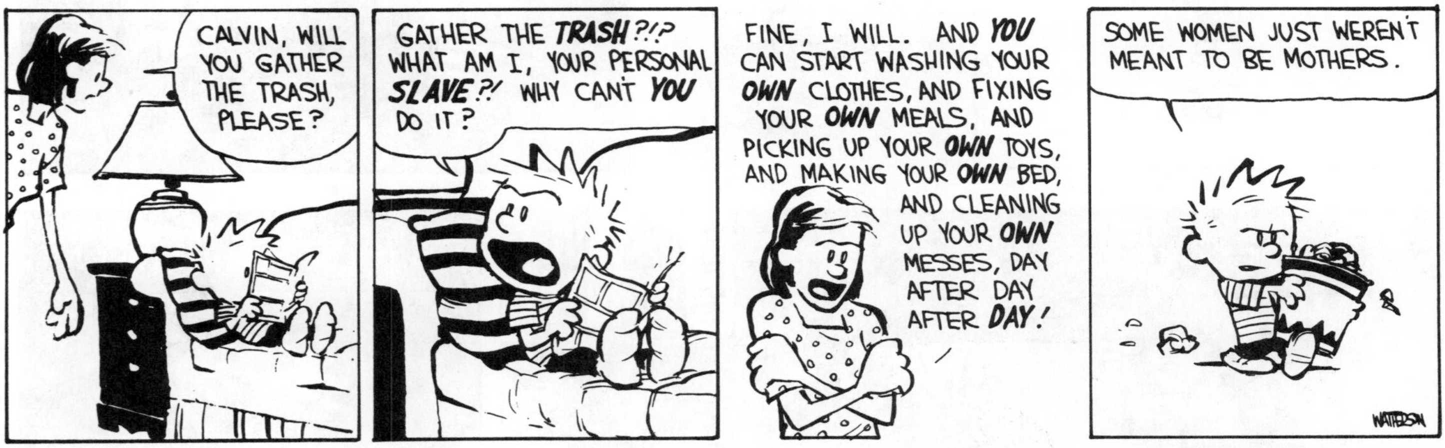
CALVIN, WILL YOU GATHER THE TRASH, PLEASE?
GATHER THE TRASH?!? WHAT AM I, YOUR PERSONAL SLAVE?! WHY CAN'T YOU DO IT?
FINE, I WILL. AND YOU CAN START WASHING YOUR OWN CLOTHES, AND FIXING YOUR OWN MEALS, AND PICKING UP YOUR OWN TOYS, AND MAKING YOUR OWN BED, AND CLEANING UP YOUR OWN MESSES, DAY AFTER DAY AFTER DAY!
SOME WOMEN JUST WEREN'T MEANT TO BE MOTHERS.
WATTERSON

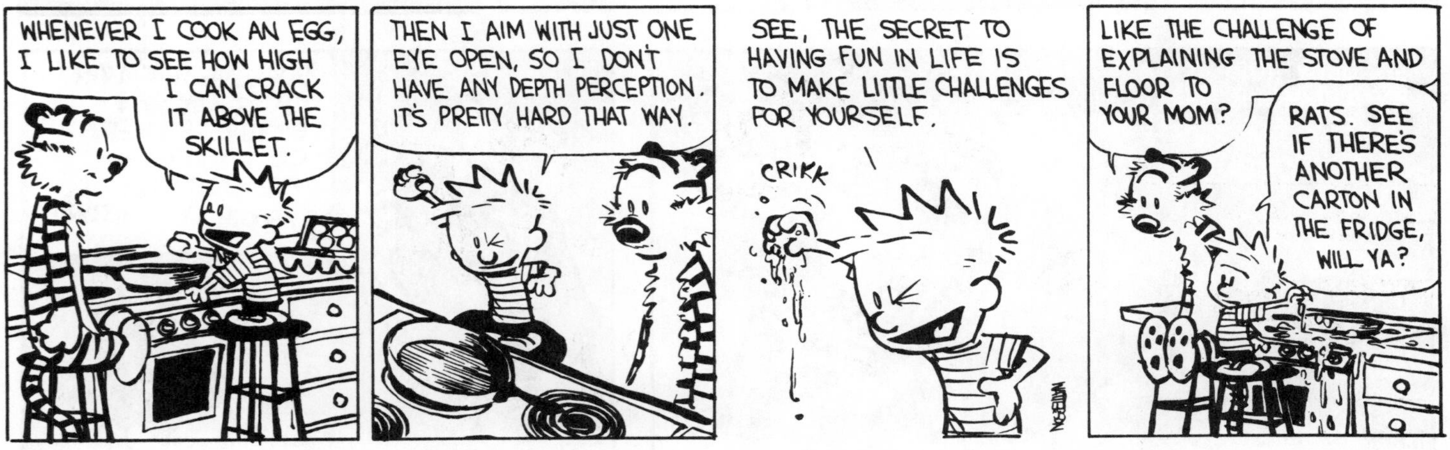
WHENEVER I COOK AN EGG, I LIKE TO SEE HOW HIGH I CAN CRACK IT ABOVE THE SKILLET.
THEN I AIM WITH JUST ONE EYE OPEN, SO I DON'T HAVE ANY DEPTH PERCEPTION. IT'S PRETTY HARD THAT WAY.
SEE, THE SECRET TO HAVING FUN IN LIFE IS TO MAKE LITTLE CHALLENGES FOR YOURSELF.
CRIKK
WATTERSON
LIKE THE CHALLENGE OF EXPLAINING THE STOVE AND FLOOR TO YOUR MOM?
RATS. SEE IF THERE'S ANOTHER CARTON IN THE FRIDGE, WILL YA?

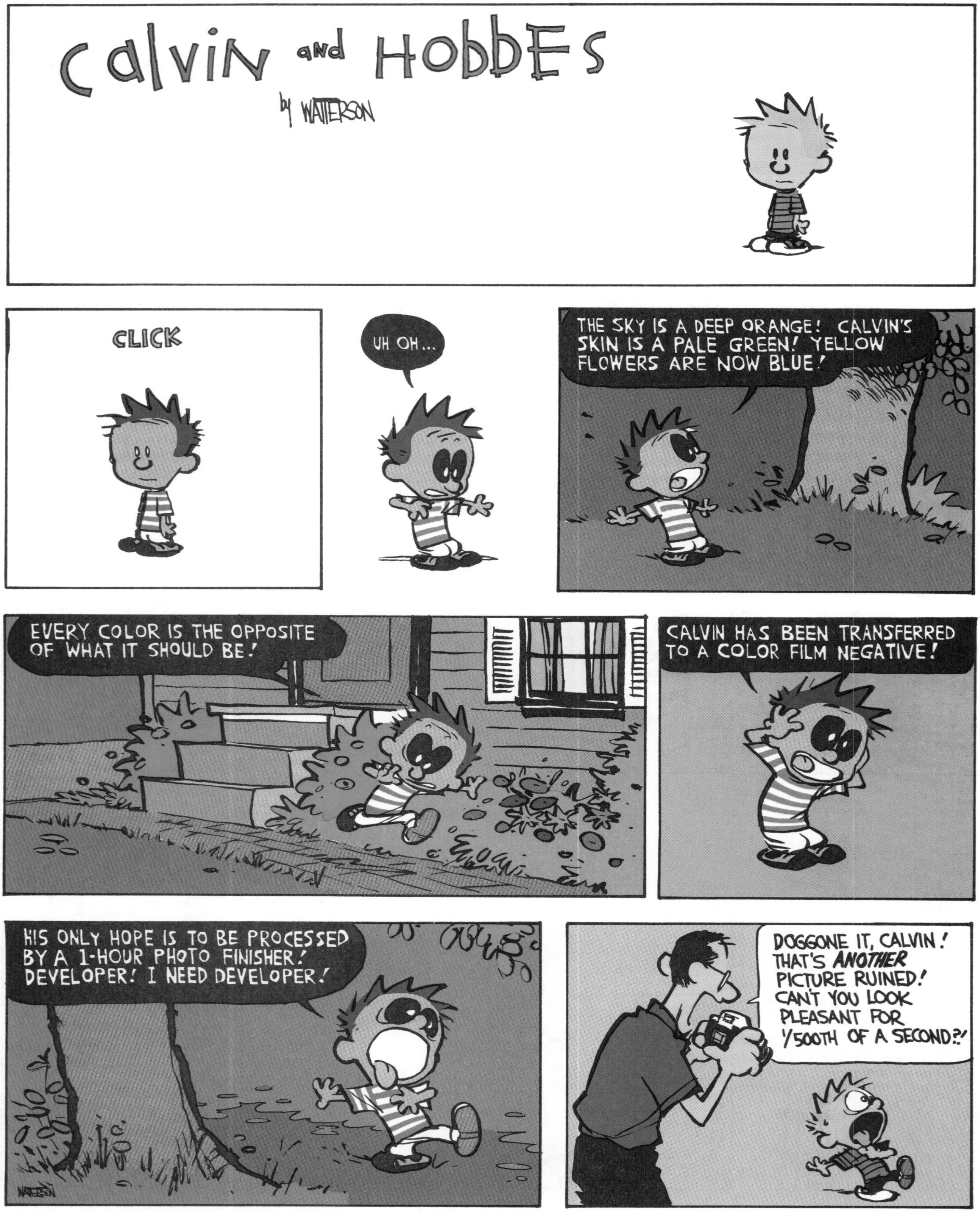

Calvin and HOBBES
by WATTERSON
CLICK
UH OH...
THE SKY IS A DEEP ORANGE! CALVIN'S SKIN IS A PALE GREEN! YELLOW FLOWERS ARE NOW BLUE!
EVERY COLOR IS THE OPPOSITE OF WHAT IT SHOULD BE!
CALVIN HAS BEEN TRANSFERRED TO A COLOR FILM NEGATIVE!
HIS ONLY HOPE IS TO BE PROCESSED BY A 1-HOUR PHOTO FINISHER! DEVELOPER! I NEED DEVELOPER!
WATTERSON
DOGGONE IT, CALVIN! THAT'S ANOTHER PICTURE RUINED! CAN'T YOU LOOK PLEASANT FOR 1/500TH OF A SECOND?!

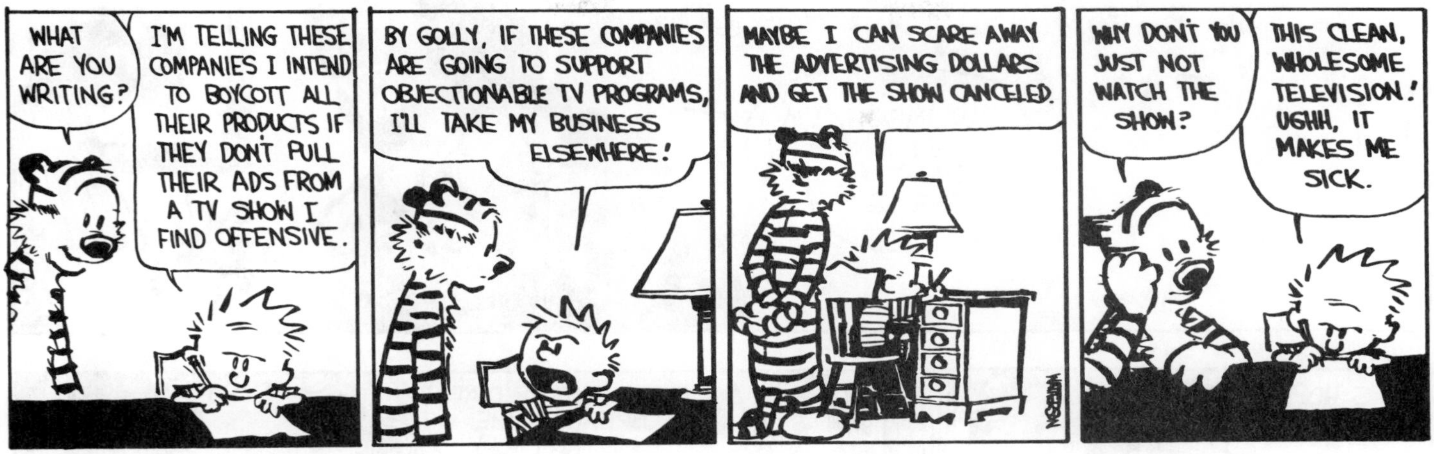
WHAT ARE YOU WRITING?
I'M TELLING THESE COMPANIES I INTEND TO BOYCOTT ALL THEIR PRODUCTS IF THEY DON'T PULL THEIR ADS FROM A TV SHOW I FIND OFFENSIVE.
BY GOLLY, IF THESE COMPANIES ARE GOING TO SUPPORT OBJECTIONABLE TV PROGRAMS, I'LL TAKE MY BUSINESS ELSEWHERE!
MAYBE I CAN SCARE AWAY THE ADVERTISING DOLLARS AND GET THE SHOW CANCELED.
WHY DON'T YOU JUST NOT WATCH THE SHOW?
THIS CLEAN, WHOLESOME TELEVISION! UGHH, IT MAKES ME SICK.

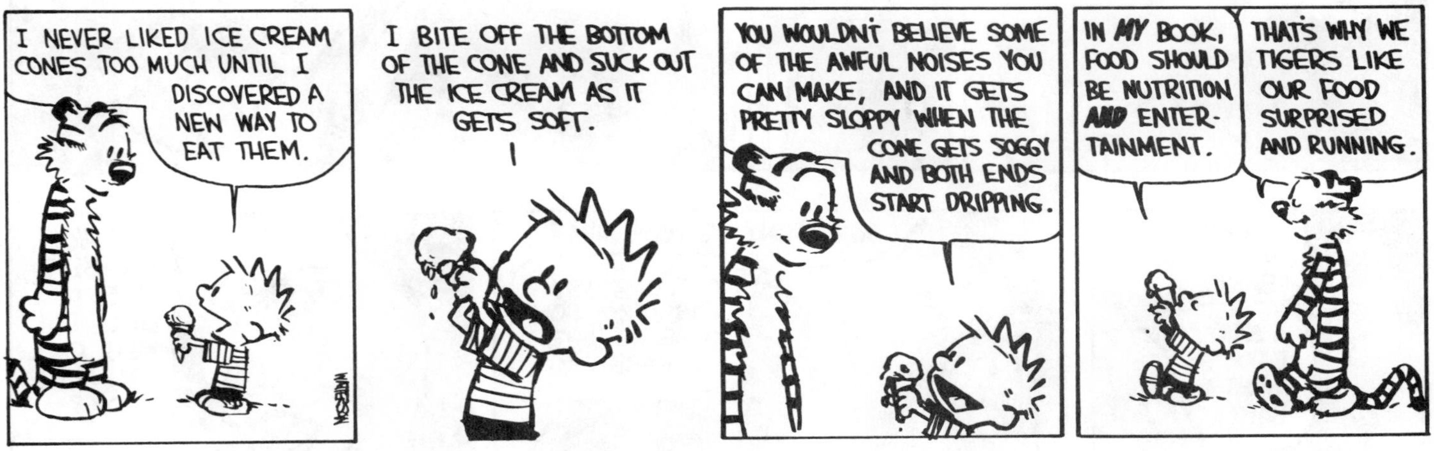
I NEVER LIKED ICE CREAM CONES TOO MUCH UNTIL I DISCOVERED A NEW WAY TO EAT THEM.
I BITE OFF THE BOTTOM OF THE CONE AND SUCK OUT THE ICE CREAM AS IT GETS SOFT.
YOU WOULDN'T BELIEVE SOME OF THE AWFUL NOISES YOU CAN MAKE, AND IT GETS PRETTY SLOPPY WHEN THE CONE GETS SOGGY AND BOTH ENDS START DRIPPING.
IN MY BOOK, FOOD SHOULD BE NUTRITION AND ENTERTAINMENT.
THAT'S WHY WE TIGERS LIKE OUR FOOD SURPRISED AND RUNNING.

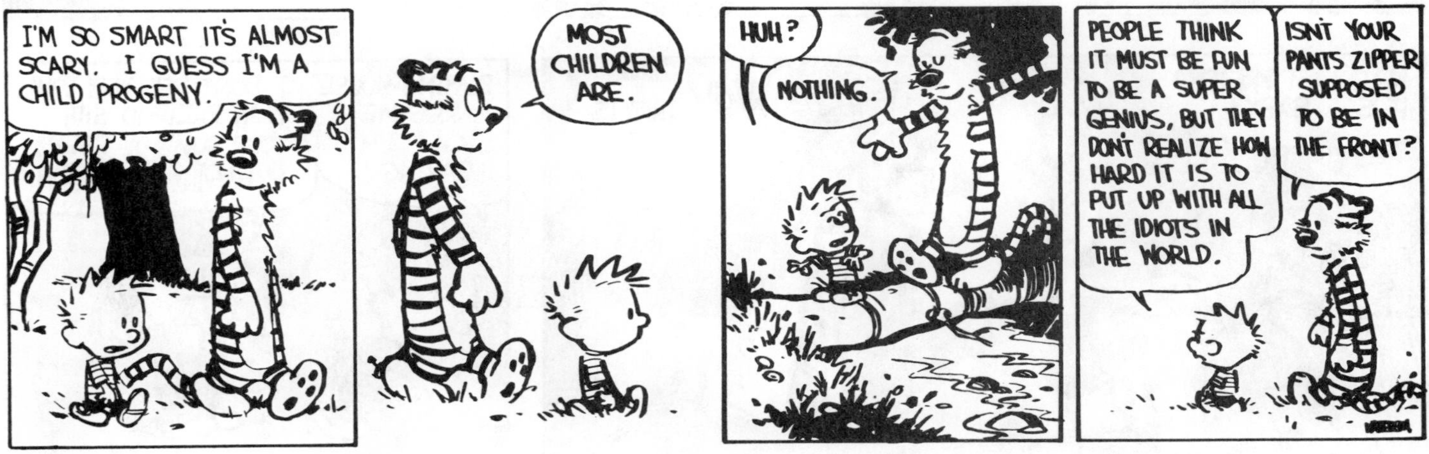
I'M SO SMART IT'S ALMOST SCARY. I GUESS I'M A CHILD PROGENY.
MOST CHILDREN ARE.
HUH?
NOTHING.
PEOPLE THINK IT MUST BE FUN TO BE A SUPER GENIUS, BUT THEY DON'T REALIZE HOW HARD IT IS TO PUT UP WITH ALL THE IDIOTS IN THE WORLD.
ISN'T YOUR PANTS ZIPPER SUPPOSED TO BE IN THE FRONT?

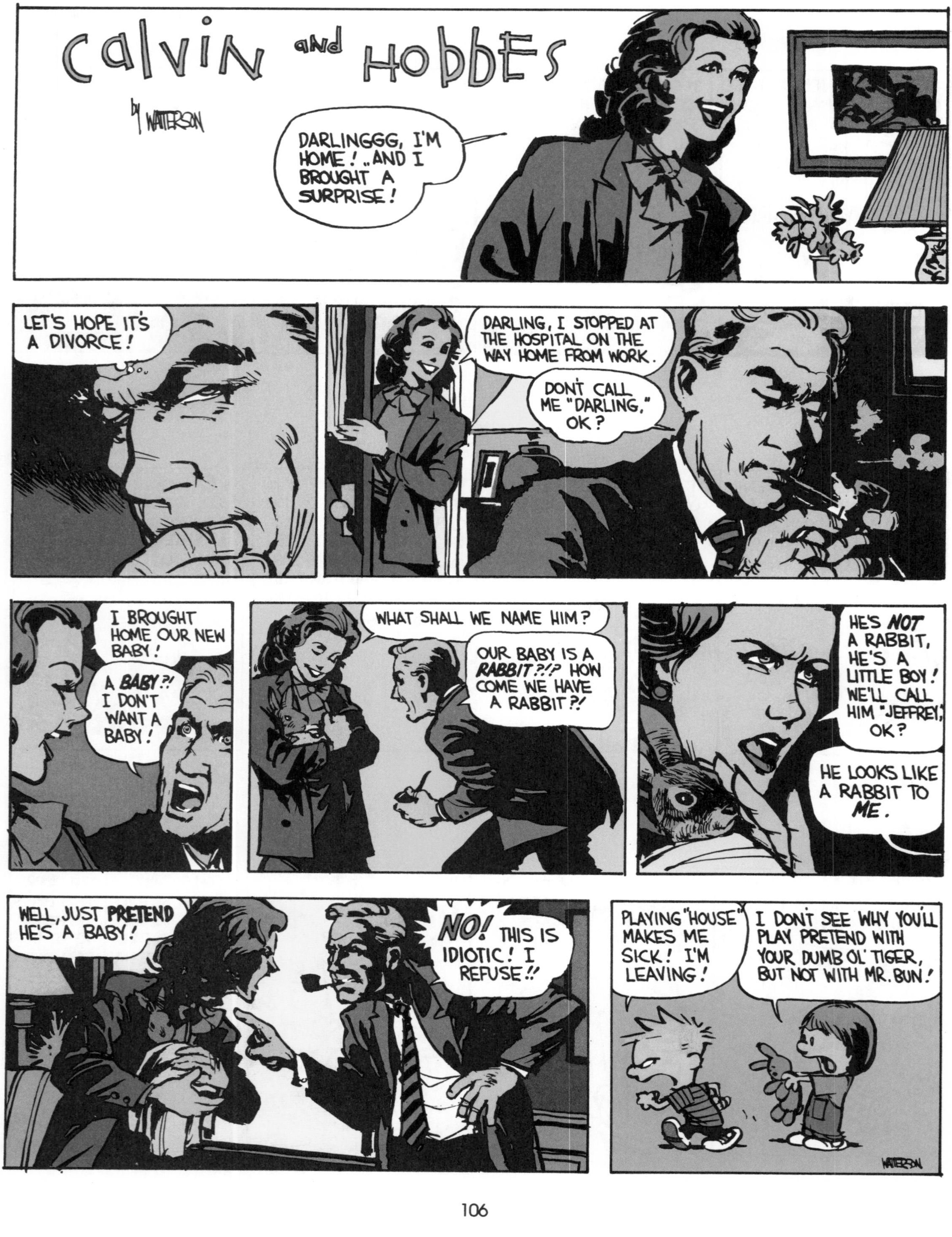
Calvin and HOBBES
by WATTERSON
DARLINGGG, I'M HOME! ..AND I BROUGHT A SURPRISE!
LET'S HOPE IT'S A DIVORCE!
DARLING, I STOPPED AT THE HOSPITAL ON THE WAY HOME FROM WORK.
DON'T CALL ME "DARLING," OK?
I BROUGHT HOME OUR NEW BABY!
A BABY?! I DON'T WANT A BABY!
WHAT SHALL WE NAME HIM?
OUR BABY IS A RABBIT?!? HOW COME WE HAVE A RABBIT?!
HE'S NOT A RABBIT, HE'S A LITTLE BOY! WE'LL CALL HIM "JEFFREY," OK?
HE LOOKS LIKE A RABBIT TO ME.
WELL, JUST PRETEND HE'S A BABY!
NO! THIS IS IDIOTIC! I REFUSE!!
PLAYING "HOUSE" MAKES ME SICK! I'M LEAVING!
I DON'T SEE WHY YOU'LL PLAY PRETEND WITH YOUR DUMB OL' TIGER, BUT NOT WITH MR. BUN!
WATTERSON

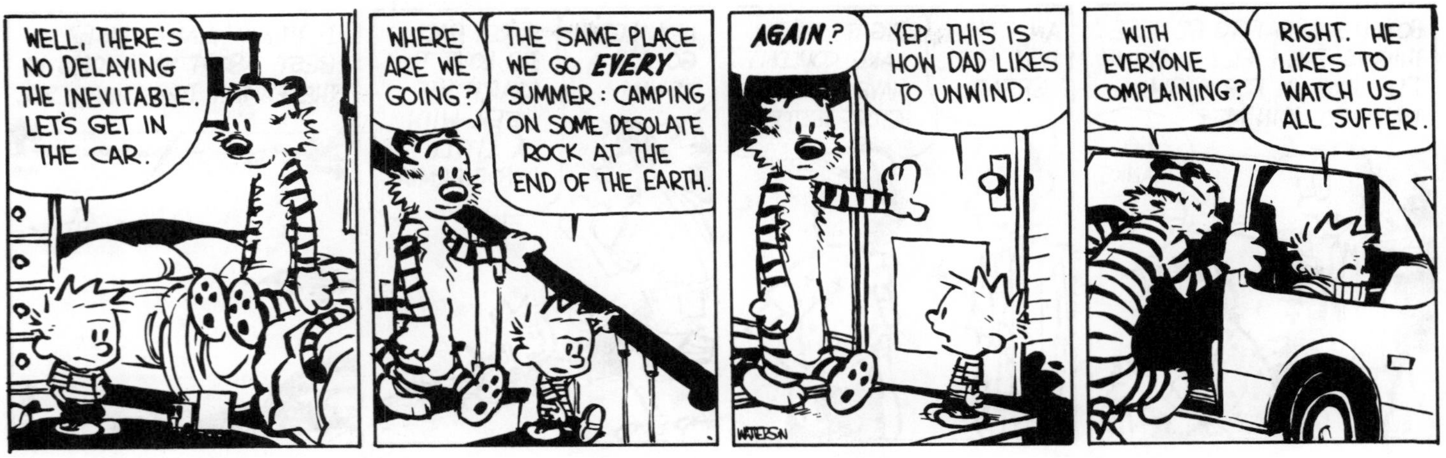
WELL, THERE'S NO DELAYING THE INEVITABLE. LET'S GET IN THE CAR.
WHERE ARE WE GOING?
THE SAME PLACE WE GO **EVERY** SUMMER: CAMPING ON SOME DESOLATE ROCK AT THE END OF THE EARTH.
AGAIN?
YEP. THIS IS HOW DAD LIKES TO UNWIND.
WITH EVERYONE COMPLAINING?
RIGHT. HE LIKES TO WATCH US ALL SUFFER.

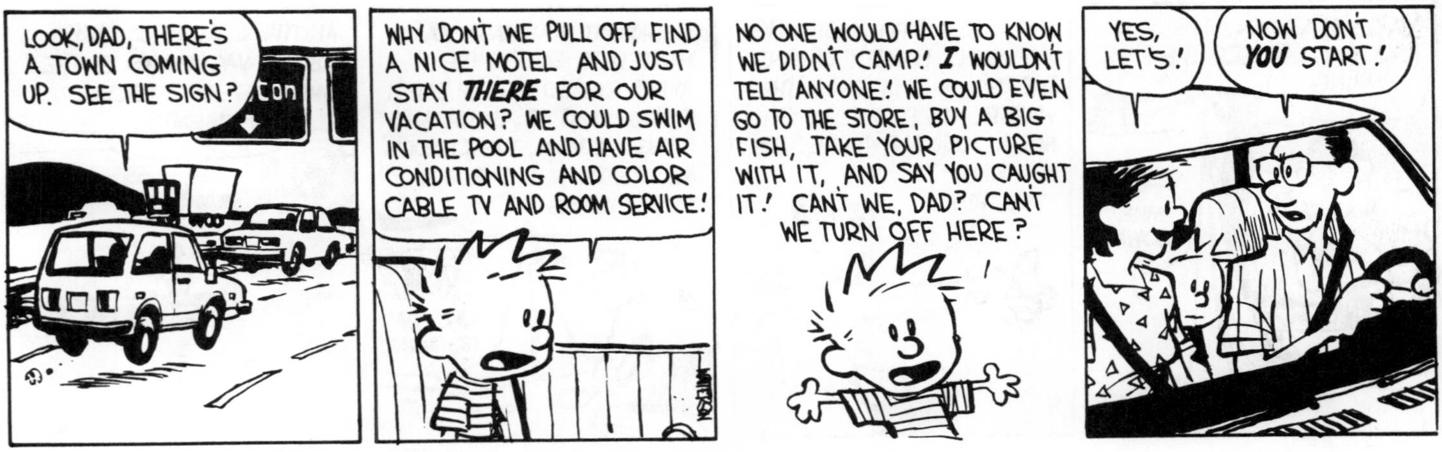
LOOK, DAD, THERE'S A TOWN COMING UP. SEE THE SIGN?
WHY DON'T WE PULL OFF, FIND A NICE MOTEL AND JUST STAY **THERE** FOR OUR VACATION? WE COULD SWIM IN THE POOL AND HAVE AIR CONDITIONING AND COLOR CABLE TV AND ROOM SERVICE!
NO ONE WOULD HAVE TO KNOW WE DIDN'T CAMP! **I** WOULDN'T TELL ANYONE! WE COULD EVEN GO TO THE STORE, BUY A BIG FISH, TAKE YOUR PICTURE WITH IT, AND SAY YOU CAUGHT IT! CAN'T WE, DAD? CAN'T WE TURN OFF HERE?
YES, LET'S!
NOW DON'T **YOU** START!

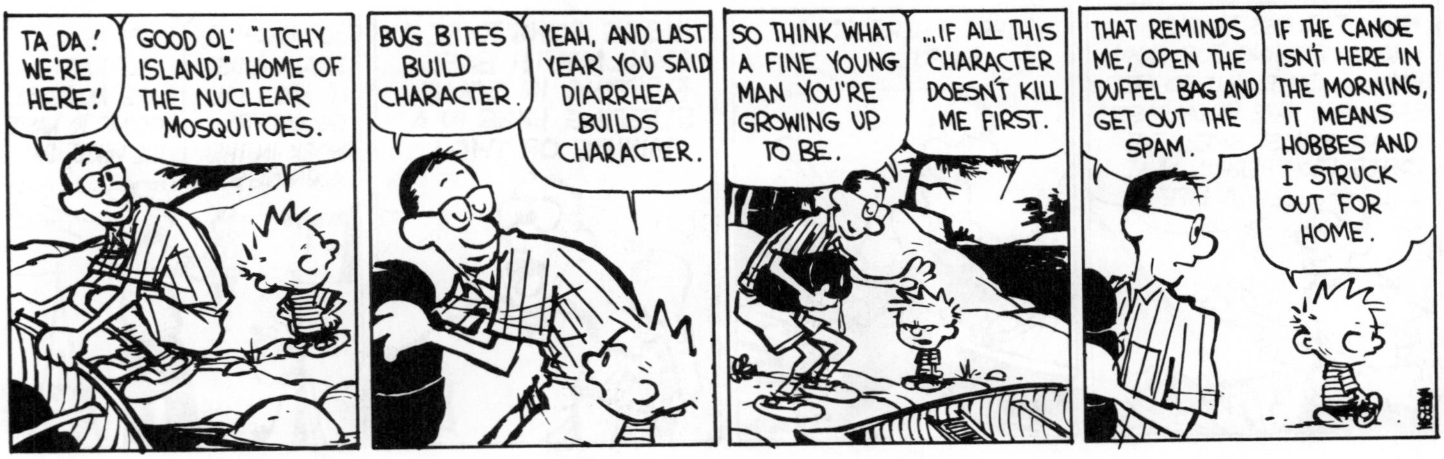
TA DA! WE'RE HERE!
GOOD OL' "ITCHY ISLAND," HOME OF THE NUCLEAR MOSQUITOES.
BUG BITES BUILD CHARACTER.
YEAH, AND LAST YEAR YOU SAID DIARRHEA BUILDS CHARACTER.
SO THINK WHAT A FINE YOUNG MAN YOU'RE GROWING UP TO BE.
...IF ALL THIS CHARACTER DOESN'T KILL ME FIRST.
THAT REMINDS ME, OPEN THE DUFFEL BAG AND GET OUT THE SPAM.
IF THE CANOE ISN'T HERE IN THE MORNING, IT MEANS HOBBES AND I STRUCK OUT FOR HOME.

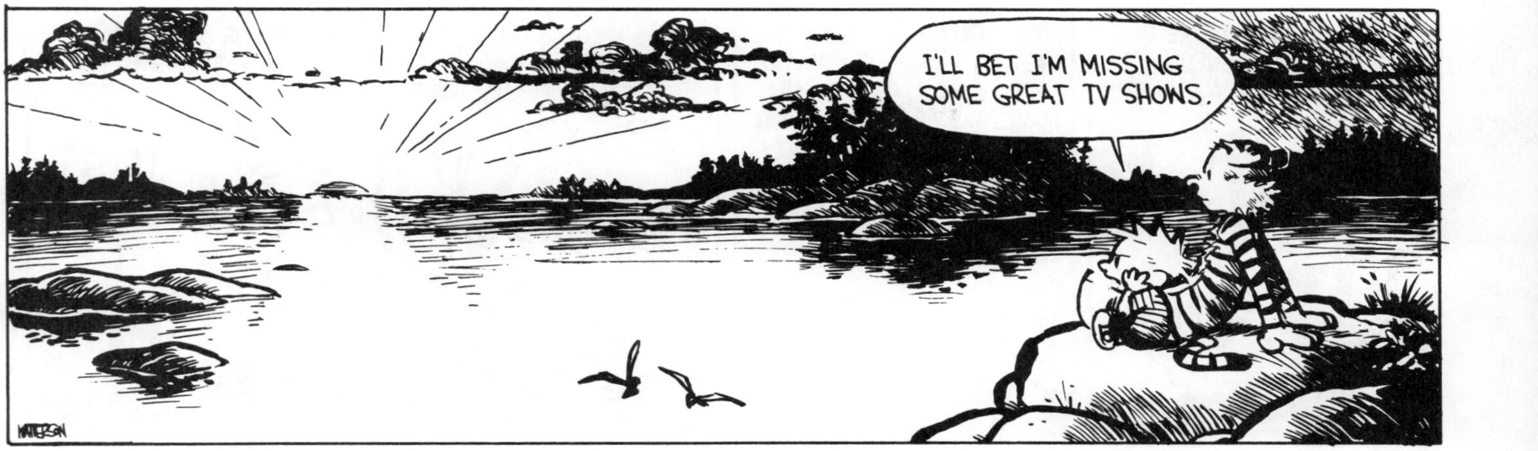
I'LL BET I'M MISSING SOME GREAT TV SHOWS.

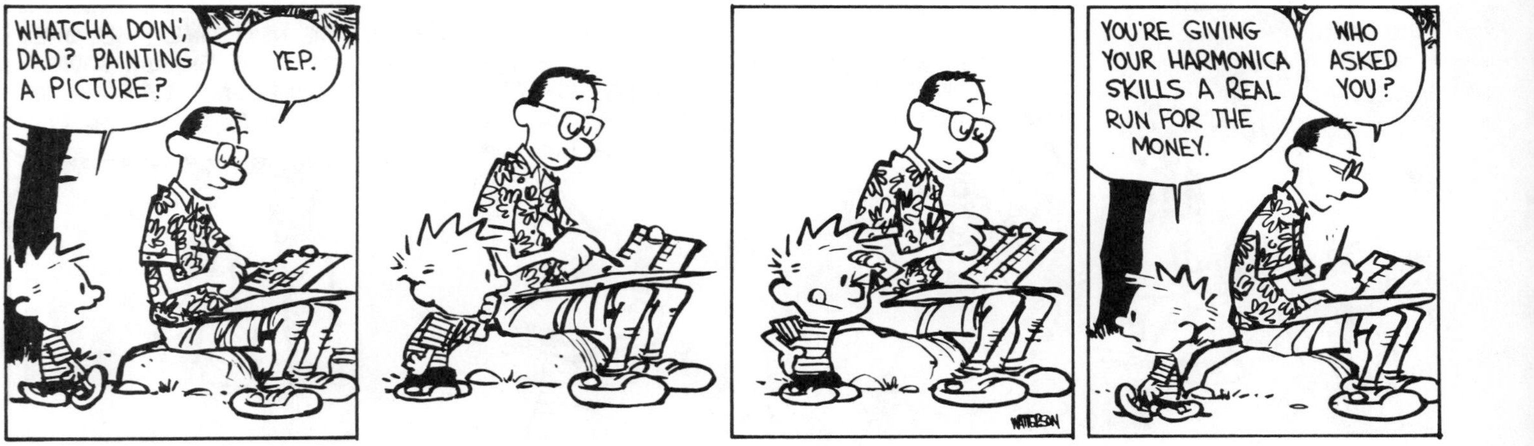
WHATCHA DOIN', DAD? PAINTING A PICTURE?
YEP.
YOU'RE GIVING YOUR HARMONICA SKILLS A REAL RUN FOR THE MONEY.
WHO ASKED YOU?

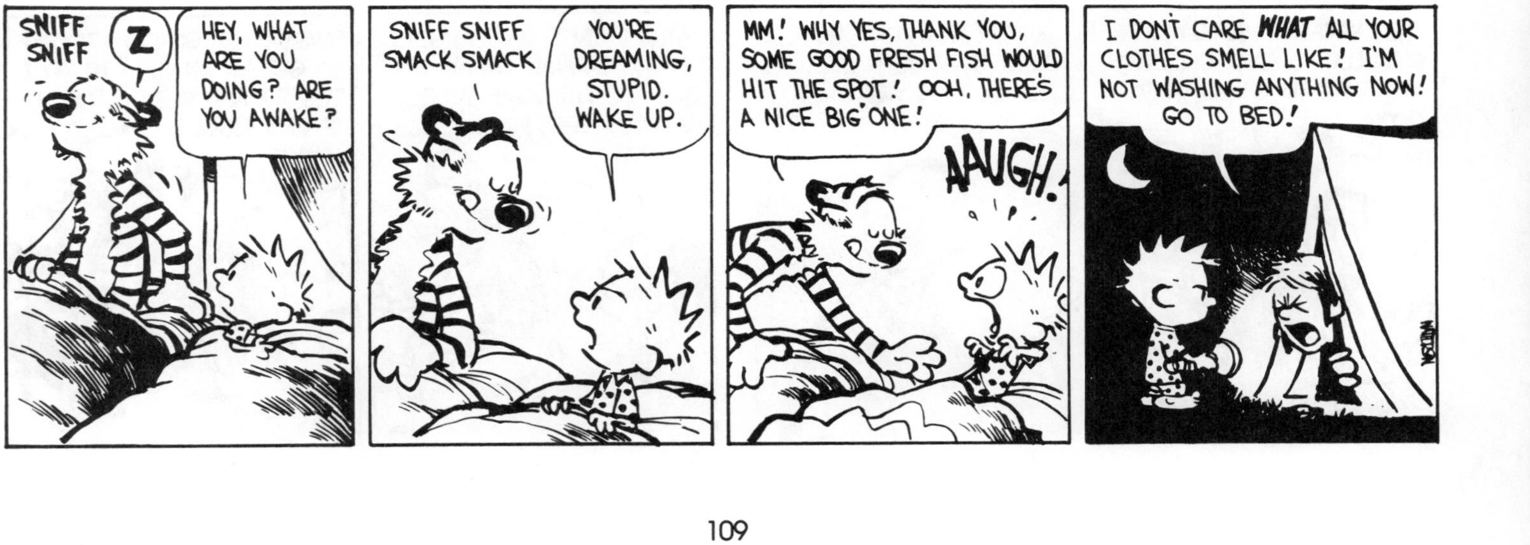
SNIFF SNIFF
Z
HEY, WHAT ARE YOU DOING? ARE YOU AWAKE?
SNIFF SNIFF SMACK SMACK
YOU'RE DREAMING, STUPID. WAKE UP.
MM! WHY YES, THANK YOU, SOME GOOD FRESH FISH WOULD HIT THE SPOT! OOH, THERE'S A NICE BIG ONE!
AAUGH!
I DON'T CARE **WHAT** ALL YOUR CLOTHES SMELL LIKE! I'M NOT WASHING ANYTHING NOW! GO TO BED!

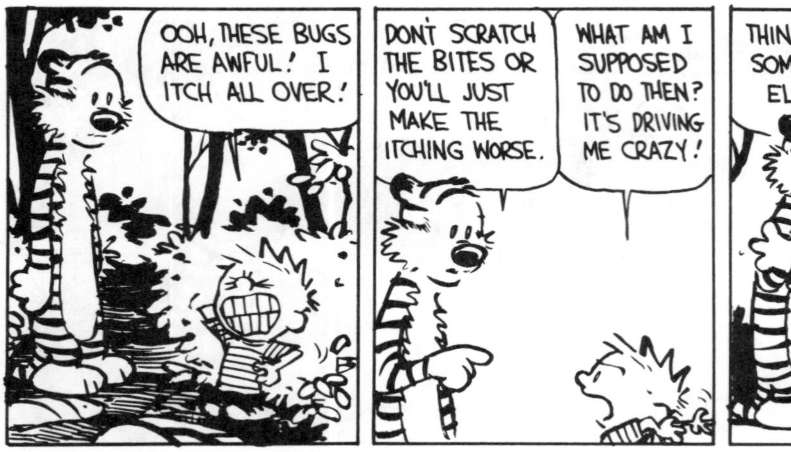
OOH, THESE BUGS ARE AWFUL! I ITCH ALL OVER!
DON'T SCRATCH THE BITES OR YOU'LL JUST MAKE THE ITCHING WORSE.
WHAT AM I SUPPOSED TO DO THEN? IT'S DRIVING ME CRAZY!
THINK ABOUT SOMETHING ELSE.
SOMETHING ELSE?! LIKE WHAT??
LIKE MAYBE STEPPING OUT OF ALL THAT POISON IVY.
I HATE THIS PLACE!

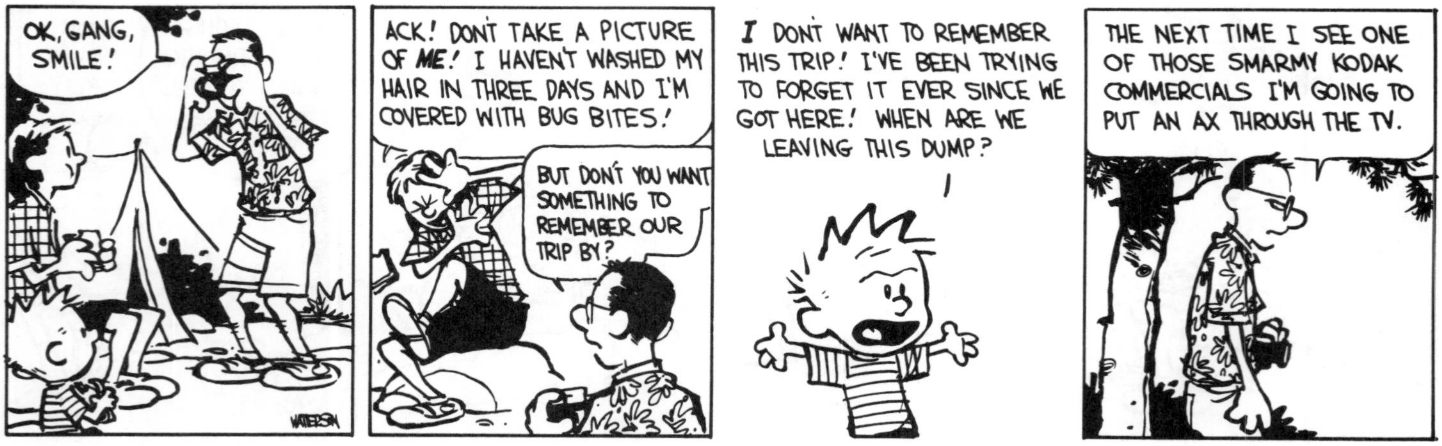
OK, GANG, SMILE!
ACK! DON'T TAKE A PICTURE OF *ME*! I HAVEN'T WASHED MY HAIR IN THREE DAYS AND I'M COVERED WITH BUG BITES!
BUT DON'T YOU WANT SOMETHING TO REMEMBER OUR TRIP BY?
I DON'T WANT TO REMEMBER THIS TRIP! I'VE BEEN TRYING TO FORGET IT EVER SINCE WE GOT HERE! WHEN ARE WE LEAVING THIS DUMP?
THE NEXT TIME I SEE ONE OF THOSE SMARMY KODAK COMMERCIALS I'M GOING TO PUT AN AX THROUGH THE TV.

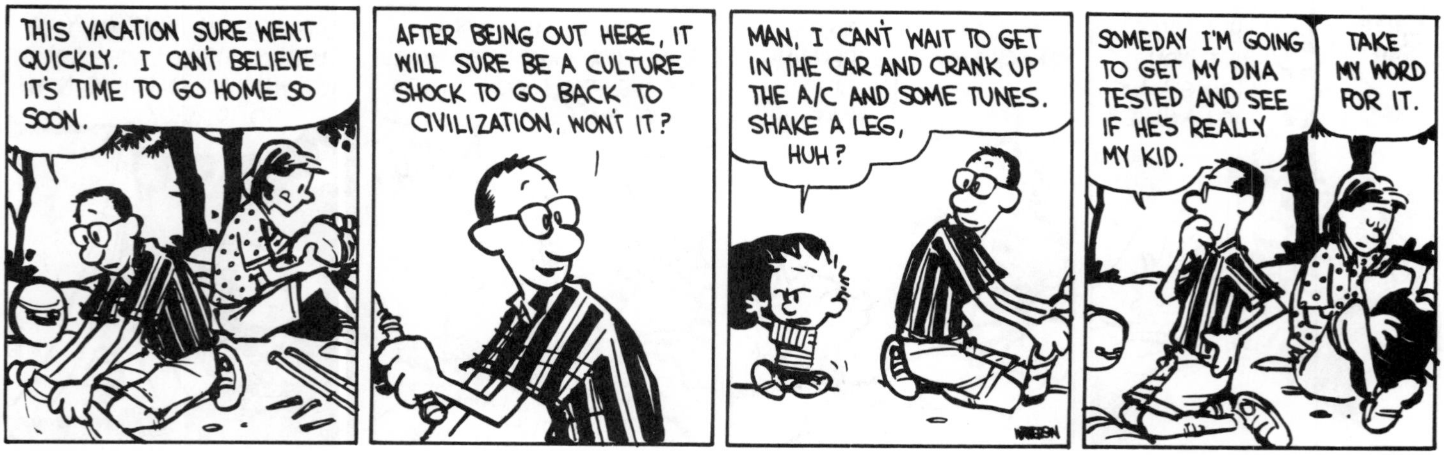
THIS VACATION SURE WENT QUICKLY. I CAN'T BELIEVE IT'S TIME TO GO HOME SO SOON.
AFTER BEING OUT HERE, IT WILL SURE BE A CULTURE SHOCK TO GO BACK TO CIVILIZATION, WON'T IT?
MAN, I CAN'T WAIT TO GET IN THE CAR AND CRANK UP THE A/C AND SOME TUNES. SHAKE A LEG, HUH?
SOMEDAY I'M GOING TO GET MY DNA TESTED AND SEE IF HE'S REALLY MY KID.
TAKE MY WORD FOR IT.

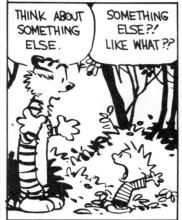

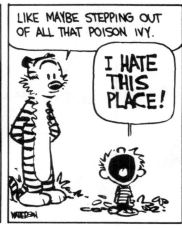

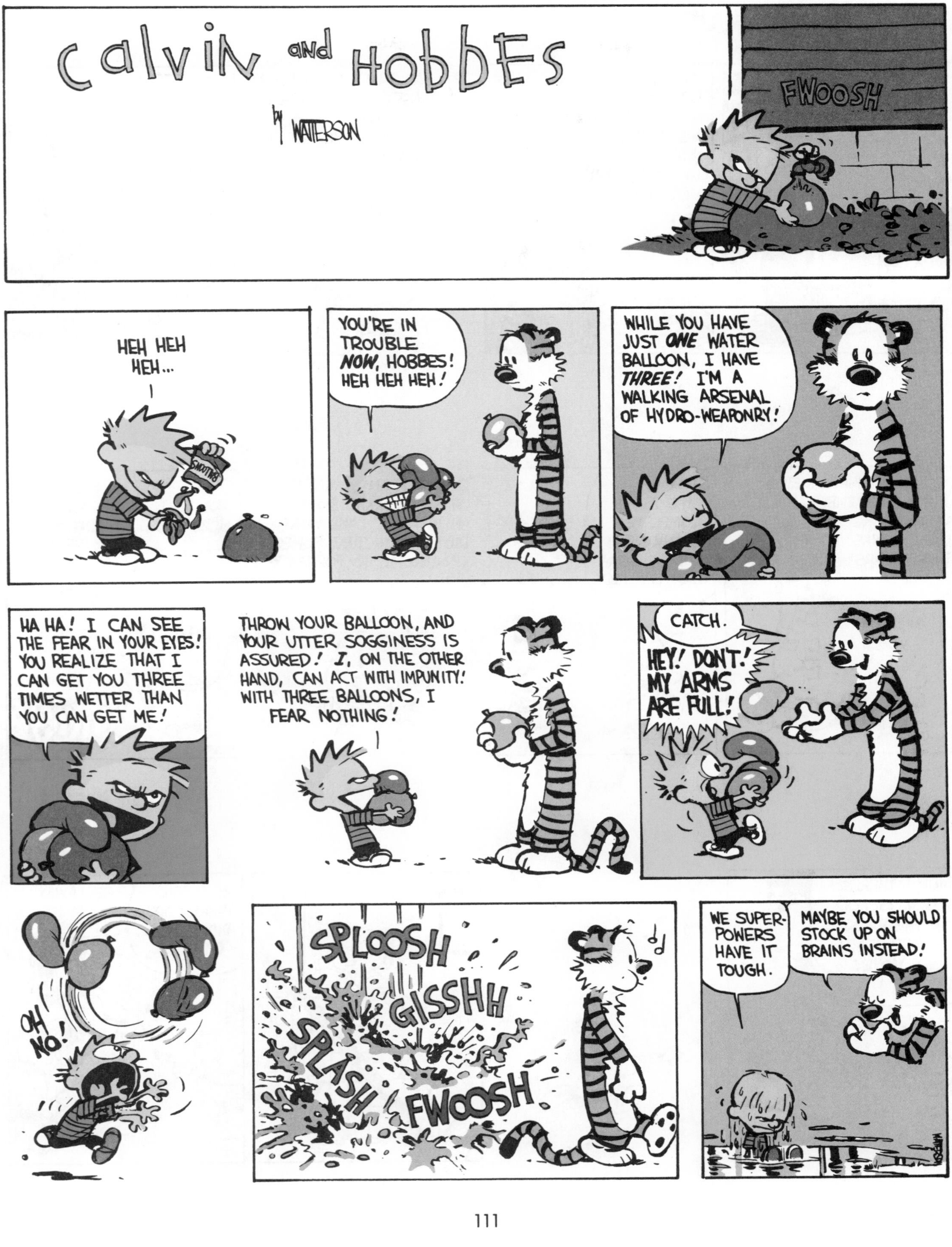
Calvin and Hobbes
by WATTERSON
FWOOSH
HEH HEH HEH...
YOU'RE IN TROUBLE NOW, HOBBES! HEH HEH HEH!
WHILE YOU HAVE JUST ONE WATER BALLOON, I HAVE THREE! I'M A WALKING ARSENAL OF HYDRO-WEAPONRY!
HA HA! I CAN SEE THE FEAR IN YOUR EYES! YOU REALIZE THAT I CAN GET YOU THREE TIMES WETTER THAN YOU CAN GET ME!
THROW YOUR BALLOON, AND YOUR UTTER SOGGINESS IS ASSURED! I, ON THE OTHER HAND, CAN ACT WITH IMPUNITY! WITH THREE BALLOONS, I FEAR NOTHING!
CATCH.
HEY! DON'T! MY ARMS ARE FULL!
OH NO!
SPLOOSH
GISSHH
SPLASH
FWOOSH
WE SUPER-POWERS HAVE IT TOUGH.
MAYBE YOU SHOULD STOCK UP ON BRAINS INSTEAD!

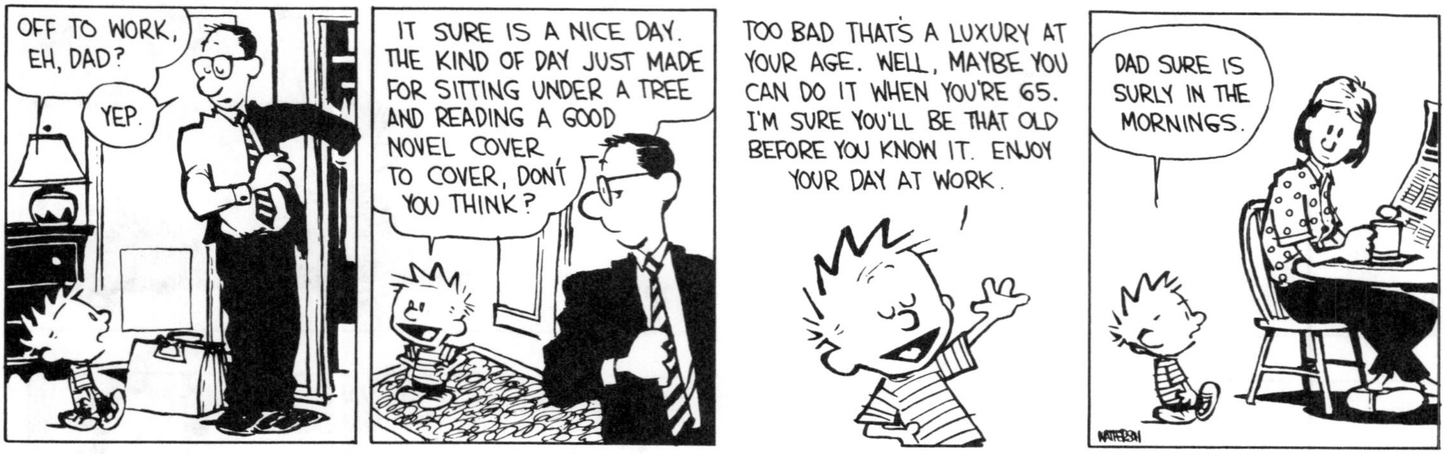
OFF TO WORK, EH, DAD?
YEP.
IT SURE IS A NICE DAY. THE KIND OF DAY JUST MADE FOR SITTING UNDER A TREE AND READING A GOOD NOVEL COVER TO COVER, DON'T YOU THINK?
TOO BAD THAT'S A LUXURY AT YOUR AGE. WELL, MAYBE YOU CAN DO IT WHEN YOU'RE 65. I'M SURE YOU'LL BE THAT OLD BEFORE YOU KNOW IT. ENJOY YOUR DAY AT WORK.
DAD SURE IS SURLY IN THE MORNINGS.

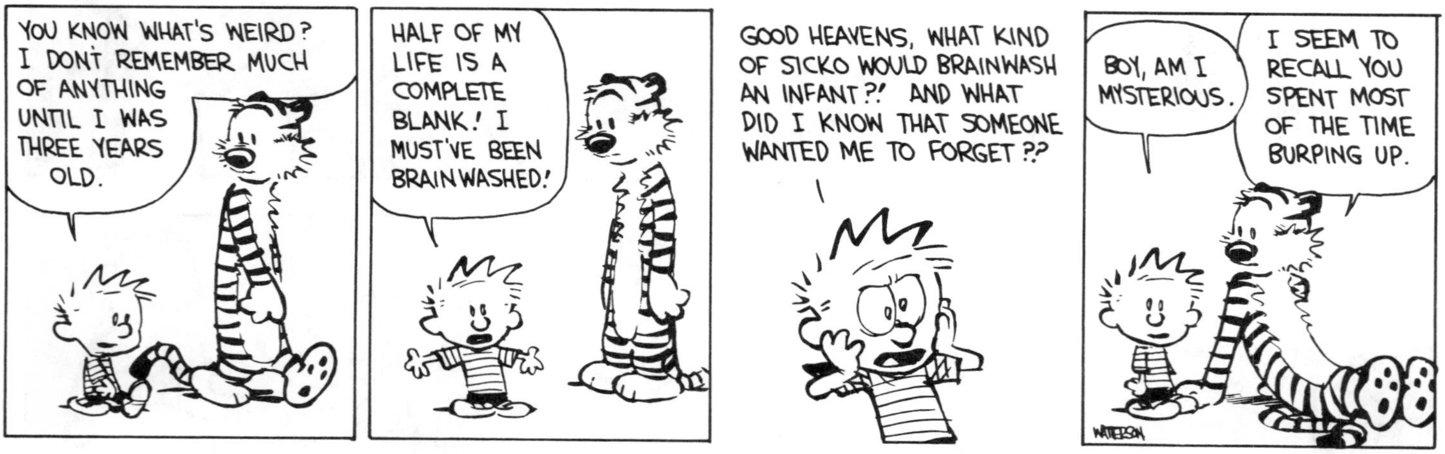
YOU KNOW WHAT'S WEIRD? I DON'T REMEMBER MUCH OF ANYTHING UNTIL I WAS THREE YEARS OLD.
HALF OF MY LIFE IS A COMPLETE BLANK! I MUST'VE BEEN BRAINWASHED!
GOOD HEAVENS, WHAT KIND OF SICKO WOULD BRAINWASH AN INFANT?! AND WHAT DID I KNOW THAT SOMEONE WANTED ME TO FORGET??
BOY, AM I MYSTERIOUS.
I SEEM TO RECALL YOU SPENT MOST OF THE TIME BURPING UP.

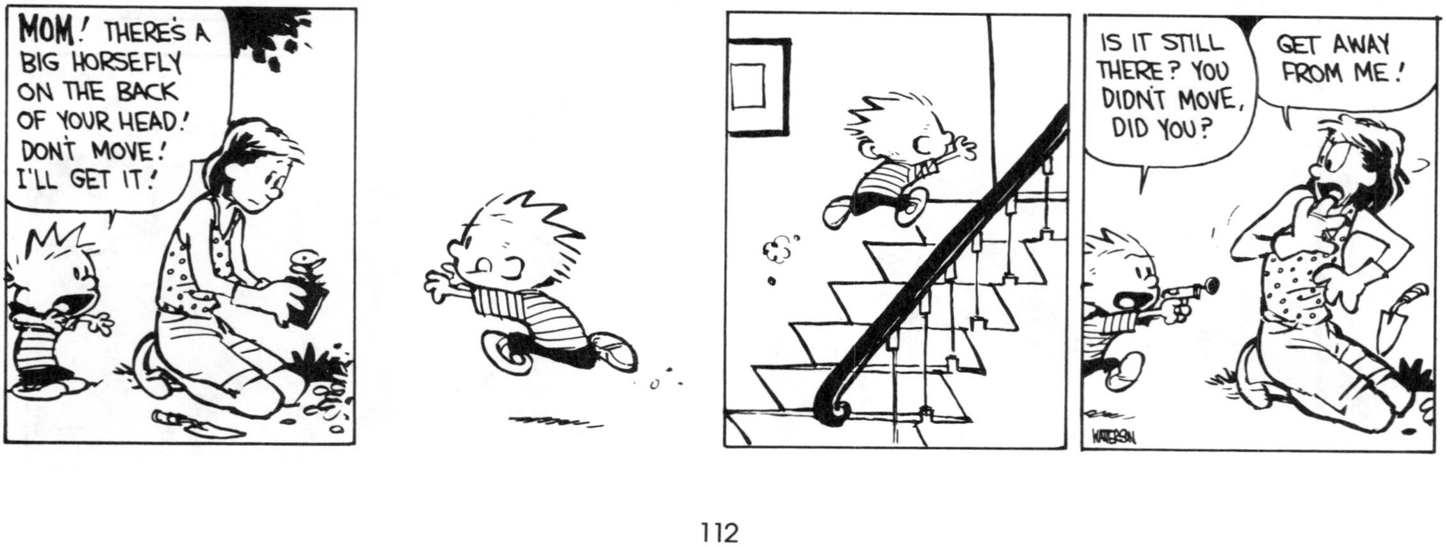
MOM! THERE'S A BIG HORSEFLY ON THE BACK OF YOUR HEAD! DON'T MOVE! I'LL GET IT!
IS IT STILL THERE? YOU DIDN'T MOVE, DID YOU?
GET AWAY FROM ME!

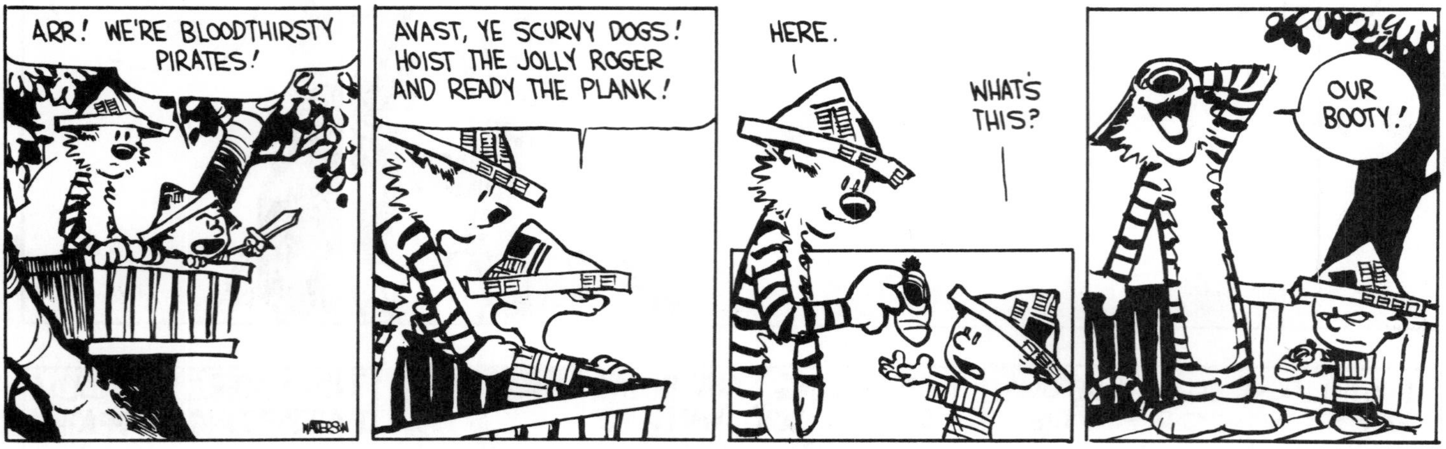
ARR! WE'RE BLOODTHIRSTY PIRATES!
AVAST, YE SCURVY DOGS! HOIST THE JOLLY ROGER AND READY THE PLANK!
HERE.
WHAT'S THIS?
OUR BOOTY!
WATTERSON

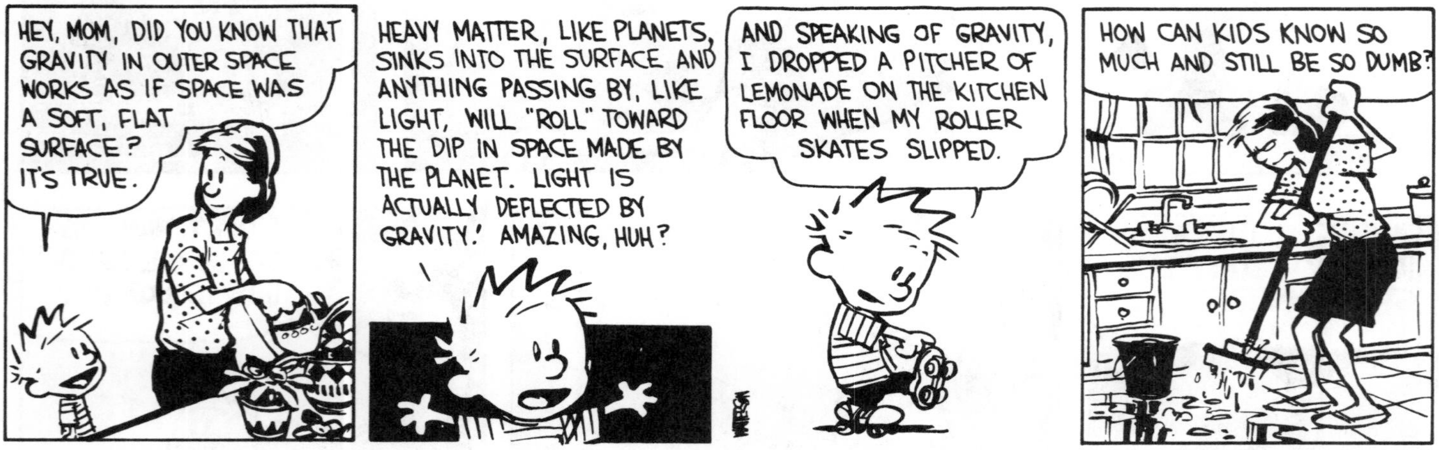
HEY, MOM, DID YOU KNOW THAT GRAVITY IN OUTER SPACE WORKS AS IF SPACE WAS A SOFT, FLAT SURFACE? IT'S TRUE.
HEAVY MATTER, LIKE PLANETS, SINKS INTO THE SURFACE AND ANYTHING PASSING BY, LIKE LIGHT, WILL "ROLL" TOWARD THE DIP IN SPACE MADE BY THE PLANET. LIGHT IS ACTUALLY DEFLECTED BY GRAVITY! AMAZING, HUH?
WATTERSON
AND SPEAKING OF GRAVITY, I DROPPED A PITCHER OF LEMONADE ON THE KITCHEN FLOOR WHEN MY ROLLER SKATES SLIPPED.
HOW CAN KIDS KNOW SO MUCH AND STILL BE SO DUMB?

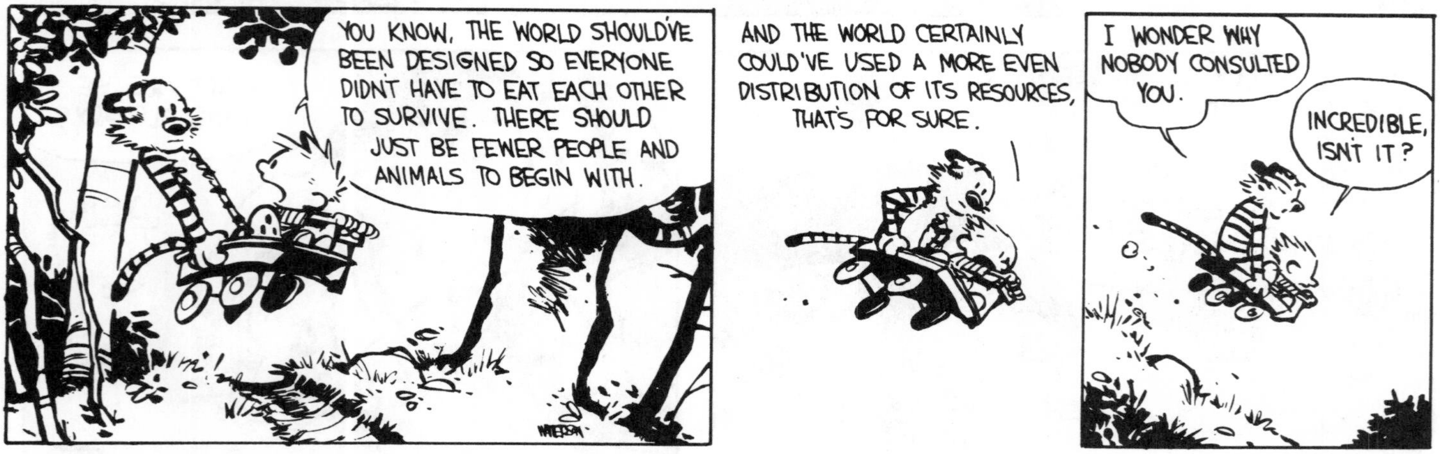
YOU KNOW, THE WORLD SHOULD'VE BEEN DESIGNED SO EVERYONE DIDN'T HAVE TO EAT EACH OTHER TO SURVIVE. THERE SHOULD JUST BE FEWER PEOPLE AND ANIMALS TO BEGIN WITH.
WATTERSON
AND THE WORLD CERTAINLY COULD'VE USED A MORE EVEN DISTRIBUTION OF ITS RESOURCES, THAT'S FOR SURE.
I WONDER WHY NOBODY CONSULTED YOU.
INCREDIBLE, ISN'T IT?

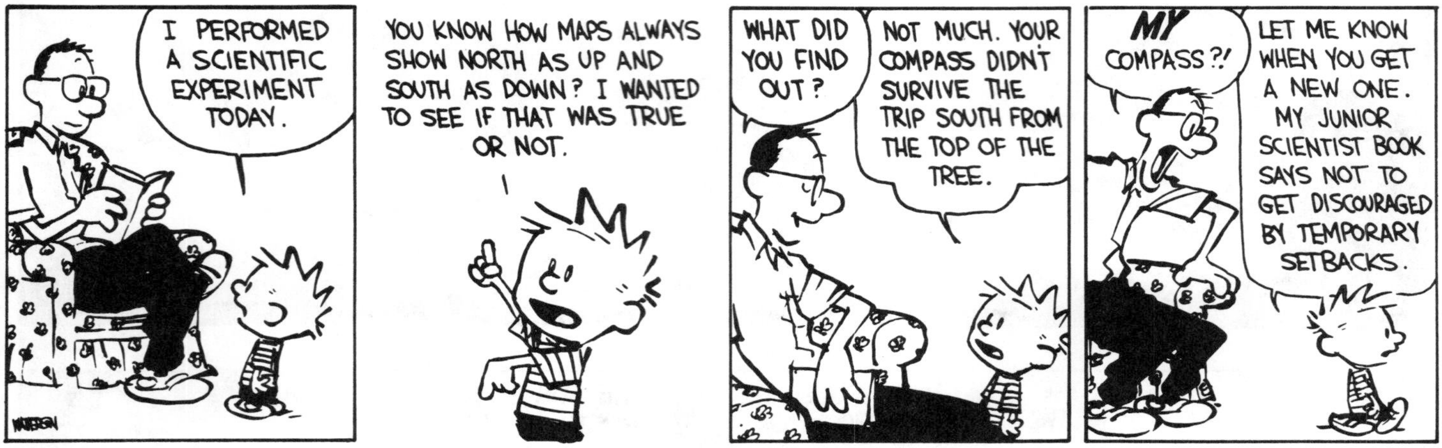
I PERFORMED A SCIENTIFIC EXPERIMENT TODAY.
YOU KNOW HOW MAPS ALWAYS SHOW NORTH AS UP AND SOUTH AS DOWN? I WANTED TO SEE IF THAT WAS TRUE OR NOT.
WHAT DID YOU FIND OUT?
NOT MUCH. YOUR COMPASS DIDN'T SURVIVE THE TRIP SOUTH FROM THE TOP OF THE TREE.
MY COMPASS?!
LET ME KNOW WHEN YOU GET A NEW ONE. MY JUNIOR SCIENTIST BOOK SAYS NOT TO GET DISCOURAGED BY TEMPORARY SETBACKS.
WATTERSON

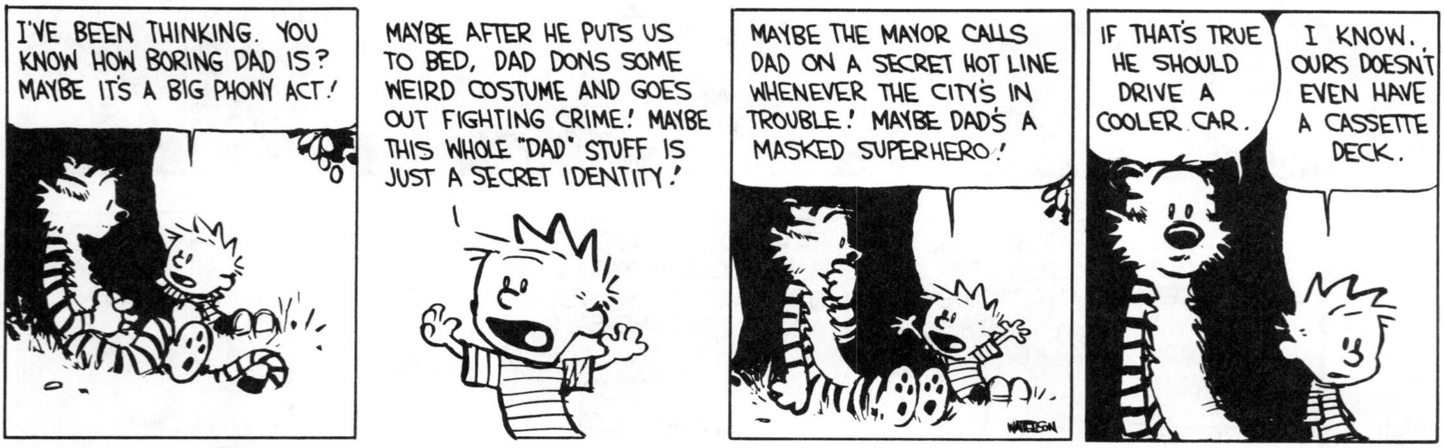
I'VE BEEN THINKING. YOU KNOW HOW BORING DAD IS? MAYBE IT'S A BIG PHONY ACT!
MAYBE AFTER HE PUTS US TO BED, DAD DONS SOME WEIRD COSTUME AND GOES OUT FIGHTING CRIME! MAYBE THIS WHOLE "DAD" STUFF IS JUST A SECRET IDENTITY!
MAYBE THE MAYOR CALLS DAD ON A SECRET HOT LINE WHENEVER THE CITY'S IN TROUBLE! MAYBE DAD'S A MASKED SUPERHERO!
IF THAT'S TRUE HE SHOULD DRIVE A COOLER CAR.
I KNOW. OURS DOESN'T EVEN HAVE A CASSETTE DECK.
WATTERSON

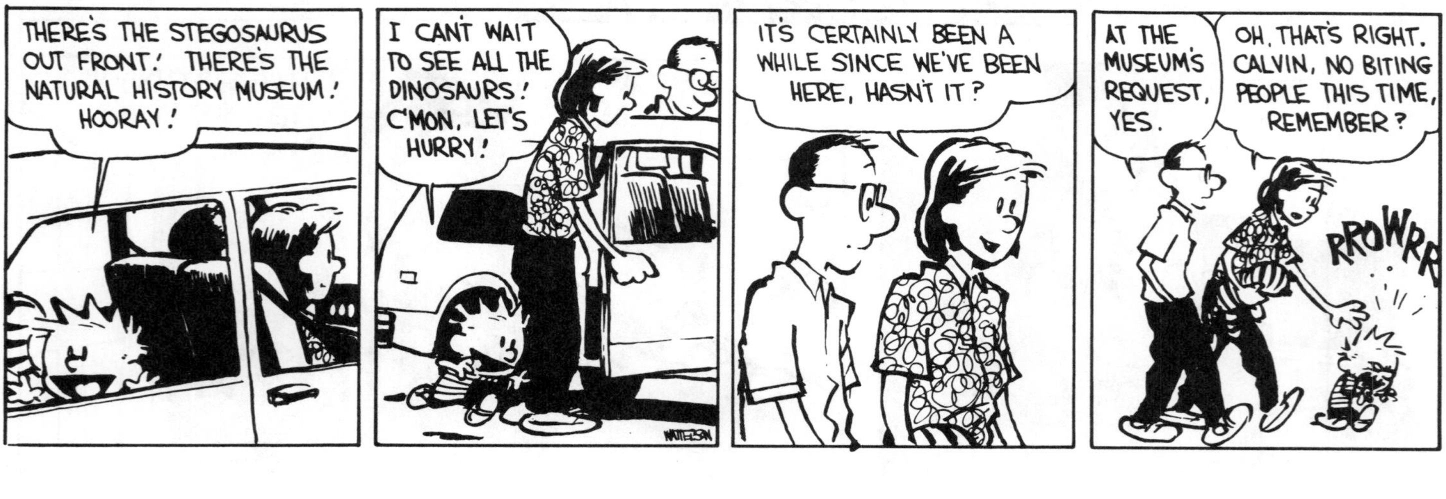
THERE'S THE STEGOSAURUS OUT FRONT! THERE'S THE NATURAL HISTORY MUSEUM! HOORAY!
I CAN'T WAIT TO SEE ALL THE DINOSAURS! C'MON, LET'S HURRY!
WATTERSON
IT'S CERTAINLY BEEN A WHILE SINCE WE'VE BEEN HERE, HASN'T IT?
AT THE MUSEUM'S REQUEST, YES.
OH, THAT'S RIGHT. CALVIN, NO BITING PEOPLE THIS TIME, REMEMBER?
RROWRR

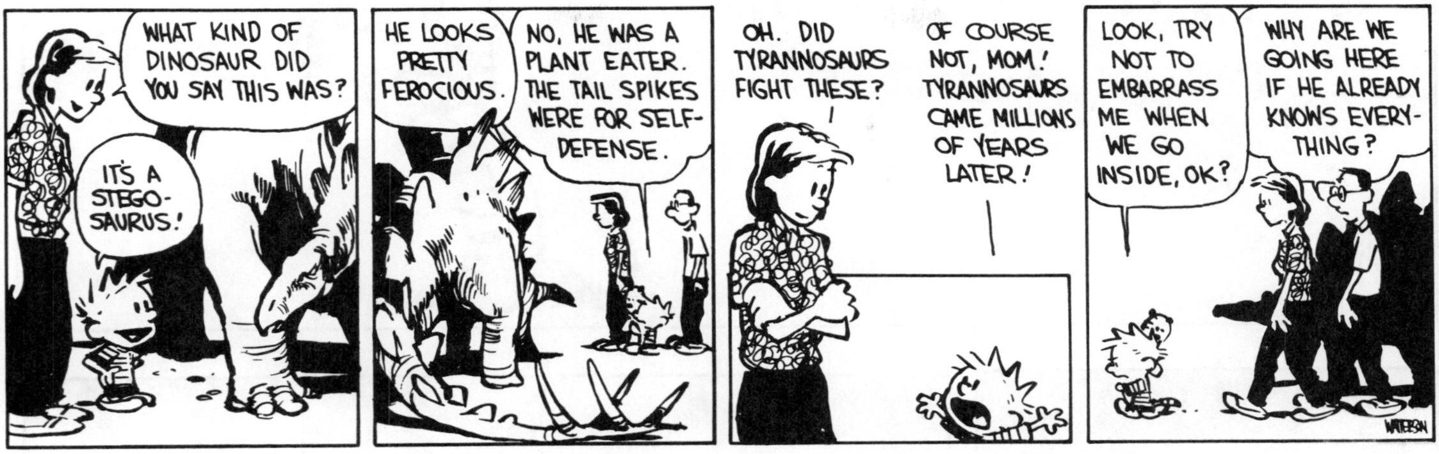
WHAT KIND OF DINOSAUR DID YOU SAY THIS WAS?
IT'S A STEGOSAURUS!
HE LOOKS PRETTY FEROCIOUS.
NO, HE WAS A PLANT EATER. THE TAIL SPIKES WERE FOR SELF-DEFENSE.
OH. DID TYRANNOSAURS FIGHT THESE?
OF COURSE NOT, MOM! TYRANNOSAURS CAME MILLIONS OF YEARS LATER!
LOOK, TRY NOT TO EMBARRASS ME WHEN WE GO INSIDE, OK?
WHY ARE WE GOING HERE IF HE ALREADY KNOWS EVERYTHING?
WATTERSON

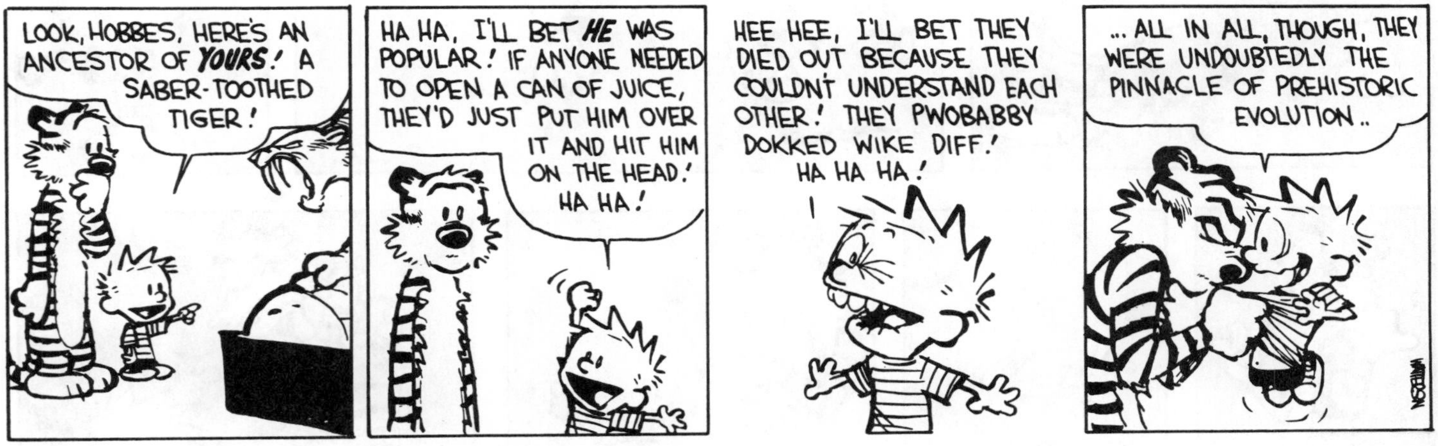
LOOK, HOBBES, HERE'S AN ANCESTOR OF YOURS! A SABER-TOOTHED TIGER!
HA HA, I'LL BET HE WAS POPULAR! IF ANYONE NEEDED TO OPEN A CAN OF JUICE, THEY'D JUST PUT HIM OVER IT AND HIT HIM ON THE HEAD! HA HA!
HEE HEE, I'LL BET THEY DIED OUT BECAUSE THEY COULDN'T UNDERSTAND EACH OTHER! THEY PWOBABBY DOKKED WIKE DIFF! HA HA HA!
... ALL IN ALL, THOUGH, THEY WERE UNDOUBTEDLY THE PINNACLE OF PREHISTORIC EVOLUTION ..
WATTERSON

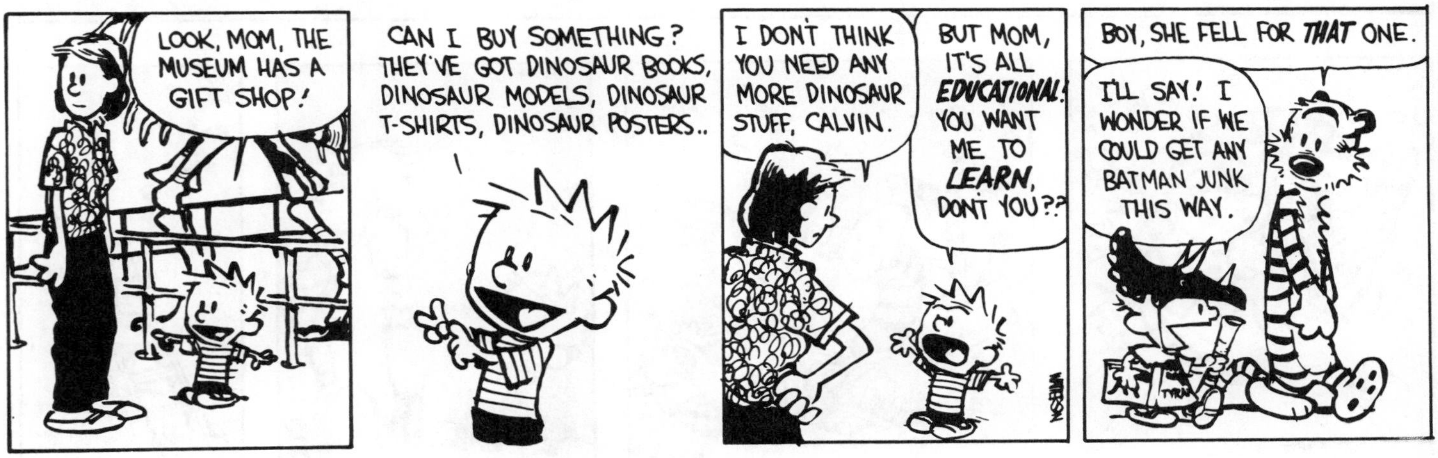
LOOK, MOM, THE MUSEUM HAS A GIFT SHOP!
CAN I BUY SOMETHING? THEY'VE GOT DINOSAUR BOOKS, DINOSAUR MODELS, DINOSAUR T-SHIRTS, DINOSAUR POSTERS..
I DON'T THINK YOU NEED ANY MORE DINOSAUR STUFF, CALVIN.
BUT MOM, IT'S ALL EDUCATIONAL! YOU WANT ME TO LEARN, DON'T YOU??
WATTERSON
BOY, SHE FELL FOR THAT ONE.
I'LL SAY! I WONDER IF WE COULD GET ANY BATMAN JUNK THIS WAY.

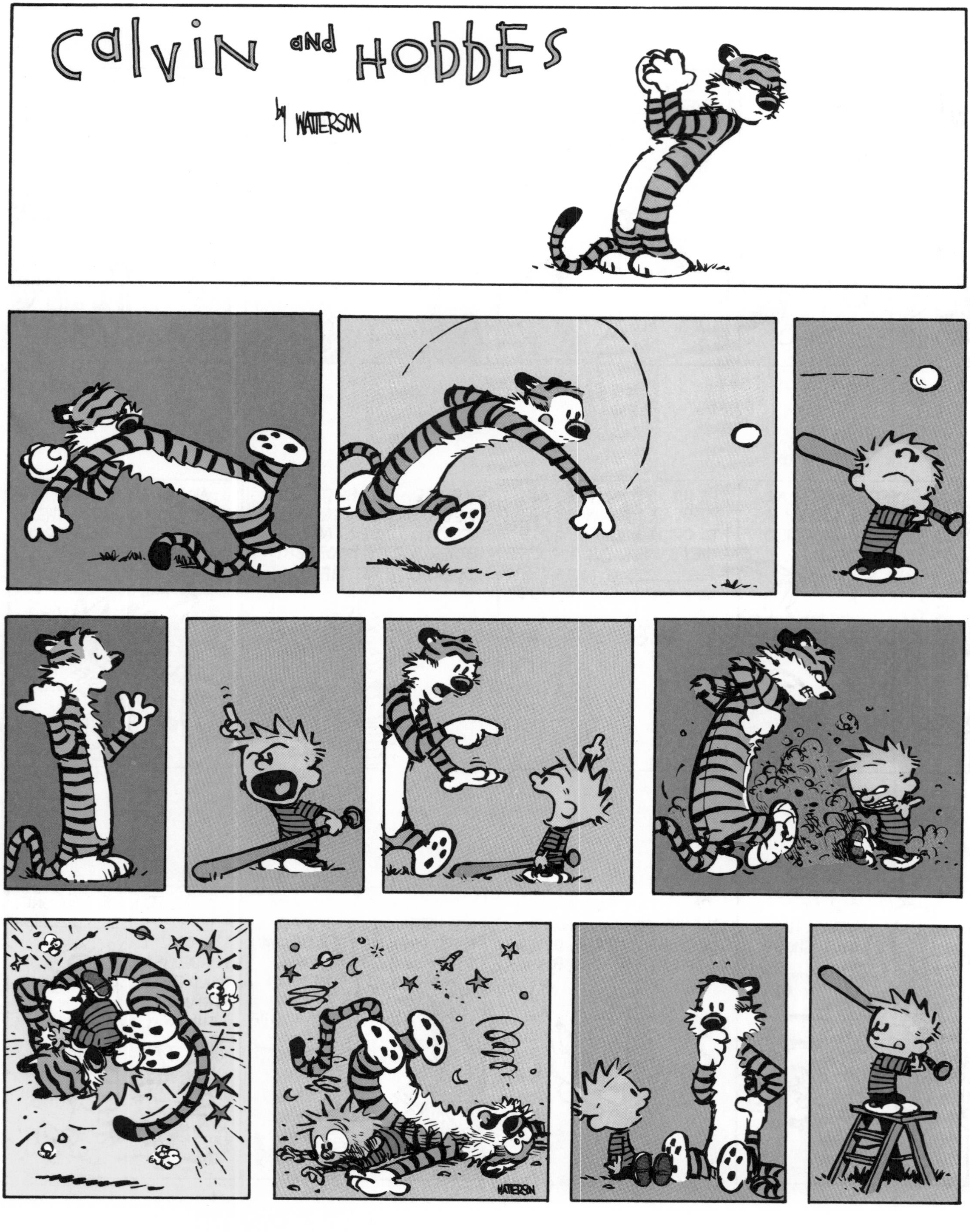
Calvin and HOBBES
by WATTERSON
WATTERSON

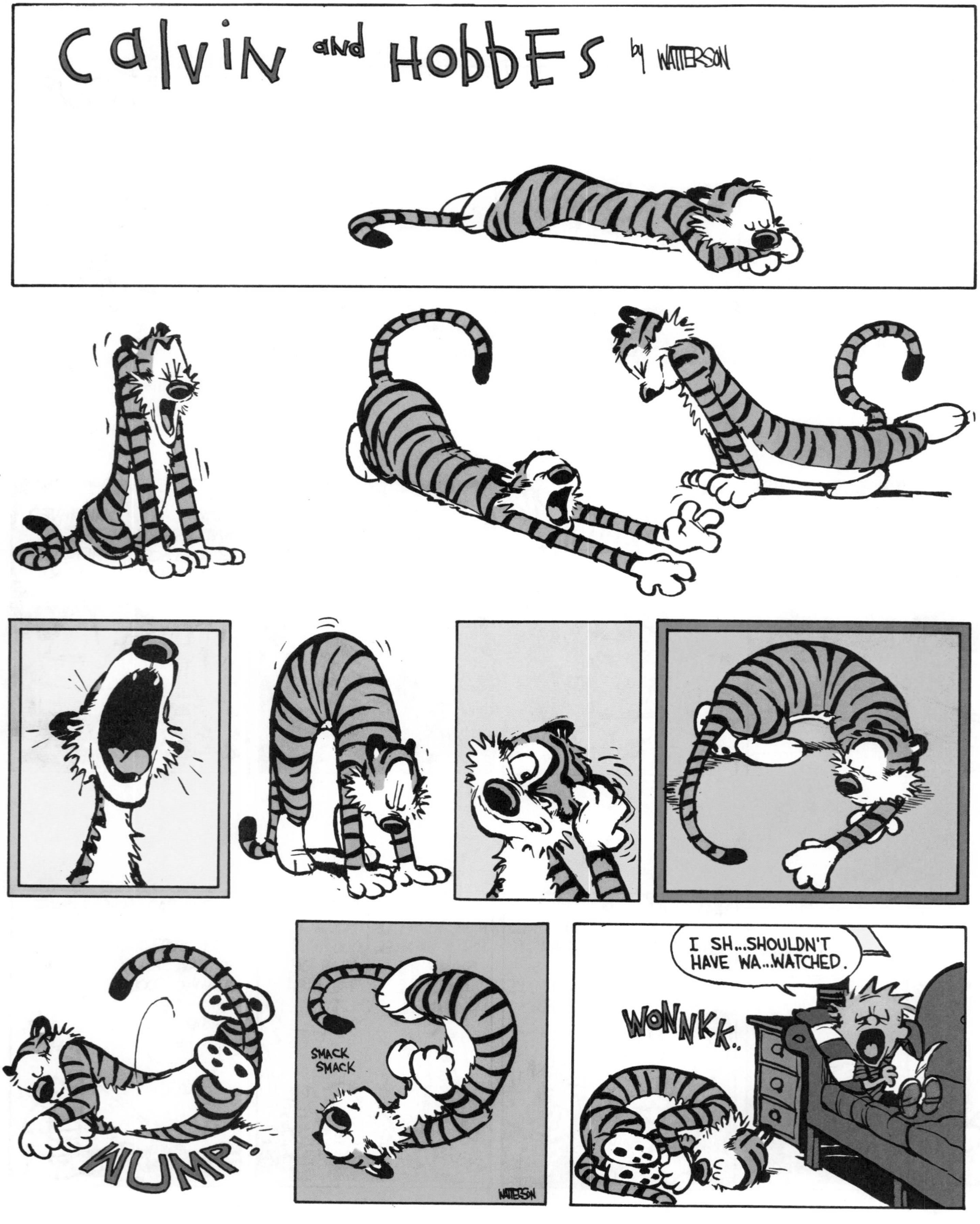
Calvin and HOBBES
by WATTERSON
WUMP!
SMACK
SMACK
WATTERSON
WONNKK..
I SH...SHOULDN'T HAVE WA...WATCHED.

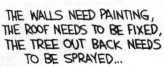

CALVIN and HOBBES by WATTERSON

A 30-TON BRONTOSAURUS

... IS ABOUT TO FACE A PREMATURE EXTINCTION!

THE ALLOSAURUS, FEARSOME PREDATOR OF THE JURASSIC, STALKS HIS PREY!

THE HERD OF BRONTOSAURS IS UNAWARE OF HIS PRESENCE!

SPOTTING A STRAGGLER, THE ALLOSAURUS LUNGES!

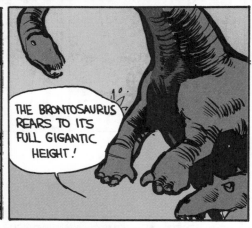

THE BRONTOSAURUS REARS TO ITS FULL GIGANTIC HEIGHT!

WHAT INDUCES AN ALLOSAURUS TO ATTACK A MONSTER MORE THAN TWICE HIS OWN SIZE??

I'M HUNGRY!

THE HAMBURGERS ARE COOKING! NOW GET OFF ME!

122

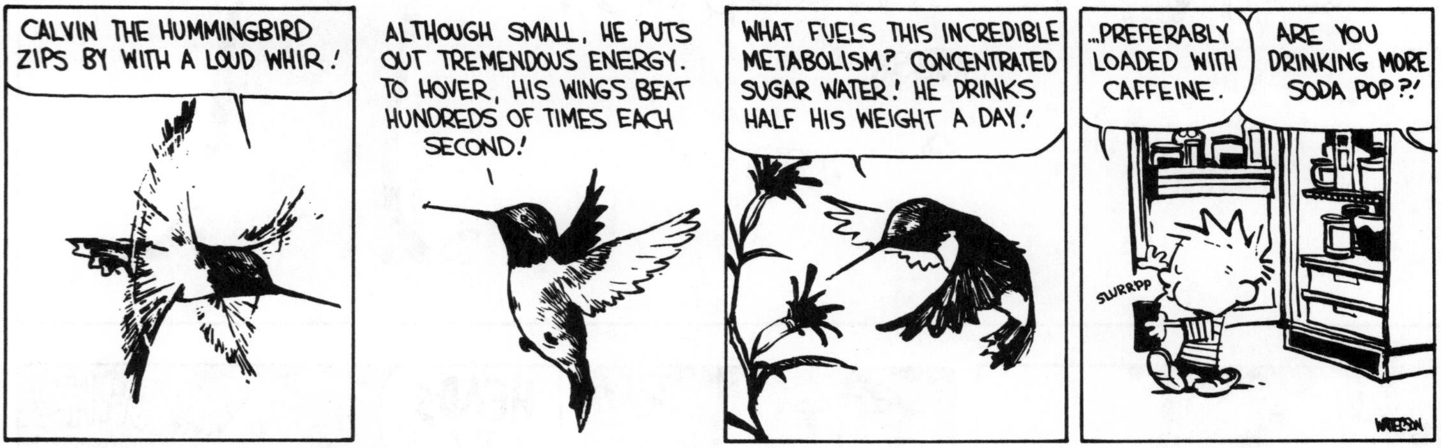
CALVIN THE HUMMINGBIRD ZIPS BY WITH A LOUD WHIR!
ALTHOUGH SMALL, HE PUTS OUT TREMENDOUS ENERGY. TO HOVER, HIS WINGS BEAT HUNDREDS OF TIMES EACH SECOND!
WHAT FUELS THIS INCREDIBLE METABOLISM? CONCENTRATED SUGAR WATER! HE DRINKS HALF HIS WEIGHT A DAY!
...PREFERABLY LOADED WITH CAFFEINE.
ARE YOU DRINKING MORE SODA POP?!
SLURRPP
WATTERSON

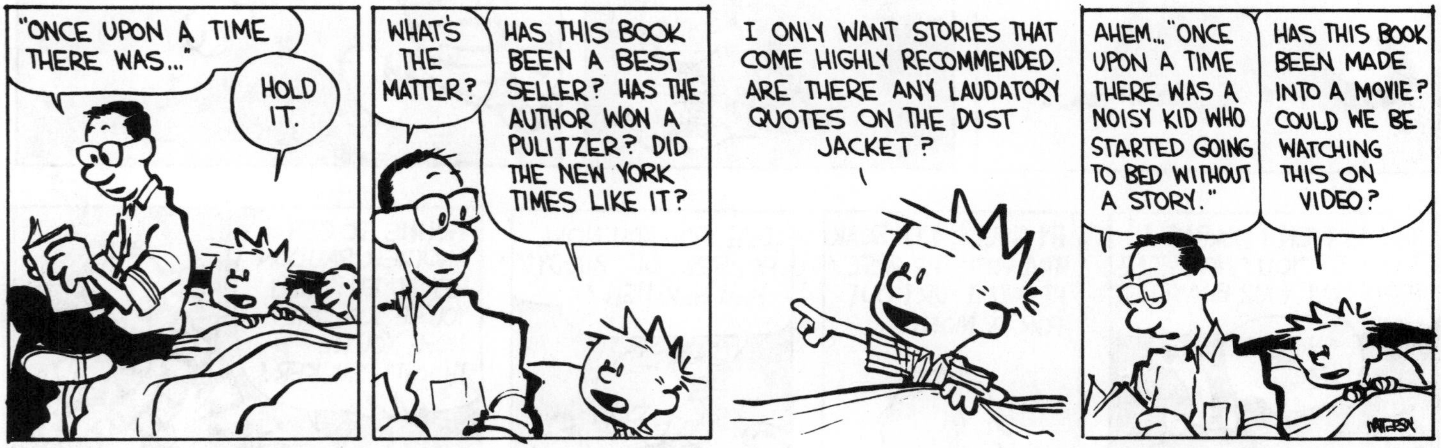
"ONCE UPON A TIME THERE WAS..."
HOLD IT.
WHAT'S THE MATTER?
HAS THIS BOOK BEEN A BEST SELLER? HAS THE AUTHOR WON A PULITZER? DID THE NEW YORK TIMES LIKE IT?
I ONLY WANT STORIES THAT COME HIGHLY RECOMMENDED. ARE THERE ANY LAUDATORY QUOTES ON THE DUST JACKET?
AHEM... "ONCE UPON A TIME THERE WAS A NOISY KID WHO STARTED GOING TO BED WITHOUT A STORY."
HAS THIS BOOK BEEN MADE INTO A MOVIE? COULD WE BE WATCHING THIS ON VIDEO?
WATTERSON

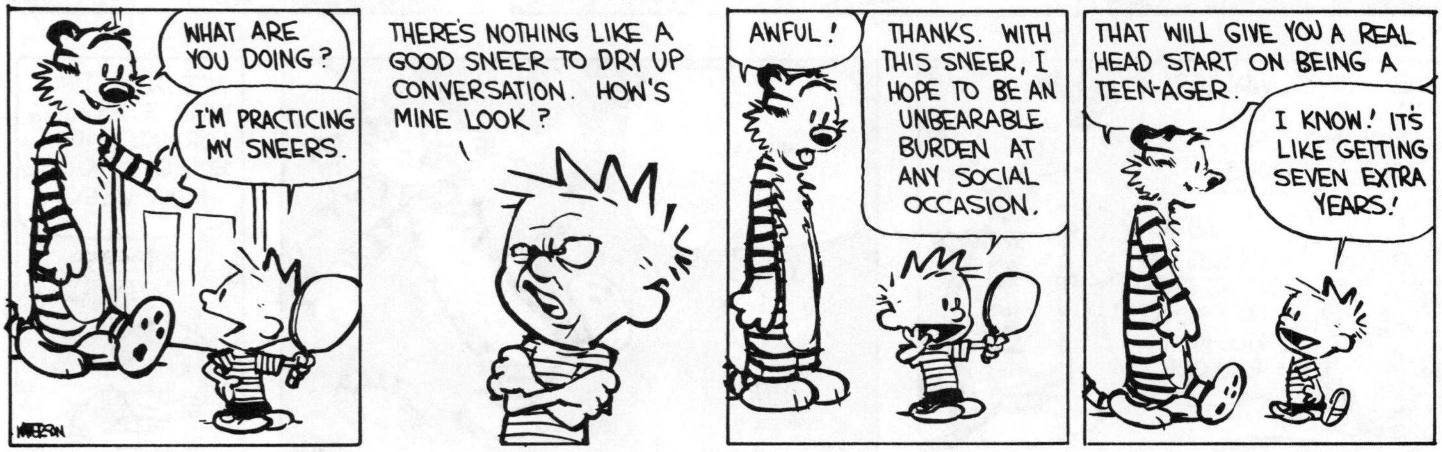
WHAT ARE YOU DOING?
I'M PRACTICING MY SNEERS.
THERE'S NOTHING LIKE A GOOD SNEER TO DRY UP CONVERSATION. HOW'S MINE LOOK?
AWFUL!
THANKS. WITH THIS SNEER, I HOPE TO BE AN UNBEARABLE BURDEN AT ANY SOCIAL OCCASION.
THAT WILL GIVE YOU A REAL HEAD START ON BEING A TEEN-AGER.
I KNOW! IT'S LIKE GETTING SEVEN EXTRA YEARS!
WATTERSON

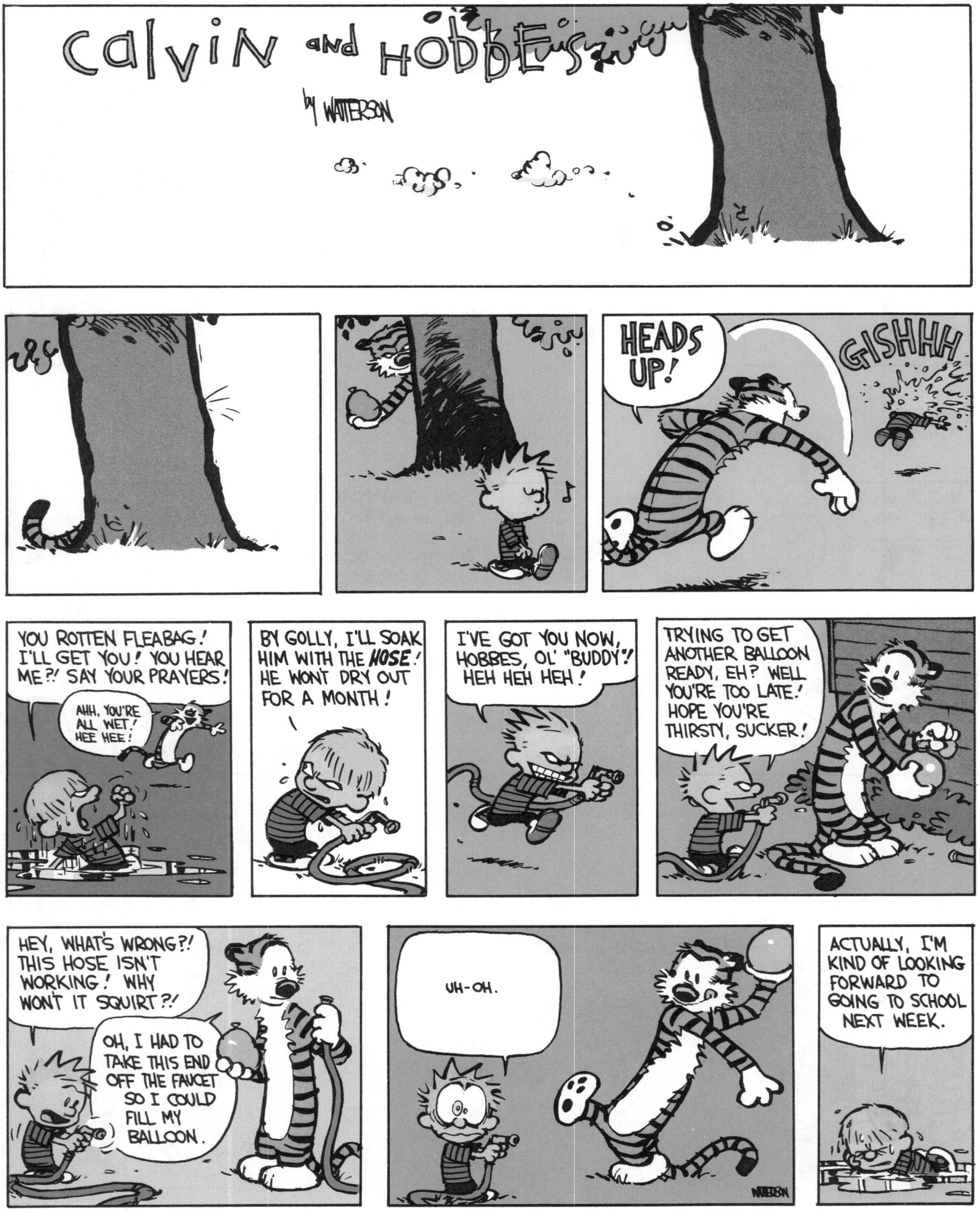
Calvin and HOBBES
by WATTERSON
HEADS UP!
GISHHH
YOU ROTTEN FLEABAG! I'LL GET YOU! YOU HEAR ME?! SAY YOUR PRAYERS!
AHH, YOU'RE ALL WET! HEE HEE!
BY GOLLY, I'LL SOAK HIM WITH THE HOSE! HE WON'T DRY OUT FOR A MONTH!
I'VE GOT YOU NOW, HOBBES, OL' "BUDDY"! HEH HEH HEH!
TRYING TO GET ANOTHER BALLOON READY, EH? WELL YOU'RE TOO LATE! HOPE YOU'RE THIRSTY, SUCKER!
HEY, WHAT'S WRONG?! THIS HOSE ISN'T WORKING! WHY WON'T IT SQUIRT?!
OH, I HAD TO TAKE THIS END OFF THE FAUCET SO I COULD FILL MY BALLOON.
UH-OH.
WATTERSON
ACTUALLY, I'M KIND OF LOOKING FORWARD TO GOING TO SCHOOL NEXT WEEK.

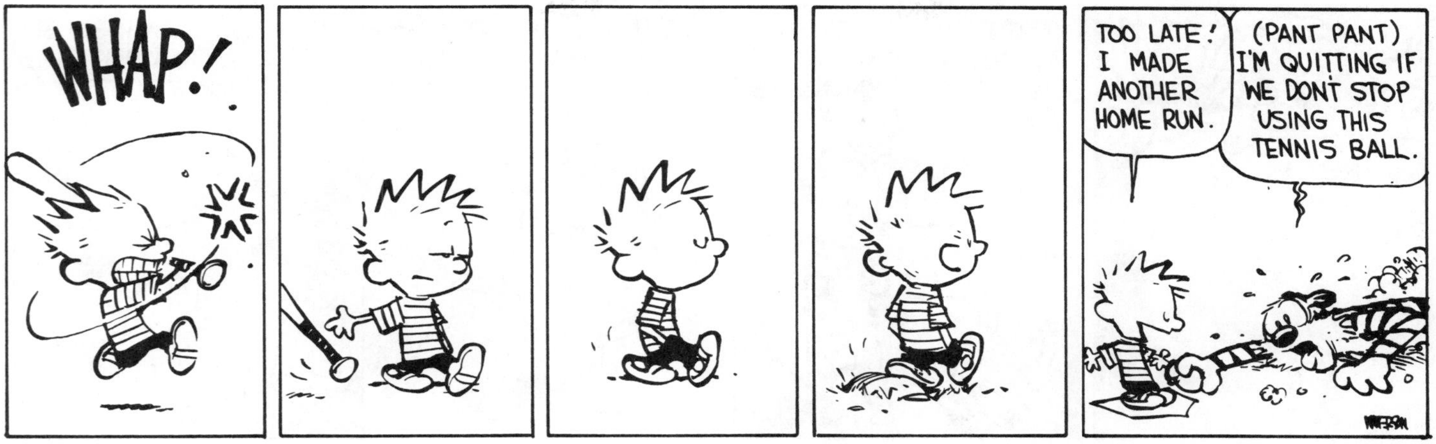
WHAP!
TOO LATE! I MADE ANOTHER HOME RUN.
(PANT PANT) I'M QUITTING IF WE DON'T STOP USING THIS TENNIS BALL.

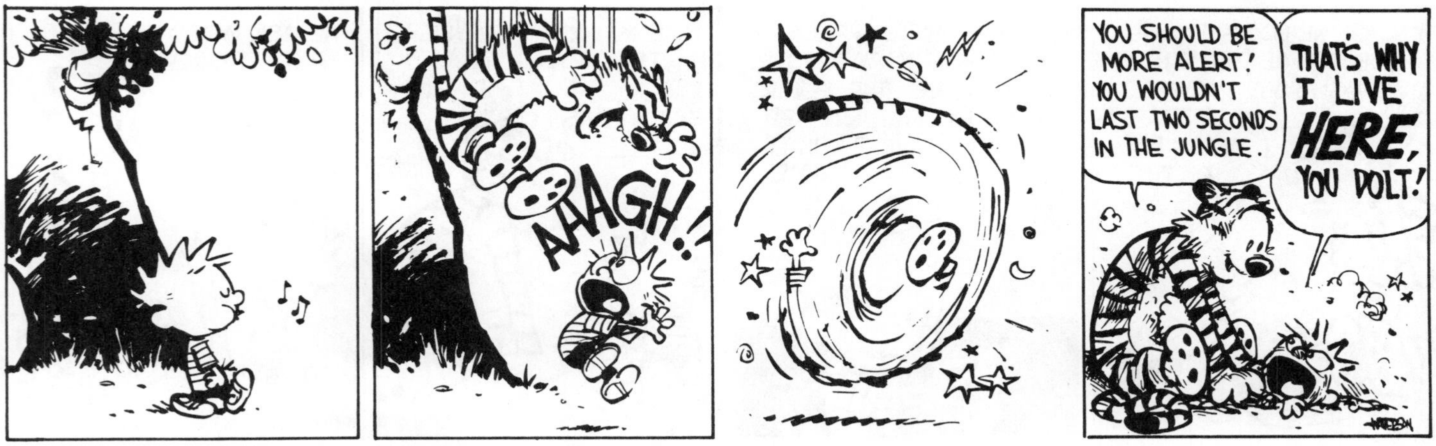
AAAGH!!
YOU SHOULD BE MORE ALERT! YOU WOULDN'T LAST TWO SECONDS IN THE JUNGLE.
THAT'S WHY I LIVE *HERE*, YOU DOLT!

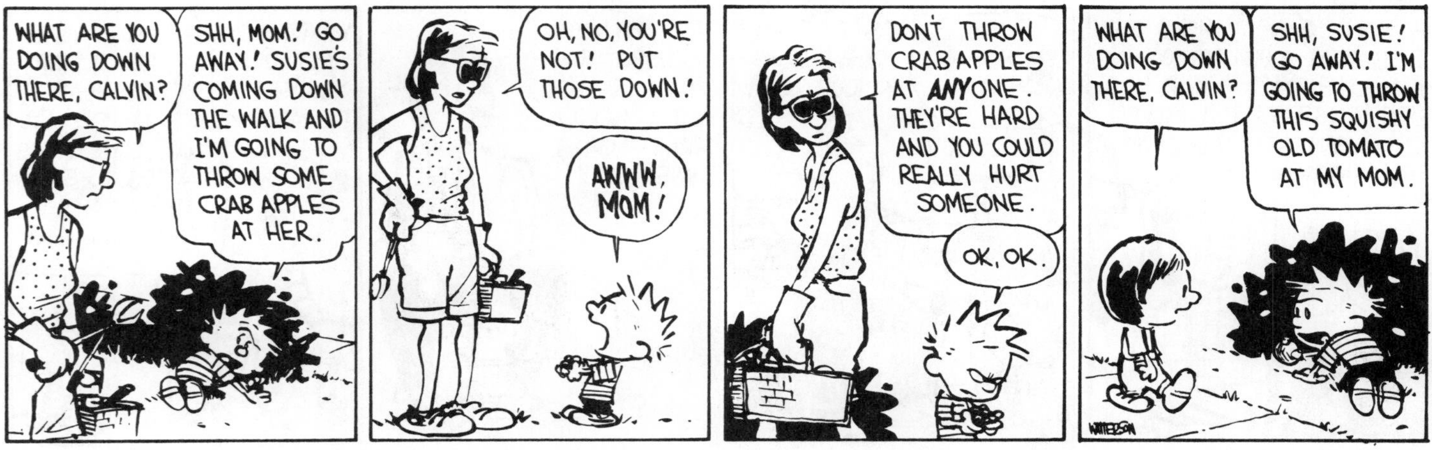
WHAT ARE YOU DOING DOWN THERE, CALVIN?
SHH, MOM! GO AWAY! SUSIE'S COMING DOWN THE WALK AND I'M GOING TO THROW SOME CRAB APPLES AT HER.
OH, NO, YOU'RE NOT! PUT THOSE DOWN!
AWWW, MOM!
DON'T THROW CRAB APPLES AT *ANY*ONE. THEY'RE HARD AND YOU COULD REALLY HURT SOMEONE.
OK, OK.
WHAT ARE YOU DOING DOWN THERE, CALVIN?
SHH, SUSIE! GO AWAY! I'M GOING TO THROW THIS SQUISHY OLD TOMATO AT MY MOM.

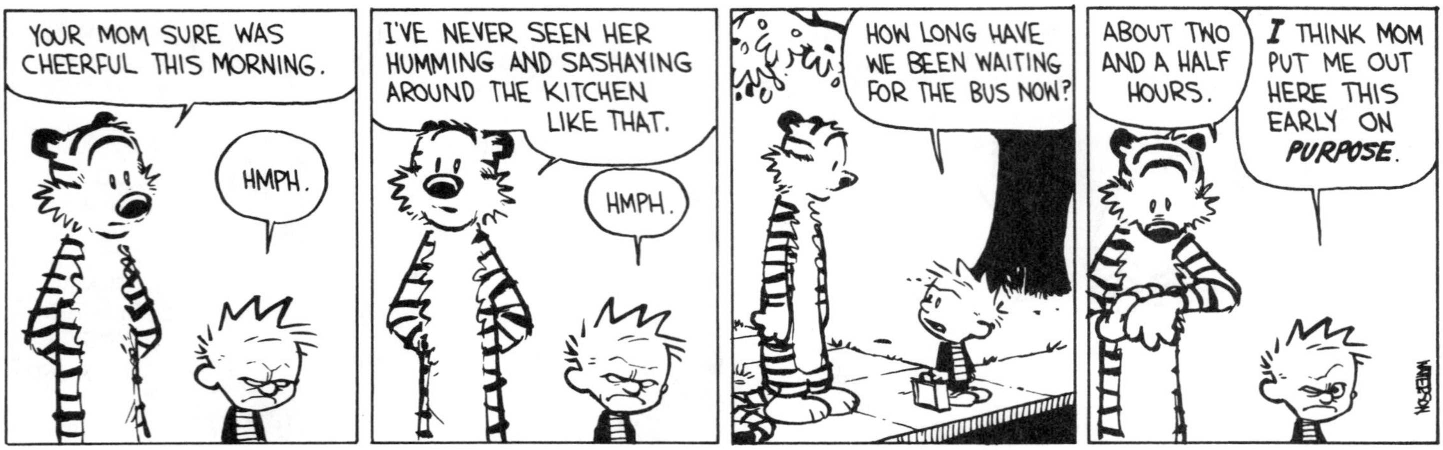
YOUR MOM SURE WAS CHEERFUL THIS MORNING.
HMPH.
I'VE NEVER SEEN HER HUMMING AND SASHAYING AROUND THE KITCHEN LIKE THAT.
HMPH.
HOW LONG HAVE WE BEEN WAITING FOR THE BUS NOW?
ABOUT TWO AND A HALF HOURS.
I THINK MOM PUT ME OUT HERE THIS EARLY ON PURPOSE.

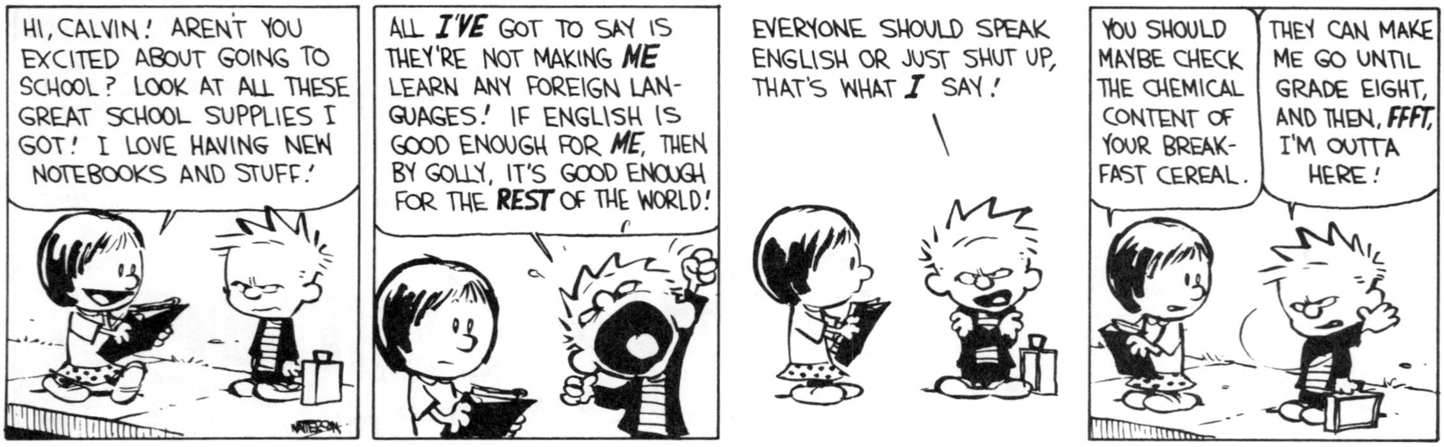
HI, CALVIN! AREN'T YOU EXCITED ABOUT GOING TO SCHOOL? LOOK AT ALL THESE GREAT SCHOOL SUPPLIES I GOT! I LOVE HAVING NEW NOTEBOOKS AND STUFF!
ALL I'VE GOT TO SAY IS THEY'RE NOT MAKING ME LEARN ANY FOREIGN LANGUAGES! IF ENGLISH IS GOOD ENOUGH FOR ME, THEN BY GOLLY, IT'S GOOD ENOUGH FOR THE REST OF THE WORLD!
EVERYONE SHOULD SPEAK ENGLISH OR JUST SHUT UP, THAT'S WHAT I SAY!
YOU SHOULD MAYBE CHECK THE CHEMICAL CONTENT OF YOUR BREAKFAST CEREAL.
THEY CAN MAKE ME GO UNTIL GRADE EIGHT, AND THEN, FFFT, I'M OUTTA HERE!

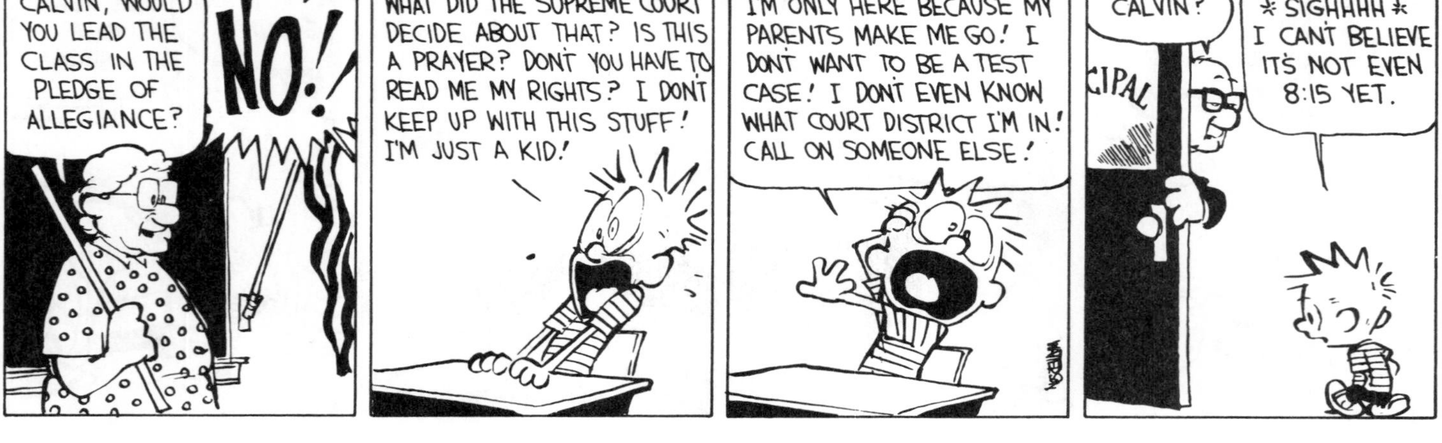
CALVIN, WOULD YOU LEAD THE CLASS IN THE PLEDGE OF ALLEGIANCE?
NO!!
WHAT DID THE SUPREME COURT DECIDE ABOUT THAT? IS THIS A PRAYER? DON'T YOU HAVE TO READ ME MY RIGHTS? I DON'T KEEP UP WITH THIS STUFF! I'M JUST A KID!
I'M ONLY HERE BECAUSE MY PARENTS MAKE ME GO! I DON'T WANT TO BE A TEST CASE! I DON'T EVEN KNOW WHAT COURT DISTRICT I'M IN! CALL ON SOMEONE ELSE!
CIPAL
CALVIN?
* SIGHHHH * I CAN'T BELIEVE IT'S NOT EVEN 8:15 YET.

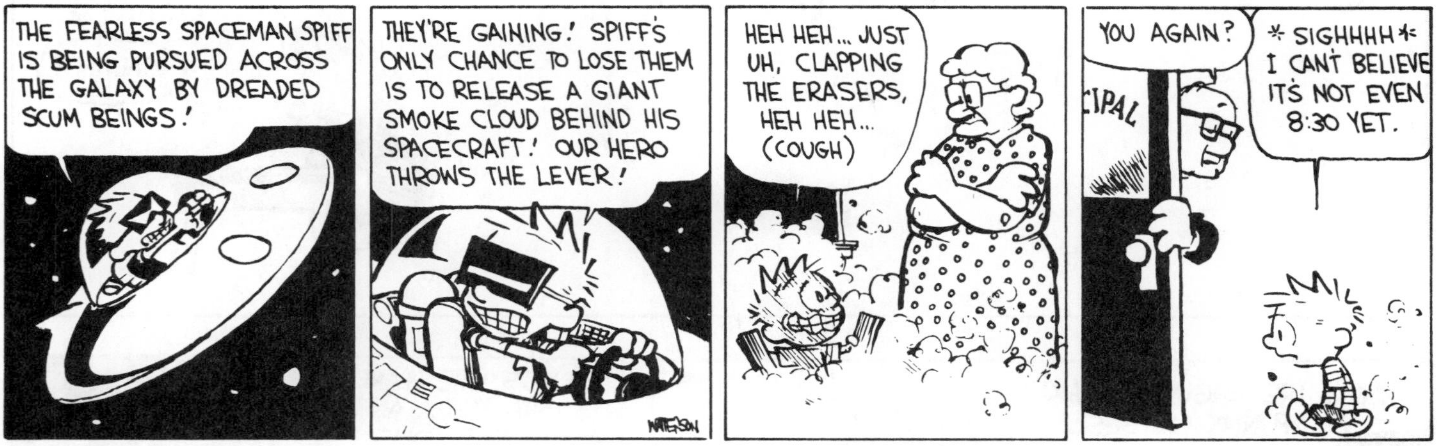
THE FEARLESS SPACEMAN SPIFF IS BEING PURSUED ACROSS THE GALAXY BY DREADED SCUM BEINGS!
THEY'RE GAINING! SPIFF'S ONLY CHANCE TO LOSE THEM IS TO RELEASE A GIANT SMOKE CLOUD BEHIND HIS SPACECRAFT! OUR HERO THROWS THE LEVER!
HEH HEH... JUST UH, CLAPPING THE ERASERS, HEH HEH... (COUGH)
YOU AGAIN?
SIGHHHH I CAN'T BELIEVE IT'S NOT EVEN 8:30 YET.

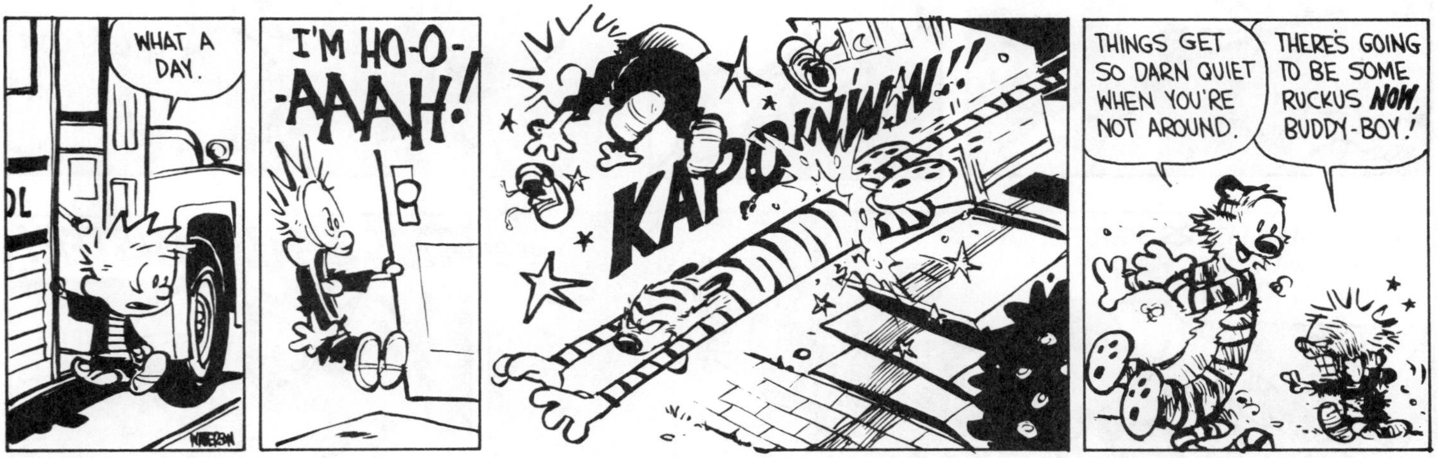
WHAT A DAY.
I'M HO-O--AAAH!
KAPOINWW!!
THINGS GET SO DARN QUIET WHEN YOU'RE NOT AROUND.
THERE'S GOING TO BE SOME RUCKUS NOW, BUDDY-BOY!

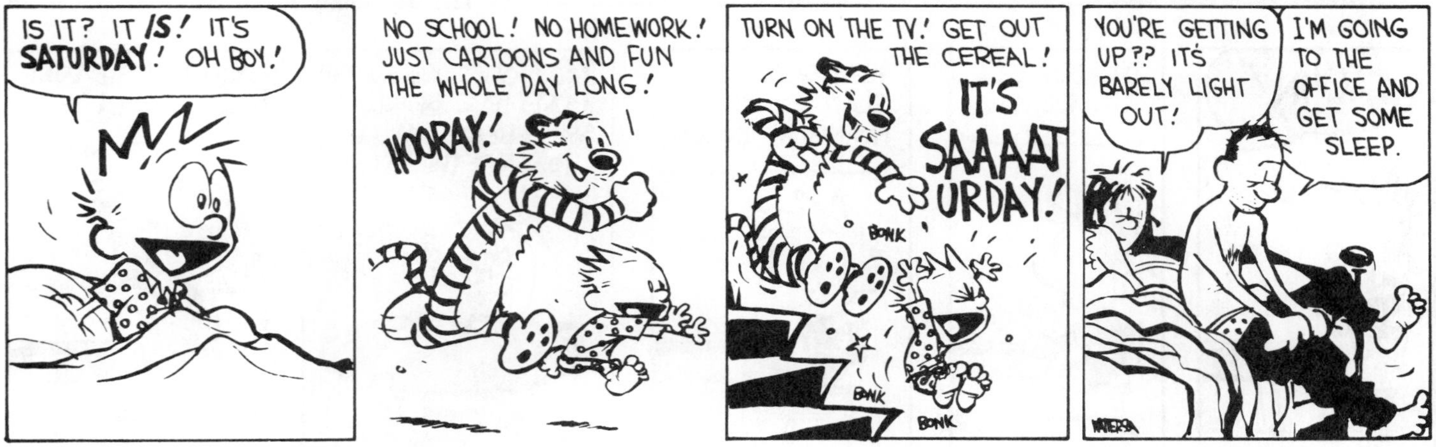
IS IT? IT IS! IT'S SATURDAY! OH BOY!
NO SCHOOL! NO HOMEWORK! JUST CARTOONS AND FUN THE WHOLE DAY LONG!
HOORAY!
TURN ON THE TV! GET OUT THE CEREAL!
IT'S SAAAAT URDAY!
BONK
BONK
BONK
YOU'RE GETTING UP?? IT'S BARELY LIGHT OUT!
I'M GOING TO THE OFFICE AND GET SOME SLEEP.

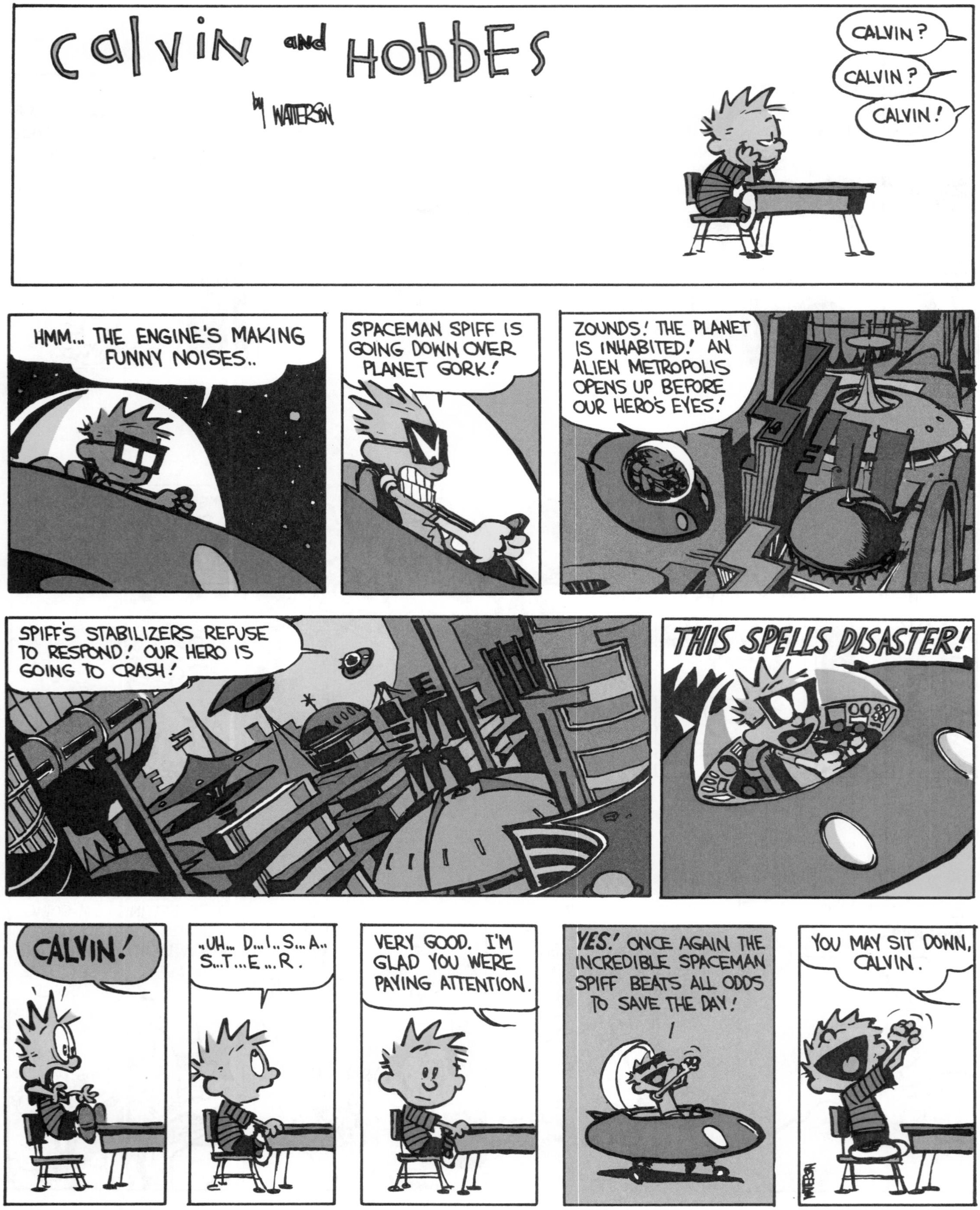
Calvin and HOBBES
by WATTERSON
CALVIN?
CALVIN?
CALVIN!
HMM... THE ENGINE'S MAKING FUNNY NOISES..
SPACEMAN SPIFF IS GOING DOWN OVER PLANET GORK!
ZOUNDS! THE PLANET IS INHABITED! AN ALIEN METROPOLIS OPENS UP BEFORE OUR HERO'S EYES!
SPIFF'S STABILIZERS REFUSE TO RESPOND! OUR HERO IS GOING TO CRASH!
THIS SPELLS DISASTER!
CALVIN!
..UH... D...I...S... A... S...T...E...R.
VERY GOOD. I'M GLAD YOU WERE PAYING ATTENTION.
YES! ONCE AGAIN THE INCREDIBLE SPACEMAN SPIFF BEATS ALL ODDS TO SAVE THE DAY!
YOU MAY SIT DOWN, CALVIN.

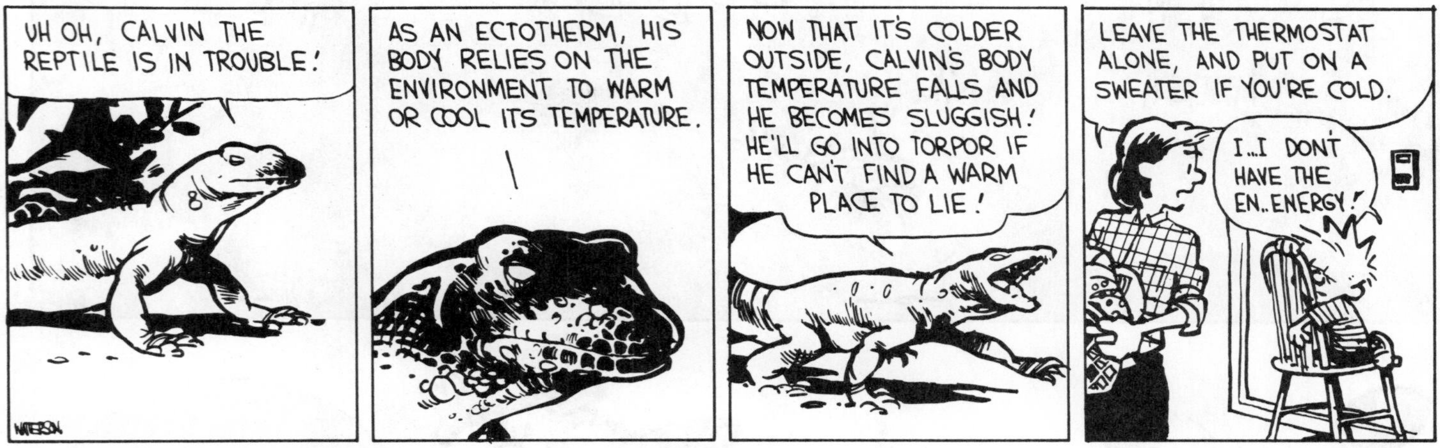
UH OH, CALVIN THE REPTILE IS IN TROUBLE!
AS AN ECTOTHERM, HIS BODY RELIES ON THE ENVIRONMENT TO WARM OR COOL ITS TEMPERATURE.
NOW THAT IT'S COLDER OUTSIDE, CALVIN'S BODY TEMPERATURE FALLS AND HE BECOMES SLUGGISH! HE'LL GO INTO TORPOR IF HE CAN'T FIND A WARM PLACE TO LIE!
LEAVE THE THERMOSTAT ALONE, AND PUT ON A SWEATER IF YOU'RE COLD.
I...I DON'T HAVE THE EN..ENERGY!

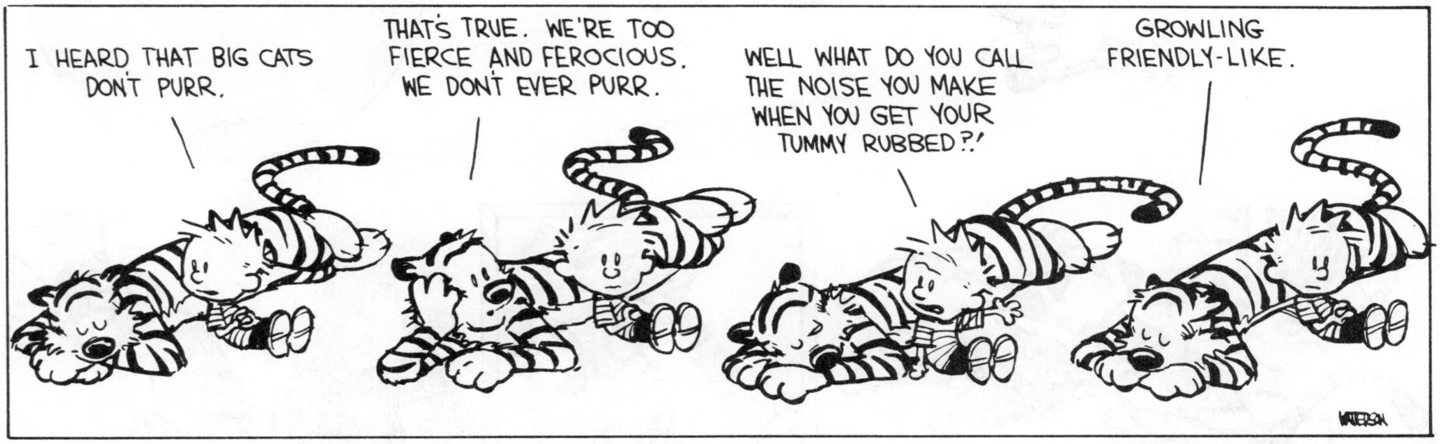
I HEARD THAT BIG CATS DON'T PURR.
THAT'S TRUE. WE'RE TOO FIERCE AND FEROCIOUS. WE DON'T EVER PURR.
WELL WHAT DO YOU CALL THE NOISE YOU MAKE WHEN YOU GET YOUR TUMMY RUBBED?!
GROWLING FRIENDLY-LIKE.

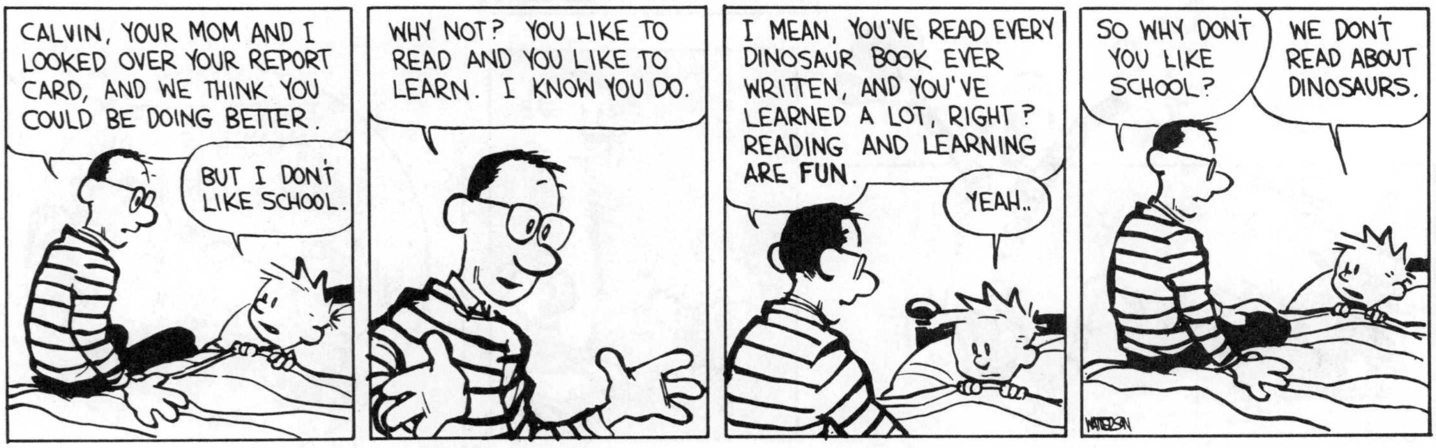
CALVIN, YOUR MOM AND I LOOKED OVER YOUR REPORT CARD, AND WE THINK YOU COULD BE DOING BETTER.
BUT I DON'T LIKE SCHOOL.
WHY NOT? YOU LIKE TO READ AND YOU LIKE TO LEARN. I KNOW YOU DO.
I MEAN, YOU'VE READ EVERY DINOSAUR BOOK EVER WRITTEN, AND YOU'VE LEARNED A LOT, RIGHT? READING AND LEARNING ARE FUN.
YEAH..
SO WHY DON'T YOU LIKE SCHOOL?
WE DON'T READ ABOUT DINOSAURS.

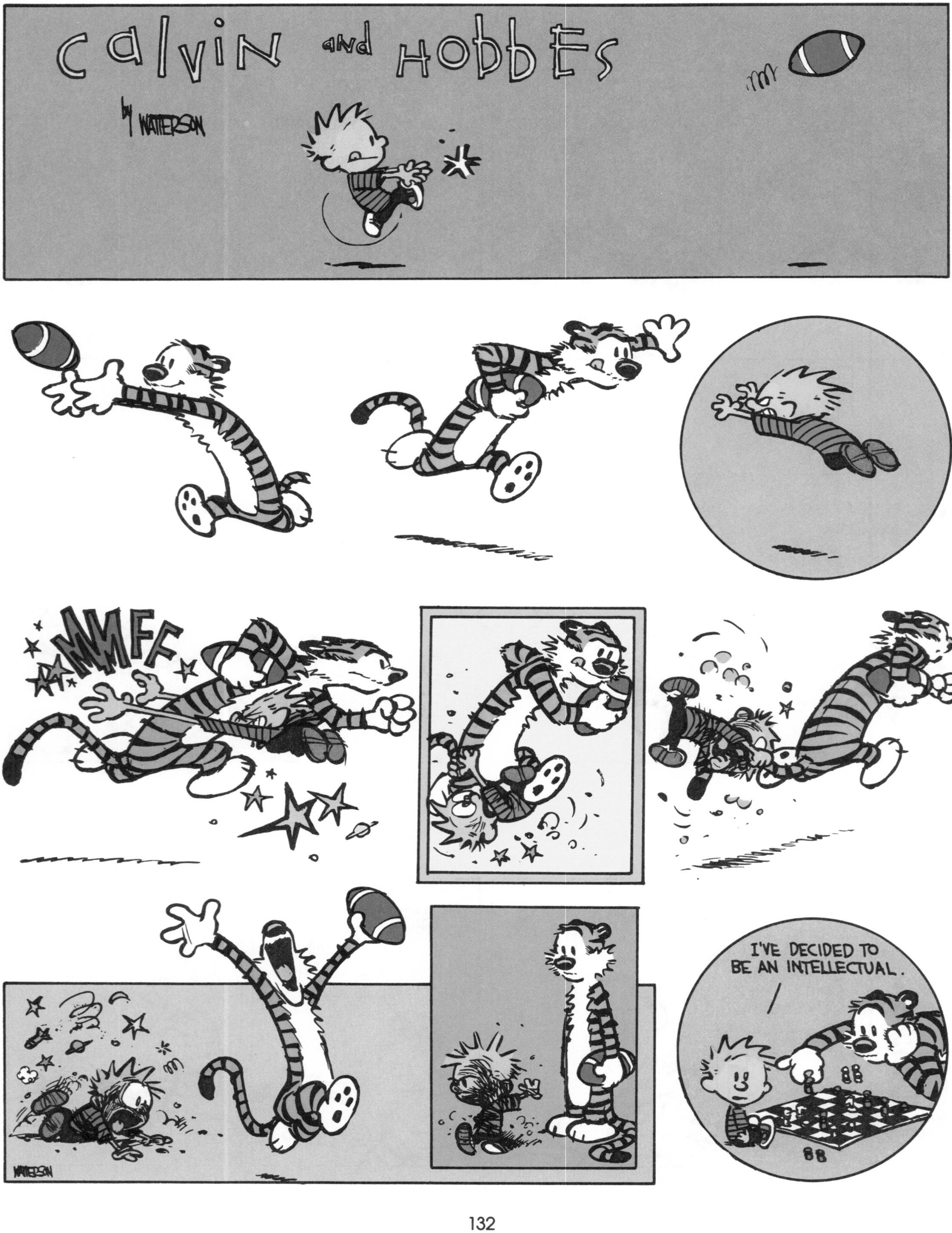
Calvin and HOBBES
by WATTERSON
MMFF
WATTERSON
I'VE DECIDED TO BE AN INTELLECTUAL.

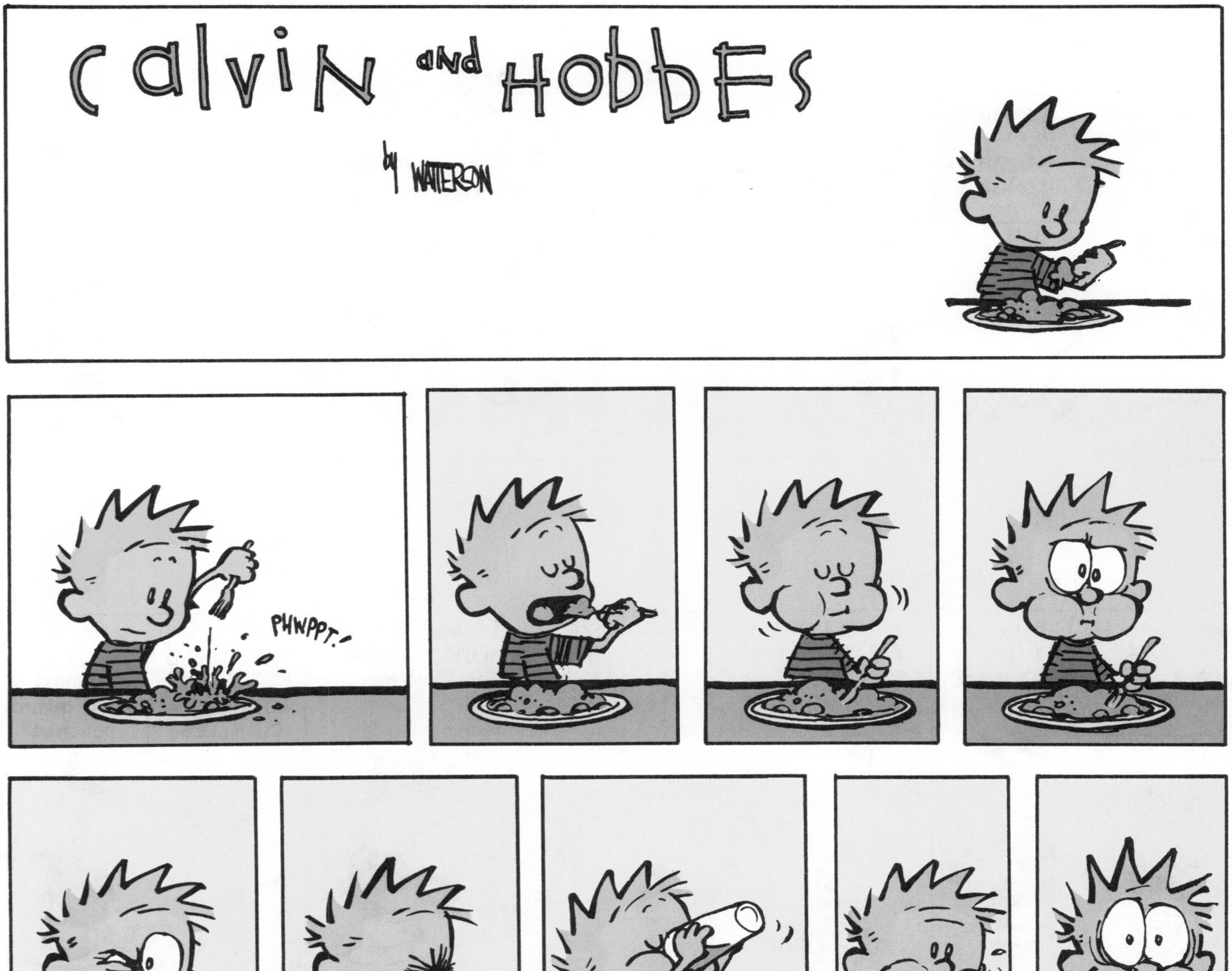
Calvin and HOBBES
by WATTERSON
PHWPPT!
THPWIPBTH
AHHH..
DEAR, SOMETIME I WANT YOU TO LOOK AT THAT DISCOLORED SPOT ON THE RUG. IT SEEMS TO BE GETTING BIGGER ALL THE TIME.
MAY I LEAVE THE TABLE? LIKE RIGHT NOW?

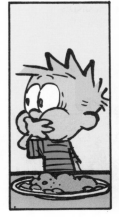

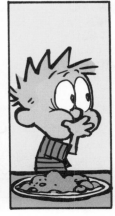

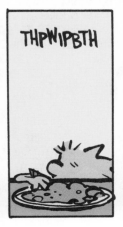

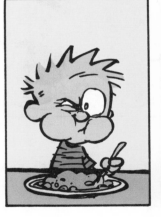

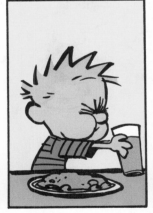

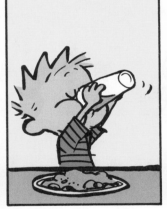

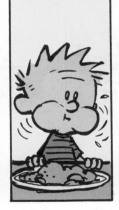

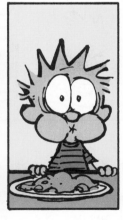

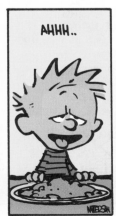

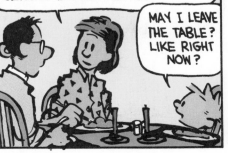

134

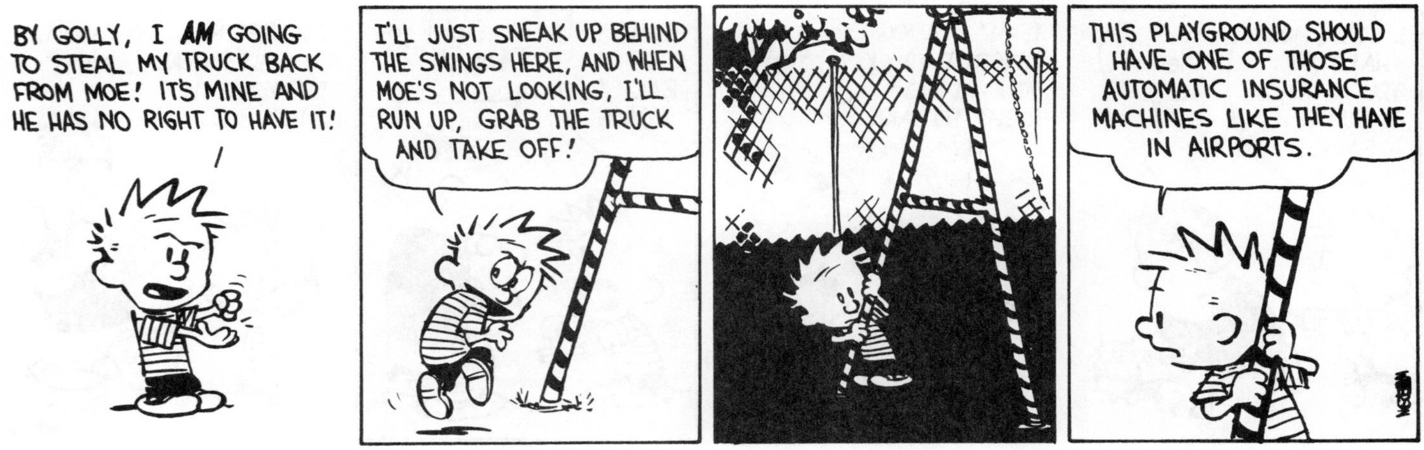
BY GOLLY, I AM GOING TO STEAL MY TRUCK BACK FROM MOE! IT'S MINE AND HE HAS NO RIGHT TO HAVE IT!
I'LL JUST SNEAK UP BEHIND THE SWINGS HERE, AND WHEN MOE'S NOT LOOKING, I'LL RUN UP, GRAB THE TRUCK AND TAKE OFF!
THIS PLAYGROUND SHOULD HAVE ONE OF THOSE AUTOMATIC INSURANCE MACHINES LIKE THEY HAVE IN AIRPORTS.

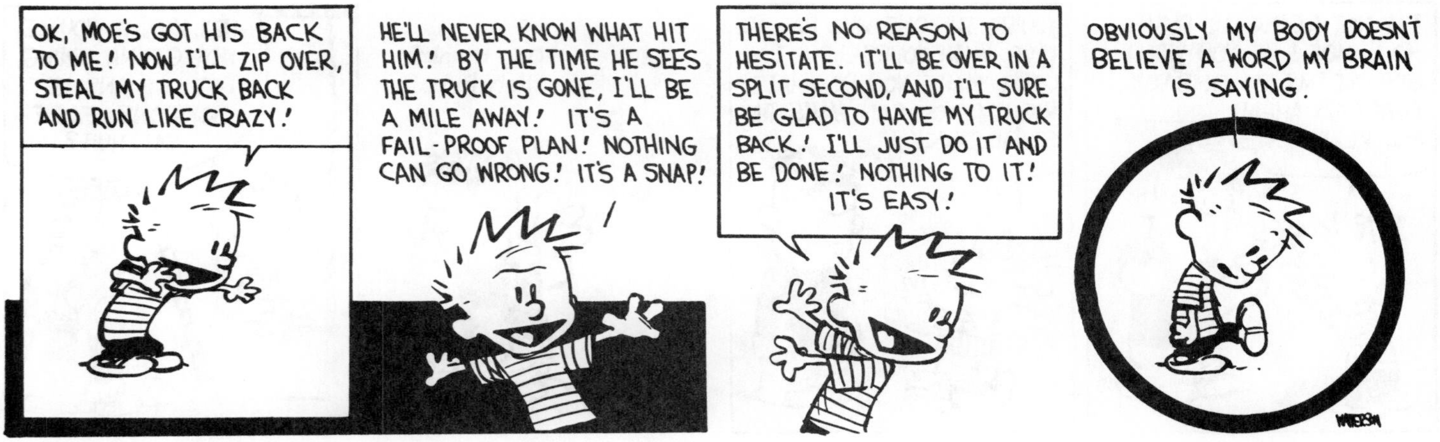
OK, MOE'S GOT HIS BACK TO ME! NOW I'LL ZIP OVER, STEAL MY TRUCK BACK AND RUN LIKE CRAZY!
HE'LL NEVER KNOW WHAT HIT HIM! BY THE TIME HE SEES THE TRUCK IS GONE, I'LL BE A MILE AWAY! IT'S A FAIL-PROOF PLAN! NOTHING CAN GO WRONG! IT'S A SNAP!
THERE'S NO REASON TO HESITATE. IT'LL BE OVER IN A SPLIT SECOND, AND I'LL SURE BE GLAD TO HAVE MY TRUCK BACK! I'LL JUST DO IT AND BE DONE! NOTHING TO IT! IT'S EASY!
OBVIOUSLY MY BODY DOESN'T BELIEVE A WORD MY BRAIN IS SAYING.

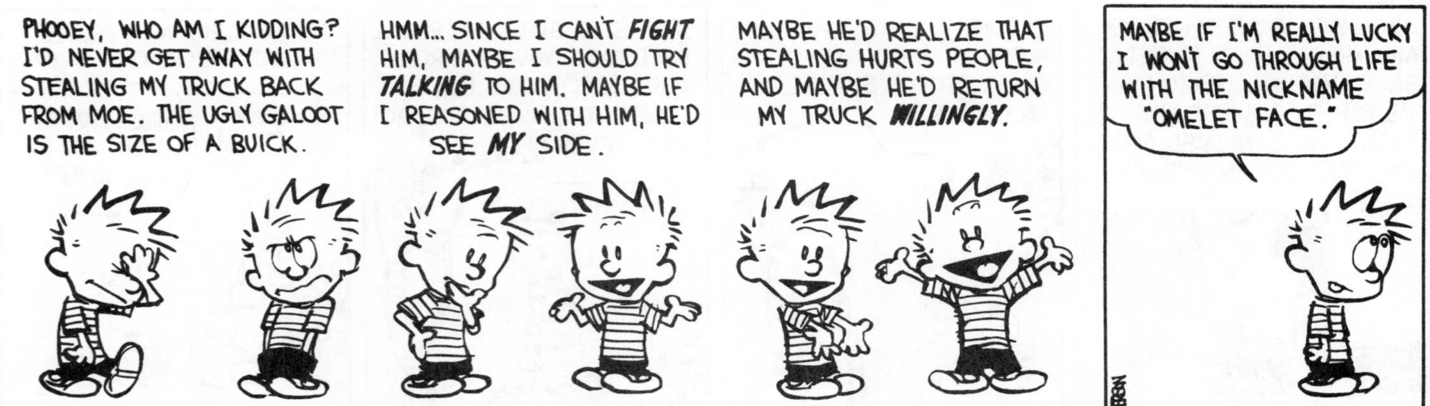
PHOOEY, WHO AM I KIDDING? I'D NEVER GET AWAY WITH STEALING MY TRUCK BACK FROM MOE. THE UGLY GALOOT IS THE SIZE OF A BUICK.
HMM... SINCE I CAN'T FIGHT HIM, MAYBE I SHOULD TRY TALKING TO HIM. MAYBE IF I REASONED WITH HIM, HE'D SEE MY SIDE.
MAYBE HE'D REALIZE THAT STEALING HURTS PEOPLE, AND MAYBE HE'D RETURN MY TRUCK WILLINGLY.
MAYBE IF I'M REALLY LUCKY I WON'T GO THROUGH LIFE WITH THE NICKNAME "OMELET FACE."

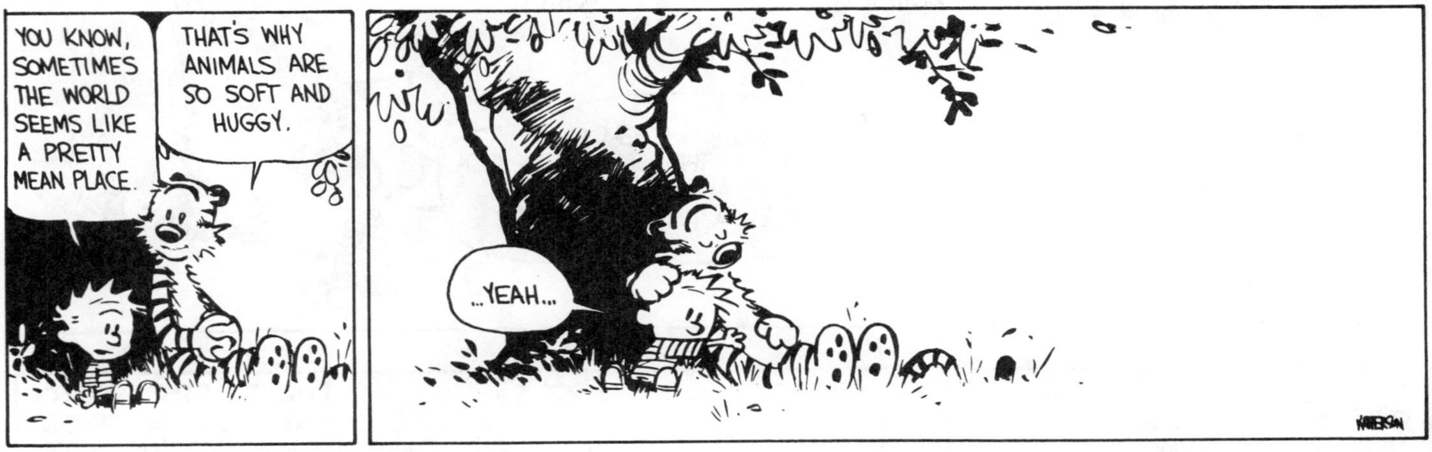
YOU KNOW, SOMETIMES THE WORLD SEEMS LIKE A PRETTY MEAN PLACE.
THAT'S WHY ANIMALS ARE SO SOFT AND HUGGY.
...YEAH...
WATTERSON

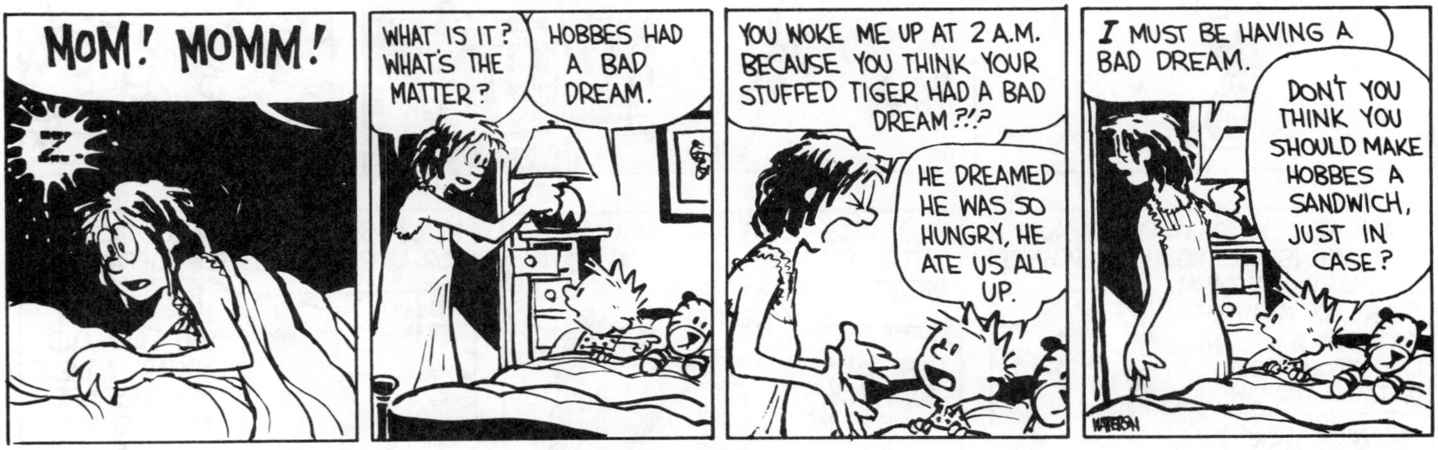
MOM! MOMM!
WHAT IS IT? WHAT'S THE MATTER?
HOBBES HAD A BAD DREAM.
YOU WOKE ME UP AT 2 A.M. BECAUSE YOU THINK YOUR STUFFED TIGER HAD A BAD DREAM?!?
HE DREAMED HE WAS SO HUNGRY, HE ATE US ALL UP.
I MUST BE HAVING A BAD DREAM.
DON'T YOU THINK YOU SHOULD MAKE HOBBES A SANDWICH, JUST IN CASE?
WATTERSON

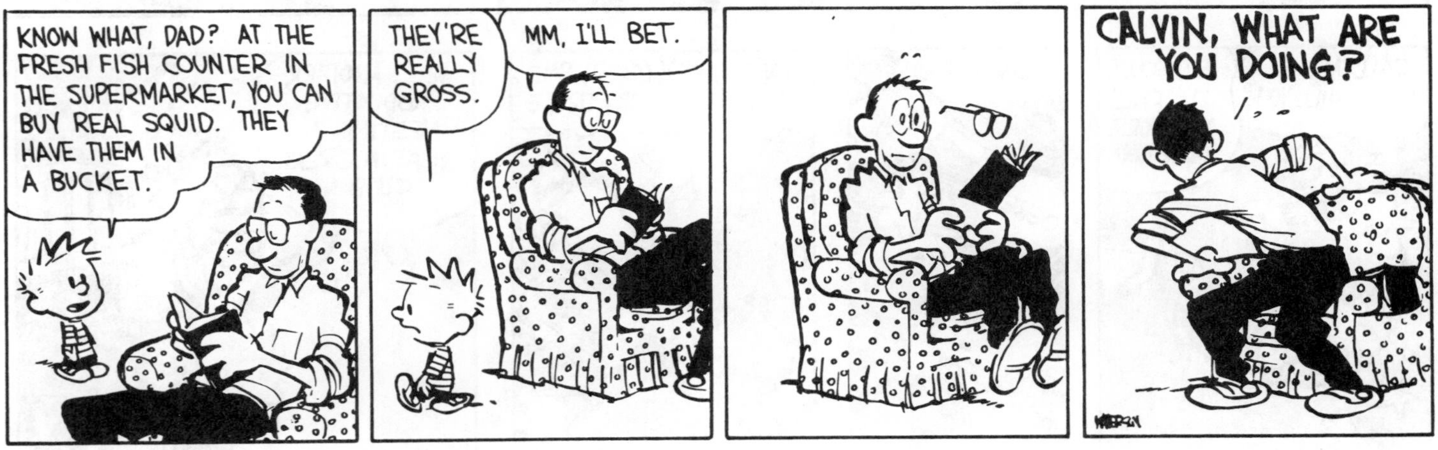
KNOW WHAT, DAD? AT THE FRESH FISH COUNTER IN THE SUPERMARKET, YOU CAN BUY REAL SQUID. THEY HAVE THEM IN A BUCKET.
THEY'RE REALLY GROSS.
MM, I'LL BET.
CALVIN, WHAT ARE YOU DOING?
WATTERSON

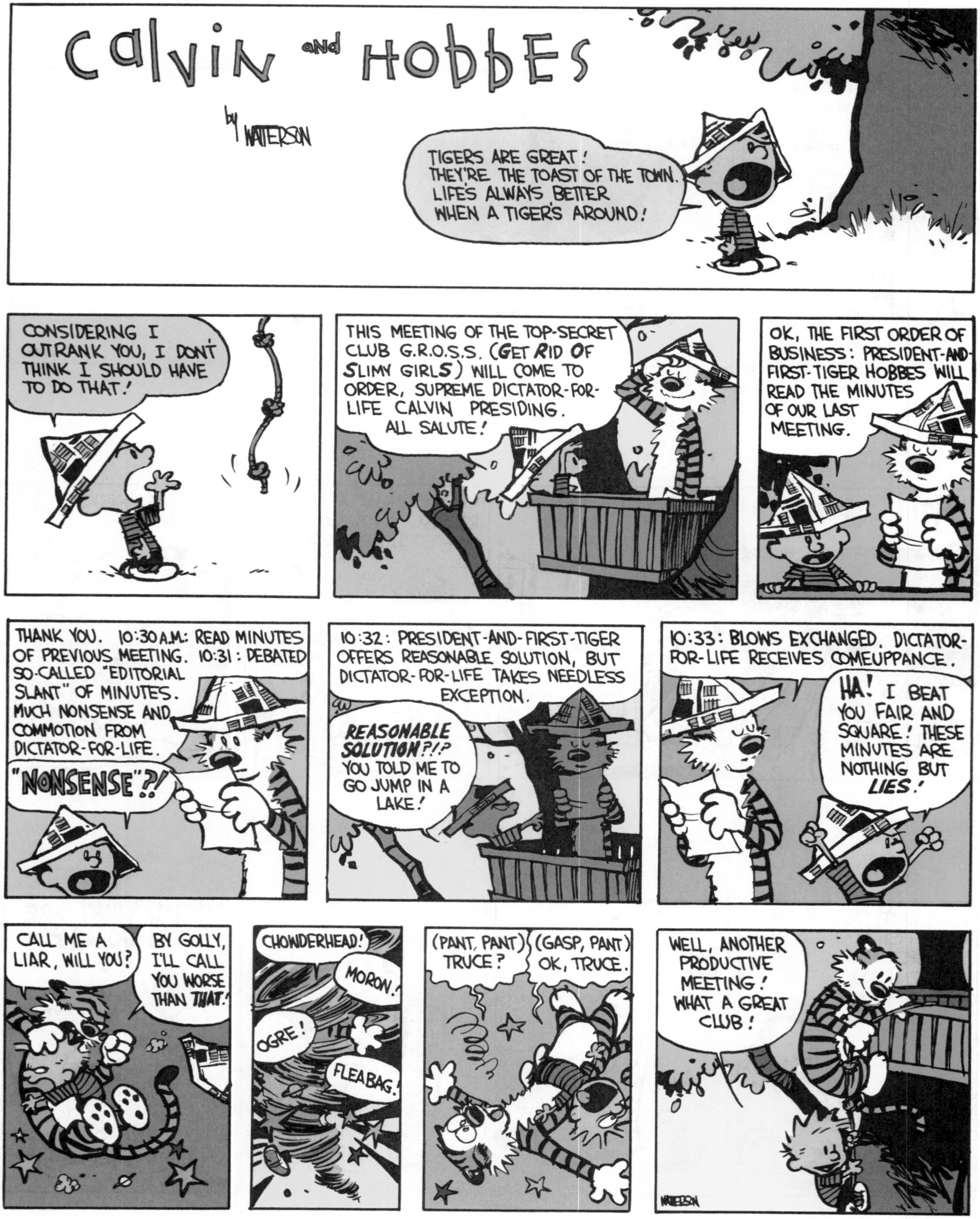
Calvin and Hobbes
by WATTERSON
TIGERS ARE GREAT! THEY'RE THE TOAST OF THE TOWN. LIFE'S ALWAYS BETTER WHEN A TIGER'S AROUND!
CONSIDERING I OUTRANK YOU, I DON'T THINK I SHOULD HAVE TO DO THAT!
THIS MEETING OF THE TOP-SECRET CLUB G.R.O.S.S. (GET RID OF SLIMY GIRLS) WILL COME TO ORDER, SUPREME DICTATOR-FOR-LIFE CALVIN PRESIDING. ALL SALUTE!
OK, THE FIRST ORDER OF BUSINESS: PRESIDENT-AND-FIRST-TIGER HOBBES WILL READ THE MINUTES OF OUR LAST MEETING.
THANK YOU. 10:30 A.M.: READ MINUTES OF PREVIOUS MEETING. 10:31: DEBATED SO-CALLED "EDITORIAL SLANT" OF MINUTES. MUCH NONSENSE AND COMMOTION FROM DICTATOR-FOR-LIFE.
"NONSENSE"?!
10:32: PRESIDENT-AND-FIRST-TIGER OFFERS REASONABLE SOLUTION, BUT DICTATOR-FOR-LIFE TAKES NEEDLESS EXCEPTION.
REASONABLE SOLUTION?!? YOU TOLD ME TO GO JUMP IN A LAKE!
10:33: BLOWS EXCHANGED. DICTATOR-FOR-LIFE RECEIVES COMEUPPANCE.
HA! I BEAT YOU FAIR AND SQUARE! THESE MINUTES ARE NOTHING BUT LIES!
CALL ME A LIAR, WILL YOU?
BY GOLLY, I'LL CALL YOU WORSE THAN THAT!
CHOWDERHEAD!
MORON!
OGRE!
FLEABAG!
(PANT, PANT) TRUCE?
(GASP, PANT) OK, TRUCE.
WELL, ANOTHER PRODUCTIVE MEETING! WHAT A GREAT CLUB!
WATTERSON

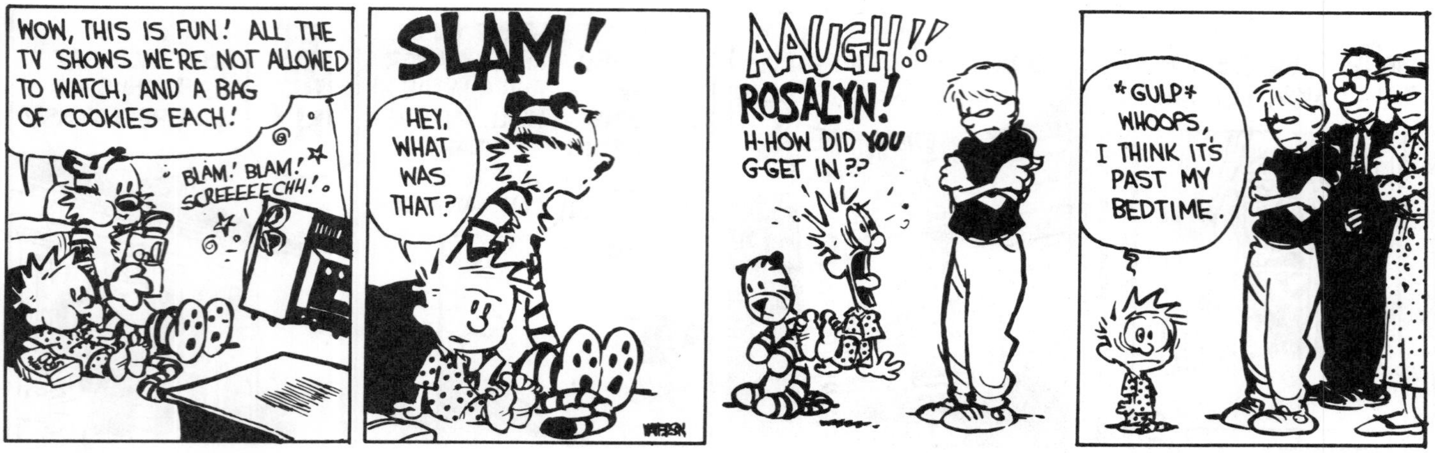
WOW, THIS IS FUN! ALL THE TV SHOWS WE'RE NOT ALLOWED TO WATCH, AND A BAG OF COOKIES EACH!
BLAM! BLAM! SCREEEEECHH!
SLAM!
HEY, WHAT WAS THAT?
AAUGH!!
ROSALYN! H-HOW DID YOU G-GET IN ??
GULP WHOOPS, I THINK IT'S PAST MY BEDTIME.

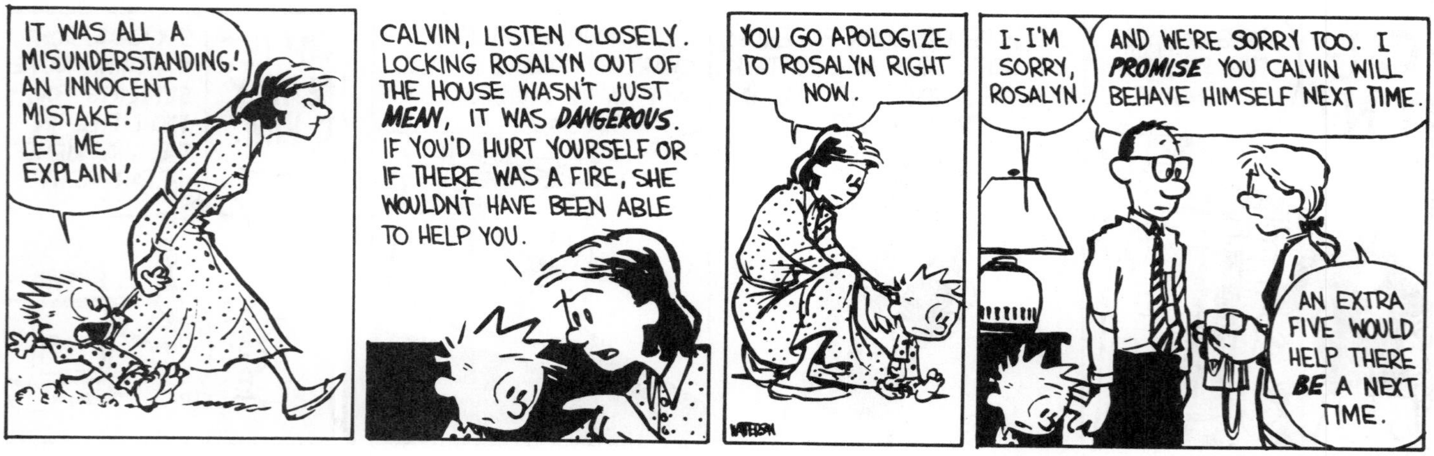
IT WAS ALL A MISUNDERSTANDING! AN INNOCENT MISTAKE! LET ME EXPLAIN!
CALVIN, LISTEN CLOSELY. LOCKING ROSALYN OUT OF THE HOUSE WASN'T JUST MEAN, IT WAS DANGEROUS. IF YOU'D HURT YOURSELF OR IF THERE WAS A FIRE, SHE WOULDN'T HAVE BEEN ABLE TO HELP YOU.
YOU GO APOLOGIZE TO ROSALYN RIGHT NOW.
I-I'M SORRY, ROSALYN.
AND WE'RE SORRY TOO. I PROMISE YOU CALVIN WILL BEHAVE HIMSELF NEXT TIME.
AN EXTRA FIVE WOULD HELP THERE BE A NEXT TIME.

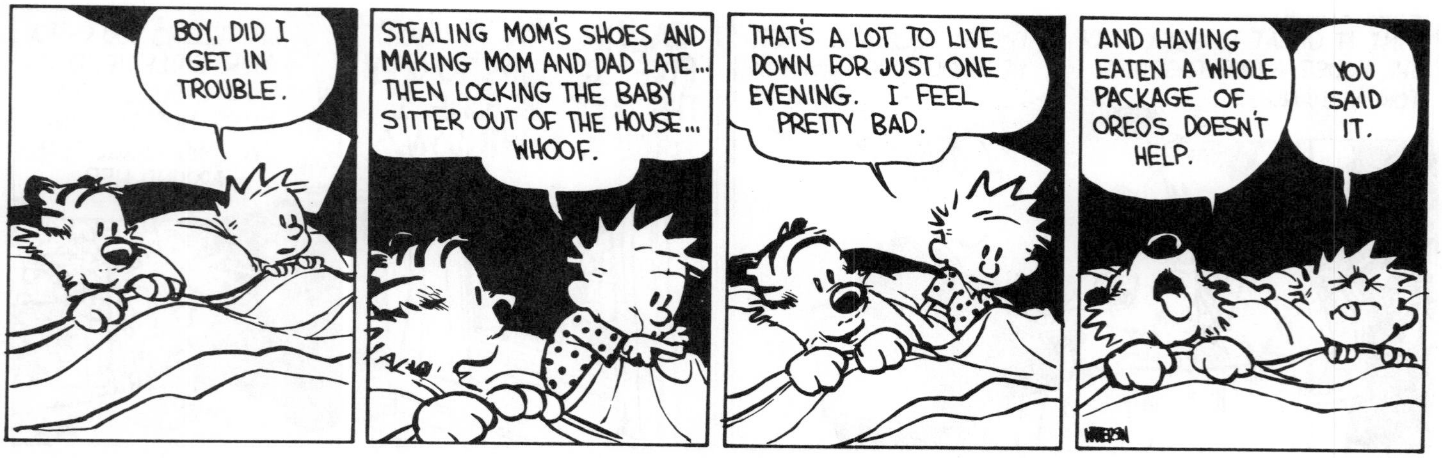
BOY, DID I GET IN TROUBLE.
STEALING MOM'S SHOES AND MAKING MOM AND DAD LATE... THEN LOCKING THE BABY SITTER OUT OF THE HOUSE... WHOOF.
THAT'S A LOT TO LIVE DOWN FOR JUST ONE EVENING. I FEEL PRETTY BAD.
AND HAVING EATEN A WHOLE PACKAGE OF OREOS DOESN'T HELP.
YOU SAID IT.

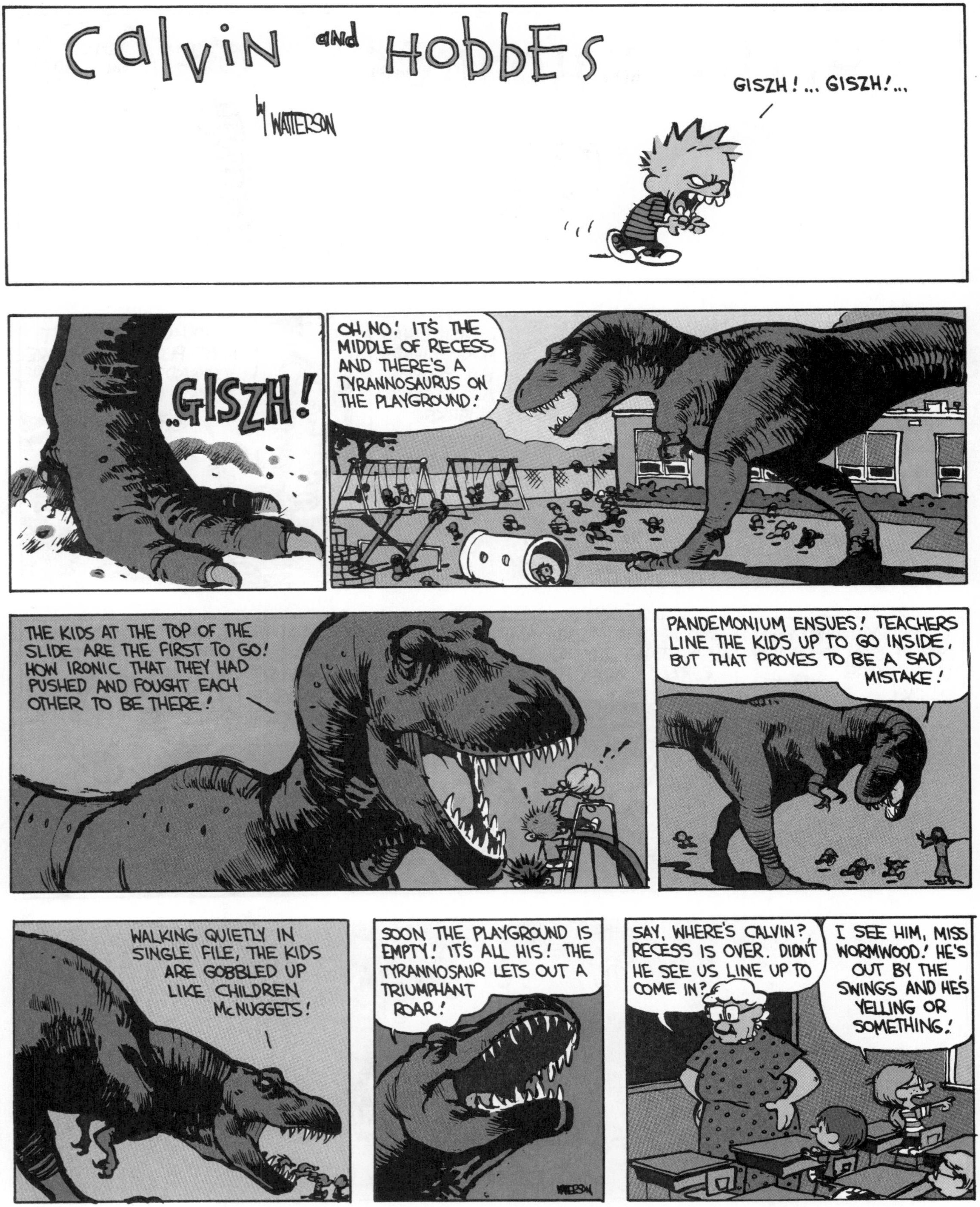
Calvin and HOBBES
by WATTERSON
GISZH! ... GISZH! ...
..GISZH!
OH, NO! IT'S THE MIDDLE OF RECESS AND THERE'S A TYRANNOSAURUS ON THE PLAYGROUND!
THE KIDS AT THE TOP OF THE SLIDE ARE THE FIRST TO GO! HOW IRONIC THAT THEY HAD PUSHED AND FOUGHT EACH OTHER TO BE THERE!
PANDEMONIUM ENSUES! TEACHERS LINE THE KIDS UP TO GO INSIDE, BUT THAT PROVES TO BE A SAD MISTAKE!
WALKING QUIETLY IN SINGLE FILE, THE KIDS ARE GOBBLED UP LIKE CHILDREN McNUGGETS!
SOON THE PLAYGROUND IS EMPTY! IT'S ALL HIS! THE TYRANNOSAUR LETS OUT A TRIUMPHANT ROAR!
SAY, WHERE'S CALVIN? RECESS IS OVER. DIDN'T HE SEE US LINE UP TO COME IN?
I SEE HIM, MISS WORMWOOD! HE'S OUT BY THE SWINGS AND HE'S YELLING OR SOMETHING!
WATTERSON

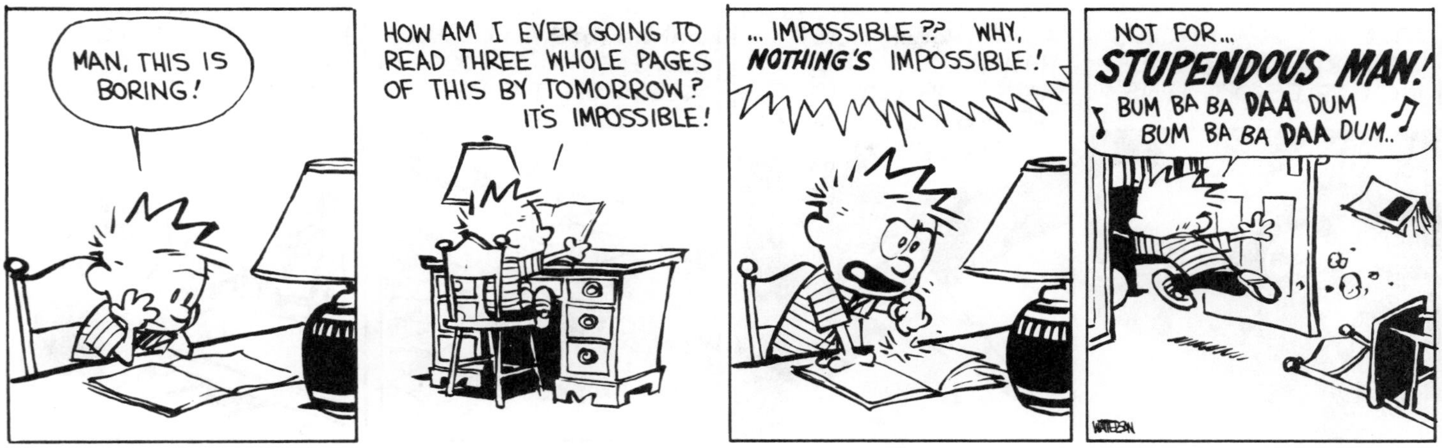
MAN, THIS IS BORING!
HOW AM I EVER GOING TO READ THREE WHOLE PAGES OF THIS BY TOMORROW? IT'S IMPOSSIBLE!
... IMPOSSIBLE?? WHY, NOTHING'S IMPOSSIBLE!
NOT FOR... STUPENDOUS MAN!
BUM BA BA DAA DUM BUM BA BA DAA DUM..
WATTERSON

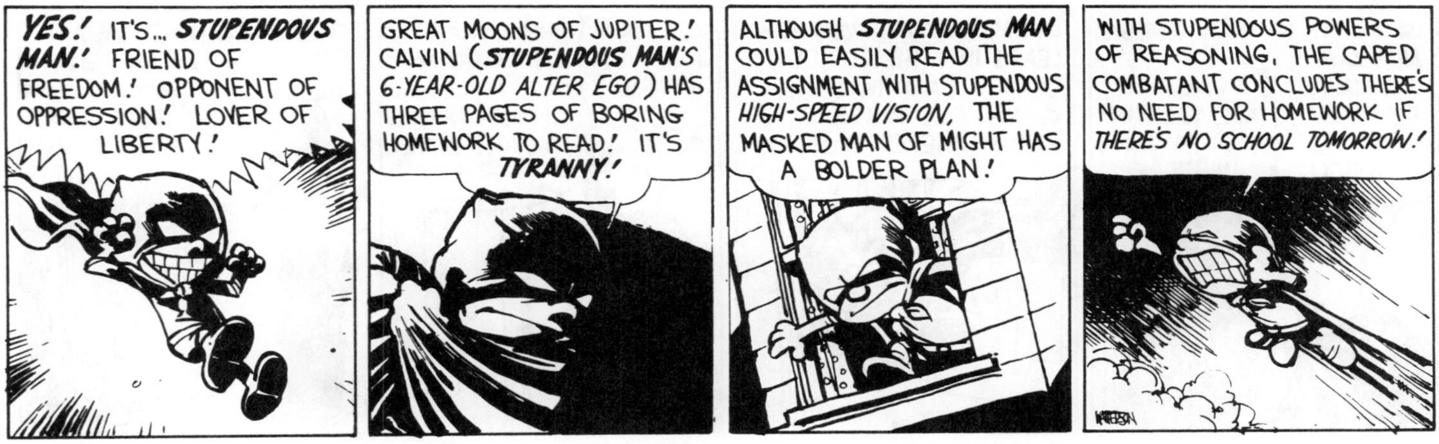
YES! IT'S... STUPENDOUS MAN! FRIEND OF FREEDOM! OPPONENT OF OPPRESSION! LOVER OF LIBERTY!
GREAT MOONS OF JUPITER! CALVIN (STUPENDOUS MAN'S 6-YEAR-OLD ALTER EGO) HAS THREE PAGES OF BORING HOMEWORK TO READ! IT'S TYRANNY!
ALTHOUGH STUPENDOUS MAN COULD EASILY READ THE ASSIGNMENT WITH STUPENDOUS HIGH-SPEED VISION, THE MASKED MAN OF MIGHT HAS A BOLDER PLAN!
WITH STUPENDOUS POWERS OF REASONING, THE CAPED COMBATANT CONCLUDES THERE'S NO NEED FOR HOMEWORK IF THERE'S NO SCHOOL TOMORROW!
WATTERSON

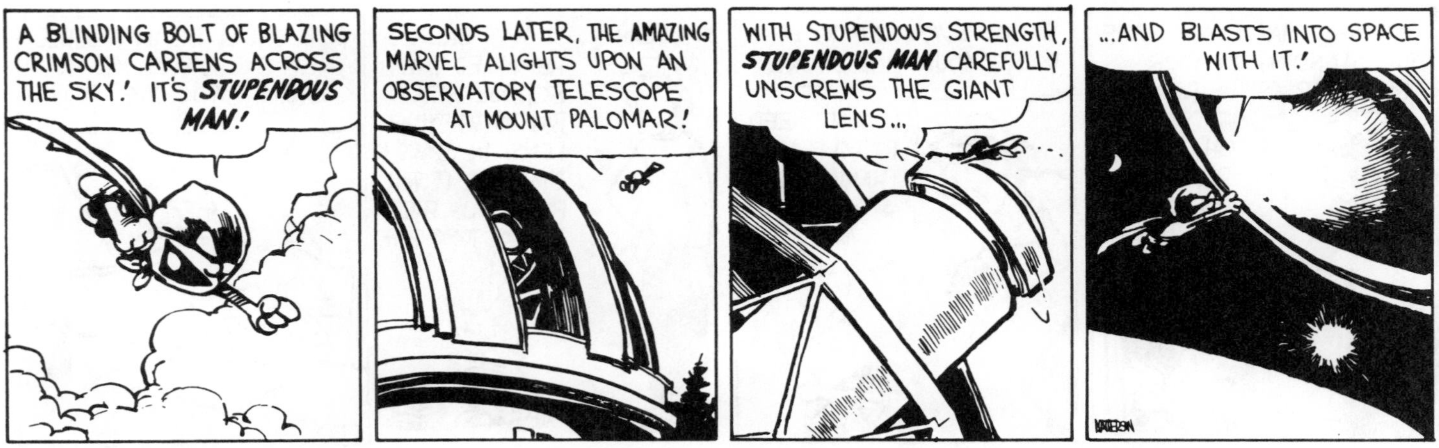
A BLINDING BOLT OF BLAZING CRIMSON CAREENS ACROSS THE SKY! IT'S STUPENDOUS MAN!
SECONDS LATER, THE AMAZING MARVEL ALIGHTS UPON AN OBSERVATORY TELESCOPE AT MOUNT PALOMAR!
WITH STUPENDOUS STRENGTH, STUPENDOUS MAN CAREFULLY UNSCREWS THE GIANT LENS...
...AND BLASTS INTO SPACE WITH IT!
WATTERSON

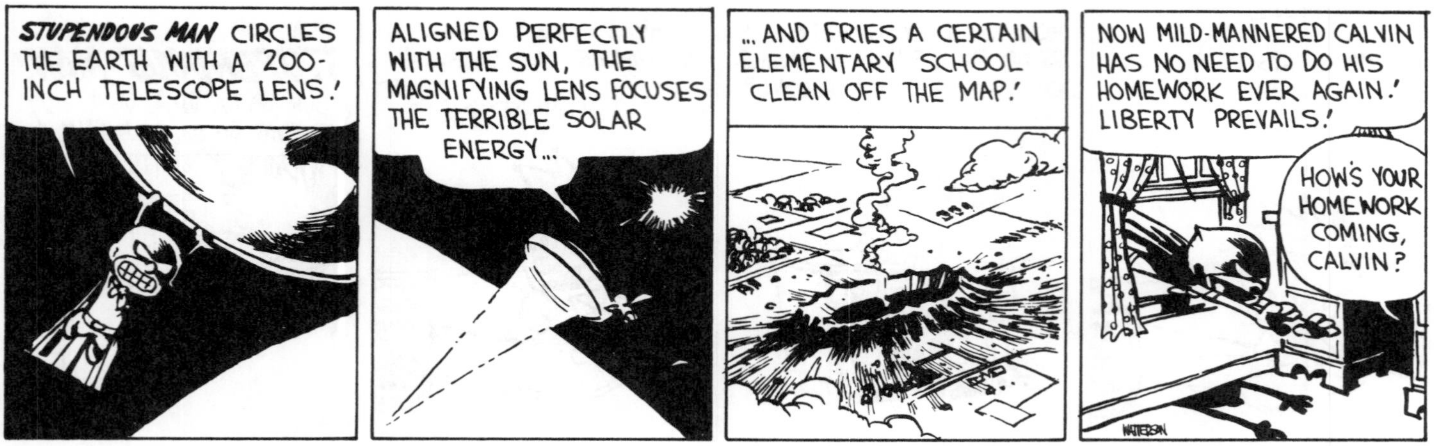
STUPENDOUS MAN CIRCLES THE EARTH WITH A 200-INCH TELESCOPE LENS!
ALIGNED PERFECTLY WITH THE SUN, THE MAGNIFYING LENS FOCUSES THE TERRIBLE SOLAR ENERGY...
...AND FRIES A CERTAIN ELEMENTARY SCHOOL CLEAN OFF THE MAP!
NOW MILD-MANNERED CALVIN HAS NO NEED TO DO HIS HOMEWORK EVER AGAIN! LIBERTY PREVAILS!
HOW'S YOUR HOMEWORK COMING, CALVIN?
WATTERSON

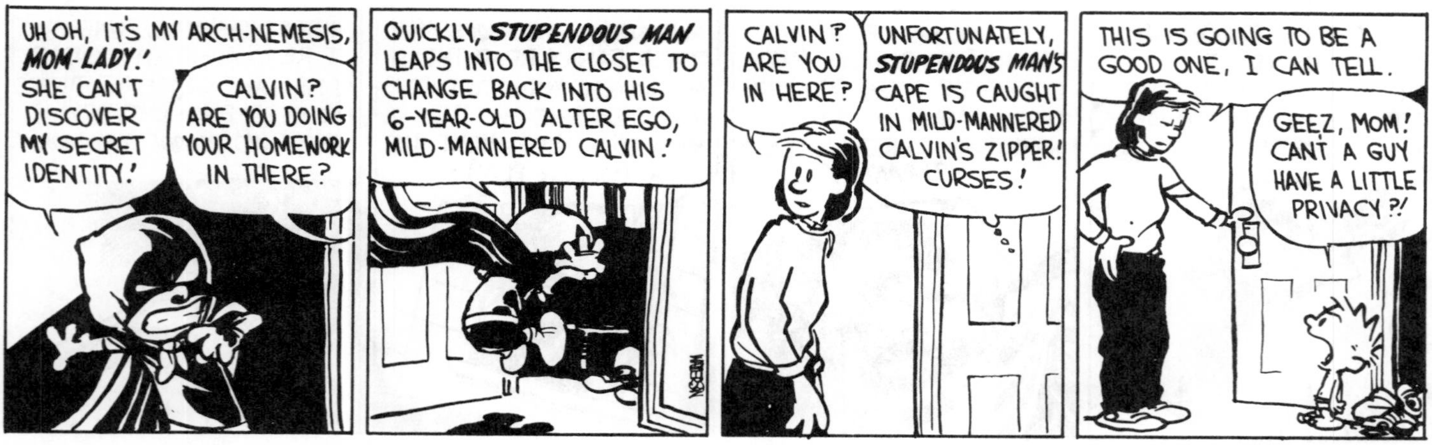
UH OH, IT'S MY ARCH-NEMESIS, MOM-LADY! SHE CAN'T DISCOVER MY SECRET IDENTITY!
CALVIN? ARE YOU DOING YOUR HOMEWORK IN THERE?
QUICKLY, STUPENDOUS MAN LEAPS INTO THE CLOSET TO CHANGE BACK INTO HIS 6-YEAR-OLD ALTER EGO, MILD-MANNERED CALVIN!
WATTERSON
CALVIN? ARE YOU IN HERE?
UNFORTUNATELY, STUPENDOUS MAN'S CAPE IS CAUGHT IN MILD-MANNERED CALVIN'S ZIPPER! CURSES!
THIS IS GOING TO BE A GOOD ONE, I CAN TELL.
GEEZ, MOM! CAN'T A GUY HAVE A LITTLE PRIVACY?!

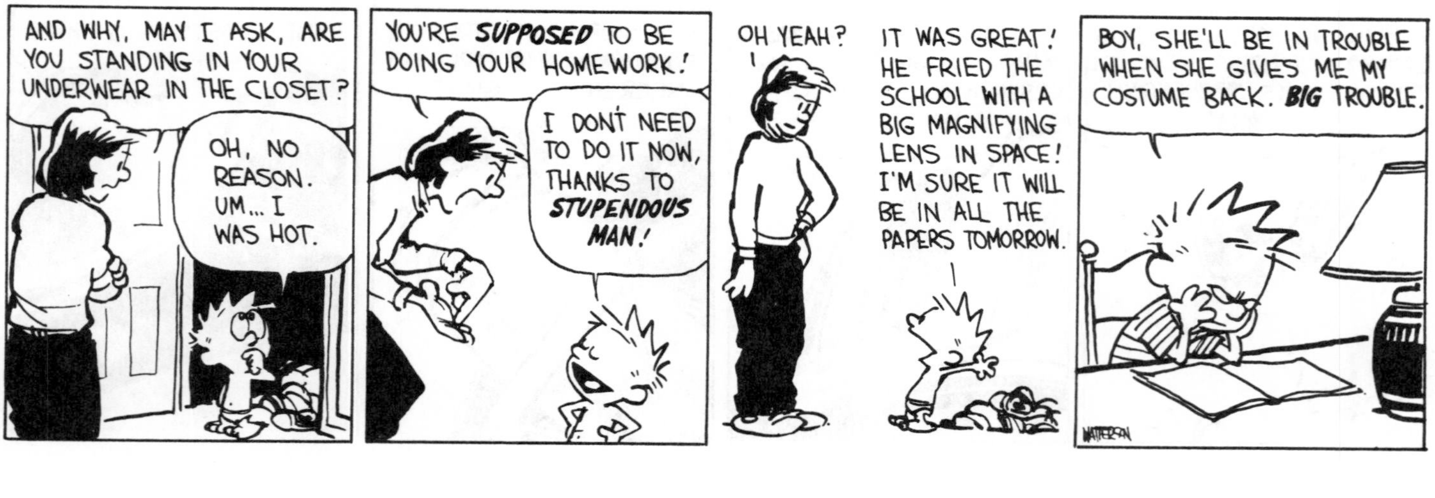
AND WHY, MAY I ASK, ARE YOU STANDING IN YOUR UNDERWEAR IN THE CLOSET?
OH, NO REASON. UM... I WAS HOT.
YOU'RE SUPPOSED TO BE DOING YOUR HOMEWORK!
I DON'T NEED TO DO IT NOW, THANKS TO STUPENDOUS MAN!
OH YEAH?
IT WAS GREAT! HE FRIED THE SCHOOL WITH A BIG MAGNIFYING LENS IN SPACE! I'M SURE IT WILL BE IN ALL THE PAPERS TOMORROW.
BOY, SHE'LL BE IN TROUBLE WHEN SHE GIVES ME MY COSTUME BACK. BIG TROUBLE.
WATTERSON

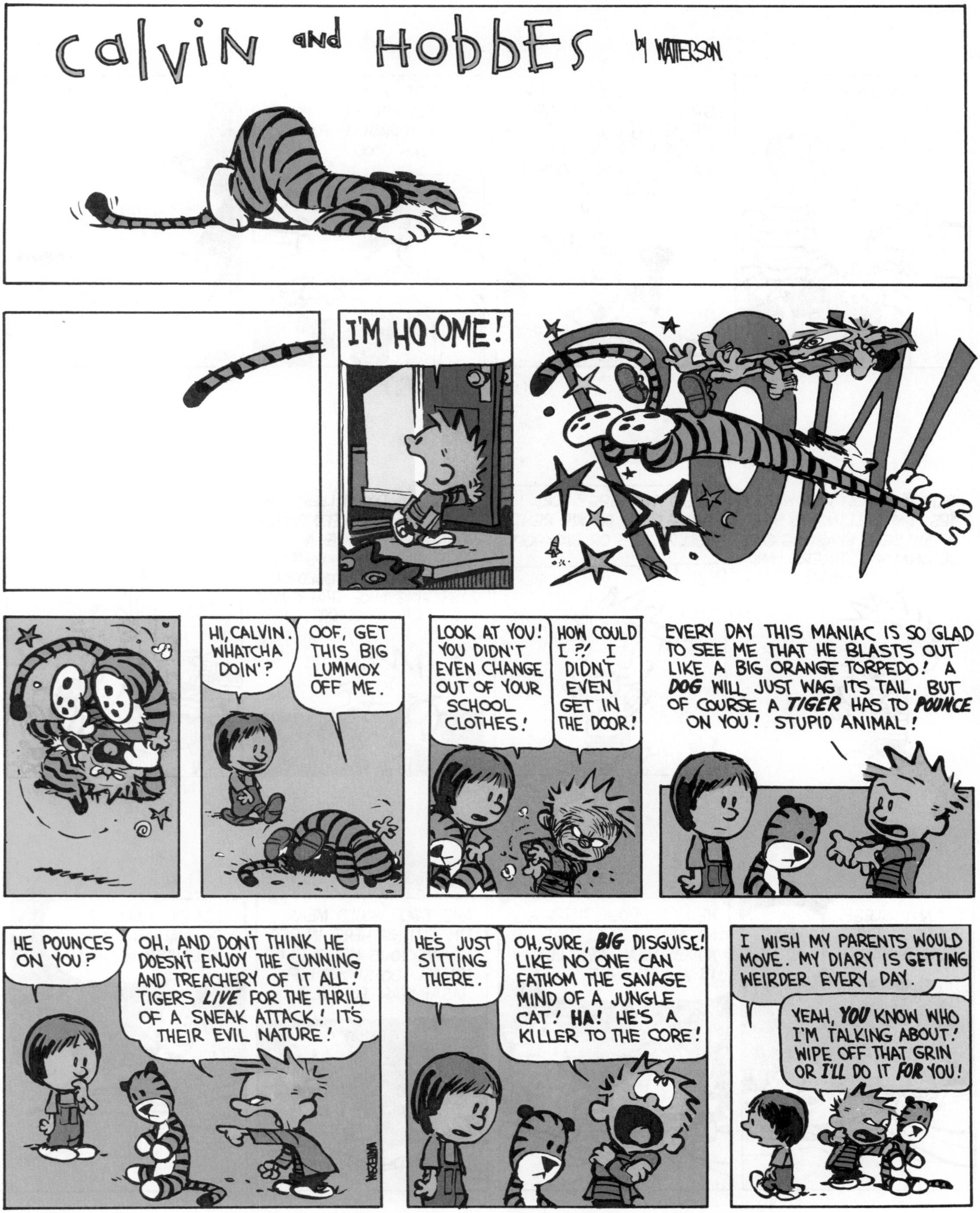

Calvin and Hobbes
by WATTERSON
I'M HO-OME!
POW
HI, CALVIN. WHATCHA DOIN'?
OOF, GET THIS BIG LUMMOX OFF ME.
LOOK AT YOU! YOU DIDN'T EVEN CHANGE OUT OF YOUR SCHOOL CLOTHES!
HOW COULD I ?! I DIDN'T EVEN GET IN THE DOOR!
EVERY DAY THIS MANIAC IS SO GLAD TO SEE ME THAT HE BLASTS OUT LIKE A BIG ORANGE TORPEDO! A DOG WILL JUST WAG ITS TAIL, BUT OF COURSE A TIGER HAS TO POUNCE ON YOU! STUPID ANIMAL!
HE POUNCES ON YOU?
OH, AND DON'T THINK HE DOESN'T ENJOY THE CUNNING AND TREACHERY OF IT ALL! TIGERS LIVE FOR THE THRILL OF A SNEAK ATTACK! IT'S THEIR EVIL NATURE!
WATTERSON
HE'S JUST SITTING THERE.
OH, SURE, BIG DISGUISE! LIKE NO ONE CAN FATHOM THE SAVAGE MIND OF A JUNGLE CAT! HA! HE'S A KILLER TO THE CORE!
I WISH MY PARENTS WOULD MOVE. MY DIARY IS GETTING WEIRDER EVERY DAY.
YEAH, YOU KNOW WHO I'M TALKING ABOUT! WIPE OFF THAT GRIN OR I'LL DO IT FOR YOU!

148

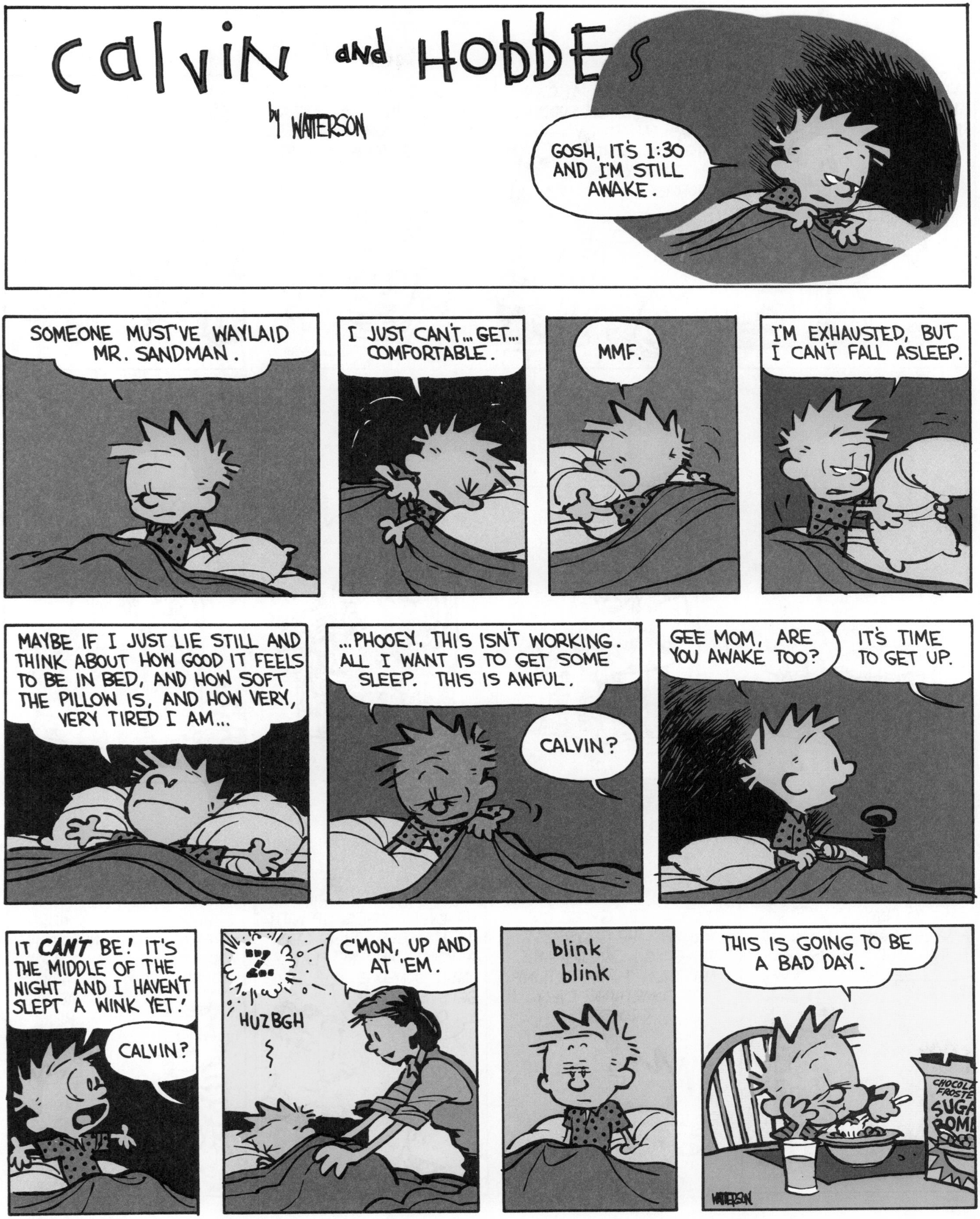
Calvin and HOBBES
by WATTERSON
GOSH, IT'S 1:30 AND I'M STILL AWAKE.
SOMEONE MUST'VE WAYLAID MR. SANDMAN.
I JUST CAN'T... GET... COMFORTABLE.
MMF.
I'M EXHAUSTED, BUT I CAN'T FALL ASLEEP.
MAYBE IF I JUST LIE STILL AND THINK ABOUT HOW GOOD IT FEELS TO BE IN BED, AND HOW SOFT THE PILLOW IS, AND HOW VERY, VERY TIRED I AM...
...PHOOEY, THIS ISN'T WORKING. ALL I WANT IS TO GET SOME SLEEP. THIS IS AWFUL.
CALVIN?
GEE MOM, ARE YOU AWAKE TOO?
IT'S TIME TO GET UP.
IT CAN'T BE! IT'S THE MIDDLE OF THE NIGHT AND I HAVEN'T SLEPT A WINK YET!
CALVIN?
HUZBGH
C'MON, UP AND AT 'EM.
blink
blink
THIS IS GOING TO BE A BAD DAY.
WATTERSON

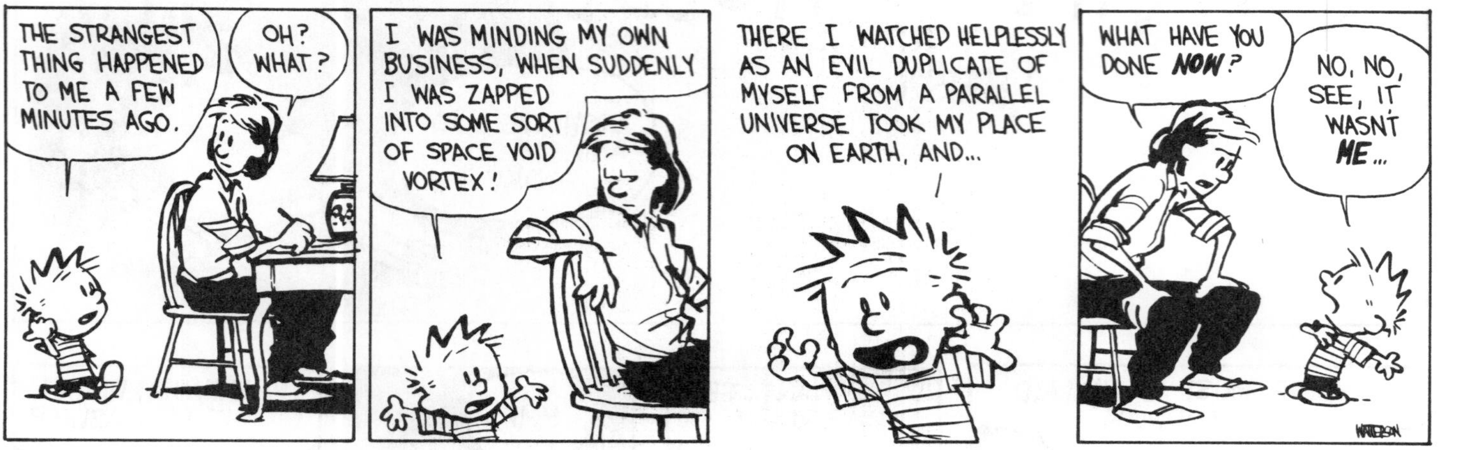
THE STRANGEST THING HAPPENED TO ME A FEW MINUTES AGO.
OH? WHAT?
I WAS MINDING MY OWN BUSINESS, WHEN SUDDENLY I WAS ZAPPED INTO SOME SORT OF SPACE VOID VORTEX!
THERE I WATCHED HELPLESSLY AS AN EVIL DUPLICATE OF MYSELF FROM A PARALLEL UNIVERSE TOOK MY PLACE ON EARTH, AND...
WHAT HAVE YOU DONE NOW?
NO, NO, SEE, IT WASN'T ME...
WATTERSON

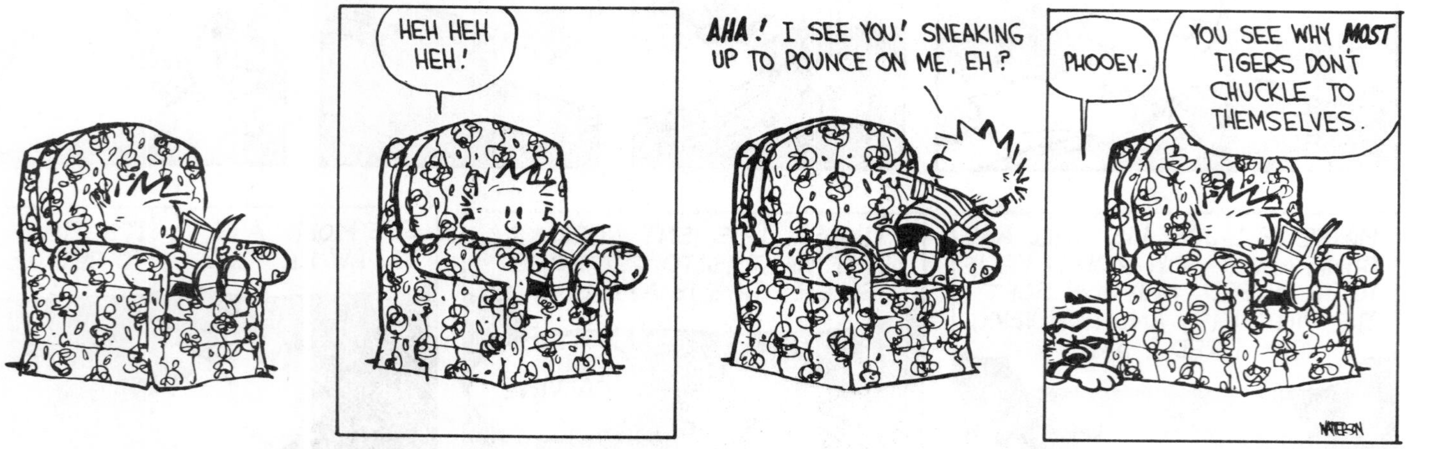
HEH HEH HEH!
AHA! I SEE YOU! SNEAKING UP TO POUNCE ON ME, EH?
PHOOEY.
YOU SEE WHY MOST TIGERS DON'T CHUCKLE TO THEMSELVES.
WATTERSON

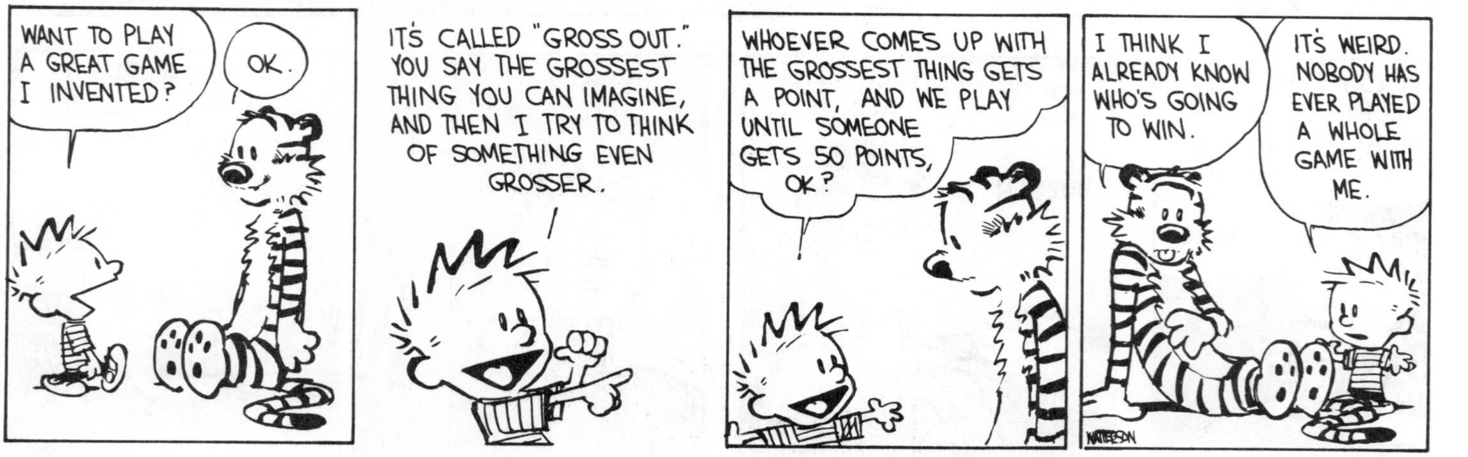
WANT TO PLAY A GREAT GAME I INVENTED?
OK.
IT'S CALLED "GROSS OUT." YOU SAY THE GROSSEST THING YOU CAN IMAGINE, AND THEN I TRY TO THINK OF SOMETHING EVEN GROSSER.
WHOEVER COMES UP WITH THE GROSSEST THING GETS A POINT, AND WE PLAY UNTIL SOMEONE GETS 50 POINTS, OK?
I THINK I ALREADY KNOW WHO'S GOING TO WIN.
IT'S WEIRD. NOBODY HAS EVER PLAYED A WHOLE GAME WITH ME.
WATTERSON

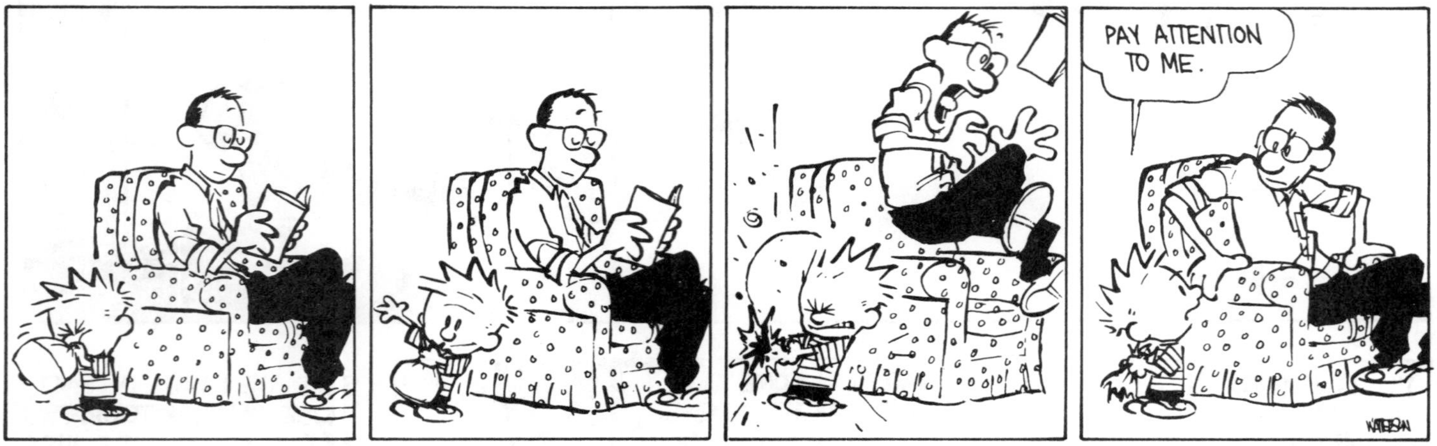

PAY ATTENTION TO ME.

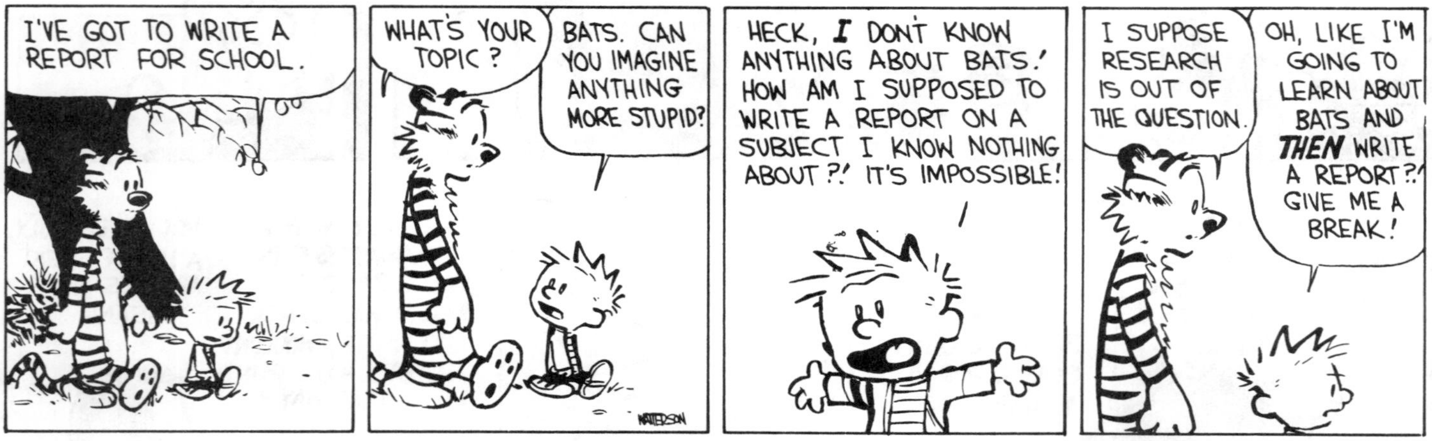

I'VE GOT TO WRITE A REPORT FOR SCHOOL.
WHAT'S YOUR TOPIC?
BATS. CAN YOU IMAGINE ANYTHING MORE STUPID?
HECK, I DON'T KNOW ANYTHING ABOUT BATS! HOW AM I SUPPOSED TO WRITE A REPORT ON A SUBJECT I KNOW NOTHING ABOUT?! IT'S IMPOSSIBLE!
I SUPPOSE RESEARCH IS OUT OF THE QUESTION.
OH, LIKE I'M GOING TO LEARN ABOUT BATS AND THEN WRITE A REPORT?! GIVE ME A BREAK!

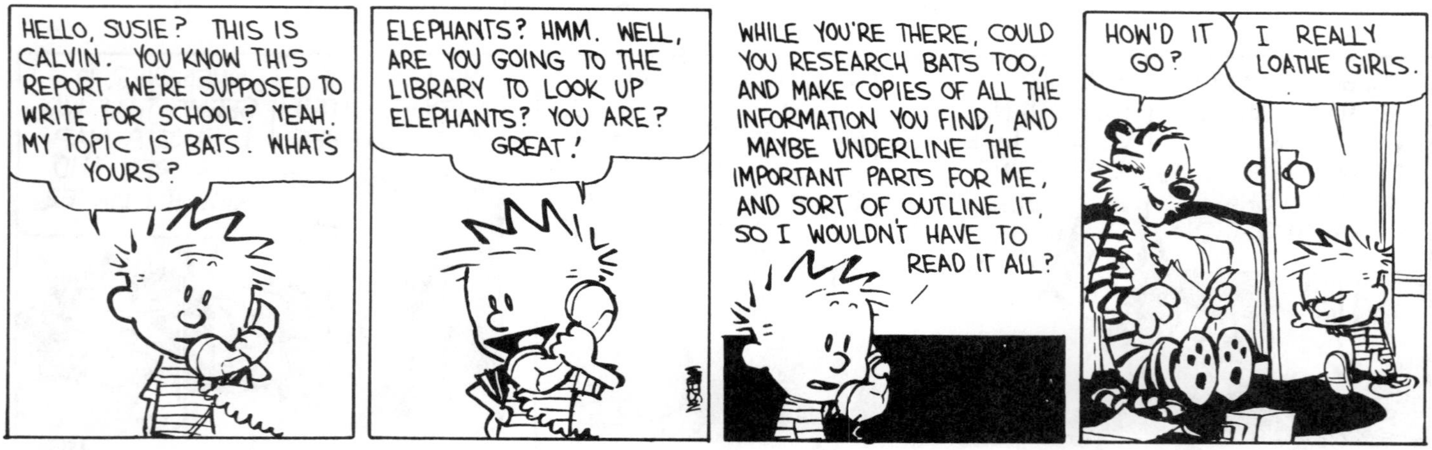

HELLO, SUSIE? THIS IS CALVIN. YOU KNOW THIS REPORT WE'RE SUPPOSED TO WRITE FOR SCHOOL? YEAH. MY TOPIC IS BATS. WHAT'S YOURS?
ELEPHANTS? HMM. WELL, ARE YOU GOING TO THE LIBRARY TO LOOK UP ELEPHANTS? YOU ARE? GREAT!
WHILE YOU'RE THERE, COULD YOU RESEARCH BATS TOO, AND MAKE COPIES OF ALL THE INFORMATION YOU FIND, AND MAYBE UNDERLINE THE IMPORTANT PARTS FOR ME, AND SORT OF OUTLINE IT, SO I WOULDN'T HAVE TO READ IT ALL?
HOW'D IT GO?
I REALLY LOATHE GIRLS.

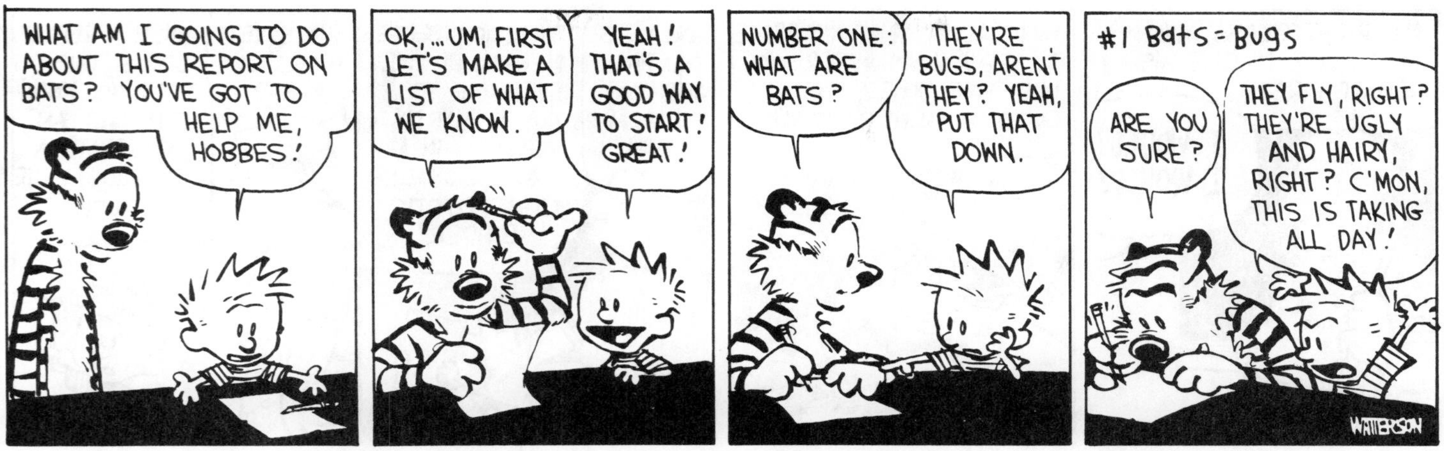
WHAT AM I GOING TO DO ABOUT THIS REPORT ON BATS? YOU'VE GOT TO HELP ME, HOBBES!
OK, ... UM, FIRST LET'S MAKE A LIST OF WHAT WE KNOW.
YEAH! THAT'S A GOOD WAY TO START! GREAT!
NUMBER ONE: WHAT ARE BATS?
THEY'RE BUGS, AREN'T THEY? YEAH, PUT THAT DOWN.
#1 Bats = Bugs
ARE YOU SURE?
THEY FLY, RIGHT? THEY'RE UGLY AND HAIRY, RIGHT? C'MON, THIS IS TAKING ALL DAY!
WATTERSON

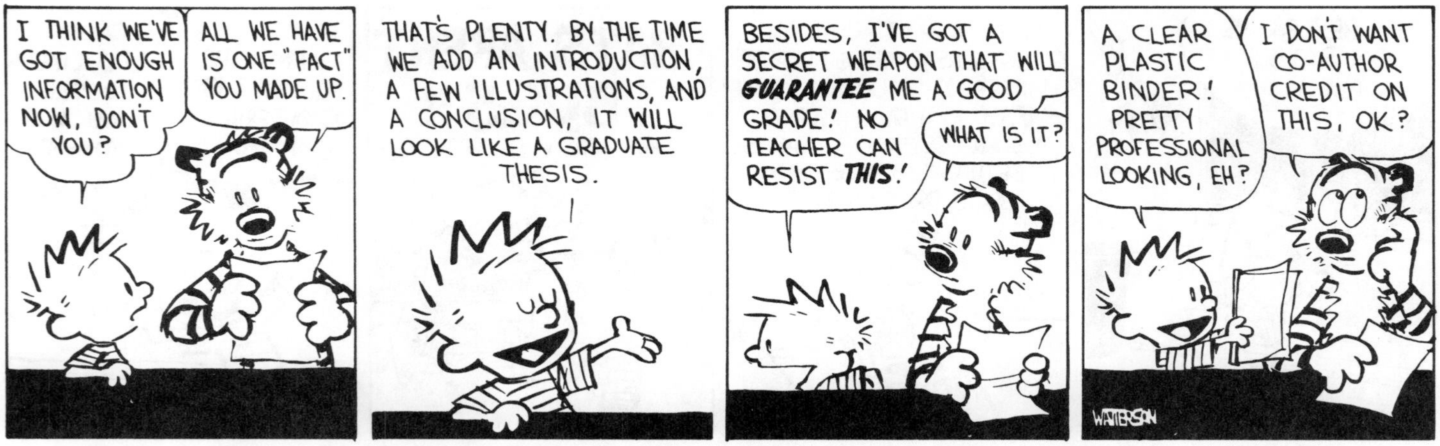
I THINK WE'VE GOT ENOUGH INFORMATION NOW, DON'T YOU?
ALL WE HAVE IS ONE "FACT" YOU MADE UP.
THAT'S PLENTY. BY THE TIME WE ADD AN INTRODUCTION, A FEW ILLUSTRATIONS, AND A CONCLUSION, IT WILL LOOK LIKE A GRADUATE THESIS.
BESIDES, I'VE GOT A SECRET WEAPON THAT WILL GUARANTEE ME A GOOD GRADE! NO TEACHER CAN RESIST THIS!
WHAT IS IT?
A CLEAR PLASTIC BINDER! PRETTY PROFESSIONAL LOOKING, EH?
I DON'T WANT CO-AUTHOR CREDIT ON THIS, OK?
WATTERSON

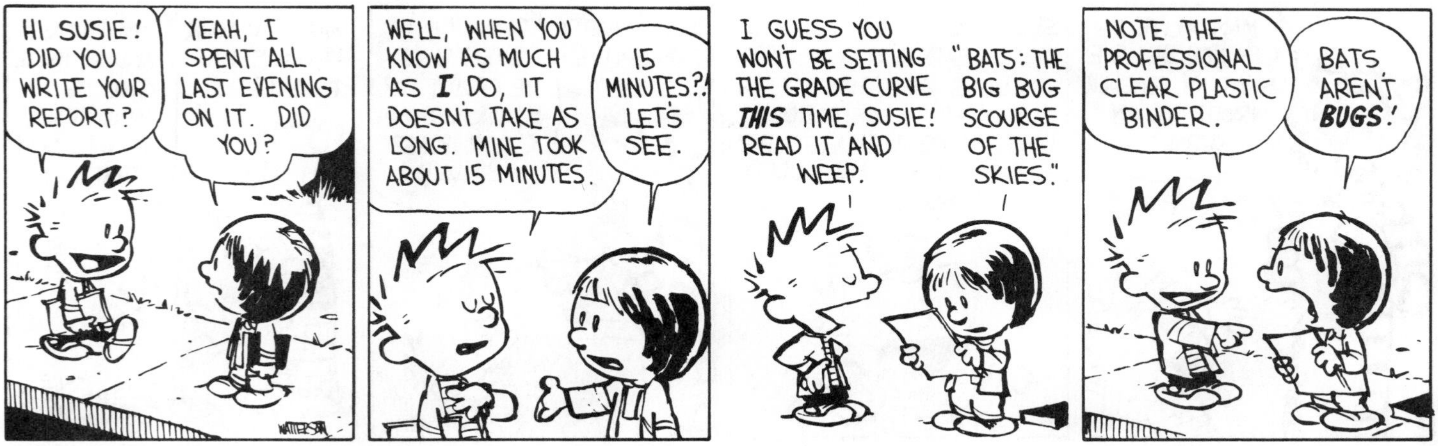
HI SUSIE! DID YOU WRITE YOUR REPORT?
YEAH, I SPENT ALL LAST EVENING ON IT. DID YOU?
WATTERSON
WELL, WHEN YOU KNOW AS MUCH AS I DO, IT DOESN'T TAKE AS LONG. MINE TOOK ABOUT 15 MINUTES.
15 MINUTES?! LET'S SEE.
I GUESS YOU WON'T BE SETTING THE GRADE CURVE THIS TIME, SUSIE! READ IT AND WEEP.
"BATS: THE BIG BUG SCOURGE OF THE SKIES."
NOTE THE PROFESSIONAL CLEAR PLASTIC BINDER.
BATS AREN'T BUGS!

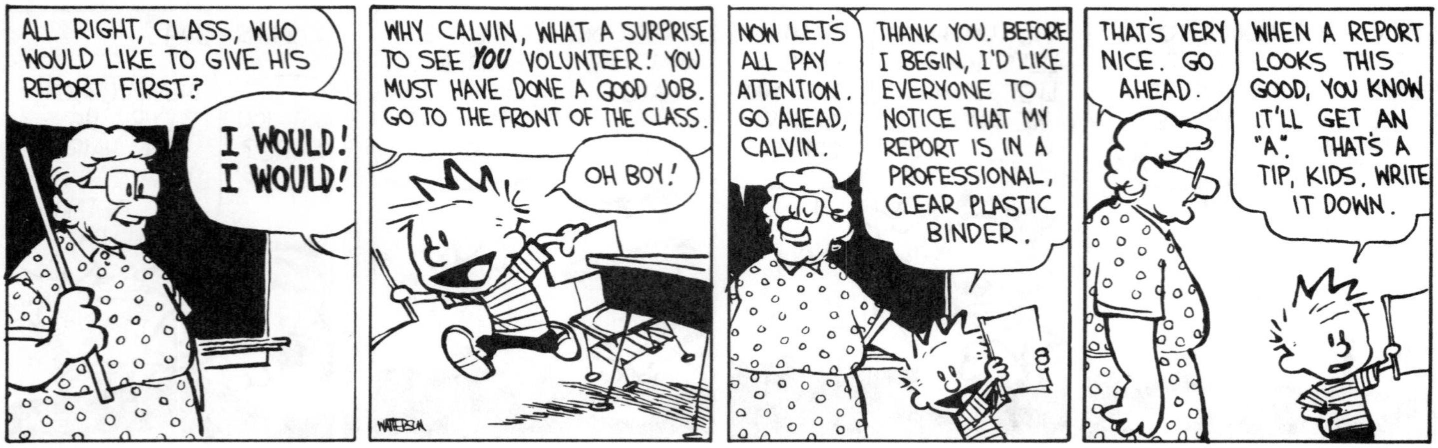
ALL RIGHT, CLASS, WHO WOULD LIKE TO GIVE HIS REPORT FIRST?
I WOULD! I WOULD!
WHY CALVIN, WHAT A SURPRISE TO SEE *YOU* VOLUNTEER! YOU MUST HAVE DONE A GOOD JOB. GO TO THE FRONT OF THE CLASS.
OH BOY!
NOW LET'S ALL PAY ATTENTION. GO AHEAD, CALVIN.
THANK YOU. BEFORE I BEGIN, I'D LIKE EVERYONE TO NOTICE THAT MY REPORT IS IN A PROFESSIONAL, CLEAR PLASTIC BINDER.
THAT'S VERY NICE. GO AHEAD.
WHEN A REPORT LOOKS THIS GOOD, YOU KNOW IT'LL GET AN "A". THAT'S A TIP, KIDS. WRITE IT DOWN.

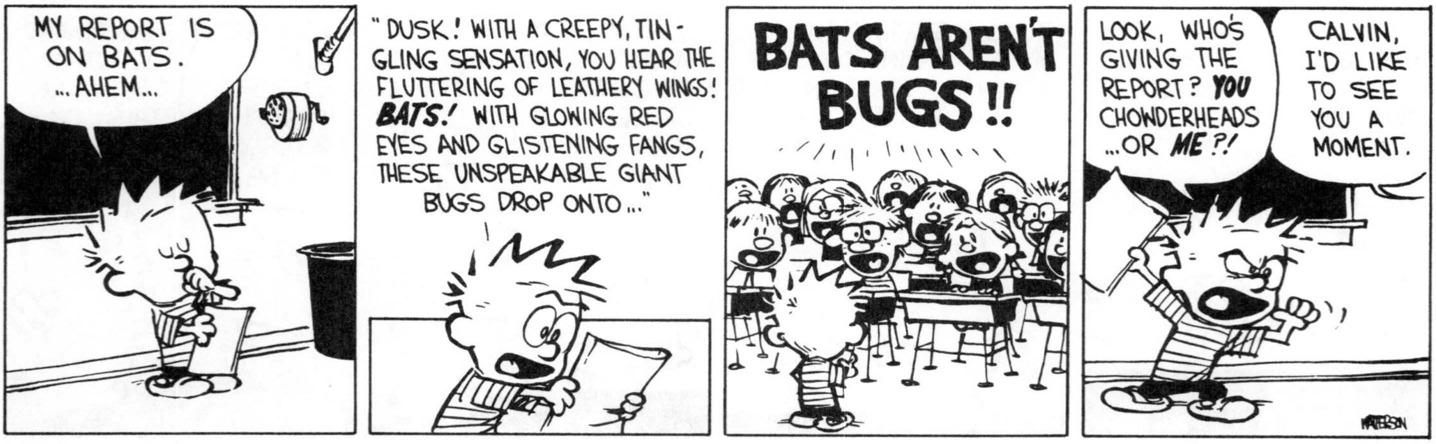
MY REPORT IS ON BATS. ...AHEM...
"DUSK! WITH A CREEPY, TINGLING SENSATION, YOU HEAR THE FLUTTERING OF LEATHERY WINGS! *BATS!* WITH GLOWING RED EYES AND GLISTENING FANGS, THESE UNSPEAKABLE GIANT BUGS DROP ONTO..."
BATS AREN'T BUGS!!
LOOK, WHO'S GIVING THE REPORT? *YOU* CHOWDERHEADS ...OR *ME*?!
CALVIN, I'D LIKE TO SEE YOU A MOMENT.

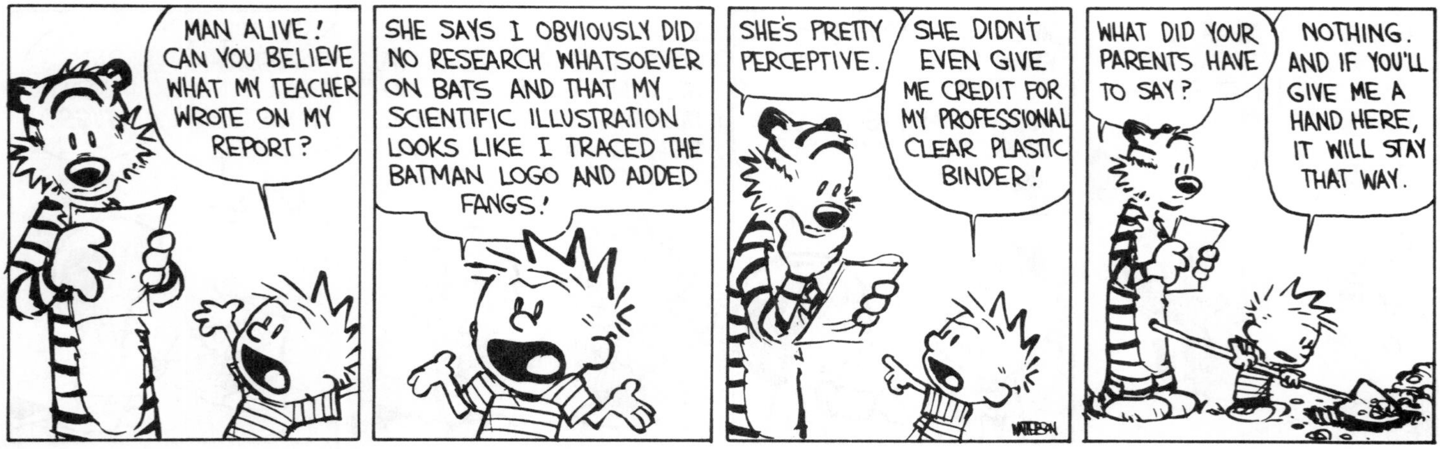
MAN ALIVE! CAN YOU BELIEVE WHAT MY TEACHER WROTE ON MY REPORT?
SHE SAYS I OBVIOUSLY DID NO RESEARCH WHATSOEVER ON BATS AND THAT MY SCIENTIFIC ILLUSTRATION LOOKS LIKE I TRACED THE BATMAN LOGO AND ADDED FANGS!
SHE'S PRETTY PERCEPTIVE.
SHE DIDN'T EVEN GIVE ME CREDIT FOR MY PROFESSIONAL CLEAR PLASTIC BINDER!
WHAT DID YOUR PARENTS HAVE TO SAY?
NOTHING. AND IF YOU'LL GIVE ME A HAND HERE, IT WILL STAY THAT WAY.

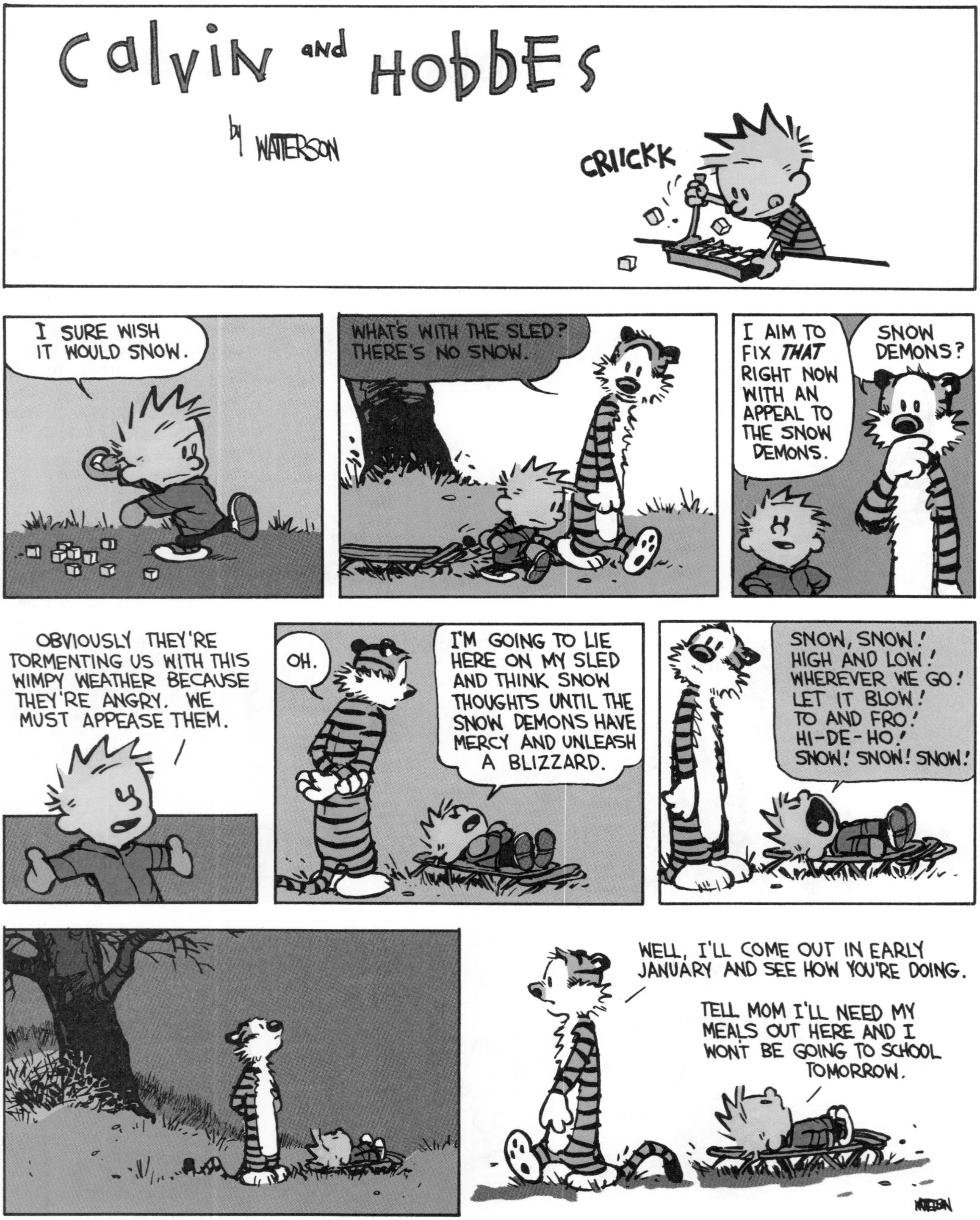
Calvin and Hobbes
by WATTERSON
CRIICKK
I SURE WISH IT WOULD SNOW.
WHAT'S WITH THE SLED? THERE'S NO SNOW.
I AIM TO FIX THAT RIGHT NOW WITH AN APPEAL TO THE SNOW DEMONS.
SNOW DEMONS?
OBVIOUSLY THEY'RE TORMENTING US WITH THIS WIMPY WEATHER BECAUSE THEY'RE ANGRY. WE MUST APPEASE THEM.
OH.
I'M GOING TO LIE HERE ON MY SLED AND THINK SNOW THOUGHTS UNTIL THE SNOW DEMONS HAVE MERCY AND UNLEASH A BLIZZARD.
SNOW, SNOW! HIGH AND LOW! WHEREVER WE GO! LET IT BLOW! TO AND FRO! HI-DE-HO! SNOW! SNOW! SNOW!
WELL, I'LL COME OUT IN EARLY JANUARY AND SEE HOW YOU'RE DOING.
TELL MOM I'LL NEED MY MEALS OUT HERE AND I WON'T BE GOING TO SCHOOL TOMORROW.
WATTERSON

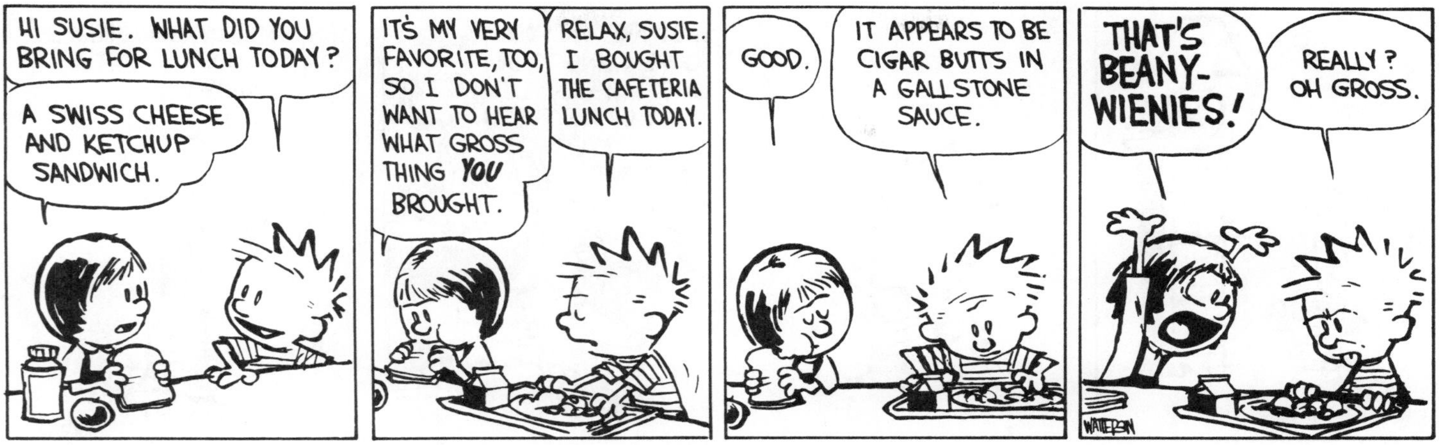
HI SUSIE. WHAT DID YOU BRING FOR LUNCH TODAY?
A SWISS CHEESE AND KETCHUP SANDWICH.
IT'S MY VERY FAVORITE, TOO, SO I DON'T WANT TO HEAR WHAT GROSS THING *YOU* BROUGHT.
RELAX, SUSIE. I BOUGHT THE CAFETERIA LUNCH TODAY.
GOOD.
IT APPEARS TO BE CIGAR BUTTS IN A GALLSTONE SAUCE.
THAT'S BEANY-WIENIES!
REALLY? OH GROSS.

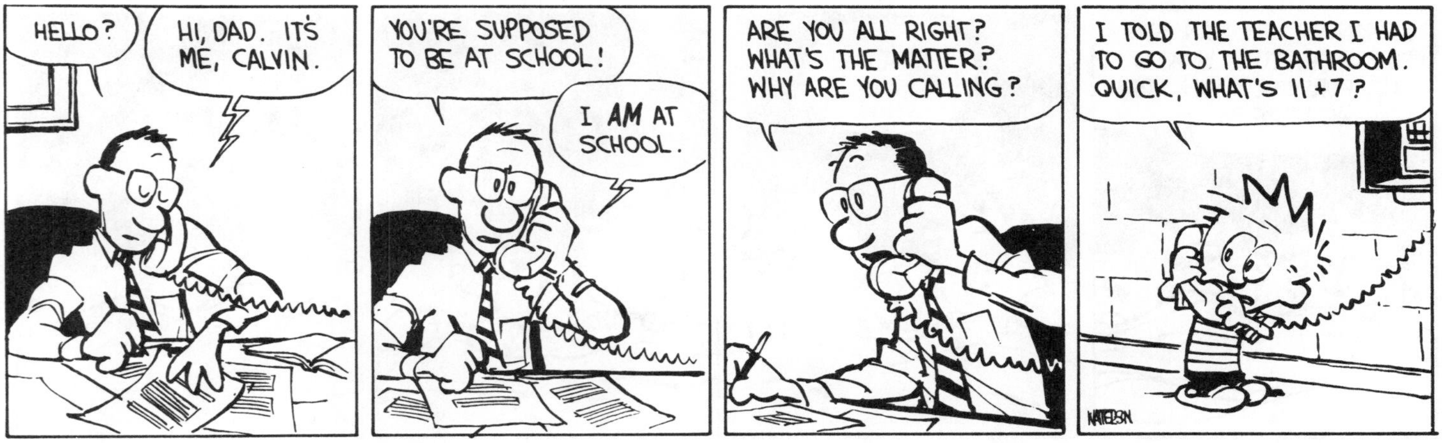
HELLO?
HI, DAD. IT'S ME, CALVIN.
YOU'RE SUPPOSED TO BE AT SCHOOL!
I *AM* AT SCHOOL.
ARE YOU ALL RIGHT? WHAT'S THE MATTER? WHY ARE YOU CALLING?
I TOLD THE TEACHER I HAD TO GO TO THE BATHROOM. QUICK, WHAT'S 11 + 7?

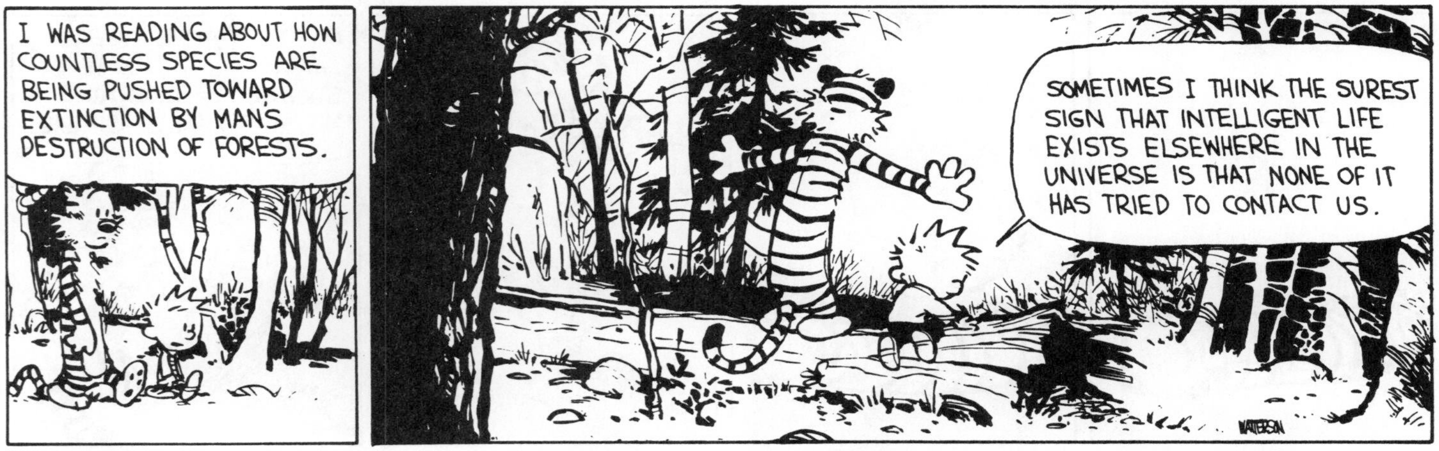
I WAS READING ABOUT HOW COUNTLESS SPECIES ARE BEING PUSHED TOWARD EXTINCTION BY MAN'S DESTRUCTION OF FORESTS.
SOMETIMES I THINK THE SUREST SIGN THAT INTELLIGENT LIFE EXISTS ELSEWHERE IN THE UNIVERSE IS THAT NONE OF IT HAS TRIED TO CONTACT US.

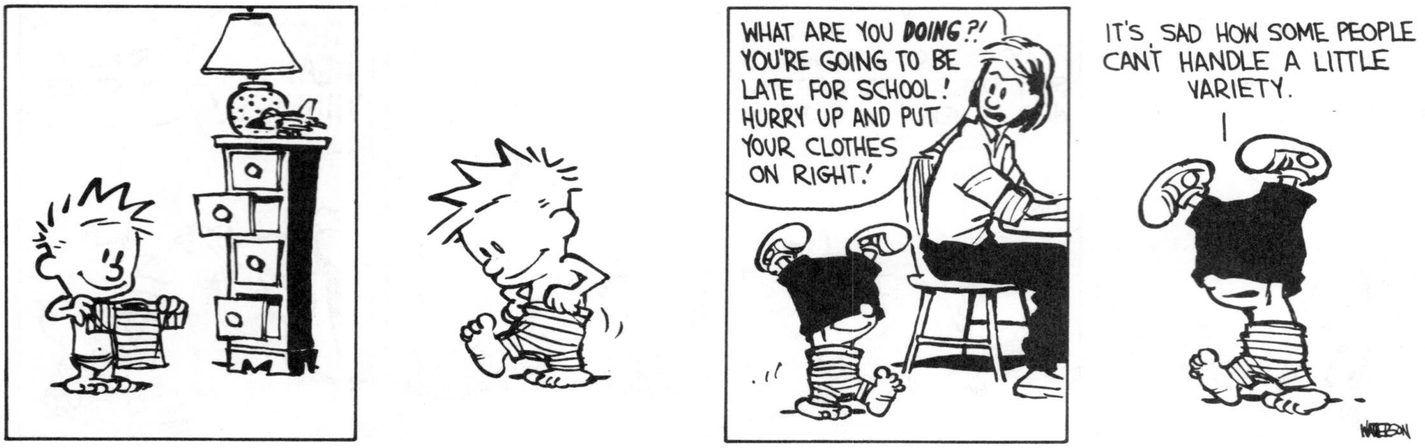
WHAT ARE YOU DOING?! YOU'RE GOING TO BE LATE FOR SCHOOL! HURRY UP AND PUT YOUR CLOTHES ON RIGHT!
IT'S SAD HOW SOME PEOPLE CAN'T HANDLE A LITTLE VARIETY.

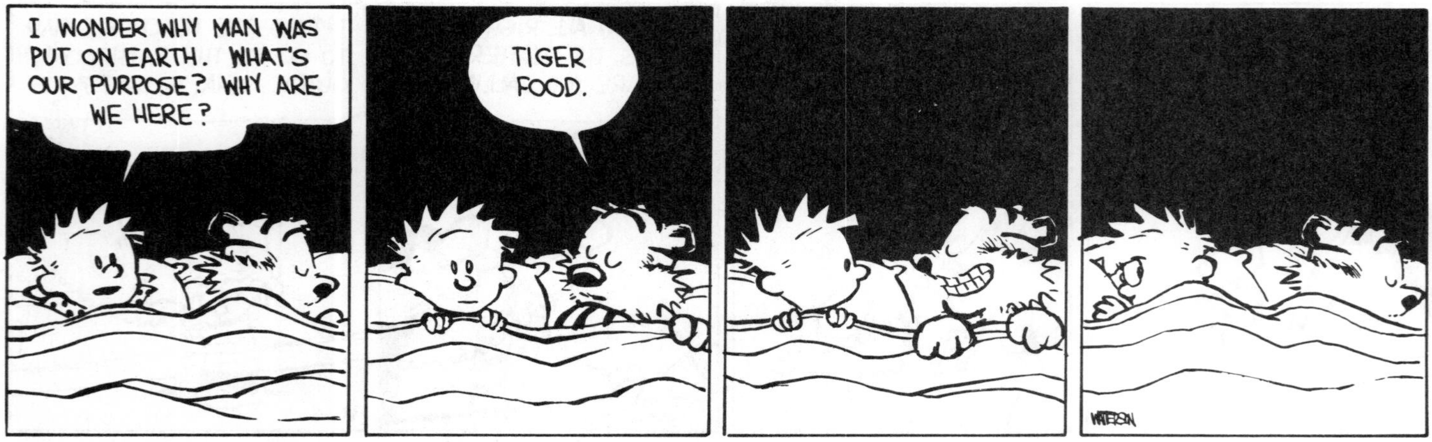
I WONDER WHY MAN WAS PUT ON EARTH. WHAT'S OUR PURPOSE? WHY ARE WE HERE?
TIGER FOOD.

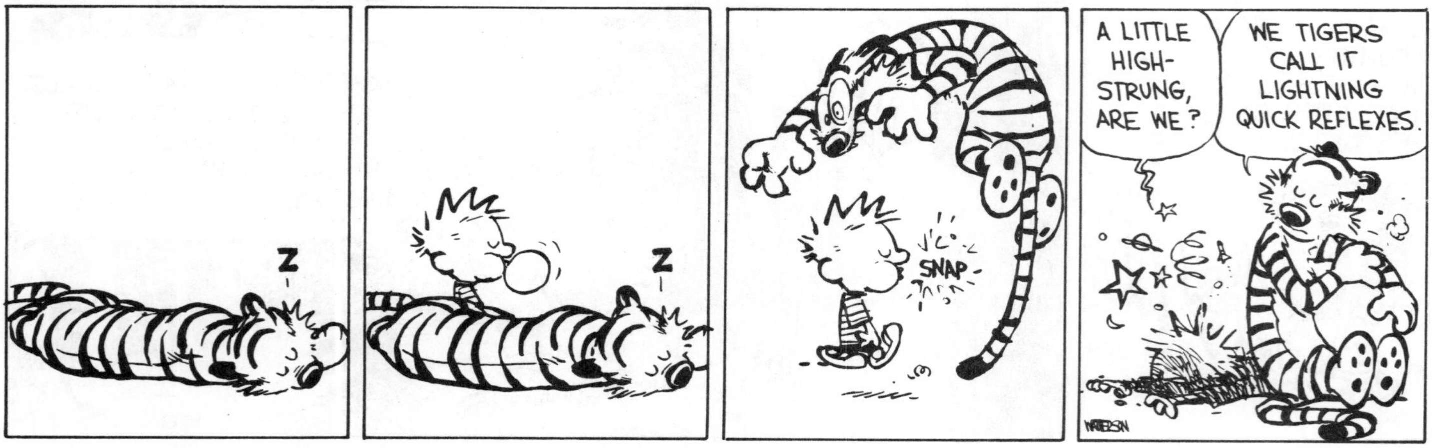
Z
Z
SNAP
A LITTLE HIGH-STRUNG, ARE WE?
WE TIGERS CALL IT LIGHTNING QUICK REFLEXES.

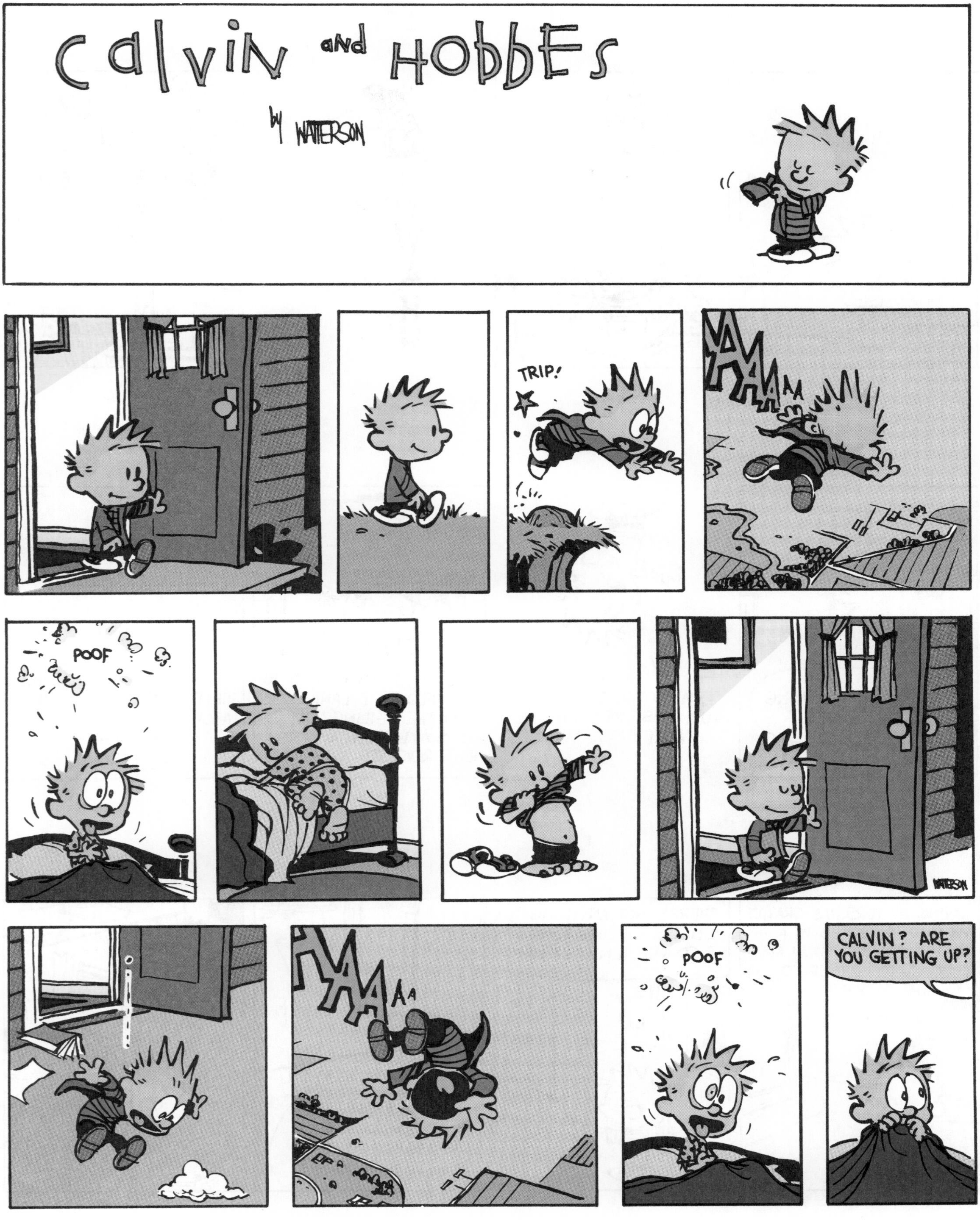
CALVIN AND HOBBES
by WATTERSON
TRIP!
AAAAAAAA
POOF
WATTERSON
AAAAA
POOF
CALVIN? ARE YOU GETTING UP?

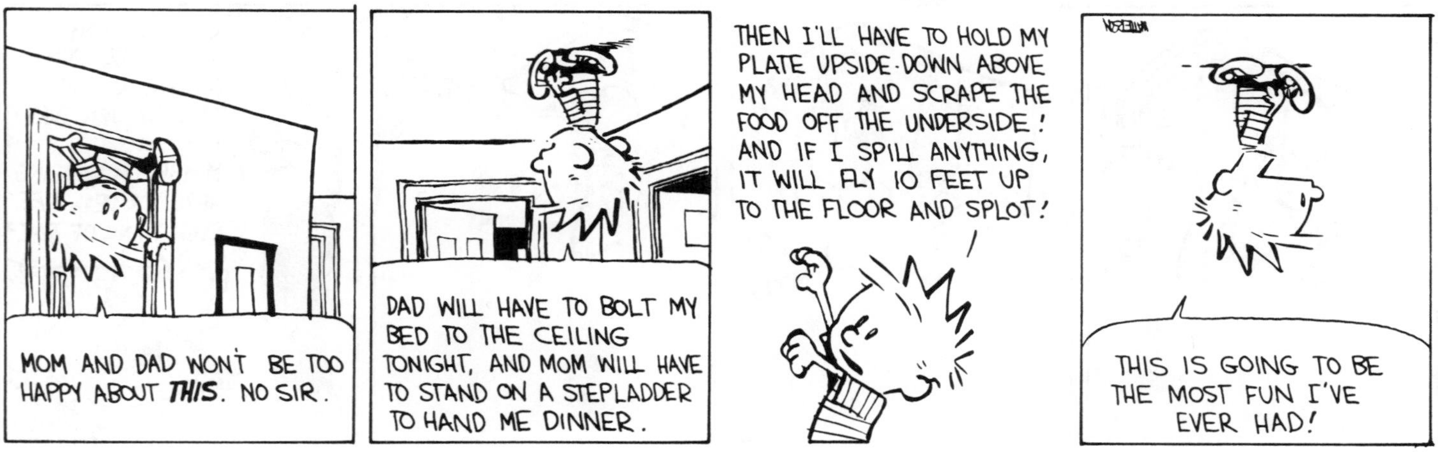
MOM AND DAD WON'T BE TOO HAPPY ABOUT **THIS**. NO SIR.
DAD WILL HAVE TO BOLT MY BED TO THE CEILING TONIGHT, AND MOM WILL HAVE TO STAND ON A STEPLADDER TO HAND ME DINNER.
THEN I'LL HAVE TO HOLD MY PLATE UPSIDE-DOWN ABOVE MY HEAD AND SCRAPE THE FOOD OFF THE UNDERSIDE! AND IF I SPILL ANYTHING, IT WILL FLY 10 FEET UP TO THE FLOOR AND SPLOT!
THIS IS GOING TO BE THE MOST FUN I'VE EVER HAD!

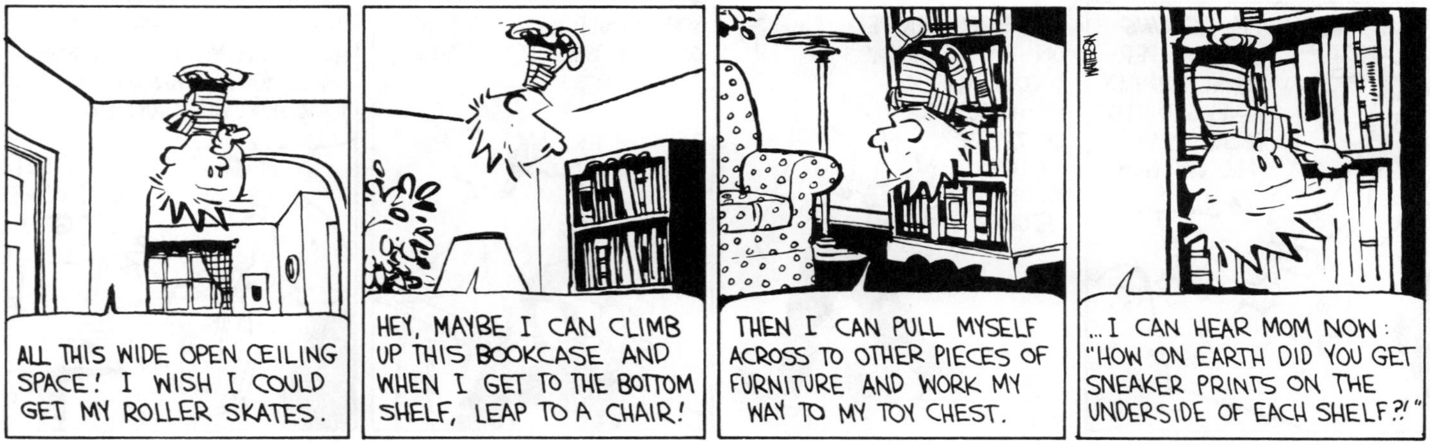
ALL THIS WIDE OPEN CEILING SPACE! I WISH I COULD GET MY ROLLER SKATES.
HEY, MAYBE I CAN CLIMB UP THIS BOOKCASE AND WHEN I GET TO THE BOTTOM SHELF, LEAP TO A CHAIR!
THEN I CAN PULL MYSELF ACROSS TO OTHER PIECES OF FURNITURE AND WORK MY WAY TO MY TOY CHEST.
...I CAN HEAR MOM NOW: "HOW ON EARTH DID YOU GET SNEAKER PRINTS ON THE UNDERSIDE OF EACH SHELF?!"

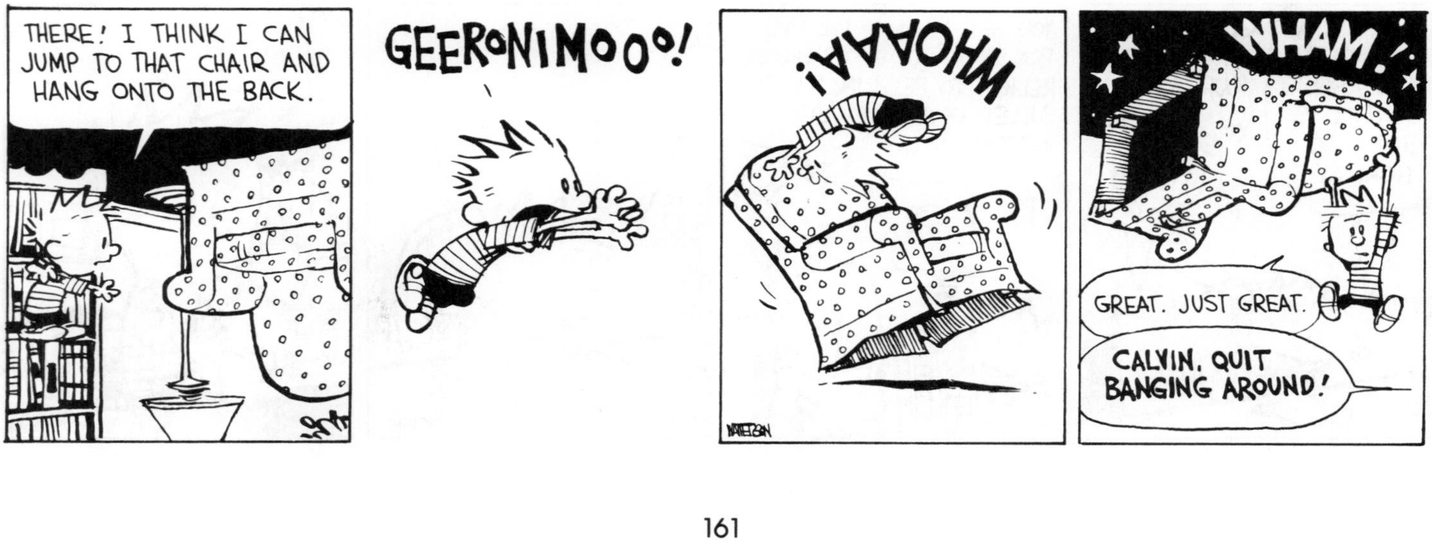
THERE! I THINK I CAN JUMP TO THAT CHAIR AND HANG ONTO THE BACK.
GEERONIMOOO!
WHOAAA!
WHAM!
GREAT. JUST GREAT.
CALVIN, QUIT BANGING AROUND!

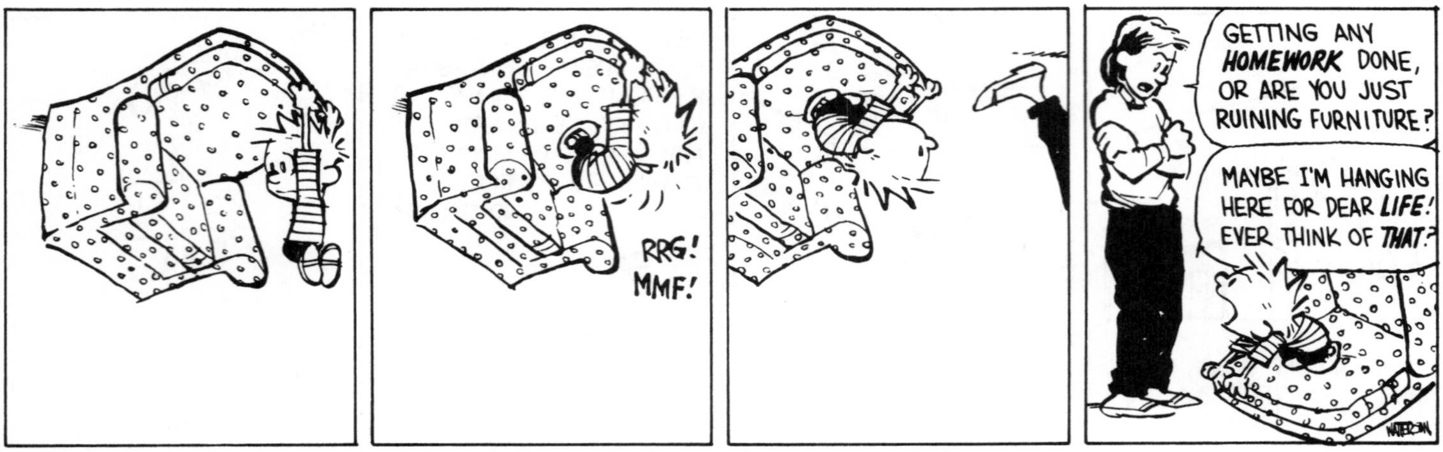
RRG! MMF!
GETTING ANY HOMEWORK DONE, OR ARE YOU JUST RUINING FURNITURE?
MAYBE I'M HANGING HERE FOR DEAR LIFE! EVER THINK OF THAT?

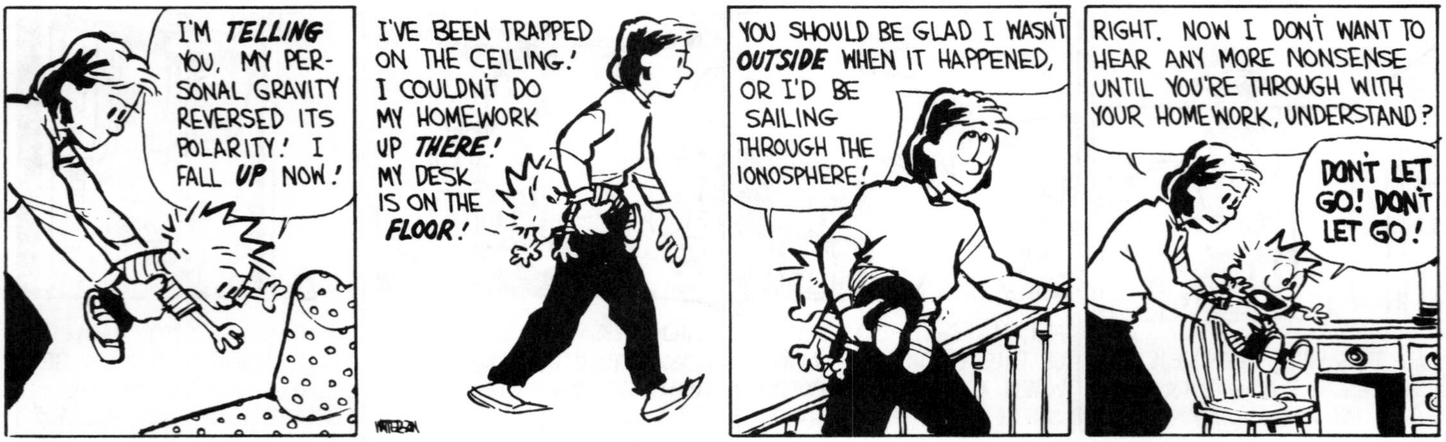
I'M TELLING YOU, MY PERSONAL GRAVITY REVERSED ITS POLARITY! I FALL UP NOW!
I'VE BEEN TRAPPED ON THE CEILING! I COULDN'T DO MY HOMEWORK UP THERE! MY DESK IS ON THE FLOOR!
YOU SHOULD BE GLAD I WASN'T OUTSIDE WHEN IT HAPPENED, OR I'D BE SAILING THROUGH THE IONOSPHERE!
RIGHT. NOW I DON'T WANT TO HEAR ANY MORE NONSENSE UNTIL YOU'RE THROUGH WITH YOUR HOMEWORK, UNDERSTAND?
DON'T LET GO! DON'T LET GO!

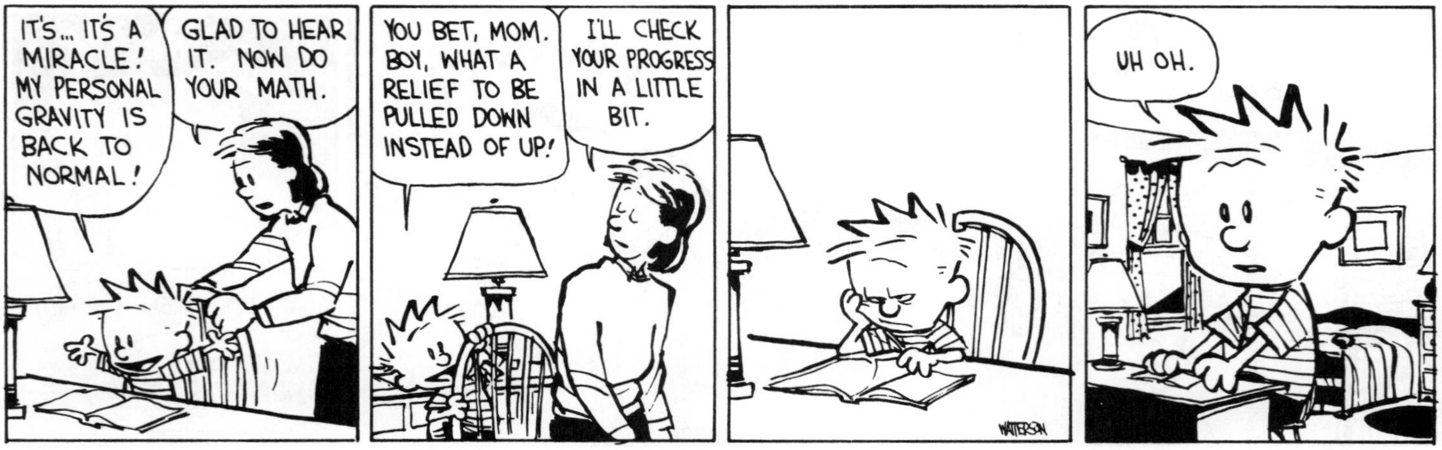
IT'S... IT'S A MIRACLE! MY PERSONAL GRAVITY IS BACK TO NORMAL!
GLAD TO HEAR IT. NOW DO YOUR MATH.
YOU BET, MOM. BOY, WHAT A RELIEF TO BE PULLED DOWN INSTEAD OF UP!
I'LL CHECK YOUR PROGRESS IN A LITTLE BIT.
UH OH.

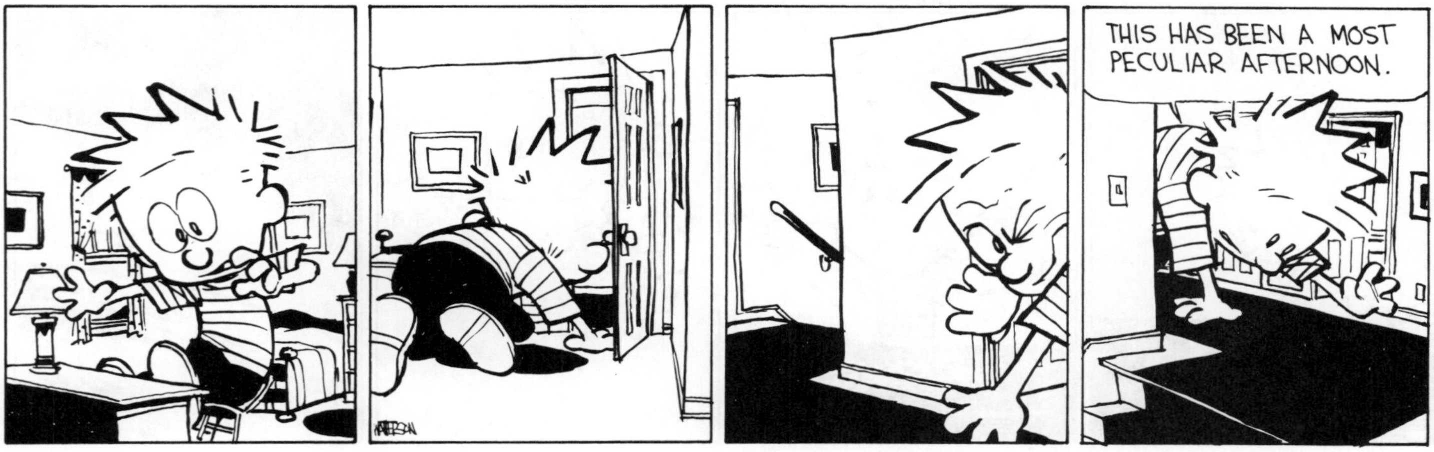
THIS HAS BEEN A MOST PECULIAR AFTERNOON.

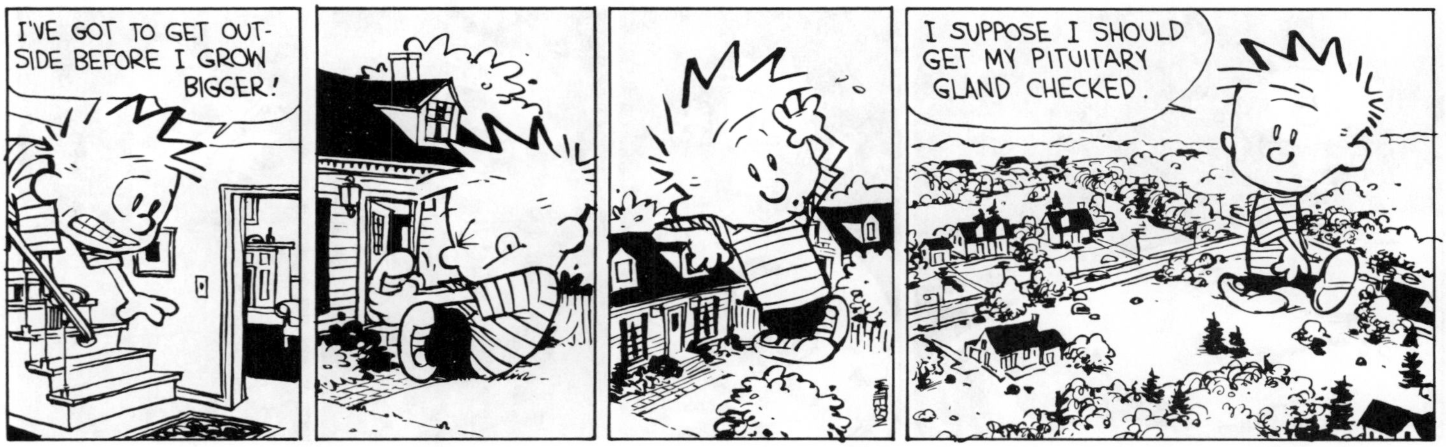
I'VE GOT TO GET OUT-SIDE BEFORE I GROW BIGGER!
I SUPPOSE I SHOULD GET MY PITUITARY GLAND CHECKED.

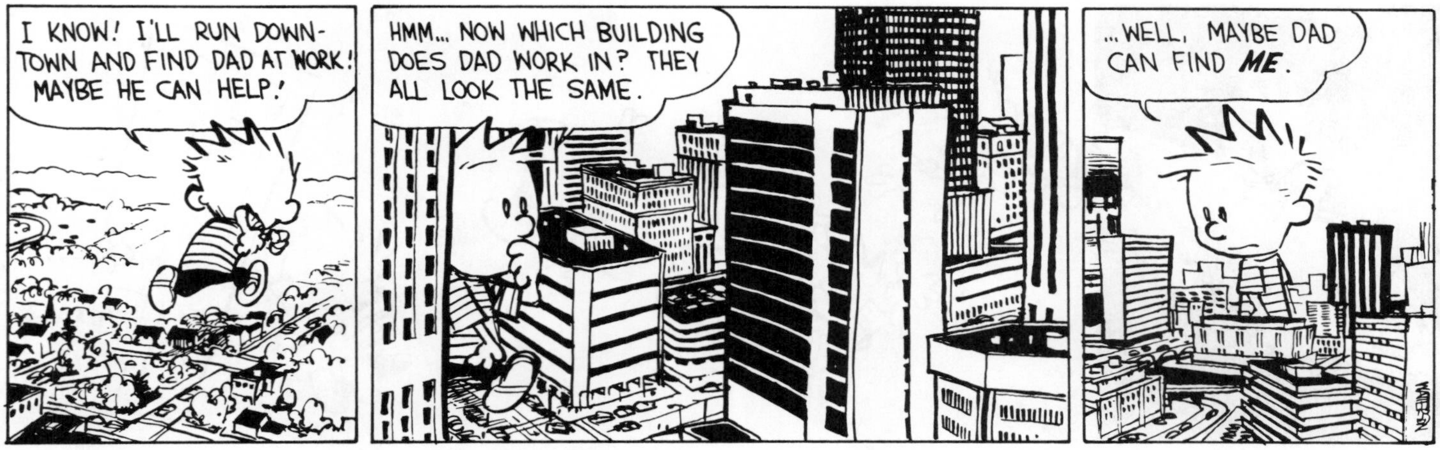
I KNOW! I'LL RUN DOWN-TOWN AND FIND DAD AT WORK! MAYBE HE CAN HELP!
HMM... NOW WHICH BUILDING DOES DAD WORK IN? THEY ALL LOOK THE SAME.
...WELL, MAYBE DAD CAN FIND **ME**.

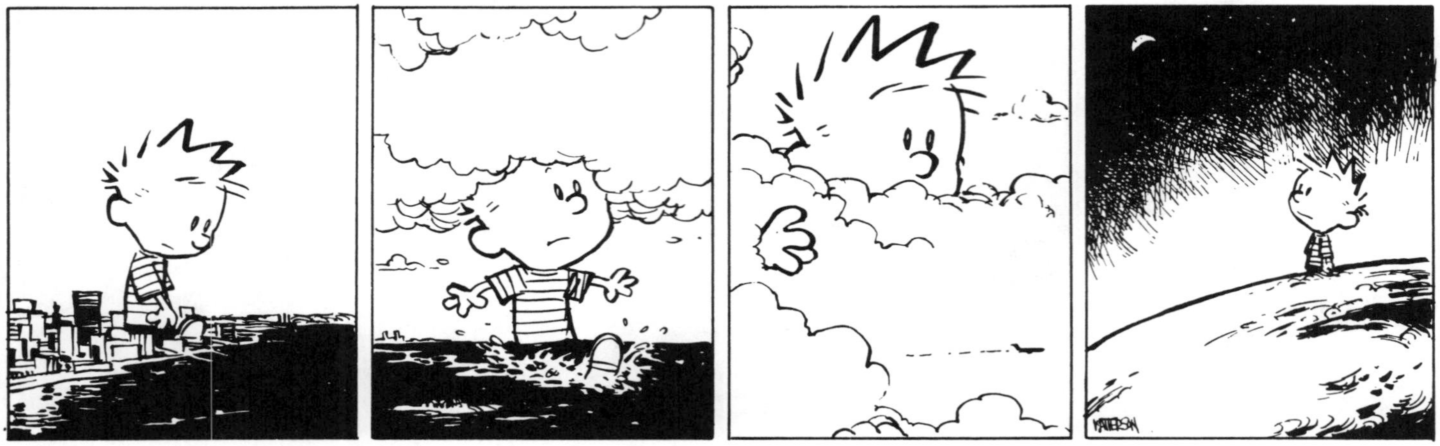

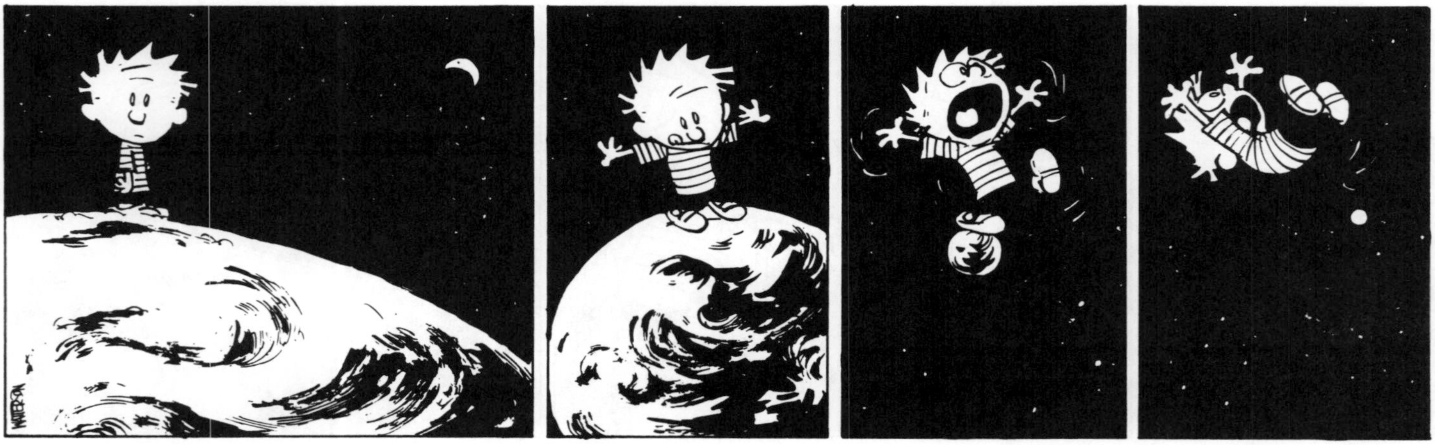

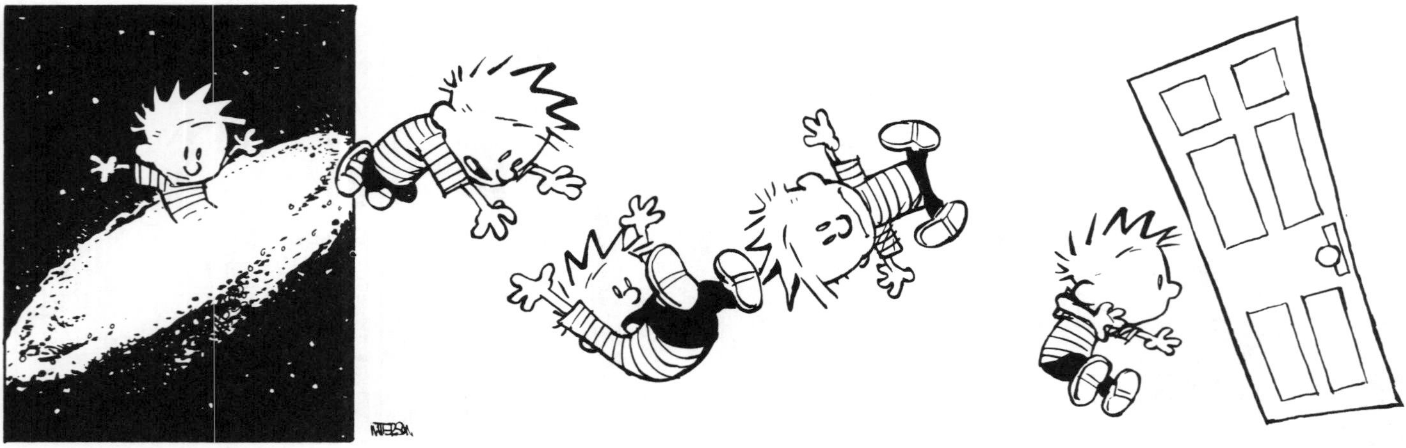

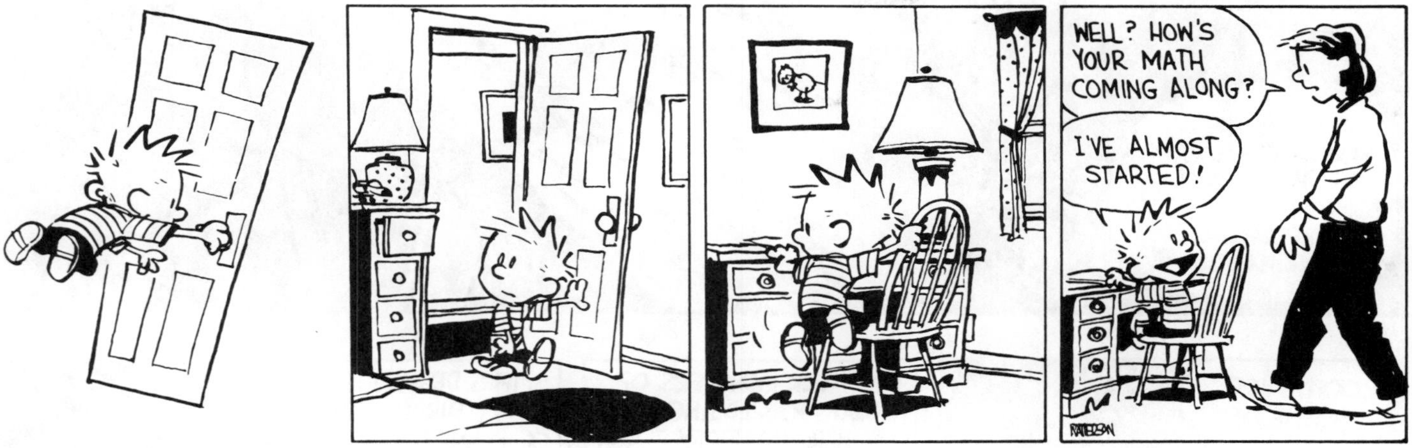
WELL? HOW'S YOUR MATH COMING ALONG?
I'VE ALMOST STARTED!

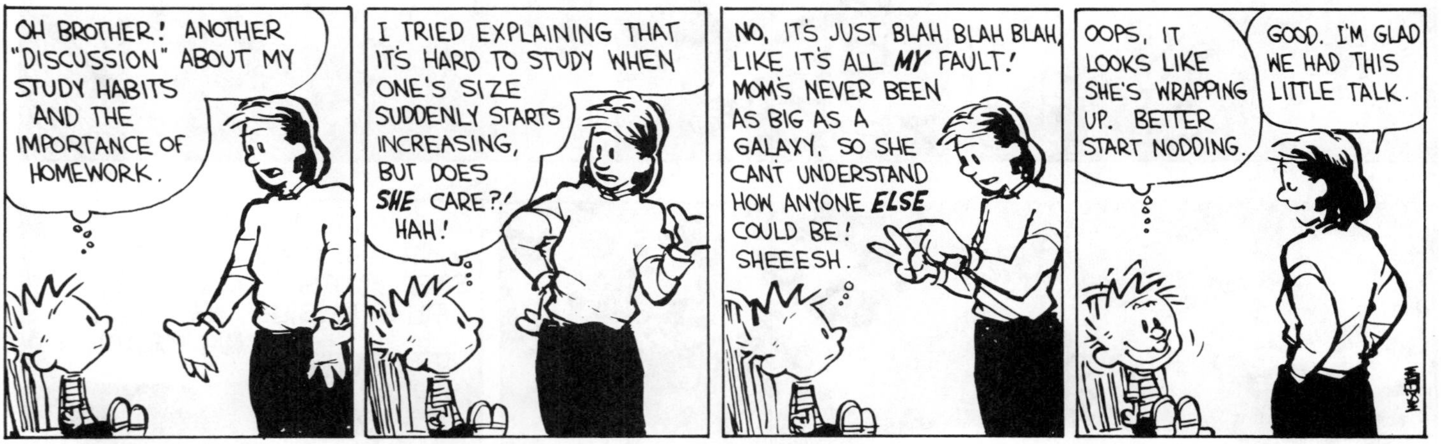
OH BROTHER! ANOTHER "DISCUSSION" ABOUT MY STUDY HABITS AND THE IMPORTANCE OF HOMEWORK.
I TRIED EXPLAINING THAT IT'S HARD TO STUDY WHEN ONE'S SIZE SUDDENLY STARTS INCREASING, BUT DOES SHE CARE?! HAH!
NO, IT'S JUST BLAH BLAH BLAH, LIKE IT'S ALL MY FAULT! MOM'S NEVER BEEN AS BIG AS A GALAXY, SO SHE CAN'T UNDERSTAND HOW ANYONE ELSE COULD BE! SHEEESH.
OOPS, IT LOOKS LIKE SHE'S WRAPPING UP. BETTER START NODDING.
GOOD. I'M GLAD WE HAD THIS LITTLE TALK.

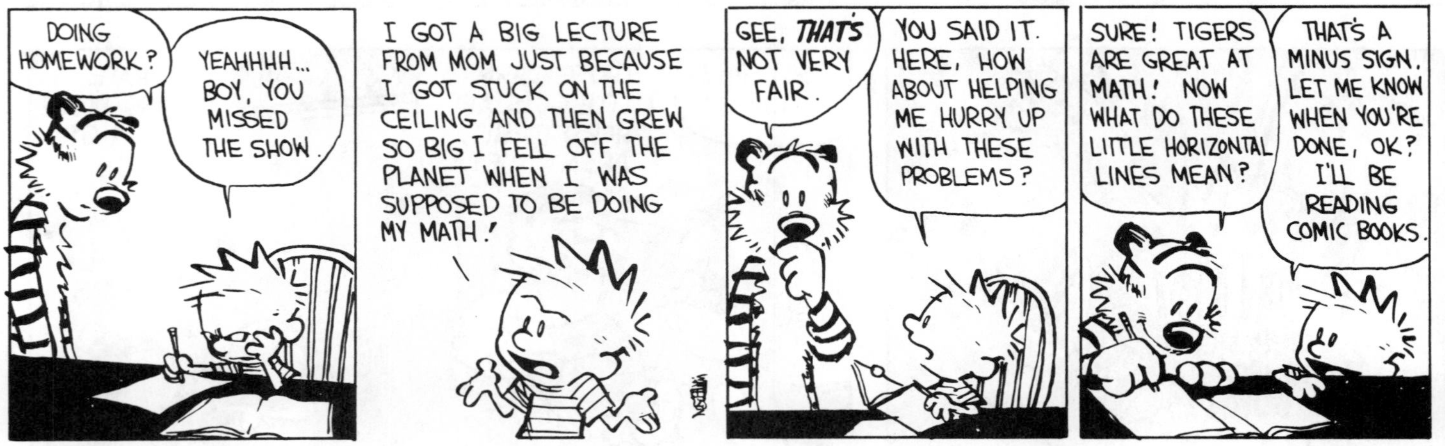
DOING HOMEWORK?
YEAHHHH... BOY, YOU MISSED THE SHOW.
I GOT A BIG LECTURE FROM MOM JUST BECAUSE I GOT STUCK ON THE CEILING AND THEN GREW SO BIG I FELL OFF THE PLANET WHEN I WAS SUPPOSED TO BE DOING MY MATH!
GEE, THAT'S NOT VERY FAIR.
YOU SAID IT. HERE, HOW ABOUT HELPING ME HURRY UP WITH THESE PROBLEMS?
SURE! TIGERS ARE GREAT AT MATH! NOW WHAT DO THESE LITTLE HORIZONTAL LINES MEAN?
THAT'S A MINUS SIGN. LET ME KNOW WHEN YOU'RE DONE, OK? I'LL BE READING COMIC BOOKS.

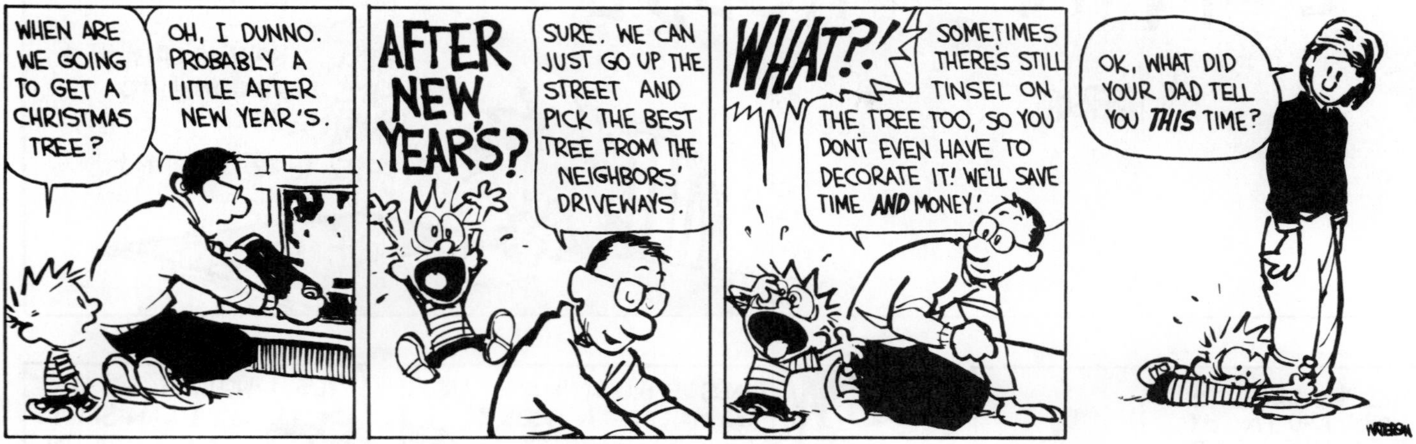
WHEN ARE WE GOING TO GET A CHRISTMAS TREE?
OH, I DUNNO. PROBABLY A LITTLE AFTER NEW YEAR'S.
AFTER NEW YEAR'S?
SURE. WE CAN JUST GO UP THE STREET AND PICK THE BEST TREE FROM THE NEIGHBORS' DRIVEWAYS.
WHAT?!
SOMETIMES THERE'S STILL TINSEL ON THE TREE TOO, SO YOU DON'T EVEN HAVE TO DECORATE IT! WE'LL SAVE TIME **AND** MONEY!
OK, WHAT DID YOUR DAD TELL YOU **THIS** TIME?

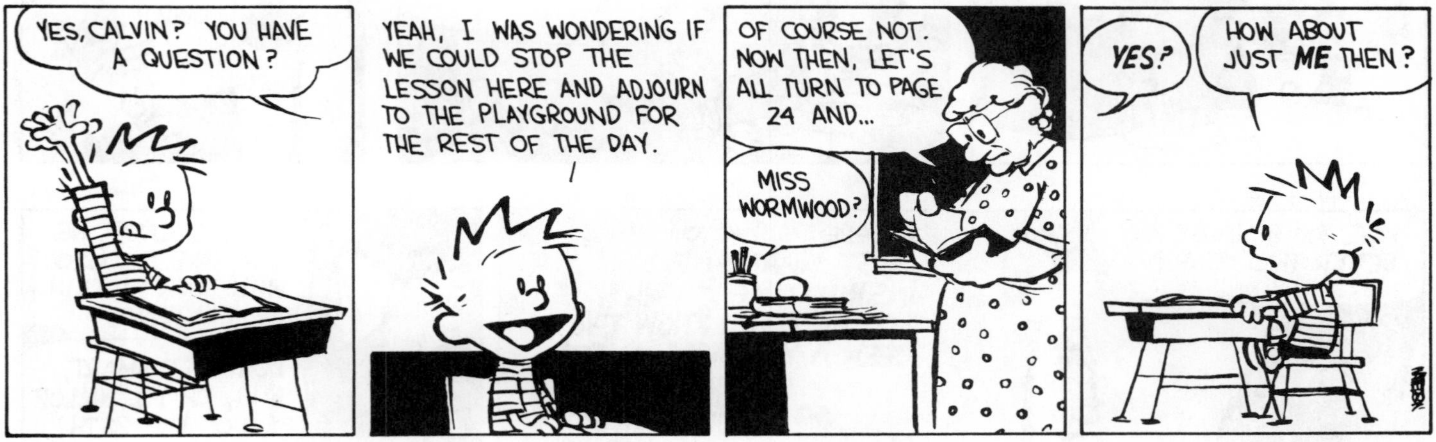
YES, CALVIN? YOU HAVE A QUESTION?
YEAH, I WAS WONDERING IF WE COULD STOP THE LESSON HERE AND ADJOURN TO THE PLAYGROUND FOR THE REST OF THE DAY.
OF COURSE NOT. NOW THEN, LET'S ALL TURN TO PAGE 24 AND...
MISS WORMWOOD?
YES?
HOW ABOUT JUST **ME** THEN?

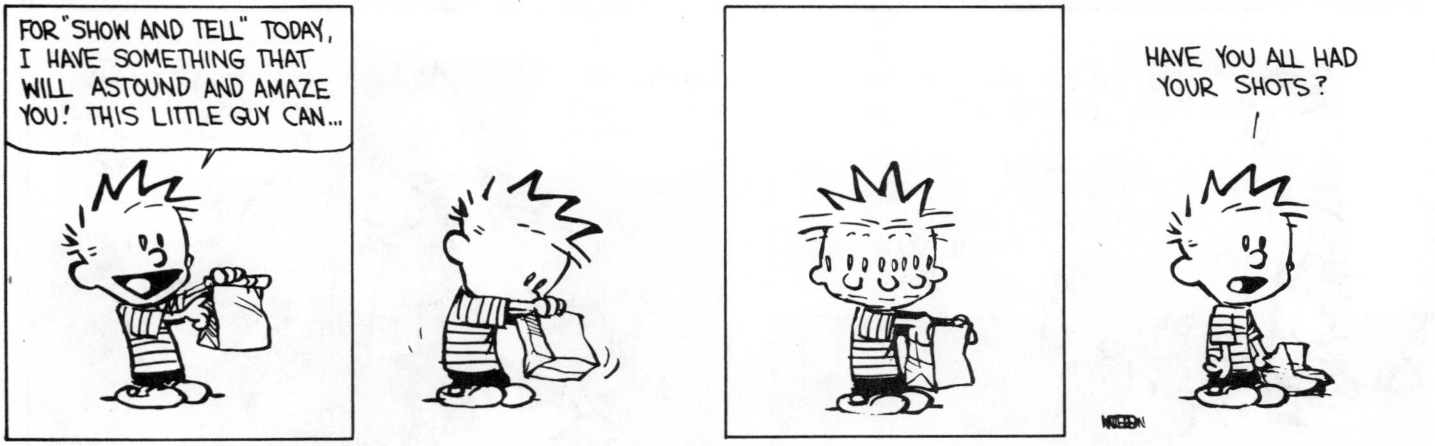
FOR "SHOW AND TELL" TODAY, I HAVE SOMETHING THAT WILL ASTOUND AND AMAZE YOU! THIS LITTLE GUY CAN...
HAVE YOU ALL HAD YOUR SHOTS?

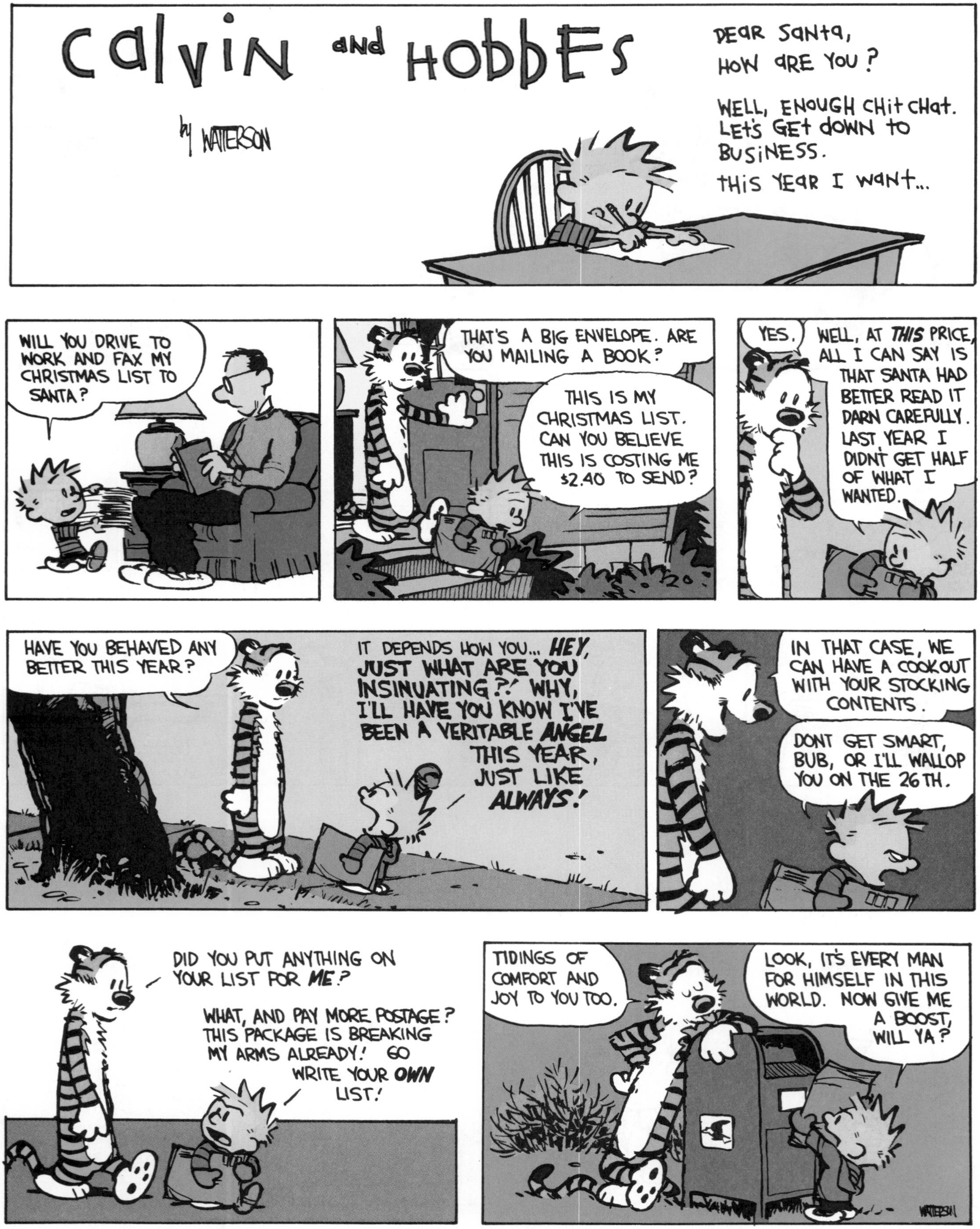
Calvin and HOBBES
by WATTERSON
DEAR SANTA, HOW ARE YOU?
WELL, ENOUGH CHIT CHAT. LET'S GET DOWN TO BUSINESS.
THIS YEAR I WANT...
WILL YOU DRIVE TO WORK AND FAX MY CHRISTMAS LIST TO SANTA?
THAT'S A BIG ENVELOPE. ARE YOU MAILING A BOOK?
THIS IS MY CHRISTMAS LIST. CAN YOU BELIEVE THIS IS COSTING ME $2.40 TO SEND?
YES.
WELL, AT THIS PRICE, ALL I CAN SAY IS THAT SANTA HAD BETTER READ IT DARN CAREFULLY. LAST YEAR I DIDN'T GET HALF OF WHAT I WANTED.
HAVE YOU BEHAVED ANY BETTER THIS YEAR?
IT DEPENDS HOW YOU... HEY, JUST WHAT ARE YOU INSINUATING?! WHY, I'LL HAVE YOU KNOW I'VE BEEN A VERITABLE ANGEL THIS YEAR, JUST LIKE ALWAYS!
IN THAT CASE, WE CAN HAVE A COOKOUT WITH YOUR STOCKING CONTENTS.
DONT GET SMART, BUB, OR I'LL WALLOP YOU ON THE 26TH.
DID YOU PUT ANYTHING ON YOUR LIST FOR ME?
WHAT, AND PAY MORE POSTAGE? THIS PACKAGE IS BREAKING MY ARMS ALREADY! GO WRITE YOUR OWN LIST!
TIDINGS OF COMFORT AND JOY TO YOU TOO.
LOOK, IT'S EVERY MAN FOR HIMSELF IN THIS WORLD. NOW GIVE ME A BOOST, WILL YA?
WATTERSON

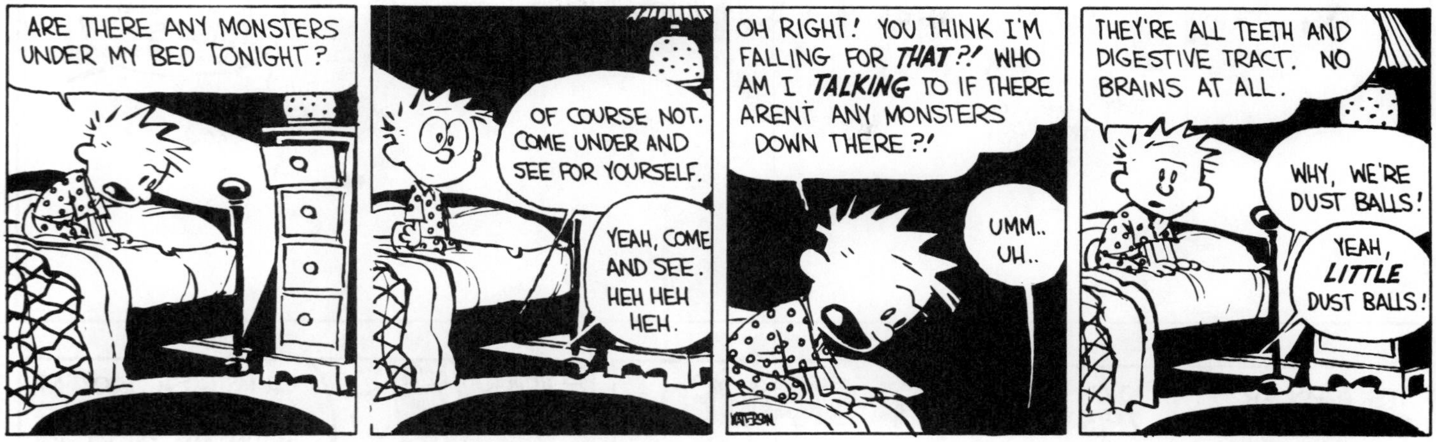
ARE THERE ANY MONSTERS UNDER MY BED TONIGHT?
OF COURSE NOT. COME UNDER AND SEE FOR YOURSELF.
YEAH, COME AND SEE. HEH HEH HEH.
OH RIGHT! YOU THINK I'M FALLING FOR THAT?! WHO AM I TALKING TO IF THERE AREN'T ANY MONSTERS DOWN THERE?!
UMM.. UH..
THEY'RE ALL TEETH AND DIGESTIVE TRACT. NO BRAINS AT ALL.
WHY, WE'RE DUST BALLS!
YEAH, LITTLE DUST BALLS!

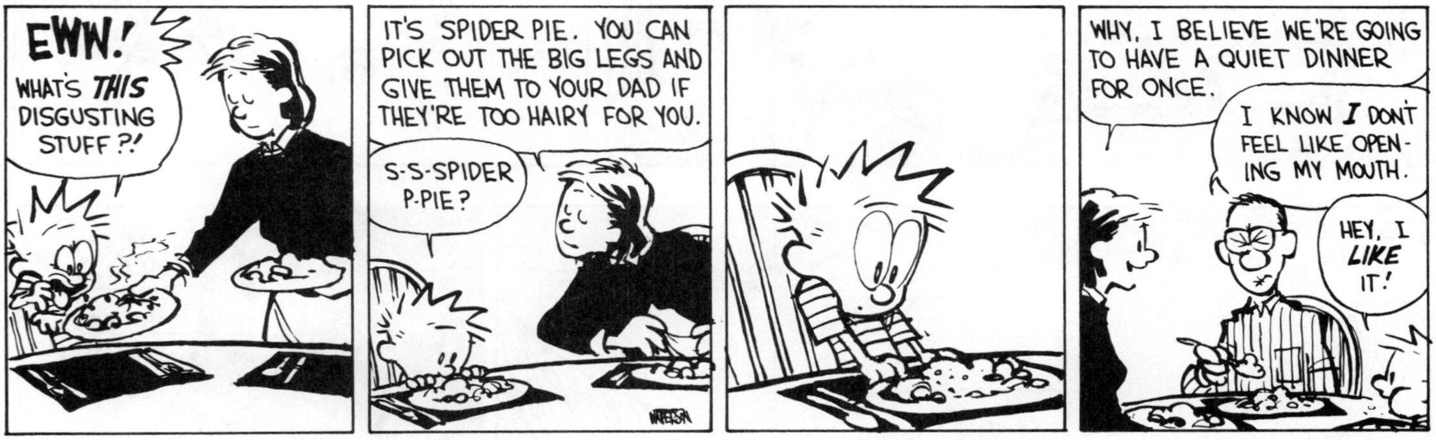
EWW!
WHAT'S THIS DISGUSTING STUFF?!
IT'S SPIDER PIE. YOU CAN PICK OUT THE BIG LEGS AND GIVE THEM TO YOUR DAD IF THEY'RE TOO HAIRY FOR YOU.
S-S-SPIDER P-PIE?
WHY, I BELIEVE WE'RE GOING TO HAVE A QUIET DINNER FOR ONCE.
I KNOW I DON'T FEEL LIKE OPENING MY MOUTH.
HEY, I LIKE IT!

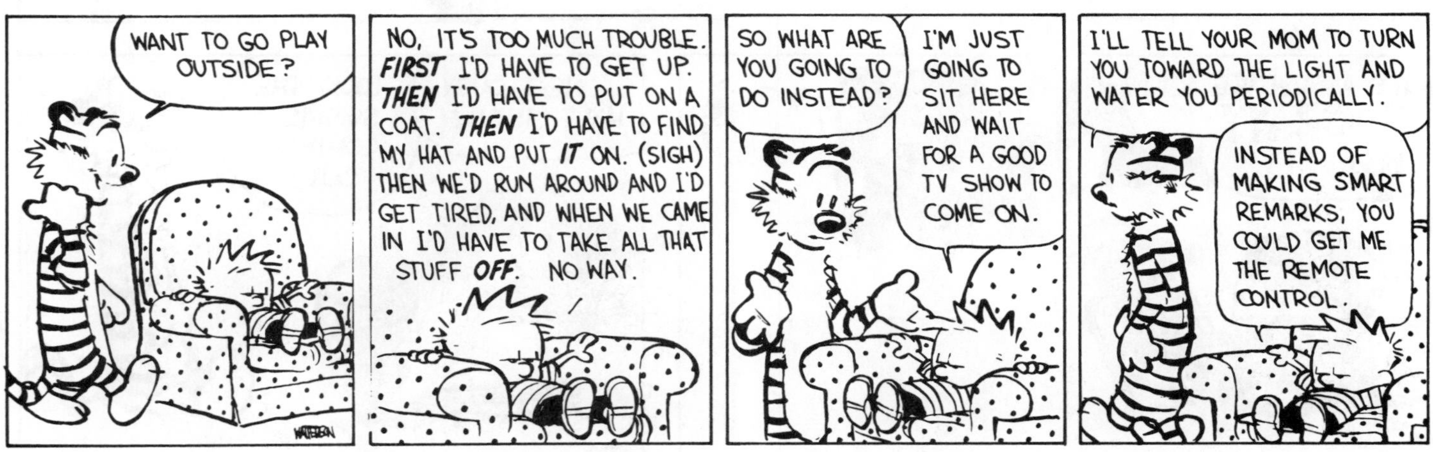
WANT TO GO PLAY OUTSIDE?
NO, IT'S TOO MUCH TROUBLE. FIRST I'D HAVE TO GET UP. THEN I'D HAVE TO PUT ON A COAT. THEN I'D HAVE TO FIND MY HAT AND PUT IT ON. (SIGH) THEN WE'D RUN AROUND AND I'D GET TIRED, AND WHEN WE CAME IN I'D HAVE TO TAKE ALL THAT STUFF OFF. NO WAY.
SO WHAT ARE YOU GOING TO DO INSTEAD?
I'M JUST GOING TO SIT HERE AND WAIT FOR A GOOD TV SHOW TO COME ON.
I'LL TELL YOUR MOM TO TURN YOU TOWARD THE LIGHT AND WATER YOU PERIODICALLY.
INSTEAD OF MAKING SMART REMARKS, YOU COULD GET ME THE REMOTE CONTROL.

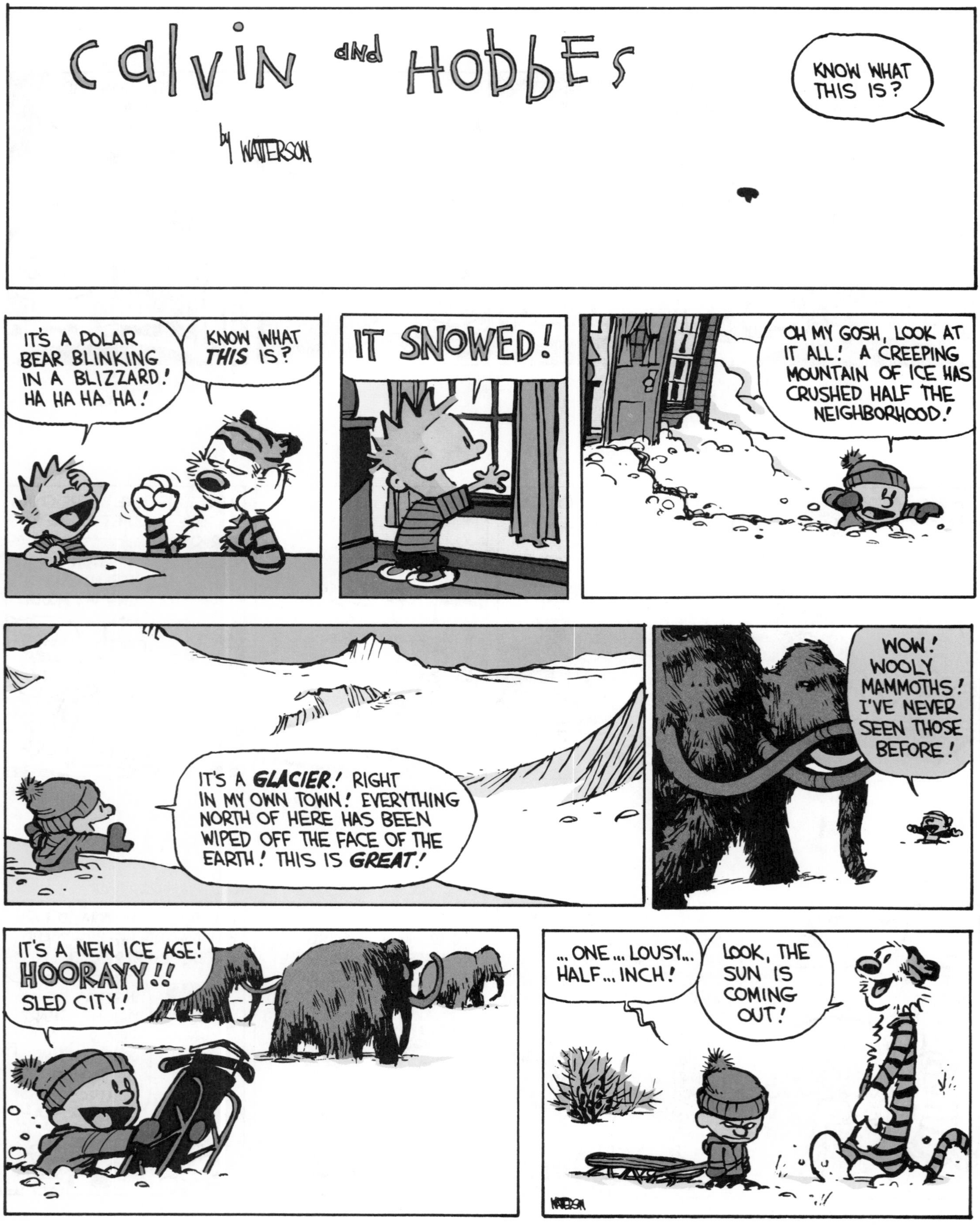
Calvin and Hobbes
by WATTERSON
KNOW WHAT THIS IS?
IT'S A POLAR BEAR BLINKING IN A BLIZZARD! HA HA HA HA!
KNOW WHAT THIS IS?
IT SNOWED!
OH MY GOSH, LOOK AT IT ALL! A CREEPING MOUNTAIN OF ICE HAS CRUSHED HALF THE NEIGHBORHOOD!
IT'S A GLACIER! RIGHT IN MY OWN TOWN! EVERYTHING NORTH OF HERE HAS BEEN WIPED OFF THE FACE OF THE EARTH! THIS IS GREAT!
WOW! WOOLY MAMMOTHS! I'VE NEVER SEEN THOSE BEFORE!
IT'S A NEW ICE AGE! HOORAYY!! SLED CITY!
LOOK, THE SUN IS COMING OUT!
... ONE ... LOUSY... HALF... INCH!
WATTERSON

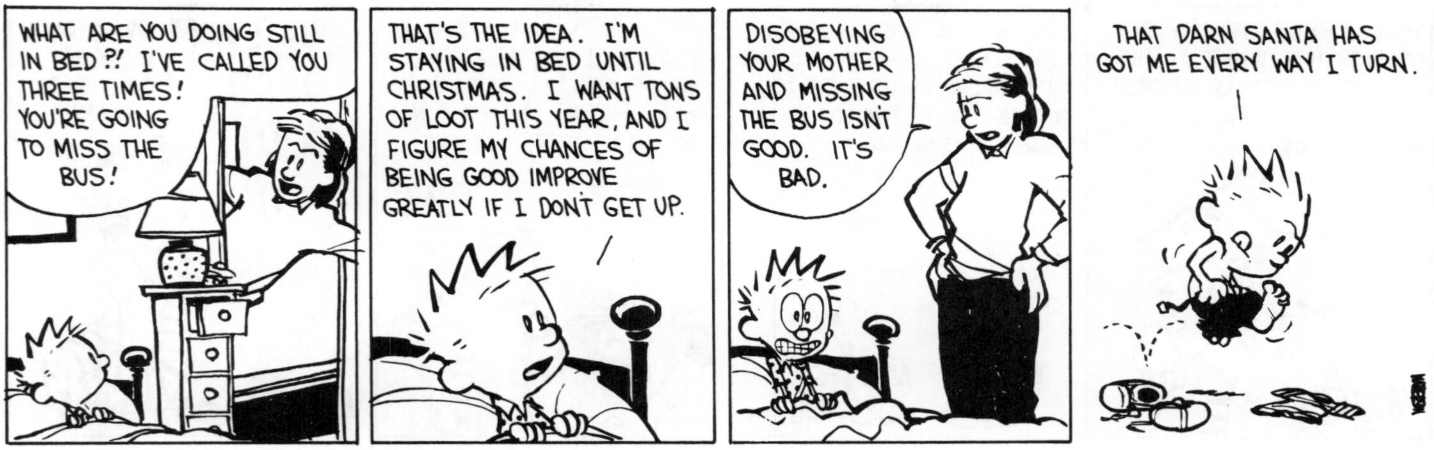
WHAT ARE YOU DOING STILL IN BED ?! I'VE CALLED YOU THREE TIMES! YOU'RE GOING TO MISS THE BUS!
THAT'S THE IDEA. I'M STAYING IN BED UNTIL CHRISTMAS. I WANT TONS OF LOOT THIS YEAR, AND I FIGURE MY CHANCES OF BEING GOOD IMPROVE GREATLY IF I DON'T GET UP.
DISOBEYING YOUR MOTHER AND MISSING THE BUS ISN'T GOOD. IT'S BAD.
THAT DARN SANTA HAS GOT ME EVERY WAY I TURN.

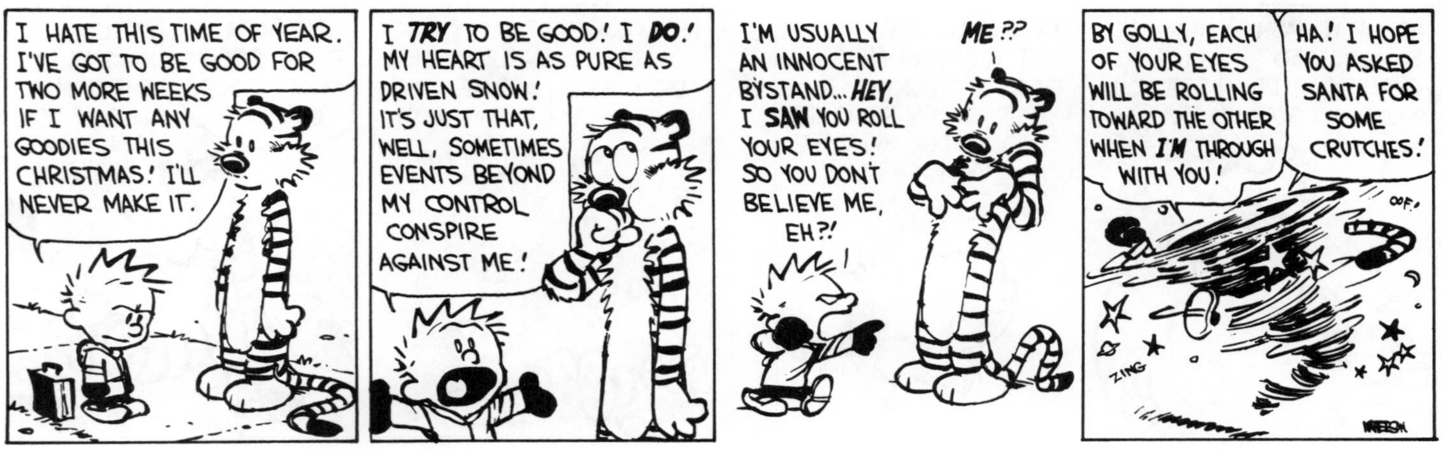
I HATE THIS TIME OF YEAR. I'VE GOT TO BE GOOD FOR TWO MORE WEEKS IF I WANT ANY GOODIES THIS CHRISTMAS! I'LL NEVER MAKE IT.
I TRY TO BE GOOD! I DO! MY HEART IS AS PURE AS DRIVEN SNOW!
IT'S JUST THAT, WELL, SOMETIMES EVENTS BEYOND MY CONTROL CONSPIRE AGAINST ME!
I'M USUALLY AN INNOCENT BYSTAND... HEY, I SAW YOU ROLL YOUR EYES! SO YOU DON'T BELIEVE ME, EH?!
ME??
BY GOLLY, EACH OF YOUR EYES WILL BE ROLLING TOWARD THE OTHER WHEN I'M THROUGH WITH YOU!
HA! I HOPE YOU ASKED SANTA FOR SOME CRUTCHES!
OOF!
ZING

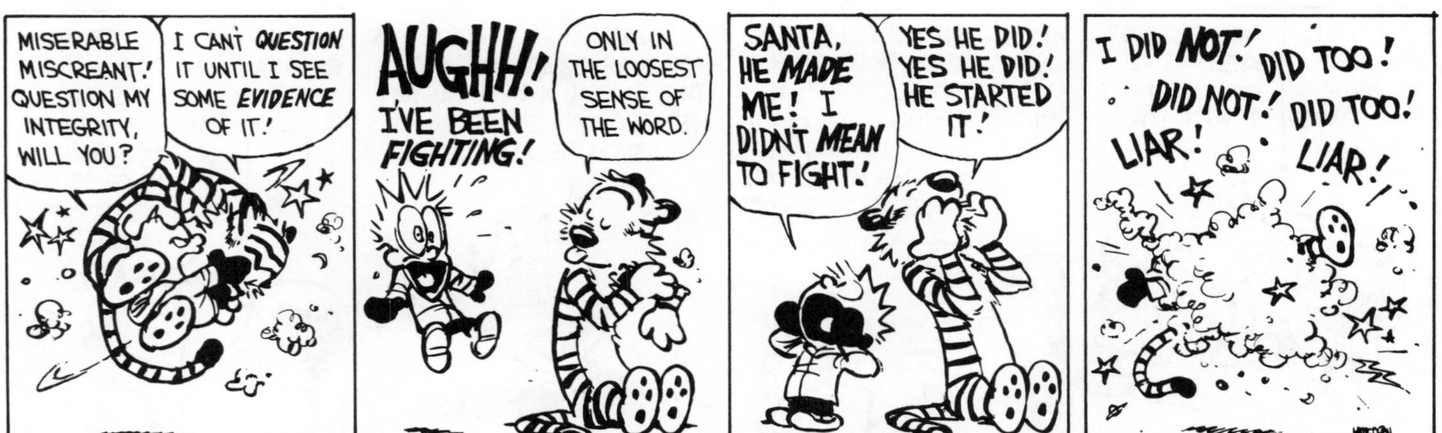
MISERABLE MISCREANT! QUESTION MY INTEGRITY, WILL YOU?
I CAN'T QUESTION IT UNTIL I SEE SOME EVIDENCE OF IT!
AUGHH! I'VE BEEN FIGHTING!
ONLY IN THE LOOSEST SENSE OF THE WORD.
SANTA, HE MADE ME! I DIDN'T MEAN TO FIGHT!
YES HE DID! YES HE DID! HE STARTED IT!
I DID NOT! DID TOO! DID NOT! DID TOO! LIAR! LIAR!

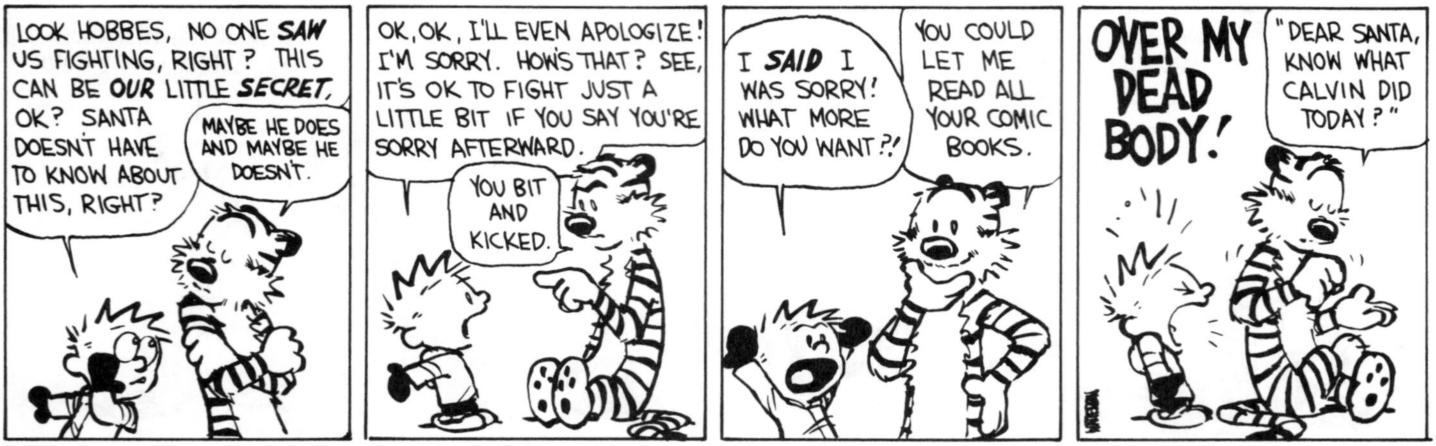
LOOK HOBBES, NO ONE SAW US FIGHTING, RIGHT? THIS CAN BE OUR LITTLE SECRET, OK? SANTA DOESN'T HAVE TO KNOW ABOUT THIS, RIGHT?
MAYBE HE DOES AND MAYBE HE DOESN'T.
OK, OK, I'LL EVEN APOLOGIZE! I'M SORRY. HOW'S THAT? SEE, IT'S OK TO FIGHT JUST A LITTLE BIT IF YOU SAY YOU'RE SORRY AFTERWARD.
YOU BIT AND KICKED.
I SAID I WAS SORRY! WHAT MORE DO YOU WANT?!
YOU COULD LET ME READ ALL YOUR COMIC BOOKS.
OVER MY DEAD BODY!
"DEAR SANTA, KNOW WHAT CALVIN DID TODAY?"

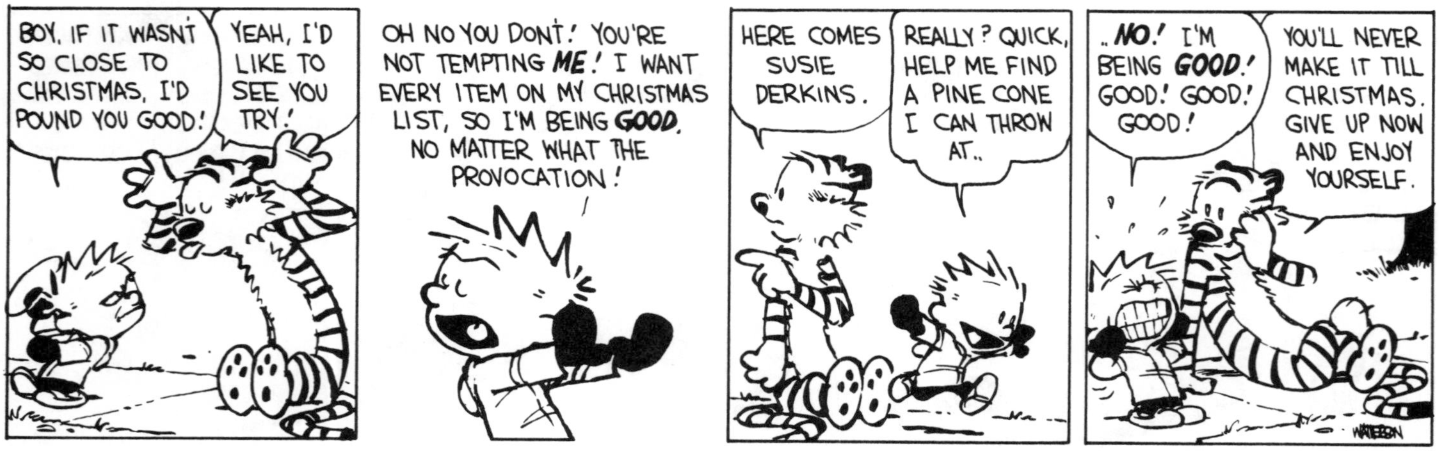
BOY, IF IT WASN'T SO CLOSE TO CHRISTMAS, I'D POUND YOU GOOD!
YEAH, I'D LIKE TO SEE YOU TRY!
OH NO YOU DON'T! YOU'RE NOT TEMPTING ME! I WANT EVERY ITEM ON MY CHRISTMAS LIST, SO I'M BEING GOOD, NO MATTER WHAT THE PROVOCATION!
HERE COMES SUSIE DERKINS.
REALLY? QUICK, HELP ME FIND A PINE CONE I CAN THROW AT..
..NO! I'M BEING GOOD! GOOD! GOOD! GOOD!
YOU'LL NEVER MAKE IT TILL CHRISTMAS. GIVE UP NOW AND ENJOY YOURSELF.

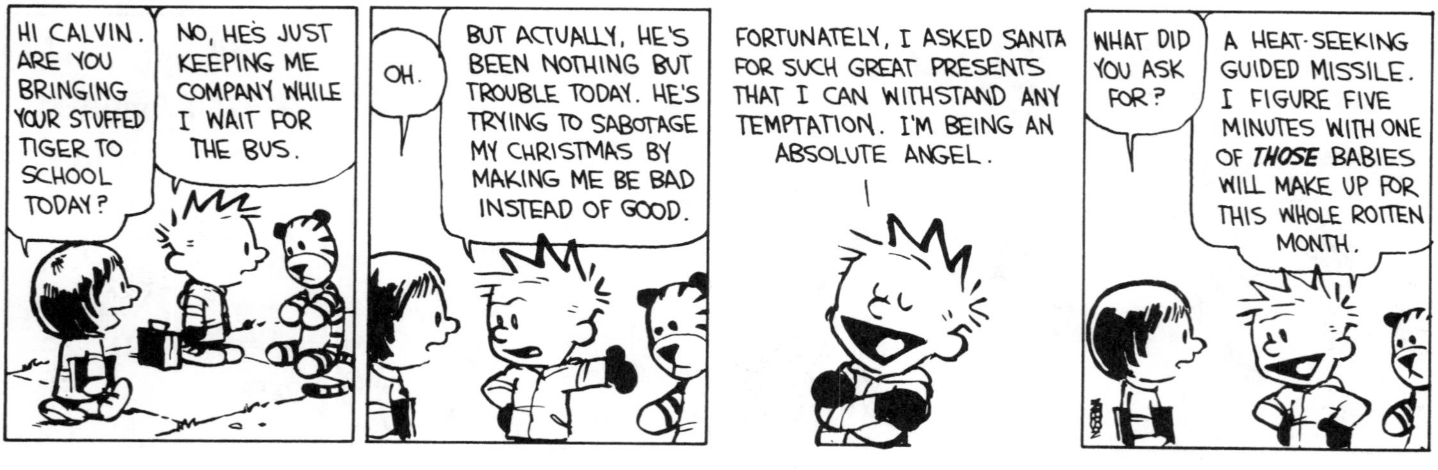
HI CALVIN. ARE YOU BRINGING YOUR STUFFED TIGER TO SCHOOL TODAY?
NO, HE'S JUST KEEPING ME COMPANY WHILE I WAIT FOR THE BUS.
OH.
BUT ACTUALLY, HE'S BEEN NOTHING BUT TROUBLE TODAY. HE'S TRYING TO SABOTAGE MY CHRISTMAS BY MAKING ME BE BAD INSTEAD OF GOOD.
FORTUNATELY, I ASKED SANTA FOR SUCH GREAT PRESENTS THAT I CAN WITHSTAND ANY TEMPTATION. I'M BEING AN ABSOLUTE ANGEL.
WHAT DID YOU ASK FOR?
A HEAT-SEEKING GUIDED MISSILE. I FIGURE FIVE MINUTES WITH ONE OF THOSE BABIES WILL MAKE UP FOR THIS WHOLE ROTTEN MONTH.

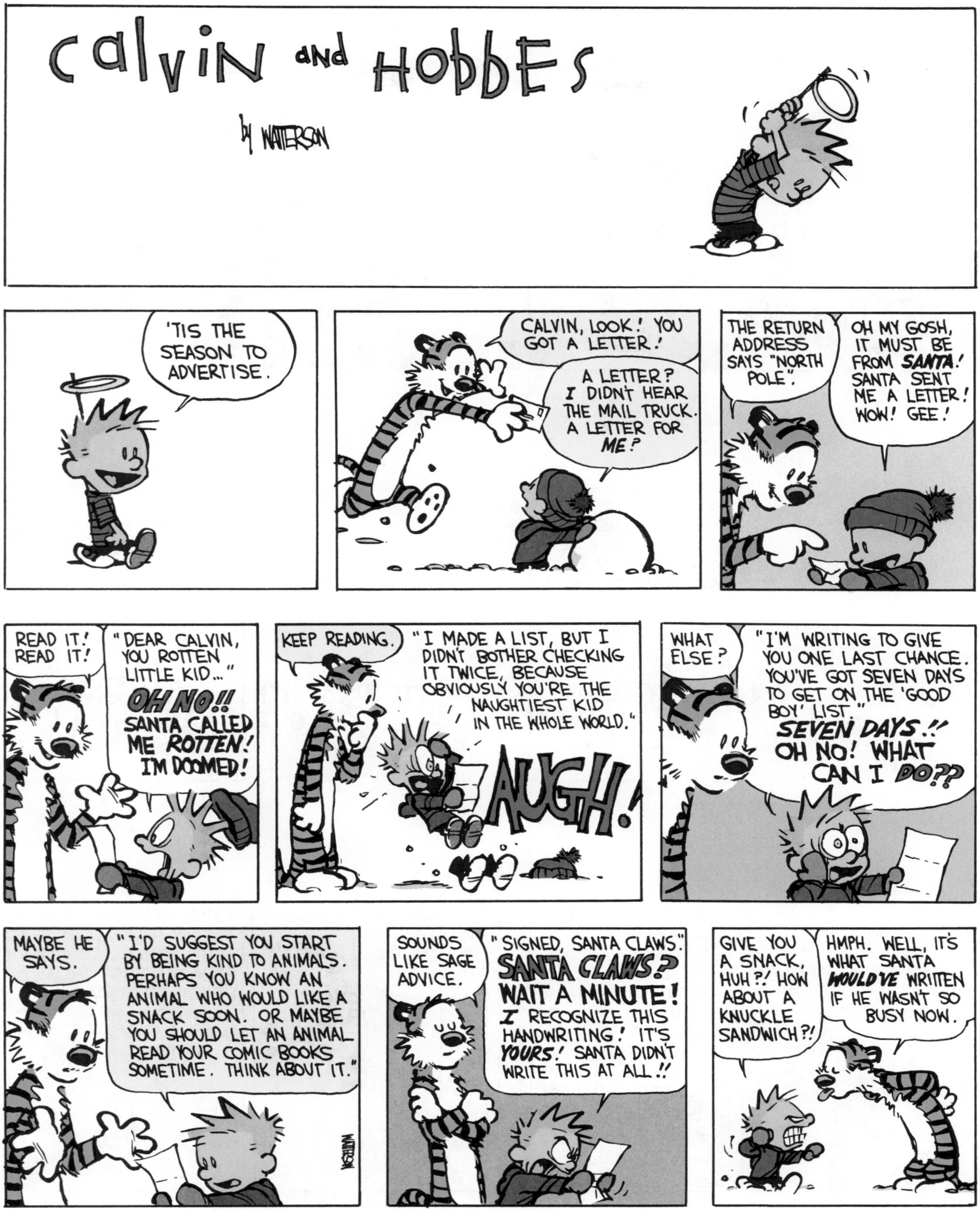
Calvin and HobbEs
by WATTERSON
'TIS THE SEASON TO ADVERTISE.
CALVIN, LOOK! YOU GOT A LETTER!
A LETTER? I DIDN'T HEAR THE MAIL TRUCK. A LETTER FOR ME?
THE RETURN ADDRESS SAYS "NORTH POLE".
OH MY GOSH, IT MUST BE FROM SANTA! SANTA SENT ME A LETTER! WOW! GEE!
READ IT! READ IT!
"DEAR CALVIN, YOU ROTTEN LITTLE KID..."
OH NO!! SANTA CALLED ME ROTTEN! I'M DOOMED!
KEEP READING.
"I MADE A LIST, BUT I DIDN'T BOTHER CHECKING IT TWICE, BECAUSE OBVIOUSLY YOU'RE THE NAUGHTIEST KID IN THE WHOLE WORLD."
AUGH!
WHAT ELSE?
"I'M WRITING TO GIVE YOU ONE LAST CHANCE. YOU'VE GOT SEVEN DAYS TO GET ON THE 'GOOD BOY' LIST."
SEVEN DAYS!! OH NO! WHAT CAN I DO??
MAYBE HE SAYS.
"I'D SUGGEST YOU START BY BEING KIND TO ANIMALS. PERHAPS YOU KNOW AN ANIMAL WHO WOULD LIKE A SNACK SOON. OR MAYBE YOU SHOULD LET AN ANIMAL READ YOUR COMIC BOOKS SOMETIME. THINK ABOUT IT."
WATTERSON
SOUNDS LIKE SAGE ADVICE.
"SIGNED, SANTA CLAWS."
SANTA CLAWS? WAIT A MINUTE! I RECOGNIZE THIS HANDWRITING! IT'S YOURS! SANTA DIDN'T WRITE THIS AT ALL!!
GIVE YOU A SNACK, HUH?! HOW ABOUT A KNUCKLE SANDWICH?!
HMPH. WELL, IT'S WHAT SANTA WOULD'VE WRITTEN IF HE WASN'T SO BUSY NOW.

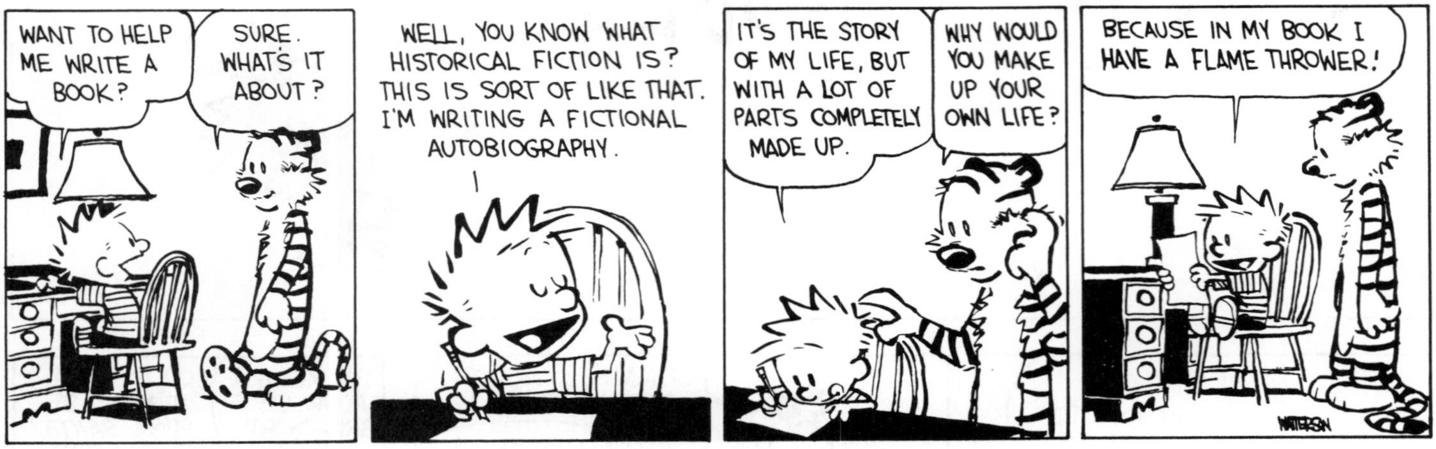
WANT TO HELP ME WRITE A BOOK?
SURE. WHAT'S IT ABOUT?
WELL, YOU KNOW WHAT HISTORICAL FICTION IS? THIS IS SORT OF LIKE THAT. I'M WRITING A FICTIONAL AUTOBIOGRAPHY.
IT'S THE STORY OF MY LIFE, BUT WITH A LOT OF PARTS COMPLETELY MADE UP.
WHY WOULD YOU MAKE UP YOUR OWN LIFE?
BECAUSE IN MY BOOK I HAVE A FLAME THROWER!

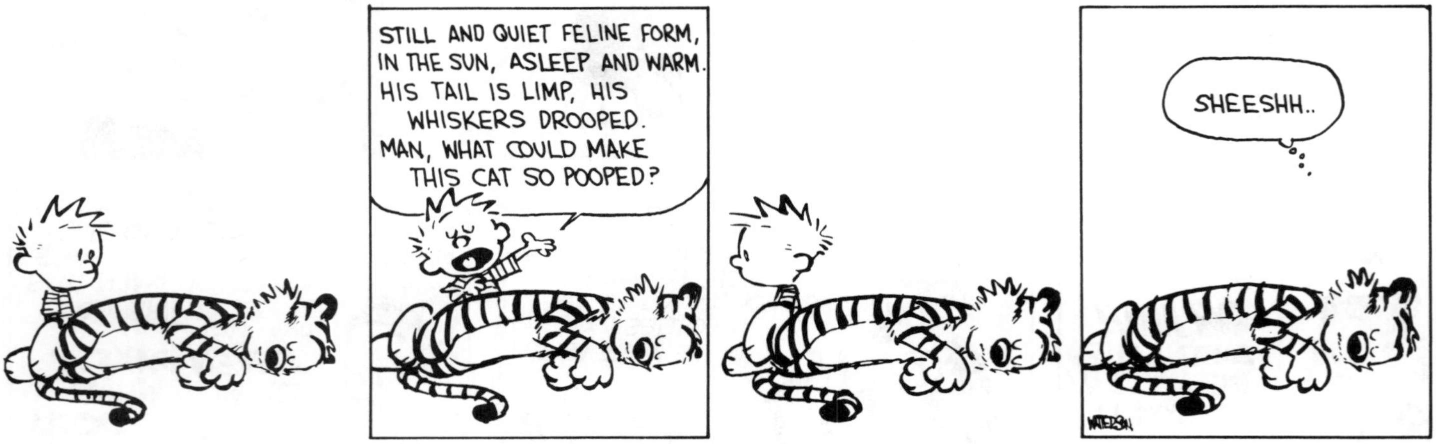
STILL AND QUIET FELINE FORM, IN THE SUN, ASLEEP AND WARM. HIS TAIL IS LIMP, HIS WHISKERS DROOPED. MAN, WHAT COULD MAKE THIS CAT SO POOPED?
SHEESHH..

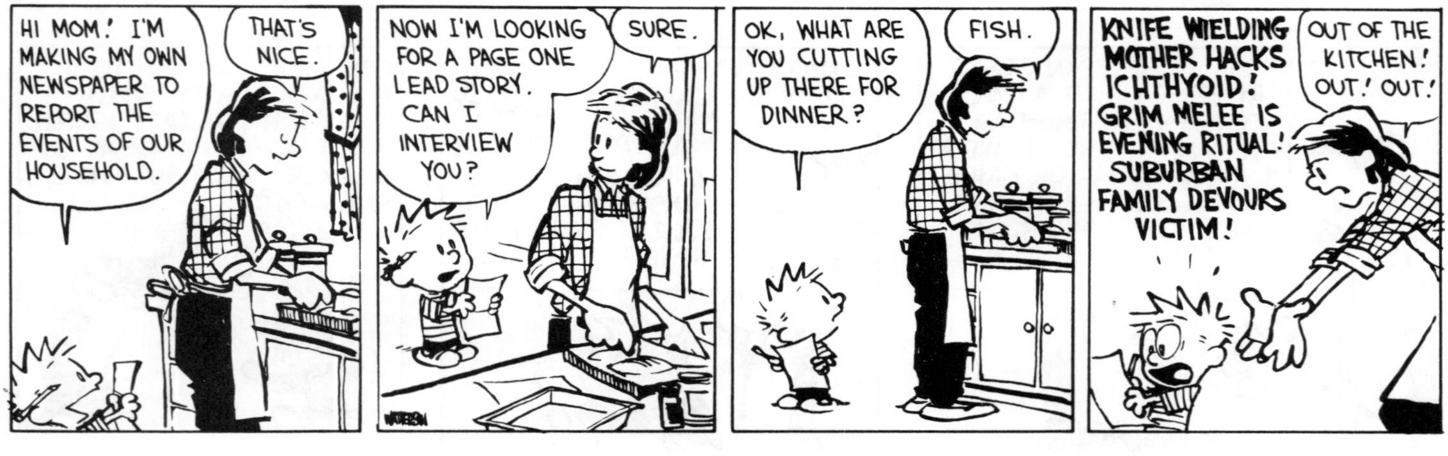
HI MOM! I'M MAKING MY OWN NEWSPAPER TO REPORT THE EVENTS OF OUR HOUSEHOLD.
THAT'S NICE.
NOW I'M LOOKING FOR A PAGE ONE LEAD STORY. CAN I INTERVIEW YOU?
SURE.
OK, WHAT ARE YOU CUTTING UP THERE FOR DINNER?
FISH.
KNIFE WIELDING MOTHER HACKS ICHTHYOID! GRIM MELEE IS EVENING RITUAL! SUBURBAN FAMILY DEVOURS VICTIM!
OUT OF THE KITCHEN! OUT! OUT!

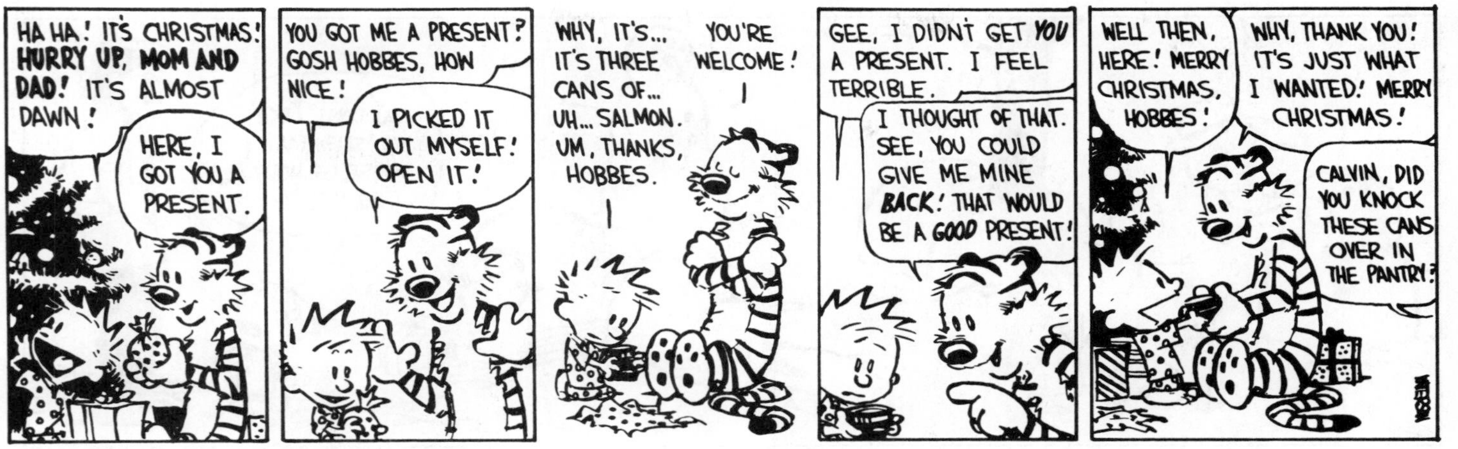
HA HA! IT'S CHRISTMAS! **HURRY UP, MOM AND DAD!** IT'S ALMOST DAWN!
HERE, I GOT YOU A PRESENT.
YOU GOT ME A PRESENT? GOSH HOBBES, HOW NICE!
I PICKED IT OUT MYSELF! OPEN IT!
WHY, IT'S... IT'S THREE CANS OF... UH... SALMON. UM, THANKS, HOBBES.
YOU'RE WELCOME!
GEE, I DIDN'T GET **YOU** A PRESENT. I FEEL TERRIBLE.
I THOUGHT OF THAT. SEE, YOU COULD GIVE ME MINE **BACK**! THAT WOULD BE A **GOOD** PRESENT!
WELL THEN, HERE! MERRY CHRISTMAS, HOBBES!
WHY, THANK YOU! IT'S JUST WHAT I WANTED! MERRY CHRISTMAS!
CALVIN, DID YOU KNOCK THESE CANS OVER IN THE PANTRY?

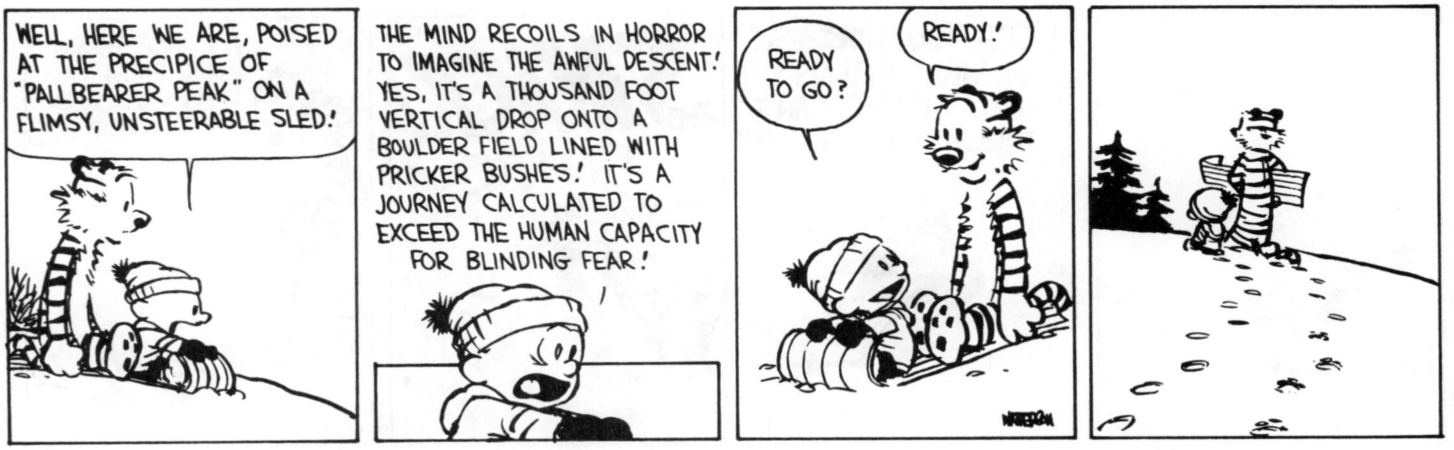
WELL, HERE WE ARE, POISED AT THE PRECIPICE OF "PALLBEARER PEAK" ON A FLIMSY, UNSTEERABLE SLED!
THE MIND RECOILS IN HORROR TO IMAGINE THE AWFUL DESCENT! YES, IT'S A THOUSAND FOOT VERTICAL DROP ONTO A BOULDER FIELD LINED WITH PRICKER BUSHES! IT'S A JOURNEY CALCULATED TO EXCEED THE HUMAN CAPACITY FOR BLINDING FEAR!
READY TO GO?
READY!

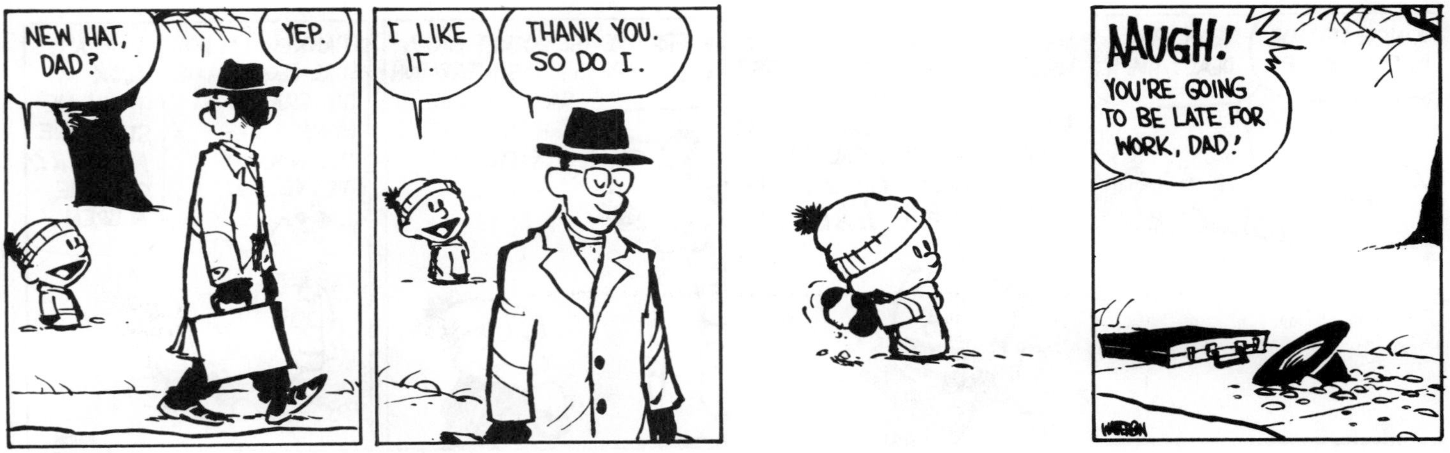
NEW HAT, DAD?
YEP.
I LIKE IT.
THANK YOU. SO DO I.
AAUGH!
YOU'RE GOING TO BE LATE FOR WORK, DAD!

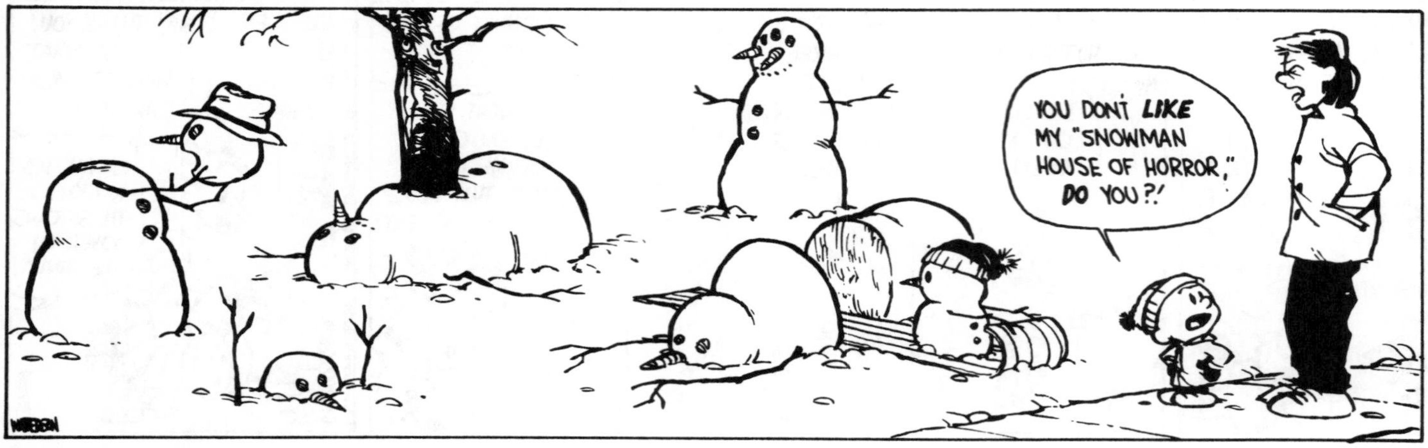
YOU DON'T **LIKE** MY "SNOWMAN HOUSE OF HORROR," **DO** YOU?!

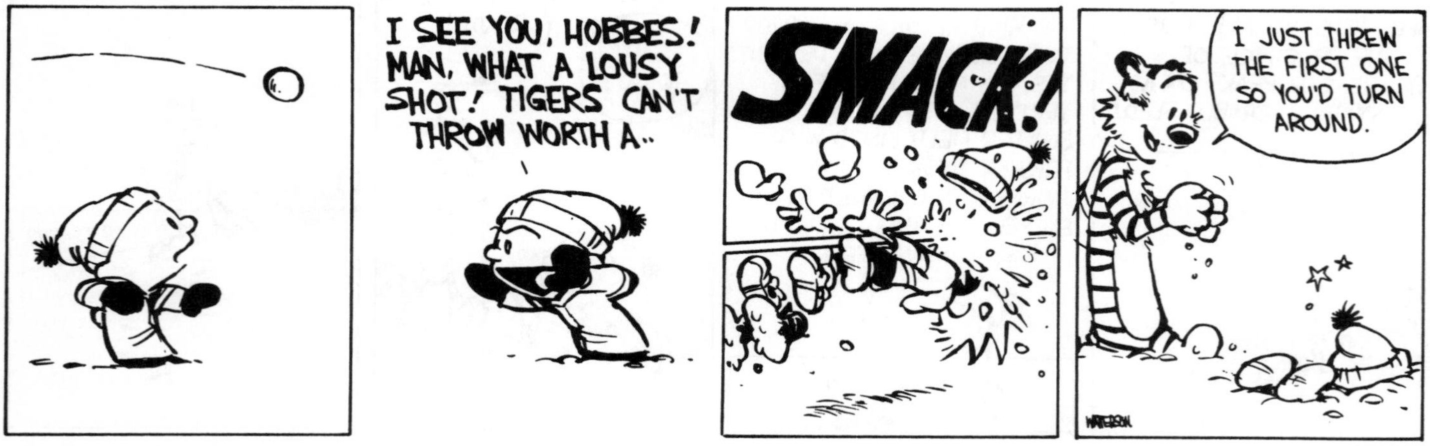
I SEE YOU, HOBBES! MAN, WHAT A LOUSY SHOT! TIGERS CAN'T THROW WORTH A..
SMACK!
I JUST THREW THE FIRST ONE SO YOU'D TURN AROUND.

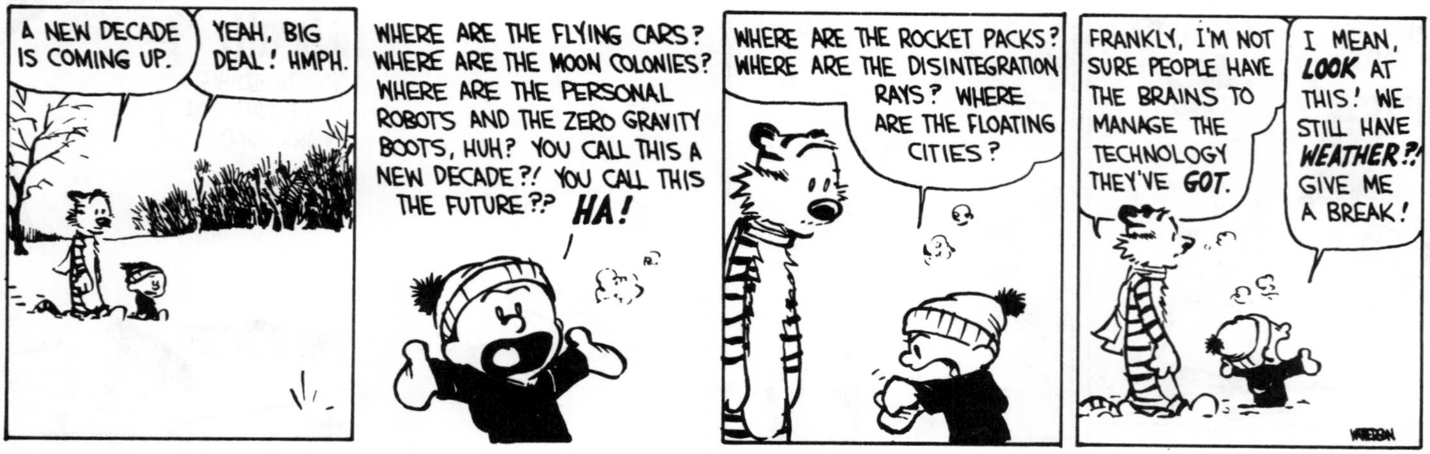
A NEW DECADE IS COMING UP.
YEAH, BIG DEAL! HMPH.
WHERE ARE THE FLYING CARS? WHERE ARE THE MOON COLONIES? WHERE ARE THE PERSONAL ROBOTS AND THE ZERO GRAVITY BOOTS, HUH? YOU CALL THIS A NEW DECADE?! YOU CALL THIS THE FUTURE?? **HA!**
WHERE ARE THE ROCKET PACKS? WHERE ARE THE DISINTEGRATION RAYS? WHERE ARE THE FLOATING CITIES?
FRANKLY, I'M NOT SURE PEOPLE HAVE THE BRAINS TO MANAGE THE TECHNOLOGY THEY'VE **GOT**.
I MEAN, **LOOK** AT THIS! WE STILL HAVE **WEATHER?!** GIVE ME A BREAK!

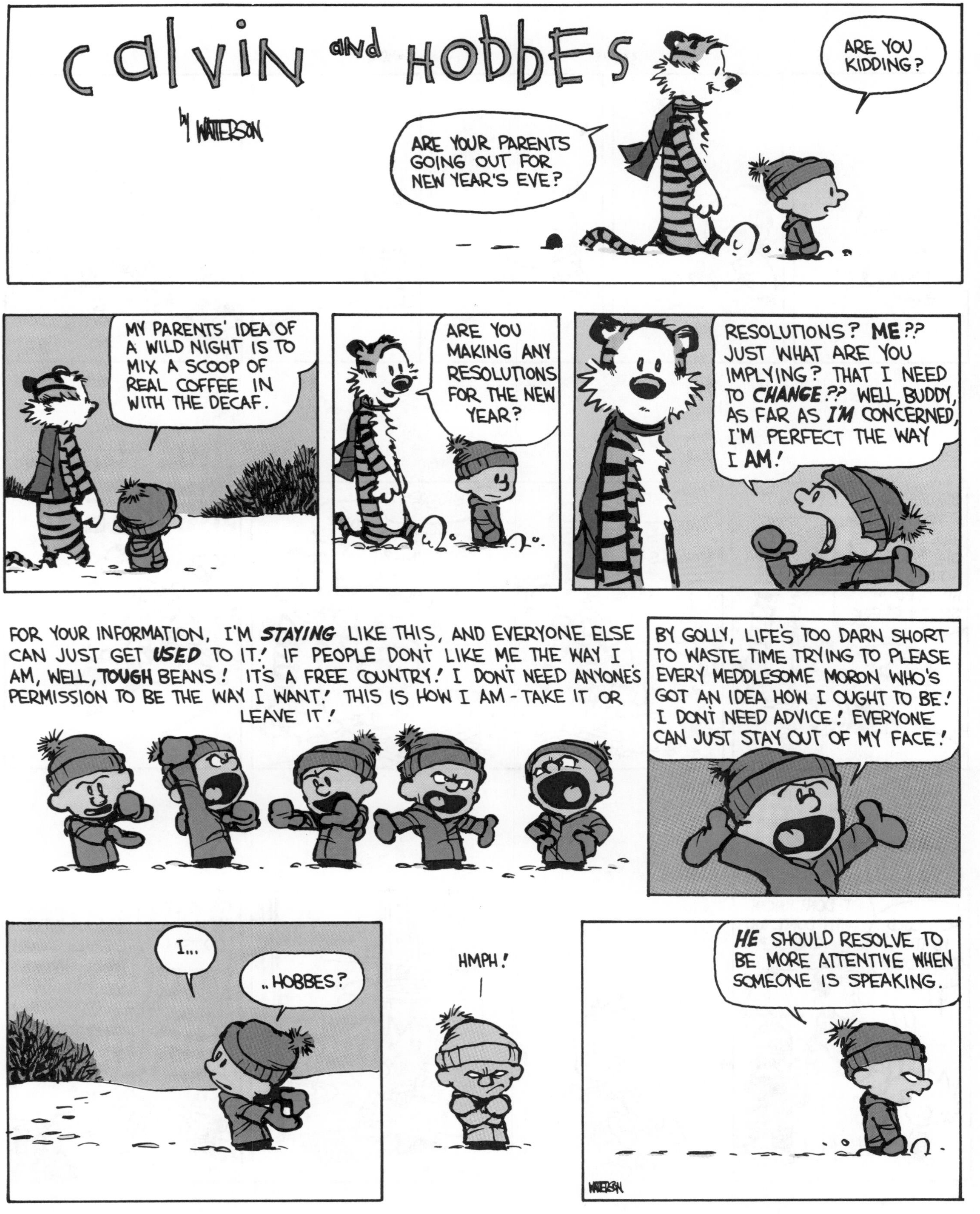
calvin and HOBBES
by WATTERSON
ARE YOUR PARENTS GOING OUT FOR NEW YEAR'S EVE?
ARE YOU KIDDING?
MY PARENTS' IDEA OF A WILD NIGHT IS TO MIX A SCOOP OF REAL COFFEE IN WITH THE DECAF.
ARE YOU MAKING ANY RESOLUTIONS FOR THE NEW YEAR?
RESOLUTIONS? ME?? JUST WHAT ARE YOU IMPLYING? THAT I NEED TO CHANGE?? WELL, BUDDY, AS FAR AS I'M CONCERNED, I'M PERFECT THE WAY I AM!
FOR YOUR INFORMATION, I'M STAYING LIKE THIS, AND EVERYONE ELSE CAN JUST GET USED TO IT! IF PEOPLE DON'T LIKE ME THE WAY I AM, WELL, TOUGH BEANS! IT'S A FREE COUNTRY! I DON'T NEED ANYONE'S PERMISSION TO BE THE WAY I WANT! THIS IS HOW I AM - TAKE IT OR LEAVE IT!
BY GOLLY, LIFE'S TOO DARN SHORT TO WASTE TIME TRYING TO PLEASE EVERY MEDDLESOME MORON WHO'S GOT AN IDEA HOW I OUGHT TO BE! I DON'T NEED ADVICE! EVERYONE CAN JUST STAY OUT OF MY FACE!
I...
..HOBBES?
HMPH!
HE SHOULD RESOLVE TO BE MORE ATTENTIVE WHEN SOMEONE IS SPEAKING.
WATTERSON

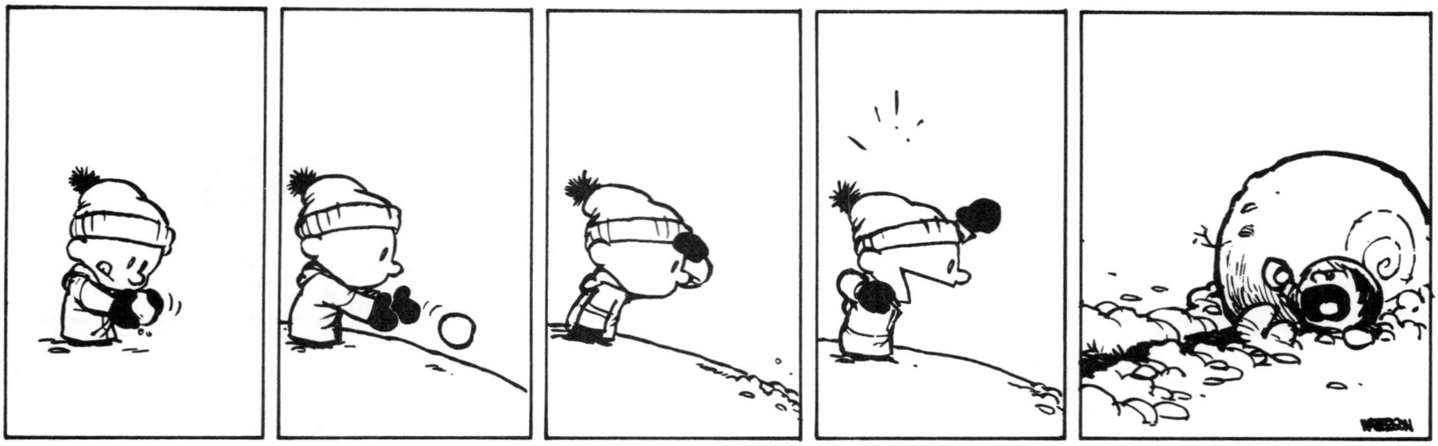

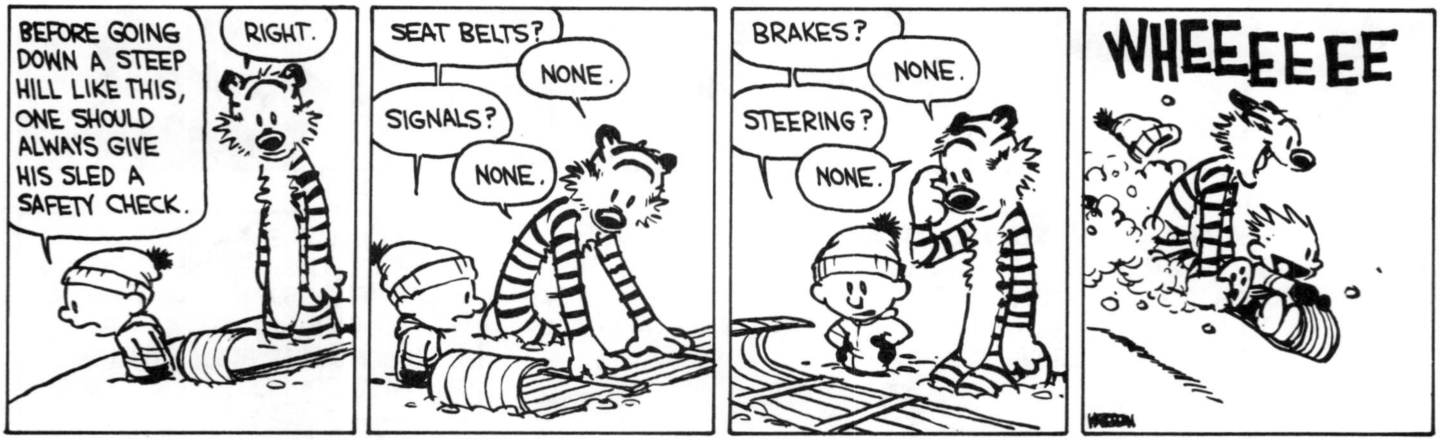

BEFORE GOING DOWN A STEEP HILL LIKE THIS, ONE SHOULD ALWAYS GIVE HIS SLED A SAFETY CHECK.
RIGHT.
SEAT BELTS?
NONE.
SIGNALS?
NONE.
BRAKES?
NONE.
STEERING?
NONE.
WHEEEEEE

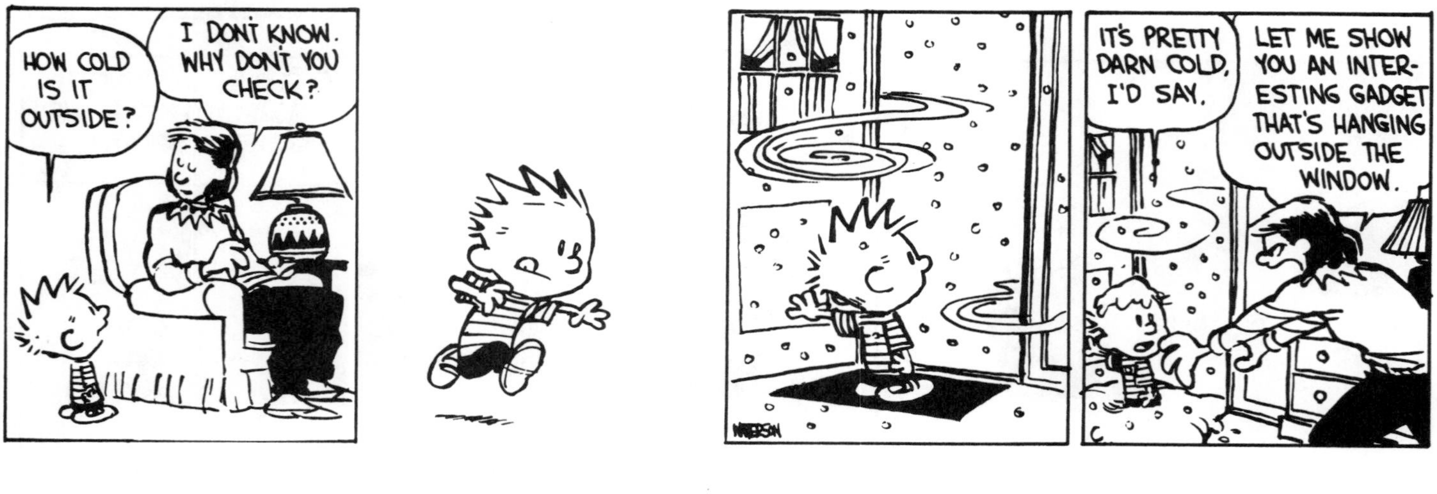

HOW COLD IS IT OUTSIDE?
I DON'T KNOW. WHY DON'T YOU CHECK?
IT'S PRETTY DARN COLD, I'D SAY.
LET ME SHOW YOU AN INTERESTING GADGET THAT'S HANGING OUTSIDE THE WINDOW.

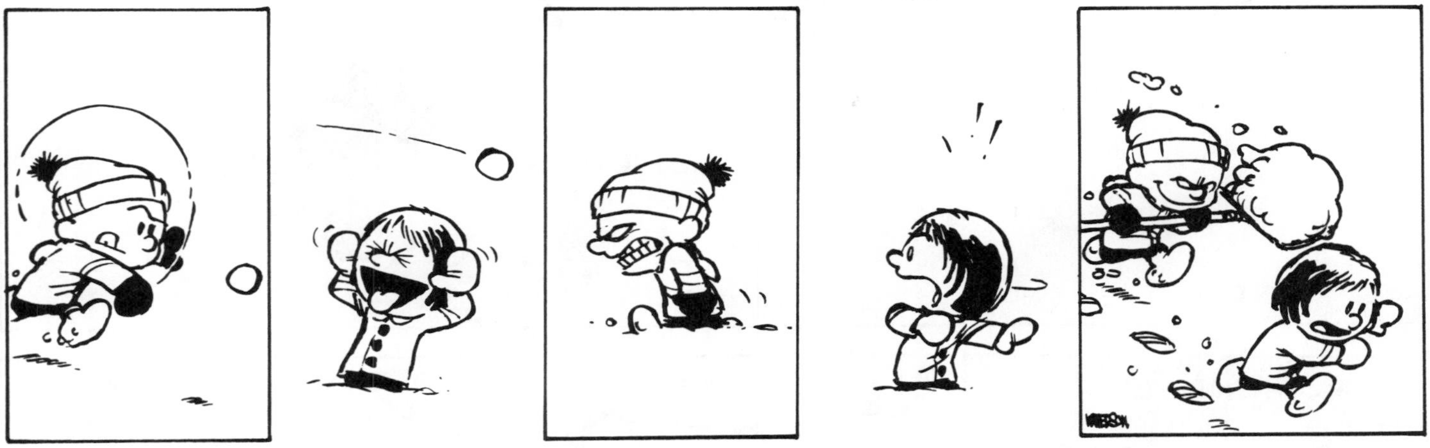

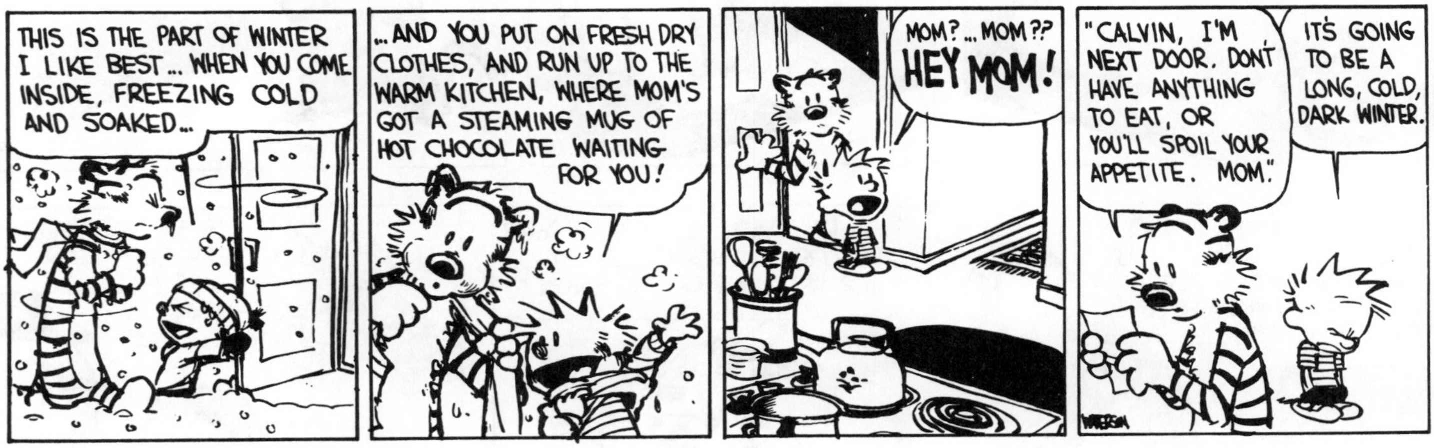
THIS IS THE PART OF WINTER I LIKE BEST... WHEN YOU COME INSIDE, FREEZING COLD AND SOAKED...
...AND YOU PUT ON FRESH DRY CLOTHES, AND RUN UP TO THE WARM KITCHEN, WHERE MOM'S GOT A STEAMING MUG OF HOT CHOCOLATE WAITING FOR YOU!
MOM? ... MOM?? HEY MOM!
"CALVIN, I'M NEXT DOOR. DON'T HAVE ANYTHING TO EAT, OR YOU'LL SPOIL YOUR APPETITE. MOM."
IT'S GOING TO BE A LONG, COLD, DARK WINTER.

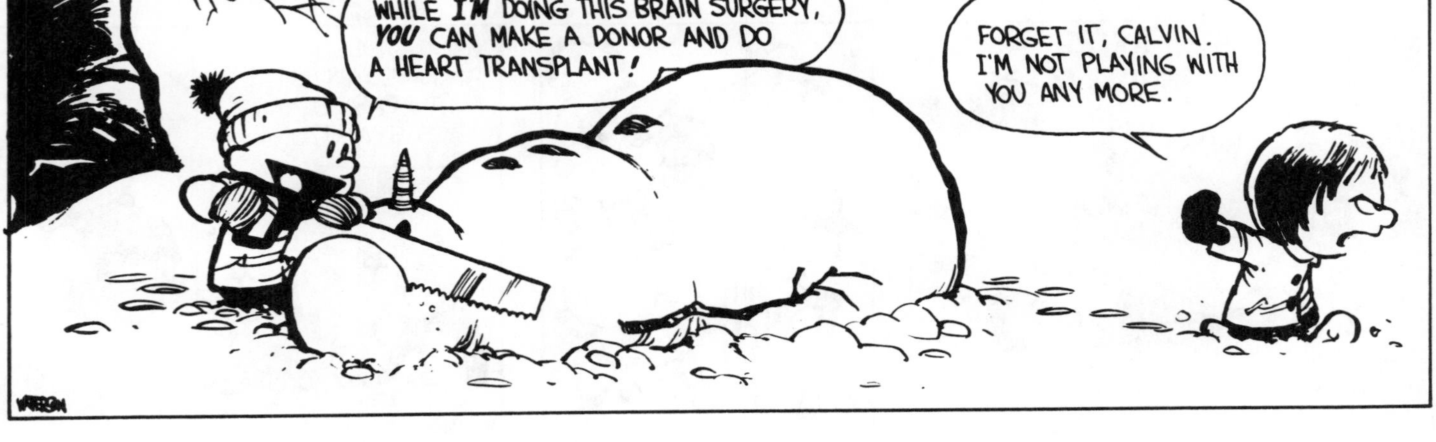
WHILE ***I'M*** DOING THIS BRAIN SURGERY, ***YOU*** CAN MAKE A DONOR AND DO A HEART TRANSPLANT!
FORGET IT, CALVIN. I'M NOT PLAYING WITH YOU ANY MORE.

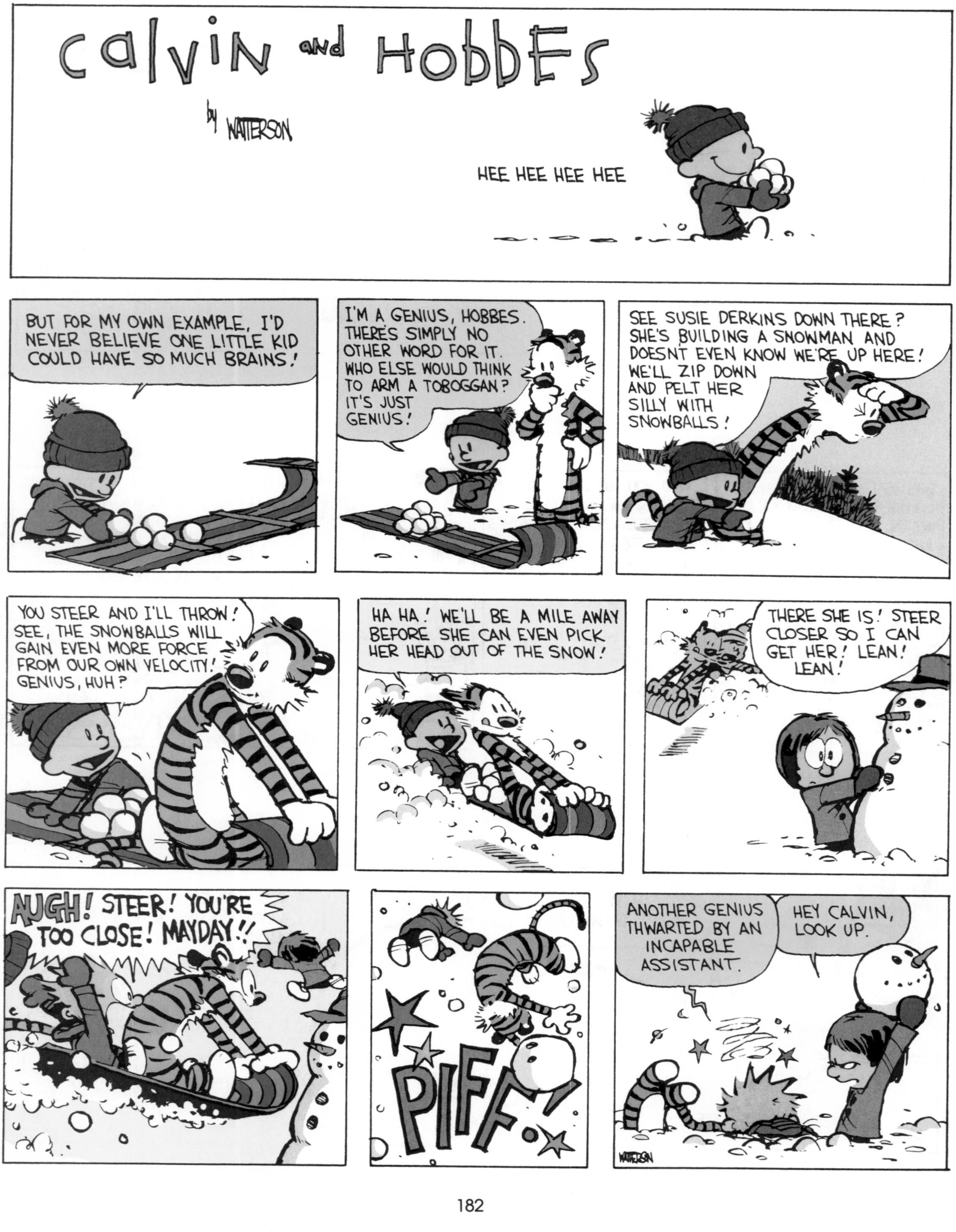
Calvin and HOBBES
by WATTERSON
HEE HEE HEE HEE
BUT FOR MY OWN EXAMPLE, I'D NEVER BELIEVE ONE LITTLE KID COULD HAVE SO MUCH BRAINS!
I'M A GENIUS, HOBBES. THERE'S SIMPLY NO OTHER WORD FOR IT. WHO ELSE WOULD THINK TO ARM A TOBOGGAN? IT'S JUST GENIUS!
SEE SUSIE DERKINS DOWN THERE? SHE'S BUILDING A SNOWMAN AND DOESN'T EVEN KNOW WE'RE UP HERE! WE'LL ZIP DOWN AND PELT HER SILLY WITH SNOWBALLS!
YOU STEER AND I'LL THROW! SEE, THE SNOWBALLS WILL GAIN EVEN MORE FORCE FROM OUR OWN VELOCITY! GENIUS, HUH?
HA HA! WE'LL BE A MILE AWAY BEFORE SHE CAN EVEN PICK HER HEAD OUT OF THE SNOW!
THERE SHE IS! STEER CLOSER SO I CAN GET HER! LEAN! LEAN!
AUGH! STEER! YOU'RE TOO CLOSE! MAYDAY!!
PIFF!
ANOTHER GENIUS THWARTED BY AN INCAPABLE ASSISTANT.
HEY CALVIN, LOOK UP.
WATTERSON

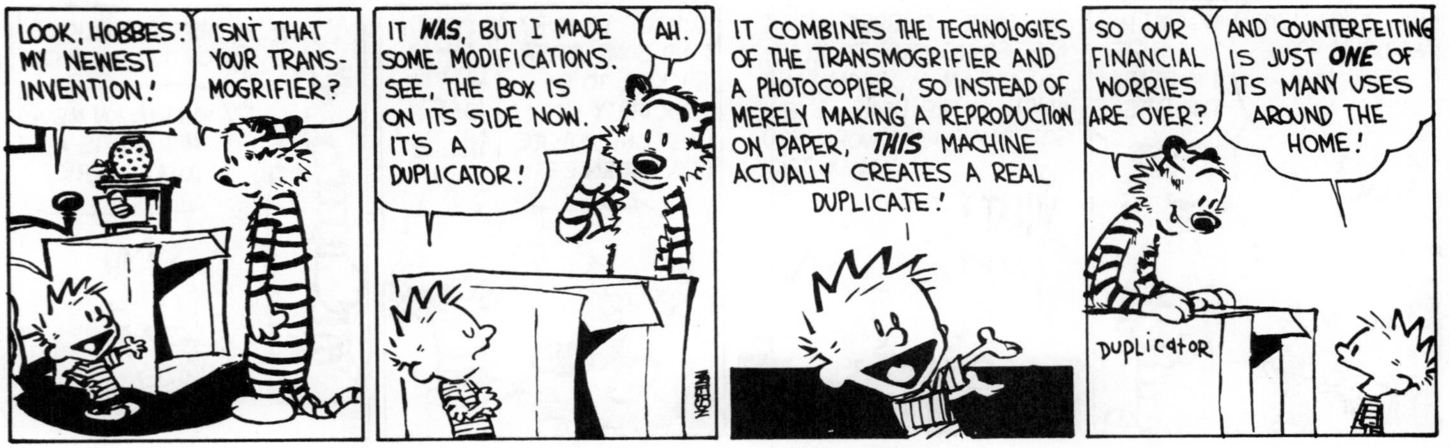
LOOK, HOBBES! MY NEWEST INVENTION!
ISN'T THAT YOUR TRANSMOGRIFIER?
IT WAS, BUT I MADE SOME MODIFICATIONS. SEE, THE BOX IS ON ITS SIDE NOW. IT'S A DUPLICATOR!
AH.
IT COMBINES THE TECHNOLOGIES OF THE TRANSMOGRIFIER AND A PHOTOCOPIER, SO INSTEAD OF MERELY MAKING A REPRODUCTION ON PAPER, THIS MACHINE ACTUALLY CREATES A REAL DUPLICATE!
SO OUR FINANCIAL WORRIES ARE OVER?
AND COUNTERFEITING IS JUST ONE OF ITS MANY USES AROUND THE HOME!
DUPLICATOR

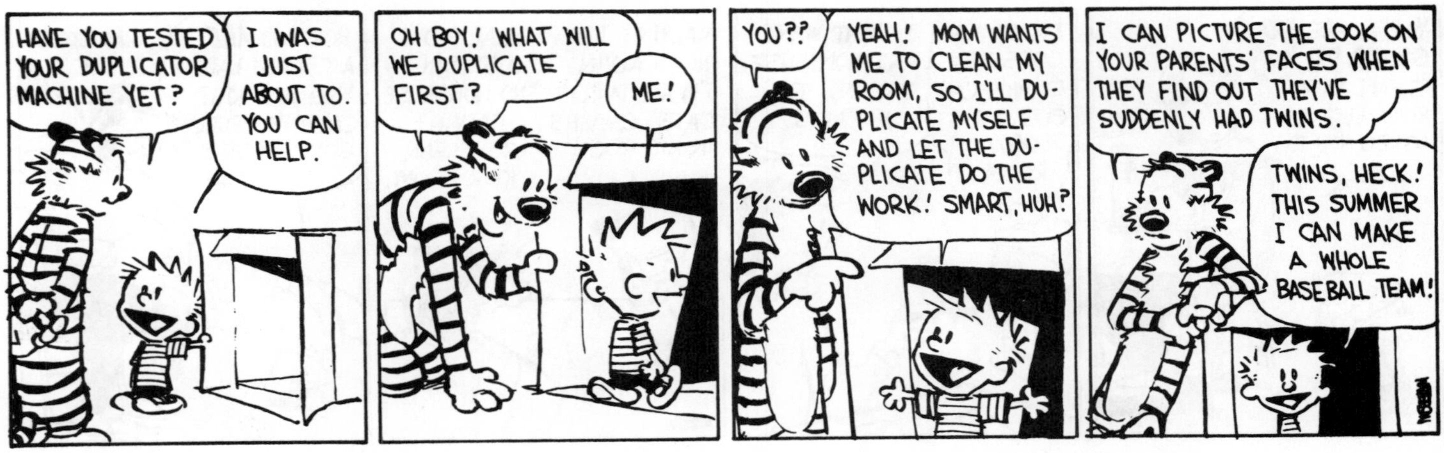
HAVE YOU TESTED YOUR DUPLICATOR MACHINE YET?
I WAS JUST ABOUT TO. YOU CAN HELP.
OH BOY! WHAT WILL WE DUPLICATE FIRST?
ME!
YOU??
YEAH! MOM WANTS ME TO CLEAN MY ROOM, SO I'LL DUPLICATE MYSELF AND LET THE DUPLICATE DO THE WORK! SMART, HUH?
I CAN PICTURE THE LOOK ON YOUR PARENTS' FACES WHEN THEY FIND OUT THEY'VE SUDDENLY HAD TWINS.
TWINS, HECK! THIS SUMMER I CAN MAKE A WHOLE BASEBALL TEAM!

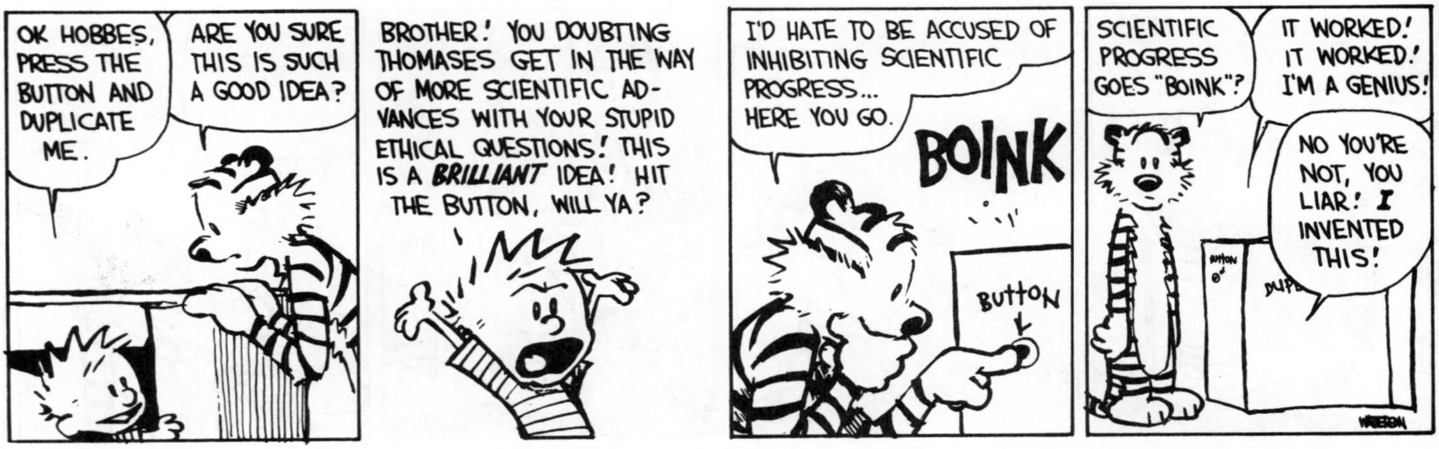
OK HOBBES, PRESS THE BUTTON AND DUPLICATE ME.
ARE YOU SURE THIS IS SUCH A GOOD IDEA?
BROTHER! YOU DOUBTING THOMASES GET IN THE WAY OF MORE SCIENTIFIC ADVANCES WITH YOUR STUPID ETHICAL QUESTIONS! THIS IS A BRILLIANT IDEA! HIT THE BUTTON, WILL YA?
I'D HATE TO BE ACCUSED OF INHIBITING SCIENTIFIC PROGRESS... HERE YOU GO.
BOINK
BUTTON
SCIENTIFIC PROGRESS GOES "BOINK"?
IT WORKED! IT WORKED! I'M A GENIUS!
NO YOU'RE NOT, YOU LIAR! I INVENTED THIS!

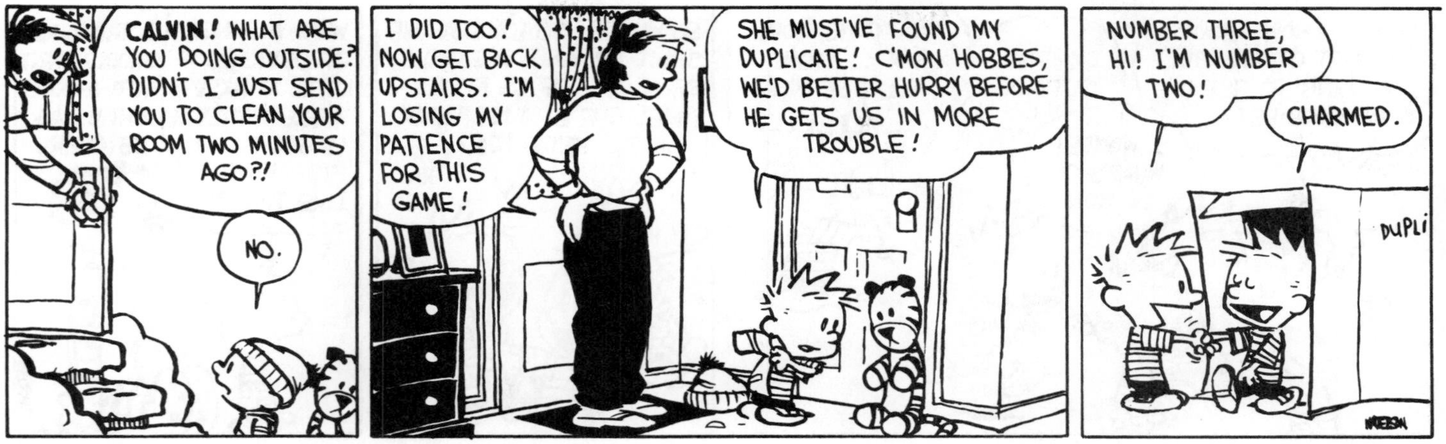
CALVIN! WHAT ARE YOU DOING OUTSIDE? DIDN'T I JUST SEND YOU TO CLEAN YOUR ROOM TWO MINUTES AGO?!
NO.
I DID TOO! NOW GET BACK UPSTAIRS. I'M LOSING MY PATIENCE FOR THIS GAME!
SHE MUST'VE FOUND MY DUPLICATE! C'MON HOBBES, WE'D BETTER HURRY BEFORE HE GETS US IN MORE TROUBLE!
NUMBER THREE, HI! I'M NUMBER TWO!
CHARMED.
DUPLI

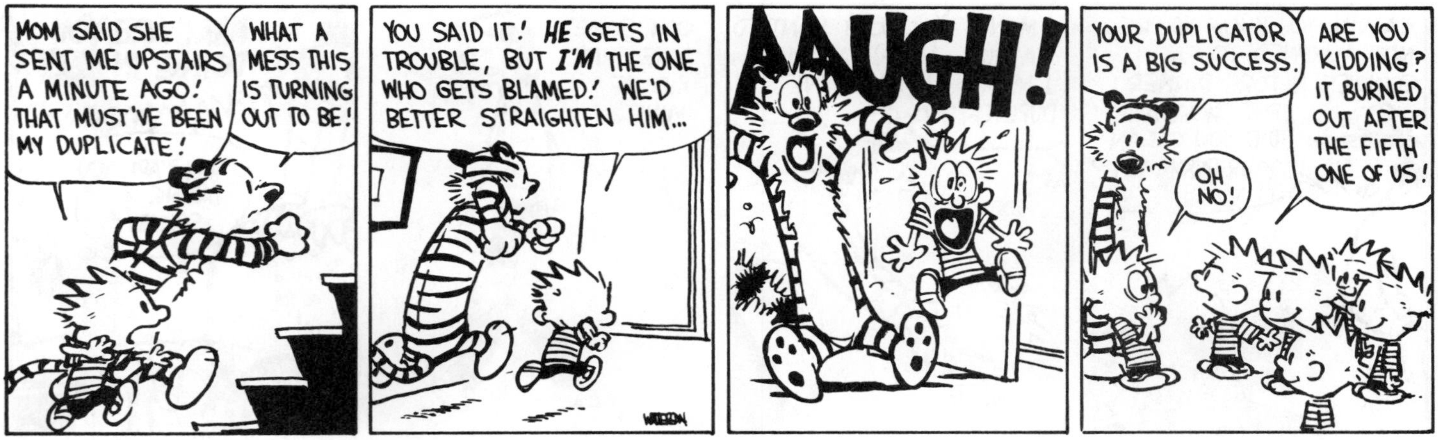
MOM SAID SHE SENT ME UPSTAIRS A MINUTE AGO! THAT MUST'VE BEEN MY DUPLICATE!
WHAT A MESS THIS IS TURNING OUT TO BE!
YOU SAID IT! HE GETS IN TROUBLE, BUT I'M THE ONE WHO GETS BLAMED! WE'D BETTER STRAIGHTEN HIM...
AAUGH!
YOUR DUPLICATOR IS A BIG SUCCESS.
ARE YOU KIDDING? IT BURNED OUT AFTER THE FIFTH ONE OF US!
OH NO!

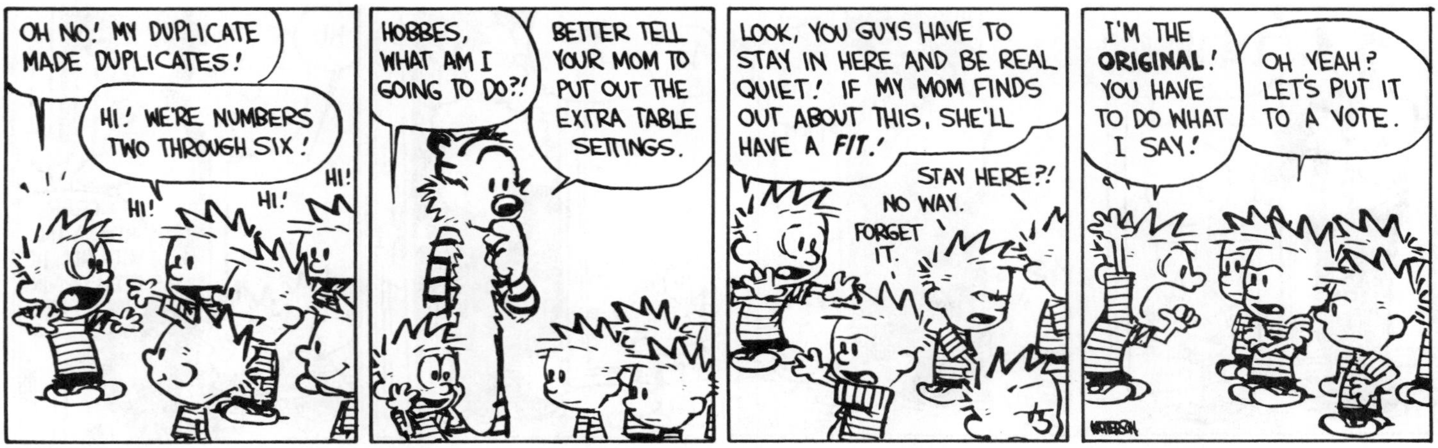
OH NO! MY DUPLICATE MADE DUPLICATES!
HI! WE'RE NUMBERS TWO THROUGH SIX!
HI!
HI!
HI!
HOBBES, WHAT AM I GOING TO DO?!
BETTER TELL YOUR MOM TO PUT OUT THE EXTRA TABLE SETTINGS.
LOOK, YOU GUYS HAVE TO STAY IN HERE AND BE REAL QUIET! IF MY MOM FINDS OUT ABOUT THIS, SHE'LL HAVE A FIT!
STAY HERE?!
NO WAY.
FORGET IT.
I'M THE ORIGINAL! YOU HAVE TO DO WHAT I SAY!
OH YEAH? LET'S PUT IT TO A VOTE.

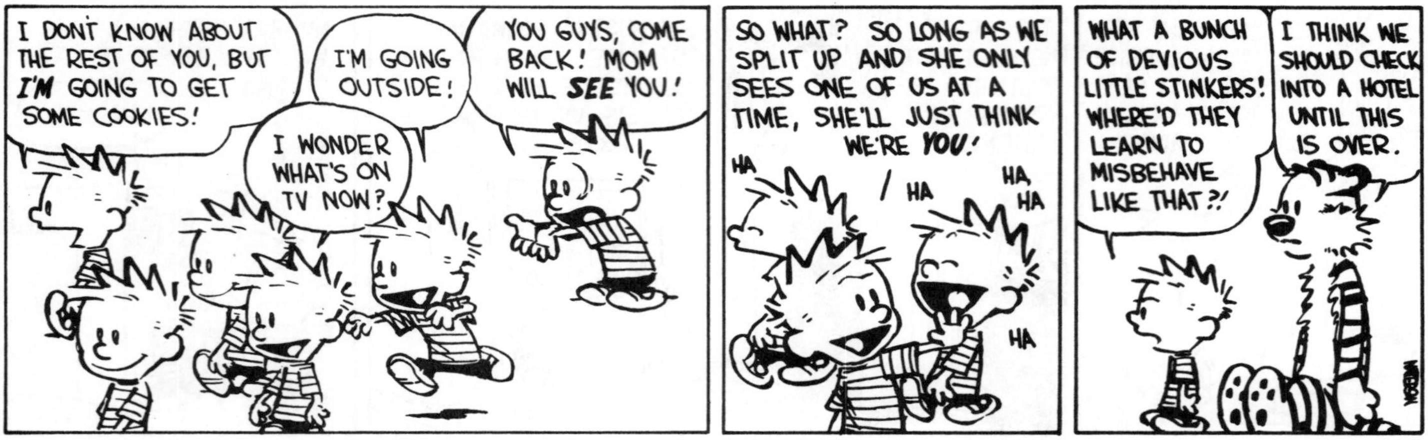
I DON'T KNOW ABOUT THE REST OF YOU, BUT I'M GOING TO GET SOME COOKIES!
I'M GOING OUTSIDE!
I WONDER WHAT'S ON TV NOW?
YOU GUYS, COME BACK! MOM WILL SEE YOU!
SO WHAT? SO LONG AS WE SPLIT UP AND SHE ONLY SEES ONE OF US AT A TIME, SHE'LL JUST THINK WE'RE YOU!
HA HA HA, HA HA
WHAT A BUNCH OF DEVIOUS LITTLE STINKERS! WHERE'D THEY LEARN TO MISBEHAVE LIKE THAT?!
I THINK WE SHOULD CHECK INTO A HOTEL UNTIL THIS IS OVER.

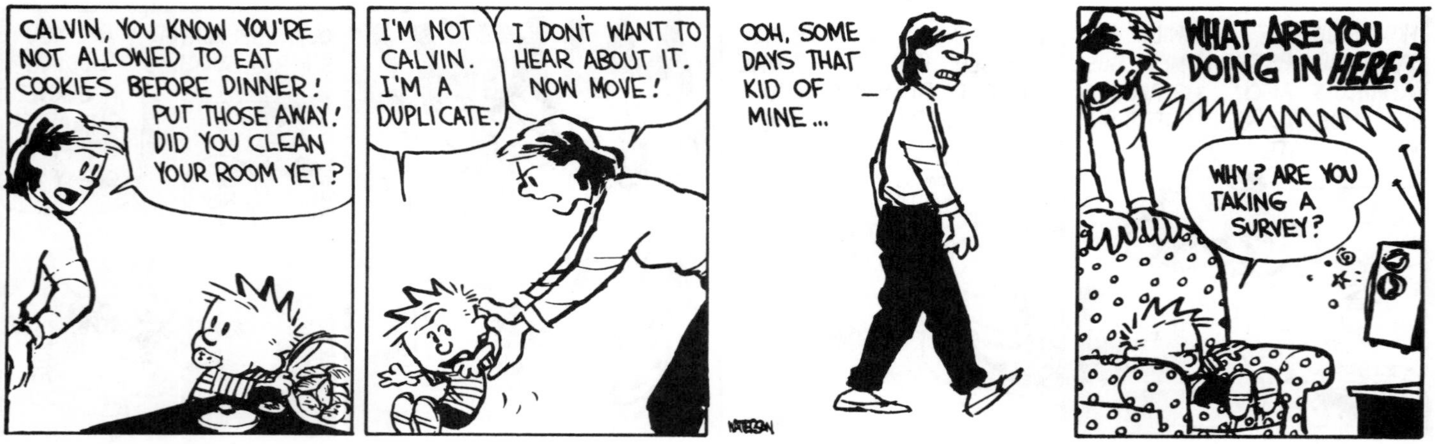
CALVIN, YOU KNOW YOU'RE NOT ALLOWED TO EAT COOKIES BEFORE DINNER! PUT THOSE AWAY! DID YOU CLEAN YOUR ROOM YET?
I'M NOT CALVIN. I'M A DUPLICATE.
I DON'T WANT TO HEAR ABOUT IT. NOW MOVE!
OOH, SOME DAYS THAT KID OF MINE...
WHAT ARE YOU DOING IN HERE?!
WHY? ARE YOU TAKING A SURVEY?

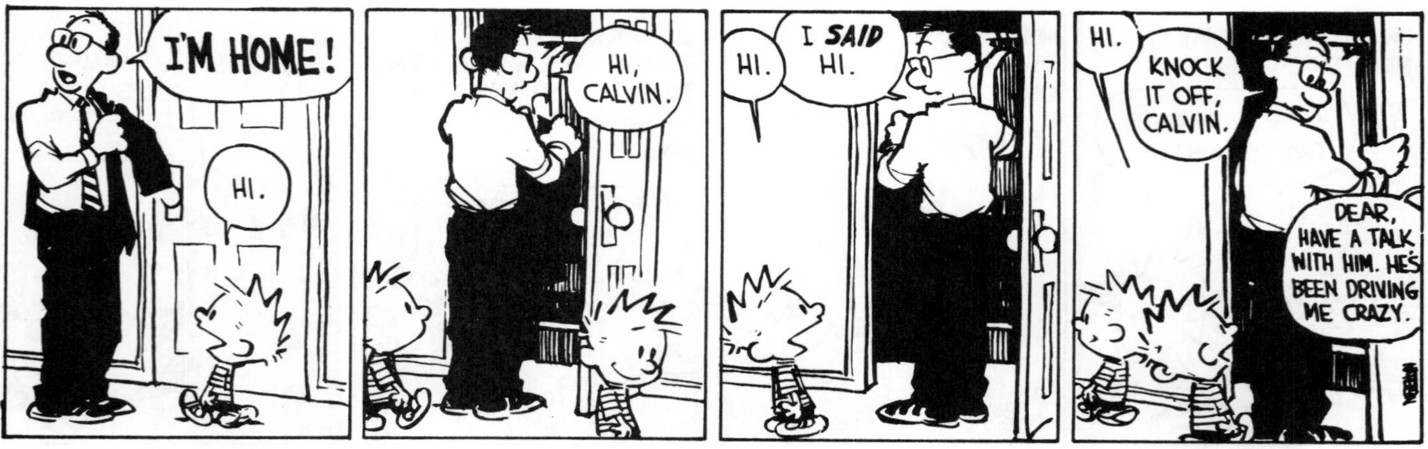
I'M HOME!
HI.
HI, CALVIN.
HI.
I SAID HI.
HI.
KNOCK IT OFF, CALVIN.
DEAR, HAVE A TALK WITH HIM. HE'S BEEN DRIVING ME CRAZY.

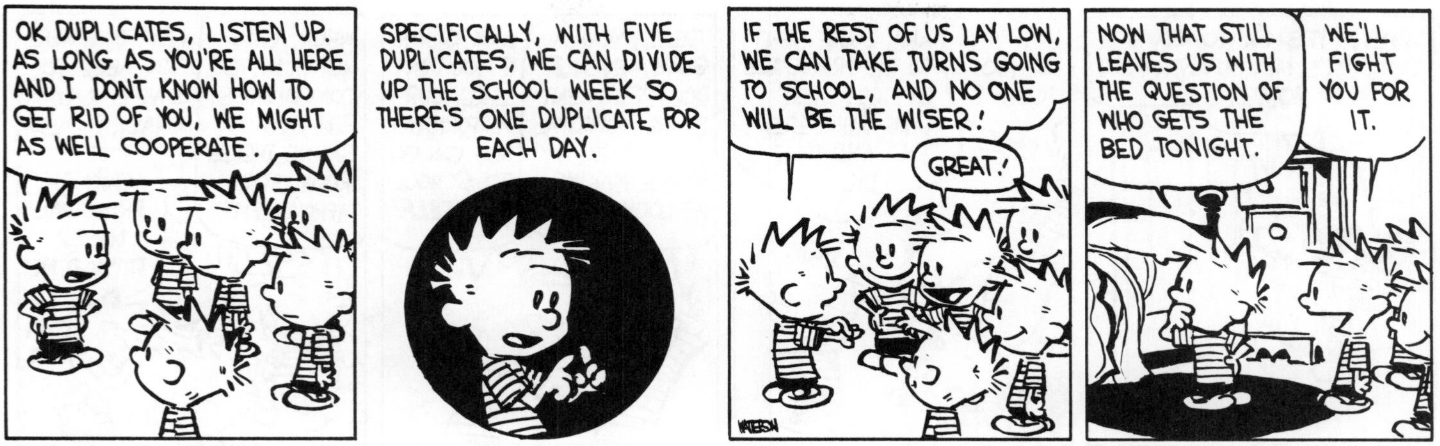
OK DUPLICATES, LISTEN UP. AS LONG AS YOU'RE ALL HERE AND I DON'T KNOW HOW TO GET RID OF YOU, WE MIGHT AS WELL COOPERATE.
SPECIFICALLY, WITH FIVE DUPLICATES, WE CAN DIVIDE UP THE SCHOOL WEEK SO THERE'S ONE DUPLICATE FOR EACH DAY.
IF THE REST OF US LAY LOW, WE CAN TAKE TURNS GOING TO SCHOOL, AND NO ONE WILL BE THE WISER!
GREAT!
NOW THAT STILL LEAVES US WITH THE QUESTION OF WHO GETS THE BED TONIGHT.
WE'LL FIGHT YOU FOR IT.

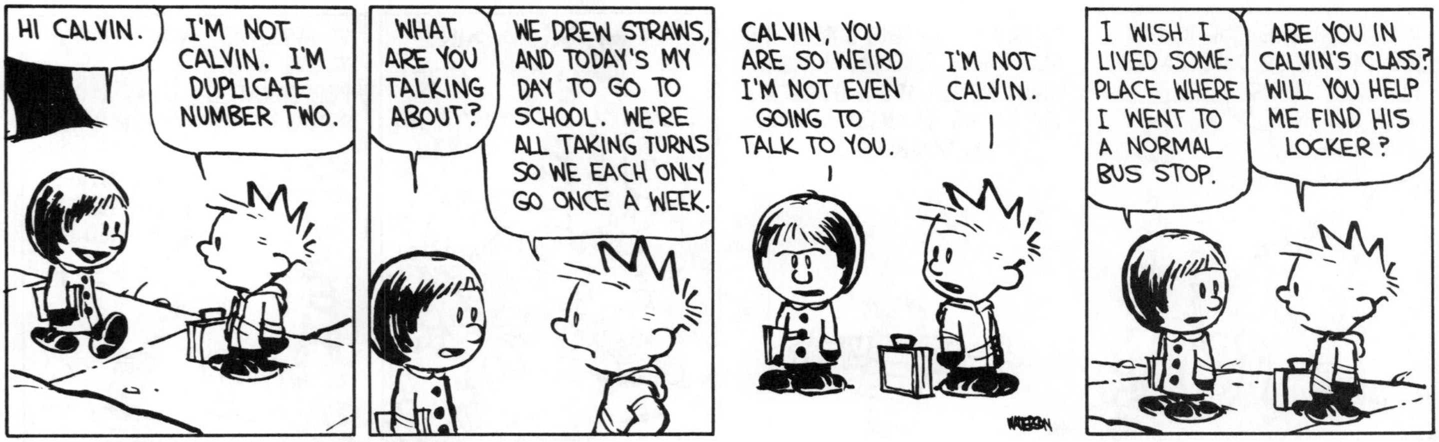
HI CALVIN.
I'M NOT CALVIN. I'M DUPLICATE NUMBER TWO.
WHAT ARE YOU TALKING ABOUT?
WE DREW STRAWS, AND TODAY'S MY DAY TO GO TO SCHOOL. WE'RE ALL TAKING TURNS SO WE EACH ONLY GO ONCE A WEEK.
CALVIN, YOU ARE SO WEIRD I'M NOT EVEN GOING TO TALK TO YOU.
I'M NOT CALVIN.
I WISH I LIVED SOME-PLACE WHERE I WENT TO A NORMAL BUS STOP.
ARE YOU IN CALVIN'S CLASS? WILL YOU HELP ME FIND HIS LOCKER?

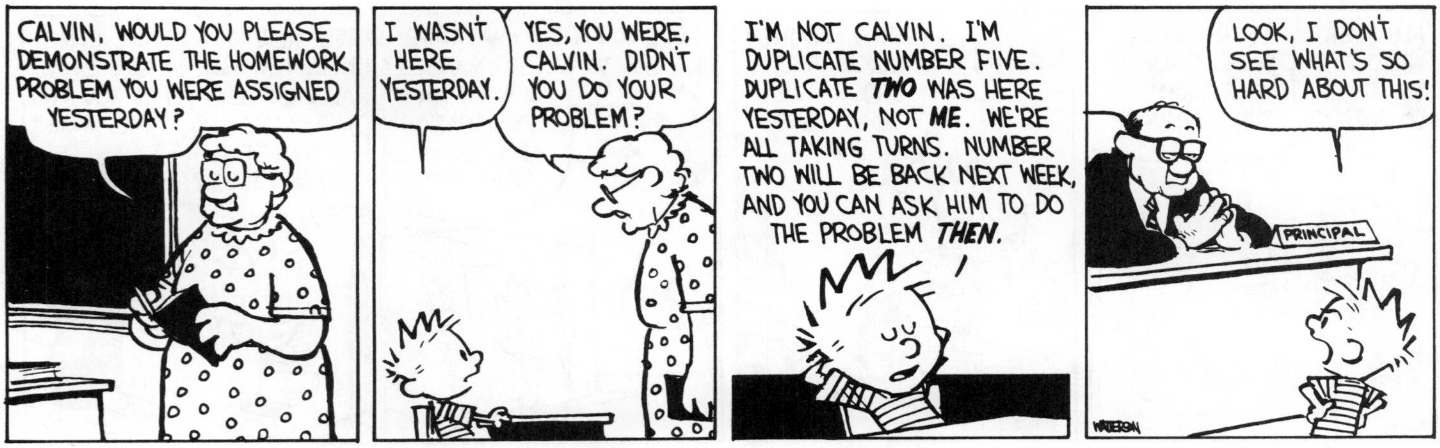
CALVIN, WOULD YOU PLEASE DEMONSTRATE THE HOMEWORK PROBLEM YOU WERE ASSIGNED YESTERDAY?
I WASN'T HERE YESTERDAY.
YES, YOU WERE, CALVIN. DIDN'T YOU DO YOUR PROBLEM?
I'M NOT CALVIN. I'M DUPLICATE NUMBER FIVE. DUPLICATE **TWO** WAS HERE YESTERDAY, NOT **ME**. WE'RE ALL TAKING TURNS. NUMBER TWO WILL BE BACK NEXT WEEK, AND YOU CAN ASK HIM TO DO THE PROBLEM **THEN**.
LOOK, I DON'T SEE WHAT'S SO HARD ABOUT THIS!
PRINCIPAL

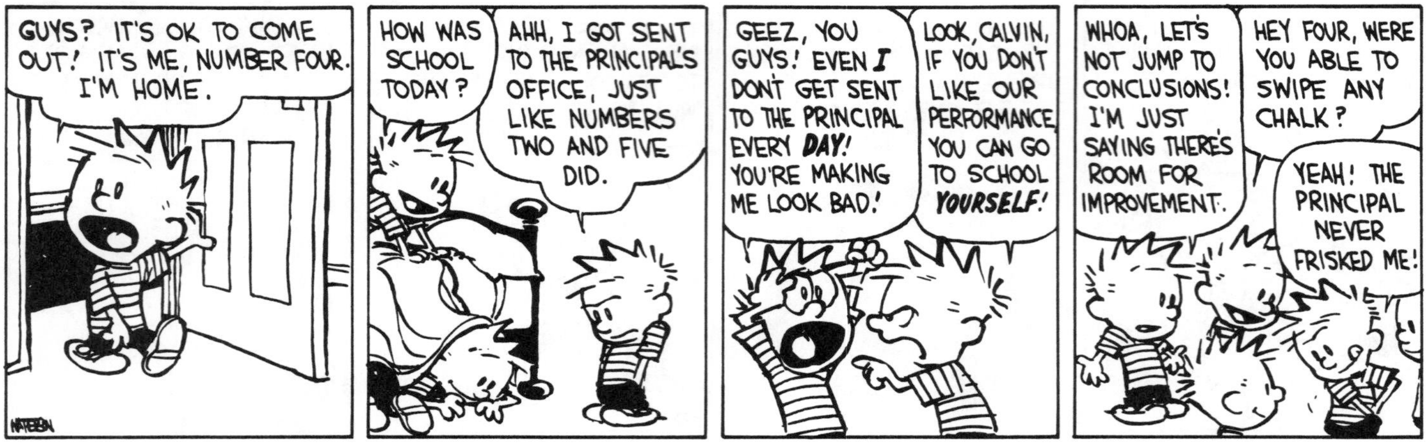
GUYS? IT'S OK TO COME OUT! IT'S ME, NUMBER FOUR. I'M HOME.
HOW WAS SCHOOL TODAY?
AHH, I GOT SENT TO THE PRINCIPAL'S OFFICE, JUST LIKE NUMBERS TWO AND FIVE DID.
GEEZ, YOU GUYS! EVEN ***I*** DON'T GET SENT TO THE PRINCIPAL EVERY ***DAY***! YOU'RE MAKING ME LOOK BAD!
LOOK, CALVIN, IF YOU DON'T LIKE OUR PERFORMANCE, YOU CAN GO TO SCHOOL ***YOURSELF***!
WHOA, LET'S NOT JUMP TO CONCLUSIONS! I'M JUST SAYING THERE'S ROOM FOR IMPROVEMENT.
HEY FOUR, WERE YOU ABLE TO SWIPE ANY CHALK?
YEAH! THE PRINCIPAL NEVER FRISKED ME!

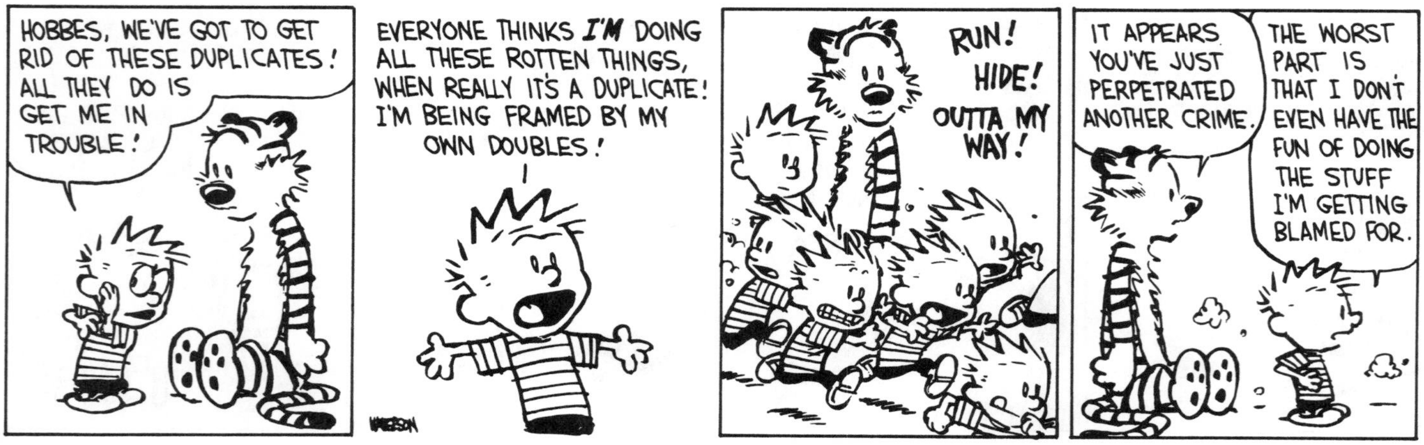
HOBBES, WE'VE GOT TO GET RID OF THESE DUPLICATES! ALL THEY DO IS GET ME IN TROUBLE!
EVERYONE THINKS ***I'M*** DOING ALL THESE ROTTEN THINGS, WHEN REALLY IT'S A DUPLICATE! I'M BEING FRAMED BY MY OWN DOUBLES!
RUN!
HIDE!
OUTTA MY WAY!
IT APPEARS YOU'VE JUST PERPETRATED ANOTHER CRIME.
THE WORST PART IS THAT I DON'T EVEN HAVE THE FUN OF DOING THE STUFF I'M GETTING BLAMED FOR.

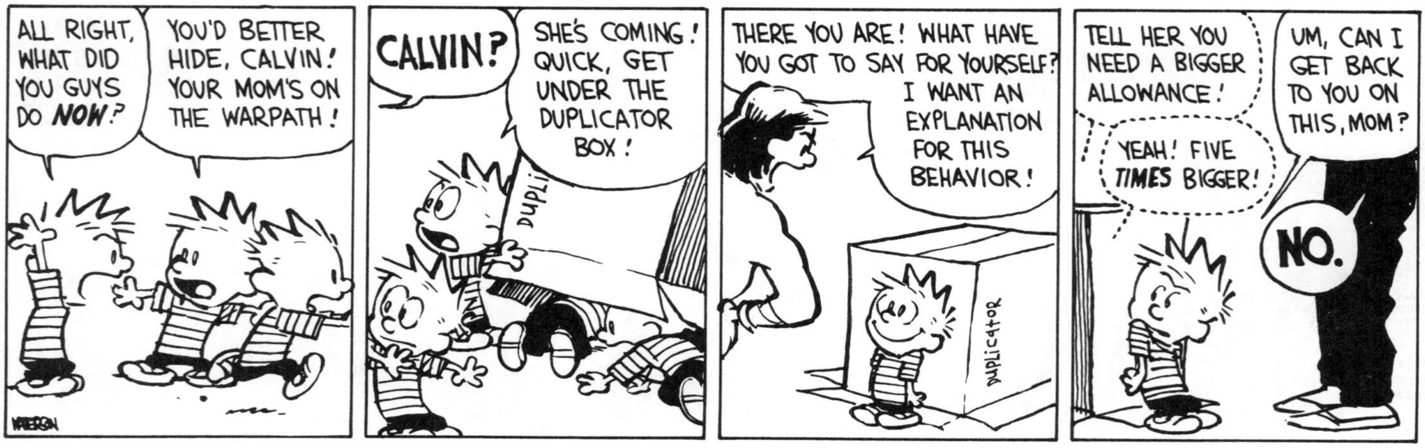
ALL RIGHT, WHAT DID YOU GUYS DO ***NOW***?
YOU'D BETTER HIDE, CALVIN! YOUR MOM'S ON THE WARPATH!
CALVIN?
SHE'S COMING! QUICK, GET UNDER THE DUPLICATOR BOX!
DUPLI
THERE YOU ARE! WHAT HAVE YOU GOT TO SAY FOR YOURSELF? I WANT AN EXPLANATION FOR THIS BEHAVIOR!
DUPLICATOR
TELL HER YOU NEED A BIGGER ALLOWANCE!
YEAH! FIVE ***TIMES*** BIGGER!
UM, CAN I GET BACK TO YOU ON THIS, MOM?
NO.

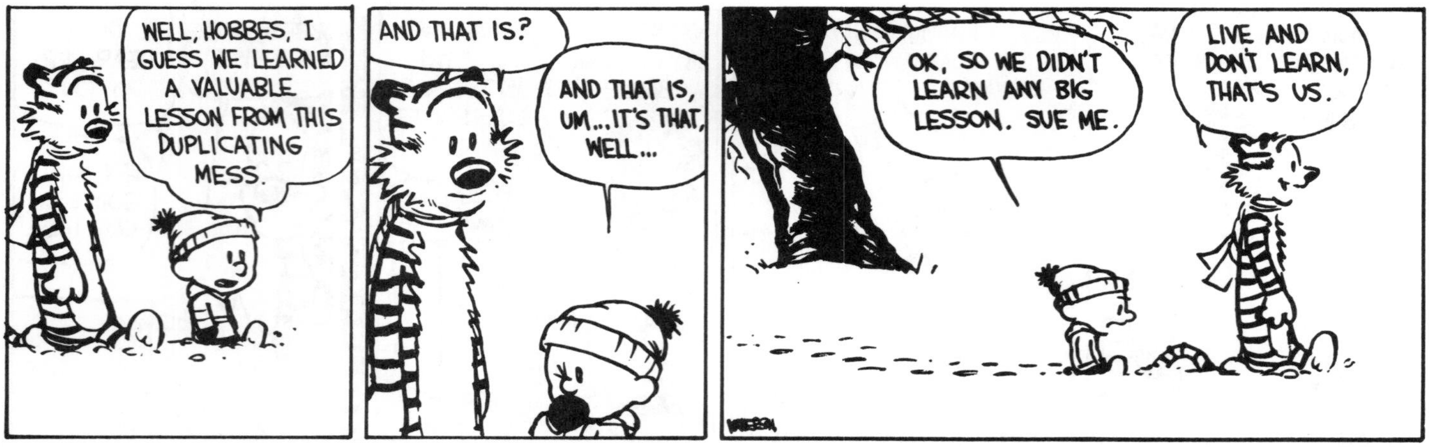
WELL, HOBBES, I GUESS WE LEARNED A VALUABLE LESSON FROM THIS DUPLICATING MESS.
AND THAT IS?
AND THAT IS, UM...IT'S THAT, WELL...
OK, SO WE DIDN'T LEARN ANY BIG LESSON. SUE ME.
LIVE AND DON'T LEARN, THAT'S US.

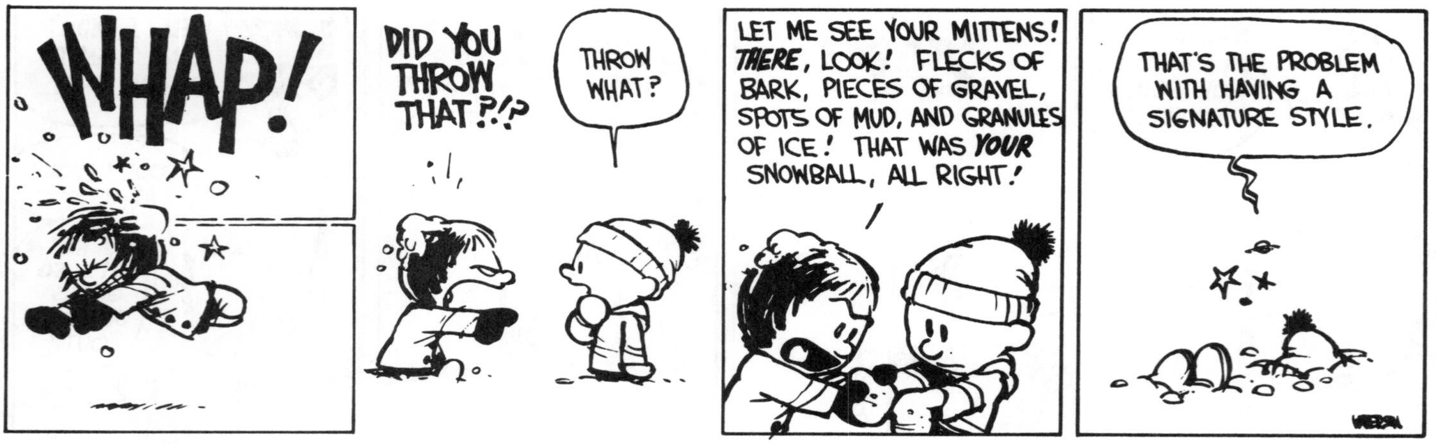
WHAP!
DID YOU THROW THAT?!?
THROW WHAT?
LET ME SEE YOUR MITTENS! THERE, LOOK! FLECKS OF BARK, PIECES OF GRAVEL, SPOTS OF MUD, AND GRANULES OF ICE! THAT WAS YOUR SNOWBALL, ALL RIGHT!
THAT'S THE PROBLEM WITH HAVING A SIGNATURE STYLE.

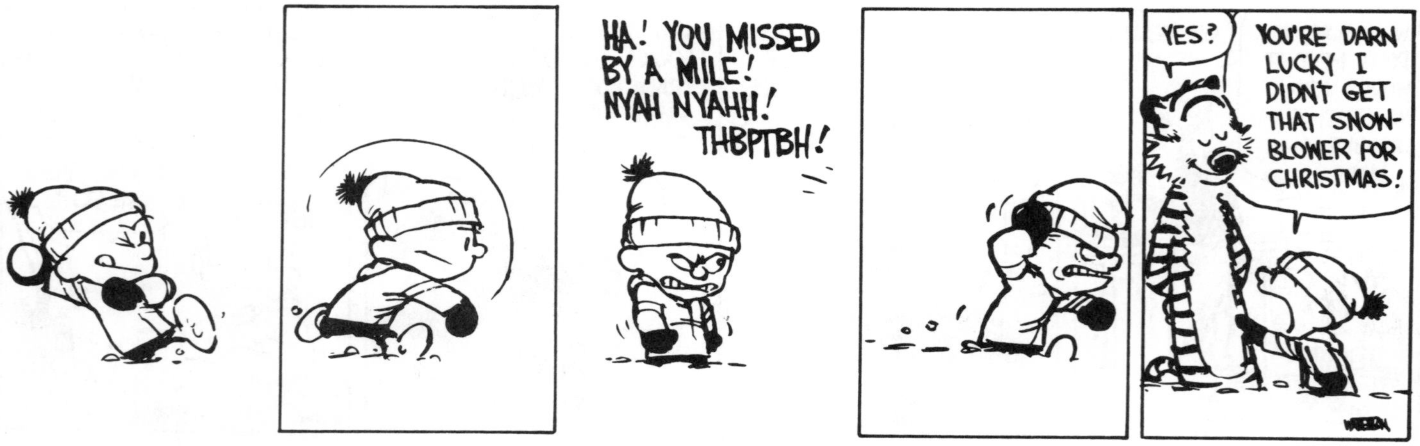
HA! YOU MISSED BY A MILE! NYAH NYAHH! THBPTBH!
YES?
YOU'RE DARN LUCKY I DIDN'T GET THAT SNOW-BLOWER FOR CHRISTMAS!

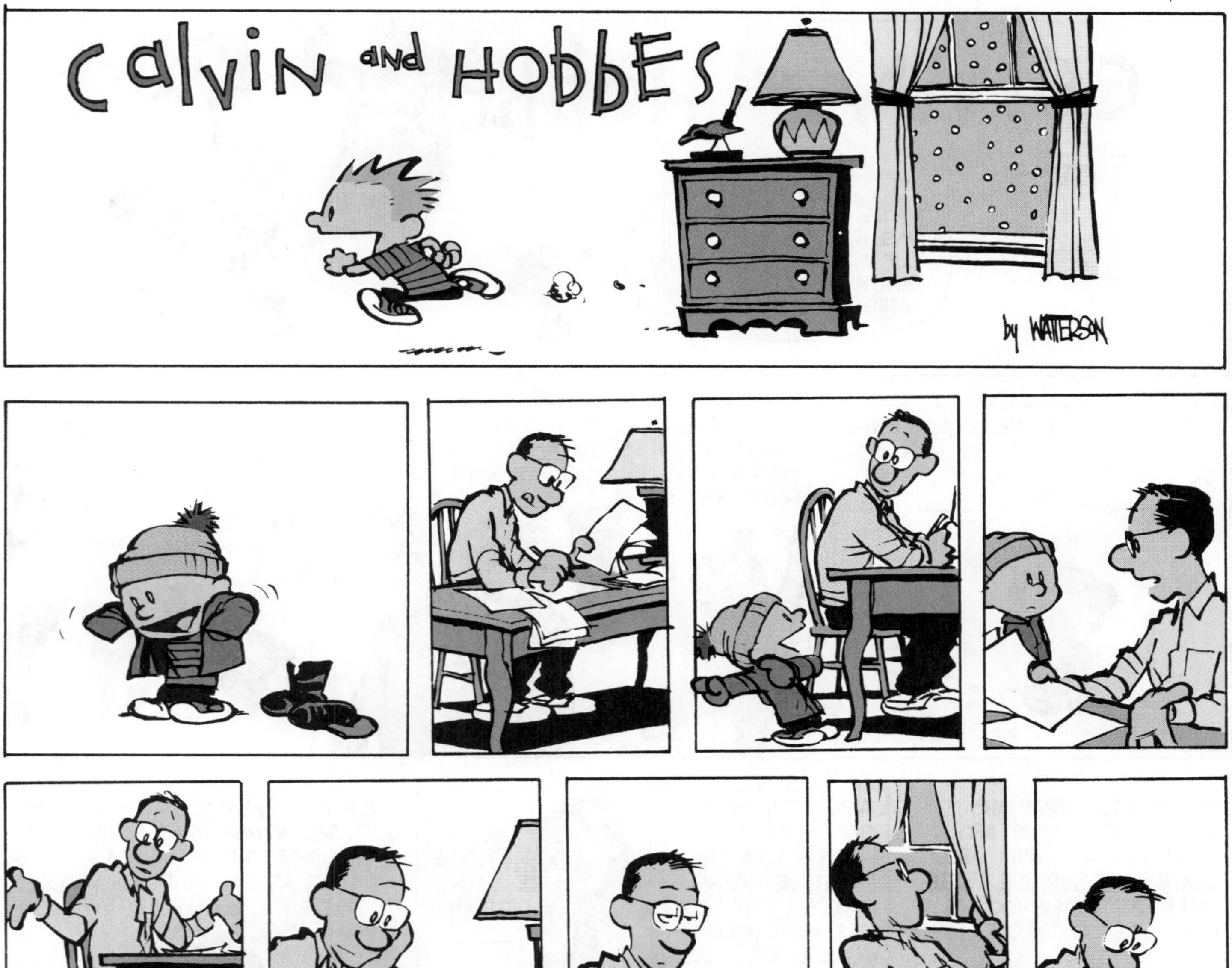
Calvin and HOBBES
by WATTERSON
WATTERSON

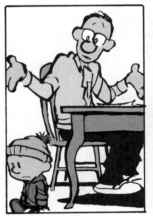

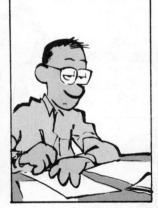

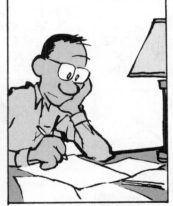

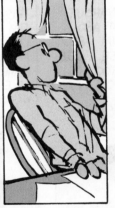

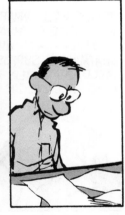

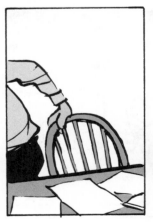

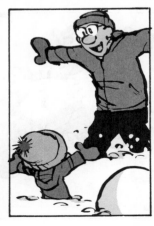

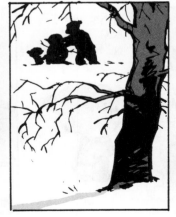

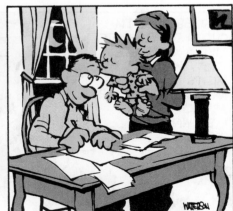

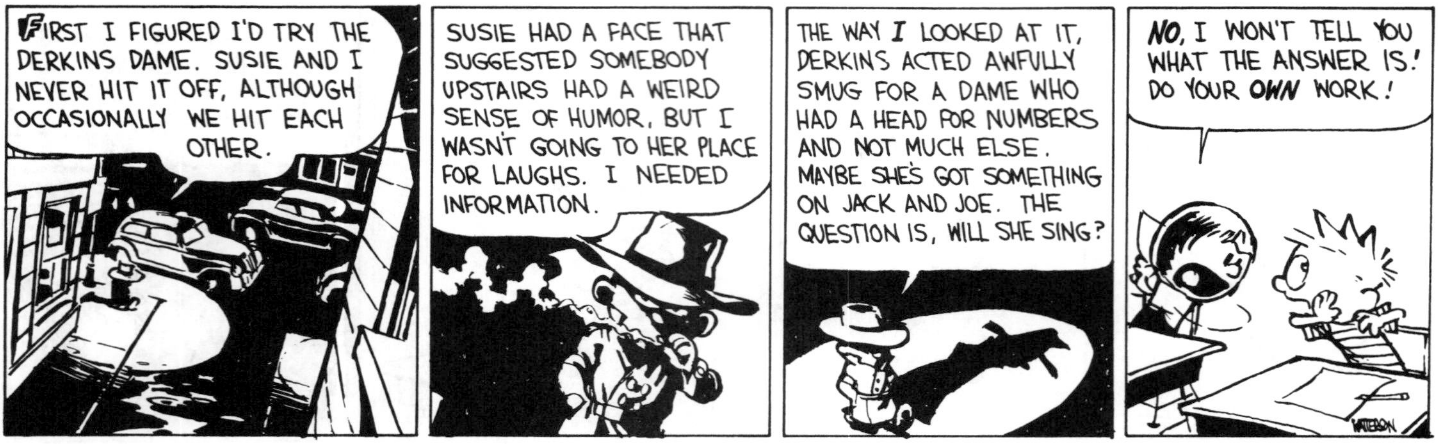
FIRST I FIGURED I'D TRY THE DERKINS DAME. SUSIE AND I NEVER HIT IT OFF, ALTHOUGH OCCASIONALLY WE HIT EACH OTHER.
SUSIE HAD A FACE THAT SUGGESTED SOMEBODY UPSTAIRS HAD A WEIRD SENSE OF HUMOR, BUT I WASN'T GOING TO HER PLACE FOR LAUGHS. I NEEDED INFORMATION.
THE WAY I LOOKED AT IT, DERKIN'S ACTED AWFULLY SMUG FOR A DAME WHO HAD A HEAD FOR NUMBERS AND NOT MUCH ELSE. MAYBE SHE'S GOT SOMETHING ON JACK AND JOE. THE QUESTION IS, WILL SHE SING?
NO, I WON'T TELL YOU WHAT THE ANSWER IS! DO YOUR OWN WORK!

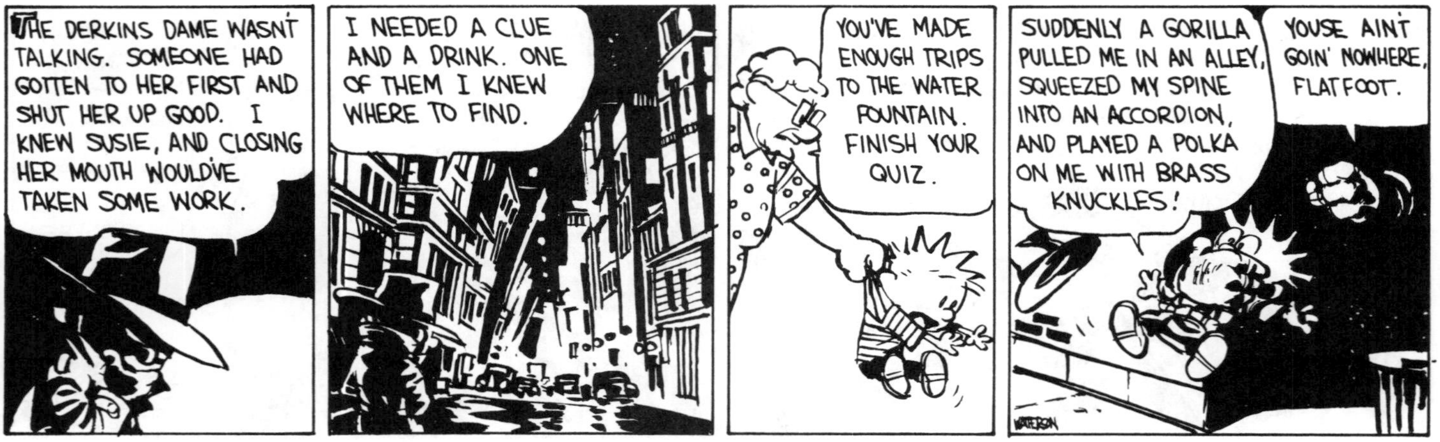
THE DERKINS DAME WASN'T TALKING. SOMEONE HAD GOTTEN TO HER FIRST AND SHUT HER UP GOOD. I KNEW SUSIE, AND CLOSING HER MOUTH WOULD'VE TAKEN SOME WORK.
I NEEDED A CLUE AND A DRINK. ONE OF THEM I KNEW WHERE TO FIND.
YOU'VE MADE ENOUGH TRIPS TO THE WATER FOUNTAIN. FINISH YOUR QUIZ.
SUDDENLY A GORILLA PULLED ME IN AN ALLEY, SQUEEZED MY SPINE INTO AN ACCORDION, AND PLAYED A POLKA ON ME WITH BRASS KNUCKLES!
YOUSE AIN'T GOIN' NOWHERE, FLATFOOT.

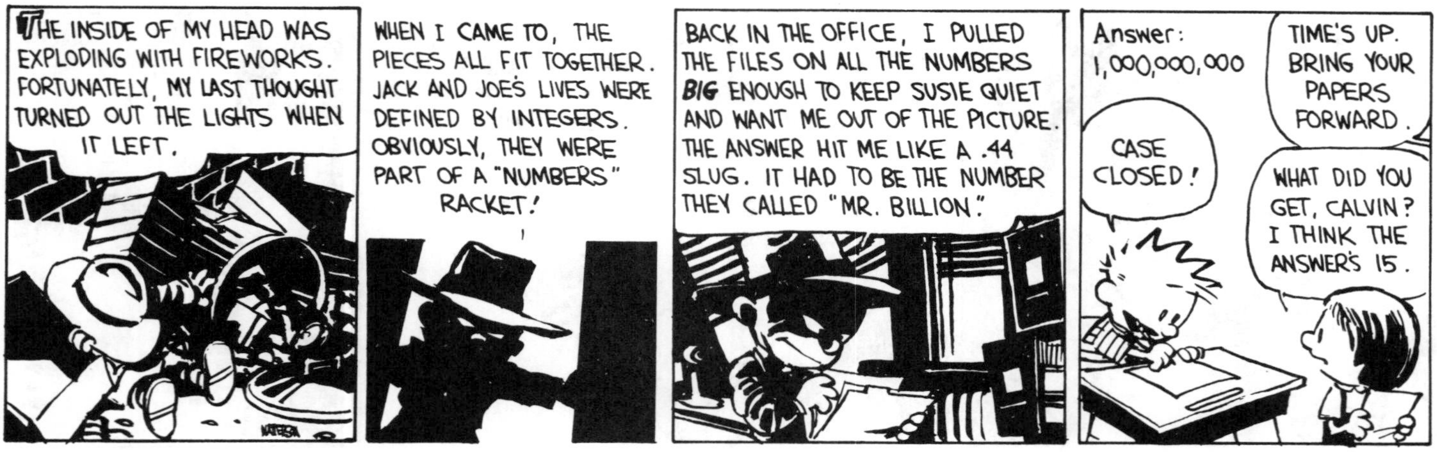
THE INSIDE OF MY HEAD WAS EXPLODING WITH FIREWORKS. FORTUNATELY, MY LAST THOUGHT TURNED OUT THE LIGHTS WHEN IT LEFT.
WHEN I CAME TO, THE PIECES ALL FIT TOGETHER. JACK AND JOE'S LIVES WERE DEFINED BY INTEGERS. OBVIOUSLY, THEY WERE PART OF A "NUMBERS" RACKET!
BACK IN THE OFFICE, I PULLED THE FILES ON ALL THE NUMBERS BIG ENOUGH TO KEEP SUSIE QUIET AND WANT ME OUT OF THE PICTURE. THE ANSWER HIT ME LIKE A .44 SLUG. IT HAD TO BE THE NUMBER THEY CALLED "MR. BILLION."
Answer: 1,000,000,000
TIME'S UP. BRING YOUR PAPERS FORWARD.
CASE CLOSED!
WHAT DID YOU GET, CALVIN? I THINK THE ANSWER'S 15.

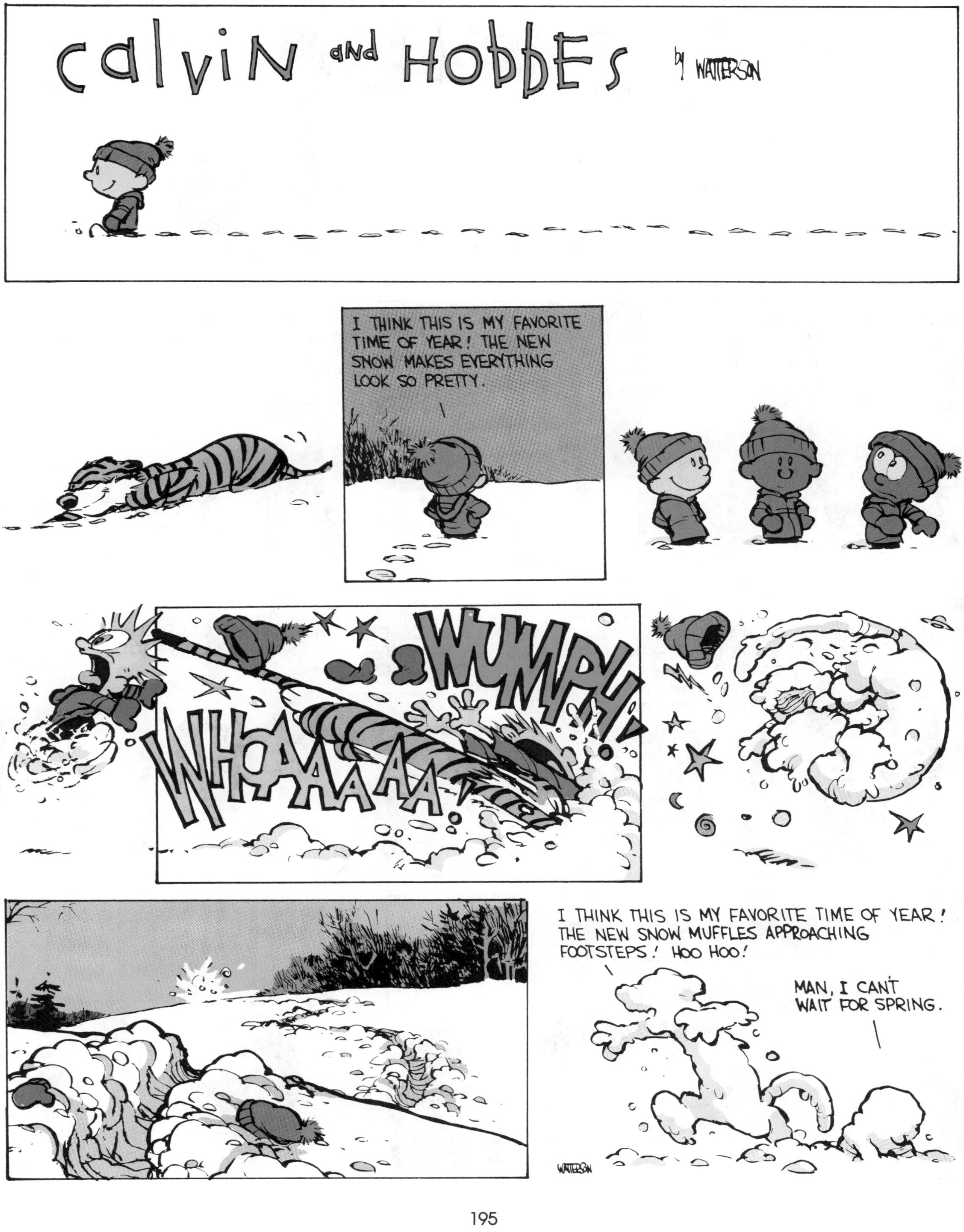
Calvin and HOBBES
by WATTERSON
I THINK THIS IS MY FAVORITE TIME OF YEAR! THE NEW SNOW MAKES EVERYTHING LOOK SO PRETTY.
WUMPH!
WHOAAAAAA!
I THINK THIS IS MY FAVORITE TIME OF YEAR! THE NEW SNOW MUFFLES APPROACHING FOOTSTEPS! HOO HOO!
MAN, I CAN'T WAIT FOR SPRING.
WATTERSON

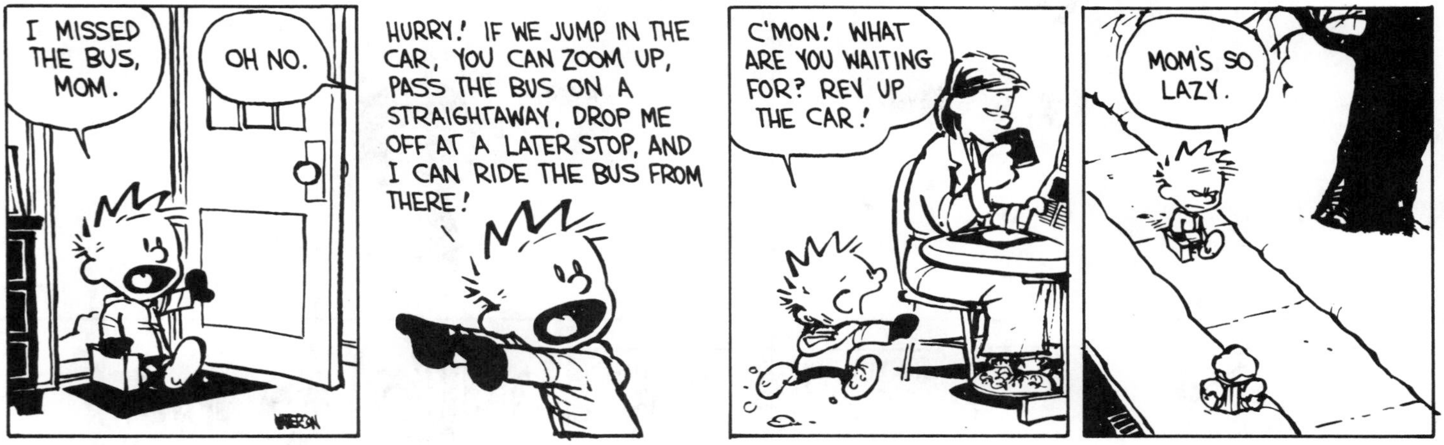
I MISSED THE BUS, MOM.
OH NO.
HURRY! IF WE JUMP IN THE CAR, YOU CAN ZOOM UP, PASS THE BUS ON A STRAIGHTAWAY, DROP ME OFF AT A LATER STOP, AND I CAN RIDE THE BUS FROM THERE!
C'MON! WHAT ARE YOU WAITING FOR? REV UP THE CAR!
MOM'S SO LAZY.

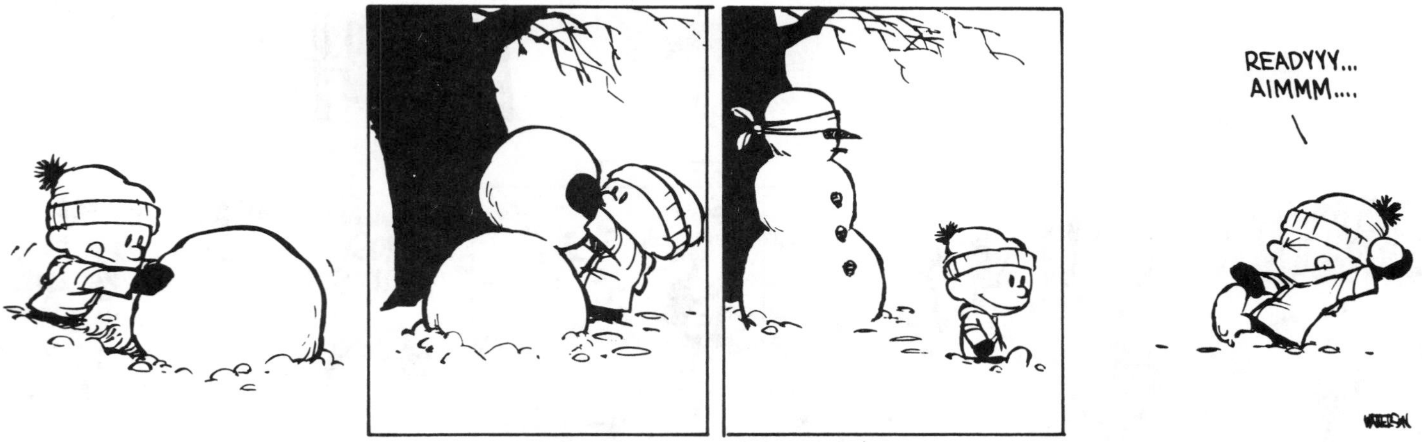
READYYY... AIMMM....

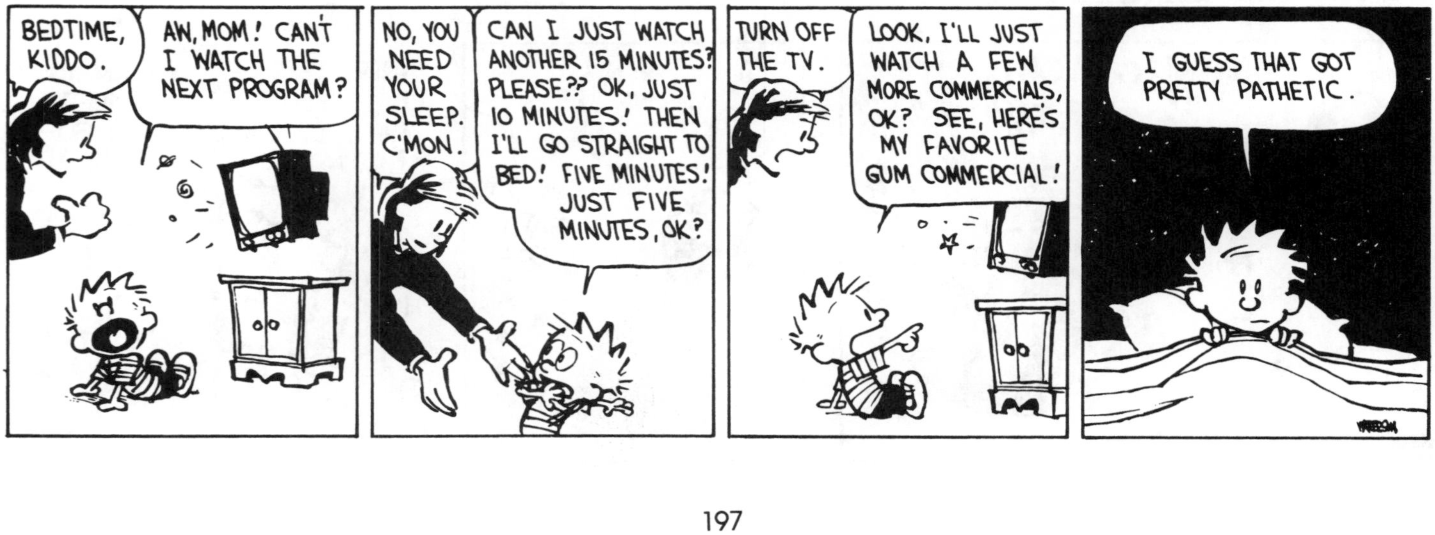
BEDTIME, KIDDO.
AW, MOM! CAN'T I WATCH THE NEXT PROGRAM?
NO, YOU NEED YOUR SLEEP. C'MON.
CAN I JUST WATCH ANOTHER 15 MINUTES? PLEASE?? OK, JUST 10 MINUTES! THEN I'LL GO STRAIGHT TO BED! FIVE MINUTES! JUST FIVE MINUTES, OK?
TURN OFF THE TV.
LOOK, I'LL JUST WATCH A FEW MORE COMMERCIALS, OK? SEE, HERE'S MY FAVORITE GUM COMMERCIAL!
I GUESS THAT GOT PRETTY PATHETIC.

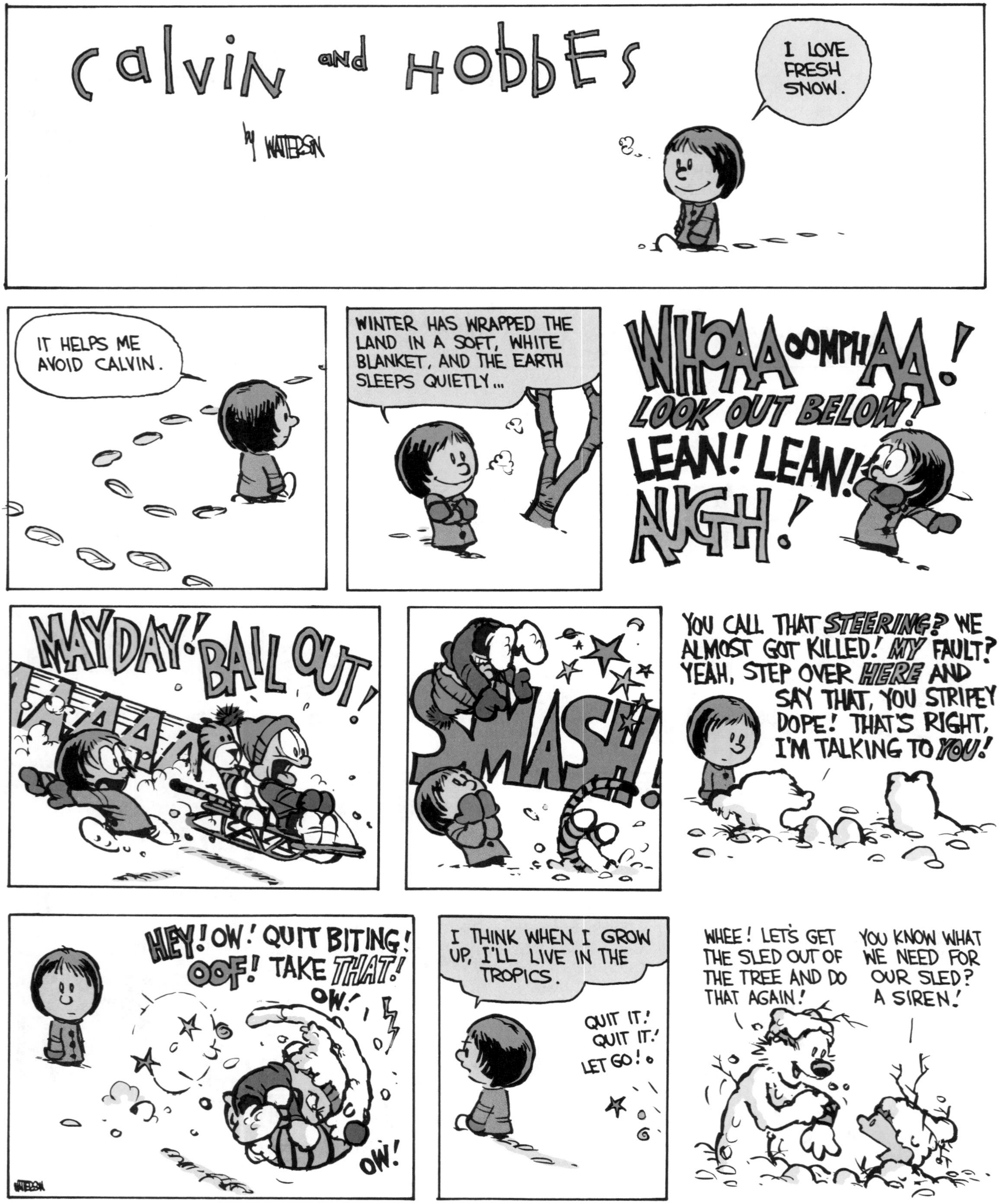
Calvin and HOBBES
by WATTERSON
I LOVE FRESH SNOW.
IT HELPS ME AVOID CALVIN.
WINTER HAS WRAPPED THE LAND IN A SOFT, WHITE BLANKET, AND THE EARTH SLEEPS QUIETLY...
WHOAAOOMPHAA!
LOOK OUT BELOW!
LEAN! LEAN!
AUGH!
MAYDAY! BAIL OUT!
SMASH!
YOU CALL THAT STEERING? WE ALMOST GOT KILLED! MY FAULT? YEAH, STEP OVER HERE AND SAY THAT, YOU STRIPEY DOPE! THAT'S RIGHT, I'M TALKING TO YOU!
HEY! OW! QUIT BITING! OOF! TAKE THAT! OW! OW!
WATTERSON
I THINK WHEN I GROW UP, I'LL LIVE IN THE TROPICS.
QUIT IT! QUIT IT! LET GO!
WHEE! LET'S GET THE SLED OUT OF THE TREE AND DO THAT AGAIN!
YOU KNOW WHAT WE NEED FOR OUR SLED? A SIREN!

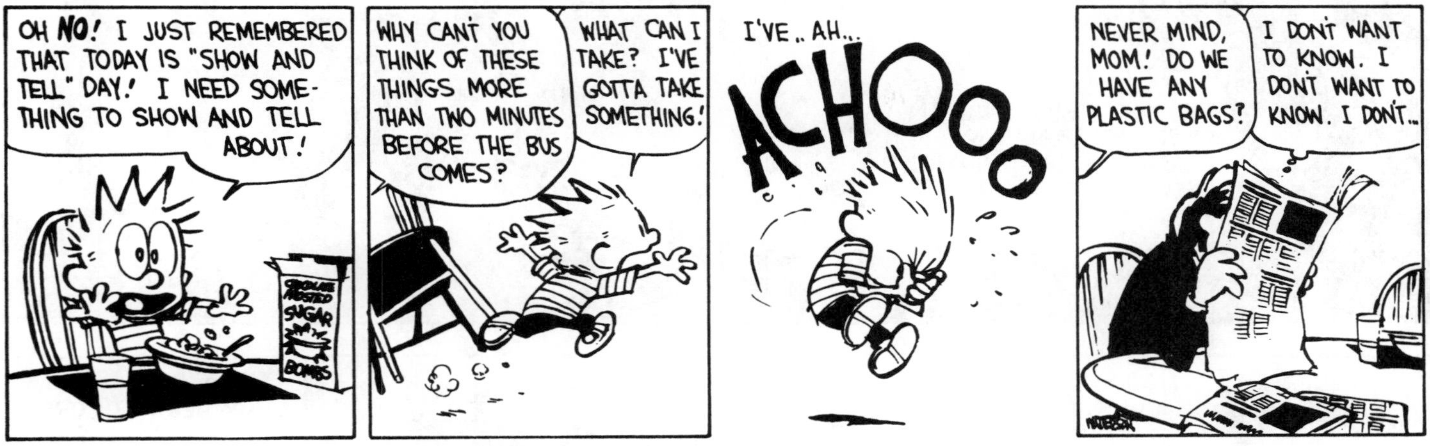
OH NO! I JUST REMEMBERED THAT TODAY IS "SHOW AND TELL" DAY! I NEED SOMETHING TO SHOW AND TELL ABOUT!
SUGAR BOMBS
WHY CAN'T YOU THINK OF THESE THINGS MORE THAN TWO MINUTES BEFORE THE BUS COMES?
WHAT CAN I TAKE? I'VE GOTTA TAKE SOMETHING!
I'VE.. AH..
ACHOOO
NEVER MIND, MOM! DO WE HAVE ANY PLASTIC BAGS?
I DON'T WANT TO KNOW. I DON'T WANT TO KNOW. I DON'T..

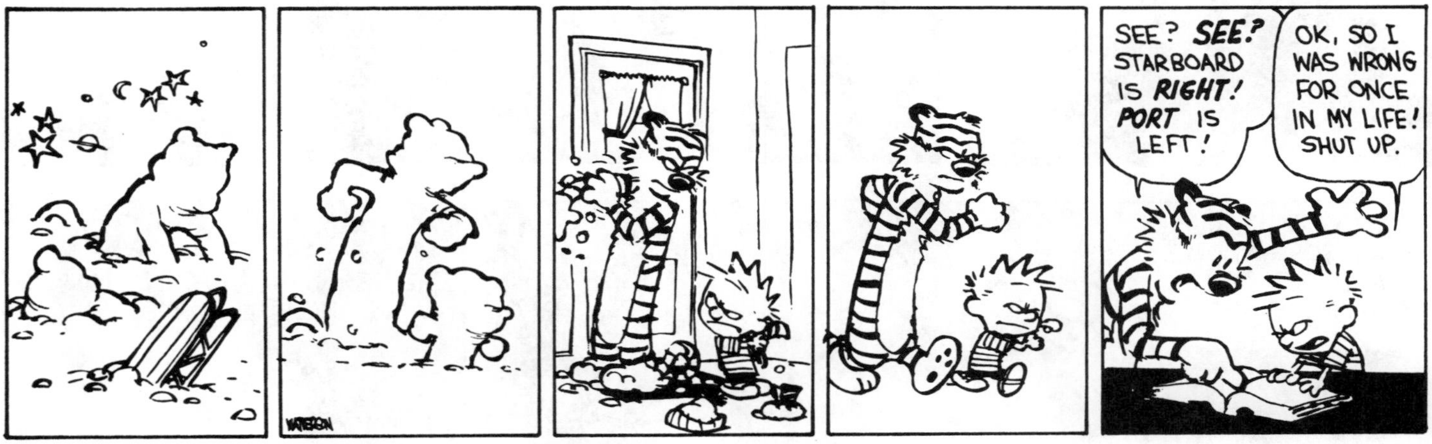
SEE? SEE? STARBOARD IS RIGHT! PORT IS LEFT!
OK, SO I WAS WRONG FOR ONCE IN MY LIFE! SHUT UP.

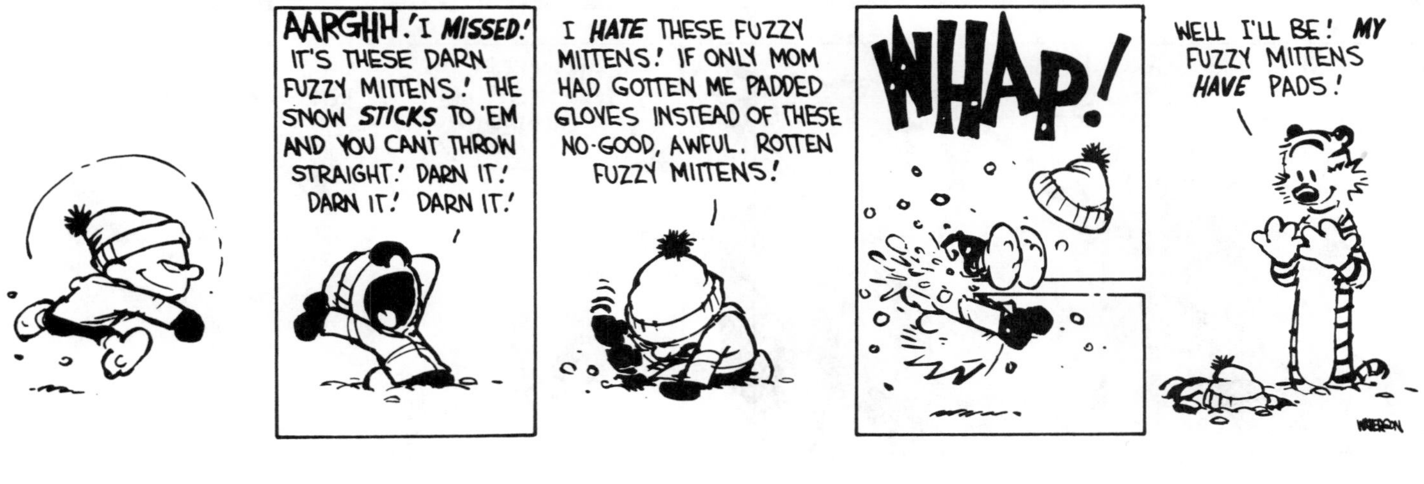
AARGHH! I MISSED! IT'S THESE DARN FUZZY MITTENS! THE SNOW STICKS TO 'EM AND YOU CAN'T THROW STRAIGHT! DARN IT! DARN IT! DARN IT!
I HATE THESE FUZZY MITTENS! IF ONLY MOM HAD GOTTEN ME PADDED GLOVES INSTEAD OF THESE NO-GOOD, AWFUL, ROTTEN FUZZY MITTENS!
WHAP!
WELL I'LL BE! MY FUZZY MITTENS HAVE PADS!

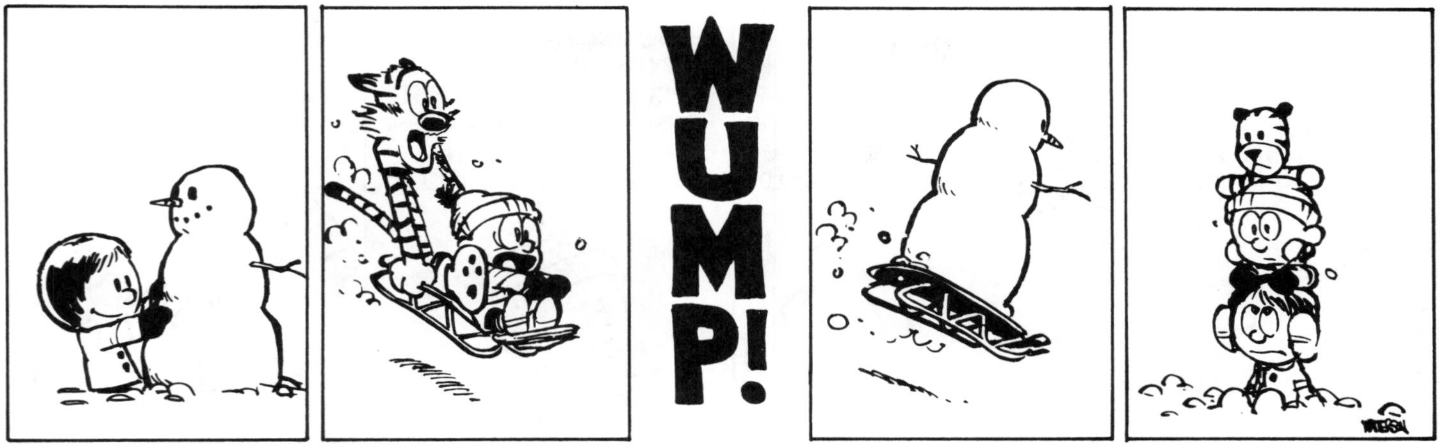
WUMP!

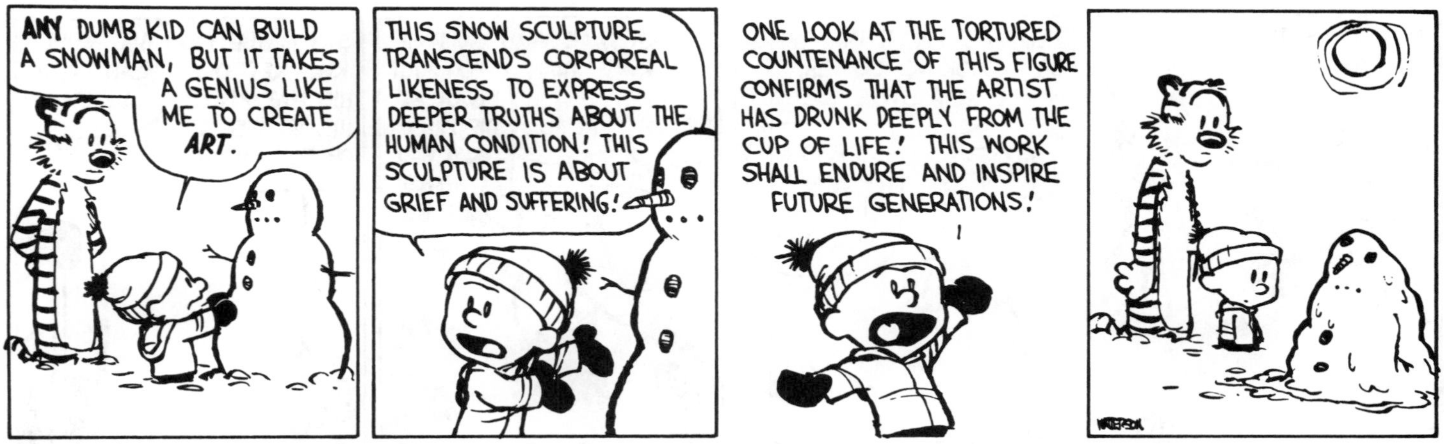
ANY DUMB KID CAN BUILD A SNOWMAN, BUT IT TAKES A GENIUS LIKE ME TO CREATE ART.
THIS SNOW SCULPTURE TRANSCENDS CORPOREAL LIKENESS TO EXPRESS DEEPER TRUTHS ABOUT THE HUMAN CONDITION! THIS SCULPTURE IS ABOUT GRIEF AND SUFFERING!
ONE LOOK AT THE TORTURED COUNTENANCE OF THIS FIGURE CONFIRMS THAT THE ARTIST HAS DRUNK DEEPLY FROM THE CUP OF LIFE! THIS WORK SHALL ENDURE AND INSPIRE FUTURE GENERATIONS!

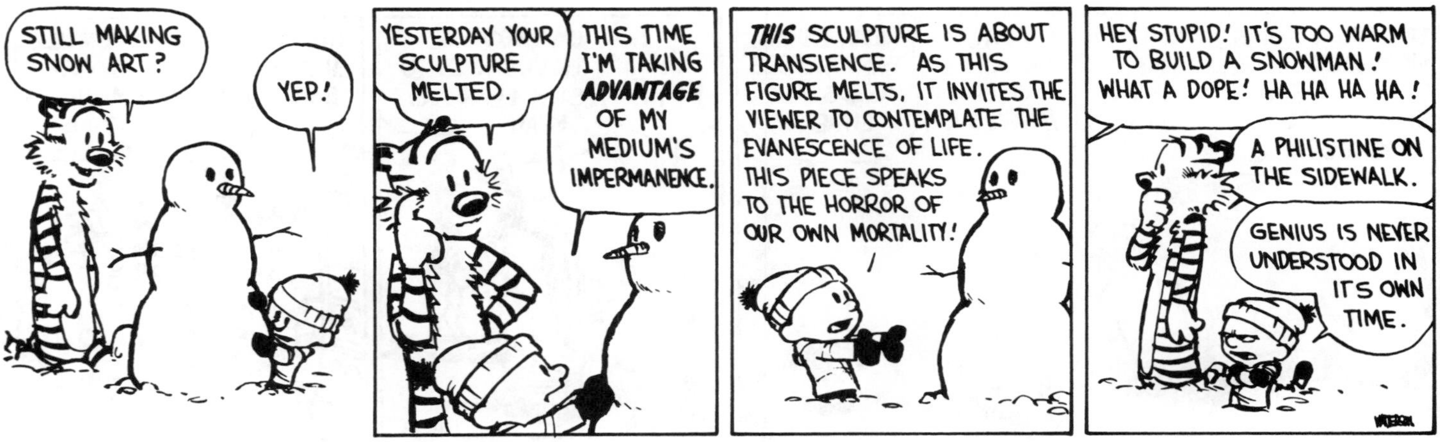
STILL MAKING SNOW ART?
YEP!
YESTERDAY YOUR SCULPTURE MELTED.
THIS TIME I'M TAKING ADVANTAGE OF MY MEDIUM'S IMPERMANENCE.
THIS SCULPTURE IS ABOUT TRANSIENCE. AS THIS FIGURE MELTS, IT INVITES THE VIEWER TO CONTEMPLATE THE EVANESCENCE OF LIFE. THIS PIECE SPEAKS TO THE HORROR OF OUR OWN MORTALITY!
HEY STUPID! IT'S TOO WARM TO BUILD A SNOWMAN! WHAT A DOPE! HA HA HA HA!
A PHILISTINE ON THE SIDEWALK.
GENIUS IS NEVER UNDERSTOOD IN ITS OWN TIME.

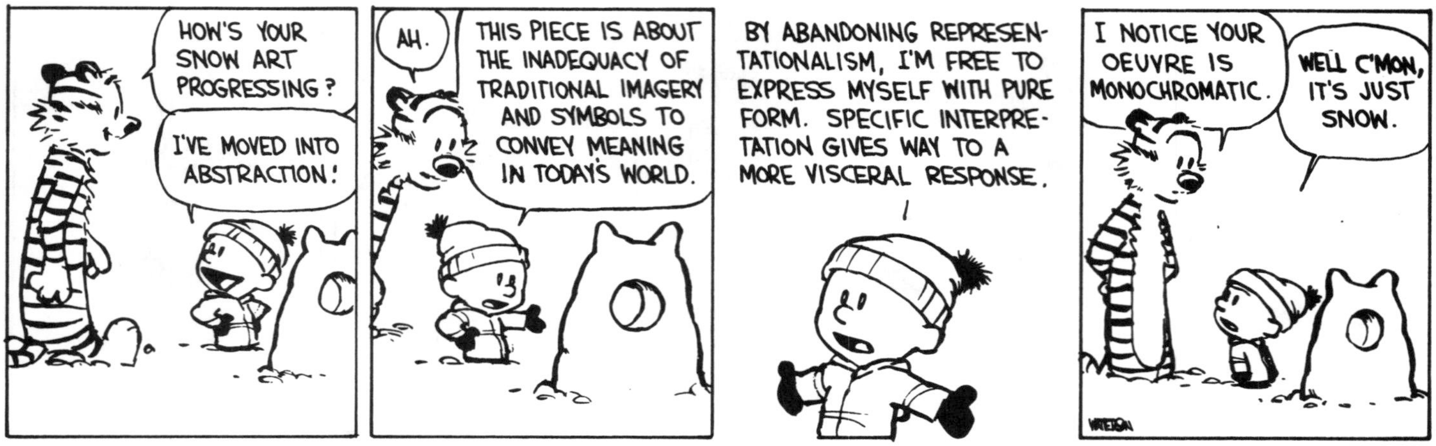
HOW'S YOUR SNOW ART PROGRESSING?
I'VE MOVED INTO ABSTRACTION!
AH.
THIS PIECE IS ABOUT THE INADEQUACY OF TRADITIONAL IMAGERY AND SYMBOLS TO CONVEY MEANING IN TODAY'S WORLD.
BY ABANDONING REPRESENTATIONALISM, I'M FREE TO EXPRESS MYSELF WITH PURE FORM. SPECIFIC INTERPRETATION GIVES WAY TO A MORE VISCERAL RESPONSE.
I NOTICE YOUR OEUVRE IS MONOCHROMATIC.
WELL C'MON, IT'S JUST SNOW.

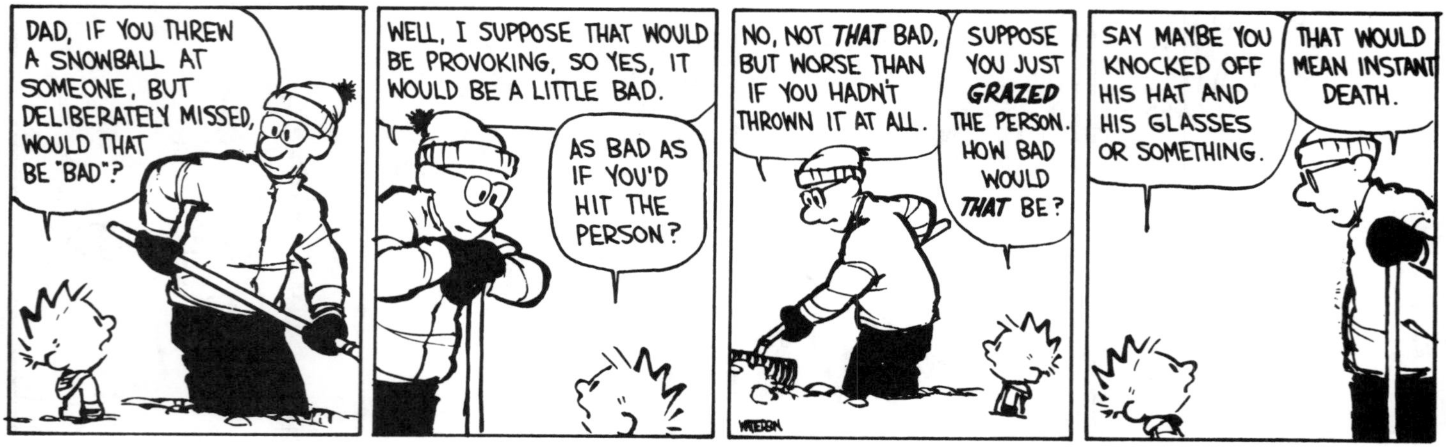
DAD, IF YOU THREW A SNOWBALL AT SOMEONE, BUT DELIBERATELY MISSED, WOULD THAT BE "BAD"?
WELL, I SUPPOSE THAT WOULD BE PROVOKING, SO YES, IT WOULD BE A LITTLE BAD.
AS BAD AS IF YOU'D HIT THE PERSON?
NO, NOT *THAT* BAD, BUT WORSE THAN IF YOU HADN'T THROWN IT AT ALL.
SUPPOSE YOU JUST *GRAZED* THE PERSON. HOW BAD WOULD *THAT* BE?
SAY MAYBE YOU KNOCKED OFF HIS HAT AND HIS GLASSES OR SOMETHING.
THAT WOULD MEAN INSTANT DEATH.

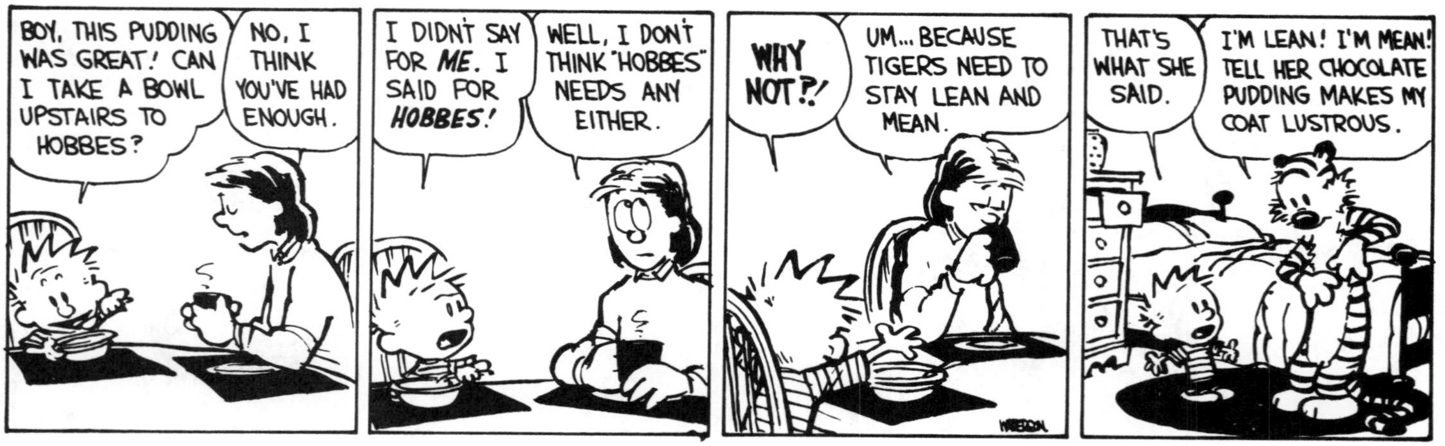
BOY, THIS PUDDING WAS GREAT! CAN I TAKE A BOWL UPSTAIRS TO HOBBES?
NO, I THINK YOU'VE HAD ENOUGH.
I DIDN'T SAY FOR *ME*. I SAID FOR *HOBBES*!
WELL, I DON'T THINK "HOBBES" NEEDS ANY EITHER.
WHY NOT?!
UM... BECAUSE TIGERS NEED TO STAY LEAN AND MEAN.
THAT'S WHAT SHE SAID.
I'M LEAN! I'M MEAN! TELL HER CHOCOLATE PUDDING MAKES MY COAT LUSTROUS.

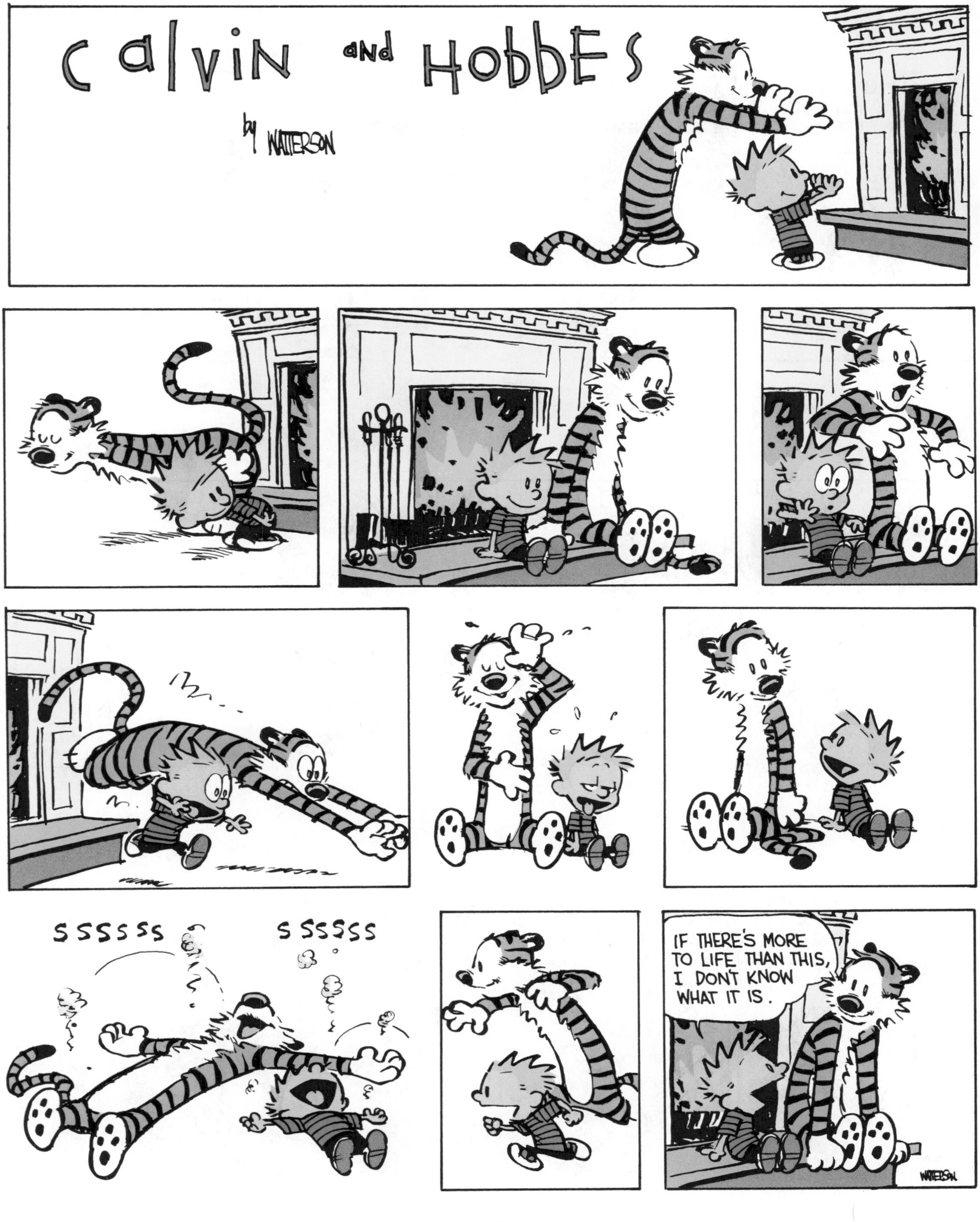
Calvin and HOBBES
by WATTERSON
SSSSSS
SSSSSS
IF THERE'S MORE TO LIFE THAN THIS, I DON'T KNOW WHAT IT IS.
WATTERSON

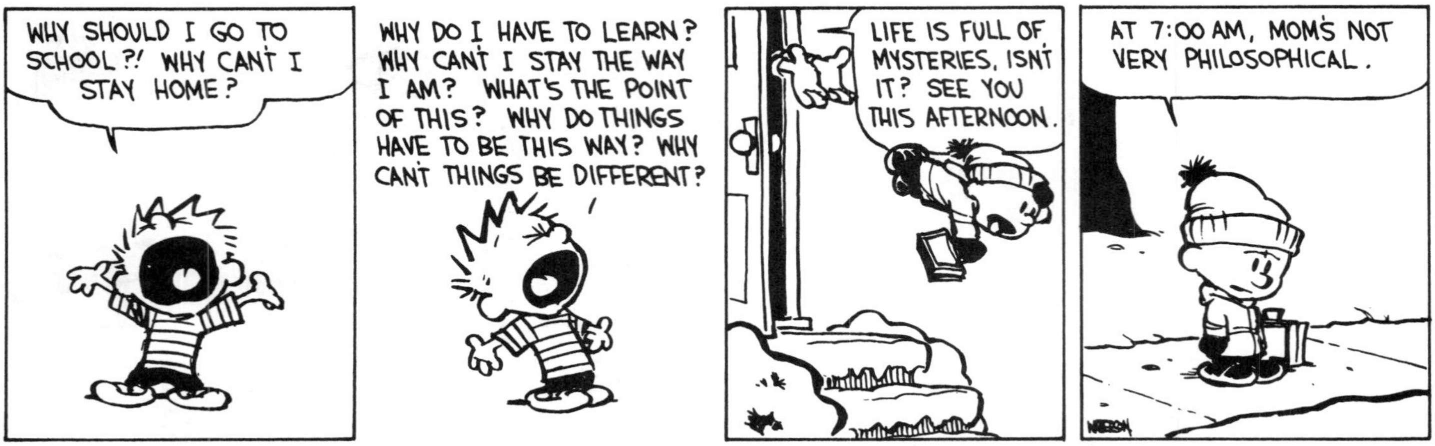
WHY SHOULD I GO TO SCHOOL?! WHY CAN'T I STAY HOME?
WHY DO I HAVE TO LEARN? WHY CAN'T I STAY THE WAY I AM? WHAT'S THE POINT OF THIS? WHY DO THINGS HAVE TO BE THIS WAY? WHY CAN'T THINGS BE DIFFERENT?
LIFE IS FULL OF MYSTERIES, ISN'T IT? SEE YOU THIS AFTERNOON.
AT 7:00 AM, MOM'S NOT VERY PHILOSOPHICAL.

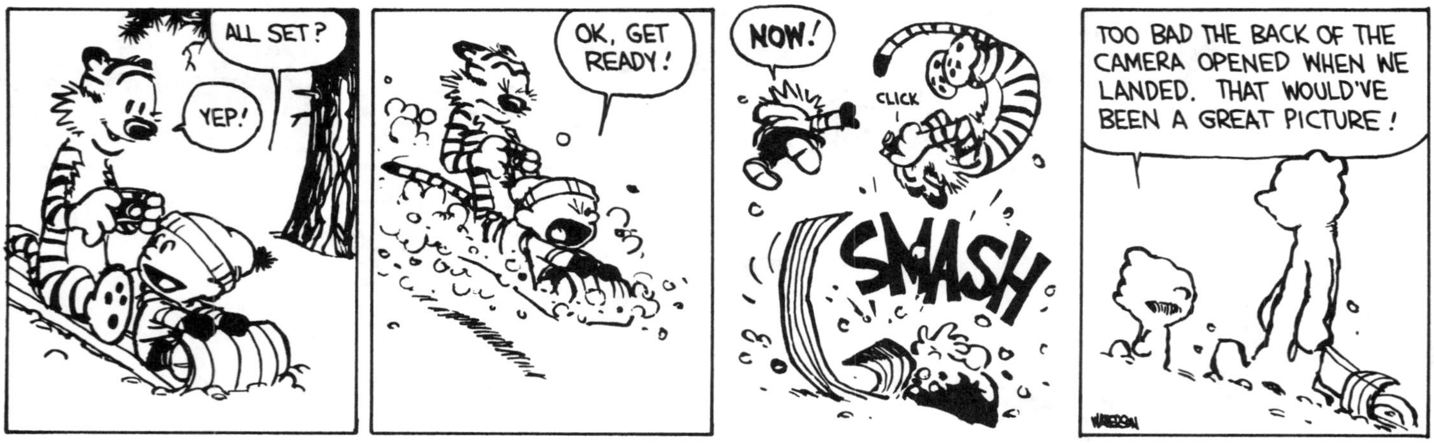
ALL SET?
YEP!
OK, GET READY!
NOW!
CLICK
SMASH
TOO BAD THE BACK OF THE CAMERA OPENED WHEN WE LANDED. THAT WOULD'VE BEEN A GREAT PICTURE!

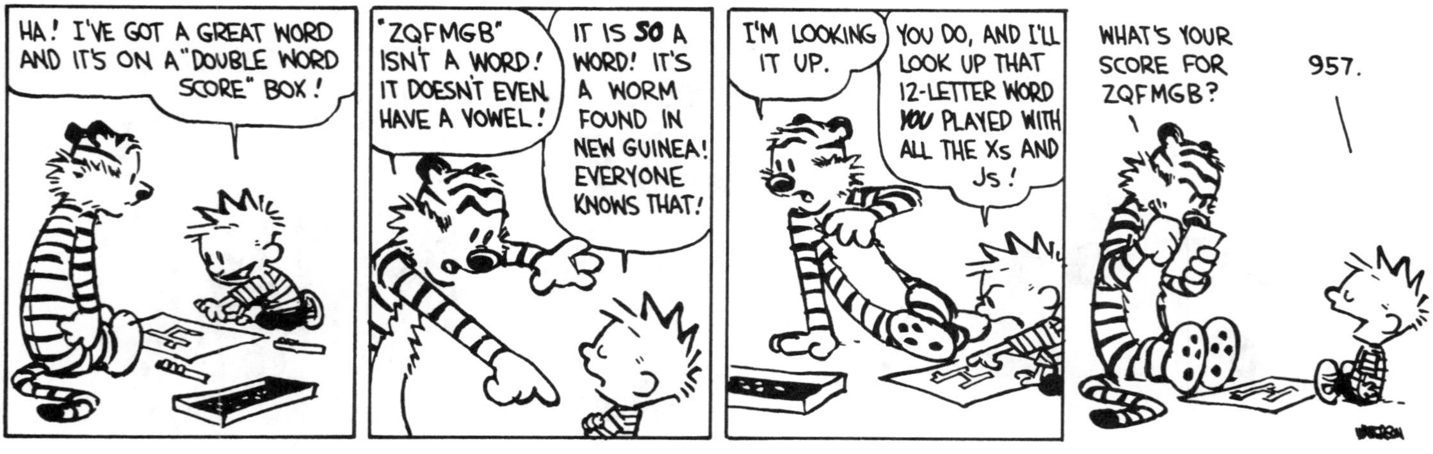
HA! I'VE GOT A GREAT WORD AND IT'S ON A "DOUBLE WORD SCORE" BOX!
"ZQFMGB" ISN'T A WORD! IT DOESN'T EVEN HAVE A VOWEL!
IT IS SO A WORD! IT'S A WORM FOUND IN NEW GUINEA! EVERYONE KNOWS THAT!
I'M LOOKING IT UP.
YOU DO, AND I'LL LOOK UP THAT 12-LETTER WORD YOU PLAYED WITH ALL THE Xs AND Js!
WHAT'S YOUR SCORE FOR ZQFMGB?
957.

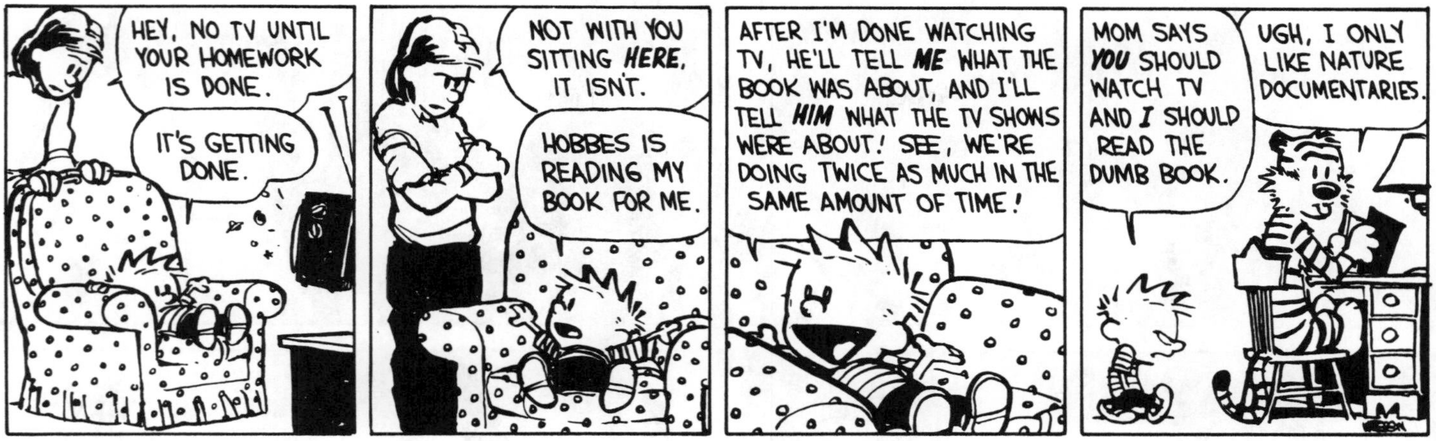
HEY, NO TV UNTIL YOUR HOMEWORK IS DONE.
IT'S GETTING DONE.
NOT WITH YOU SITTING HERE, IT ISN'T.
HOBBES IS READING MY BOOK FOR ME.
AFTER I'M DONE WATCHING TV, HE'LL TELL ME WHAT THE BOOK WAS ABOUT, AND I'LL TELL HIM WHAT THE TV SHOWS WERE ABOUT! SEE, WE'RE DOING TWICE AS MUCH IN THE SAME AMOUNT OF TIME!
MOM SAYS YOU SHOULD WATCH TV AND I SHOULD READ THE DUMB BOOK.
UGH, I ONLY LIKE NATURE DOCUMENTARIES.

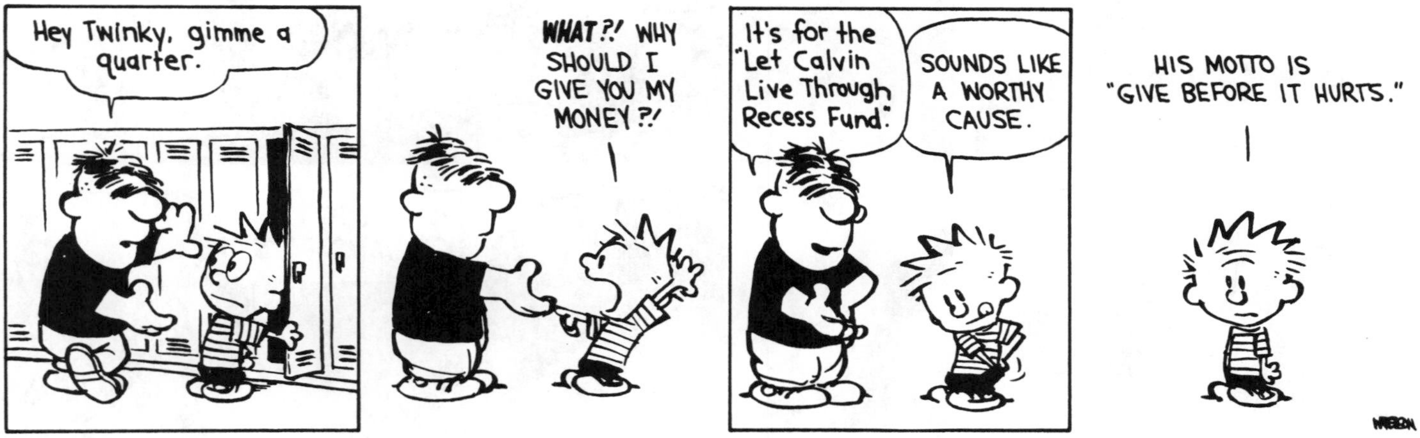
Hey Twinky, gimme a quarter.
WHAT?! WHY SHOULD I GIVE YOU MY MONEY?!
It's for the "Let Calvin Live Through Recess Fund."
SOUNDS LIKE A WORTHY CAUSE.
HIS MOTTO IS "GIVE BEFORE IT HURTS."

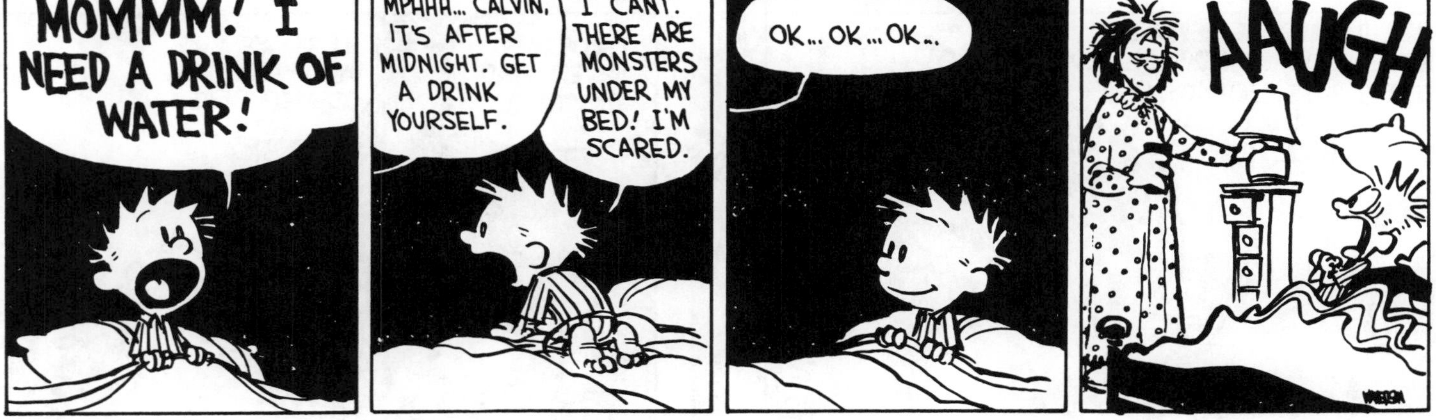
MOMMM! I NEED A DRINK OF WATER!
MPHHH... CALVIN, IT'S AFTER MIDNIGHT. GET A DRINK YOURSELF.
I CAN'T. THERE ARE MONSTERS UNDER MY BED! I'M SCARED.
OK... OK... OK...
AAUGH

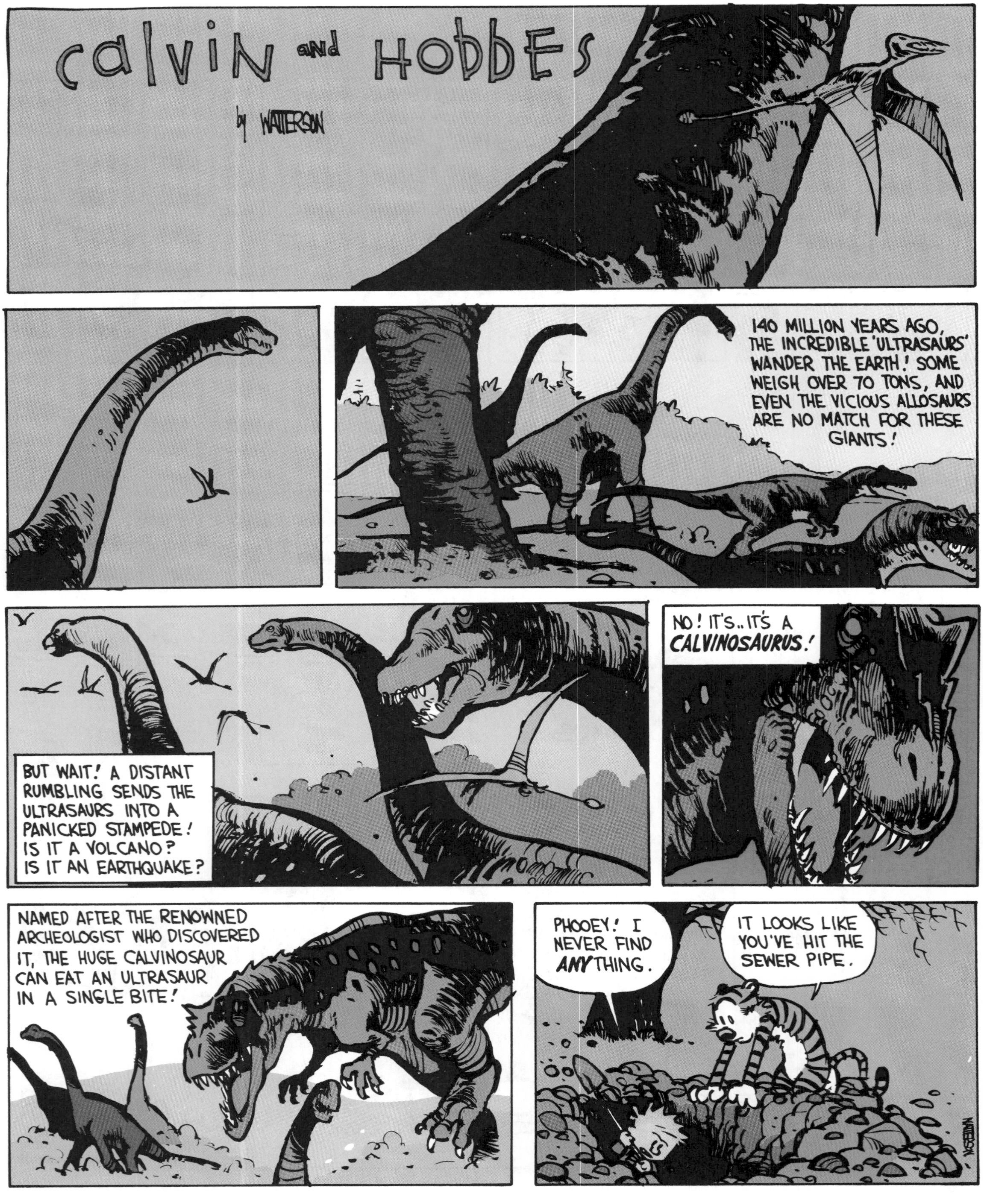
Calvin and HOBBES
by WATTERSON
140 MILLION YEARS AGO, THE INCREDIBLE 'ULTRASAURS' WANDER THE EARTH! SOME WEIGH OVER 70 TONS, AND EVEN THE VICIOUS ALLOSAURS ARE NO MATCH FOR THESE GIANTS!
BUT WAIT! A DISTANT RUMBLING SENDS THE ULTRASAURS INTO A PANICKED STAMPEDE! IS IT A VOLCANO? IS IT AN EARTHQUAKE?
NO! IT'S.. IT'S A ***CALVINOSAURUS!***
NAMED AFTER THE RENOWNED ARCHEOLOGIST WHO DISCOVERED IT, THE HUGE CALVINOSAUR CAN EAT AN ULTRASAUR IN A SINGLE BITE!
PHOOEY! I NEVER FIND ***ANY***THING.
IT LOOKS LIKE YOU'VE HIT THE SEWER PIPE.

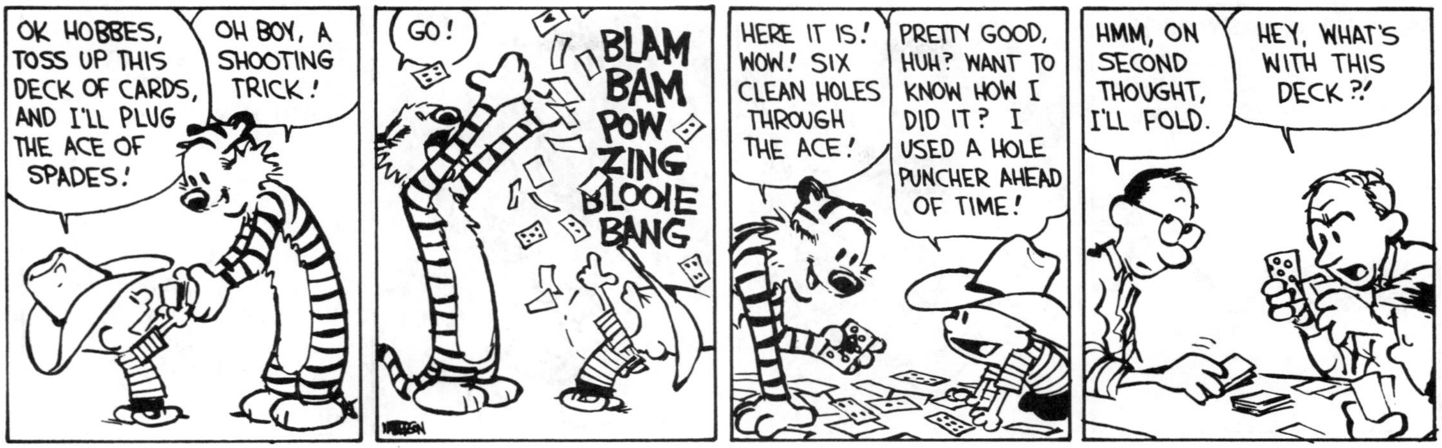
OK HOBBES, TOSS UP THIS DECK OF CARDS, AND I'LL PLUG THE ACE OF SPADES!
OH BOY, A SHOOTING TRICK!
GO!
BLAM BAM POW ZING BLOOIE BANG
HERE IT IS! WOW! SIX CLEAN HOLES THROUGH THE ACE!
PRETTY GOOD, HUH? WANT TO KNOW HOW I DID IT? I USED A HOLE PUNCHER AHEAD OF TIME!
HMM, ON SECOND THOUGHT, I'LL FOLD.
HEY, WHAT'S WITH THIS DECK?!

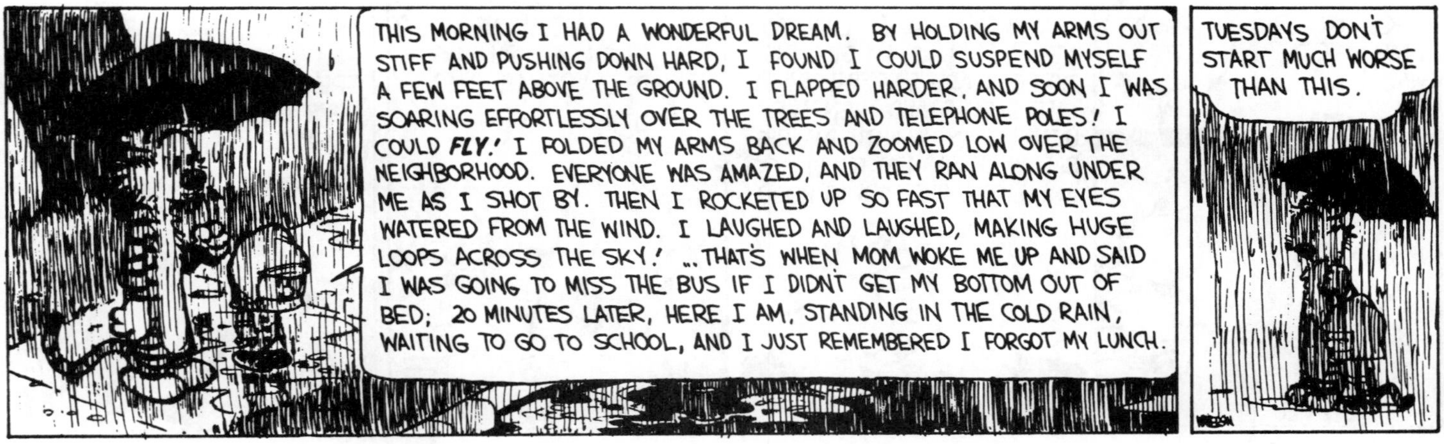
THIS MORNING I HAD A WONDERFUL DREAM. BY HOLDING MY ARMS OUT STIFF AND PUSHING DOWN HARD, I FOUND I COULD SUSPEND MYSELF A FEW FEET ABOVE THE GROUND. I FLAPPED HARDER, AND SOON I WAS SOARING EFFORTLESSLY OVER THE TREES AND TELEPHONE POLES! I COULD FLY! I FOLDED MY ARMS BACK AND ZOOMED LOW OVER THE NEIGHBORHOOD. EVERYONE WAS AMAZED, AND THEY RAN ALONG UNDER ME AS I SHOT BY. THEN I ROCKETED UP SO FAST THAT MY EYES WATERED FROM THE WIND. I LAUGHED AND LAUGHED, MAKING HUGE LOOPS ACROSS THE SKY! ...THAT'S WHEN MOM WOKE ME UP AND SAID I WAS GOING TO MISS THE BUS IF I DIDN'T GET MY BOTTOM OUT OF BED; 20 MINUTES LATER, HERE I AM, STANDING IN THE COLD RAIN, WAITING TO GO TO SCHOOL, AND I JUST REMEMBERED I FORGOT MY LUNCH.
TUESDAYS DON'T START MUCH WORSE THAN THIS.

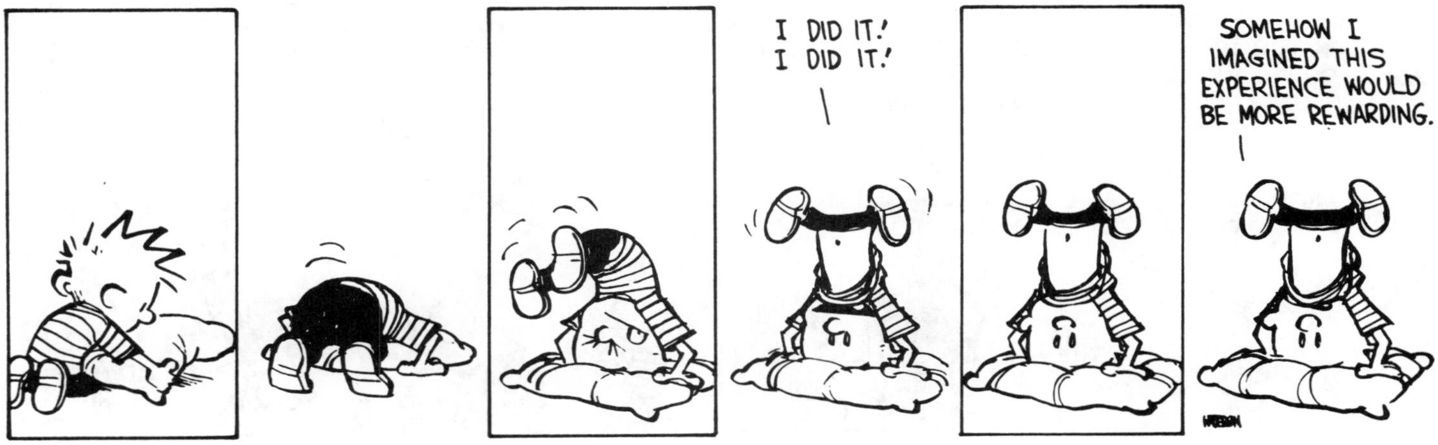
I DID IT! I DID IT!
SOMEHOW I IMAGINED THIS EXPERIENCE WOULD BE MORE REWARDING.

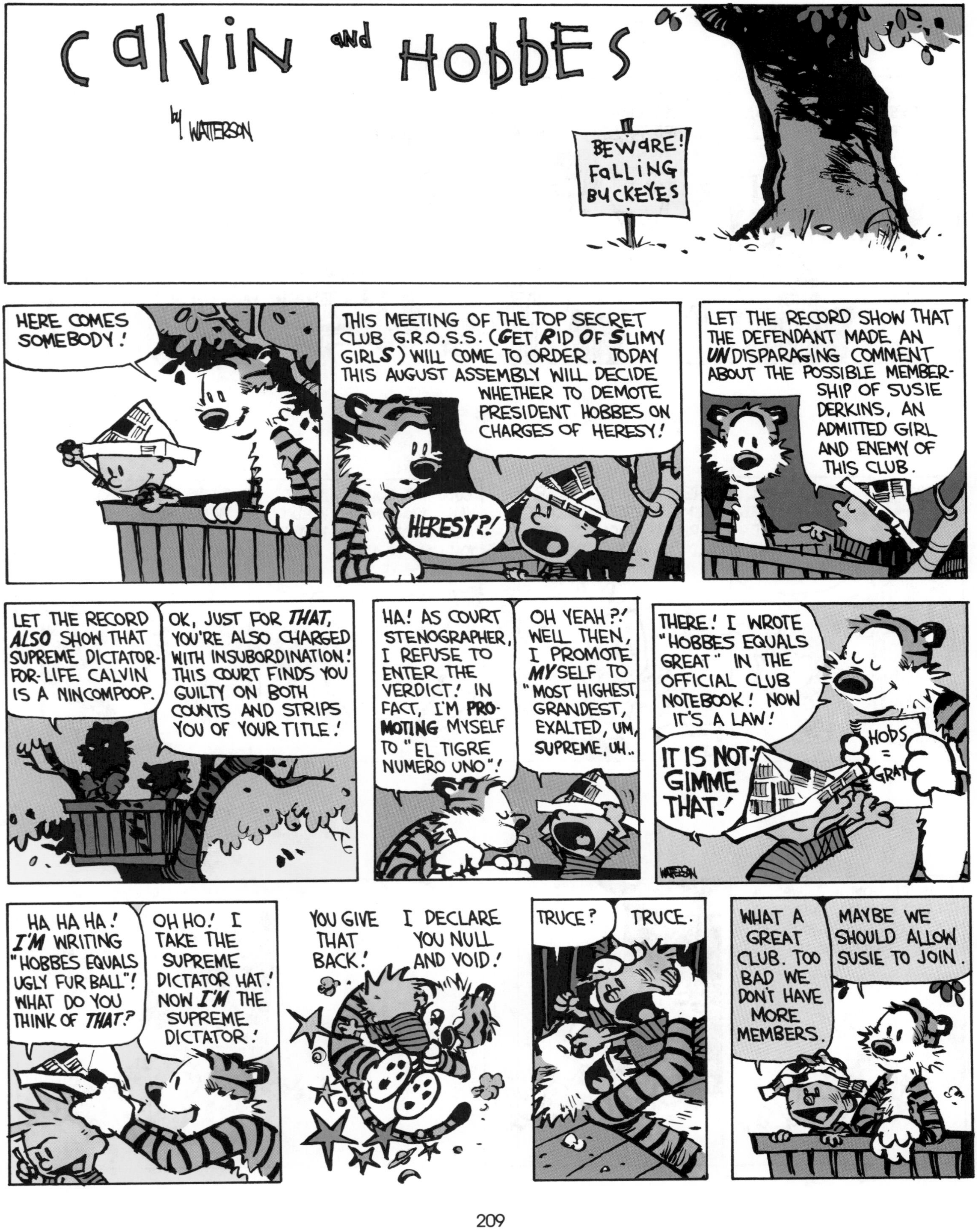
Calvin and HOBBES
by WATTERSON
BEWARE! FALLING BUCKEYES
HERE COMES SOMEBODY!
THIS MEETING OF THE TOP SECRET CLUB G.R.O.S.S. (GET RID OF SLIMY GIRLS) WILL COME TO ORDER. TODAY THIS AUGUST ASSEMBLY WILL DECIDE WHETHER TO DEMOTE PRESIDENT HOBBES ON CHARGES OF HERESY!
HERESY?!
LET THE RECORD SHOW THAT THE DEFENDANT MADE AN UNDISPARAGING COMMENT ABOUT THE POSSIBLE MEMBERSHIP OF SUSIE DERKINS, AN ADMITTED GIRL AND ENEMY OF THIS CLUB.
LET THE RECORD ALSO SHOW THAT SUPREME DICTATOR-FOR-LIFE CALVIN IS A NINCOMPOOP.
OK, JUST FOR THAT, YOU'RE ALSO CHARGED WITH INSUBORDINATION! THIS COURT FINDS YOU GUILTY ON BOTH COUNTS AND STRIPS YOU OF YOUR TITLE!
HA! AS COURT STENOGRAPHER, I REFUSE TO ENTER THE VERDICT! IN FACT, I'M PROMOTING MYSELF TO "EL TIGRE NUMERO UNO"!
OH YEAH?! WELL THEN, I PROMOTE MYSELF TO "MOST HIGHEST, GRANDEST, EXALTED, UM, SUPREME, UH..
THERE! I WROTE "HOBBES EQUALS GREAT" IN THE OFFICIAL CLUB NOTEBOOK! NOW IT'S A LAW!
HOBS = GRAT
IT IS NOT! GIMME THAT!
WATTERSON
HA HA HA! I'M WRITING "HOBBES EQUALS UGLY FUR BALL"! WHAT DO YOU THINK OF THAT?
OH HO! I TAKE THE SUPREME DICTATOR HAT! NOW I'M THE SUPREME DICTATOR!
YOU GIVE THAT BACK!
I DECLARE YOU NULL AND VOID!
TRUCE?
TRUCE.
WHAT A GREAT CLUB. TOO BAD WE DON'T HAVE MORE MEMBERS.
MAYBE WE SHOULD ALLOW SUSIE TO JOIN.

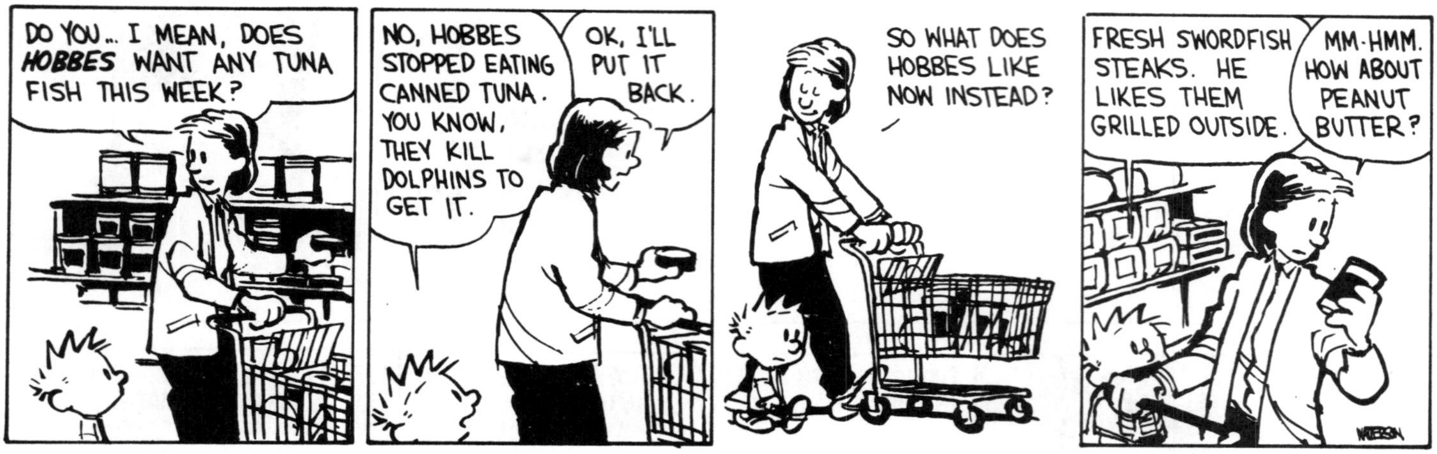
DO YOU... I MEAN, DOES *HOBBES* WANT ANY TUNA FISH THIS WEEK?
NO, HOBBES STOPPED EATING CANNED TUNA. YOU KNOW, THEY KILL DOLPHINS TO GET IT.
OK, I'LL PUT IT BACK.
SO WHAT DOES HOBBES LIKE NOW INSTEAD?
FRESH SWORDFISH STEAKS. HE LIKES THEM GRILLED OUTSIDE.
MM-HMM. HOW ABOUT PEANUT BUTTER?

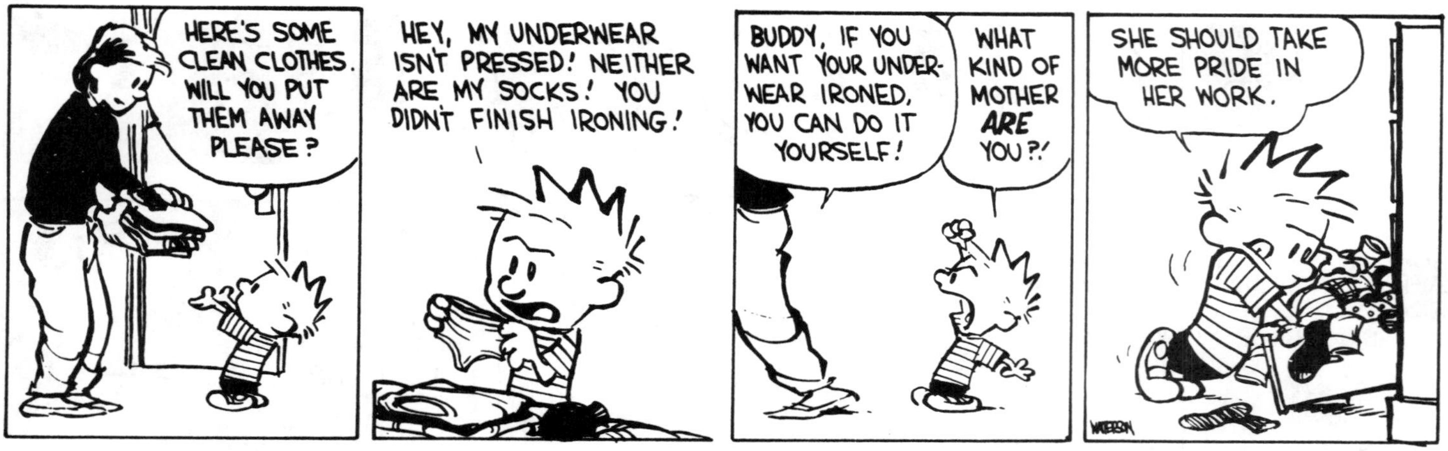
HERE'S SOME CLEAN CLOTHES. WILL YOU PUT THEM AWAY PLEASE?
HEY, MY UNDERWEAR ISN'T PRESSED! NEITHER ARE MY SOCKS! YOU DIDN'T FINISH IRONING!
BUDDY, IF YOU WANT YOUR UNDERWEAR IRONED, YOU CAN DO IT YOURSELF!
WHAT KIND OF MOTHER *ARE* YOU?!
SHE SHOULD TAKE MORE PRIDE IN HER WORK.

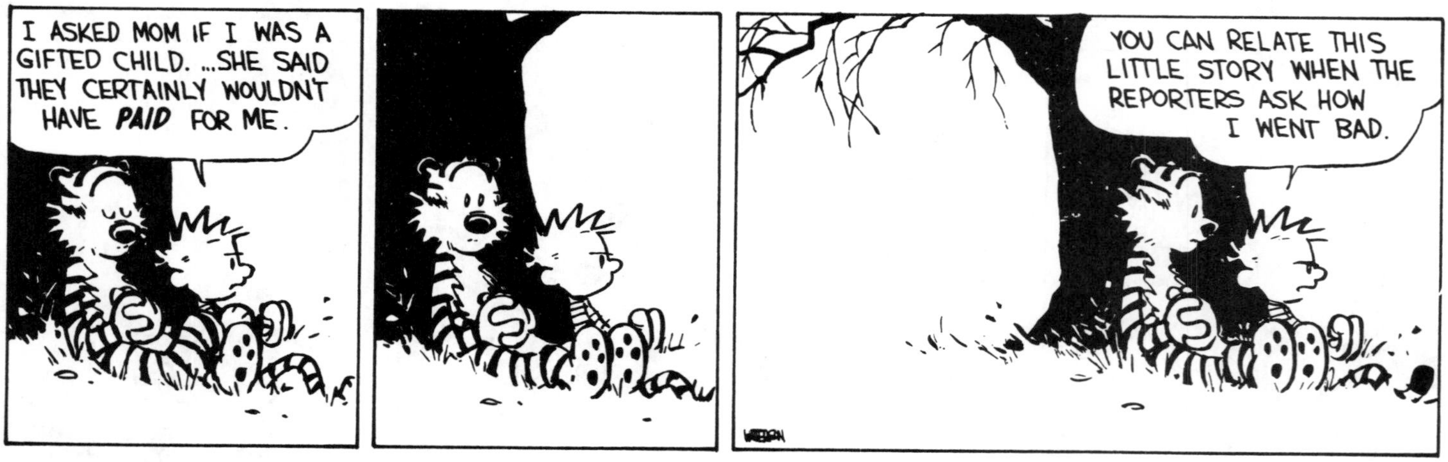
I ASKED MOM IF I WAS A GIFTED CHILD. ...SHE SAID THEY CERTAINLY WOULDN'T HAVE *PAID* FOR ME.
YOU CAN RELATE THIS LITTLE STORY WHEN THE REPORTERS ASK HOW I WENT BAD.

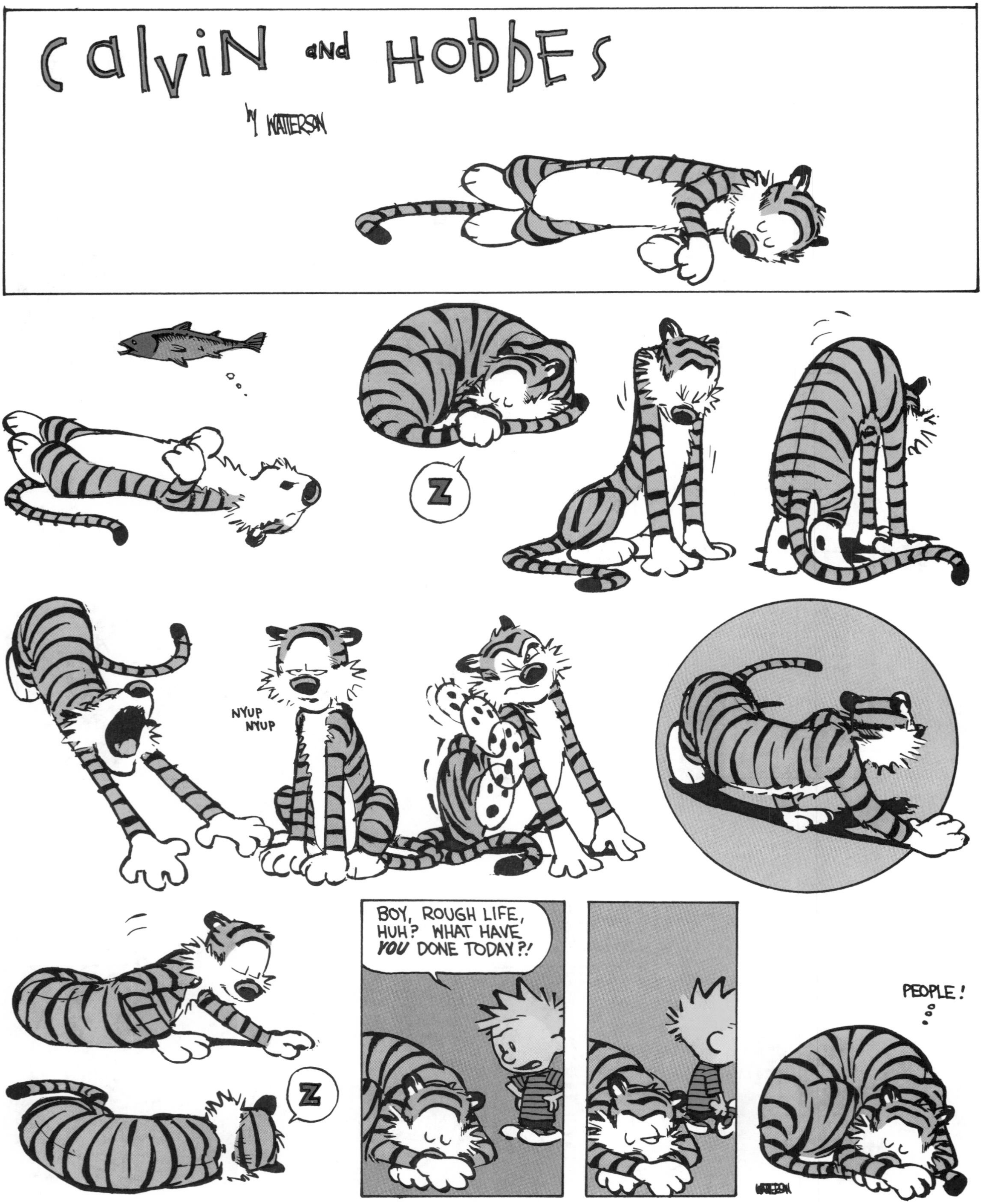
Calvin and HOBBES
by WATTERSON
Z
NYUP NYUP
Z
BOY, ROUGH LIFE, HUH? WHAT HAVE YOU DONE TODAY?!
PEOPLE!
WATTERSON

I GET THE FEELING THERE WAS NO RIGHT ANSWER TO THAT QUESTION.

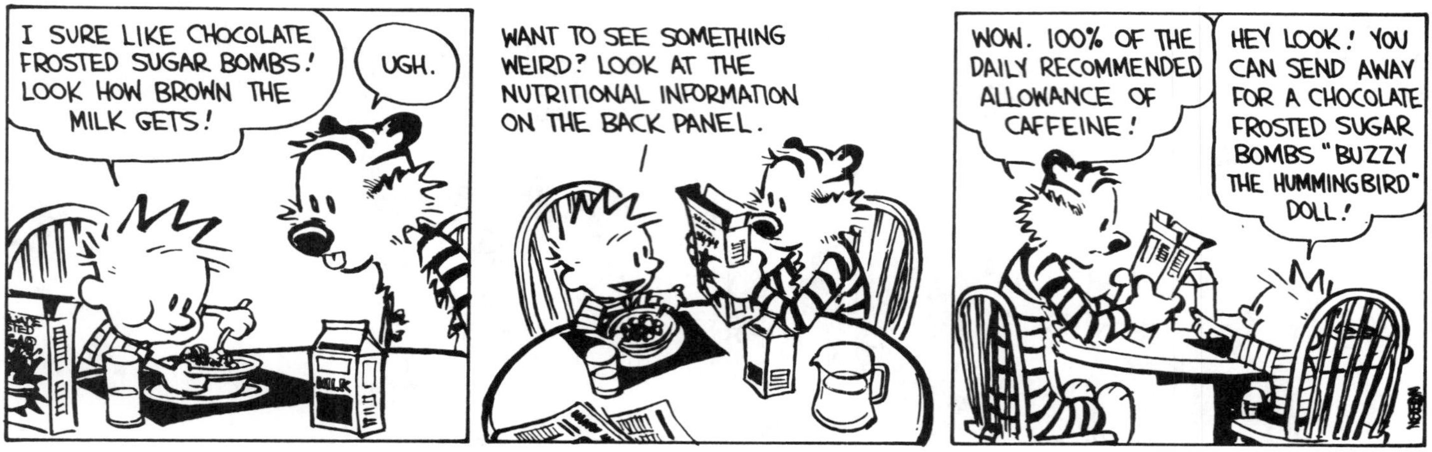
I SURE LIKE CHOCOLATE FROSTED SUGAR BOMBS! LOOK HOW BROWN THE MILK GETS!
UGH.
WANT TO SEE SOMETHING WEIRD? LOOK AT THE NUTRITIONAL INFORMATION ON THE BACK PANEL.
WOW. 100% OF THE DAILY RECOMMENDED ALLOWANCE OF CAFFEINE!
HEY LOOK! YOU CAN SEND AWAY FOR A CHOCOLATE FROSTED SUGAR BOMBS "BUZZY THE HUMMINGBIRD" DOLL!

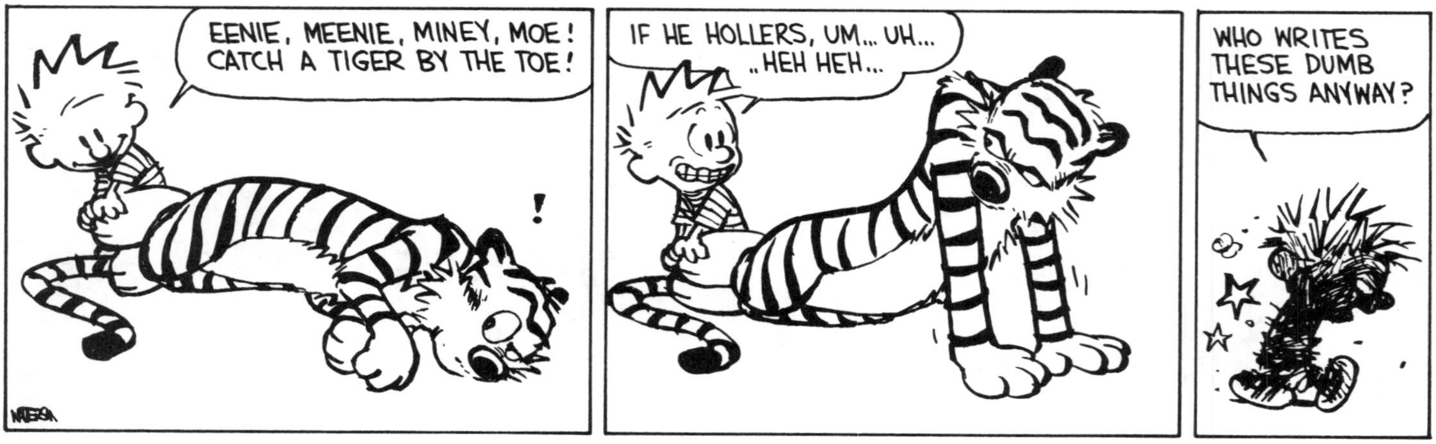
EENIE, MEENIE, MINEY, MOE! CATCH A TIGER BY THE TOE!
!
IF HE HOLLERS, UM... UH... ..HEH HEH...
WHO WRITES THESE DUMB THINGS ANYWAY?

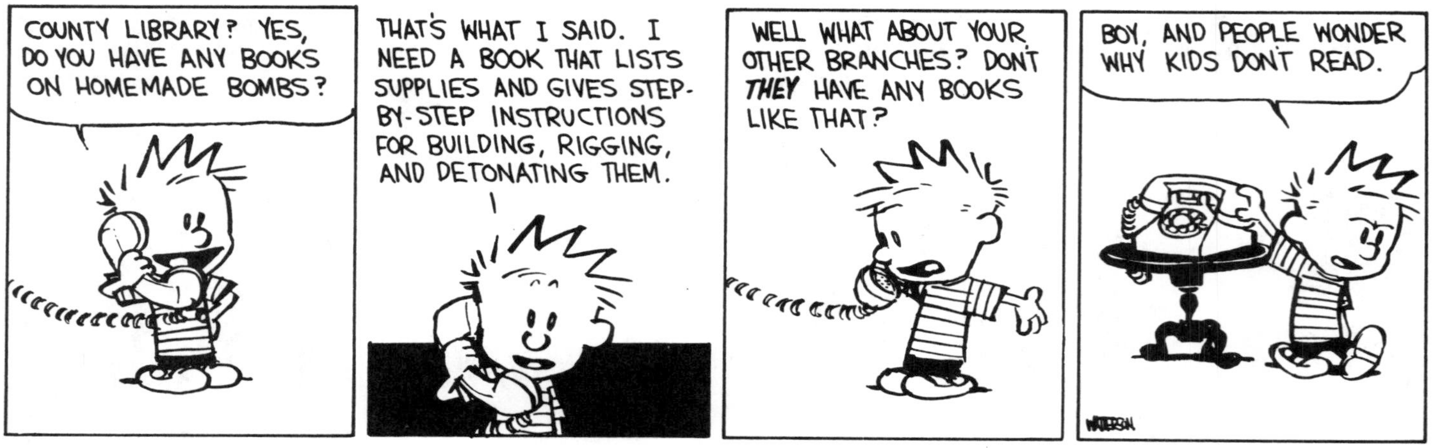
COUNTY LIBRARY? YES, DO YOU HAVE ANY BOOKS ON HOMEMADE BOMBS?
THAT'S WHAT I SAID. I NEED A BOOK THAT LISTS SUPPLIES AND GIVES STEP-BY-STEP INSTRUCTIONS FOR BUILDING, RIGGING, AND DETONATING THEM.
WELL WHAT ABOUT YOUR OTHER BRANCHES? DON'T *THEY* HAVE ANY BOOKS LIKE THAT?
BOY, AND PEOPLE WONDER WHY KIDS DON'T READ.

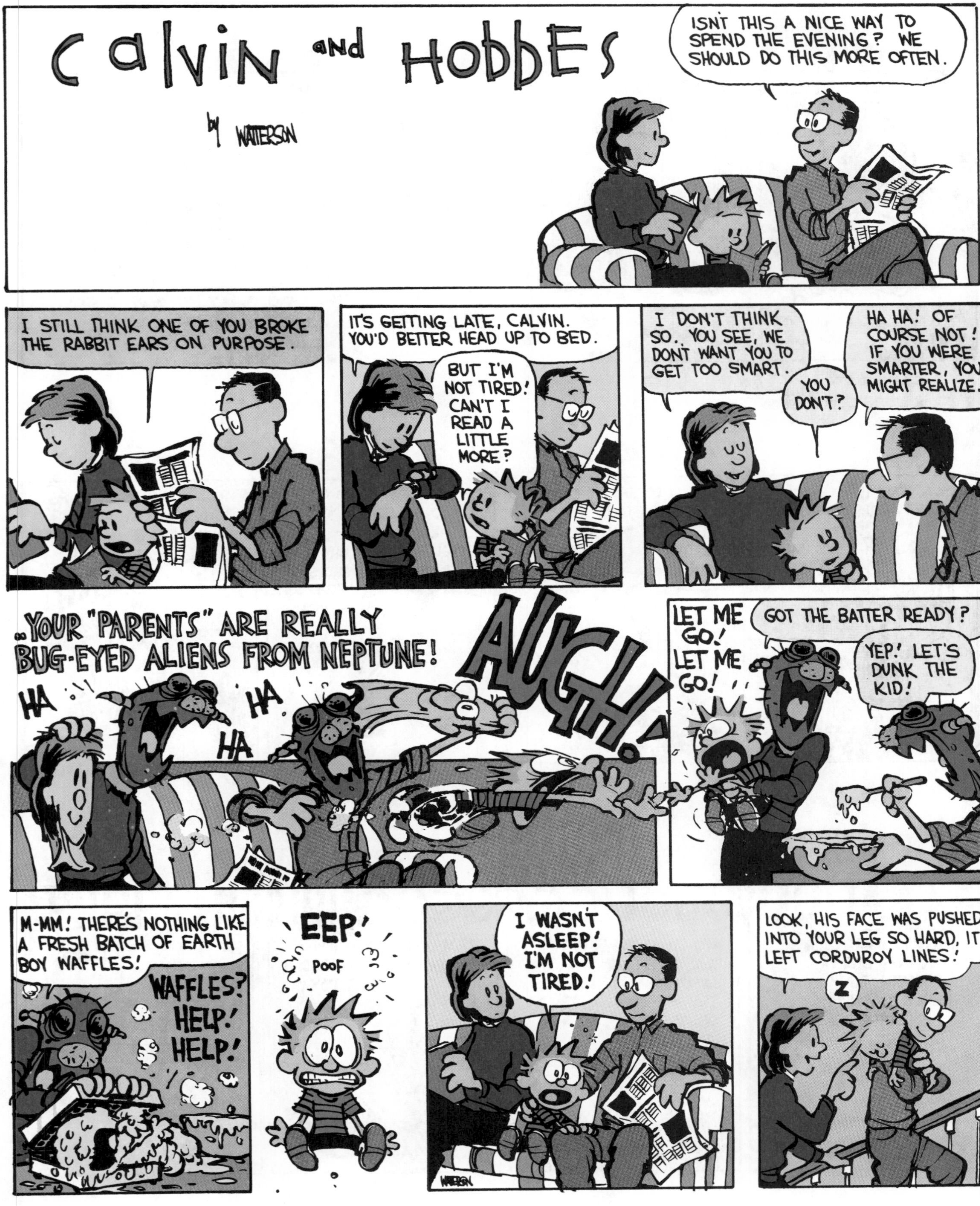
Calvin and Hobbes
by WATTERSON
ISN'T THIS A NICE WAY TO SPEND THE EVENING? WE SHOULD DO THIS MORE OFTEN.
I STILL THINK ONE OF YOU BROKE THE RABBIT EARS ON PURPOSE.
IT'S GETTING LATE, CALVIN. YOU'D BETTER HEAD UP TO BED.
BUT I'M NOT TIRED! CAN'T I READ A LITTLE MORE?
I DON'T THINK SO. YOU SEE, WE DON'T WANT YOU TO GET TOO SMART.
YOU DON'T?
HA HA! OF COURSE NOT! IF YOU WERE SMARTER, YOU MIGHT REALIZE..
..YOUR "PARENTS" ARE REALLY BUG-EYED ALIENS FROM NEPTUNE!
HA
HA
HA
AUGH!
LET ME GO! LET ME GO!
GOT THE BATTER READY?
YEP! LET'S DUNK THE KID!
M-MM! THERE'S NOTHING LIKE A FRESH BATCH OF EARTH BOY WAFFLES!
WAFFLES? HELP! HELP!
EEP!
POOF
I WASN'T ASLEEP! I'M NOT TIRED!
WATTERSON
LOOK, HIS FACE WAS PUSHED INTO YOUR LEG SO HARD, IT LEFT CORDUROY LINES!
Z

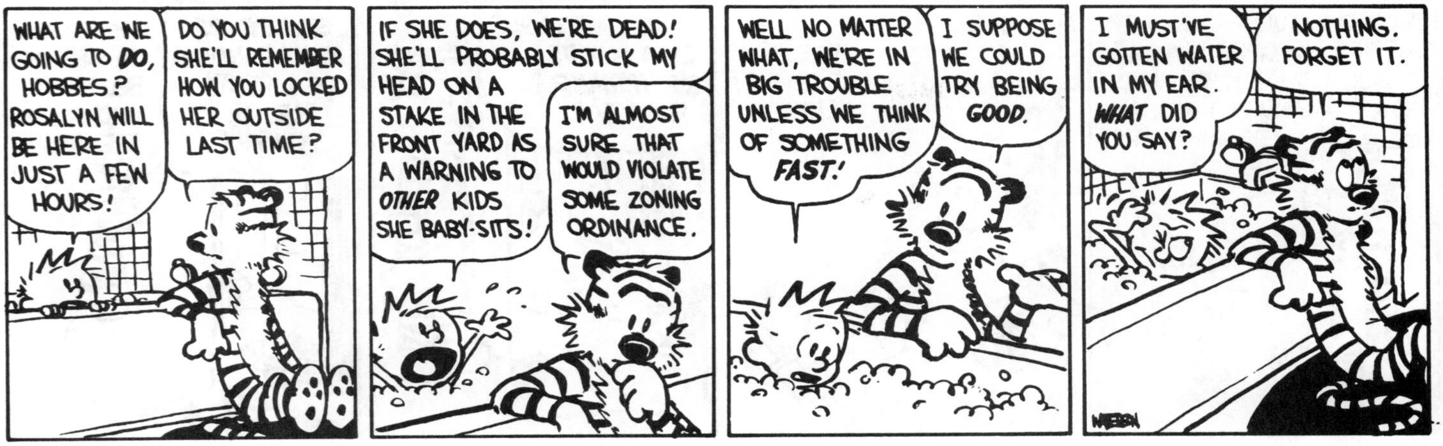
WHAT ARE WE GOING TO *DO*, HOBBES? ROSALYN WILL BE HERE IN JUST A FEW HOURS!
DO YOU THINK SHE'LL REMEMBER HOW YOU LOCKED HER OUTSIDE LAST TIME?
IF SHE DOES, WE'RE DEAD! SHE'LL PROBABLY STICK MY HEAD ON A STAKE IN THE FRONT YARD AS A WARNING TO *OTHER* KIDS SHE BABY-SITS!
I'M ALMOST SURE THAT WOULD VIOLATE SOME ZONING ORDINANCE.
WELL NO MATTER WHAT, WE'RE IN BIG TROUBLE UNLESS WE THINK OF SOMETHING *FAST*!
I SUPPOSE WE COULD TRY BEING *GOOD*.
I MUST'VE GOTTEN WATER IN MY EAR. *WHAT* DID YOU SAY?
NOTHING. FORGET IT.

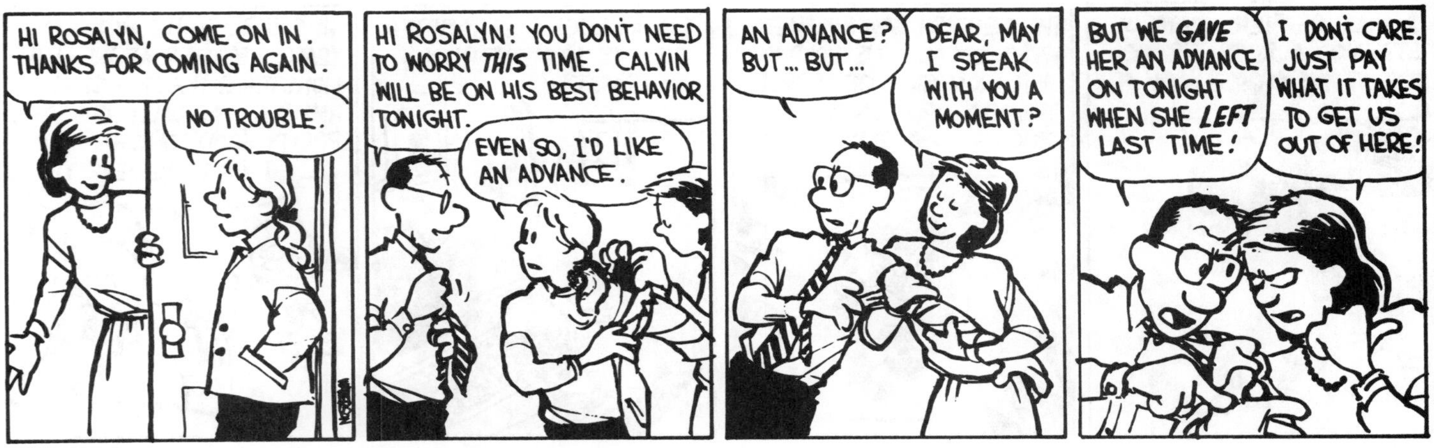
HI ROSALYN, COME ON IN. THANKS FOR COMING AGAIN.
NO TROUBLE.
HI ROSALYN! YOU DON'T NEED TO WORRY *THIS* TIME. CALVIN WILL BE ON HIS BEST BEHAVIOR TONIGHT.
EVEN SO, I'D LIKE AN ADVANCE.
AN ADVANCE? BUT... BUT...
DEAR, MAY I SPEAK WITH YOU A MOMENT?
BUT WE *GAVE* HER AN ADVANCE ON TONIGHT WHEN SHE *LEFT* LAST TIME!
I DON'T CARE. JUST PAY WHAT IT TAKES TO GET US OUT OF HERE!

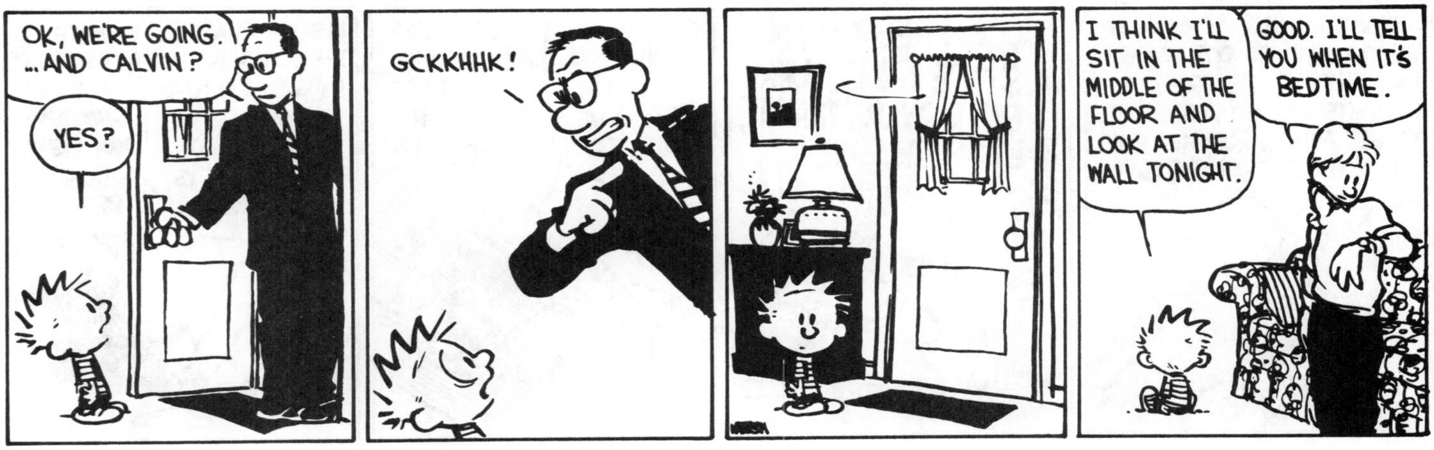
OK, WE'RE GOING. ...AND CALVIN?
YES?
GCKKHHK!
I THINK I'LL SIT IN THE MIDDLE OF THE FLOOR AND LOOK AT THE WALL TONIGHT.
GOOD. I'LL TELL YOU WHEN IT'S BEDTIME.

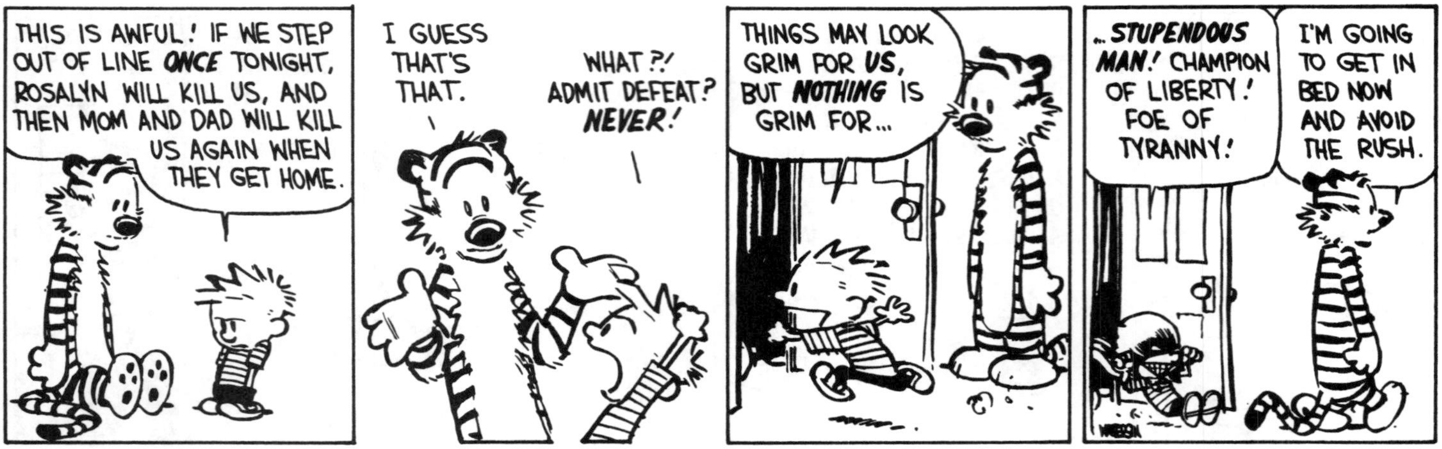
THIS IS AWFUL! IF WE STEP OUT OF LINE ONCE TONIGHT, ROSALYN WILL KILL US, AND THEN MOM AND DAD WILL KILL US AGAIN WHEN THEY GET HOME.
I GUESS THAT'S THAT.
WHAT ?! ADMIT DEFEAT? NEVER!
THINGS MAY LOOK GRIM FOR US, BUT NOTHING IS GRIM FOR...
...STUPENDOUS MAN! CHAMPION OF LIBERTY! FOE OF TYRANNY!
I'M GOING TO GET IN BED NOW AND AVOID THE RUSH.

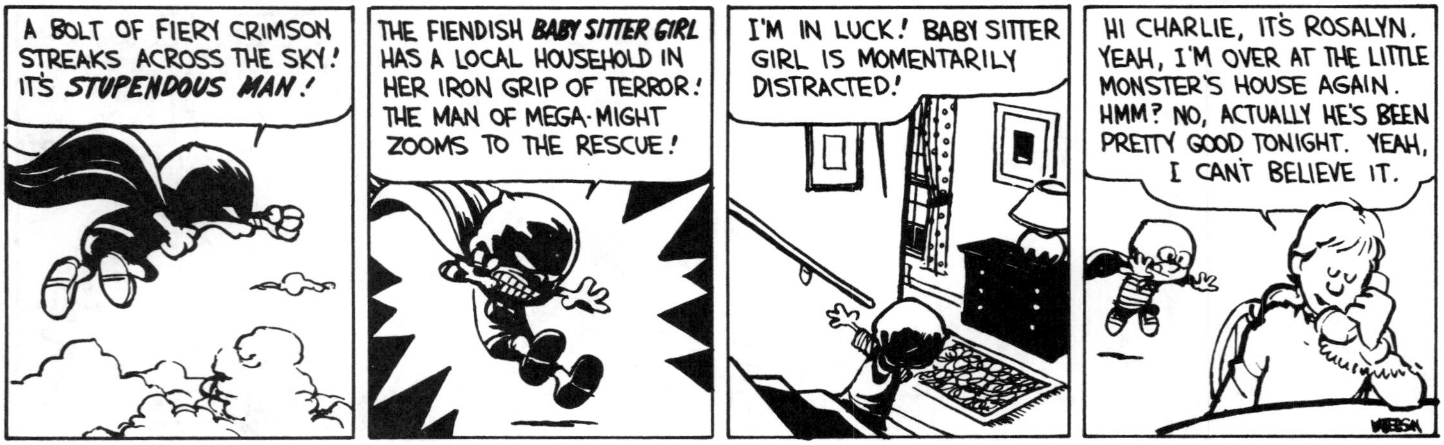
A BOLT OF FIERY CRIMSON STREAKS ACROSS THE SKY! IT'S STUPENDOUS MAN!
THE FIENDISH BABY SITTER GIRL HAS A LOCAL HOUSEHOLD IN HER IRON GRIP OF TERROR! THE MAN OF MEGA-MIGHT ZOOMS TO THE RESCUE!
I'M IN LUCK! BABY SITTER GIRL IS MOMENTARILY DISTRACTED!
HI CHARLIE, IT'S ROSALYN. YEAH, I'M OVER AT THE LITTLE MONSTER'S HOUSE AGAIN. HMM? NO, ACTUALLY HE'S BEEN PRETTY GOOD TONIGHT. YEAH, I CAN'T BELIEVE IT.

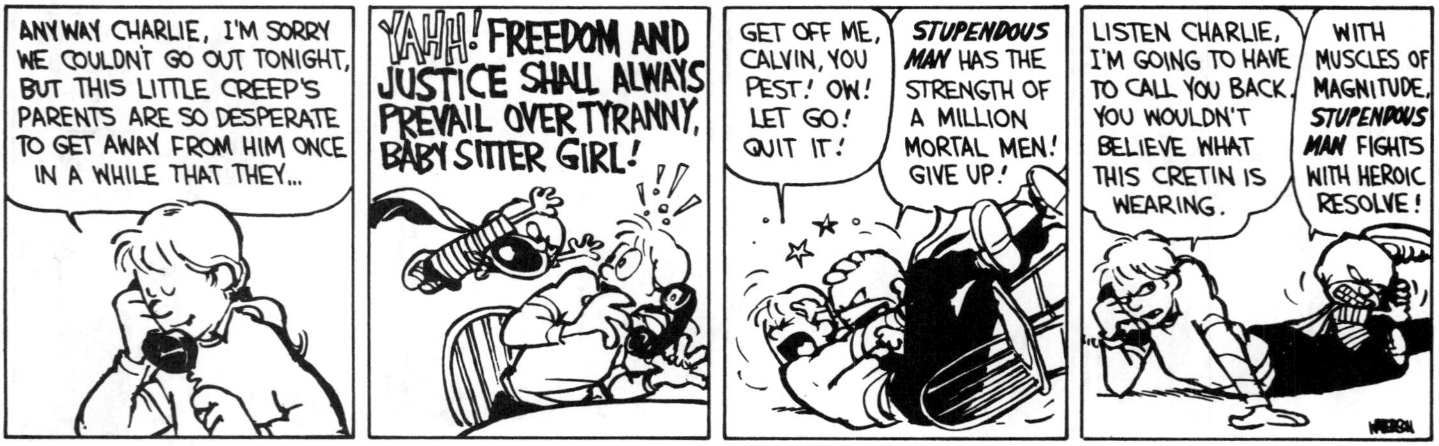
ANYWAY CHARLIE, I'M SORRY WE COULDN'T GO OUT TONIGHT, BUT THIS LITTLE CREEP'S PARENTS ARE SO DESPERATE TO GET AWAY FROM HIM ONCE IN A WHILE THAT THEY...
YAHH! FREEDOM AND JUSTICE SHALL ALWAYS PREVAIL OVER TYRANNY, BABY SITTER GIRL!
!?!
GET OFF ME, CALVIN, YOU PEST! OW! LET GO! QUIT IT!
STUPENDOUS MAN HAS THE STRENGTH OF A MILLION MORTAL MEN! GIVE UP!
LISTEN CHARLIE, I'M GOING TO HAVE TO CALL YOU BACK. YOU WOULDN'T BELIEVE WHAT THIS CRETIN IS WEARING.
WITH MUSCLES OF MAGNITUDE, STUPENDOUS MAN FIGHTS WITH HEROIC RESOLVE!

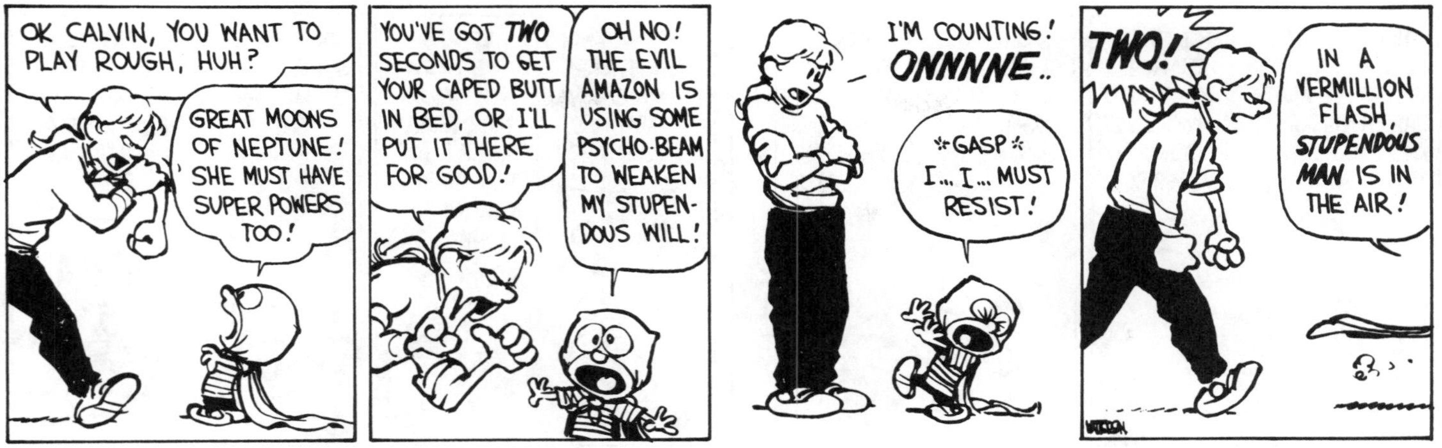
OK CALVIN, YOU WANT TO PLAY ROUGH, HUH?
GREAT MOONS OF NEPTUNE! SHE MUST HAVE SUPER POWERS TOO!
YOU'VE GOT **TWO** SECONDS TO GET YOUR CAPED BUTT IN BED, OR I'LL PUT IT THERE FOR GOOD!
OH NO! THE EVIL AMAZON IS USING SOME PSYCHO-BEAM TO WEAKEN MY STUPENDOUS WILL!
I'M COUNTING! **ONNNNE**..
GASP I... I... MUST RESIST!
TWO!
IN A VERMILLION FLASH, ***STUPENDOUS MAN*** IS IN THE AIR!

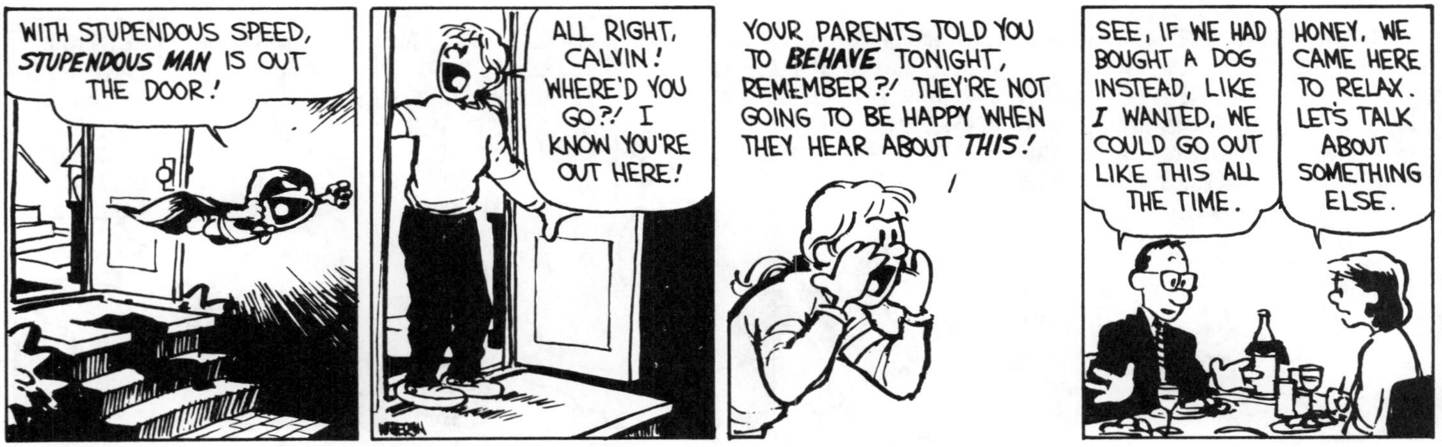
WITH STUPENDOUS SPEED, ***STUPENDOUS MAN*** IS OUT THE DOOR!
ALL RIGHT, CALVIN! WHERE'D YOU GO?! I KNOW YOU'RE OUT HERE!
YOUR PARENTS TOLD YOU TO ***BEHAVE*** TONIGHT, REMEMBER?! THEY'RE NOT GOING TO BE HAPPY WHEN THEY HEAR ABOUT ***THIS***!
SEE, IF WE HAD BOUGHT A DOG INSTEAD, LIKE ***I*** WANTED, WE COULD GO OUT LIKE THIS ALL THE TIME.
HONEY, WE CAME HERE TO RELAX. LET'S TALK ABOUT SOMETHING ELSE.

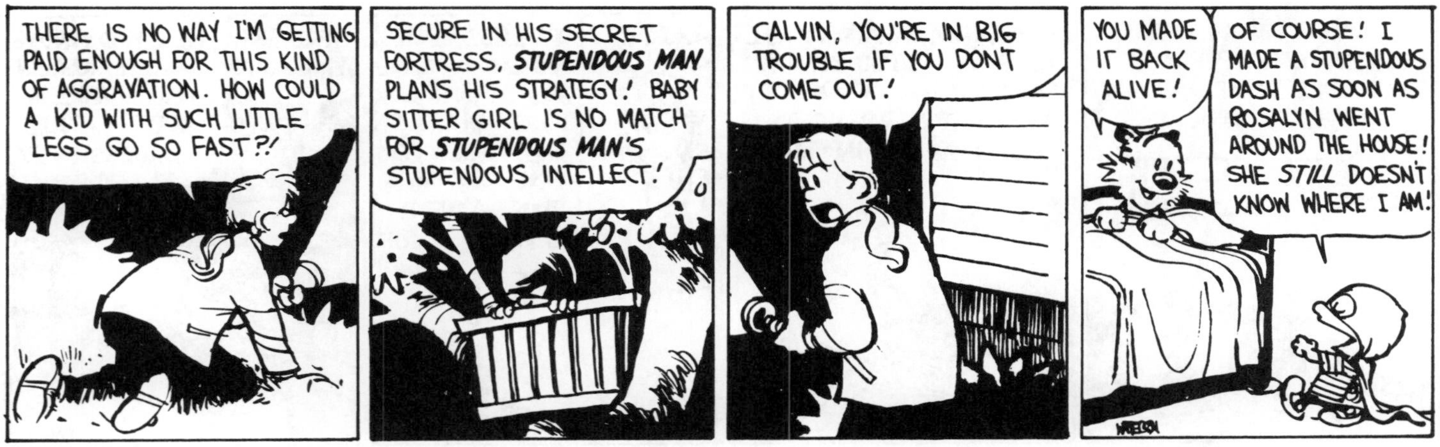
THERE IS NO WAY I'M GETTING PAID ENOUGH FOR THIS KIND OF AGGRAVATION. HOW COULD A KID WITH SUCH LITTLE LEGS GO SO FAST?!
SECURE IN HIS SECRET FORTRESS, ***STUPENDOUS MAN*** PLANS HIS STRATEGY! BABY SITTER GIRL IS NO MATCH FOR ***STUPENDOUS MAN'S*** STUPENDOUS INTELLECT!
CALVIN, YOU'RE IN BIG TROUBLE IF YOU DON'T COME OUT!
YOU MADE IT BACK ALIVE!
OF COURSE! I MADE A STUPENDOUS DASH AS SOON AS ROSALYN WENT AROUND THE HOUSE! SHE ***STILL*** DOESN'T KNOW WHERE I AM!

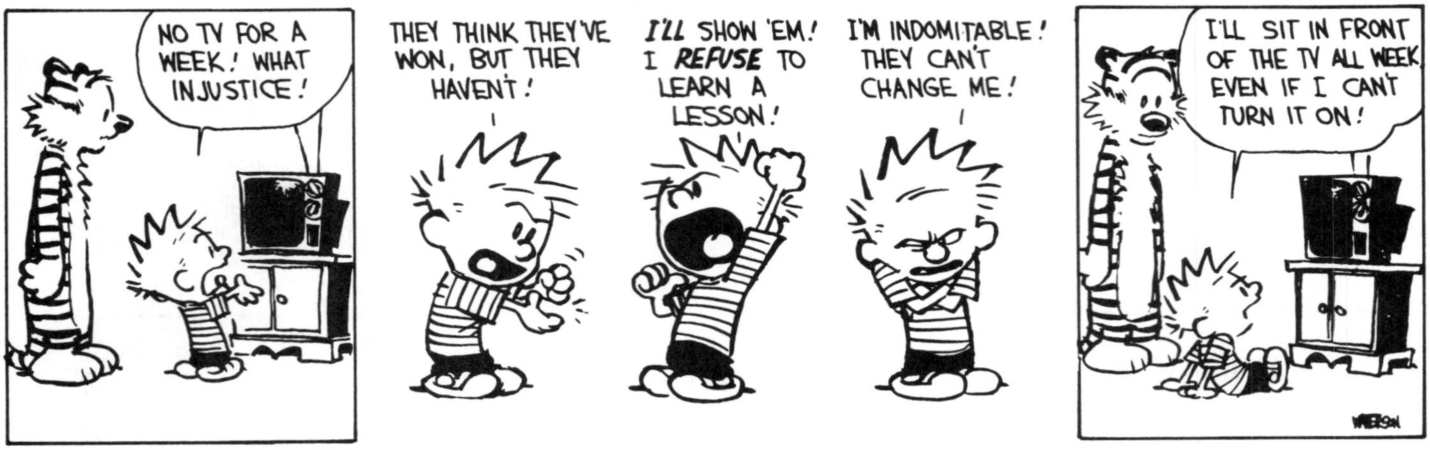
NO TV FOR A WEEK! WHAT INJUSTICE!
THEY THINK THEY'VE WON, BUT THEY HAVEN'T!
I'LL SHOW 'EM! I *REFUSE* TO LEARN A LESSON!
I'M INDOMITABLE! THEY CAN'T CHANGE ME!
I'LL SIT IN FRONT OF THE TV ALL WEEK, EVEN IF I CAN'T TURN IT ON!

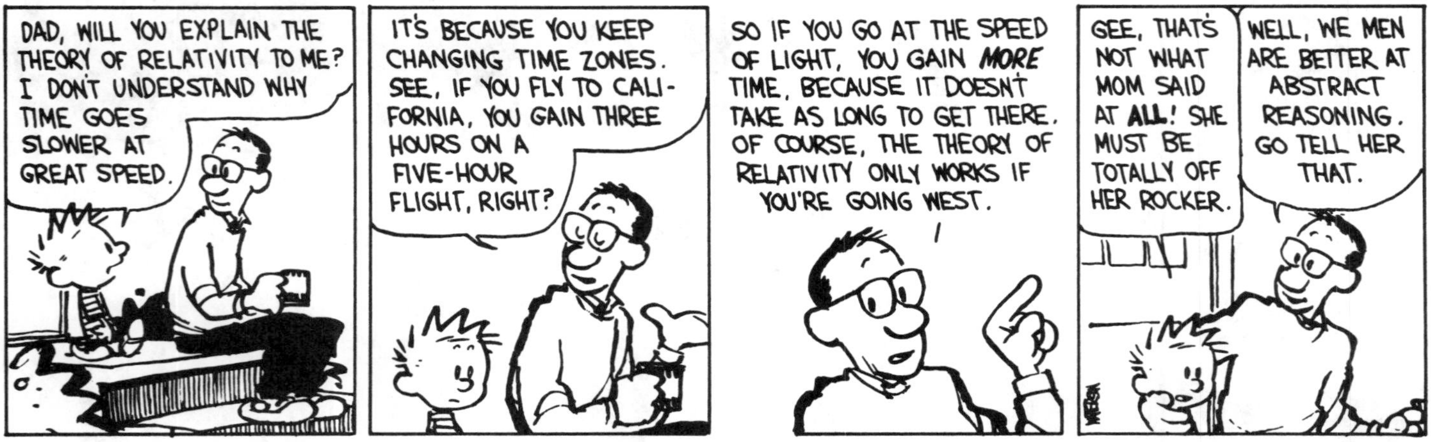
DAD, WILL YOU EXPLAIN THE THEORY OF RELATIVITY TO ME? I DON'T UNDERSTAND WHY TIME GOES SLOWER AT GREAT SPEED.
IT'S BECAUSE YOU KEEP CHANGING TIME ZONES. SEE, IF YOU FLY TO CALIFORNIA, YOU GAIN THREE HOURS ON A FIVE-HOUR FLIGHT, RIGHT?
SO IF YOU GO AT THE SPEED OF LIGHT, YOU GAIN *MORE* TIME, BECAUSE IT DOESN'T TAKE AS LONG TO GET THERE. OF COURSE, THE THEORY OF RELATIVITY ONLY WORKS IF YOU'RE GOING WEST.
GEE, THAT'S NOT WHAT MOM SAID AT **ALL**! SHE MUST BE TOTALLY OFF HER ROCKER.
WELL, WE MEN ARE BETTER AT ABSTRACT REASONING. GO TELL HER THAT.

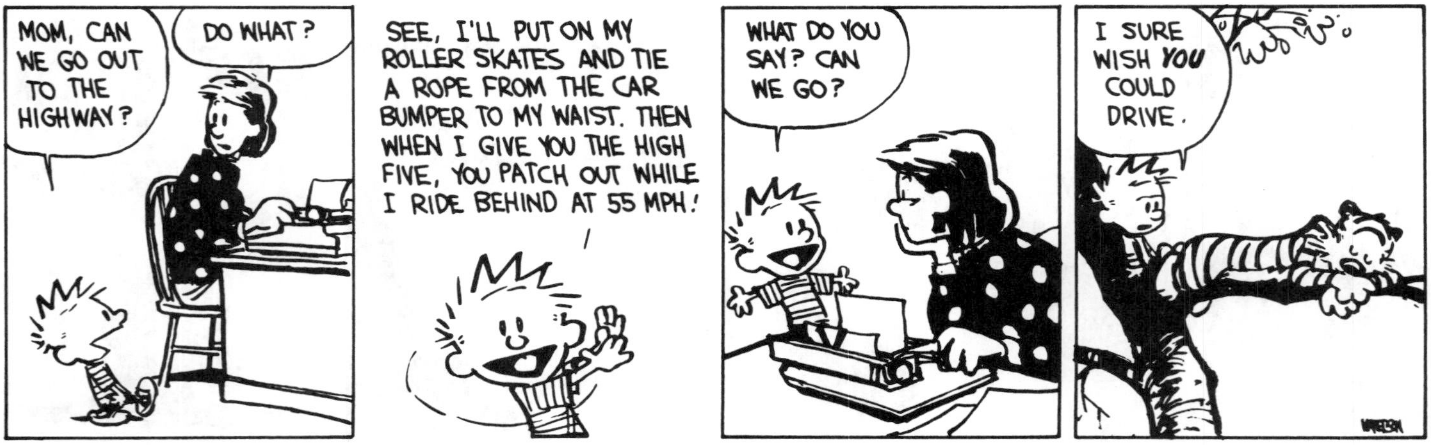
MOM, CAN WE GO OUT TO THE HIGHWAY?
DO WHAT?
SEE, I'LL PUT ON MY ROLLER SKATES AND TIE A ROPE FROM THE CAR BUMPER TO MY WAIST. THEN WHEN I GIVE YOU THE HIGH FIVE, YOU PATCH OUT WHILE I RIDE BEHIND AT 55 MPH!
WHAT DO YOU SAY? CAN WE GO?
I SURE WISH *YOU* COULD DRIVE.

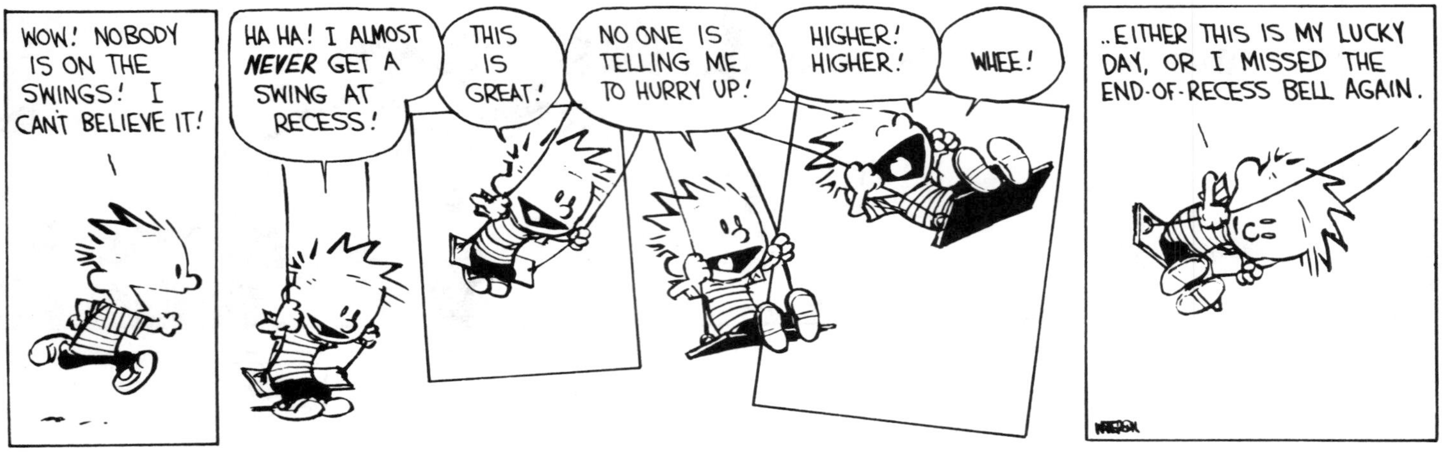
WOW! NOBODY IS ON THE SWINGS! I CAN'T BELIEVE IT!
HA HA! I ALMOST *NEVER* GET A SWING AT RECESS!
THIS IS GREAT!
NO ONE IS TELLING ME TO HURRY UP!
HIGHER! HIGHER!
WHEE!
..EITHER THIS IS MY LUCKY DAY, OR I MISSED THE END-OF-RECESS BELL AGAIN.

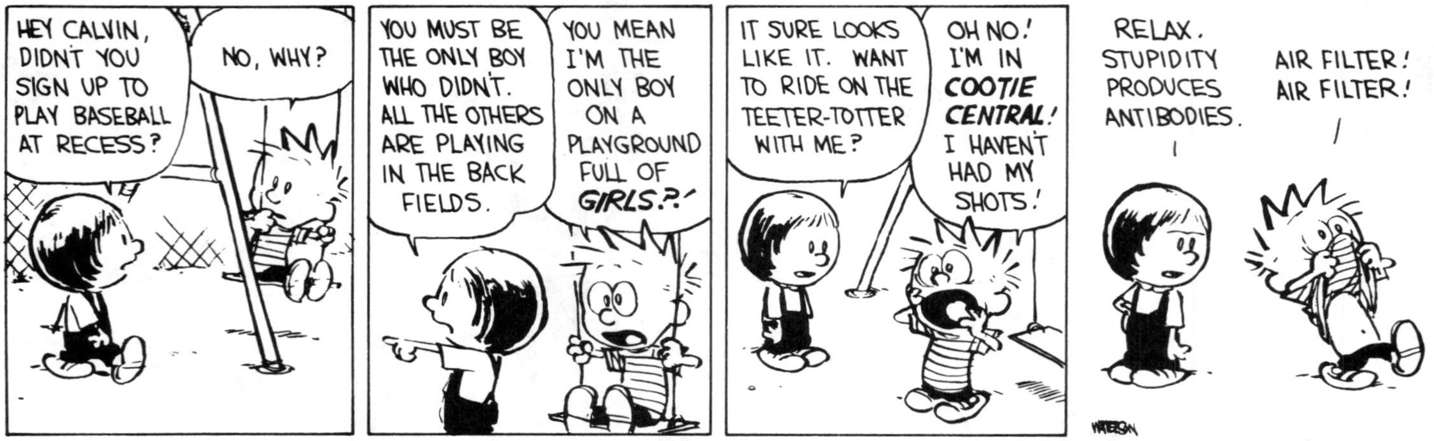
HEY CALVIN, DIDN'T YOU SIGN UP TO PLAY BASEBALL AT RECESS?
NO, WHY?
YOU MUST BE THE ONLY BOY WHO DIDN'T. ALL THE OTHERS ARE PLAYING IN THE BACK FIELDS.
YOU MEAN I'M THE ONLY BOY ON A PLAYGROUND FULL OF *GIRLS*?!
IT SURE LOOKS LIKE IT. WANT TO RIDE ON THE TEETER-TOTTER WITH ME?
OH NO! I'M IN *COOTIE CENTRAL*! I HAVEN'T HAD MY SHOTS!
RELAX. STUPIDITY PRODUCES ANTIBODIES.
AIR FILTER! AIR FILTER!

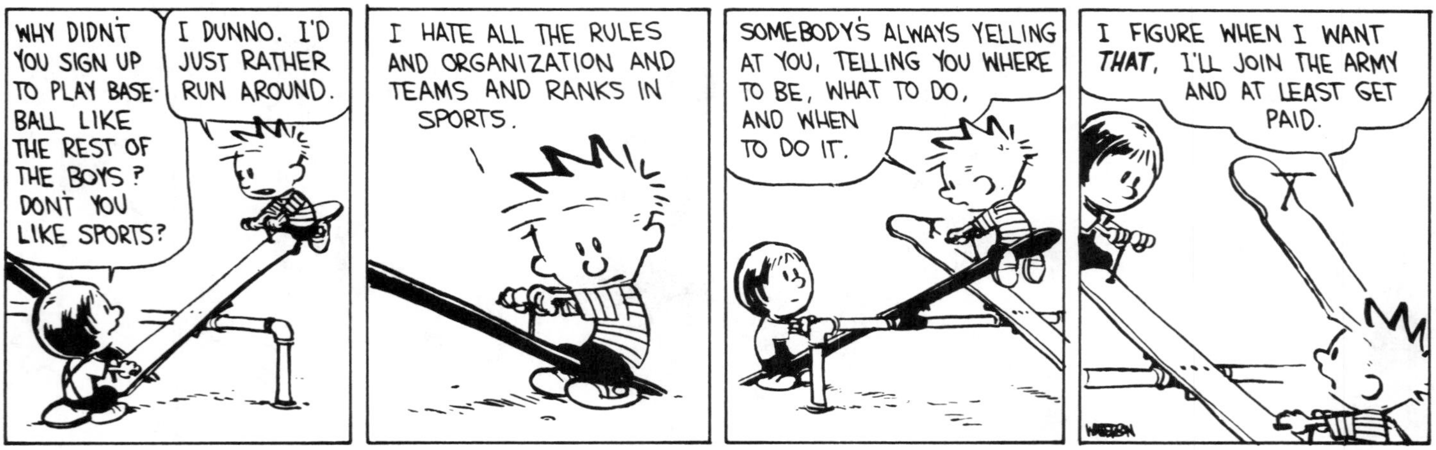
WHY DIDN'T YOU SIGN UP TO PLAY BASE-BALL LIKE THE REST OF THE BOYS? DON'T YOU LIKE SPORTS?
I DUNNO. I'D JUST RATHER RUN AROUND.
I HATE ALL THE RULES AND ORGANIZATION AND TEAMS AND RANKS IN SPORTS.
SOMEBODY'S ALWAYS YELLING AT YOU, TELLING YOU WHERE TO BE, WHAT TO DO, AND WHEN TO DO IT.
I FIGURE WHEN I WANT *THAT*, I'LL JOIN THE ARMY AND AT LEAST GET PAID.

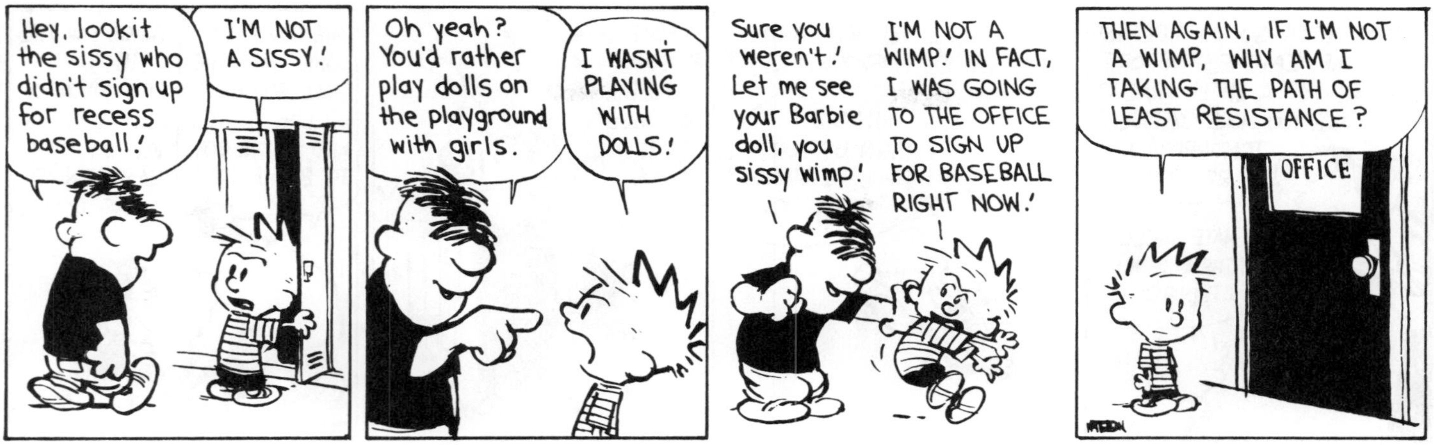
Hey, lookit the sissy who didn't sign up for recess baseball!
I'M NOT A SISSY!
Oh yeah? You'd rather play dolls on the playground with girls.
I WASN'T PLAYING WITH DOLLS!
Sure you weren't! Let me see your Barbie doll, you sissy wimp!
I'M NOT A WIMP! IN FACT, I WAS GOING TO THE OFFICE TO SIGN UP FOR BASEBALL RIGHT NOW!
THEN AGAIN, IF I'M NOT A WIMP, WHY AM I TAKING THE PATH OF LEAST RESISTANCE?
OFFICE

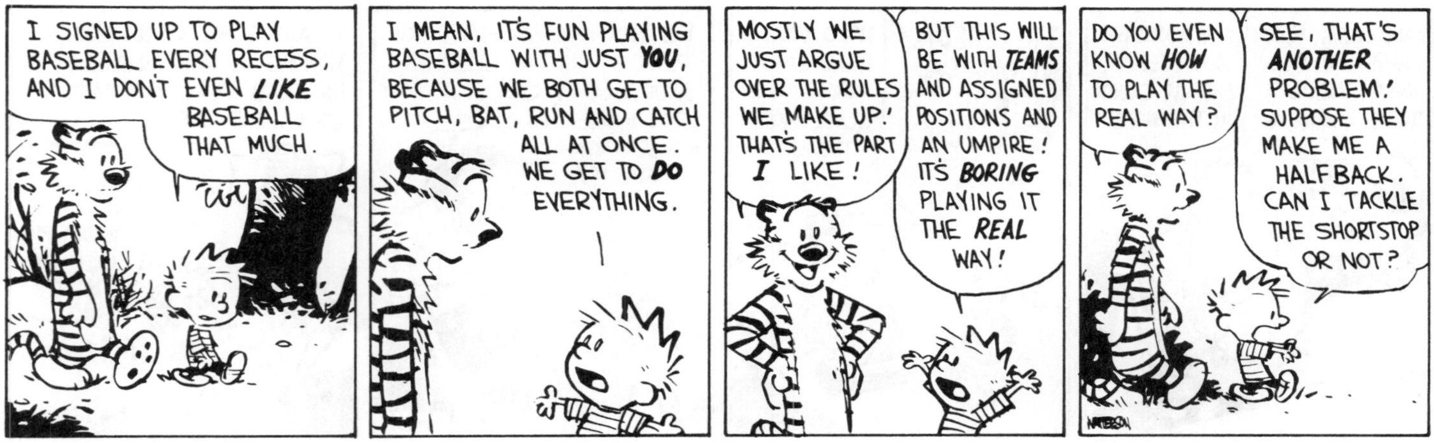
I SIGNED UP TO PLAY BASEBALL EVERY RECESS, AND I DON'T EVEN LIKE BASEBALL THAT MUCH.
I MEAN, IT'S FUN PLAYING BASEBALL WITH JUST YOU, BECAUSE WE BOTH GET TO PITCH, BAT, RUN AND CATCH ALL AT ONCE. WE GET TO DO EVERYTHING.
MOSTLY WE JUST ARGUE OVER THE RULES WE MAKE UP! THAT'S THE PART I LIKE!
BUT THIS WILL BE WITH TEAMS AND ASSIGNED POSITIONS AND AN UMPIRE! IT'S BORING PLAYING IT THE REAL WAY!
DO YOU EVEN KNOW HOW TO PLAY THE REAL WAY?
SEE, THAT'S ANOTHER PROBLEM! SUPPOSE THEY MAKE ME A HALFBACK. CAN I TACKLE THE SHORTSTOP OR NOT?

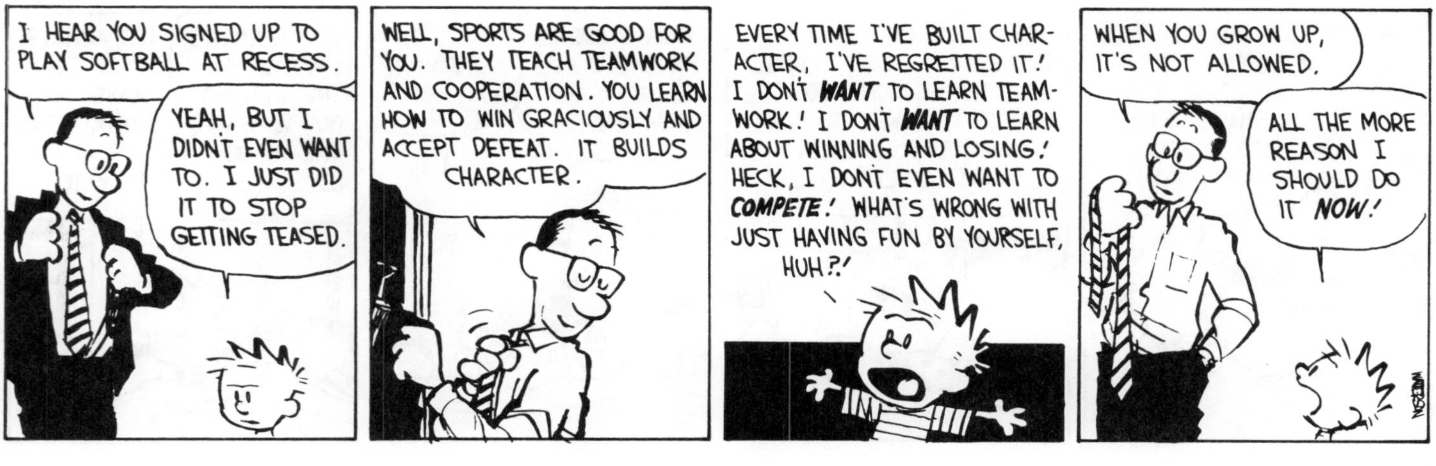
I HEAR YOU SIGNED UP TO PLAY SOFTBALL AT RECESS.
YEAH, BUT I DIDN'T EVEN WANT TO. I JUST DID IT TO STOP GETTING TEASED.
WELL, SPORTS ARE GOOD FOR YOU. THEY TEACH TEAMWORK AND COOPERATION. YOU LEARN HOW TO WIN GRACIOUSLY AND ACCEPT DEFEAT. IT BUILDS CHARACTER.
EVERY TIME I'VE BUILT CHARACTER, I'VE REGRETTED IT! I DON'T WANT TO LEARN TEAMWORK! I DON'T WANT TO LEARN ABOUT WINNING AND LOSING! HECK, I DON'T EVEN WANT TO COMPETE! WHAT'S WRONG WITH JUST HAVING FUN BY YOURSELF, HUH?!
WHEN YOU GROW UP, IT'S NOT ALLOWED.
ALL THE MORE REASON I SHOULD DO IT NOW!

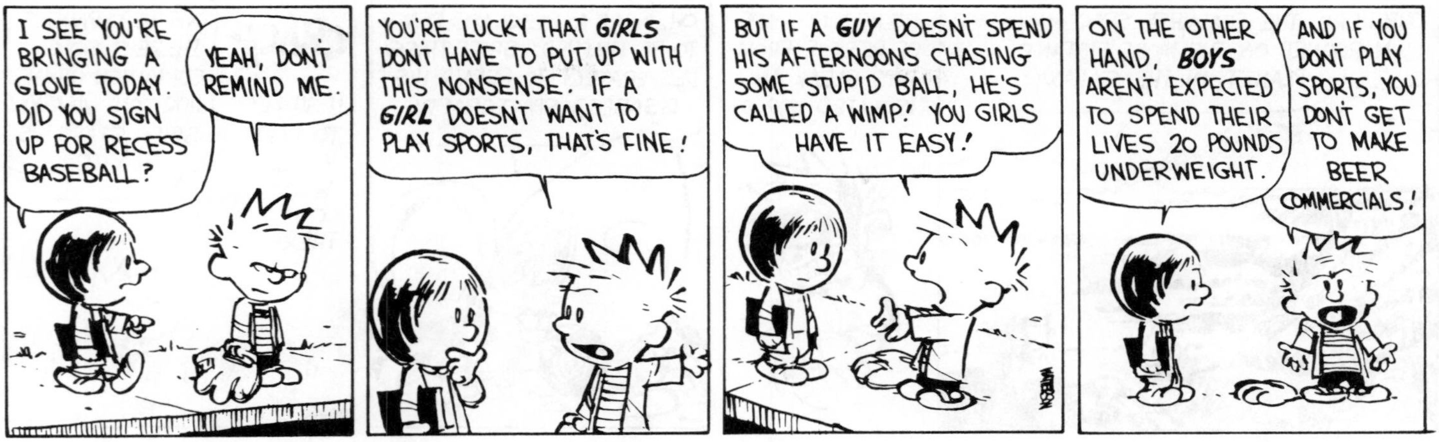
I SEE YOU'RE BRINGING A GLOVE TODAY. DID YOU SIGN UP FOR RECESS BASEBALL?
YEAH, DON'T REMIND ME.
YOU'RE LUCKY THAT GIRLS DON'T HAVE TO PUT UP WITH THIS NONSENSE. IF A GIRL DOESN'T WANT TO PLAY SPORTS, THAT'S FINE!
BUT IF A GUY DOESN'T SPEND HIS AFTERNOONS CHASING SOME STUPID BALL, HE'S CALLED A WIMP! YOU GIRLS HAVE IT EASY!
ON THE OTHER HAND, BOYS AREN'T EXPECTED TO SPEND THEIR LIVES 20 POUNDS UNDERWEIGHT.
AND IF YOU DON'T PLAY SPORTS, YOU DON'T GET TO MAKE BEER COMMERCIALS!

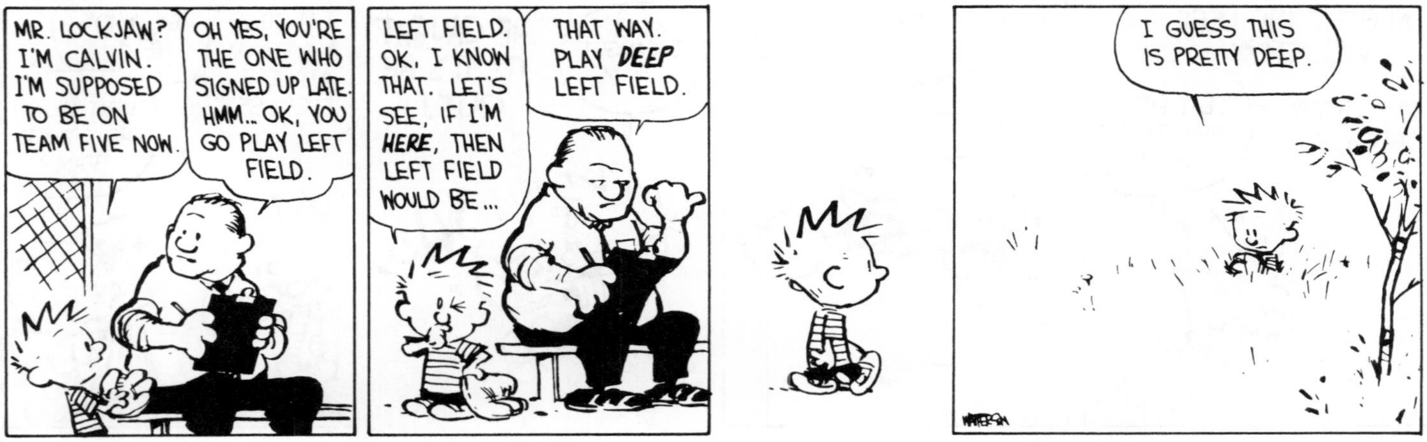
MR. LOCKJAW? I'M CALVIN. I'M SUPPOSED TO BE ON TEAM FIVE NOW.
OH YES, YOU'RE THE ONE WHO SIGNED UP LATE. HMM.. OK, YOU GO PLAY LEFT FIELD.
LEFT FIELD. OK, I KNOW THAT. LET'S SEE, IF I'M HERE, THEN LEFT FIELD WOULD BE...
THAT WAY. PLAY DEEP LEFT FIELD.
I GUESS THIS IS PRETTY DEEP.

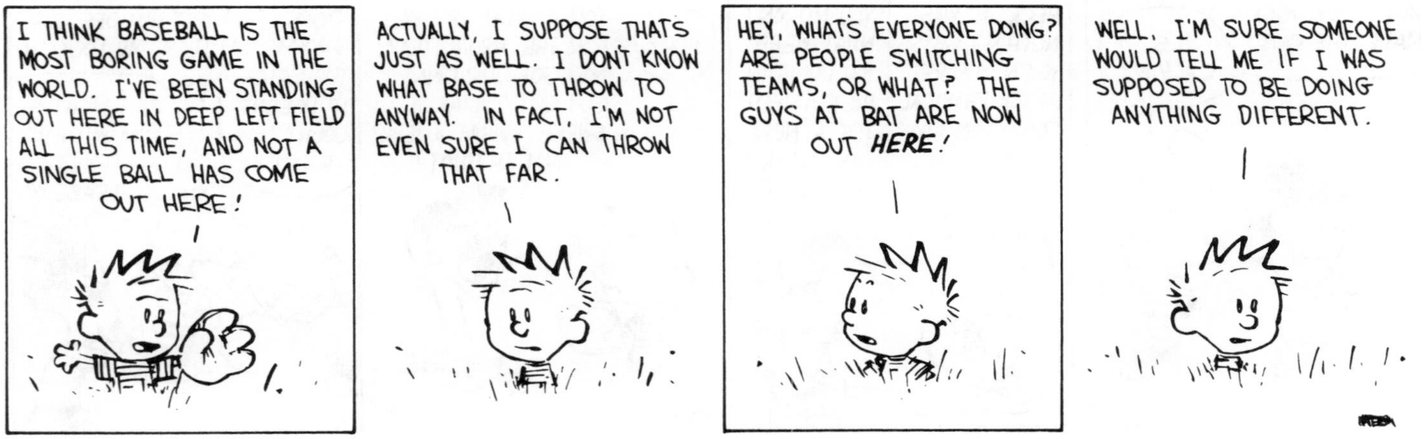
I THINK BASEBALL IS THE MOST BORING GAME IN THE WORLD. I'VE BEEN STANDING OUT HERE IN DEEP LEFT FIELD ALL THIS TIME, AND NOT A SINGLE BALL HAS COME OUT HERE!
ACTUALLY, I SUPPOSE THAT'S JUST AS WELL. I DON'T KNOW WHAT BASE TO THROW TO ANYWAY. IN FACT, I'M NOT EVEN SURE I CAN THROW THAT FAR.
HEY, WHAT'S EVERYONE DOING? ARE PEOPLE SWITCHING TEAMS, OR WHAT? THE GUYS AT BAT ARE NOW OUT HERE!
WELL, I'M SURE SOMEONE WOULD TELL ME IF I WAS SUPPOSED TO BE DOING ANYTHING DIFFERENT.

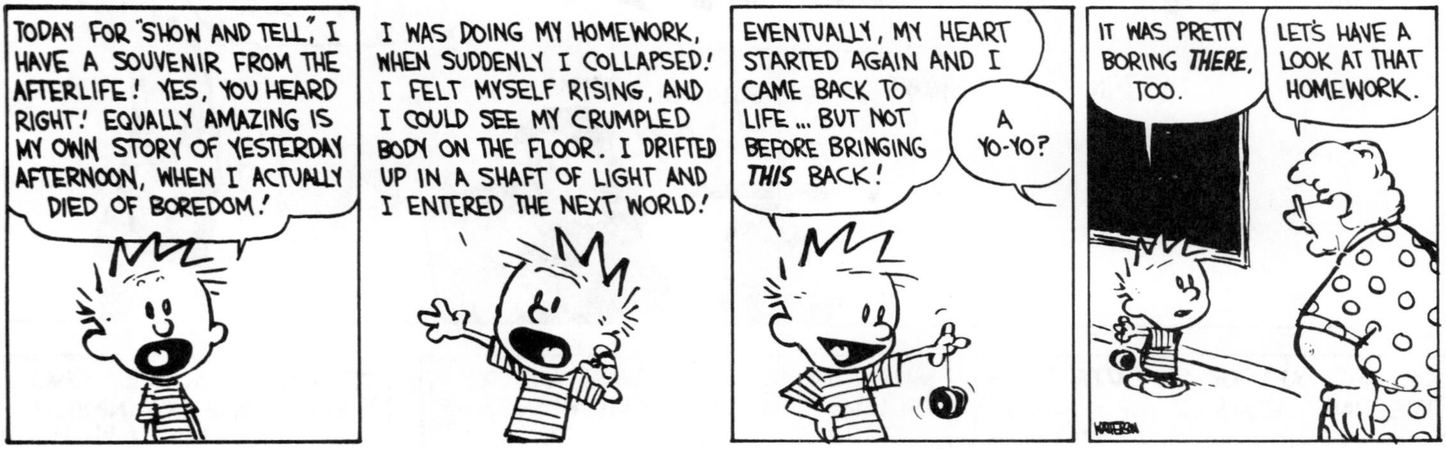
TODAY FOR "SHOW AND TELL," I HAVE A SOUVENIR FROM THE AFTERLIFE! YES, YOU HEARD RIGHT! EQUALLY AMAZING IS MY OWN STORY OF YESTERDAY AFTERNOON, WHEN I ACTUALLY DIED OF BOREDOM!
I WAS DOING MY HOMEWORK, WHEN SUDDENLY I COLLAPSED! I FELT MYSELF RISING, AND I COULD SEE MY CRUMPLED BODY ON THE FLOOR. I DRIFTED UP IN A SHAFT OF LIGHT AND I ENTERED THE NEXT WORLD!
EVENTUALLY, MY HEART STARTED AGAIN AND I CAME BACK TO LIFE ... BUT NOT BEFORE BRINGING THIS BACK!
A YO-YO?
IT WAS PRETTY BORING THERE, TOO.
LET'S HAVE A LOOK AT THAT HOMEWORK.

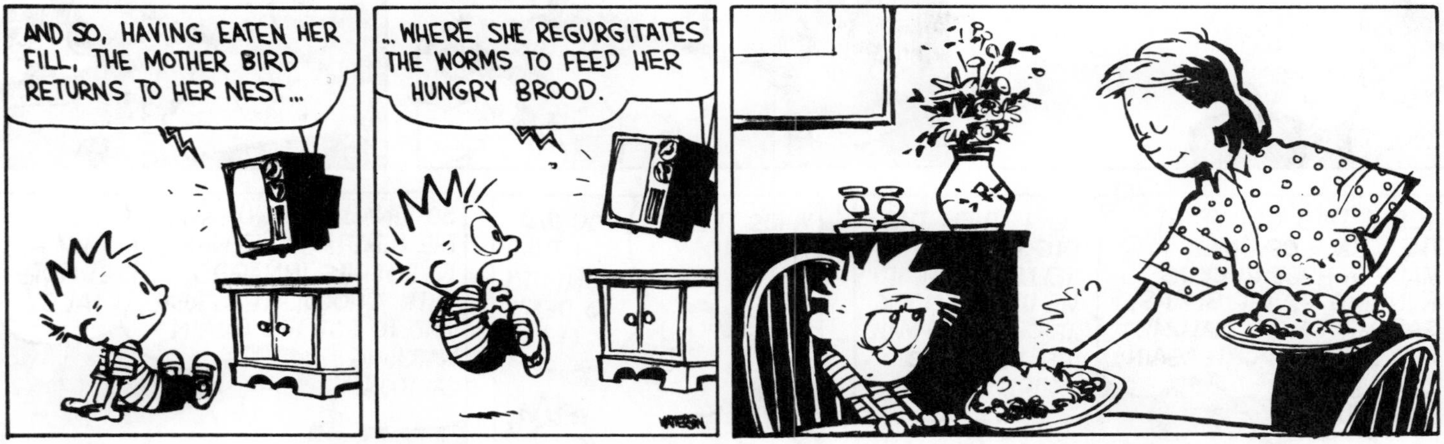
AND SO, HAVING EATEN HER FILL, THE MOTHER BIRD RETURNS TO HER NEST...
...WHERE SHE REGURGITATES THE WORMS TO FEED HER HUNGRY BROOD.

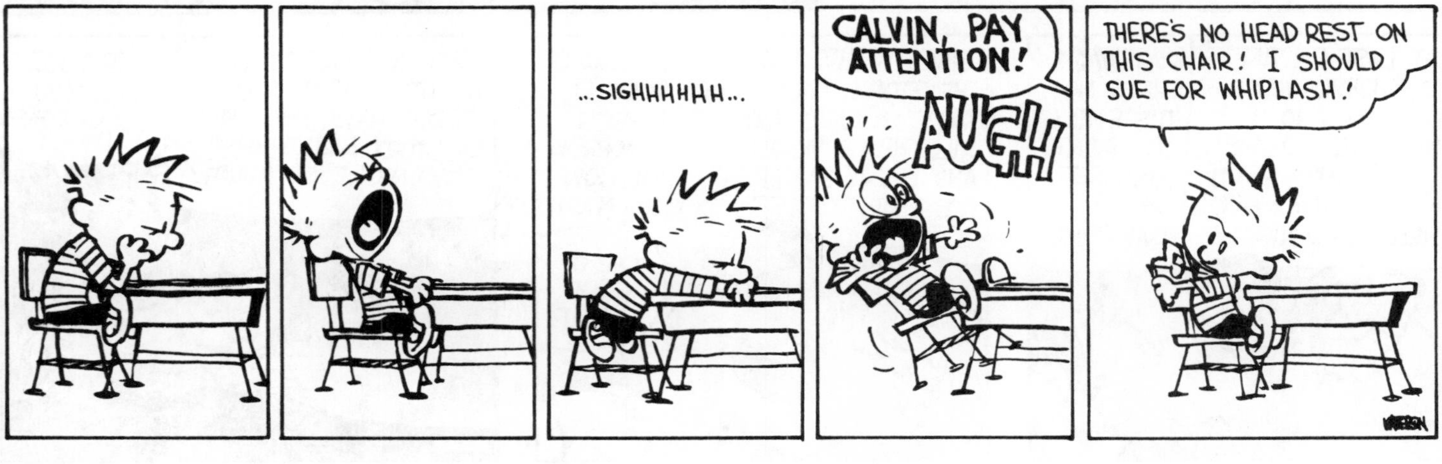
...SIGHHHHHH...
CALVIN, PAY ATTENTION!
AUGH
THERE'S NO HEAD REST ON THIS CHAIR! I SHOULD SUE FOR WHIPLASH!

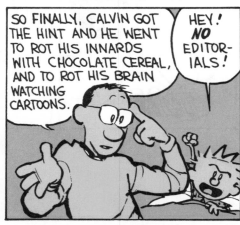

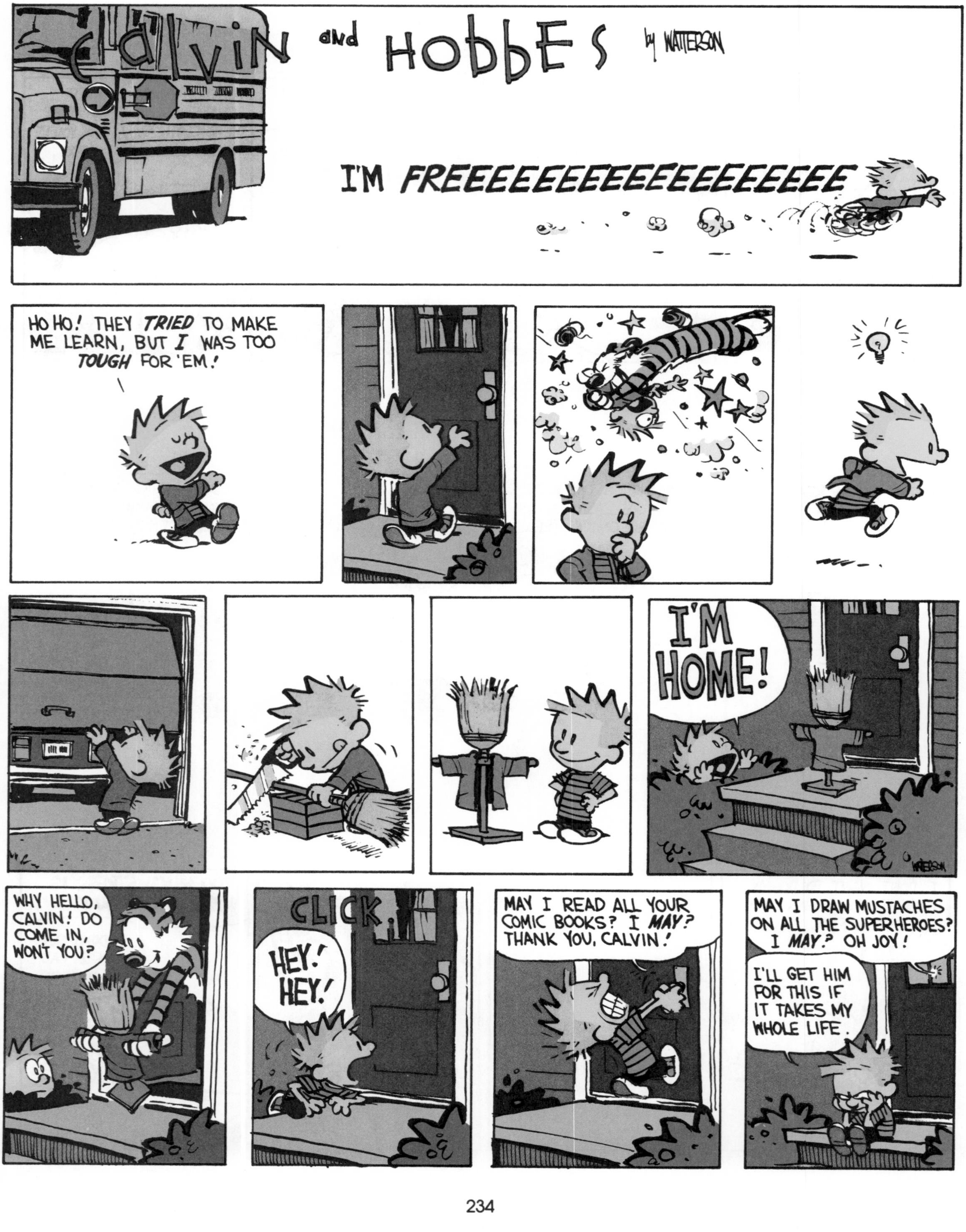
Calvin and HOBBES by WATTERSON
I'M FREEEEEEEEEEEEEEEEEEE
HO HO! THEY TRIED TO MAKE ME LEARN, BUT I WAS TOO TOUGH FOR 'EM!
I'M HOME!
WATTERSON
WHY HELLO, CALVIN! DO COME IN, WON'T YOU?
CLICK
HEY! HEY!
MAY I READ ALL YOUR COMIC BOOKS? I MAY? THANK YOU, CALVIN!
MAY I DRAW MUSTACHES ON ALL THE SUPERHEROES? I MAY? OH JOY!
I'LL GET HIM FOR THIS IF IT TAKES MY WHOLE LIFE.

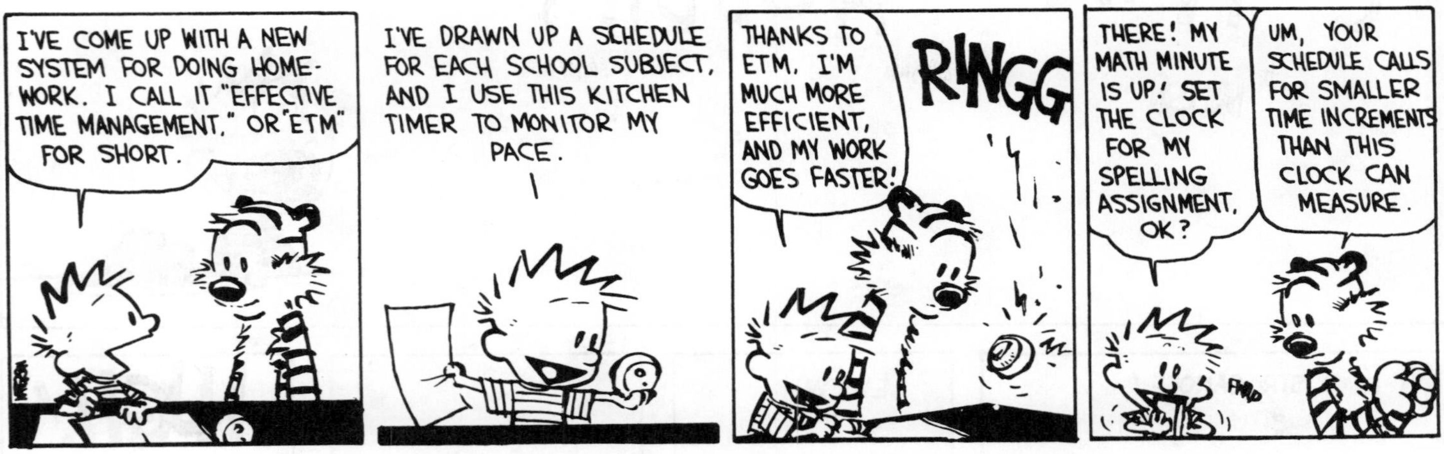
I'VE COME UP WITH A NEW SYSTEM FOR DOING HOME-WORK. I CALL IT "EFFECTIVE TIME MANAGEMENT," OR "ETM" FOR SHORT.
I'VE DRAWN UP A SCHEDULE FOR EACH SCHOOL SUBJECT, AND I USE THIS KITCHEN TIMER TO MONITOR MY PACE.
THANKS TO ETM, I'M MUCH MORE EFFICIENT, AND MY WORK GOES FASTER!
RINGG
THERE! MY MATH MINUTE IS UP! SET THE CLOCK FOR MY SPELLING ASSIGNMENT, OK?
UM, YOUR SCHEDULE CALLS FOR SMALLER TIME INCREMENTS THAN THIS CLOCK CAN MEASURE.

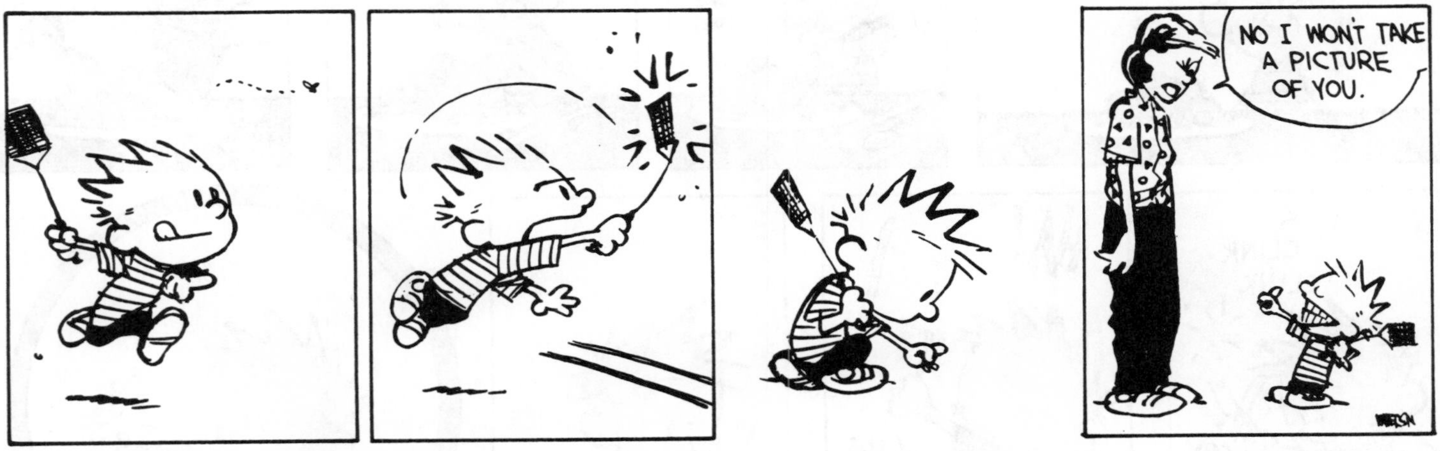
NO I WON'T TAKE A PICTURE OF YOU.

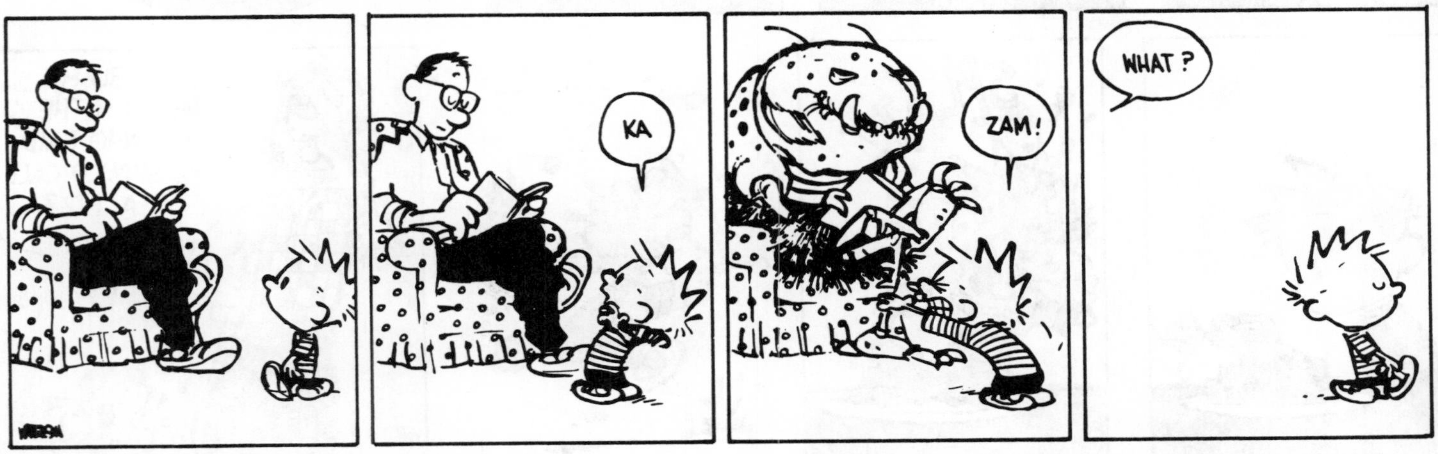
KA
ZAM!
WHAT?

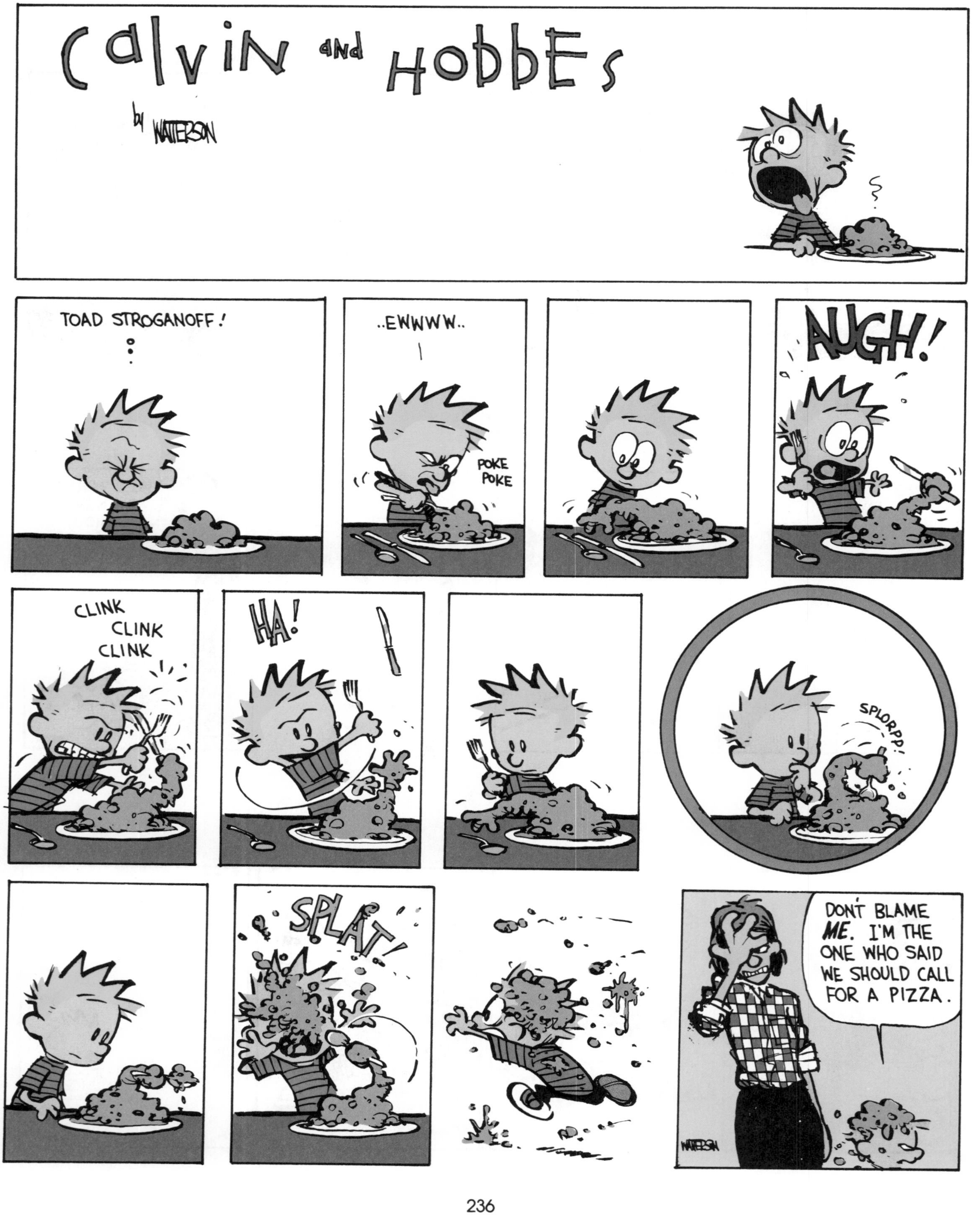
Calvin and Hobbes
by WATTERSON
TOAD STROGANOFF!
..EWWWW..
POKE POKE
AUGH!
CLINK CLINK CLINK
HA!
SPLORPP!
SPLAT!
DON'T BLAME ME. I'M THE ONE WHO SAID WE SHOULD CALL FOR A PIZZA.
WATTERSON

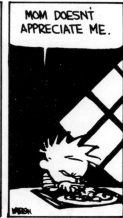

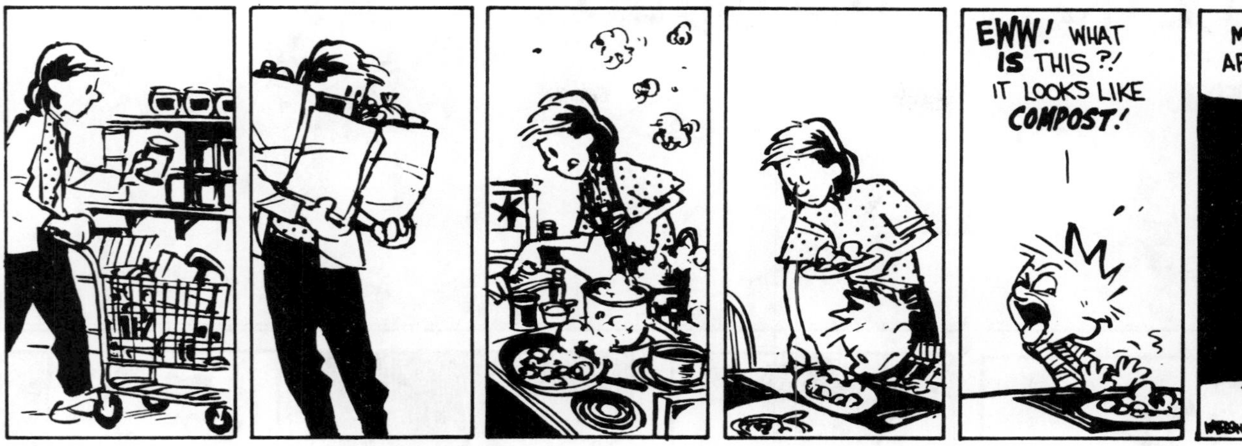
EWW! WHAT IS THIS?! IT LOOKS LIKE COMPOST!
MOM DOESN'T APPRECIATE ME.

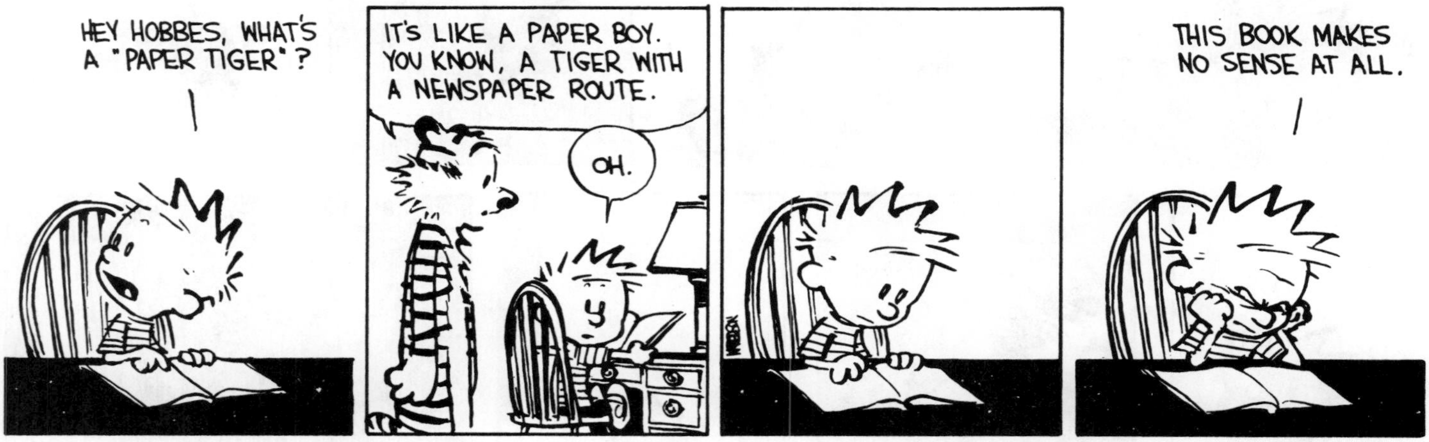
HEY HOBBES, WHAT'S A "PAPER TIGER"?
IT'S LIKE A PAPER BOY. YOU KNOW, A TIGER WITH A NEWSPAPER ROUTE.
OH.
THIS BOOK MAKES NO SENSE AT ALL.

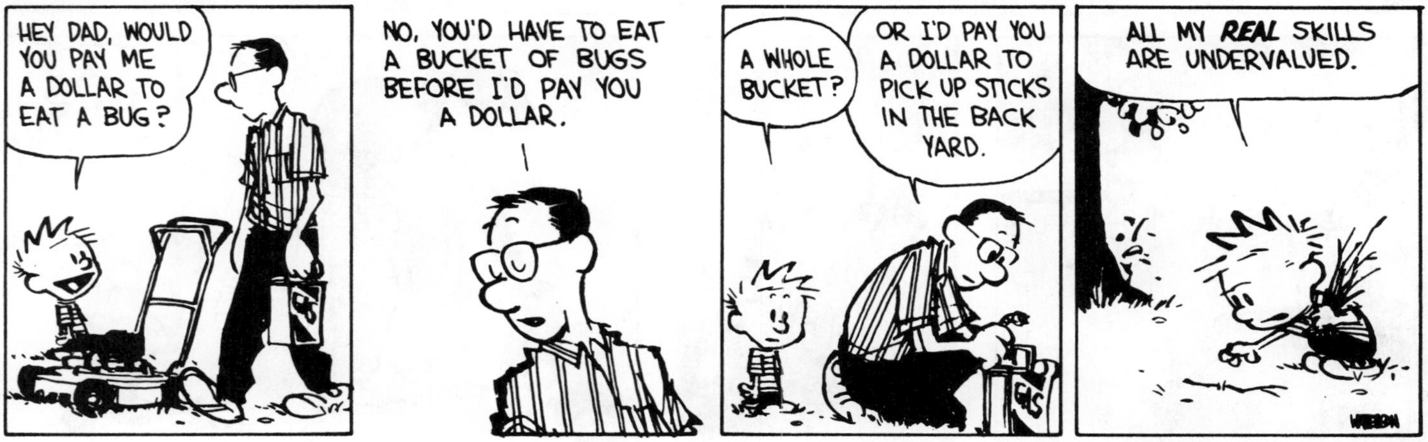
HEY DAD, WOULD YOU PAY ME A DOLLAR TO EAT A BUG?
NO, YOU'D HAVE TO EAT A BUCKET OF BUGS BEFORE I'D PAY YOU A DOLLAR.
A WHOLE BUCKET?
OR I'D PAY YOU A DOLLAR TO PICK UP STICKS IN THE BACK YARD.
ALL MY REAL SKILLS ARE UNDERVALUED.

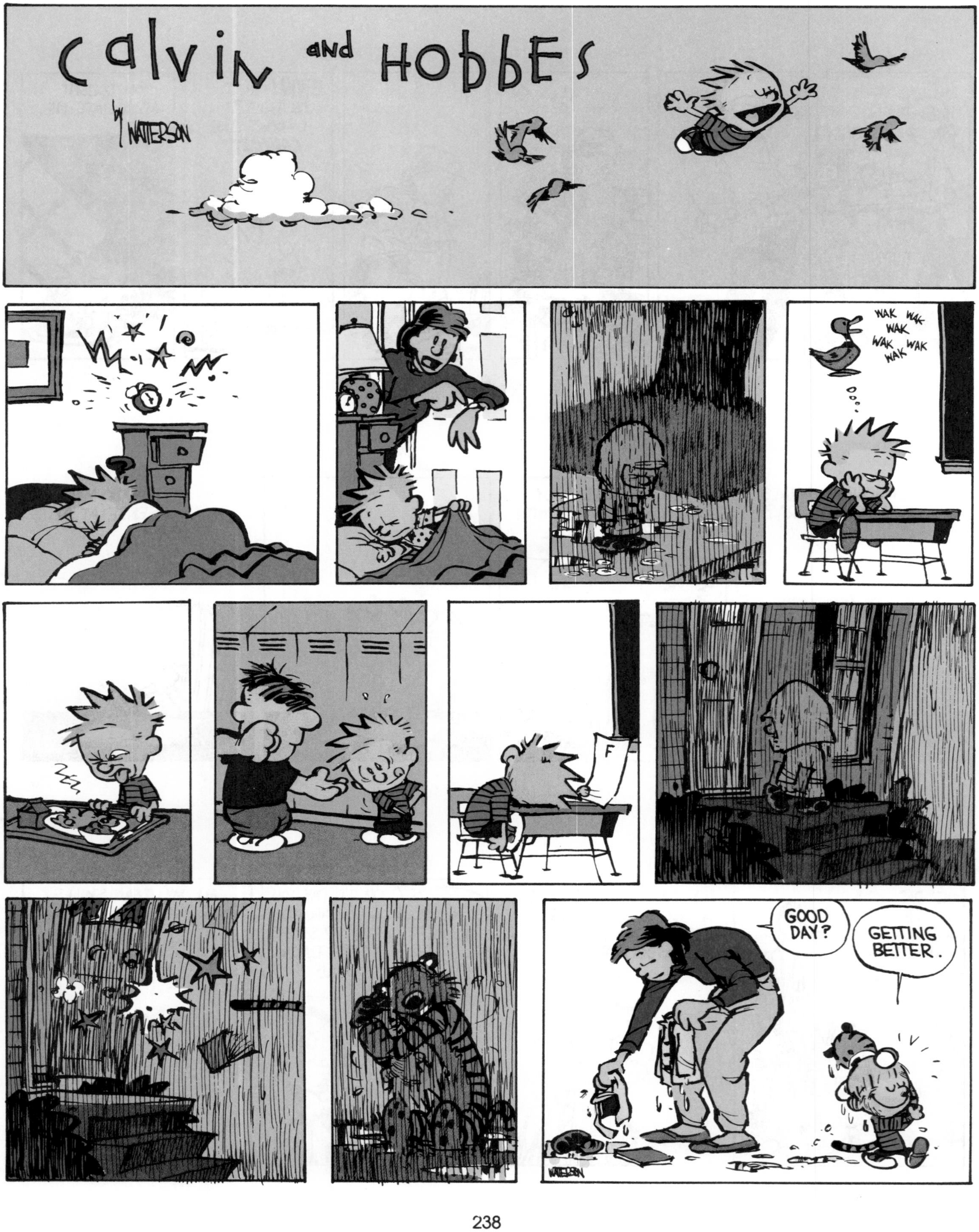
Calvin and HOBBES
by WATTERSON
WAK WAK WAK WAK WAK WAK
F
GOOD DAY?
GETTING BETTER.

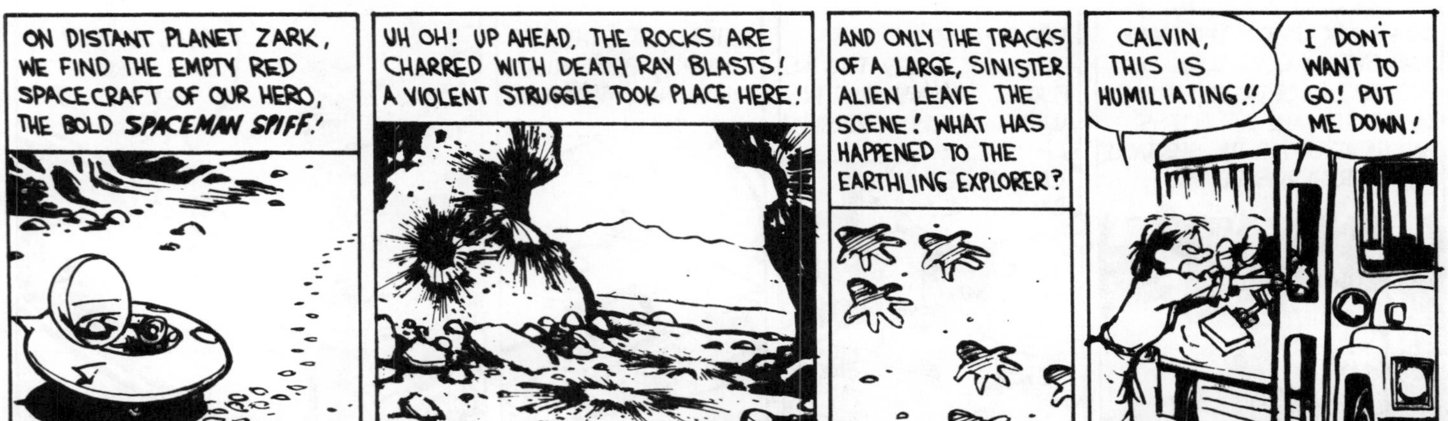
ON DISTANT PLANET ZARK, WE FIND THE EMPTY RED SPACECRAFT OF OUR HERO, THE BOLD SPACEMAN SPIFF!
UH OH! UP AHEAD, THE ROCKS ARE CHARRED WITH DEATH RAY BLASTS! A VIOLENT STRUGGLE TOOK PLACE HERE!
AND ONLY THE TRACKS OF A LARGE, SINISTER ALIEN LEAVE THE SCENE! WHAT HAS HAPPENED TO THE EARTHLING EXPLORER?
CALVIN, THIS IS HUMILIATING!!
I DON'T WANT TO GO! PUT ME DOWN!

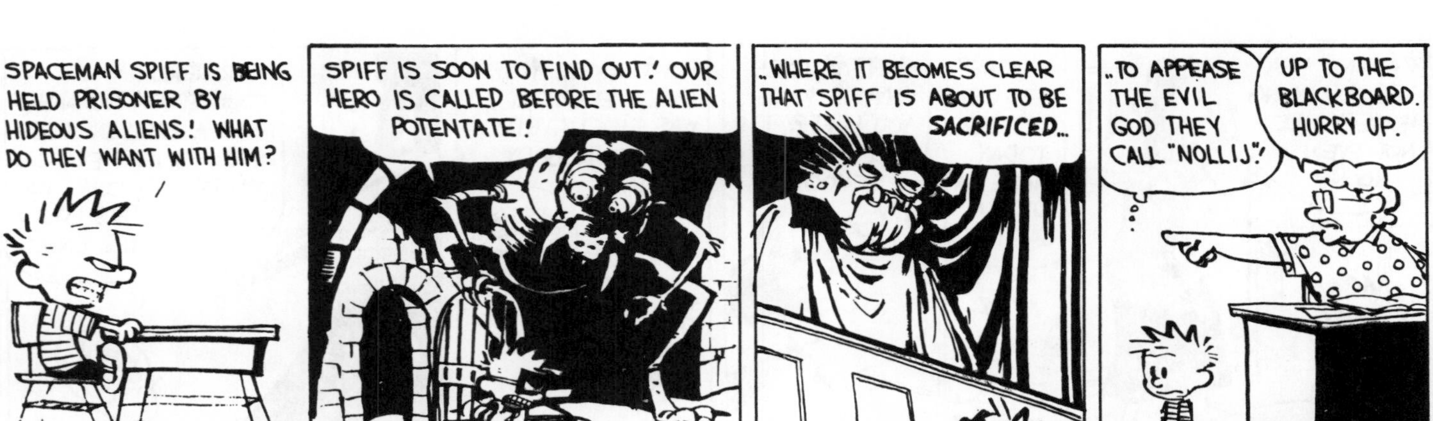
SPACEMAN SPIFF IS BEING HELD PRISONER BY HIDEOUS ALIENS! WHAT DO THEY WANT WITH HIM?
SPIFF IS SOON TO FIND OUT! OUR HERO IS CALLED BEFORE THE ALIEN POTENTATE!
..WHERE IT BECOMES CLEAR THAT SPIFF IS ABOUT TO BE SACRIFICED...
..TO APPEASE THE EVIL GOD THEY CALL "NOLLIJ"!
UP TO THE BLACKBOARD. HURRY UP.

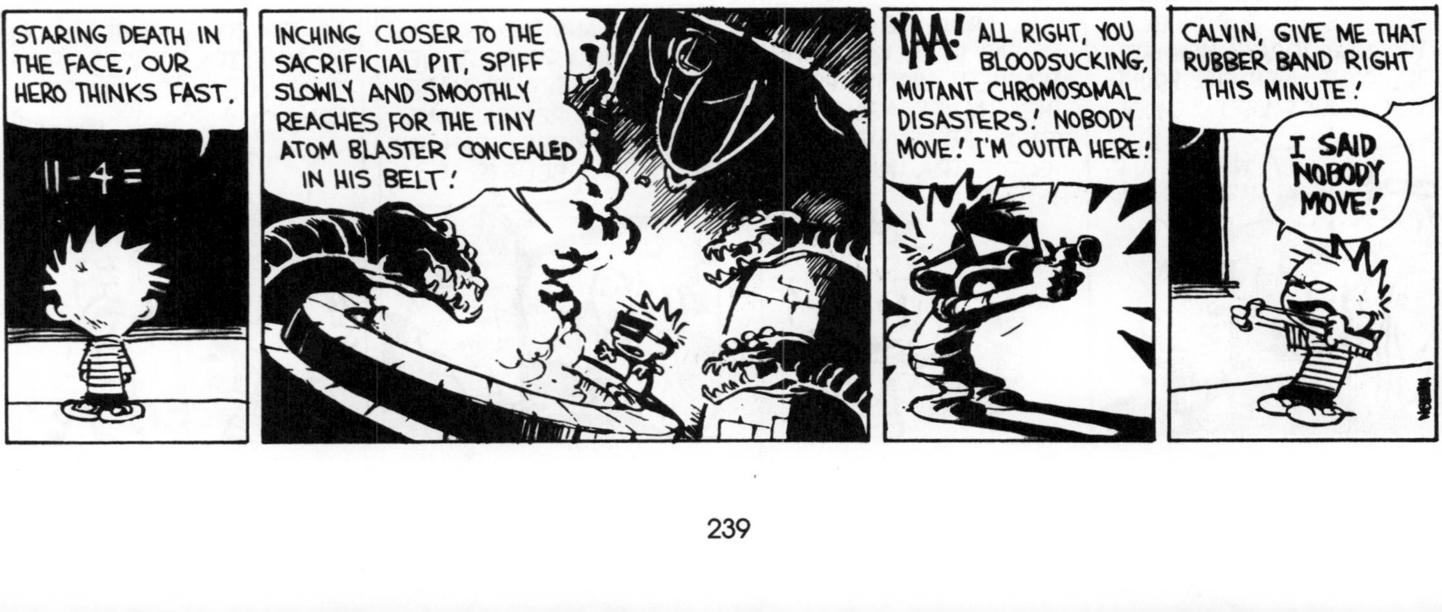
STARING DEATH IN THE FACE, OUR HERO THINKS FAST.
11 - 4 =
INCHING CLOSER TO THE SACRIFICIAL PIT, SPIFF SLOWLY AND SMOOTHLY REACHES FOR THE TINY ATOM BLASTER CONCEALED IN HIS BELT!
YAA! ALL RIGHT, YOU BLOODSUCKING, MUTANT CHROMOSOMAL DISASTERS! NOBODY MOVE! I'M OUTTA HERE!
CALVIN, GIVE ME THAT RUBBER BAND RIGHT THIS MINUTE!
I SAID NOBODY MOVE!

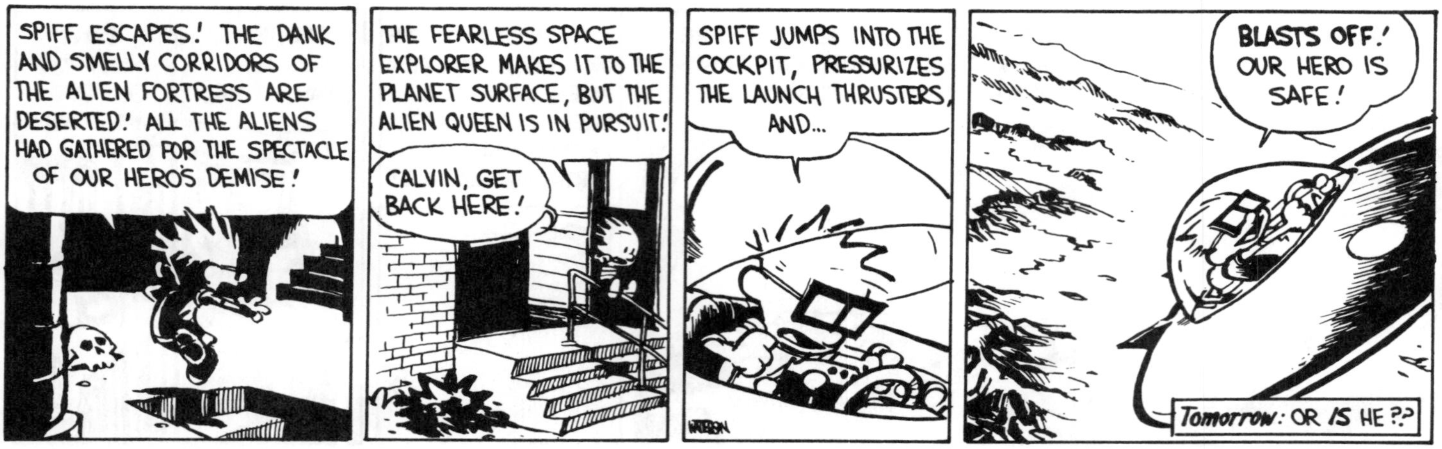
SPIFF ESCAPES! THE DANK AND SMELLY CORRIDORS OF THE ALIEN FORTRESS ARE DESERTED! ALL THE ALIENS HAD GATHERED FOR THE SPECTACLE OF OUR HERO'S DEMISE!
THE FEARLESS SPACE EXPLORER MAKES IT TO THE PLANET SURFACE, BUT THE ALIEN QUEEN IS IN PURSUIT!
CALVIN, GET BACK HERE!
SPIFF JUMPS INTO THE COCKPIT, PRESSURIZES THE LAUNCH THRUSTERS, AND...
BLASTS OFF! OUR HERO IS SAFE!
Tomorrow: OR IS HE?!?

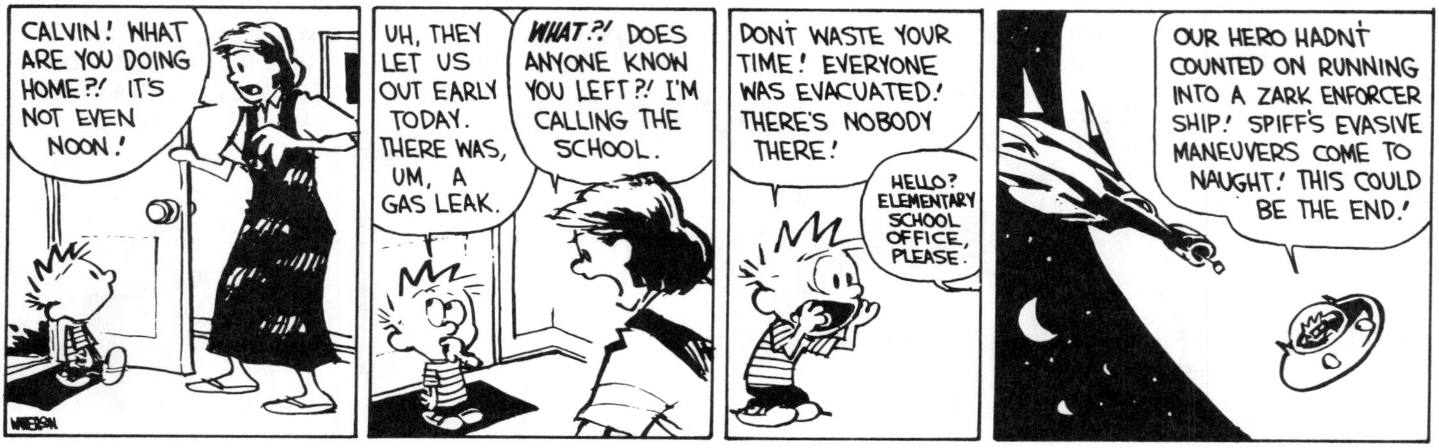
CALVIN! WHAT ARE YOU DOING HOME?! IT'S NOT EVEN NOON!
UH, THEY LET US OUT EARLY TODAY. THERE WAS, UM, A GAS LEAK.
WHAT?! DOES ANYONE KNOW YOU LEFT?! I'M CALLING THE SCHOOL.
DON'T WASTE YOUR TIME! EVERYONE WAS EVACUATED! THERE'S NOBODY THERE!
HELLO? ELEMENTARY SCHOOL OFFICE, PLEASE.
OUR HERO HADN'T COUNTED ON RUNNING INTO A ZARK ENFORCER SHIP! SPIFF'S EVASIVE MANEUVERS COME TO NAUGHT! THIS COULD BE THE END!

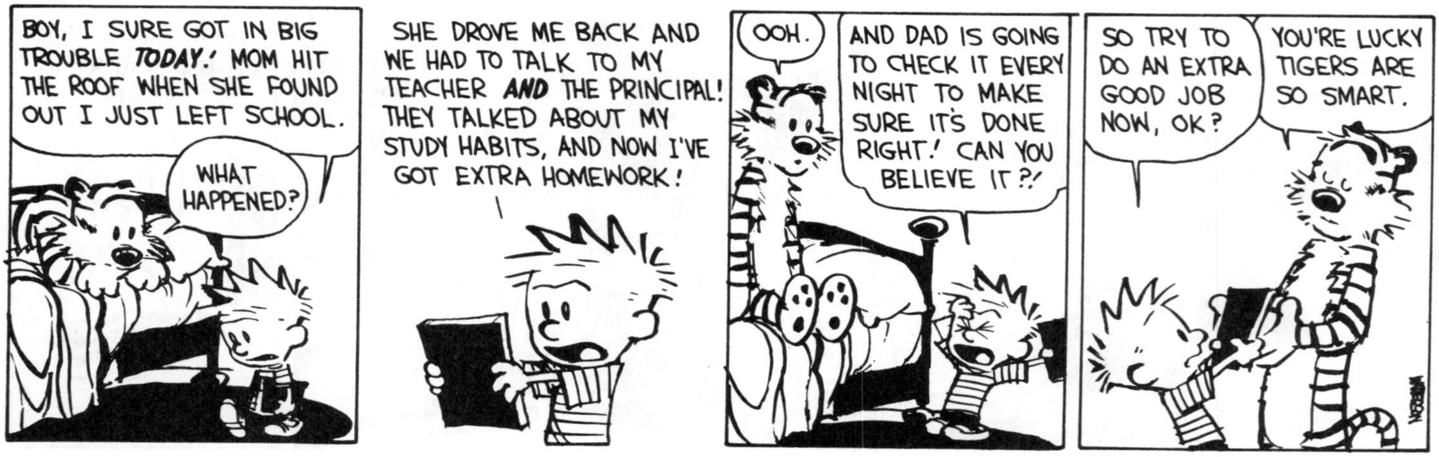
BOY, I SURE GOT IN BIG TROUBLE TODAY! MOM HIT THE ROOF WHEN SHE FOUND OUT I JUST LEFT SCHOOL.
WHAT HAPPENED?
SHE DROVE ME BACK AND WE HAD TO TALK TO MY TEACHER AND THE PRINCIPAL! THEY TALKED ABOUT MY STUDY HABITS, AND NOW I'VE GOT EXTRA HOMEWORK!
OOH.
AND DAD IS GOING TO CHECK IT EVERY NIGHT TO MAKE SURE IT'S DONE RIGHT! CAN YOU BELIEVE IT?!
SO TRY TO DO AN EXTRA GOOD JOB NOW, OK?
YOU'RE LUCKY TIGERS ARE SO SMART.

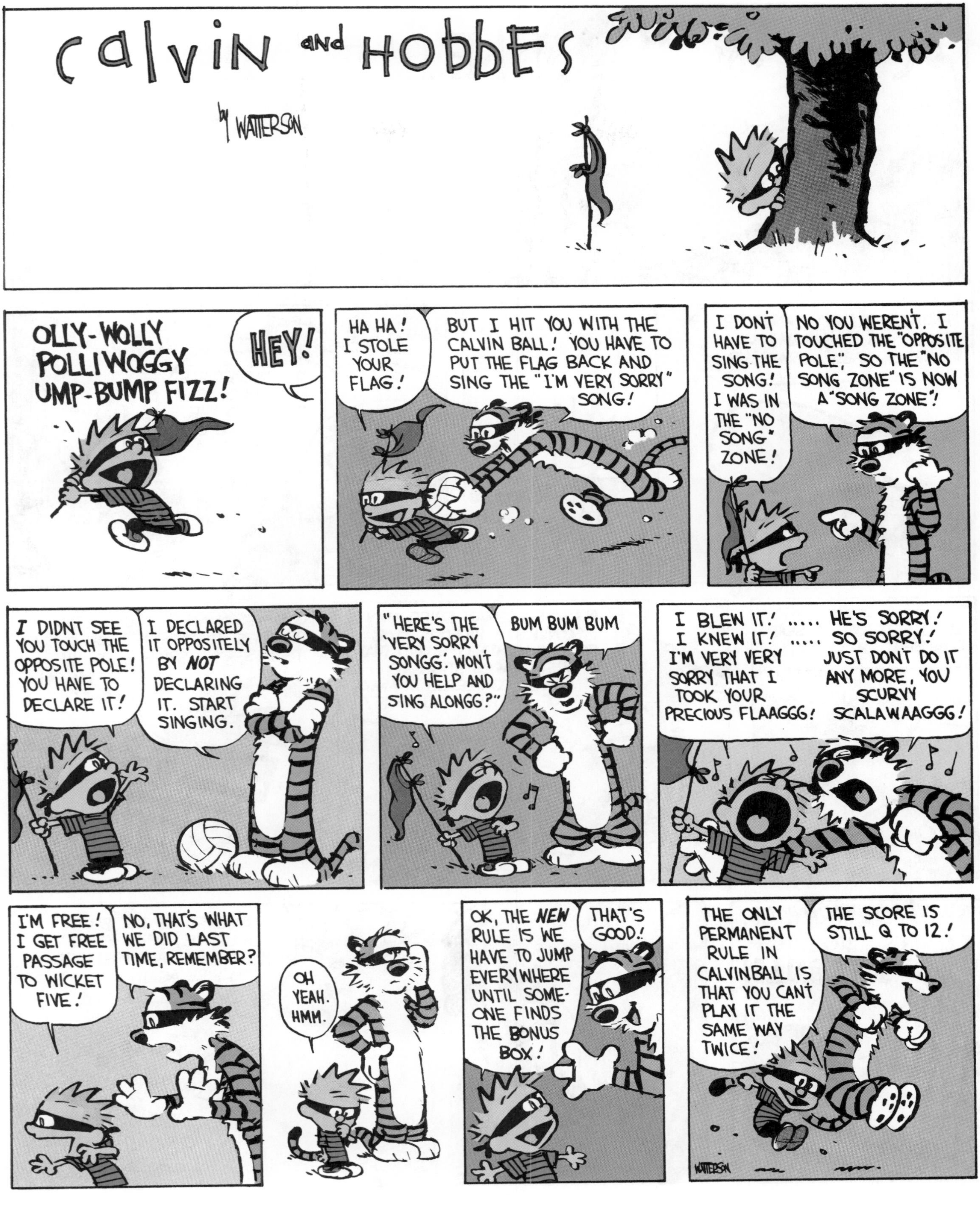
Calvin and HOBBES
by WATTERSON
OLLY-WOLLY POLLIWOGGY UMP-BUMP FIZZ!
HEY!
HA HA! I STOLE YOUR FLAG!
BUT I HIT YOU WITH THE CALVIN BALL! YOU HAVE TO PUT THE FLAG BACK AND SING THE "I'M VERY SORRY" SONG!
I DON'T HAVE TO SING THE SONG! I WAS IN THE "NO SONG" ZONE!
NO YOU WEREN'T. I TOUCHED THE "OPPOSITE POLE," SO THE "NO SONG ZONE" IS NOW A "SONG ZONE"!
I DIDNT SEE YOU TOUCH THE OPPOSITE POLE! YOU HAVE TO DECLARE IT!
I DECLARED IT OPPOSITELY BY NOT DECLARING IT. START SINGING.
"HERE'S THE 'VERY SORRY SONGG.' WON'T YOU HELP AND SING ALONGG?"
BUM BUM BUM
I BLEW IT! ..... HE'S SORRY! I KNEW IT! ..... SO SORRY! I'M VERY VERY SORRY THAT I TOOK YOUR PRECIOUS FLAAGGG! JUST DON'T DO IT ANY MORE, YOU SCURVY SCALAWAAGGG!
I'M FREE! I GET FREE PASSAGE TO WICKET FIVE!
NO, THAT'S WHAT WE DID LAST TIME, REMEMBER?
OH YEAH. HMM.
OK, THE NEW RULE IS WE HAVE TO JUMP EVERYWHERE UNTIL SOMEONE FINDS THE BONUS BOX!
THAT'S GOOD!
THE ONLY PERMANENT RULE IN CALVINBALL IS THAT YOU CAN'T PLAY IT THE SAME WAY TWICE!
THE SCORE IS STILL Q TO 12!
WATTERSON

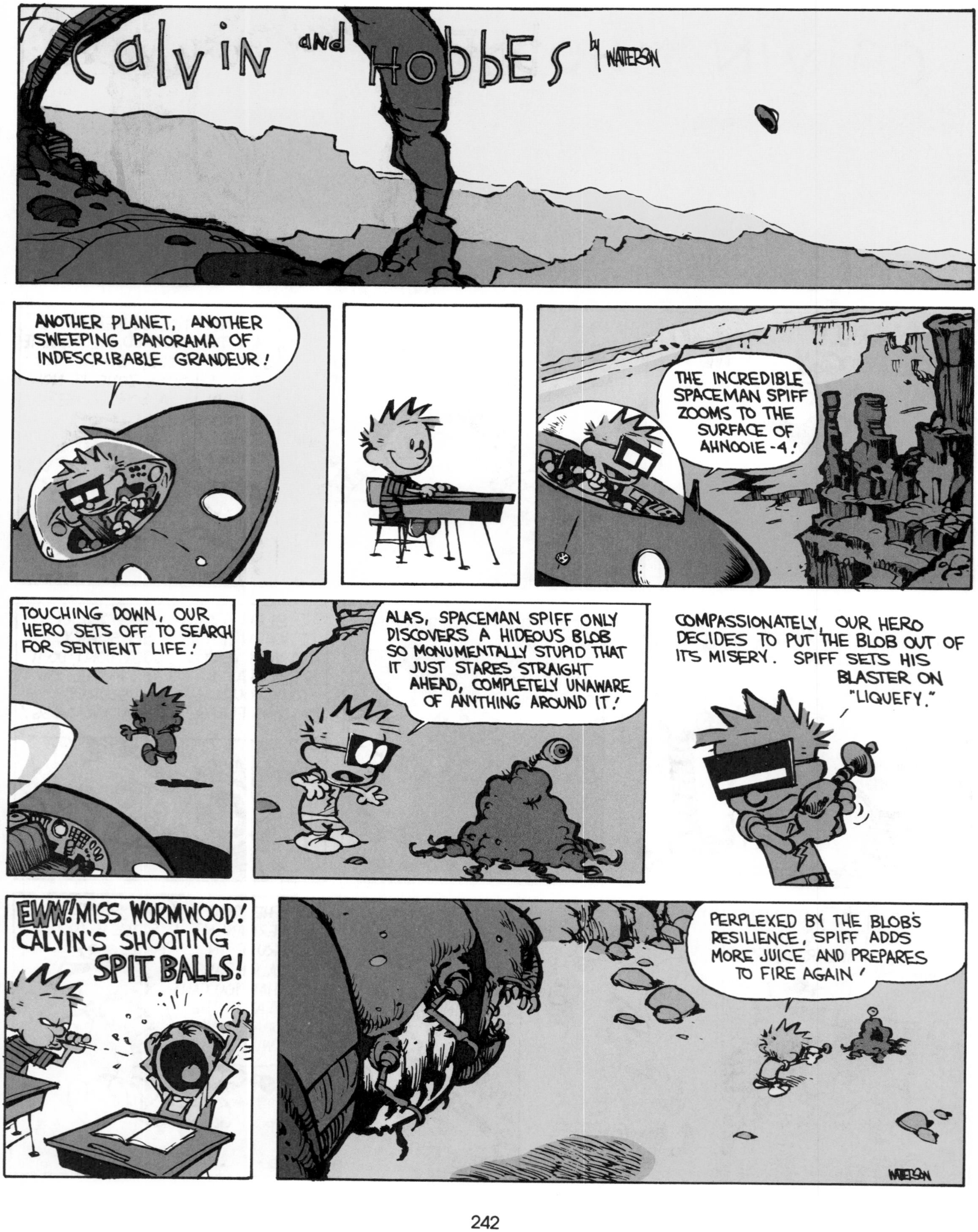

Calvin and HobbES by WATTERSON
ANOTHER PLANET, ANOTHER SWEEPING PANORAMA OF INDESCRIBABLE GRANDEUR!
THE INCREDIBLE SPACEMAN SPIFF ZOOMS TO THE SURFACE OF AHNOOIE-4!
TOUCHING DOWN, OUR HERO SETS OFF TO SEARCH FOR SENTIENT LIFE!
ALAS, SPACEMAN SPIFF ONLY DISCOVERS A HIDEOUS BLOB SO MONUMENTALLY STUPID THAT IT JUST STARES STRAIGHT AHEAD, COMPLETELY UNAWARE OF ANYTHING AROUND IT!
COMPASSIONATELY, OUR HERO DECIDES TO PUT THE BLOB OUT OF ITS MISERY. SPIFF SETS HIS BLASTER ON "LIQUEFY."
EWW! MISS WORMWOOD! CALVIN'S SHOOTING SPIT BALLS!
PERPLEXED BY THE BLOB'S RESILIENCE, SPIFF ADDS MORE JUICE AND PREPARES TO FIRE AGAIN!
WATTERSON

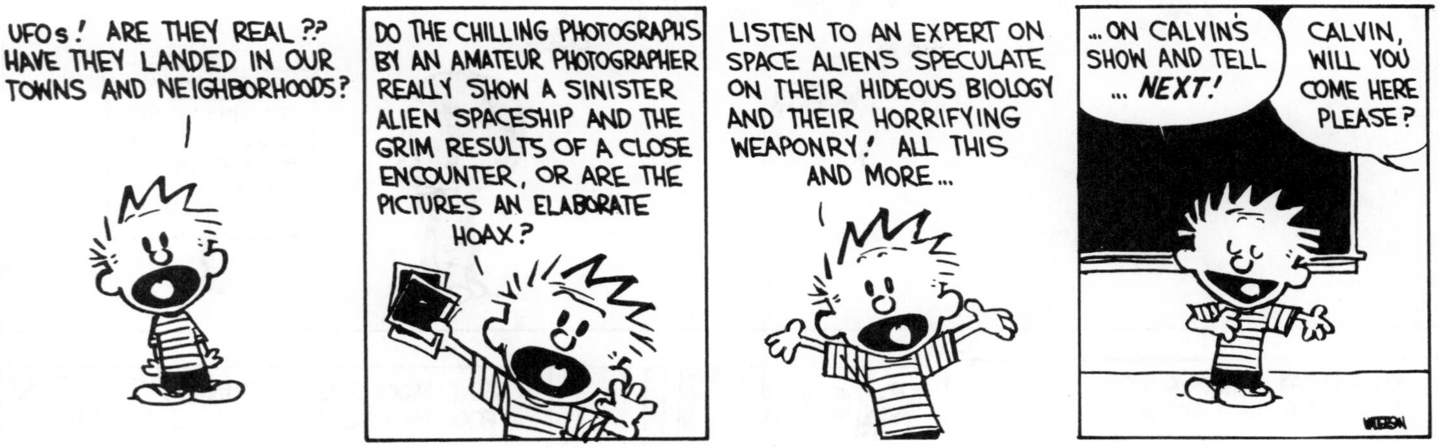
UFOs! ARE THEY REAL?? HAVE THEY LANDED IN OUR TOWNS AND NEIGHBORHOODS?
DO THE CHILLING PHOTOGRAPHS BY AN AMATEUR PHOTOGRAPHER REALLY SHOW A SINISTER ALIEN SPACESHIP AND THE GRIM RESULTS OF A CLOSE ENCOUNTER, OR ARE THE PICTURES AN ELABORATE HOAX?
LISTEN TO AN EXPERT ON SPACE ALIENS SPECULATE ON THEIR HIDEOUS BIOLOGY AND THEIR HORRIFYING WEAPONRY! ALL THIS AND MORE...
...ON CALVIN'S SHOW AND TELL ... NEXT!
CALVIN, WILL YOU COME HERE PLEASE?

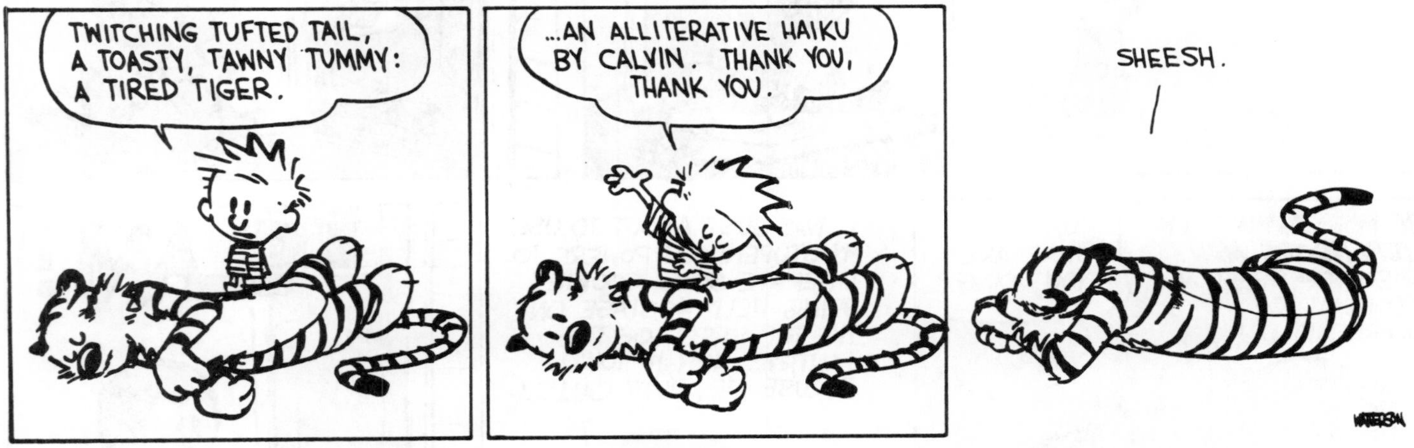
TWITCHING TUFTED TAIL, A TOASTY, TAWNY TUMMY: A TIRED TIGER.
...AN ALLITERATIVE HAIKU BY CALVIN. THANK YOU, THANK YOU.
SHEESH.

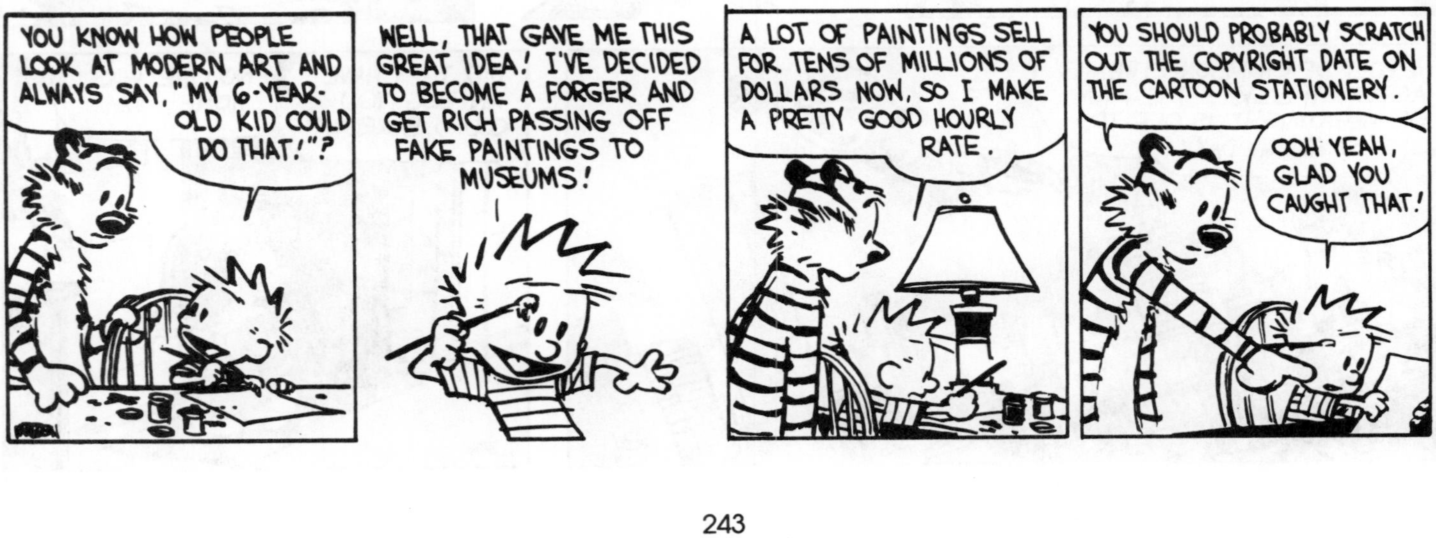
YOU KNOW HOW PEOPLE LOOK AT MODERN ART AND ALWAYS SAY, "MY 6-YEAR-OLD KID COULD DO THAT!"?
WELL, THAT GAVE ME THIS GREAT IDEA! I'VE DECIDED TO BECOME A FORGER AND GET RICH PASSING OFF FAKE PAINTINGS TO MUSEUMS!
A LOT OF PAINTINGS SELL FOR TENS OF MILLIONS OF DOLLARS NOW, SO I MAKE A PRETTY GOOD HOURLY RATE.
YOU SHOULD PROBABLY SCRATCH OUT THE COPYRIGHT DATE ON THE CARTOON STATIONERY.
OOH YEAH, GLAD YOU CAUGHT THAT!

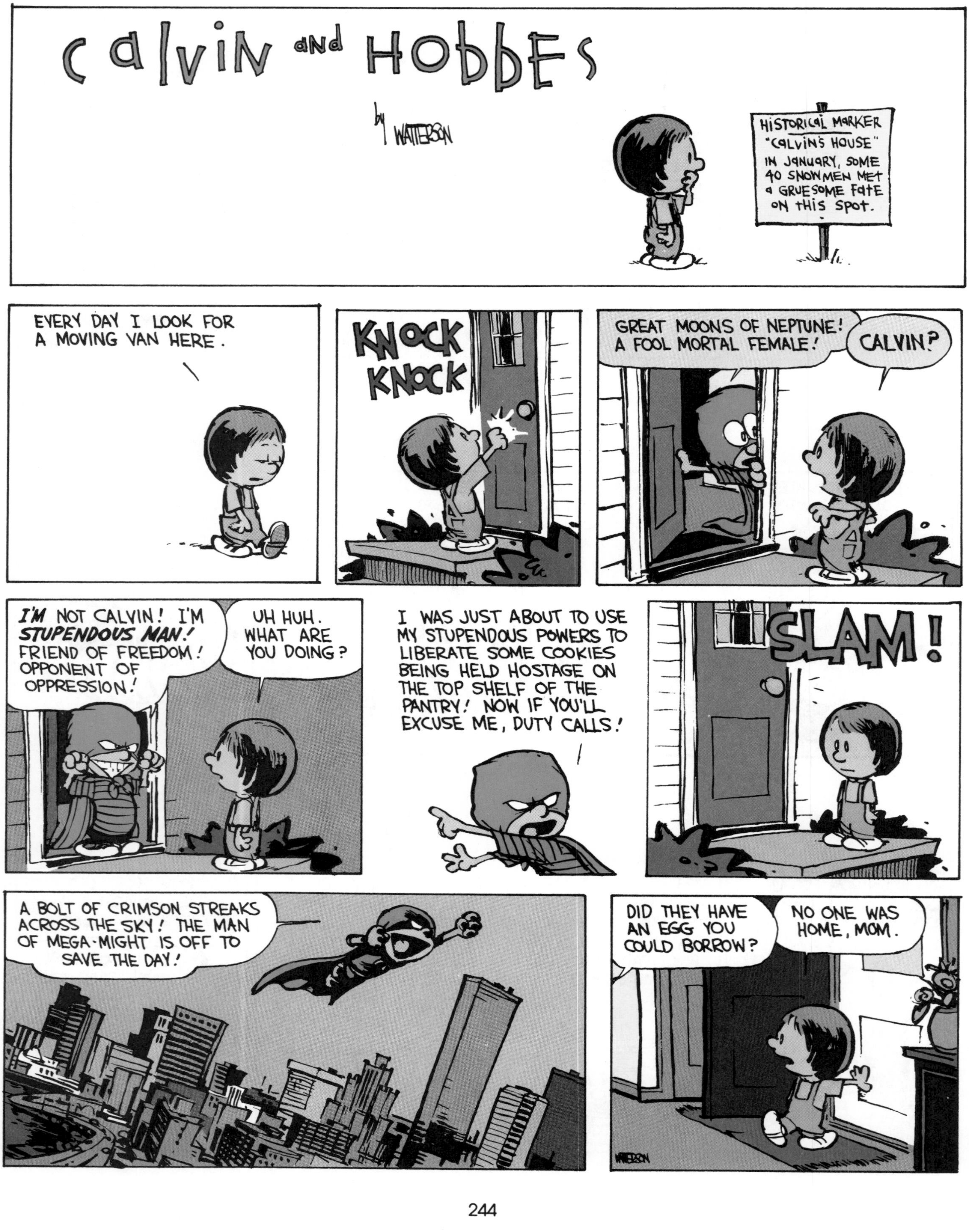

Calvin and Hobbes
by WATTERSON
HISTORICAL MARKER "CALVIN'S HOUSE" IN JANUARY, SOME 40 SNOWMEN MET A GRUESOME FATE ON THIS SPOT.
EVERY DAY I LOOK FOR A MOVING VAN HERE.
KNOCK KNOCK
GREAT MOONS OF NEPTUNE! A FOOL MORTAL FEMALE!
CALVIN?
I'M NOT CALVIN! I'M STUPENDOUS MAN! FRIEND OF FREEDOM! OPPONENT OF OPPRESSION!
UH HUH. WHAT ARE YOU DOING?
I WAS JUST ABOUT TO USE MY STUPENDOUS POWERS TO LIBERATE SOME COOKIES BEING HELD HOSTAGE ON THE TOP SHELF OF THE PANTRY! NOW IF YOU'LL EXCUSE ME, DUTY CALLS!
SLAM!
A BOLT OF CRIMSON STREAKS ACROSS THE SKY! THE MAN OF MEGA-MIGHT IS OFF TO SAVE THE DAY!
DID THEY HAVE AN EGG YOU COULD BORROW?
NO ONE WAS HOME, MOM.
WATTERSON

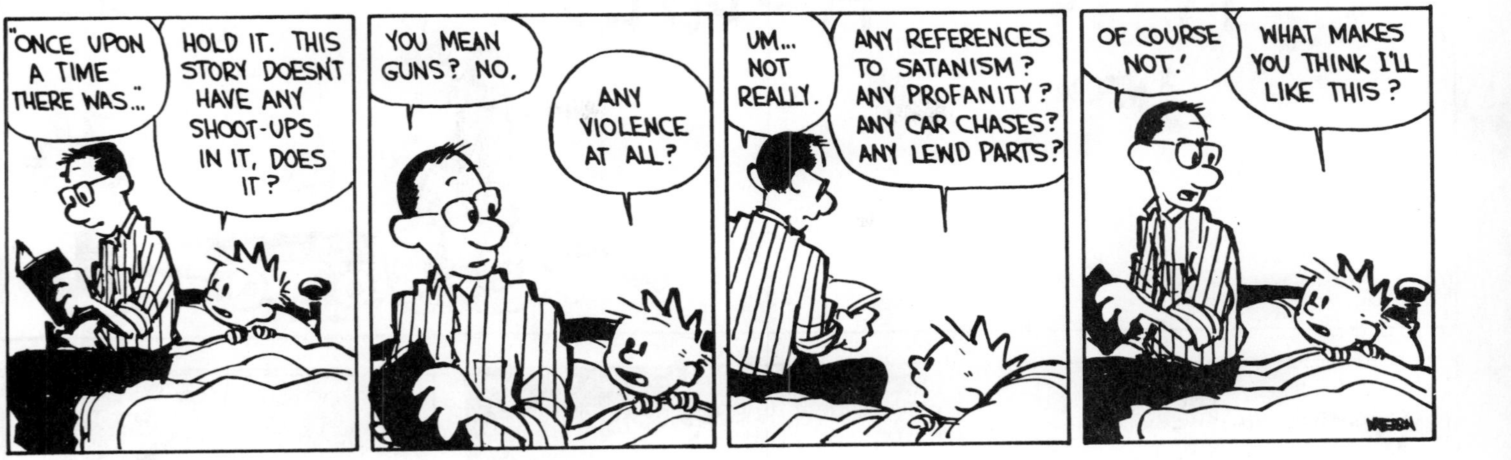
"ONCE UPON A TIME THERE WAS..."
HOLD IT. THIS STORY DOESN'T HAVE ANY SHOOT-UPS IN IT, DOES IT?
YOU MEAN GUNS? NO.
ANY VIOLENCE AT ALL?
UM... NOT REALLY.
ANY REFERENCES TO SATANISM? ANY PROFANITY? ANY CAR CHASES? ANY LEWD PARTS?
OF COURSE NOT!
WHAT MAKES YOU THINK I'LL LIKE THIS?

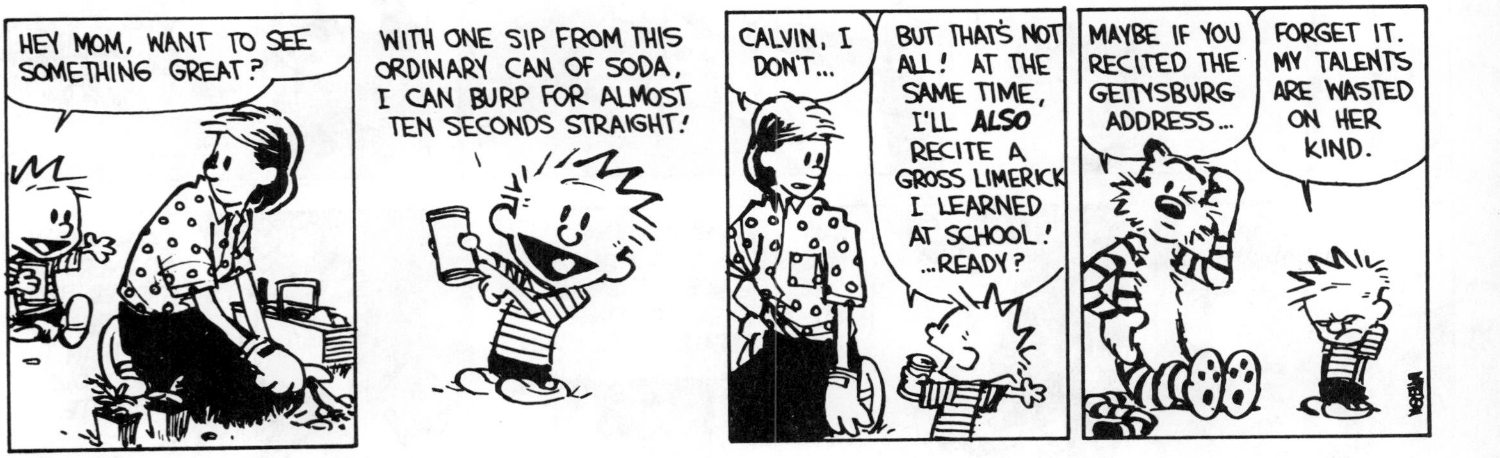
HEY MOM, WANT TO SEE SOMETHING GREAT?
WITH ONE SIP FROM THIS ORDINARY CAN OF SODA, I CAN BURP FOR ALMOST TEN SECONDS STRAIGHT!
CALVIN, I DON'T...
BUT THAT'S NOT ALL! AT THE SAME TIME, I'LL ALSO RECITE A GROSS LIMERICK I LEARNED AT SCHOOL! ...READY?
MAYBE IF YOU RECITED THE GETTYSBURG ADDRESS...
FORGET IT. MY TALENTS ARE WASTED ON HER KIND.

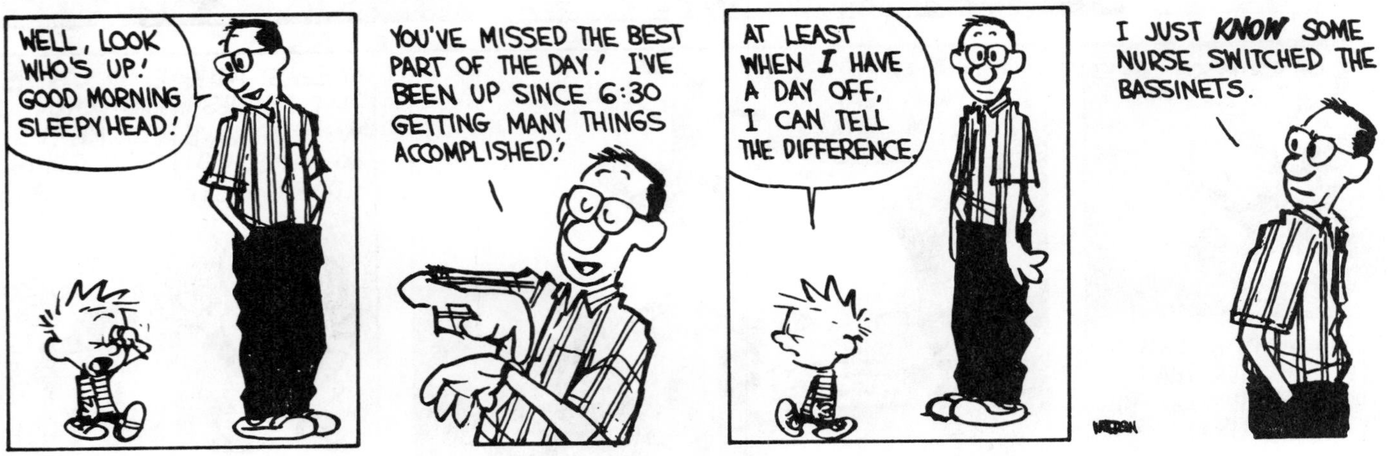
WELL, LOOK WHO'S UP! GOOD MORNING SLEEPYHEAD!
YOU'VE MISSED THE BEST PART OF THE DAY! I'VE BEEN UP SINCE 6:30 GETTING MANY THINGS ACCOMPLISHED!
AT LEAST WHEN I HAVE A DAY OFF, I CAN TELL THE DIFFERENCE.
I JUST KNOW SOME NURSE SWITCHED THE BASSINETS.

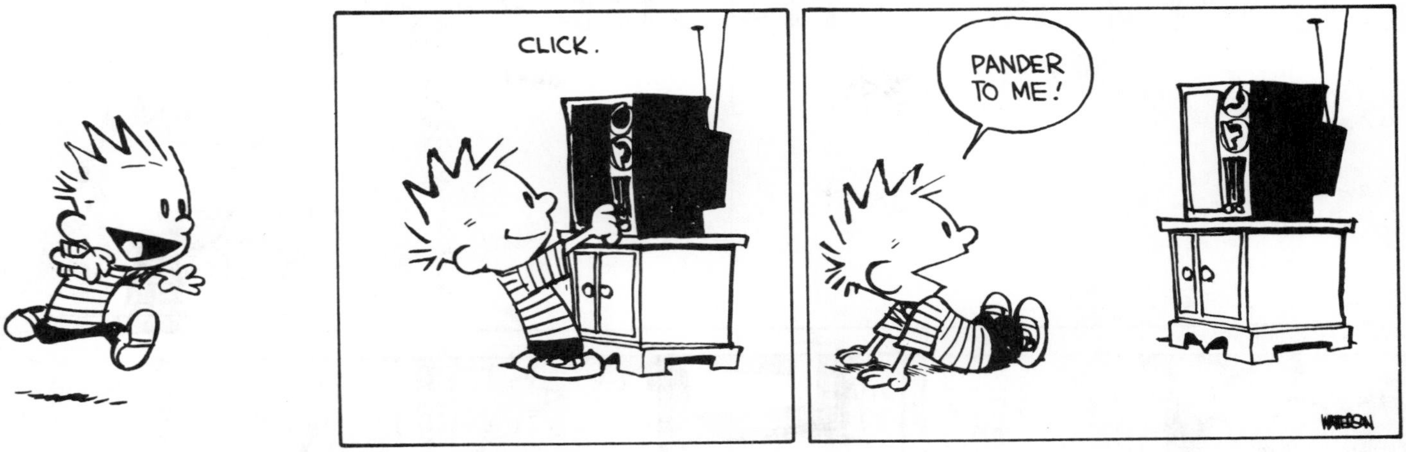
CLICK.
PANDER TO ME!

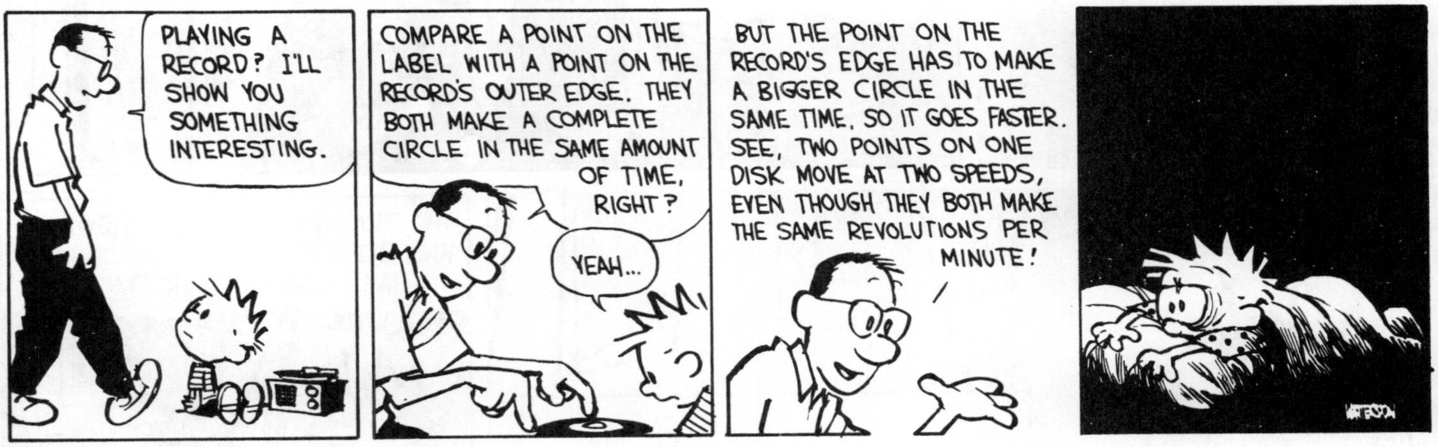
PLAYING A RECORD? I'LL SHOW YOU SOMETHING INTERESTING.
COMPARE A POINT ON THE LABEL WITH A POINT ON THE RECORD'S OUTER EDGE. THEY BOTH MAKE A COMPLETE CIRCLE IN THE SAME AMOUNT OF TIME, RIGHT?
YEAH...
BUT THE POINT ON THE RECORD'S EDGE HAS TO MAKE A BIGGER CIRCLE IN THE SAME TIME, SO IT GOES FASTER. SEE, TWO POINTS ON ONE DISK MOVE AT TWO SPEEDS, EVEN THOUGH THEY BOTH MAKE THE SAME REVOLUTIONS PER MINUTE!

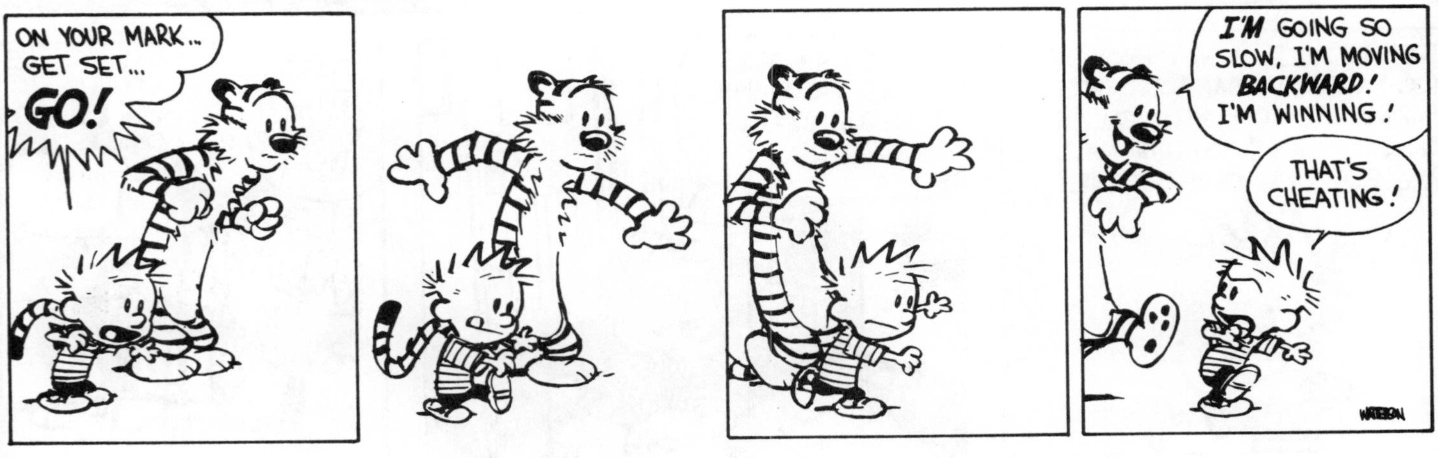
ON YOUR MARK... GET SET...
GO!
I'M GOING SO SLOW, I'M MOVING BACKWARD! I'M WINNING!
THAT'S CHEATING!

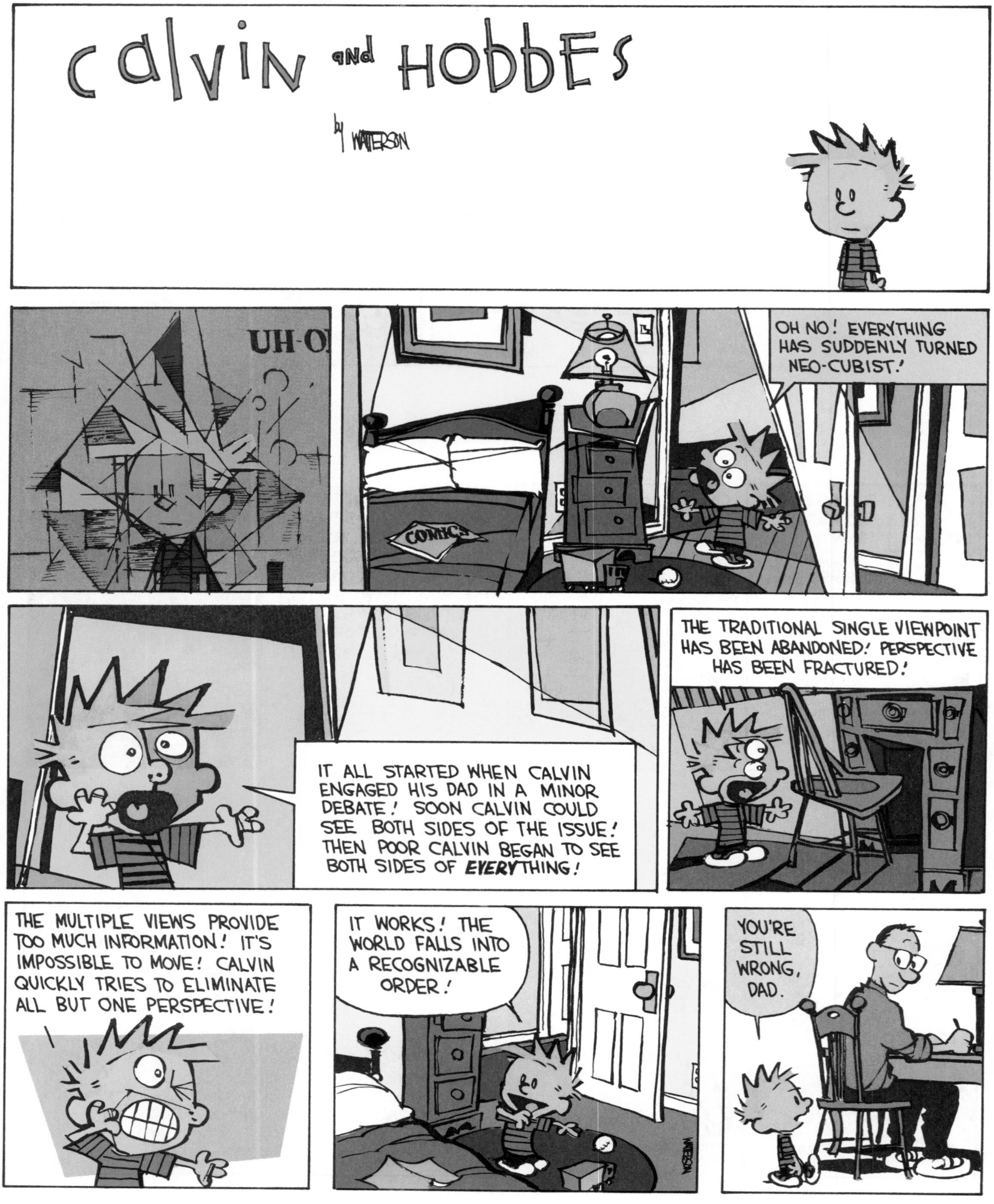
Calvin and HOBBES
by WATTERSON
UH-O
COMICS
OH NO! EVERYTHING HAS SUDDENLY TURNED NEO-CUBIST!
IT ALL STARTED WHEN CALVIN ENGAGED HIS DAD IN A MINOR DEBATE! SOON CALVIN COULD SEE BOTH SIDES OF THE ISSUE! THEN POOR CALVIN BEGAN TO SEE BOTH SIDES OF EVERYTHING!
THE TRADITIONAL SINGLE VIEWPOINT HAS BEEN ABANDONED! PERSPECTIVE HAS BEEN FRACTURED!
THE MULTIPLE VIEWS PROVIDE TOO MUCH INFORMATION! IT'S IMPOSSIBLE TO MOVE! CALVIN QUICKLY TRIES TO ELIMINATE ALL BUT ONE PERSPECTIVE!
IT WORKS! THE WORLD FALLS INTO A RECOGNIZABLE ORDER!
WATTERSON
YOU'RE STILL WRONG, DAD.

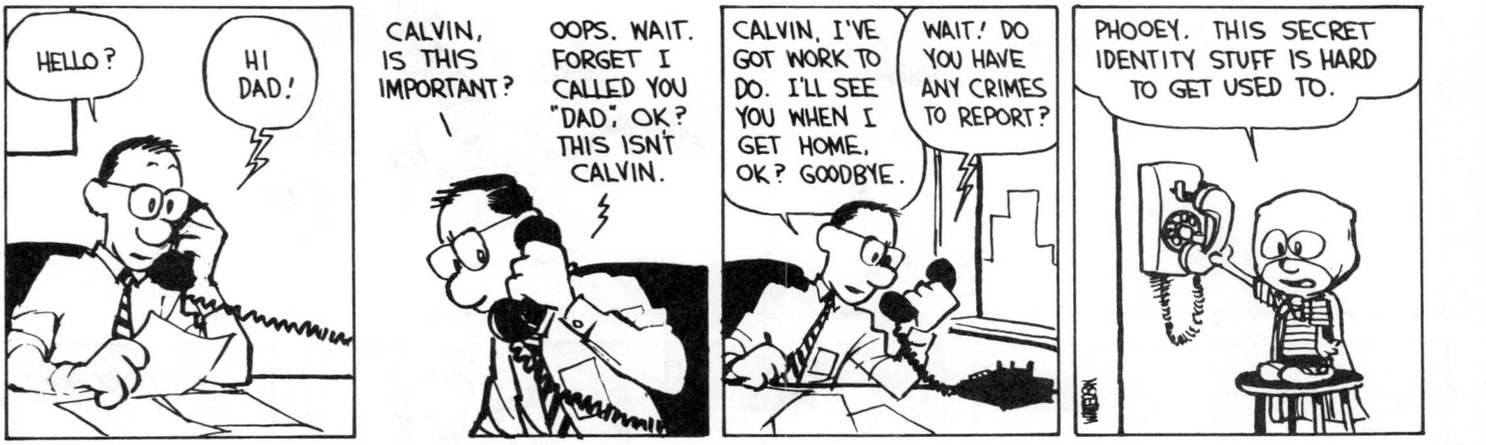
HELLO?
HI DAD!
CALVIN, IS THIS IMPORTANT?
OOPS. WAIT. FORGET I CALLED YOU "DAD," OK? THIS ISN'T CALVIN.
CALVIN, I'VE GOT WORK TO DO. I'LL SEE YOU WHEN I GET HOME. OK? GOODBYE.
WAIT! DO YOU HAVE ANY CRIMES TO REPORT?
PHOOEY. THIS SECRET IDENTITY STUFF IS HARD TO GET USED TO.

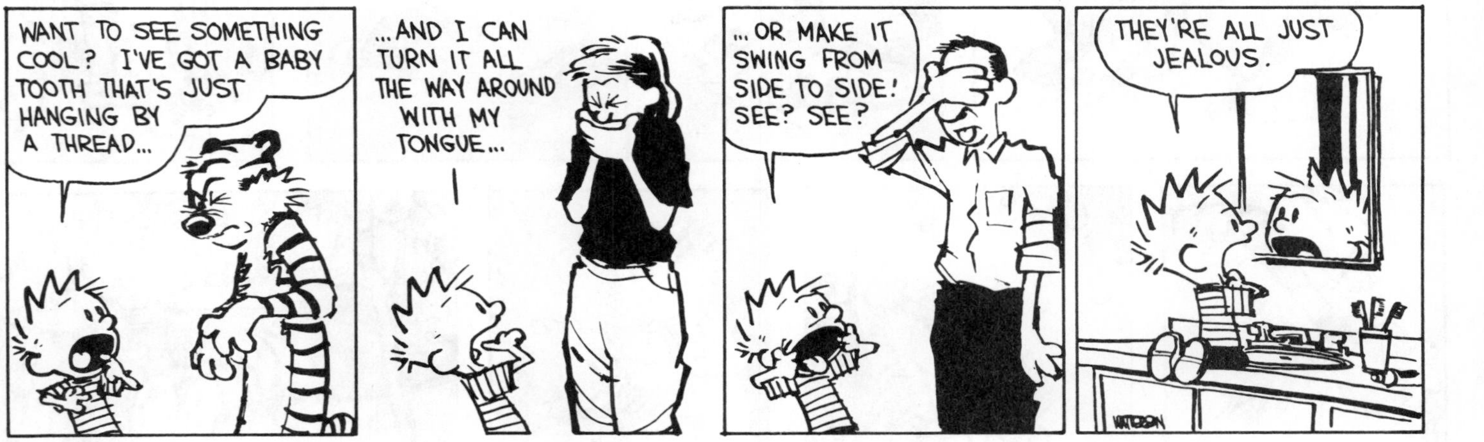
WANT TO SEE SOMETHING COOL? I'VE GOT A BABY TOOTH THAT'S JUST HANGING BY A THREAD...
...AND I CAN TURN IT ALL THE WAY AROUND WITH MY TONGUE...
...OR MAKE IT SWING FROM SIDE TO SIDE! SEE? SEE?
THEY'RE ALL JUST JEALOUS.

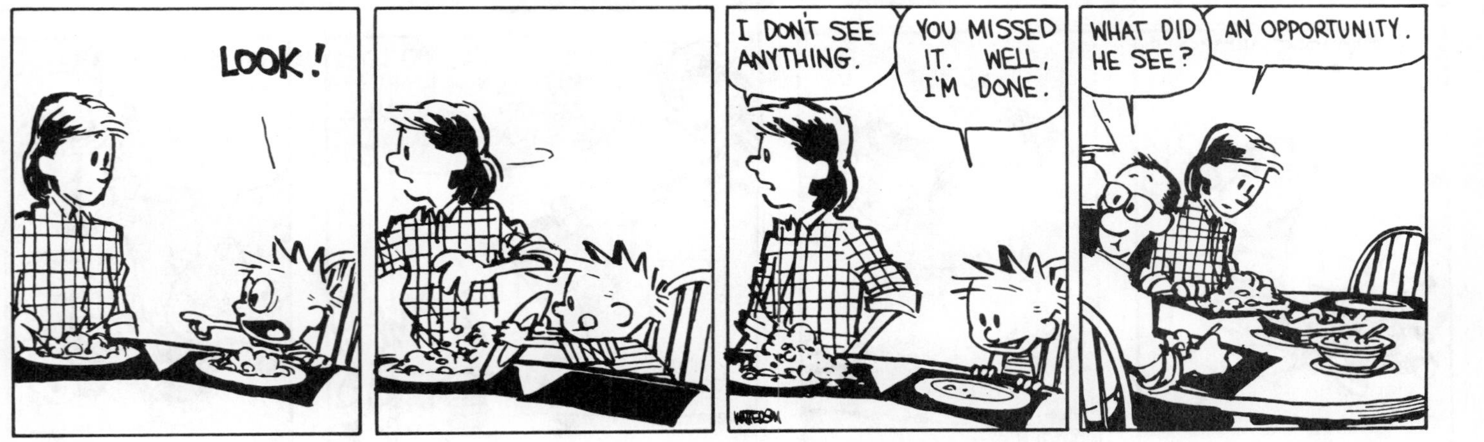
LOOK!
I DON'T SEE ANYTHING.
YOU MISSED IT. WELL, I'M DONE.
WHAT DID HE SEE?
AN OPPORTUNITY.

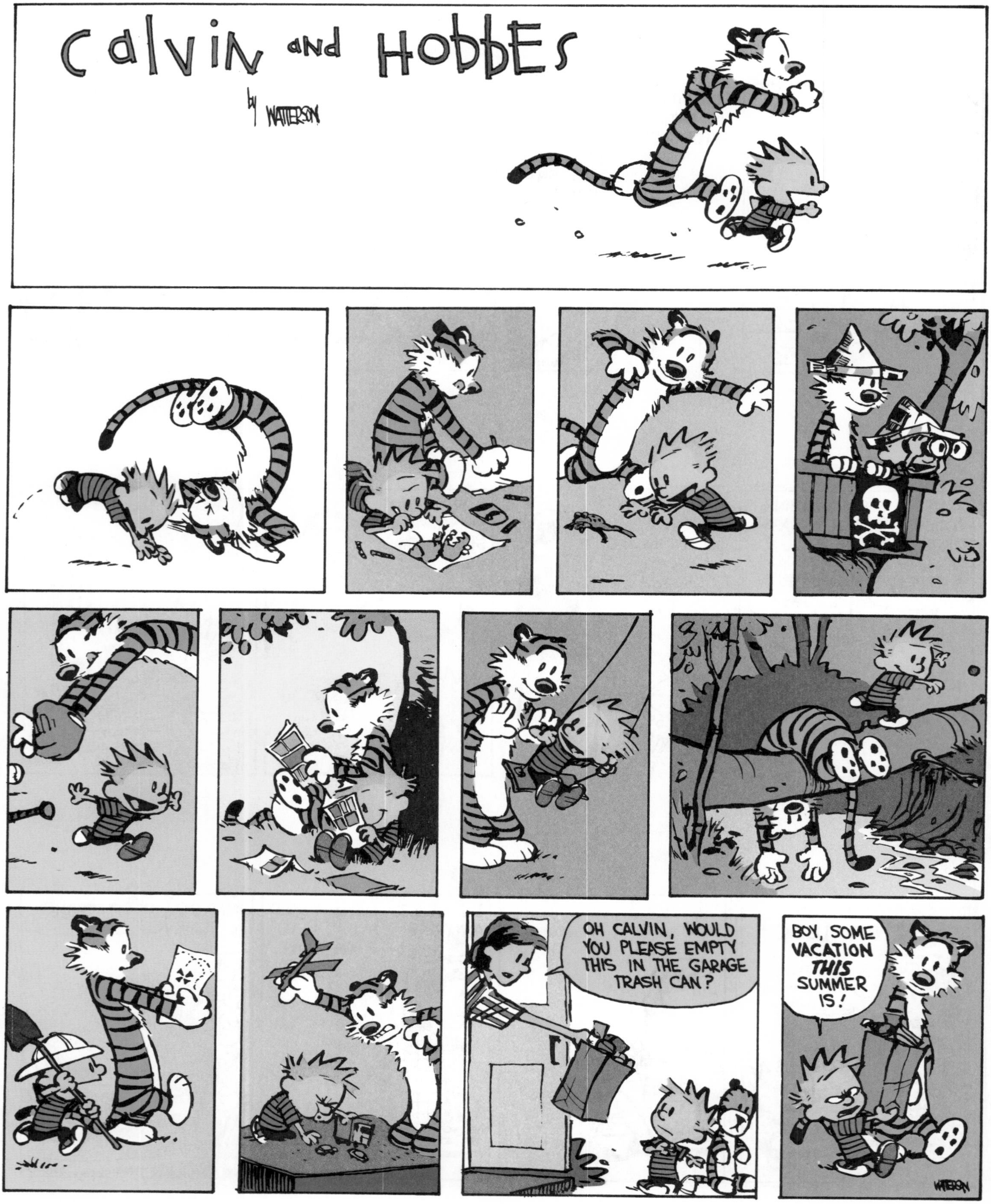
Calvin and HOBBES
by WATTERSON
OH CALVIN, WOULD YOU PLEASE EMPTY THIS IN THE GARAGE TRASH CAN?
BOY, SOME VACATION THIS SUMMER IS!
WATTERSON

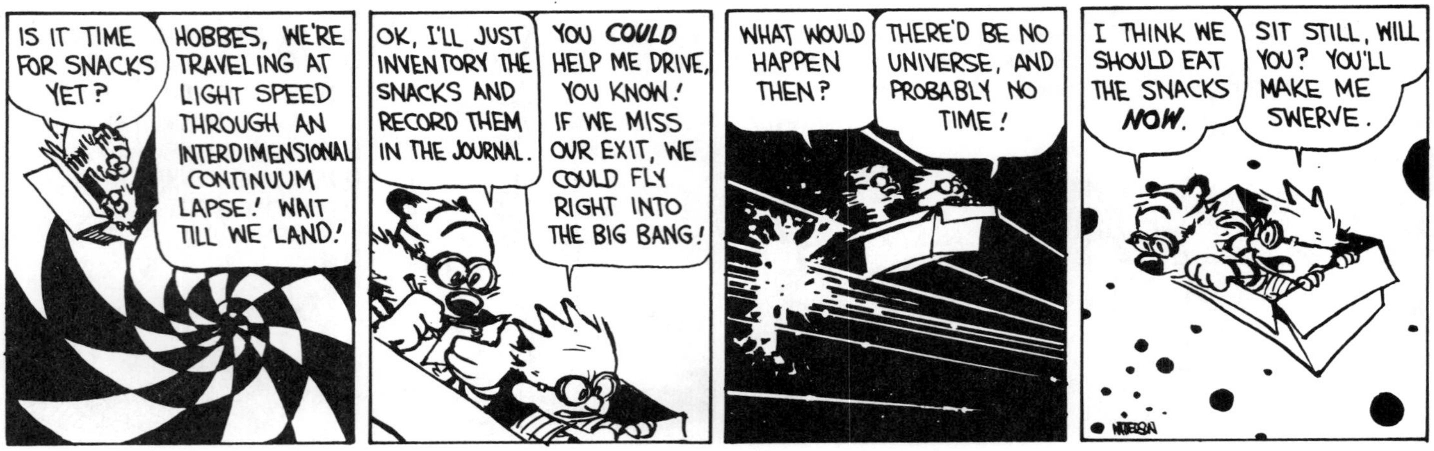
IS IT TIME FOR SNACKS YET?
HOBBES, WE'RE TRAVELING AT LIGHT SPEED THROUGH AN INTERDIMENSIONAL CONTINUUM LAPSE! WAIT TILL WE LAND!
OK, I'LL JUST INVENTORY THE SNACKS AND RECORD THEM IN THE JOURNAL.
YOU **COULD** HELP ME DRIVE, YOU KNOW! IF WE MISS OUR EXIT, WE COULD FLY RIGHT INTO THE BIG BANG!
WHAT WOULD HAPPEN THEN?
THERE'D BE NO UNIVERSE, AND PROBABLY NO TIME!
I THINK WE SHOULD EAT THE SNACKS ***NOW***.
SIT STILL, WILL YOU? YOU'LL MAKE ME SWERVE.
WATTERSON

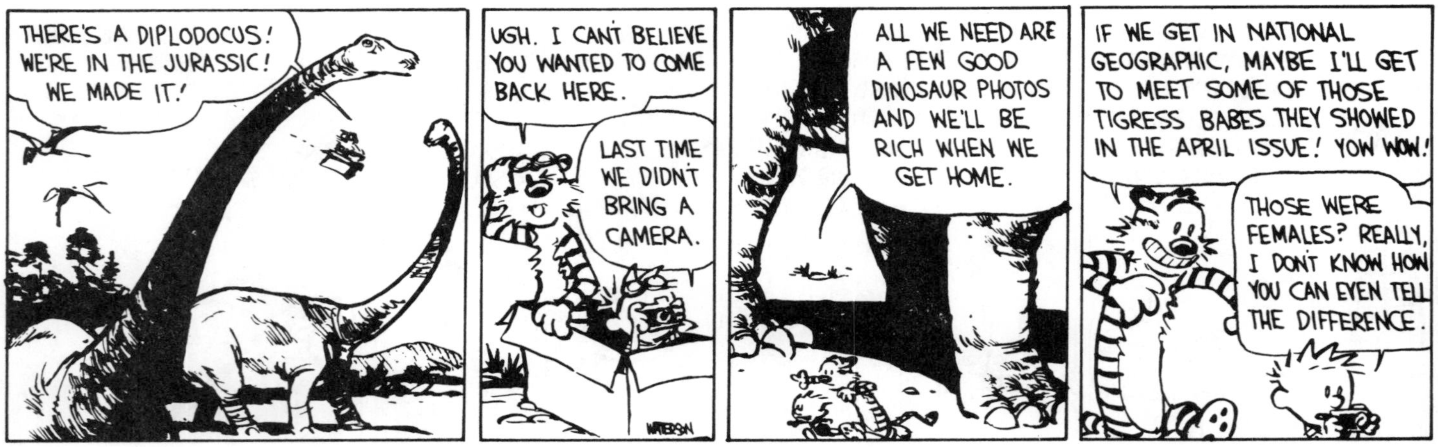
THERE'S A DIPLODOCUS! WE'RE IN THE JURASSIC! WE MADE IT!
UGH. I CAN'T BELIEVE YOU WANTED TO COME BACK HERE.
LAST TIME WE DIDN'T BRING A CAMERA.
WATTERSON
ALL WE NEED ARE A FEW GOOD DINOSAUR PHOTOS AND WE'LL BE RICH WHEN WE GET HOME.
IF WE GET IN NATIONAL GEOGRAPHIC, MAYBE I'LL GET TO MEET SOME OF THOSE TIGRESS BABES THEY SHOWED IN THE APRIL ISSUE! YOW WOW!
THOSE WERE FEMALES? REALLY, I DON'T KNOW HOW YOU CAN EVEN TELL THE DIFFERENCE.

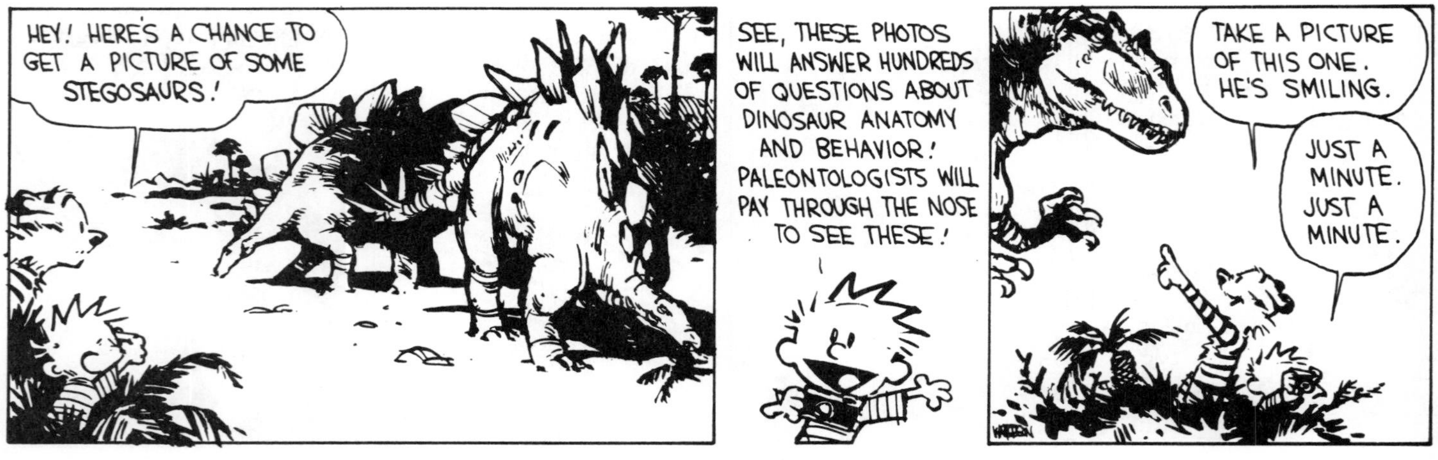
HEY! HERE'S A CHANCE TO GET A PICTURE OF SOME STEGOSAURS!
SEE, THESE PHOTOS WILL ANSWER HUNDREDS OF QUESTIONS ABOUT DINOSAUR ANATOMY AND BEHAVIOR! PALEONTOLOGISTS WILL PAY THROUGH THE NOSE TO SEE THESE!
TAKE A PICTURE OF THIS ONE. HE'S SMILING.
JUST A MINUTE. JUST A MINUTE.
WATTERSON

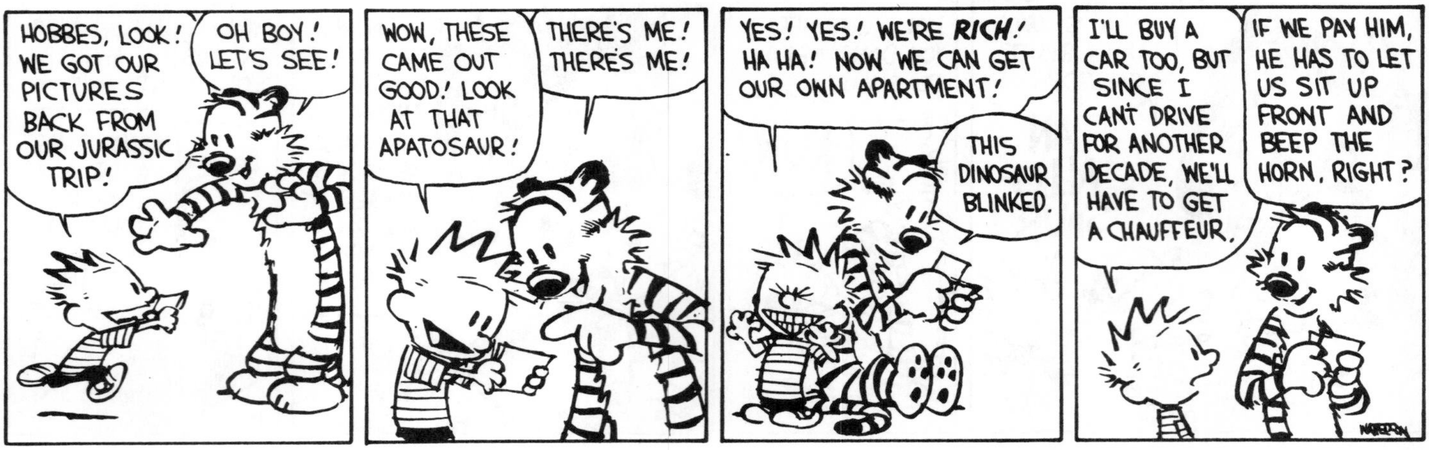
HOBBES, LOOK! WE GOT OUR PICTURES BACK FROM OUR JURASSIC TRIP!
OH BOY! LET'S SEE!
WOW, THESE CAME OUT GOOD! LOOK AT THAT APATOSAUR!
THERE'S ME! THERE'S ME!
YES! YES! WE'RE RICH! HA HA! NOW WE CAN GET OUR OWN APARTMENT!
THIS DINOSAUR BLINKED.
I'LL BUY A CAR TOO, BUT SINCE I CAN'T DRIVE FOR ANOTHER DECADE, WE'LL HAVE TO GET A CHAUFFEUR.
IF WE PAY HIM, HE HAS TO LET US SIT UP FRONT AND BEEP THE HORN, RIGHT?

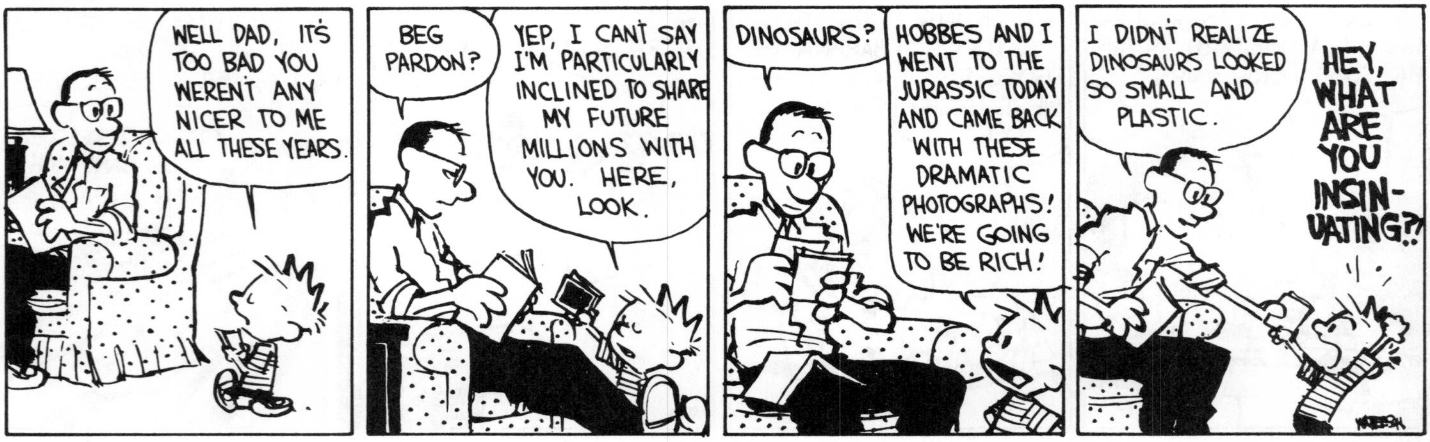
WELL DAD, IT'S TOO BAD YOU WEREN'T ANY NICER TO ME ALL THESE YEARS.
BEG PARDON?
YEP, I CAN'T SAY I'M PARTICULARLY INCLINED TO SHARE MY FUTURE MILLIONS WITH YOU. HERE, LOOK.
DINOSAURS?
HOBBES AND I WENT TO THE JURASSIC TODAY AND CAME BACK WITH THESE DRAMATIC PHOTOGRAPHS! WE'RE GOING TO BE RICH!
I DIDN'T REALIZE DINOSAURS LOOKED SO SMALL AND PLASTIC.
HEY, WHAT ARE YOU INSIN-UATING?!

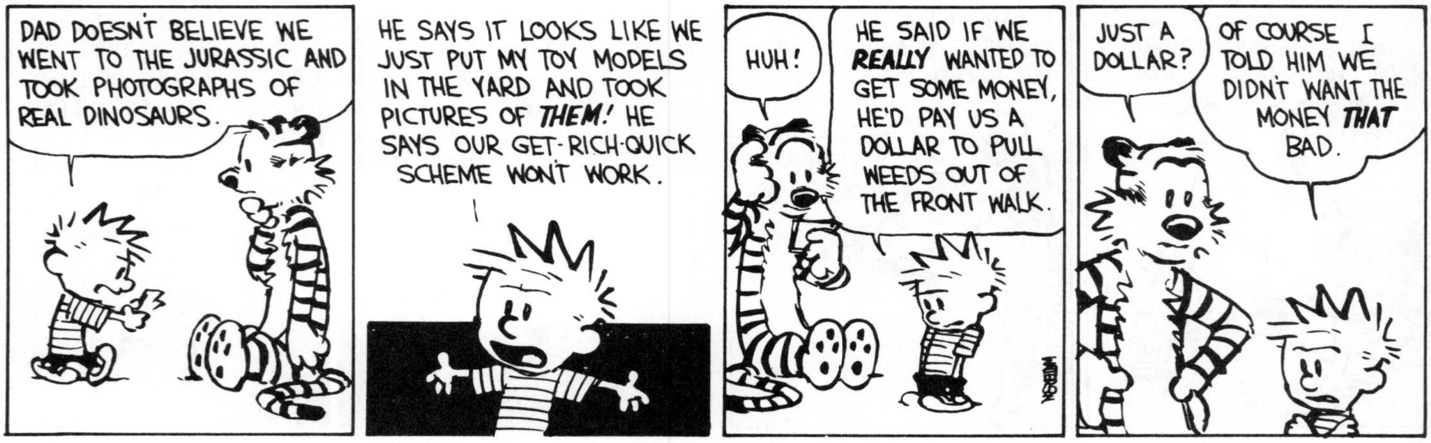
DAD DOESN'T BELIEVE WE WENT TO THE JURASSIC AND TOOK PHOTOGRAPHS OF REAL DINOSAURS.
HE SAYS IT LOOKS LIKE WE JUST PUT MY TOY MODELS IN THE YARD AND TOOK PICTURES OF THEM! HE SAYS OUR GET-RICH-QUICK SCHEME WON'T WORK.
HUH!
HE SAID IF WE REALLY WANTED TO GET SOME MONEY, HE'D PAY US A DOLLAR TO PULL WEEDS OUT OF THE FRONT WALK.
JUST A DOLLAR?
OF COURSE I TOLD HIM WE DIDN'T WANT THE MONEY THAT BAD.

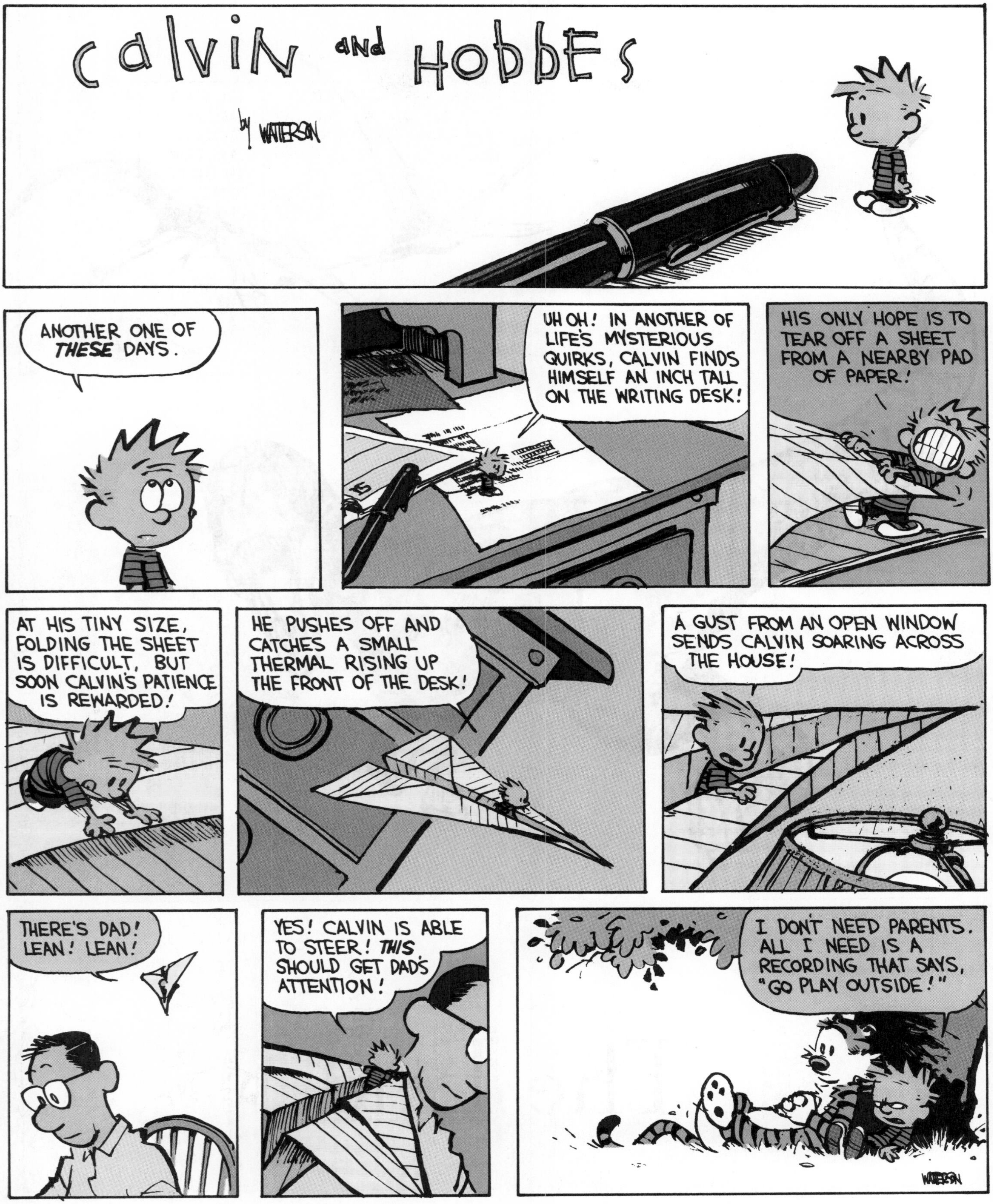
Calvin and HOBBES
by WATERSON
ANOTHER ONE OF *THESE* DAYS.
UH OH! IN ANOTHER OF LIFE'S MYSTERIOUS QUIRKS, CALVIN FINDS HIMSELF AN INCH TALL ON THE WRITING DESK!
HIS ONLY HOPE IS TO TEAR OFF A SHEET FROM A NEARBY PAD OF PAPER!
AT HIS TINY SIZE, FOLDING THE SHEET IS DIFFICULT, BUT SOON CALVIN'S PATIENCE IS REWARDED!
HE PUSHES OFF AND CATCHES A SMALL THERMAL RISING UP THE FRONT OF THE DESK!
A GUST FROM AN OPEN WINDOW SENDS CALVIN SOARING ACROSS THE HOUSE!
THERE'S DAD! LEAN! LEAN!
YES! CALVIN IS ABLE TO STEER! *THIS* SHOULD GET DAD'S ATTENTION!
I DON'T NEED PARENTS. ALL I NEED IS A RECORDING THAT SAYS, "GO PLAY OUTSIDE!"
WATERSON

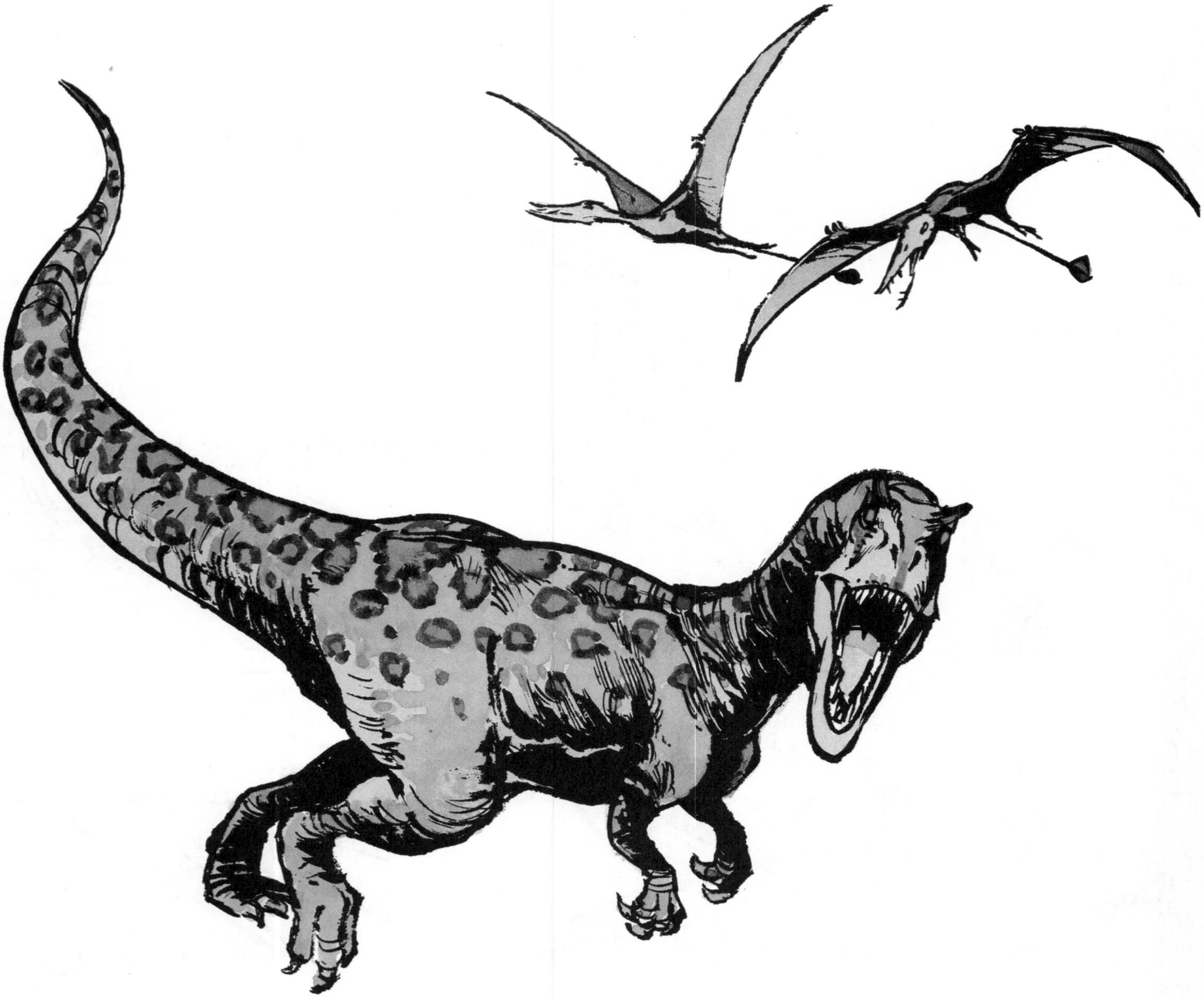

The End